Automated Face Analysis:
Emerging Technologies and Research

T0336180

Daijin Kim
Pohang University of Science & Technology, Korea

Jaewon Sung
Digital Media Research Lab, LG Electronics, Korea

MEDICAL INFORMATION SCIENCE REFERENCE

Hershey · New York

Director of Editorial Content:	Kristin Klinger
Senior Managing Editor:	Jamie Snavely
Managing Editor:	Jeff Ash
Assistant Managing Editor:	Carole Coulson
Typesetter:	Jeff Ash
Cover Design:	Lisa Tosheff
Printed at:	Yurchak Printing Inc.

Published in the United States of America by
Information Science Reference (an imprint of IGI Global)
701 E. Chocolate Avenue, Suite 200
Hershey PA 17033
Tel: 717-533-8845
Fax: 717-533-8661
E-mail: cust@igi-global.com
Web site: http://www.igi-global.com/reference

and in the United Kingdom by
Information Science Reference (an imprint of IGI Global)
3 Henrietta Street
Covent Garden
London WC2E 8LU
Tel: 44 20 7240 0856
Fax: 44 20 7379 0609
Web site: http://www.eurospanbookstore.com

Library of Congress Cataloging-in-Publication Data=

Daijin, Kim, 1959-

Automated face analysis : emerging technologies and research / by Daijin Kim and Jaewon Sung.

p. cm.

Summary: "This book provides related theoretical background to understand the overall configuration and challenging problem of automated face analysis systems"--Provided by publisher.

Includes bibliographical references and index.

ISBN 978-1-60566-216-9 (hardcover : alk. paper) -- ISBN 978-1-60566-217-6 (ebook)

1. Human face recognition (Computer science) I. Sung, Jaewon. II. Title.

TA1650.D355 2009

006.3'7--dc22

2008040441

British Cataloguing in Publication Data
A Cataloguing in Publication record for this book is available from the British Library.

All work contributed to this book is new, previously-unpublished material. The views expressed in this book are those of the authors, but not necessarily of the publisher.

Table of Contents

Preface

According to neuropsychology, the human face is believed to be the most important means for human communication among all social communication instruments. Of the information that the human face carries, the identity information is the most valuable. By recognizing the idenity of a person, we feel comfortable with their familiar face, sometimes uncomfortable with unfamiliar ones as when a baby cries when a strange face shows up, and recall our memories what we have talked with the person, which brings rich backgrounds and context information for smooth conversation.

Facial expressions provide an important means of non-verbal comunication in human communcation. They reflect the internal emotional state of the individual including a smile (happy), a frown (worry), a glare (anger), a snarl (anger), a stare (curiosity), a grimace (pain), ecstasy, anger, fear, doubt, confidence and threat. Besides these, facial gestures provide other non-verbal communication in human communications. By their nodding, shaking, dozzing, or winking, we can under-stand the intention or status of the other person. Sometimes, we express a sad or frustrated feeling by just looking down or looking up at the sky without moving the face for a while.

Since Takeo Kanade began to develop a face recognition algorithm 30 years ago, many researchers have performed research of automated face analysis extensively and achieved a great number of remarkable accomplishments. Thanks to their en-deavour, the automated face analysis technique has been widely applied to many fields such as biometircs, security and surveillance systems, clinical psychology and psychiatry, biomedical applications, human computer interaction (HCI), hu-man robot interaction (HRI), lip reading (to assist the speech recognition in noisy environments), low bit rate video coding of the face for telecommunication, avatar systems, and entertainment.

This book was written to meet three primary requirements. First, we want to put together all related subjects such as face and eye detection, face modeling, face tracking, face recognition, facial expression recognition, and facial gesture recogni-tion into this book. Second, we provide the introductory theoretical backgrounds for each subject, which help the reader's understanding greatly. Third, beyond the faces, we add some other subjects such as the human detection, hand gesture recognition, and body gesture recognition, which are closely related to the automated face analysis.

The book is intended for students and practioners who plan to work in the automated face analysis field or who want to become familiar with state-of-the-art automated face analysis. This book provides plenty of references for scientists and engineers working in related research fields such as image processing, computer vision, biometrics, security, computer graphics, human-computer interaction (HCI), human-robots interaction (HRI), or the computer game industry. We have also provided the summary of many current databases and demonstration systems; of face, eye, facial expression, and gesture, in Appnedix A and B, respectively, which are essential for doing the related researches. The material fits a variety of categories such as advanced tutorial, guide to the current technology, and state-of-the-art survey.

The book consists of eight chapters, covering all the major components and subareas required to understand the emerging technologies and research in automated face analysis. Each chapter focuses on a specific part of the automated face analysis, introduces the required theoretical background, reviews the related up-to-date techniques, presents the experimental results, and points out challenges and future research directions.

Chapter I presents the roles of the face in human communication and the goals of the automated face analysis.

Chapter II presents the face and detection including the theorectial background such as the AdaBoost learning technique and the modified census transform (MCT). We emphasize how to improve the face and eye detection performance by introducing the face certainty map and the MCT. We also introduce the face disguise discrimination technique using the AdaBoost learning of eye/non-eye and/or mouth/non-mouth.

Chapter III presents face modeling including the theoretical background such as the active shape models (ASMs) and the active appearance models (AAMs). We emphasize how to make the face modeling robust by introducing stereo-based AAM, view-basee AAM, and a unified gradient-based approach for combining ASM into AAM.

Chapter IV presents face tracking including the theoretical background such as particle filters, the cylindrical head model (CHM), and the incremental PCA (IPCA). We emphasize how to make the face tracking robust to the changes of background, pose, illumination, and moving speed by introducing: background-robust face tracking using AAM and ACM, pose-robust face tracking using AAM and CHM, illumination-robust face tracking using AAM and IPCA, and fast and robust face tracking using AAM in particle filter framework.

Chapter V presents face recognition including the theoretical background such as the mixture models, the embedded hidden Markov models (HMMs), the local feature analysis (LFA), the tensor analysis, and the 3D morphable models (3D MM). We present a variety of face recognition methods using the mixture model, the embedded HMM, the LFA, the tensor-based AAM, and the 3D MM, and compare the pros and cons of each face recognition method.

Chapter VI presents the facial expression recognition including the theoretical background such as the generalized discriminant analysis (GDA), the bilinear models, and the relative expression image. We present the facial expression recognition using the AAM features and the GDA, and the natural facial expression recognition using the differential-AAM and the manifold learning. Also, we present the facial expression synthesis using the AAM and the bilinear model.

Chapter VII presents the facial gesture recognition including the theoretical background such as the hidden Markov model (HMM). We present how to recognize facial gestures like nodding, denying, and blinking by combining CHM and HMM and apply it to control a TV set.

Chapter VIII presents the human detection, the hand gesture recognition, and the body gesture recognition beyond the automated face analysis, including the theoretical background such as the scale adaptive filters (SAFs) and the iterative closest point (ICP) algorithm. We present a variety of the human motion analysis techniques such as the human detection using the pose-robust SAFs, the hand gesture rcognition using MEI and MHI, the 2D body gesture recognition using the forward spotting accumulative HMMs, and the 3D body gesture recognition using 3D articulated human body model.

Acknowledgment

The authors would like to thank deeply Dr. Takeo Kanade who has encouraged and supported us during the write-up of the manuscript. In particular, the first author greatly appreciates the very insightful discussions and feedback that he gave during his one year's stay at the CMU. The second author would like to express many thanks to all past and current students who carried out the experiments and wrote many valuable manuscripts. Also, the second author is also very much indebted to his family for the strong support they have provided while putting together the material of the manuscript.

The material presented in this book is the result of research performing during last 10 years involving many researchers besides the authors. We would like to acknowledge the financial support from: the Intelligent Robotics Development Program funded by one of the 21st Century Frontier R&D Programs, funded by the Ministry of Science and Technology of Korea; the Lab of Excellency Project funded by the Ministry of Education and Human Resources Development (MOE); the Ministry of Commerce, Industry and Energy (MOCIE) and the Ministry of Labor (MOLAB); the Biometrics Engineering Research Center (BERC) Program at Yonsei University funded by the Korea Science and Engineering Foundation (KOSEF); and the Regional Technology Innovation Program funded by the Ministry of Commerce, Industry and Energy (MOCIE), and many other programs.

Chapter I
Introduction

1.1 ROLES OF THE FACE IN THE HUMAN COMMUNICATION

Communication between one human and another is the hallmark of our species. According to neuropsychology, the human face is the primary tool in human communication among all social communication instruments (Perry et al., 1998). One of the most important pieces of information that the human face carries may be the identity. By recognizing the identity of a person, we can feel comfortable with familiar faces, sometimes uncomfortable with unfamiliar ones (as when a baby cries when a strange face shows up), and recall our memories of conversations with the person, which brings rich backgrounds and context information for smooth conversation.

Moreover, a constellation of findings, from neuroscience, psychology, and cognitive science suggests that emotion plays a surprising critical role in rational and intelligent behavior (Damasio, 1994). Scientists have amassed evidence that emotional skills are a basic component of intelligence, especially for learning preferences and adapting to what is important (Salovey and Mayer, 1990). Emotion modulates almost all modes of human communication including: word choice, tone of voice, facial expression, gestural behaviors, posture, skin temperature and clamminess, respiration, and muscle tension. Emotions can significantly change a message; sometimes it is not what was said that was most important, but how it was said.

Due to the remarkable expressive communication capacity of the face that has been refined during the thousands of generations, facial expressions have the capacity to reflect the internal emotional state of the individual including smiling, frowning, glaring, snarling, ignoring, staring, and even "come here" or "get lost." The face expresses pain, ecstasy, anger, fear, doubt, confidence and threat. Surprisingly, these kinds of non-verbal messages take up a large portion of the whole communicative message in face-to-face human communication: 55% of the messsage is transferred by facial expression, while only 7% is due to linguistic language, and 38% is due to paralanguage (Mehrabian, 1968).

Besides the identification and emotion of the face, facial gestures provide many kinds of messages in human communication. We can understand the intension or status of others by looking if the other is nodding, shaking, dozzing, or winking. Sometimes, we express sad or frustrated feelings by just looking down or looking up at the sky without moving for a while. These behaviors do not belong to the facial expressions but they provide abundant messages to others. Therefore, the abilities to perceive and understand others' emotion from their faces are crucial functions of the fast and smooth social interaction.

1.2 GOALS OF THE AUTOMATED FACE ANALYSIS

Machines may not need all of the communication skills that people need; however, there is evidence that machines will require at least some of these skills to appear intelligent when interacting with people. A relevant theory is that of Reeves and Nass (1996) at Stanford. Human-computer interaction is inherently natural and social, following the basics of human-human interaction. For example, if a piece of technology talks to you but never listens to you, then it is likely to annoy you, analogous to the situation where a human talks to you but never listens to you. Nass and Reeves conducted dozens of experiments of classical human-human interaction, taking out one of the humans and putting in a computer, and finding that the basic human-human results still holds.

In general, the aforementioned human communication skills include many modalities such as visual, and autotory channels. Among the many skills, this book concentrates on the skills that are based on visual sensing of the human eyes. Thus, the ultimate goal of the automated face analysis that researchers dream of is to catch all the visual messages that a human face brings, and to understand the meaning of them, and to automatically react to the human in an appropriate and natural way so that the human can easily communicate with any computer, robot, or machine as the human communicates with another human.

Since Kanade (Kanade, 1973) began to develop a face recognition algorithm 30 years ago, many researchers have extended the research area of computer vision to include face detection, face tracking, facial expression recognition, and facial gesture recognition. Nowadays, due to their remarkable achievments (although they are not perfect) and the enhancement in hardware performance, the face detection, face recognition, and facial expression recognition techniques have begun to commercialize. For example, there are numerous commercial companies that sell their own face recognition techniques and there is a famous competition for these companies, the face recognition vendor test (FRVT) that is held in the U.S.. The facial expression recognition techniques are curently being applied to digital cameras, where the digital cameras equipped with the facial expression recognition technique automatically detect multiple faces and release their shutter automatically when the faces smile.

The automated face analysis technique can be used on a wide variety of applications including: security systems, clinical psychology and psychiatry, biomedical applications, human computer interaction (HCI), human robot interaction (HRI), lip reading to assist the speech recognition in noisy environments, low bit rate video coding of the face for telecommunication, avatar systems, and entertainment.

Automated face analysis is a complex task because physiognomies of faces vary from one indiviaual to another quite considerably due to different age, ethnicity, gender, facial hair, cosmetic products and occluding objects such as glasses and hair. However, faces appear disparate because of pose and lighting changes. Such variations have to be addressed at different stages of automated face analysis system (Fasel and Luettin, 2003). Because solving all the difficulties at a time, we took the 'divide and conquer' approach in this book. We grouped the problems into eight representative cetegories that are the subject of each part: (1) face and eye detection, (2) face modeling, (3) face tracking, (4) face recognition, (5) facial expression recognition, (6) facial gesture recognition and (7) human motion analysis beyond the face.

The benefits of the 'divide and conquer' can be found on the fact that required functions of commercial systems are different from each other according to their target applications. For example, the facial expression recognition and facial gesture recogntion are not the essential requirements of the access control system at the gate. Likewise, many application systems can be built by selecting one or a combination of functions that are suitable for their specific purpose.

Fig. 1.2.1 shows a general structure of the automated face analysis system, where the system is divided into the aforementioned 7 subjects. The face and eye detection is the most fundamental task of automated face analysis because it tells if there is a face to analyze and where the face is located in the input image. The detection results are used to initialize the face model. Various kinds of face models can be selected according to the goal of analysis because different sets of features can be extracted from different face models, where the features can scale, rotation, location, 2D shape, 3D shape, texture, color, and so on. In general, the features of the face model are represented by a set of parameters and initialzing the face model means finding proper values of the parameters. However, if the input is video data, then using a face tracking algorithm is a better choice than applying the face and eye detection algorithm for the next input images because face tracking algorithms are usually more efficient than face detection algorithms that search for the face in the whole input image. The face tracking algorithm searches optimum values of the model parameters around the previous values and adjust the model parameters with the new optimum values. Once the face model is well fitted to an input image, the three recognition algorithms such as face recognition, facial expression recognition, and facial gesture recognition algorithms extract features from the face model and recognizes the identity, facial expression, and facial gesture of the face.

Figure 1.2.1. Structure of automated face analysis systems

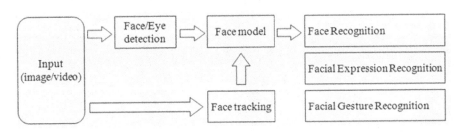

The automated human motion analysis system also has similar components to the automated face analysis system, i.e., the system requires human detection, human model, human tracking, and human motion analysis components. .

Many techniques of the automated face analysis system are already commercialized. One of the most well known applications is for security. Access control or gate control systems at homes, airports, and buildings use face detection and recognition technique. Such technique can also be used for ATM (automatic teller machine) to keep unauthorized people from withdrawing the money. The automated face analysis technique can be applied to various fields and situations. You can foresee the results of plastic surgery without expensive and painful operations. Your car will alarms when you doze. Your camera will catch smiling faces. The ATM (automatic teller machine) will prevent unautorized people from withdrawing the money. You can choose the pictures with a specific friend in your digital album using face image-based search engine. Eventually, the robots in your home will be equipped with all the techniques introduced in this book; They will recognize your face, feeling and behavior as your friends do.

1.3 REFERENCES

Damasio, A. R. (1994). *Descartes' error: emotion, reason, and the human brain*. New York: Gosset/Putnam Press.

Fasel, B., & Luettin, J. (2003). Automatic facial expression analysis: a survey, Pattern Recognition, *36*, 259-275.

Kanade, T. (1973). *Picture processing by computer complex and recognition of human faces*. Ph.D. thesis, Kyoto University.

Mehrabian, A. (1968). Communication without words. *Psychology Today, 2*(4), 53-56.

Perry, B. D., Czyzewski, D., Lopez, M., Spiller, L., & Treadwell-Deering, D. (1998). Neuropsychologic impact of facial deformities in children-neurodevelopmental role of the face in communication and bonding. *Clinics in Plastic Surgery, 25*, 587-597.

Reeves, B., & Nass, C. (1996). *The media equation*. Cambridge Univ. Press, Center for the Study of Language and Information.

Salovey, P., & Mayer, J. D. (1990). Emotional intelligence. *Imagination, Cognition and Personality, 9*(3), 185-211.

Chapter II
Face and Eye Detection

Face detection is the most fundamental step for the research on image-based automated face analysis such as face tracking, face recognition, face authentication, facial expression recognition and facial gesture recognition. When a novel face image is given we must know where the face is located, and how large the scale is to limit our concern to the face patch in the image and normalize the scale and orientation of the face patch.

Usually, the face detection results are not stable; the scale of the detected face rectangle can be larger or smaller than that of the real face in the image. Therefore, many researchers use eye detectors to obtain stable normalized face images. Because the eyes have salient patterns in the human face image, they can be located stably and used for face image normalization. The eye detection becomes more important when we want to apply model-based face image analysis approaches. Most of the model-based approaches use non-linear optimization algorithms to fit their face models to a face image, which require a good initialization for successful convergence of the fitting algorithm. Using the detected eye locations, the face models can be located more accurately by placing the face models so that the two eyes of the face models match to the detected two eyes in the image. Generally, initializing the face models using the detected eye locations give more accurate initialzation results than just using the detected face rectanlge.

Over the past few years, a number of new face detection techniques have been proposed. These techniques are categorized as appearance-based approaches. The main idea of appearance-based methods is scanning windows and classifying the window as either face or nonface. Numerous classifiers have been tried to classify face and nonface.

Sung and Poggio (1998) proposed a distribution-based face detector. These methods partitioned the face distribution into 6 clusters and nonface distribution into 6 clusters in the PCA subspace, and classified face and nonfaces based on distances which is computed between a candidate subwindow and its projection onto the PCA subspace for each of the 12 clusters. Rowley et al., (1998) reported a Neural Networks-based face detector. An ensemble of Neural Networks works on pixel intensities of candidate regions. Each network has different networks with retinal connections to compute the spatial relationships of facial features and then merge from individual networks to final classifier. Féraud et al., (1997) developed the Constrained Generative Model (CGM) based face detector. CGMs are auto-associative connected Multi-Layer Perceptrons (MLP) which are trained to perform a non-linear PCA. The reconstruction errors of the CGMs classify face and nonface. Yang et.al., (2000) proposed the Sparse Networks of Windows (SNoW) based face detector. SNoW is a single layer Neural Network that use the Littlestone's Winnow update rule (Littlestone, 1988). SNoW learning uses boolean features that encode the intensity and positions of pixels.

The above proposed methods provide accurate performance (few false alarms), but all of these methods need a lot of computation time (more than one second) to process an image. This is a big limitation for real-time face detection applications. To overcome this problem, Viola and Jones (2001) proposed the first real-time face detection method. Instead of using pixel information, they used a set of simple features that can be computed at any position and scale in constant time. The algorithm is a booting-based method which shows very good results both in terms of accuracy and speed.

Automatic face analysis requires a stable and accurate normalization step, where the scaled and rotated face in an input image is transformed to a reference scale and orientation. The eyes in the face have been widely used in the face normalization step because they are one of the stable and reliable features of the face (Hsu et al., 2002).

Brunelli and Poggio (1993) and Beymer (1994) detected the eyes using the template matching algorithm, which measures the similarity between the template image and an input image. Pentland et al., (1994) used the eigenspace method to detect the eyes, which showed better eye detection performance than the template matching method. Kawaguchi et al., (2000) described an eye detection algorithm based on Hough transform. Jesorsky et al., (2001) used the Hausdorff distance and Multi-layer Perceptron for finding the eye center. It searches for the best match between the model edge images and segmented input images accroding to the Hausdorff distance. Kawaguchi and Rizon (2003) detected the iris using the intensity and the edge information. Ma et al.. (2004) proposed a three stage method for eye localization based on AdaBoost classifiers which detects face region, two eyes and eye-pair. The positions of three pairs are used for eye localization. Hamouz et al., (2005) proposes a feature-based method which consists of some sub-steps. As the first step, the faces are searched using Gabor filters and the response matrix. After this step, further refinement requires: face hypothesis generation, registration, and appearance verification. Finally, this method verifies the obtained candidate configurations by SVM. Wang et al., (2005) used AdaBoost algorithm which overcome the limited discriminant capability of Haar wavelet. In this paper, to extract more effective features, the Recursive Nonparametric Discriminant Analysis is used. It provides sample weights useful for the AdaBoost algorithm. Fasel et al., (2005) proposed a generative framework for eye localization. This algorithm uses GentleBoost trained Haar-like features. Song et al., (2006) used the binary edge images.

The most recent eye detection algorithms are based on the AdaBoost learning algorithm and SVM classifier (Campadelli et al., 2007); because AdaBoost algorithm and SVM algorithm have good generalization capabilities.

This chapter is organized into five parts: (1) a representative AdaBoost learning algorithm that classifies a given image patch into a face class or a non-face class, (2) a representative illumination-robust feature extracting method like MCT, (3) the face detection using the face certainty map, (4) a robust eye detection using MCT-based feature correlation, and (5) an application using the face and eye detection, the face disguise discrimination using the AdaBoost learning.

2.1 ADABOOST

The *AdaBoost* is a kind of adaptive boosting method. It finds a set of optimal weak classifiers that are made of simple ranglular filters. The weak classifier can be represented as

$$h_j = \begin{cases} 1 & if \ p_j f_j(x) < p_j \theta_j, \\ 0 & otherwise, \end{cases} \qquad (2.1.1)$$

where f, θ and p are a simple rectangular filter, a threshold and a parity, respectively. The learning steps of the adaBoost can be summarized as follows (Viola and Jones, 2001; Freund and Schapire, 1995).

1. Prepare two sets of training images, where the two sets consists of object data and non-object data, respectively.
2. Set the weights of all the training images uniformly and set iteration index t = 1.
3. Compute the error rate of each classifier using the training images as

$$\varepsilon_j = \sum_i w_j \mid h_j(x_i) - y_i \mid \qquad (2.1.2)$$

where i and j are the index of the training images and the index of weak classifiers, respectively.
4. Select a weak classifier that has the lowest error rate.
5. Update the weights of the training images as

$$w_{t+1,i} = w_{t,i} \beta_t^{1-e_i} \qquad (2.1.3)$$

where $\beta_t = \dfrac{\varepsilon_t}{1-\varepsilon_t}$ and we set e_i as

$$e_i = \begin{cases} 0 & if \ a \ training \ image \ \mathrm{x}_i \ is \ classified \ correctly, \\ 1 & otherwise, \end{cases} \qquad (2.1.4)$$

6. Normalize the weights $w_{t,i}$ so that the sum of them become 1.
7. Check the iteration index $\underline{t}$.
   If $(t < T)$ Set $t = t + 1$ and go to step 3.
8. Compute the final strong classifier value as

$$h(x) = \begin{cases} 1 & \sum_{t=1}^{T} \alpha_t h_t(x) \geq \frac{1}{2}\sum_{t=1}^{T}\alpha_t \\ 0 & otherwise \end{cases}$$

(2.1.5)

where $\alpha = \log\left(\frac{1}{\beta_t}\right)$.

In order to compute the rectangular filter f_j rapidly, we define the *integral image* (Crow, 1984). The integral image at a location (i, j) is defined by the sum of the pixels above and up to the left of (i, j) as

$$ii(i,j) = \sum_{i' \leq i, j' \leq j} i(i', j')$$

(2.1.6)

where $ii(i,j)$ is the integral image at a location (i, j) and $i(i', j')$ is the pixel value of original image. The integral image can be the following iterative manner as

$$s(i,j) = s(i, j-1) + i(i, j)$$
$$ii(i,j) = ii(i-1, j) + s(i, j)$$

(2.1.7)

where $s(i,j)$ is the cumulative row sum and initially $s(i, -1) = 0$, $ii(-1, j) = 0$. Fig. 2.1.1 shows how to compute the rectangular filter using the integral image. The sum of region D can be compute by a simple computation as $ii(x_4, y_4) + ii(x_1, y_1) - (ii(x_2, y_2) + ii(x_3, y_3))$.

We use a cascaded *AdaBoost* detector where each cascade step is trained by the adaBoost learning. The cascaded AdaBoost detector enables a fast object detection because a sub-window can be thrown away without preceding to the next the stage whenever it fails to be an object. Fig. 2.1.2 illustrates an example of the cascaded AdaBoost detector.

A detailed explanation of building the cascaded AdaBoost detector is given below (Viola and Jones, 2001).

1. Initialize the values of parameters d, f and F_{target} that denote the maximum acceptable false positive rate per layer, the minimum acceptable detection rate per layer and overall false positive rate.
2. Prepare both training and validation sets of positive and negative examples.
3. Set $F_0 = 1.0$, $D_0 = 1.0$ and $i = 1$, where F_0, D_0 and i are overall false positive rate, overall detection rate and the cascade step, respectively.

Figure 2.1.1. An example of computing the rectangular filter using integral image

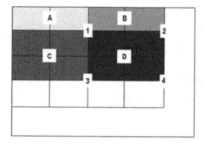

Figure 2.1.2. An example of the cascaded AdaBoost detector

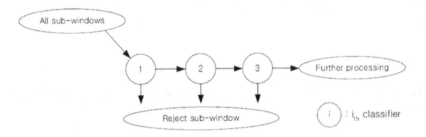

4.   Iterate the below procedure until $F_i \leq F_{target}$, where F_i is the false positive rate of the *i*th cascade step.
   A.   Set $n_i = 1$ and $F_i = F_{i-1}$, where n_i is the number of trained classifier in the *i*th cascade step.
   B.   Train a classifier with n_i features using adaBoost algorithm with a training set of positive and negative examples.
   C.   Evaluate current cascaded adaBoost detector on a validation set to compute the F_i and D_i.
   D.   Decrease the threshold for the *i*th detector until the current cascaded adaBoost detector has a detection rate of at least $d \times D_{i-1}$.

   Viola and Jones (2002) have successfully applied the AdaBoost learning algorithm to the face detection problem, where the weak classifiers for the Adaboost learning were simple Haar filter-like features. The weak point of the AdaBoost is that it take long time in the learning stage. When there are lots of candidate weak classifiers, the AdaBoost learning tries to find the optimum combination of the weak classifiers and the weighting variable for the selected weak classifiers. However, once the strong classifier is learned, the application of the strong classifier to the test image can be done very efficiently.

2.2 MODIFIED CENSUS TRANSFORM

Zabin and Woodfill (1996) proposed an illumination insensitive local image transform method called *census transform* (CT) which is an ordered set of comparisons of pixel intensities in a local neighborhood representing which pixels have lesser intensity than the center. The *Modified Census Transform (MCT)* is a non-parametric local transform which modifies the census transform (Fröba and Ernst, 2004). It is an ordered set of comparisons of pixel intensities in a local neighborhood representing which pixels have lesser intensity than the mean of pixel intensities. Let $N(\mathbf{x})$ be a spatial neighborhood of the pixel at $\mathbf{x}$ and $N'(\mathbf{x})$ include the pixel at $\mathbf{x}$, i.e., $N'(\mathbf{x}) = \{\mathbf{x} \cup N(\mathbf{x})\}$. Let $I(\mathbf{x})$ and $\bar{I}(\mathbf{x})$ be the pixel intensity at $\mathbf{x}$ and the mean of pixel intensity at $\mathbf{x}$ over the $N'(\mathbf{x})$, respectively. Then, the MCT of the pixel at $\mathbf{x}$ is defined as

$$\Gamma(\mathbf{x}) = \bigotimes_{y \in N'(\mathbf{x})} C(\bar{I}(\mathbf{x}), I(\mathbf{y})), \tag{2.2.1}$$

where C is a comparison function as

$$C(\bar{I}(\mathbf{x}), I(\mathbf{y})) = \begin{cases} 1 & if\ \bar{I}(\mathbf{x}) < I(\mathbf{y}), \\ 0 & otherwise, \end{cases} \qquad (2.2.2)$$

and $\otimes$ denotes a concatenation operator. If we consider a 3×3 neighborhood, the *MCT* provides a total of 511 different local structure patterns.

When we consider the 2D image, the MCT of the pixel at (x, y) can be computed by a summation:

$$\Gamma(x, y) = \sum_{x'=x-1}^{x+1} \sum_{y'=y-1}^{y+1} 2^{3(x-x'+1)+(y-y'+1)} C(\bar{I}(x, y), I(x', y')), \qquad (2.2.3)$$

where $\bar{I}(x, y)$ is the mean of 3×3 neighborhood pixel intensities of the pixel at (x, y) in the image and $C(\bar{I}(x, y), I(x', y'))$ is a comparison function as

$$C(\bar{I}(x, y), I(x', y')) = \begin{cases} 1 & if\ \bar{I}(x, y) < I(x', y'), \\ 0 & otherwise. \end{cases} \qquad (2.2.4)$$

However, the MCT is very sensitive to a subtle change of pixel intensity in the local region or the camera noise. Fig. 2.2.1 (a) illustrates a typical example of the conventional MCT. As you see, the pixel intensity values within the 3×3 neighborhood are almost similar, but the conventional MCT produces '1' at the upper right corner because the intensity value is slightly larger than the mean value. To solve this sensitivity problem, we devise the existing MCT by adding a small constant value $\delta I (=2\ or\ 3)$ to the mean intensity as

$$\Gamma(x, y) = \sum_{x'=x-1}^{x+1} \sum_{y'=y-1}^{y+1} 2^{3(x-x'+1)+(y-y'+1)} C(\bar{I}(x, y) + \delta I, I(x', y')), \qquad (2.2.5)$$

where $C(\bar{I}(x, y), I(x', y'))$ is a modified comparison function as

$$C(\bar{I}(x, y) + \delta I, I(x', y')) = \begin{cases} 1 & if\ \bar{I}(x, y) + \delta I < I(x', y'), \\ 0 & otherwise. \end{cases} \qquad (2.2.6)$$

Fig. 2.2.1 (b) illustrates an insensitive MCT that is not sensitive to a subtle change within the 3×3 neighborhood of the pixel at (x, y), where the MCT values are all zeros in the 3×3 neighborhood even though there is a small variation in the pixel intensities of the neighborhood.

Fröba and Ernst (2004) have successfully applied the *MCT* image transformation algorithm for illumination robust face detection problem. Because the MCT is a local image transformation algorithm, they are sensitive to local noises. Recently, the idea of MCT is extened to a more general concept like the local binary pattern (LBP), where the image scale is considered as wavelet analysis.

Figure 2.2.1. Comparison of the conventional MCT and insensitive MCT

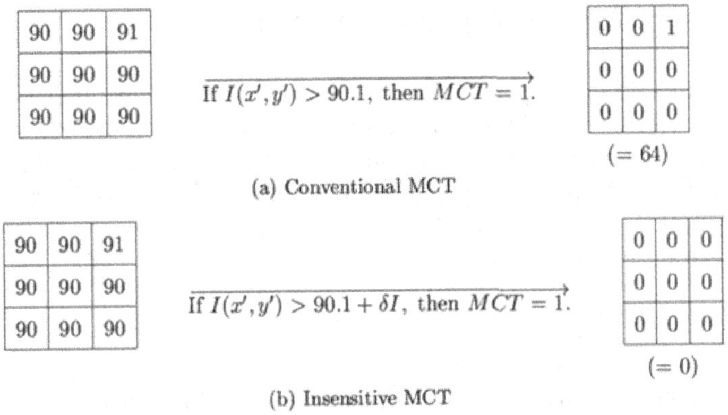

90	90	91
90	90	90
90	90	90

$$\overrightarrow{\text{If } I(x',y') > 90.1, \text{ then } MCT = 1.}$$

0	0	1
0	0	0
0	0	0

$(= 64)$

(a) Conventional MCT

90	90	91
90	90	90
90	90	90

$$\overrightarrow{\text{If } I(x',y') > 90.1 + \delta I, \text{ then } MCT = 1.}$$

0	0	0
0	0	0
0	0	0

$(= 0)$

(b) Insensitive MCT

2.3 FACE DETECTION USING FACE CERTAINTY MAP

The *face detection* has the following intrinsic difficulties. First, face is not a rigid object, i.e., every person has different facial shape and different form/location of facial features such as eyes, nose, and mouth. Second, face of the same person looks different as the facial expression, facial pose, and illumination condition changes. Finally, it is impossible to train infinite number of all non-face patterns. Consequently, unexpected false acceptance or false rejection could be occurred.

The procedure of face detection could be divided as preprocessing step, face detection step, and postprocessing step. First, for the preprocessing step, illumination compensation techniques like histogram equalization (Sung, 1996), normalization to zero mean and unit variance on the analysis window (Viola and Jones, 2002), and modified census transform (Fröba and Ernst, 2004) have been proposed. Second, for the face detection step, many classification algorithms have been proposed to classify the face and non-face patterns such as skin color based approaches (Yang and Waibel, 1996; Dai and Nakano, 1996), SVM (Osuna, 1998; Mohan et al., 2001), Gaussian mixture model (Sung and Poggio, 1998), maximum likelihood (Schneiderman and Kanade, 2000), neural network (Rowley et al., 1998; Mohan et al., 2001), and AdaBoost (Viola and Jones, 2002; Fröba and Ernst, 2004). Finally, for postprocessing step, the algorithms usually group detected faces which is located in the similar position. Then, they select only one face from each face group and determine the size, location, and rotation of the selected face. These methods usually show good performance, but have difficulties in learning every non-face patterns in natural scene. In addition, these methods are somewhat slow due to much computation steps.

In this section, we present a novel face detection algorithm, where the overall procedures are presented in Fig. 2.3.1 For preprocessing step, we revise the modified census transform to compensate the sensitivity to the change of pixel values. For face detection step, we propose difference of pyramid (DoP) images for fast face detection. Finally, for postprocessing step, we propose *face certainty map (FCM)* which contains facial information such as facial size, location, rotation, and confidence value to reduce false acceptance rate (FAR) with constant detection performance.

2.3.1 Preprocessing Step

2.3.1.1 Revised Modified Census Transform

Zabin and Woodfill (1996) proposed an illumination insensitive local transform method called census transform (CT) which is an ordered set of comparisons of pixel intensities in a local neighborhood representing which pixels have lesser intensity than the center. Let $N(x)$ define a local spatial neighborhood of the pixel at x so that $x \notin N(x)$, a comparison function $C(I(x), I(x'))$ be 1 if $I(x) < I(x')$, and $\otimes$ denote the concatenation operation, then the census transform at x is defined as

$$T(x) = \bigotimes_{y \in N} C(I(x), I(y)).$$ (2.3.1)

The CT is a local image trnasformation method to obtain an illumination insentivene features (Zabin and Woodfill, 1996). Since census transform transforms pixel values by comparison with center pixel value, it can not transforms the pixel values equal to center pixel value. Fröba and Ernst (2004) proposed modified census transform (MCT) to solve this problem. Let $N'(x)$ be a local spatial neighborhood of the pixel at x so that $N'(x) = N(x) \cup x$. The intensity mean on this neighborhood is denoted by $\bar{I}(x)$. With this, they formulate the modified census transform as

$$\Gamma(x) = \bigotimes_{y \in N'} C(\bar{I}(x), I(y)),$$ (2.3.2)

where $\otimes$ denote the concatenation operation.

Using Eq. (2.3.2), they could determine all of the 511 structure kernels defined on a 3×3 neighborhood, while CT has only 256 structure kernels. However, as you can see in Fig. 2.3.2 (a), MCT is sensitive to subtle changes of pixel values in local region. To solve this problem, we revised MCT by addition of a small value $\delta I (=2 \text{ or } 3)$ as

Figure 2.3.1. Overall procedure of the face detection algorithm

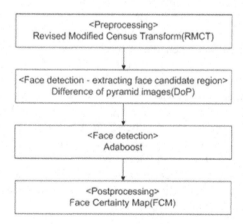

$$\Upsilon(x) = \bigotimes_{y \in N'} C(\overline{I}(x) + \delta I, I(y)).$$
   (2.3.3)

We call Eq. (2.3.3) as *revised modified census transform (RMCT)*, which transforms the pixel values to one of 511 patterns in 3 × 3 neighborhood. Since the local pixel value changes in 3 × 3 neighborhood is insensitive to illumination change, this transform is robust to illumination change. Fig. 2.3.2 (b) shows that a small noise in the neighborhood pixels does not affect the transformed result. Moreover, since *RMCT* has regular patterns which can represent facial features, it is good to classify face and non-face patterns.

2.3.2 Face Detection Step

2.3.2.1 Face Detection Using RMCT and AdaBoost

In this section, we present a novel face detection algorithm using *RMCT* and AdaBoost. RMCT transforms the pixel values to one of 511 patterns in 3 × 3 neighborhood. Then, using the training images transformed by RMCT, we construct the weak classifier which classifies the face and non-face patterns and the strong classifier which is the linear combination of weak classifiers. The weak classifier consists of the set of feature locations and the confidence values for each RMCT pattern.

In the test phase, we scan the image plane by shifting the scanning window and obtain the confidence value for strong classifier in each window location. Then, we determine the window location as face region, when the confidence value is above the threshold.

Moreover, we construct the multi-stage classifier cascade for the fast face detection. We expect that the image patches which contain background are rejected from early stage of cascade. Accordingly, the detection speed may increase (Viola and Jones, 2002; Fröba and Ernst, 2004). For training multi-stage classifier cascade, the non-face training images for first classifier are composed of arbitrary non-face images, while that of later classifiers are composed of the images which is falsely accepted by the former classifiers.

Figure 2.3.2. Comparison of MCT and RMCT

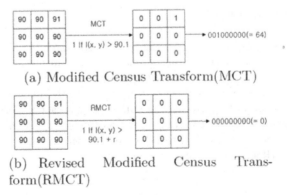

(a) Modified Census Transform(MCT)

(b) Revised   Modified   Census   Transform(RMCT)

2.3.2.2 Speed Up the Algorithm

The face detector analyzes image patches of pre-defined size. Each window has to be classified either as a face or non-face. In order to detect faces in the input image, conventional face detection algorithms have been carried out by scanning all possible analysis windows. In addition, to find faces of various size, the image is repeatedly down-scaled with a pre-defined scaling factor. This is done until the scaled image is smaller than the sub window size. Although face detection by this full-search algorithm shows optimal performance, it is computationally expensive and slow.

To solve this problem, we propose difference of pyramid (DoP) images coupled with two-dimensional logarithmic search. First, we obtain face candidate region using DoP. Since the algorithm does not search the whole input image but the face candidate region, we expect it will reduce the computational time.

Extracting face candidate region using motion difference has been adopted for fast face detection in many previous works. However this method assumes that the location of camera is fixed and the background image is constant. Accordingly, it is difficult to adopt this method to still image or image sequence from moving camera. We propose difference of pyramid images (DoP) for compensating this problem. In order to obtain face candidate region using motion difference, at least two images are required such as background image and input image or image of previous frame and image of current frame. However, we can obtain the face candidate region from the single image using DoP, since it is computed not from image sequence but from single image. Thus, we are able to adopt this algorithm to still image and image sequence from moving camera as well.

Many face detection algorithms construct several numbers of down-scaled pyramid images and then scan each pyramid image using scanning window with pre-defined size. In this paper, we construct n down-scaled images which constitute an image pyramid. Then, we obtain n-1 DoP image by subtract ith pyramid image from (i-1)th pyramid image. Since the size of ith pyramid image and (i-1)th pyramid image are different, we first align each image with the center point then obtain the DoP image by subtracting corresponding pixel points. Since plain background has little changes in DoP image, we can perform fast face detection. The pixel points in DoP image which have higher value than threshold are selected as face candidate region. Fig. 2.3.3 shows some example images of DoP.

2.3.3 Postprocessing Step

2.3.3.1 Face Certainty Map

To minimize *false acceptance rate (FAR)* and *false rejection rate (FRR)*, existing face detection algorithms concentrate on learning optimal model parameters and devising optimal detection algorithm. However, since the model parameters are determined by the face and non-face images in the training set, it is not guaranteed that the algorithms work well for novel images. In addition, there are infinite number of non-face patterns in real-world, accordingly it is almost impossible to train every non-face patterns in natural scene. As a result, the face detection algorithms, which showed good performance during the training phase, show high FRR and FAR in real environment.

Figure 2.3.3. Difference of pyramid images

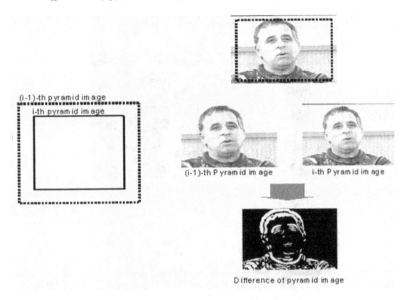

The face detector we described in the previous section determines the image patch in the current scanning window as face when the confidence value is above the threshold and determines it as non-face when the confidence value is beyond the threshold. We call the scanning window of which the confidence value is above the threshold as detected face window. Fig. 2.3.4 shows some examples of the face detection algorithm explained in the previous section: the rectangles in each figure represent the detected face windows. We can see that while the face regions are detected perfectly, there are several falsely accepted regions. In addition, when we investigate the figures precisely, there are numbers of detected face windows near real face region, while few detected face windows are near falsely accepted regions. With this observation, we propose face certainty map (FCM) which can reduce FAR with constant detection performance and no additional training.

As you can see in Fig. 2.3.5, there are multiple detected face windows, even though there is only one face in the input image. For real face region, there are detected face windows with same location but different scale (Fig. 2.3.5 (a)) and detected face windows with same scale but different location (Fig. 2.3.5 (b)). However, falsely accepted regions do not show this property. Consequently, we can determine the regions where multiple detected face windows are overlapped as face region and the regions with no overlapped detected face windows as falsely accepted region. By adopting this methodology, we can reduce FAR greatly.

From now on, we explain how to adopt FCM to the face detection. The detailed explanation of the procedure is given below.

- For each scanning window centered at (x, y), we compute the confidence value.

$$H_i(\Upsilon) = \sum_{p \in S_i} h_p(\Upsilon(p)), \qquad (2.3.4)$$

Figure 2.3.4. Face detection results without FCM

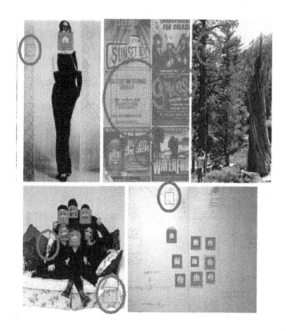

where *i* represents the *i*th cascade, *p* represents the *p*th feature location, and S_i is the set of feature locations, respectively.

- The cumukated confidence value for all *n* cascade is represented by a summation as

$$S(x,y) = \sum_{i=1}^{n} H_i(\Upsilon),$$

(2.3.5)

where $H_i(\Upsilon)$ has a certain value when it is above threshold for all *i*. Otherwise, it is 0.

Figure 2.3.5. (a) Detected face windows which have the same center point (C1) but different scale, (b) Detected face windows which have the same scale but different center point

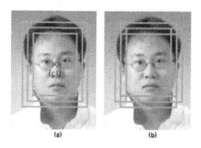

We compute the cumulated confidence value for every pixel position in the image.

- We also compute Eq. (2.3.5) for all pyramid images, then we have $S_p(x, y), p = 1, \ldots, m$, where m is the total number of constructed pyramid images and the pixel locations (x, y) of each down-scaled pyramid image are translated to its corresponding original image locations.

- The FCM for location (x, y) consists of four items such as $S_{max}(x, y)$, $W_{max}(x, y)$, $H_{max}(x, y)$, and $C(x, y)$ $S_{max}(x, y)$ is the maximum confidence value among $S_p(x, y), p = 1, \ldots, m$, $W_{max}(x, y)$ and $H_{max}(x, y)$ is the width and height of the detected face window which has the maximum confidence value, and $C(x, y)$ is the confidence value cumulated for all m pyramid images

$$C(x, y) = \sum\nolimits_{p=1}^{m} S_p(x, y).$$

- Since we constructed FCM, we can determine the face region using it. First, we look for the values above threshold in $S_{max}(x, y)$. Then we determine the location (x, y) as the center of face when $C(x, y)$ is above threshold. The non-face region where the maximum confidence value is above threshold is not classified as a face region, since $C(x, y)$ is lower than the threshold. Consequently, we can reduce the FAR using our FCM.

2.3.4 Experimental Results and Discussion

For constructing training face data, we gathered 17,000 face images from internet and Postech DB (Kim et al., 2001a). Gathered face images contain multiple human species, variety of illumination conditions, and expression variation. Each image is aligned by eye location, and we resize images to 22 × 22 base resolution. In addition, for the robustness to image rotation, we generated another 25,060 face images by rotating gathered face images to -3, 0, 3 degrees.

For non-face training data, we collected 5,000 images which include no face image from internet. Then, we extracted image patches from collected internet images by random size and position. After that, we generated 60,000 non-face images by resizing extracted image patches to the same scale of training face images. We used these 60,000 non-face images as the training non-face data for the first stage of cascade. For the next stages of cascade, we used non-face data which are considered as face image by the previous cascade(i.e. we used false positives of previous cascade as training non-face data for training current cascade). A validation training data set is used for obtaining threshold value and stop condition of each stage of cascade. The validation set face and non-face images exclude the images used for training. We constructed validation set of 15,000 face images and 25,000 non-face images by the same way as we used for training data.

For each cascade, we preprocessed each face and non-face image using RMCT. Then we chose the feature positions for classification (S_i) and obtained classification value($H_i(\Upsilon)$) and threshold value (T_i) for each position. We constructed the face detector with 4 cascade and the maximal number of allowed position for each cascade is 40, 80, 160, and 400, respectively. In addition, the RMCT is defined 511 patterns in 3 × 3 neighborhood. Accordingly, we can not apply the 3 × 3 RMCT to the training images which have the size 22 × 22. Thus, we excluded the outer areas of each image and used the inner 20 × 20 areas of it.

We tested our algorithm on CMU+MIT frontal face test set. Fig. 2.3.6 and Table 2.3.1 represent the results of face detection. When we used the FCM, the reduction of FAR is ten times better than the cascade AdaBoost detector with the same detection rate, while the detection time is almost the same. The cascade AdaBoot detector needs computations for grouping and eliminating overlapped face candidate region, whereas the face detector using the FCM needs the small computation for FCM. Operating on 320 by 240 pixel images, faces are detected at 23 frames per second on the conventional 3.2 GHz Intel Pentium IV system and 6 frames per second on OMAP5912 (ARM9 system).

2.4 EYE DETECTION USING MCT-BASED FEATURE CORRELATION

Automatice face analysis applications require stable and accurate normalization step, where the scaled and rotated face in an input image is transformed to a reference scale and orientation. The eyes in the face have been widely used in the face normalization step because they are one of the stable and reliable features of the face (Hsu et al., 2002). Thus, it is very important to detect and localize the eyes of the face (Samal and Iyengar, 1992).

Brunelli and Poggio (1993) and Beymer (1994) detected the eyes using the template matching algorithm, which measures the similarity between the template image and an input image. Pentland et al. (1994) used the eigenspace method to detect the eyes, which showed better eye detection performance than the template matching method. However, its detection performance is largely dependent on the choice of training images. Kawaguchi and Rizon (2003) detected the iris using the intensity and the edge information. Song et al. (2006) used the binary edge images. They included many technique such as the feature template, template matching, separability filter, and binary valley extraction, and so on. Unfortenately, their algorithm required different parameters on different data sets. Resultantly, their method is not intuitive and not simple.

If we have a reliable face detector, then looking for the eyes in the detected face region instead of searching for the eyes in the entire input image is more natural and intuitive method. Fortunately, there were remarkable achievements in the face detection research. Viola and Jones (2001) proposed a robust face detection method using AdaBoost learning algorithm, which showed its good generalization capability (Freund and Schapire, 1999). Fröba and Ernst (2004) used the AdaBoost algorithm with a modified version of the census transform (MCT), which is very robust to the illumination change.

Table 2.3.1. Results of face detection

Detector	Number of False Detection
RMCT, AdaBoost and FCM	3
RMCT and AdaBoost	93
Viola-Jones	78
Rowley-Baluja-Kanade	167
Bernhard Froba	27

Figure 2.3.6. Face detection results using the FCM

In this section, a novel eye detection algorithm is presented, which uses a MCT-based AdaBoost training method to detect the eyes and a *MCT-based pattern* correlation map to verify and correct the eye detection result. Although we limit the eye search area to the inside of the face that is obatined by a face detector, there exist many obstacles. Sometimes, the eyebrows or hairs can be identified as the eyes due to their similar looks to the eyes, which can result the false alarm of the detection method. This false alarm problem can be alleviated by a novel eye verification process that determines whether the detected eyes are true eye or not.

The eye verification method employs the correlation map based on the MCT-based pattern correlation. It is built by sliding a detected eye over the eye region of the opposite side and computing the correlation value in term of the Hamming distance of the MCT-based patterns between the detected eye patch and the corresponding patch in the opposite eye region. When an eye correctly (or falsely) detected, the correlation map does (or not) provide a noticeable peak. In other word, we can verify whether the detected eye is true or false depending on the existence of the noticeable peak in the correlation map.

Using this property of the correlation map, we can correct the falsely detected eye using the peak position in the correlation map of the opposite eye as follows. Assume that one eye is correctly detected and the other eye is falsely detected. Then, the correlation map of the correctly detected eye provides the noticeable peak that corresponds to the true location of the falsely detected eye. Of course, we fail to detect the eyes when both eyes are verified as the falsely detected eyes.

Fig. 2.4.1 shows a flowchart of our novel eye detection method. First, it detects the face region using the MCT-based AdaBoost face detector. Second, it detects the eye patches using the MCT-based AdaBoost eye detector. Third, it verifies whether the detected eye patch is true or false using the correlation map based on the MCT-based pattern correlation. Fourth, the falsely detected eye is corrected by the noticeable peak in the correlation map of the correctly detected eye.

2.4.1 AdaBoost Training with MCT-Based Eye Features

We present the eye detection method using the AdaBoost training with MCT-based eye features. In the AdaBoost training, we construct the weak classifier which classifies the eye and non-eye pattern and then construct the strong classifier which is the linear combination of weak classifiers.

The weak classifier tries to find the lookup table that represents the confidence weight for each MCT value at a specific pixel location and the strong classifier integrates the confidence weights through the entire image to identify the input eye image. Fröba and Ernst (2004) used a cascade of AdaBoost classifiers that consisted of four stages to accelerate the detection time. However, we use one stage AdaBoost classifier because the cascade AdaBoost classifier can degrade the detection rate and it does not take a long time to detect the eyes due to its small size. A detailed description of the AdaBoost Training with MCT-based eye features is given by the Table 2.4.1 and the Table 2.4.2.

In the test phase, we scan the eye region by moving a 12×8 size of the scanning window and obtain the confidence value corresponding to the current window location using the strong classifier. Then, we determine the window location whose confident value is maximum as the location of the detected eye. Our MCT-based AdaBoost training has been performed using only the left eye and non-eye training images. So, when we are trying to detect the right eye, we need to flip the right subregion of the face image.

2.4.2 Eye Verification

As mentioned earlier, the eye detection using the strong classifier with the AdaBoost Training with MCT-based eye features can produce the false detection near the eyebrows or the boundary of hair and forehead in particular. To remove this false detection, we devise an eye verification whether the detected eye is true or false using the MCT-based pattern correlation based on symmetrical property of the human face.

Figure 2.4.1. Flow chart of the eye detection algorithm

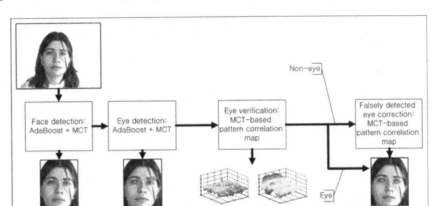

2.4.2.1 MCT-Based Pattern Correlation

The MCT represents the local intensity variation of several neighboring pixels around a given pixel in an ordered bit pattern. So, the decoded value of the MCT is

$$\sum_{i=0}^{8} b_i 2^{8-i},$$

where b_i is a binary value (0 or 1) at the i-th location. (See Fig. 2.4.2 (a)). Therefore, The MCT values can be very different even though the only one pixel location is different each other as shown in Fig. 2.4.2, where the MCT values of (b) and (c) are 146 and 402, respectively. Also, the MCT is not an entity of magnitude but a pattern of local intensity variation between a pixel and its neighboring pixels. So, the decoded value of the MCT is not appropriate for measuring the difference between two MCT patterns. To solve this problem, we propose the idea of the MCT-based pattern and the MCT-based pattern correlation based on the Hamming distance that measures the difference between two MCT-based patterns.

The MCT-based pattern $p(x, y)$ at the pixel position (x, y) is a binary representation of the 3×3 pixels in the determined order, from the upper left pixel to the lower right pixel as

$$P(x, y) = [b_0, b_1 \dots b_8], \tag{2.4.1}$$

where $\bar{I}(x, y)$ is a binary value that is obtained by the modified comparison function as

$$b_{3(y'-y+1)+(x'-x+1)} = C(\bar{I}(x, y) + \alpha, I(x', y')), \tag{2.4.2}$$

where $x' = \{t \mid t \in \{x-1, x, x+1\}\}$ and $y' = \{t \mid t \in \{y-1, y, y+1\}\}$.

We propose the MCT-based pattern correlation to compute the similarity between two different *MCT-based patterns*. It is based on the Hamming distance that counts the number of positions whose binary values are equal between two MCT-based patterns. For example, the Hamming distance between 100010101 and 111010101 is 2. Then, the MCT-based pattern correlation between image A and image B is defined as

Table 2.4.1. AdaBoost training with MCT-based eye features

- Prepare N_e training images of eye and $N_{\bar{e}}$ training images of non-eye.
- Perform the MCT to all eye and non-eye images. Let Γ_i^e and $\Gamma_j^{\bar{e}}$ be the generated features of eye and non-eye, respectively, where $i = 1, ..., N_e$ and $j = 1, ..., N_{\bar{e}}$.
- Initialize the weights of training eye and non-eye images uniformly:

$$D_1^e(i) = \frac{1}{2N_e},$$

$$D_1^{\bar{e}}(j) = \frac{1}{2N_{\bar{e}}}.$$

- For each iteration $t = 1,...,T$
  generate weak classifiers using Table 2.4.2.
- The elementary classifier of a pixel **x** can be obtained by linear combination of the
  weak classifiers as

$$h_{x_t}(\gamma) = \sum_t \alpha_t w_{x_t}(\gamma).$$

- The strong classifier is computed as

$$H(\Gamma) = \sum_{x_t} h_{x_t}(\Gamma(x_t)).$$

$$\rho = \frac{1}{N} \sum_{x,y} \rho_{x,y}, \tag{2.4.3}$$

where N is the number of pixels in the image and $\rho_{x,y}$ is the MCT-based pattern correlation at the pixel position (x, y) as

$$\rho_{x,y} = \frac{1}{9}(9 - HammingDistance(P_A(x,y), P_B(x,y))), \tag{2.4.4}$$

where $P_A(x, y)$ and $P_B(x, y)$ are the MCT-based patterns of the image A and B, respectively.

Similarly, the conventional image correlation between image A and image B is defined as

$$\rho = \frac{(\sum_{x,y} I_A(x,y)I_B(x,y))^2}{\sum_{x,y} I_A(x,y)^2 \sum_{x,y} I_B(x,y)^2}, \tag{2.4.5}$$

where $I_A(x, y)$ and $I_A(x, y)$ are the image intensity values of the image A and B at the pixel position (x, y), respectively.

Because the *MCT-based pattern* is robust to change of the illuminations, the MCT-based pattern correlation is also robust to the illumination changes. Fig. 2.4.3 shows five different face images with different illuminations. Table 2.4.3 compares the conventional image correlation with histogram equalization and the MCT-based pattern correlation between two image pairs. The table shows that (1) the mean of the MCT-based pattern correlation is higher than that of the conventional image correlation and (2) the variance of the MCT-based pattern correlation is much smaller than that of the conventional image correlation.

Table 2.4.2. A procedure for generating weak classifiers

---

1. Generate the lookup tables for each MCT value from eye images and non-eye images:

$$g_t^e(\mathbf{x},\gamma) = \sum_i D_t^e(i)I(\Gamma_i^e(\mathbf{x}) = \gamma),$$

$$g_t^{\bar{e}}(\mathbf{x},\gamma) = \sum_j D_t^{\bar{e}}(j)I(\Gamma_j^{\bar{e}}(\mathbf{x}) = \gamma),$$

where $I()$ is the indicator function which takes 1 if the argument is true and takes 0 otherwise.

2. Calculate the error δ_t for each look-up table:

$$\delta(\mathbf{x}) = \sum_\gamma \min(g_t^e(\mathbf{x},\gamma), g_t^{\bar{e}}(\mathbf{x},\gamma))$$

3. Select the best position $\mathbf{x}_t$ at each iteration t:

$$\mathbf{x}_t = \begin{cases} \mathbf{x} \mid \delta_t(\mathbf{x}) = \min_\mathbf{x}(\delta_t(\mathbf{x})) & \text{if } |S_t| < N_\mathbf{x}, \\ \mathbf{x} \mid \delta_t(\mathbf{x}) = \min_{\mathbf{x} \in S}(\delta_t(\mathbf{x})) & \text{otherwise,} \end{cases}$$

where N_x is the maximum number of positions and S_t is the set of positions that are already chosen until the iteration t. So, $S_t = S_{t-1} \cup \{\mathbf{x}_t\}$.

4. Create the lookup table for the weak classifier at the iteration t and position $\mathbf{x}$:

$$w_{\mathbf{x}_t}(\gamma) = \begin{cases} 0 & \text{if } g_t^e(\mathbf{x}_t,\gamma) > g_t^{\bar{e}}(\mathbf{x}_t,\gamma), \\ 1 & \text{otherwise.} \end{cases}$$

5. Compute a weight parameter for each iteration t as

$$\alpha_t = \frac{1}{2}\ln(\frac{1-\delta_t}{\delta_t})$$

6. Update the weights of training eye and non-eye images as

$$D_{t+1}^e(i) = \frac{D_t^e(i)}{z_{t+1}} \times \begin{cases} e^{-\alpha_t} & \text{if } w_{\mathbf{x}_t}(\Gamma_i^e(x)) = 0, \\ e^{\alpha_t} & \text{otherwise,} \end{cases}$$

$$D_{t+1}^{\bar{e}}(j) = \frac{D_t^{\bar{e}}(j)}{z_{t+1}} \times \begin{cases} e^{-\alpha_t} & \text{if } w_{\mathbf{x}_t}(\Gamma_j^{\bar{e}}(x)) = 1, \\ e^{\alpha_t} & \text{otherwise,} \end{cases}$$

where z_{t+1} is a normalization factor as

$$z_{t+1} = \sum_i D_{t+1}^e(i) + \sum_j D_{t+1}^{\bar{e}}(j).$$

Figure 2.4.2 Examples of the MCT-based patterns

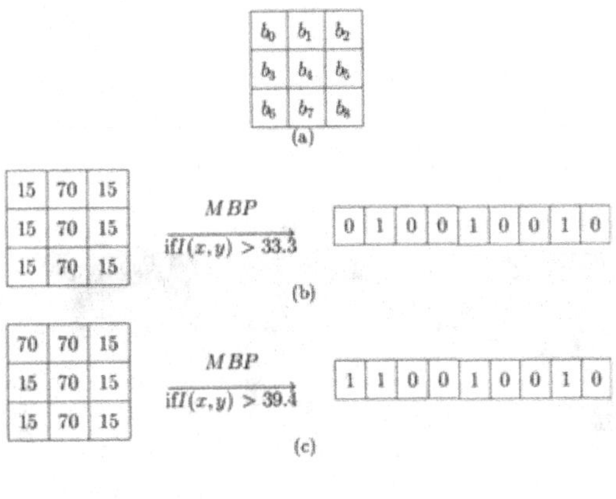

This implies that the MCT-based pattern is more robust to the change of illuminations than the conventional image correlation.

We can make the MCT-based pattern correlation map by flipping and sliding the detected eye patch of one side over the eye region of the opposite side and computing the MCT-based pattern correlation (or the conventional image correlation) at each pixel location. Fig. 2.4.4 shows two example images, where (a) and (b) are the eye region of one example image that has the constant illumination condition over the eye region and the flipped image patch of the left eye, respectively, and (c) and (d) are the eye region of the other example image that has the different illumination over the left and right eye subregion and the flipped image patch of the left eye, respectively.

Fig. 2.4.5 (a) and (b) show the conventional image correlation map and the MCT-based pattern correlation map between Fig. 2.4.4 (a) and (b), respectively. As you see, there are two noticeable peaks at the positions of the left and right eye. This implies that two correlation maps are working well when the illumination condition keeps constant over the eye region. Similarly, Fig. 2.4.5 (c) and (d) show the conventional image correlation map and the MCT-based pattern correlation map between Fig. 2.4.4 (c) and (d), respectively. As you can see, the conventional image correlation map produces the highest peak at the left eye and the MCT-based pattern correlation map produces the highest peak at the right eye. This implies that the MCT-based pattern correlation map is robust to the change of illumination when the illumination condition is varying over the left and right eye subregion.

2.4.2.2 Eye/Non-Eye Classification

The detected left and right eye patch can be either eye or non-eye, respectively. In this work, they are classified into eye or non-eye depending on the existence of a noticeable peak in the MCT-based correlation map as follows. If there is a noticeable peak in the MCT-based correlation map, the detected eye patch is an eye. Otherwise, the detected eye patch is a non-eye.

Since the strong classifier produces two detected eye patches on the left and right eye subregions, respectively, we build two different MCT-based pattern correlation maps as

- **Case 1:** Left eye correlation map that is the MCT-based pattern correlation map between the detected left eye patch and the right subregion of the face image,
- **Case 2:** Right eye correlation map that is the MCT-based pattern correlation map between the detected right eye patch and the left subregion of the face image.

Figure 2.4.3. Five face images with different illuminations

Table 2.4.3. Comparison between the conventional image correlation with histogram equalization and the MCT-based pattern correlation

	Conventional Image correlation With HIST.EQ.	MCT-based pattern correlation
Face image 1 and face image 2	0.873	0.896
Face image 1 and face image 3	0.902	0.862
Face image 1 and face image 4	0.889	0.883
Face image 1 and face image 5	0.856	0.839
Face image 2 and face image 3	0.659	0.827
Face image 2 and face image 4	0.795	0.890
Face image 2 and face image 5	0.788	0.849
Face image 3 and face image 4	0.846	0.870
Face image 3 and face image 5	0.794	0.865
Face image 4 and face image 3	0.627	0.808
Mean	0.803	0.859
Variance	0.094	0.028

We want to show how the MCT-based pattern correlation maps of the correctly detected eye and the falsely detected eye are different each other. Three images in Fig. 2.4.6 are taken to build the left eye correlation map (Case 1), where they are (a) a right eye subregion, (b) a flipped image patch of the correctly detected left eye, and (c) a flipped image patch of the falsely detected left eye (in this case, eyebrow), respectively.

Fig. 2.4.7 shows the correlation maps of (a) the correctly detected left eye patch and (b) the falsely detected left eye patch, respectively. As you see, two correlation maps look very different each other: the true eye patch produces a noticeable peak at the right eye position while the non-eye patch (eyebrow) does not produces any noticeable peak over the entire right eye subregion. From this fact, we need an effective way of finding a noticeable peak

Figure 2.4.4. Two different eye region image patches and their flipped eye image patch of the left eye

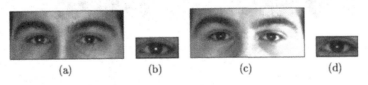

| (a) | (b) | (c) | (d) |

---

in the correlation map in order to decide whether the detected eye patch is eye or non-eye. In this work, we consider a simple way of peak finding based on two predetermined correlation values.

The novel eye/non-eye classification method is given below. First, we re-scale the correlation map whose the highest peak value becomes 1. Second, we overlay a peak finding window W_{peak} with a size of w × h at the position with the highest value in the correlation map, where w and h are the width and the height of the detected eye patch. Fig. 2.4.8 shows the peak finding windows overlayed over the contour of the correlation maps. Third, we classify whether the detected eye $E_{detected}$ patch is eye or non-eye according to the following rule as

$$E_{detected} = \begin{cases} eye & if\ R < \tau, \\ non-eye & otherwise, \end{cases} \qquad (2.4.6)$$

where τ and R are a given threshold and the high correlation ratio, which is defined by a ratio of the number of pixel positions whose correlation value is greater than a given threshold value ρ_t over the number of total pixel positions within the peak finding window W_{peak} as

$$R = \frac{1}{N}\sum_{u'=u-w/2}^{u+w/2}\sum_{v'=v-h/2}^{v+h/2} C(\rho(u',v'),\rho_t), \qquad (2.4.7)$$

where N is the number of total pixel positions of W_{peak} and C is an comparison function as

Figure 2.4.5. Two examples of the conventional image correlation map and the MCT-based pattern correlation map

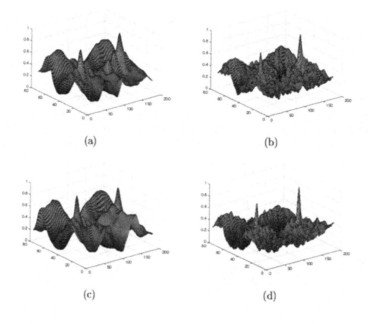

(a)   (b)

(c)   (d)

Figure 2.4.6. A typical example of the right eye subregion, the detected eye and non-eye in the left eye subregion

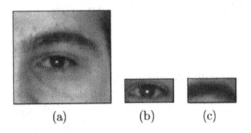

(a)   (b)   (c)

$$C(\rho(u',v'),\rho_t) = \begin{cases} 1 & if \ \rho(u',v') > \rho_t, \\ 0 & otherwise. \end{cases} \qquad (2.4.8)$$

2.4.2.3 Falsely Detected Eye Correction

After eye verification, we have four different classification results on the left and right eye regions: (1) eye and eye, (2) eye and non-eye, (3) non-eye and eye, and (4) non-eye and non-eye. In the first and fourth case, we succeed and fail to detect two eyes, respectively.

In the fourth case, there is no way to detect the eyes. However, in the case of the second and third cases, we can correct the falsely detected eye as follows. In the second case, we can locate the falsely detected right eye using the peak position of the correlation map of the correctly detected left eye. Similarly, in the third case, we can locate the falsely detected left eye using the peak position of the correlation map of the correctly detected right eye.

Fig. 2.4.9 shows an example of the falsely detected eye correction, where (a) and (b) show the eye region images before and after falsely detected eye correction, respectively. In Fig. 2.4.9 (a), *A*, *B*, and *C* represent the correctly detected left eye, the falsely detected right eye, and the true right eye, respectively. As you see in Fig. 2.4.9 (b), the falsely detected right eye is corrected well. Fig. 2.4.10 shows the correlation maps where (a) and (b)

Figure 2.4.7. Correlation maps of eye and non-eye

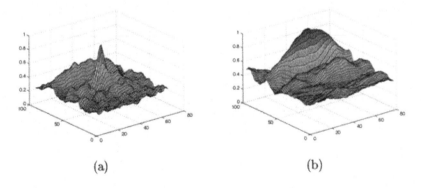

(a)   (b)

are the correlation maps using the correctly detected left eye and the falsely detected right eye, respectively.

2.4.3 Experimental Results and Discussion

2.4.3.1 Database

For the AdaBoost Training with MCT-based eye features, we used two face databases such as Asian Face Image Database PF01 (Kim et al. 2001a) and XM2VTS Database (XM2VTSDB) (Luettin and Maitre, 1998) and prepared 3,400 eye images and 220,000 non-eye images whose size is 12 × 8. For evaluating the novel eye detection method, we used two face databases such as the University of Bern face database (Achermann, 1995) and the AR face database (Martinez and Benavente, 1998).

As a measure of eye detection, we define the eye detection rate as

$$r_{eye} = \frac{1}{N}\sum_{i=1}^{N} d_i,$$

(2.4.9)

where N is the total number of the test eye images and d_i is an indicator function of successful detection as

$$d_i = \begin{cases} 1 & if\ max(\delta_l,\delta_r) < R_{iris}, \\ 0 & otherwise, \end{cases}$$

(2.4.10)

where and δ_l and δ_r are the distance between the center of the detected left eye and the center of the real left eye, and the distance between the center of the detected right eye and the center of the real right eye, respectively, and T_{iris} is a radius of the eye's iris.

It is important to normalize the training eye images for the AdaBoost Training with MCT-based eye features. The normalization process has been performed by the following. First, we rotate the training eye images such that the eye axis connecting two iris center points becomes horizontal. Second, we re-scale the horizontal size of the eye image such

Figure 2.4.8. The peak finding windows overlayed over the contours of the correlation maps

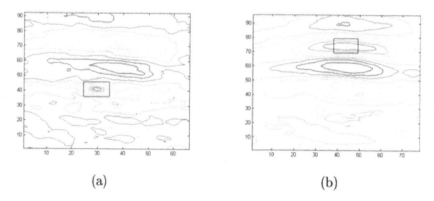

(a)   (b)

Copyright © 2009, IGI Global, distributing in print or electronic forms without written permission of IGI Global is prohibited.

Figure 2.4.9. An example of the falsely detected eye correction

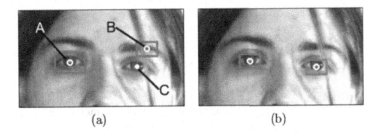

(a)   (b)

Figure 2.4.10. Correlation maps corresponding to (a) eye and (b) non-eye

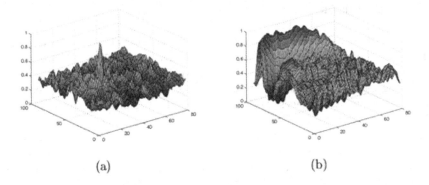

(a)   (b)

that the distance between the iris center point and the inner point along the horizontal line is equal to the predetermined size of the eye model. Third, we re-scale the vertical size of the eye image in the same scale. The predetermined size of the eye model is given in Fig. 2.4.11.

In the test databases, the accurate of the our face detection algorithm is 100%. So, we analyze only the accurate of the novel eye detection method in the experiments.

2.4.3.2 Experiments Using Bern Images

The University of Bern face database (Achermann, 1995) consists of 300 face images (30 peoples × 10 different views), where each image has a size of 512 × 342. We take 150 face images without spectacles as the test images. Fig. 2.4.12 and Fig. 2.4.13 show some Bern images whose eyes are correctly and falsely detected by the strong classifier that is obtained by the AdaBoost Training with MCT-based eye features, respectively, where the boxes represent the detected eye patches and the white circles represent the center of the detected eye patches. Fig. 2.4.14 shows one example of falsely detected eye correction by the novel eye correction method, where the left and right figures represent the eye detection results before and after falsely detected eye correction, respectively.

Table 2.4.3 compares the detection performance of various eye detection methods. As you see, the novel eye detection method outperforms other existing methods except the Song and Liu's eye detection method (Song et. al, 2006). However, they used the same face

Figure 2.4.11. Eye model

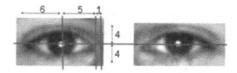

database for training and testing, but the novel eye detection method used the different face database for training and testing. This implies that the detection performance of the novel eye detection method is more reliable than that of the Song and Liu's eye detection method.

2.4.3.3 Experiments in AR Images

The AR face database (Martinez and Benavente, 1998) consists of over 3000 face images (126 peoples, 26 different conditions) whose each image size is 768 × 576. We take two subsets of the AR face database called AR-63 and AR-564. The AR-63 face database contains 63 images (twenty-one people × three different facial expressions) and the AR-564 face database includes 564 images (94 peoples × 6 conditions (3 different facial expressions and 3 different illuminations)).

Fig. 2.4.15 and Fig. 2.4.16 show some AR images whose eyes are correctly and falsely detected by the strong classifier that is obtained by the AdaBoost Training with MCT-based eye features, respectively, where the boxes represent the detected eye patches and the white circles represent the center of the detected eye patches. Fig. 2.4.17 shows four examples of falsely detected eye correction by the novel eye correction method, where (a) and (b) represent the eye detection results before and after falsely detected eye correction, respectively.

Table 2.4.4 compares the detection performance of various eye detection methods. As you see, the novel eye detection method shows better eye detection rate than other existing methods and we the improvement of eye detection rate in the case of AR-564

Figure 2.4.12. Some examples of the correctly detected eyes in the Bern face database

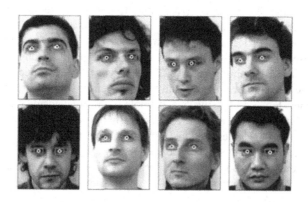

Fig. 2.4.13. Some examples of the falsely detected eyes in the Bern face database

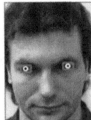

Figure 2.4.14. An example of falsely detected eye correction

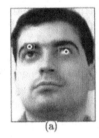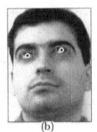

face database is bigger than that in the case of AR-63 face database. This implies that the novel eye detection method works well under various conditions than other existing eye detection methods.

Table 2.4.5 shows the detailed description of eye detection results of different categories in the AR-564 face database when the novel eye detection is applied. As you see, there is a little improvement of eye detection rate in some categories such as smile and left illumination and the eye correction method increases the eye detection rate by 0.8%, which corresponds to the eye correction of four face images.

2.5 FACE DISGUISE DISCRIMINATION USING ADABOOST LEARNING

Because of the increasing number of financial automation machinery such as the Automated Teller Machine (ATM) and the Cash Dispenser (CD), not only the convenience of accessing the financial transactions but also the illegal financial transactions are increased. Where an illegal financial transactions are attempting financial transactions by an user who has a stolen cash card or a stolen credit card. Because biometric information has not possibility of robbery, using biometric information is a solution to restrict the illegal financial transaction.

According to *"Financial success for biometrics?, Biometric Technology Today, April, 2005,"* many approaches which are the fingerprint verification (Jain, et al., 1997), iris

Table 2.4.3. Comparisons of various eye detection methods using the Bern face database

Algorithms	Eye detection rate (%)
Eye detection using the MCT-based AdaBoost training	98.0
Novel method using the falsely detected eye correction	98.7
Song and Liu	98.7
Kawaguchi and Rizon	95.3
Template matching	77.9
Eigenface method using 50 training samples	90.7
Eigenface method using 100 training samples	93.3

verification (Daugman, 2004), vein verification (Im, et al., 2001), signature verification (Plamondon, et al., 2000), keystroke dynamics (Bleha, et al., 1990) are used to verify customer's identity at the ATM. These methods have not only the advantage of the substitution of the identification card such as a cash card or a credit card but also restricting the illegal financial transaction when cards lost. But many people does not use these methods, because of refusal feeling about collecting biometric information.

For this reason, we study the prevention method for the illegal financial transaction. In general, CCTV captures face images of the ATM users. If an illegal financial transaction occurs, captured images are used in order to grasp the suspect. But captured images are not reliable if the customer wears a mask or a sun-glass on his face. If we know the wearing mask or sun-glass on his face, we can restrict a his financial transaction. This chapter describes the facial disguise algorithm of the ATM or the CD user.

Fig. 2.4.15. Some examples of the correctly detected eyes in AR-564 face database

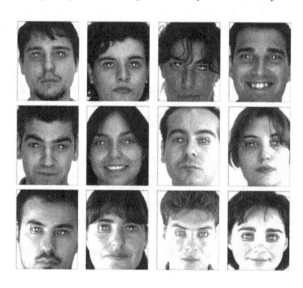

Figure 2.4.16. Some examples of the falsely detected eyes in AR-564 face database

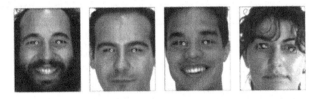

Fig. 2.4.17. Four examples of the falsely detected eye correction

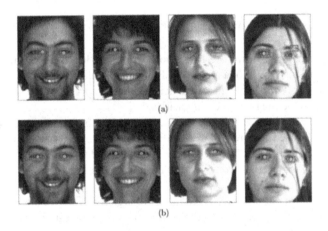

In this section, we use AdaBoost with the modified census transform (MCT) (Freund and Schapire, 1999; Fröba and Ernst, 2004) due to its simplicity of learning and high speed of detection. Fig. 2.5.1 shows a overview of the facial disguise discrimination method. First, it detects the face region using MCT-based AdaBoost face detector. Second, it divides into some subregions and it detects the eyes and the mouth using the MCT-based AdaBoost eye detector and mouth detector in input images. Finally, it discriminates eye disguise using the fraction of the number of eye images divided by the number of face images in input images. This discriminator is based on the probability of Binomial distribution. Similary, we use the number of mouth images to discriminate mouth disguise.

Table 2.4.4. Comparisons of various eye detection methods using the AR face database

Algorithms	Detection rate (%)	
	AR-63	AR-564
Eye detection using the MCT-based AdaBoost training	96.8	98.0
Novel method using the falsely detected eye correction	98.4	98.8
Song and Liu	96.8	96.6
Kawaguchi and Rizon	96.8	-

Table 2.4.5. Detailed description of eye detection in the AR-564 face database

Category	Before correction (%)	After correction (%)
Neutral	100	100
Smile	94.7	96.8
Angry	98.9	98.9
left illumination	96.8	98.9
right illumination	98.9	98.9
both illumination	98.9	98.9

2.5.1 Facial Component Detection

The Modified Census Transform (MCT) is a non-parametric local transform which modifies the census transform by Fröba and Ernst(Fröba and Ernst, 2004). It is an ordered set of comparisons of pixel intensities in a local neighborhood representing which pixels have lesser intensity than the mean of pixel intensities.

We present the detection method for the face, the eyes and the mouth using the AdaBoost training with MCT-based features. In the AdaBoost training, we construct the weak classifier which classifies the target facial component pattern and non-target facial component pattern and then construct the strong classifier which is the linear combination of weak classifiers.

In the detection, we scan the face region, the eye region and the mouth region by moving of the scanning window and obtain the confidence value corresponding to the current window location using the strong classifier. Then, we determine the window location whose confident value is maximum as the location of the detected face, the detected eyes and the detected mouth.

2.5.2 Facial Disguise Discrimination

To discriminate the facial disguise, we use the image sequence because the using the image sequence is complement to the detection method. In the image sequence, we detect the eye and the mouth, and determine the statuse of disguise. If the number of the detected eye and mouth images is greater than the specified threshold, then the input face is the normal face. Otherwise, we are determined the disguised face of the input face. Where, the threshold value is computed by probability mass function and cumulative density function of Binomial distribution.

2.5.2.1 Eye Disguise Discrimination

To discriminate the eye disguise, we use the fraction of the number of eye images divided by the total number of face images. In other words, the eye disguise method using the image sequence and discriminates the eye disguise from the image sequence when a customer uses ATM. The eye disguise discriminator is defined as

Figure 2.5.1 An overview of the facial disguise discrimination method

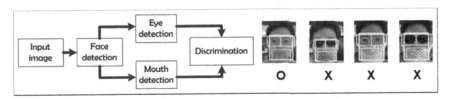

$$\Lambda_E(\mathbf{I}) = \begin{cases} normal\ eye & if\ \dfrac{ne(I)}{nf(I)} \ge \theta_E, \\ disguised\ eye & otherwise, \end{cases} \qquad (2.5.1)$$

where $\mathbf{I}$ is the image sequence, $ne(I)$ is the number of images which have detected eyes in $\mathbf{I}$, $nf(I)$ is the number of images which have a detected face in $\mathbf{I}$ and θ_E is a threshold of the $\dfrac{ne(I)}{nf(I)}$. θ_E is defined as

$$\theta_E = \frac{x}{n}, \qquad (2.5.2)$$

where n is the number of images which have a face, x is the expected number of images which have a one correct eye at least. The expected number x is calculated from the Binomial distribution. To calculate x, we use the probability of the false acceptances calculated by Binomial random variable given FAR.

The Binomial probability mass function (PMF) is defined as

$$f(x;n,p) = P\{\mathbf{y} = x\} = \binom{n}{x} p^x (1-p)^{n-x}, \qquad (2.5.3)$$

where x denotes the number of times that a certain event occurs in the n trials and p is the probability of the event occurred. The eye disguise discrimination method uses cumulative density function (CDF) because it will be defined with the probability where the event will occur from the specified interval. The CDF is defined as

$$F(x;n,p) = P\{\mathbf{y} \le x\} = \sum_{i=1}^{x} f(i;n,p) \ge c, \qquad (2.5.4)$$

where c is the confidence value. The probability is less than $1 - c$ in the n images, where the probability that the number of false detected images is greater than x.

Fig. 2.5.2 shows the PMF and the CDF of the Binomial random variable when the number of input images is 20 and the FAR of the eye detection method is 0.5.

From Fig. 2.5.2 (b), we know that the value of x, which satisfies Eq. (2.5.5), is 13.

$$P\{\mathbf{y} \le x\} \ge 0.9. \qquad (2.5.5)$$

In other words, the 90% confidence interval is [1,13]. The eye disguise discrimination method is reliable because that using the confidence interval of the CDF from FAR of the eye detection method.

The eye disguise discrimination method uses the CDF of the FAR in the eye detection method, and the CDF is defined as

$$F(x; n, p) = \sum_{i=1}^{x} \binom{n}{i} p^i (1-p)^{n-i} \geq c, \qquad (2.5.6)$$

where p is the FAR of the eye detection, c is the desired confidence of eye disguise discrimination. We can calculate x given n iteratively. Finally, the eye disguise discrimination method computes θ_e using the x.

For examples, suppose that the FAR of the eye detection method is 0.03, and the total number of input images is 50. In that case, x is 6 by Eq. (2.5.6) where the desired confidence is 99.9%. From these values, θ_E is calculated ($\theta_E = \dfrac{6}{50} = 0.12$). That is to say, the input images are decided to the normal face image when the number of the detected eye images is greater and equal than 6 in 50 input images.

2.5.2.2 Mouth Disguise Discrimination

We applied the eye disguise discrimination to the mouth disguise discrimination. The mouth disguise discriminator is defined as

$$\Lambda_M(\mathbf{I}) = \begin{cases} normal\ mouth & if\ \dfrac{nm(I)}{nf(I)} \geq \theta_M, \\ disguised\ mouth & otherwise, \end{cases} \qquad (2.5.7)$$

where $\mathbf{I}$ is the image sequence, $nm(I)$ is the number of detected mouth images in $\mathbf{I}$, $nf(I)$ is the number of detected face images in $\mathbf{I}$ and θ_M is a threshold of the $\dfrac{nm(I)}{nf(I)}$. θ_M is defined as

$$\theta_M = \dfrac{x}{n}, \qquad (2.5.8)$$

Figure 2.5.2. An example of Binomial distribution (n = 20, p = 0.5)

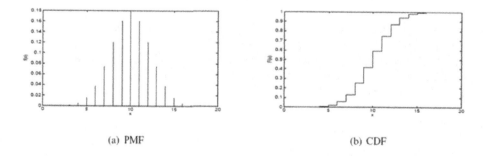

(a) PMF   (b) CDF

where n is the number of the input images, x is the expected number of images which have a one correct result at least. Because the calculation process is equivalent to the eye disguise discrimination, we omit the detailed description.

2.5.2.3 Photograph Discrimination

Sometimes, the robber uses the photograph of the another user to use a financial transaction on the automated teller machine. At this time, the eye and mouth disguise discrimination algorithms discriminate whether the input face image is a normal face image or disguised. In this section, we discriminate between the real image and the photograph by analyzes the change of images.

In general, the customer stays for a short while when he uses a automated teller machine. At this moment, if the input images are photographs, the input image will not be changed. Otherwise, the person acts moving the pupil or the winking of the eye. These peculiarities will become important factors. In this study, we use the winkling of the eye to discriminate between the real image and the photograph.

Fig. 2.5.3 (a) and Fig. 2.5.3 (b) are, repectively, an example of the real image sequence and an example of the photograph sequence. Fig. 2.5.3 (b) doesn't change of the eyelid, but Fig. 2.5.3 (a) has a visible change of the eyelid which is the winking of the eye.

To detect the closed eye, we use the AdaBoost training with the closed eye features. The photograph discriminator is defined as

$$\Lambda_P(\mathbf{I}) = \begin{cases} non\ photograph & if\ \dfrac{nce(I)}{nf(I)} \geq \theta_P, \\ photograph & otherwise, \end{cases} \qquad (2.5.9)$$

where $\mathbf{I}$ is the image sequence, $nce(I)$ is the number of images which have a detected closed eye in $\mathbf{I}$, $nf(I)$ is the number of images which have a detected face in $\mathbf{I}$ and θ_P is a threshold of the $\dfrac{nce(I)}{nf(I)}$.

But, in general, a person may be winked once during 5 seconds on the average. This means that perhaps the number of captured closed eye images is very small. For this reason, applying the confidence interval of the CDF to photograph discrimination is very difficult. So, θ_P is defined manually by many experiments.

2.5.3 Experimental Results and Discussion

For the face detection, we use 50,000 face images on the Internet. For the AdaBoost training with the MCT-based eye features, we use the asian face image database PF01 (Kim et al., 2001a) and the XM2VTS database (XM2VTSDB) (Luettin and Maitre, 1998) which are 3,400 eye images and 220,000 non-eye images whose size is 12×8. For the mouth detection, we use the asian face image database PF01 and prepared 1,800 mouth images and 15,000 non-mouth images whose size is 14×6. Similarly, we also use the asian face image database PF01 for the AdaBoost training with the MCT-based closed-eye features. It consists of 200 closed-eye images and 18,000 non-closed-eye images whose size is 12×8. To evaluate the facial disguise discrimination method, we use the AR face database

(Martinez et al., 1998) and the asian face image database PF01. The average detection time is *70ms* in Pentium 4.3GHz system.

2.5.3.1 Facial Disguise Discrimination

To evaluate facial disguise discrimination, we make a subset of the AR face database called AR-FDD that has the purpose of testing facial disguise discrimination. The AR-FDD face database contains 1086 images (96 people × 2 different conditions × 3 different illuminations × 1 or 2 sessions, some people has first session). It has 2 different conditions which are the wearing sun-glass or mask, and it consists of 3 different illuminations such as the normal illumination, the right illumination, and the left illumination.

Fig. 2.5.4 (a) shows some examples of the correct results in the AR-FDD face database by the strong classifier that is obtained by the MCT-based AdaBoost Training where the boxes represent the detected facial components(eyes, mouth). Fig. 2.5.4 (b) shows some examples of incorrect results by the strong classifier in the AR-FDD face database.

Table 2.5.1 shows the performance of the facial discrimination algorithm in the AR-FDD face database. The FRR of the eye detection is calculated in the wearing mask group, because the wearing sun-glass group has not detectable eyes. With sameness, the FRR of the mouth detection is calculated in the wearing sun-glass group. Also, false rejected result images include images which have results of the detected eye in the only one subregion.

In the AR-FDD face database, if the number of input images is 50 and the confidence is 99.9%, we calculate θ_E in the eye disguise discrimination. First, x is calculated as

$$F(x;50,0.016) = \sum_{i=1}^{x} \binom{50}{i} 0.016^i (1-0.016)^{50-i} \geq 0.999, \tag{2.5.10}$$

where x is 5 and θ_E is calculated as

$$\theta_E = \frac{x}{n} = \frac{5}{50} = 0.1. \tag{2.5.11}$$

Similarly, θ_M is computed in the mouth disguise discrimination. If the confidence is 99.9%, with Eq. (2.5.6), x is calculated as

Figure 2.5.3. Comparison between the real image sequence and the photograph sequence

(a) An example of the captured real image sequence on a camera

(b) An example of the captured photograph sequence on a camera

$$F(x;50,0.034) = \sum\nolimits_{i=1}^{x} \binom{50}{i} 0.034^{i}(1-0.034)^{50-i} \geq 0.999, \tag{2.5.12}$$

where x is 7 and θ_M is calculated as

$$\theta_M = \frac{x}{n} = \frac{7}{50} = 0.14. \tag{2.5.13}$$

2.5.3.2 Photograph Discrimination

Fig. 2.5.5 shows some correct and incorrect examples of the closed eye detection in the Asian Face Image Database PF01 and AR63 face database, where the boxes represent the detected closed eyes. In the Asian Face Image Database PF01 and AR-63 face database, the FRR and the FAR of the closed eye detection method are, respectively, 8.4%($\frac{9}{107}$) and 1.7%($\frac{3}{170}$). We apply these results to photograph discrimination.

2.5.3.3 Applications

We experiment in the cam: Logitech QuickCam Fusion. Fig 2.5.6 shows some captured images of the cam. Table 2.5.2 shows the FAR of the facial disguise discrimination using one image and the image sequence. These result shows that using image sequence with Binomial distribution's CDF of FAR is accurate and reliable for the facial disguise discrimination.

2.6 CONCLUSION

In this chapter, we explained a robust face detection algorithm using difference of pyramid (DoP) images and face certainty map (FCM). The experimental results showed that the reduction of FAR is ten times better than existing cascade AdaBoost detector while keeping detection rate and detection time almost the same. Existing AdaBoost face detection algorithms have to add more cascade stages for non-face images in order to reduce FAR. However, since it needs more weak classifier for constructing strong classifier, the processing time increases. Moreover, as the number of stages in cascade increase, FRR also increase. We were free from these drawbacks and increased detection performance by applying FCM

Figure 2.5.4. Examples of the experimental results in the AR-FDD face database

(a) Some of the correct results.   (b) Some of the incorrect results.

Table 2.5.1. The FRR and FAR of the facial disguise discrimination algorithm in the AR-FDD face database

Category	Number of total images	FRR	FAR
Eye	1086	5.5% (30 /543)	1.6% (17/1086)
Mouth	1086	7.7% (42/543)	3.4% (37/1086)

to existing AdaBoost face detection algorithm. Since we can reduce FAR, the number of stages in cascade is also minimized, while preserving the same performance as existing algorithm which has more stages of cascade. Accordingly training time and processing time is faster than existing algorithm. Furthermore, FCM can be applied to any face detection algorithm beside AdaBoost which obtains confidence value or probability.

We presented a novel eye detection method using the MCT-based pattern correlation. The method consisted of four steps. First, it detected the face region using the MCT-based AdaBoost face detector. Second, it detected the eye patches using the MCT-based AdaBoost eye detector. Third, it verified whether the detected eye patch is true or false using the correlation map based on the MCT-based pattern correlation. Fourth, the falsely detected eye was corrected by the peak position in the correlation map of the correctly detected eye.

The eye detection method can produce the false detection near the eyebrows or the boundary of hair and forehead in particular. When the existing eye detection method detects the eye in just one subregion, then it does not improve the eye detection rate. This limitations are overcome by an eye verification based on the MCT-based pattern correlation, where the falsely detected eyes are corrected. The MCT-based pattern correlation is based on the Hamming distance that measures the difference between two MCT-based patterns ,where the MCT-based pattern is a binary representation of the MCT. Also, the MCT-based pattern is robust to the illumination changes.

To verify detected eye, the eye/non-eye classification method classifies the detected eyes into eye or non-eye classes depending on the existence of a noticeable peak in the MCT-based pattern correlation map. The MCT-based pattern correlation map is built by sliding a detected eye patch over the eye region of the opposite side and computing the MCT-based pattern correlation value between the detected eye patch and the corresponding patch in the opposite eye region.The falsely detected eye correction method uses the peak position

Figure 2.5.5. Some examples of the closed eye detection

Figure 2.5.6. Some examples of the captured image from the camera

in the MCT-based pattern correlation map to correction of the falsely detected eye which is verified by the novel eye/non-eye classification method.

The experimental results show that a eye detection rate of 98.7% can be accomplished on the 150 Bern face database and 98.8% on the AR-564 database. The novel eye detection method works well under various conditions than other existing eye detection methods.

Finally, we presented the facial disguise and photograph discrimination algorithm that helps taking the reliable images with the automated teller machine. It was based on the detection methods which was trained by AdaBoost with MCT-based facial features. To discriminate facial disguise and photograph the facial disguise discrimination, we detected facial components in the image sequence as follows. First, the proposed method detected the face region using the MCT-based AdaBoost face detector. Second, it divided into some subregions and it detected the eyes and the mouth using the MCT-based AdaBoost eye detector and mouth detector.

It discriminated the eye disguise (the mouth disguise and photograph) by the fraction of the number of detected eye (mouth and closed eye) images divided by the number of face images. If the fraction is greater and equal than the threshold of the fraction, the input image sequence is determined to normal face. Where the threshold is computed by CDF from the Binomial distribution based on the FAR of the eye and the mouth. This threshold is more reliable and accurate than the user-defined threshold because that is based on the confidence interval of the Binomial distribution. The proposed facial disguise discrimination method can be applied to ATM and then it can be reduced the illegal financial transactions. And the our photograph discrimination method can be applied to ATM or the face recognition system. The facial disguise discrimination method is helpful to reduce of the illegal financial transaction on the ATM, and it helpful to increase the reliability of the face recognition system and it's applications.

Table 2.5.2. The performance of the facial disguise discrimination algorithm in application

Methods	FAR (%)
Using one image	8.5
Using image sequence with CDF of FAR	0.1

2.7 REFERENCES

Achermann, B. (1995). *The face database of university of Bern*. Institute of Computer Science and Applied Mathematics, University of Bern.

Beymer, D. (1994). Face recognition under varying pose. In *Proceedings of IEEE International Conference on Computer Vision and Pattern Recognition,* (pp. 756-761).

Bleha, S., Slivinsky, C., & Hussien, B. (1990). Computer-access security systems using keystroke dynamics. *IEEE Transaction on Pattern Analysis and Machine Intelligence, 12,* 1217-1220.

Brunelli, R., & Poggio, T. (1993). Face recognition: features versus templates. *IEEE Transactions on Pattern Analysis and Machine Intelligence, 15*(10), 1042-1052.

Campadelli, P., Lanzarotti, R., & Lipori, G. (2007). Eye localization: a survey. *The Fundamentals of Verbal and Non-verbal Communication and the Biometrical Issue NATO Science Series, 18,* IOS Press.

Dai, Y., & Nakano, Y. (1996). Face texture model based on sgld and its application in face detection in a color scene. *Pattern Recognition, 29,* 1007-1017.

Daugman, J. (2004). How iris recognition works. *IEEE Transactions on Circuits and Systems for Video Technology, 14,* 21-30.

Fasel, I., Fortenberry, B., & Movellan, J. (2005). A generative framework for real time object detection and classification. *Computer Vision and Image Understanding, 98,* 182-210.

Féraud, R., Bernier, O., & Collobert, D. (1997). A constrained generative model applied to face detection. In *Proceedings of the Fourteenth National Conference on Artificial Intelligence.*

Freund, Y., & Schapire, R. (1999). A short introduction to boosting. *Journal of Japanese Society for Artificial Intelligence, 14*(5), 771-780.

Fröba, B., & Ernst, A. (2004). Face detection with the modified census transform. In *Proceedings of IEEE International Conference on Automatic Face and Gesture Recognition,* (pp. 91-96).

Hamouz, M., Kittler, J., Kamarainen, J., Paalanen, P., Kalviainen, H., & Matas, J. (2005). Feature-based affine invariant localization of faces. *IEEE Transactions on Pattern Analysis and Machine Intelligence, 27*(9), 1490-1495.

Hsu, R., Abdel-Mottaleb, M., & Jain, A. (2002). Face detection in color images. *IEEE Transaction on Pattern Analysis and Machine Intelligence, 24*(5), 696-706.

Im, S., Park, H., Kim, Y., Han, S., Kim, S., Kang, C., & Chung, C. (2001). An biometric identification system by extracting hand vein patterns. *Journal of the Korean Physical Society, 38,* 268-272.

Jain, A., Hong, L., & Bolle, R.(1997). On-line fingerprint verification. *IEEE Transaction on Pattern Analysis and Machine Intelligence, 19,* 302-314.

Jesorsky, O., Kirchberg, K., & Frischholz, R. (2001). Robust face detection using the Hausdorff distance. *In Proceedings of Third International Conference, AVBPA 2001*, (pp. 90-95).

Kawaguchi, T., & Rizon, M. (2003). Iris detection using intensity and edge information. *Pattern Recognition, 36*(22), 549-562.

Kawaguchi, T., Hikada, D., & Rizon, M. (2000). Detection of the eyes from human faces by hough transform and separability filter. *In Proceedings of International Conference on Image Processing*, (pp. 49–52).

Kim, H. C., Sung, J. W., Je, H. M., Kim, S. K., Jun, B. J., Kim, D., & Bang, S. Y. (2001a). *Asian face image database: PF01*. Technical Report. Intelligent Multimedia Lab, Dept. of CSE, POSTECH.

Littlestone, N. (1988). Learning quickly when irrelevant attributes algorithm. *Machine Learning, 2*, 285–318.

Luettin, J., & Maitre, G. (1998). Evaluation protocol for the extended M2VTS database(XM2VTSDB). *IDIAP Communication*, 98-05, IDIAP, Martigny, Switzerland.

Ma, Y., Ding, X., Wang, Z., & Wang, N. (2004). Robust precise eye location under probabilistic framework. *In Proceedings of Sixth IEEE International Conference on Automatic Face and Gesture Recognition*, (pp. 339–344).

Martinez, A., & Benavente, R. (1998). *The AR face database*. CVC Technical Report #24.

Mohan, A., Papageorgiou, C., & Poggio, T. (2001). Example-based object detection in images by components. *IEEE Transactions on Pattern Analysis and Machine Intelligence, 23*(4) 349-361.

Osuna, E. (1998). *Support Vector Machines: Training and Applications*. PhD thesis, MIT, EE/CS Dept., Cambridge.

Pentland, A., Moghaddam, B., & Starner, T. (1994). View-based and modular eigenspaces for face recognition. *In Proceedings of IEEE International Conference on Computer Vision and Pattern Recognition*, (pp. 84-91).

Plamondon, R., & Srihari, S. (2000). On-line and off-line handwriting recognition: a comprehensive survey. *IEEE Transaction on Pattern Analysis and Machine Intelligence, 22*, 63-84.

Rowley, H., Baluja, S., & Kanade, T. (1998). Neural network-based face detection. *IEEE Transactions on Pattern Analysis and Machine Intelligence, 20*(1), 23–38.

Samal, A., & Iyengar, P. A. (1992). Automatic recognition and analysis of human faces and facial expressions: a survey. *Pattern Recognition, 25*(1), 65-77.

Schneiderman, H., & Kanade, T. (2000). A statistical method for 3d object detection applied to face and cars. *In Proceedings of Computer Vision and Pattern Recognition*, (pp. 746-751).

Song, J., Chi, Z., & Li, J. (2006). A robust eye detection method using combined binary edge and intensity information. *Pattern Recognition, 39*(6), 1110-1125.

Sung, K. (1996). *Learning and example selection for object and pattern recognition.* PhD thesis, MIT, AI Lab, Cambridge.

Sung, K., & Poggio, T. (1998). Example-based learning for view-based human face detection. *IEEE Transactions on Pattern Analysis and Machine Intelligence, 20*(1), 39–51.

Viola, P., & Jones, M. (2001). Rapid object detection using a boosted cascade of simple features. *In Proceedings of IEEE International Conference on Computer Vision and Pattern Recognition,* (pp. 511-518).

Viola, P., & Jones, M. (2002). Fast and robust classification using asymmetric adaboost and a detector cascade. *Advances in Neural Information Processing System, 14,* MIT Press, Cambridge.

Wang, P., Green, M., Ji, Q., & Wayman, J. (2005). Automatic eye detection and its validation. *In Proceedings of IEEE International Conference on Computer Vision and Pattern Recognition,* (pp. 164-171).

Yang, J., & Waibel, A. (1996). A real-time face tracker. *In Proceedings of Workshop on Application of Computer Vision,* (pp. 142-147).

Yang, M., Roth, D., & Ahuja, N. (2000). A SNoW-based face detector. *In Advances in NeuralInformation Processing Systems,* MIT Press, (pp. 855–861).

Zabih, R., & Woodfill, J. (1996). A non-parametric approach to visual correspondence. *IEEE Transactions on Pattern Analysis and Machine Intelligence.*

Chapter III
Face Modeling

In the field of computer vision, researchers have proposed many techniques for representation and analysis of the varying shape of objects, such as active contour (Kass et al., 1988) and deformable template (Yuille et al., 1989). However, the active contour, which consists of a set of points, is too flexible to limit its deformation to a reasonable amount of variations for a specific object and it does not have the ability to specify a specific shape. The deformable template, which consists of a set of parametric curves, is difficult to represent all the shape deformations of an object due to 3D rotation or self-deformations because the deformations are too complex to be explained by the combination of hand crafted simple parametric curves.

In the field of pattern recognition, researchers have focused on the analysis of texture patterns of the face image and have used many kinds of pattern analysis methods such as principal component analysis (PCA) (Turk and Pentland, 1991a, Turk and Pentland, 1991b), independent component analysis (ICA) (Bartlett et al., 2002), and wavelet decomposition (Wiskott et al., 1997). Although there were some methods that considered the shape variation of the face such as the gabor wavelet jets, they concentrated on the analysis of holistic face texture assuming they are deal with only front view face image.

Cootes and his colleagues have proposed a series of algorithms that overcome the limitations of the aforementioned shape and texture analsys methods such as the active shape model (ASM) (Cootes et al., 1995), and active appearance model (AAM) (Cootes et al., 2001d). The ASM alleviates the limitations of the previous shape analysis methods. It learns the shape variation of an object using a linear shape model from a set of training examples so that the linear shape model can produce a legal shape of the target objects without requiring the designer's prior knowledge on the target object. The AAM intelligently combined the ASM with the eigenface model, which enabled the simultaneous analysis of the shape and texture of the object. Later, the traditional AAM is further studied (Matthews and Baker, 2004a; Gross et al., 2004b) and extended to handle occlusion (Gross et al., 2004a), to incorporate 3D shape model (Xiao et al., 2004b), to fit the AAM to multiple camera images (Hu et al., 2004).

After Cootes and his colleagues proposed ASM, which mainly concentrated on the representation of the object shape, they extended the model to AAM, which can explain the shape and texture of the objects simultaneously. The ASM and AAM belong to model-based image analysis paradigm, which analyze an input image by searching for a model instance that best describes the input image; this search process is called 'fitting'. The ASM uses search-based iterative optimization and the AAM uses gradient descent iterative optimization algorithm in the model fitting process, where the model parameters are updated.

Although the ASM and AAM were developed for the purpose of medical image analysis (Cootes et al., 2005). They became popular methods in the face image analysis research field because they are good at representing the variations of the shape and texture of non-rigid objects such as the human face.

In the field of computer graphics, Blanz and Vetters (Blanz and Vetters, 1999) have proposed a *face modeling* technique, called 3D morphable model (3D MM), that learns the variations of the 3D shape and texture from detailed 3D scanning data for the synthesis of realistic 3D face models.

The 2D+3D AAM can be understood as a simplified version of 3D MM. The difference between them is that the shape model of the former consists of dozens of vertices and its model fitting algorithms are computationaly very efficient, while that of the latter consists of tens of thousands of vertices and its model fitting algorithms are far more complex than those of the former.

This chapter is organized into two parts. The first part introduces the ASMs and AAMs, which are attractive face modeling tools. Specifically, the AAMs seem to be becoming more popular than the ASM these days because they provide both the shape and texture analysis, which make the AAMs more attractive face modeling tools for the various applications that require detailed information about the shape or texture of the face. Examples of the applications are face recognition, facial expression recognition, analysing a driver's mental status to prevent him dozing, gaze tracking, lip reading, and low bit-rate video coding.

The second part introduces the recently developed algorithms that enhance the performance of the fitting algorithms and alleviate the weaknesses of the traditional AAMs. Section 3.3 explains a *stereo AAM (STAAM)* algorithm, which enhances the fitting performance of a 2D+3D AAM by fitting the 2D+3D AAM to multiple view images simultaneously using camera calibration information. Section 3.4 explains a view-based 2D+3D AAM algorithm, which can handle large pose variaions of the face by constructing multiple 2D+3D AAMs accomodating specific view angles in the training stage and selecting adequate ones according to the current view angles in the tracking stage. Section 3.5 explains a unified Gradient-based approach that combines the ASM into AAM, which utilize the characteristics of the ASMs and AAMs to enhance the accuracy of the fitting results.

3.1 ACTIVE SHAPE MODELS

Cootes et al. (1995) used the term ASM as the name of the model fitting algorithm in their paper, where the model includes a *point distribution model* (PDM). The PDM is a kind of deformable shape model that consists of a linear model to explains the shape variation of the training data. This section explains how the PDM can be constrcted from example data and how to find a set of optimal parameters of the PDM for a new input image.

3.1.1 Point Distribution Model

In the *PDM*s, a 2D shape is represented by a set of l vertices, which correspond to the salient points of a non-rigid object. The shape vector $\mathbf{s}$ consists of the coordinates of the vertices as

$$\mathbf{s} = (x_1, y_1, \ldots, x_l, y_l)^T. \tag{3.1.1}$$

The shape variation is expressed as a linear combination of a mean shape $\mathbf{s}_0$ and n shape bases $\mathbf{s}_i$ as

$$\mathbf{s} = \mathbf{s}_0 + \sum_{i=1}^{n} p_i \mathbf{s}_i, \tag{3.1.2}$$

where p_i are the shape parameters.

The mean and shape bases are learned from a set of training images using a statistical analysis technique, principal component analsys (PCA). The standard approach is to apply the PCA to a set of shape vectors that are gathered from the manually landmarked training images. The mean shape $\mathbf{s}_0$ is the mean of gathered shape vectors and the basis vectors $\mathbf{s}_i$ are the n eigenvectors corresponding to the n largest eigenvalues.

Usually, the gathered training shape vectors are aligned using the *Procrustes analysis* (Cootes et al., 2001d) before the PCA is applied to remove variations due to *similarity transformation* that scales, rotates, and translates the shape. Thus, the PCA is only concerned with the local shape deformation. Fig. 3.1.1 illustrates an example of shape bases, where the five shape bases $\mathbf{s}_1$ to $\mathbf{s}_5$ are displayed over the mean shape $\mathbf{s}_0$.

Because the PDM does not explain the similarity transformation (scaling, rotation, and translation) of the shape, we need 4 more parameters to explain the similarity transformation of the shape when we synthesize a shape using the PDM that coincident with the object in an image. The similarity transformation can be explained by 4 parameters $\mathbf{q} = \{q_1, q_2, q_3, q_4\}$ as

Figure 3.1.1 An example of shape bases, s_1 to s_5

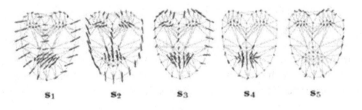

s_1 s_2 s_3 s_4 s_5

$$\begin{bmatrix} x' \\ y' \end{bmatrix} = M\big((x,y),\mathbf{q}\big) = \begin{bmatrix} q_1 & q_2 \\ -q_2 & q_1 \end{bmatrix} \begin{bmatrix} x \\ y \end{bmatrix} + \begin{bmatrix} q_3 \\ q_4 \end{bmatrix}.$$

(3.1.3)

The *PDM* is an accurate, specific, and compact deformable shape model. The PDM is an accurate model, which means that it can synthesize all valid shapes. The PDM is a specific model, which means that it excludes all invalid shapes; The invalid shapes can be excluded by simply limiting the range of the shape parameters into a certain range (usually, +/- 3 standard deviations) because the shape parameters are uncorrelated. The PDM is a compact model, which means that it uses the smallest number of parameters that are enough to describe all the shape variations.

3.1.2 Fitting the PDM to an Image

The *ASM* fitting algorithm is an iterative optimization algorithm, which consists of two steps. In the first step it searches the new location of candidate feature points that make up the vertices of the PDM in the input image. In the second step, it computes the optimal model parameters, the shape parameters **p**, and the similarity transforma parameters **q**, that best describes the candidate feature points obtained in the first step.

Assume that a set of initial model parameters are given. Then, a shape instance **s** can be synthesized using Eq. (3.1.2) and Eq. (3.1.3) Then, candidate feature points are searched along the normal direction of the vertices of the shape instance **s**. An edge-like points are searched in the early papers but later, linear local profile model is used to find the candidate feature points accurately. Once the candidate feature points are located, then new model parameters are computed as

$$\arg\min_{\mathbf{p},\mathbf{q}} \left\| \mathbf{s}' - M(\mathbf{s};\mathbf{p},\mathbf{q}) \right\|^2 ,$$

(3.1.4)

where the model parameters can be computed by linear least square estimation algorithm. Next, the new model parmameters are regarded as the initial model paramters of the next iteration. After the second step of each iteration, each shape parameter p_i is tested whether its absolution value is larger than $3\sigma_i$ (the σ_i means the standard deviation corresponding to the i-th shape paramter). If the absolution value is larger than $3\sigma_i$ then, the value is clipped not to exceed $3\sigma_i$. This clipping prevents the shape parameters become too large, which will result the synthesized model shape become too different from the shapes that are used in the training stage.

3.2 ACTIVE APPEARANCE MODELS

Active appearance models (AAMs) (Cootes and Edwards, 2001d; Matthews and Baker, 2004a) are generative, parametric models of certain visual phenomena that show both shape and appearance variations. These variations are represented by linear models that are obtained by applying the principal component analysis (PCA) to a set of collected example data. Although the original AAMs were based on 2D shape model, they are extended to incorporate 3D information such as faces moving across poses (Xiao et al.,

2004b; Hu et al., 2004). The most common application of AAMs has been face modeling (Edwards, et. al, 1998a, 1998b, 1998c) because they can represent the various face images using a compact set of parameters. This chapter briefly reviews the existing AAMs and their fitting algorithms.

3.2.1 2D Active Appearance Models

3.2.1.1 Shape Model

In 2D AAMs (Cootes and Edwards, 2001d; Matthews and Baker, 2004a), the 2D shape is represented by a triangulated 2D mesh with l vertices, which correspond to the salient points of the object. Mathematically, the shape vector $\mathbf{s}$ consists of the locations of the vertices that make up the mesh as

$$\mathbf{s} = (x_1, y_1, \ldots, x_l, y_l)^T. \tag{3.2.1}$$

In fact, the linear shape model of the AAM is exactly same with the PDM in the ASM except that there exists an pre-defined explicit mesh strucutre that is defined by the l vertices. Thus, the shape variation is expressed as a linear combination of a mean shape $\mathbf{s}_0$ and n shape bases $\mathbf{s}_i$ as

$$\mathbf{s} = \mathbf{s}_0 + \sum_{i=1}^{n} p_i \mathbf{s}_i, \tag{3.2.2}$$

where p_i are the shape parameters.

The overall procedure to build a shape model is same with the procedure of the ASM, where the training shapes are aligned using the Procrustes analysis (Cootes et al., 2001d) before PCA is applied to them and the PCA is only concerned with the local shape deformation. Fig. 3.2.1 illustrates an example of shape bases, where the five shape bases $\mathbf{s}_1$ to $\mathbf{s}_5$ are displayed over the mean shape $\mathbf{s}_0$.

3.2.1.2 Appearance Model

Once a mean shape $\mathbf{s}_0$ is obtained, the training images can be warped to the mean shape using the piece-wise affine warp (Matthews and Baker, 2004a) that is defined between the

Figure 3.2.1. An example of shape bases, $\mathbf{s}_1$ to $\mathbf{s}_5$ for a near frontal view face shape

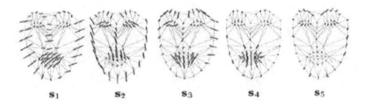

$\mathbf{s}_1$ $\mathbf{s}_2$ $\mathbf{s}_3$ $\mathbf{s}_4$ $\mathbf{s}_5$

corresponding triangles in the training image and the mean shape. These warped images are shape normalized images because they are warped to the same mesh s_0. Then, we can define the appearance as an shape normalized image $A(x)$ over the pixels x that belong to the mean shape s_0. The *appearance vector* consists of pixel intensities or color values of the appearance image arranged in lexicographical order. The appearance variation is expressed by the linear combination of a mean appearance $A_0(x)$ and m appearance bases $A_i(x)$ as

$$A(\mathbf{x}) = A_0(\mathbf{x}) + \sum_{i=1}^{m} \alpha_i A_i(\mathbf{x}), \tag{3.2.3}$$

where α_i are the appearance parameters.

As with the shape model, the appearance model is computed from a set of the manually landmarked training images by collecting the shape normalized images and applying PCA to them. The mean appearance $A_0(x)$ is the mean image of the shape normalized images and the appearance bases $A_i(x)$ are the m eivenvectors that correspond to the largest m eigenvalues. Fig. 3.2.2 illustrates an example appearance model, where the first five appearance basis images $A_1(x)$ to $A_5(x)$ are shown.

3.2.1.3 Combined vs. Independent Active Appearance Models

After Cootes and Edwards (2001d) first introduced the *combined* AAMs, Matthews and Baker (2004a) introduced *independent* AAMs. The difference is that the combined AAMs use the third PCA to the concatenated parameter vectors of the shape and appearance to utilize the correlation between the two sets of parameter vectors, while the independent AAMs treats the shape and appearance as the independent entities.

Therefore, the combined AAMs controls the appearance parameter α and shape parameter $\mathbf{p}$ using a single set of combined parameters β_i as

$$\begin{bmatrix} \mathbf{\Gamma}\boldsymbol{\alpha} \\ \mathbf{p} \end{bmatrix} = \mathbf{c}_0 + \sum_{i=1}^{k} \mathbf{c}_i \beta_i, \tag{3.2.4}$$

where $\mathbf{c}_0$ and $\mathbf{c}_i$ are the mean and ith basis vector of the combined parameter vector $\mathbf{c}$ that are obtained by applying the PCA to the combined parameter vectors and Γ is a scaled diagonal matrix to balance the different dynamic ranges of the appearance and shape parameter vectors.

This chapter focuses on the independent AAMs because it provides the clear mathematical derivations for the gradient descent fitting algorithms than the combined AAMs, where the latter uses ad hoc gradient descent fitting algorithm.

Figure 3.2.2. Examples of the five appearance bases, $A_1(x)$ to $A_5(x)$

3.2.1.4 Synthesizing Model Instance

As mentioned earlier, the AAMs are generative model. So, AAMs provide a way of synthesizing an AAM instance from the given model parameters. The synthesis is done in three steps. First, the shape normalized appearance is generated using Eq. (3.2.3) on the base shape $\mathbf{s}_0$. Second, the target shape is generated using Eq. (3.2.2) Third, the appearance on the base shape is warped to the target shape using the piece-wise affine warping.

In the second step, the 2D shape model that is used to generate the target shape cannot represent the scaling, rotation, and translation of the target shape because such variation is removed before applying the PCA to obtain the shape bases. To represent the removed scaling, rotation, and translation in the target image, extra parameters must be incorporated to the AAM. They can be incorporated by adding four special shape bases to the 2D shape model as $\mathbf{s}_{n+1} = \mathbf{s}_0 = (x_0^1, y_0^1, \ldots, x_0^l, y_0^l)'$, $\mathbf{s}_{n+2} = (-y_0^1, x_0^1, \ldots, -y_0^l, x_0^l)'$, $\mathbf{s}_{n+3} = (1^1, 0^1, \ldots, 1^l, 0^l)'$, $\mathbf{s}_{n+4} = (0^1, 1^1, \ldots, 0^l, 1^l)'$, where x_0^j and y_0^j are the jth components of x and y coordinate of the mean shape $\mathbf{s}_0$, respectively. The extra shape parameters $\mathbf{q} = (p_{n+1}, \cdots, p_{n+4})'$ represent the similarity transformation, where the first two parameters (p_{n+1}, p_{n+2}) are related to the scale and rotation, and the last two parameters (p_{n+3}, p_{n+4}) are the translations along the x and y coordinates, respectively (Matthews and Baker, 2004a).

3.2.1.5 Fitting Active Appearance Models

The problem of fitting a 2D AAM to a given image can be formulated as a searching of the appearance and shape parameters of an AAM that minimizes the following error

$$E = \sum_{x \in s_0} [\sum_{i=0}^{m} \alpha_i A_i(x) - I(W(x; p))]^2,$$
(3.2.5)

where $\alpha_0 = 1$ and W(**x**;**p**) transforms the coordinate **x** in the base shape $\mathbf{s}_0$ to the corresponding location in the target image.

Various gradient descent fitting algorithms have been proposed (Gross et al., 2003), which are extended from the LK image matching algorithm (Kanade and Lucas, 1981). Among these methods, we review the inverse compositional simultaneous update (ICSI) algorithm, which is known to show the best convergence performance and the inverse compositional project out (ICPO) algorithm, which is faster than the ICSI algorithm.

Inverse Compositional Simultaneous Update Algorithm

The *ICSI* algorithm is derived by applying the Taylor expansion to the following equation:

$$E = \sum_{\mathbf{x} \in \mathbf{s}_0} \left[\sum_{i=0}^{m} (\Delta\alpha_i + \alpha_i) A_i(\mathbf{W}(\mathbf{x};; \Delta\mathbf{p})) - I(W(\mathbf{x};; \mathbf{p}))\right]^2,$$
(3.2.6)

which is re-written Eq. (3.2.5), and the update of model parameters $\Delta\boldsymbol{\theta}^T = \{\Delta\mathbf{p}^T, \Delta\boldsymbol{\alpha}^T\}$ are computed as

$$\Delta\mathbf{\theta} = \left\{ \sum_{\mathbf{x} \in \mathbf{s}_0} \mathbf{SD}_{su}^T(\mathbf{x}) \mathbf{SD}_{su}(\mathbf{x}) \right\}^{-1} \sum_{\mathbf{x} \in \mathbf{s}_0} \mathbf{SD}_{su}^T(\mathbf{x}) E(\mathbf{x}) \qquad (3.2.7)$$

$$\mathbf{SD}_{su}(\mathbf{x}) = \left[\nabla A(\mathbf{x};;\mathbf{\alpha})^T \frac{\partial \mathbf{W}}{\partial \mathbf{p}}, A_1(\mathbf{x}), \dots, A_m(\mathbf{x}) \right], \qquad (3.2.8)$$

where $\mathbf{SD}_{su}(\mathbf{x})$ represents the steepest descent vector of the model parameters θ. The warping parameters and appearance parameters are updated as $\mathbf{W}(\mathbf{x}; \mathbf{p}) \leftarrow \mathbf{W}(\mathbf{x}; \mathbf{p}) \circ \mathbf{W}(\mathbf{x}; \Delta\mathbf{p})^{-1}$, and $\mathbf{\alpha} \leftarrow \mathbf{\alpha} + \Delta\mathbf{\alpha}$, respectively. The ICSI algorithm is slow because $\mathbf{SD}_{su}(\mathbf{x})$ in Eq. (3.2.7) depends on the varying parameters and must be recomputed at every iterations; The Hessian computation step is the most time consuming part of LK algorithms.

Inverse Compositional Project out Algorithm

The *ICPO* algorithm utilizes the orthogonal property of appearance bases, which enables the error term in Eq. (3.2.5) to be decomposed into sums of two squared error terms as in (Moghaddam and Pentland, 1997):

$$\left\| A_0 + \sum_{i=1}^m \alpha_i A_i - I^W(\mathbf{p}) \right\|_{span(A_i)}^2 + \left\| A_0 + \sum_{i=1}^m \alpha_i A_i - I^W(\mathbf{p}) \right\|_{span(A_i)^\perp}^2, \qquad (3.2.9)$$

where $I^W(\mathbf{p})$ means the vector representation of backward warped image.

The first term is defined in the subspace $span(A_i)$ that is spanned by the orthogonal appearance bases and the second term is defined in the subspace $span(A_i)^\perp$ that is orthogonal complement subspace. For any warping parameter $\mathbf{p}$, the minimum value of the first term is always zero because the term $\sum a_i A_i$ can represent any vector in $span(A_i)$. Therefore, the optimal appearance parameters can be easily computed using Eq. (5.2.3) after finding the optimal shape parameters $\mathbf{p}$. The second error term can be optimized with respect to $\mathbf{p}$ using an image matching algorithm such as the *inverse compositional Lucas Kanade* (ICLK) algorithm. Because the ICLK image matching algorithm requires just one computation of the steepest descent vector $SD(\mathbf{x})$ and the Gauss-Newton Hessian $\sum_{\mathbf{x}} SD^T(\mathbf{x}) SD(\mathbf{x})$, optimization can be done very efficiently (Gross et al., 2003).

However, the ICPO algorithm uses the steepest descent vectors and fixed Hessian matrix during iterations. This approximation is derived from the property of the orthogonality of the appearance bases and the assumption that all the appearance variations do not remain in the reconstructed image of the backward warped image although the alignment is not correct (Matthews and Baker, 2004). This assumption is usually not true. Therefore, the ICPO algorithm is the fastest algorithm among the gradient based fitting algorithms, it shows a poor fitting accuracy when compared to the ICSI algorithm. Furthermore, when the AAM is applied to model a human face, the fitting accuracy of ICPO algorithm gets worse as we include more people in the training data. See the references (Gross et. al, 2003; Gross et al. 2004b) for more detailed performance comparisons.

3.2.2 2D+3D Active Appearance Models

The 2D AAMs has been extended to model 3D shape of the object by many researchers. Xiao et al. (2004b) have proposed the *combined 2D+3D AAMs* that have an additional 3D shape model. They also proposed an efficient fitting algorithm of 2D+3D AAM by adding 3D constraints to the cost function of independent 2D AAMs. The new constraints make the 2D shape model to be a valid projection of the 3D shape model. Although the 2D shape model is built from the legal face shape data, it can generate the arbitrary shapes that do look like the face shape.

Fig. 3.2.3 shows some examples of the shapes that are generated from 2D shape model by randomly setting the shape parameters p_i. In the figure, (a)-(b) are the results when the variation of the shape parameters are limited to 3 standard deviation, and (c)-(d) are the results when the shape parameters are limited to 10 standard deviation. Usually, the shape parameters are clipped not to exceed the range of 3 standard deviations. However, Fig. 3.2.3 (a)-(b) shows that this clipping is not enough to maintain the 2D shape as a reasonable face shape.

To overcome this situation, they added the 3D constraints which reduce the number of iterations and improves the convergence performance. Furthermore, the fitting algorithm is fast because it is based on the efficient fitting algorithm of 2D AAMs (ICPO) and the added 3D constraints are computed over the 2D shape points not over the pixels. Hu et al. (2004) proposed another extension of 2D+3D AAM fitting algorithm, called multi-view AAM (MVAAM) fitting algorithm that fits a single 2D+3D AAM to multiple view images that are obtained from multiple affine cameras simultaneously.

The 2D+3D AAMs can be understood as a simplified version of 3D Morphable Models (MMs) (Blanz and Vetter, 1999). Both models use the independent two linear models to represent the variations of the 3D shape and appearance of the 3D object. In addition, they are the generative parametric models and define the error as the difference between the synthesized model image and the target image. However, 3D MMs optimize the 3D shape parameters directly with respect to the error, while 2D+3D AAMs optimize 2D shape parameters with respect to the error and the 3D shape model is used just to add the 3D constraints on the 2D shape parameters.

A 3D shape $\bar{\mathbf{s}}$ of an object is represented by a triangulated 3D mesh with $\bar{l}$ 3D vertices, which correspond to the landmark points of the 2D shape. The 3D shape variation is represented by the linear model as in the 2D shape model. Therefore, a 3D shape $\mathbf{s} = (x_1, y_1, z_1, ..., x_{\bar{l}}, y_{\bar{l}}, z_{\bar{l}})^T$ can be represented by a combination of a mean shape $\bar{\mathbf{s}}_0$ and the orthogonal shape basis $\bar{\mathbf{s}}_i$:

Figure 3.2.3. Examples of unreasonable face shapes

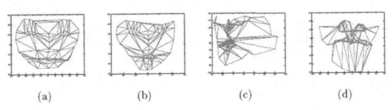

(a)   (b)   (c)   (d)

$$\bar{\mathbf{s}} = \mathbf{s}_0 + \sum\nolimits_{i=1}^{\bar{n}} \bar{p}_i \mathbf{s}_i$$

(3.2.10)

where $\bar{p}_i$ are 3D shape parameters and $\bar{n}$ is the number of 3D shape bases.

A 2D shape of an AAM is the projected shape of a rotated and translated 3D shape as

$$\mathbf{s} = P(M(\mathbf{s}; \mathbf{q}))$$

(3.2.11)

where P represents a camera projection function that models the imaging process and M represents a rigid transformation (3D rotation and 3D translation) of the 3D shape. Using the *exponential map* representation, a rigid transformation can be parameterized by 6 element vector as $\bar{\mathbf{q}} = (w_x, w_y, w_z, t_x, t_y, t_z)$, where each element describe the 3D rotation angles with respect to three axes and 3D translation (Xiao and Kanade, 2002).

Because the 2D shape of an AAM must be the 2D projected shape of a 3D shape, we can impose the following constraints on 2D shape parameters using 3D shape model as

$$\| W(\sum\nolimits_{i=0}^{n} p_i \mathbf{s}_i; \mathbf{q}) - P(M(\sum\nolimits_{i=0}^{\bar{n}} \bar{p}_i \bar{\mathbf{s}}_i; \bar{\mathbf{q}})) \|^2 = 0.$$

(3.2.12)

These constraints on the 2D AAM shape parameters $\mathbf{p}$ mean that there exist the legitimate values of $\mathbf{p}$ and $\mathbf{q}$ such that the projected 2D shape equals the 2D shape of the AAMs. These 3D constraints are added to the AAM's objective function in Eq. (3.2.5) as

$$E_{2D+3Daam} = E(\mathbf{p}, \boldsymbol{\alpha}) + k \cdot F(\mathbf{p}, \mathbf{p}, \mathbf{q}),$$

(3.2.13)

where E, F, and k are the cost function of 2D AAM in Eq. (3.2.5), the 3D constraints in Eq. (3.2.12), and a weighing variable on the 3D constraints term, respectively.

In the above two sections, we briefly reviewed two important algorithms, ASM and AAM, because we intended to provide the main idea and characteristics of the algorithms as simple as possible. However, there exists many variations of the original ASM and AAM. For the ASM, Kernel PCA (Romdhani et al., 1999) or *ICA* (Üzümcü et al., 2003) have applied to improve the shape description power. For the AAM, many kinds of fitting algorithms are proposed such as constrained AAM (Cootes and Taylor, 2001a), compressed AAM using wavelet (Wolstenholme and Taylor, 1999), and so on.

There are lots of literatures that are related to the ASM and AAM. Tim Cootes provides good materials to understand the detailed algorithms and the recent developments in ASMs and AAMs on his homepage (http://www.isbe.man.ac.uk/~bim).

3.3 AAM WITH STEREO VISION

Using the 2D+3D AAM, we can estimate the 3D shape and pose (3D rotation and translation) of the face from a single image. However, we cannot guarantee that the estimated 3D shape is precise because the inverse projection from 2D image plane to 3D space is a singular problem; when a single view image is used we can know just the directions of the rays that passing through the center of camera and the 2D pixels in the image and thus, we cannot determine the depth of the 3D points along the rays. Hu et al. (2004) proposed a fitting algorithm that fits a 2D+3D AAM to multiple view image, which we call multi-view AAM (MVAAM) fitting algorithm. The MVAAM fitting algorithm can remove the singularity problem that occurs when a single view image is used. However, the MVAAM algorithm assumed that the multiple cameras are independent, i.e., the multiple cameras had their own pose parameters and they are not constrained to be consistent between each other.

The inconsistency between the mutlple views can be alleviated by imposing more strict constrains than the 3D costraints of the MVAAM using the camera calibration information. Recent research on this approach showed that such strict constraints improve the fitting performance. Koterba et al. (2005) studied how the multiple cameras can be calibrated using the MVAAM fitting results for the weak perspective camera model and showed the effect of imposing the calibration information to the MVAAM fitting algorithm. Sung and Kim (2004, 2006d, 2006e) proposed a stereo AAM (STAAM) fitting algorithm, which is an extension of the 2D+3D AAM fitting algorithm for a calibrated stereo vision system, where calibrated multiple perspective camera models are used.

If the geometrical relationship, which is explained by the calibration information, between two cameras are known, we can reduce the number of model parameters by using one reference 3D coordinate system and one set of pose parameters, which reduces the degree of freedom in the model parameters effectively, and improves the accuracy and speed of fitting. Furthermore, the STAAM algorithm can estimate the full 6 rigid motion parameters of the head and estimate the Euclid structure of 3D shape of the face because it uses the perspective projection model. When the weak perspective projection model is used, only the affine 3D structure can be obtained.

3.3.1 Multi-View 2D+3D AAM: MVAAM

The *multi-view 2D+3D AAM* algorithm extends the existing 2D+3D AAM (Xiao et. al, 2004b) to multiple view environment where we can acquire multiple images from multiple view points looking at the same object. It is known that fitting on multiple images provides better convergence performance because information from multiple images can be integrated and the relationship of the 2D shapes in multiple views can be used to constrain the shape parameters (Hu et al., 2004; Cootes et al., 2001c).

Assume that we have two identical cameras looking an object in two different positions. The 2D shapes from each view looks different but are closely related because they are differently projected from an identical 3D shape. By this close relation, the MVAAM shares the 3D shape parameters among two different 2D shapes (Hu et al., 2004).

The 3D constraints in the MVAAM can be written as

$$\sum_{j=1}^{N} \| W(\sum_{i=0}^{n} p_i^j \mathbf{s}_i; \mathbf{q}^j) - P(M(\sum_{i=0}^{\bar{n}} \bar{p}_i \bar{\mathbf{s}}_i; \bar{\mathbf{q}}^j)) \|^2 = 0, \tag{3.3.1}$$

where j and N are the camera index and the number of cameras, respectively. As you can see, the 3D shape parameters $\bar{p}_i$ ($i = 1, 2, \cdots, \bar{n}$) eliminate the view index j because all different views share the 3D shape parameters. The cost function of the MVAAM fitting algorithm can be written as

$$E_{mvaam} = \sum_{j=1}^{N} \{ E^j(\mathbf{p}^j, \mathbf{q}^j, \mathbf{a}^j) + K \cdot F^j(\mathbf{p}^j, \mathbf{q}^j, \bar{\mathbf{q}}^j, \bar{\mathbf{p}}) \}. \tag{3.3.2}$$

3.3.2 Stereo AAM: STAAM

If we know the geometric relationship between cameras, we can enforce more strict constraints to 2D shape parameters than those of the 2D+3D AAMs. Consider two cameras whose geometric relationship is known. Then, a 3D coordinate in the reference camera can be transformed into a 3D coordinate in the other camera using the known 3D rigid transformation between two cameras. Fig. 3.3.1 shows a configuration of a stereo vision system with two cameras. There are three coordinate systems where $C1$, $C2$, and 0 correspond to the first camera, the second camera $C2$, and an object 0, respectively. The parameters $\overline{\mathbf{q}}^1$, $\overline{\mathbf{q}}^2$, and $\overline{\mathbf{q}}^{1,2}$ represent the 3D rigid transformations from 0 to the $C1$, from 0 to $C1$, and from $C1$ to $C2$, respectively. The parameters $\overline{\mathbf{q}}^1$ and $\overline{\mathbf{q}}^2$ change as the object moves while the values of $\overline{\mathbf{q}}^{1,2}$ are fixed.

For a given 3D shape $\overline{\mathbf{s}}$, the 2D shape projected to the first view image, $\mathbf{s}^1$, is

$$\mathbf{s}^1 = P(M(\overline{\mathbf{s}};\overline{\mathbf{q}}^1)), \tag{3.3.3}$$

and the 2D shape projected to the second view image, $\mathbf{s}^2$, is

$$\mathbf{s}^2 = P(M(\overline{\mathbf{s}};\overline{\mathbf{q}}^2)) = P(M(M(\overline{\mathbf{s}};\overline{\mathbf{q}}^1);\overline{\mathbf{q}}^{1,2})). \tag{3.3.4}$$

Because $\overline{\mathbf{q}}^{1,2}$ is a constant vector, $\mathbf{s}^2$ depends on the only 3D rigid transformation parameter vector $\overline{\mathbf{q}}^1$. Generally, we can determine the 2D shape in the j-th view image using the 3D rigid transformation parameter vector of the reference camera $\overline{\mathbf{q}}^1$ and the 3D rigid transformation parameter vector between the reference and the jth camera $\overline{\mathbf{q}}^{1,j}$, which is a constant vector. So, we can share the 3D rigid transformation vector among different views, which means that one set of 3D rigid transformation vector is required. In STAAM, the constraint function can be rewritten as

$$\sum_{j=1}^{N} \| W(\sum_{i=0}^{n} p_i^j \mathbf{s}_i;\mathbf{q}^j) - P(M(\sum_{i=0}^{\overline{n}} \overline{p}_i \overline{\mathbf{s}}_i;\overline{\mathbf{q}}^{1,j} \circ \overline{\mathbf{q}})) \|^2 = 0, \tag{3.3.5}$$

where $M(\cdot;\overline{\mathbf{q}}^{1,j} \circ \overline{\mathbf{q}})$ is a different notation of $M(M(\cdot;\overline{\mathbf{q}});\overline{\mathbf{q}}^{1,j})$. In Eq. (3.3.5), $\overline{\mathbf{q}}^{1,j}$ is always a constant vector and $\overline{\mathbf{q}}$ is a rigid transformation parameter vector to be estimated with respect to the first camera. As you can see, the 3D rigid transformation vectors $\overline{\mathbf{q}}^j (j=1,2,\cdot,N)$ eliminate the view index j because all different views share the 3D rigid transformation vectors.

The cost function of the STAAM can be written as

$$E_{staam} = \sum_{j=1}^{N} \{E(\mathbf{p}^j,\mathbf{q}^j,\mathbf{a}^j) + K \cdot F^j(\mathbf{p}^j,\mathbf{q}^j,\overline{\mathbf{q}},\overline{\mathbf{p}})\}, \tag{3.3.6}$$

where the constraint function F have j index because the fixed geometric relationship $\overline{\mathbf{q}}^{1,2}$ between the reference camera and j-th camera, which is different at each view, is absorbed in the constraint function.

We explain how the geometric information eliminate the ambiguity in MVAAM more intuitively. We assume that two camera positions are fixed and they are looking an identical 3D shape as in Fig. 3.3.1. For a pair of 2D shapes observed in two view, there exist one-to-one mapping function from a 2D shape in one view to a 2D shape in the other view. For a

Figure 3.3.1. Stereo vision system

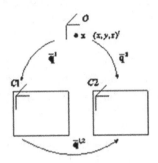

2D shape in a reference view, can any other 2D shape that is different from the physically observed 2D shape be observed in the other view ? It is impossible. The mapping function is dependent on the geometric configuration of the two cameras. However, The MVAAM algorithm allows the 3D rigid transformation parameters in each view to converge freely irrespective of other view, thus one-to-many correspondence between the fitted two 2D shapes are possible. In STAAM, this situation does not happen because the geometric relationships between the reference camera and the other cameras are fixed and the view dependent rigid transformation parameters in MVAAM are replaced by one set of rigid transformation parameters in the reference view.

When compared to the MVAAM, STAAM have the following properties, (1) more strict constraints are enforced to the 2D shape parameters enforcing one-to-one correspondence between the 2D shapes in each view, (2) full 6 rigid transformation parameters of the object can be estimated more correctly, (3) the number of model parameters are reduced by eliminating the view dependent rigid transformation parameters (4) the euclid structure of a 3D shape can be estimated while the MVAAM can estimate the 3D shape up to scale.

Stereo AAM is similar to coupled-view AAM (CVAAM) (Cootes et. al, 2001c) in that the fixed geometric relationships of the cameras are utilized. However, CVAAM does not involve 3D shape model. As a result, CVAAM cannot estimate 3D shape of the object and pose parameters (rotation angles) are estimated using an extra regression model. Moreover, CVAAM must rebuild its concatenated 2D shape model and appearance model if the relative positions of the cameras are changed.

3.3.3 Experimental Results and Discussion

To compare the fitting performance of MVAAM and STAAM, we fitted the identical images using two different algorithms from identical initial conditions and compared the fitting results. We selected 80 images from database (20 people × 4 expressions × 2 images = 80 images) and manually landmarked on both the left and right images. We obtained 2D and 3D model parameters from these data and the number of shape and appearance bases were determined to keep 95% of variation.

For each image, we computed the p^* and q^* parameter from the ground truth shape that is manually landmarked. The shape parameter p^* was perturbed such that the ith component is perturbed by $\sqrt{\lambda_i} * \sigma$, where λ_i is the eigenvalue of the linear 2D shape model. The similar transform parameter vector q^* was perturbed such that the scale, rotation, and translation values are perturbed by the Gaussian noises whose standard deviations were 0.1, 0.05 radian, 2, and 2 for scale, 0.05 for scale, rotation, horizontal translation, and vertical translation, respectively. This perturbation was done over the left and right view image independently. The 3D shape parameters $\bar{p}$ and $\bar{q}$ were initialized from these perturbed 2D AAM parameters.

Fig. 3.3.2 shows the histogram of RMS error, where the horizontal and vertical axes represent the RMS positional errors between the fitted shape and the ground truth shape in terms of pixel size and the frequency of occurrence. From this figure, we know that the RMS position error of the STAAM is smaller than that of MVAAM, where their mean values are 2 and 6 pixels, approximately.

Table 3.3.1 shows the average number of iterations and the standard deviation of the two fitting algorithms. From this table, we know that (1) the average number of iterations of the STAMM is smaller than that of the MVAAM, where the average number of iterations are 26.4 and 29.6, respectively, and (2) the STAMM shows higher standard deviation than the MVAAM, which means there is a higher chance to be reached at the convergence within a smaller number of iterations in the case of the STAMM.

Fig. 3.3.3 shows a typical example of the fitting results of the two algorithms, where the upper and lower two pictures are the fitted results of MVAAM and STAAM, respectively. In the case of MVAAM, the left view image shows a successful convergence but the right view image shows a failed convergence. In the case of STAAM, both view images show the successful convergence. All these fitting results come from the fact that the constraints of the STAAM are more strict than those of the MVAAM.

3.4 A VIEW-BASED AAM APPROACH FOR POSE-INVARIANT REPRESENTATION

Although the AAM is well suited for face image analysis, it is difficult to apply the AAM when the face changes its pose largely. When the face turn to profile view, some of the landmark points that consist of the 2D shape model become invisible, which violate the requirement of the conventional AAM that the topology of the shape model must be consistent. To deal with the pose problem, several approaches have been introduced. Cootes et al. (2002) proposed using several face models to fit an input image. They estimated the pose of an input face image by a regression technique and then fit the input face image to the face model which is close to the estimated pose. However, their approach requires pose estimation, which is another difficult problem, since the pose estimation might cause an incorrect result when the appearance of the test face image is slightly different from the training images due to different lighting conditions or different facial expressions. Gross et al. (2004a) built one copy of the shape and appearance model from a set of landmarked data that contains front view and profile view image data using principal compoent analysis with missing data (PCAMD) technique. To fit the model to arbitrarily posed face image, they adapted occlusion handling mechanism that ignores invisible parts of the face.

We propose an extension of the 2D+3D AAM to a view based approach for pose-robust face tracking. Since the view-based approach uses several 2D face image models, some additional work is needed. First, we use the *principal component analysis with missing data (PCAMD)* technique to obtain the 2D and 3D shape basis vectors since some face

Figure 3.3.2. Comparison of convergence performance in terms of positional RMS error

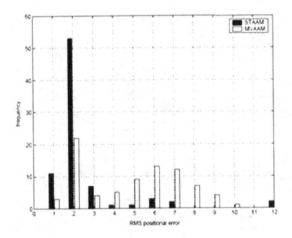

models have missing data. Second, we devise an appropriate model selection for the input face image. Our model selection method uses the pose angle that is estimated from the 2D+3D AAM directly.

3.4.1 Principal Component Analysis with Missing Data

Computer vision often uses the PCA technique (Duda et al., 2000). The conventional PCA assumes that all data components are complete. Unfortunately, the data may be incomplete in practical applications. According to multivariate statistics (Dodge, 1985), we usually replace the missing data with a specific value if the amount of missing data is small. However, this approach does not work well if a significant portion of the measurement matrix is unobserved or missing. To overcome this problem, robust statistics are employed in many papers. Here, we use the PCAMD technique (Shum et. al, 1995) to handle the missing data.

Suppose that we have a $d \times n$ measurement matrix $\mathbf{Y}$ whose rank is r and the measurement matrix is completely filled; d and n are the dimension and the number of data. Then, the PCA tries to find $\widetilde{\mathbf{U}}, \widetilde{\mathbf{S}}$ and $\widetilde{\mathbf{V}}$ that minimize the residual error given by

$$E_{PCA} = \left\| \mathbf{Y} - \mathbf{1}\mu^t - \widetilde{\mathbf{U}}\widetilde{\mathbf{S}}\widetilde{\mathbf{V}}^t \right\|^2 , \qquad (3.4.1)$$

where $\widetilde{\mathbf{U}}$ and $\widetilde{\mathbf{V}}$ are the $d \times r$ and the $n \times r$ matrices with orthogonal columns. $\widetilde{\mathbf{S}} = diag(\sigma_i)$ is a $r \times r$ diagonal matrix, μ is the maximum likelihood approximation of the mean vector,

Table 3.3.1. Comparison of convergence performance in terms of the number of iterations

Fitting algorithm	STAAM	MVAAM
average number of iterations	26.4	29.6
standard deviation	5.6	1.4

Figure 3.3.3. An illustrative example of the fitted results of two different AAMs

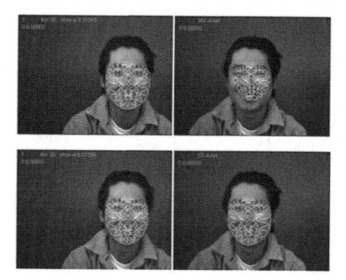

and $\mathbf{1} = (1_1,\ldots,1_d)^t$ is an *n*-tuple with all ones. The solution of this problem can be solved by the SVD of the centered data matrix $\mathbf{Y} - \mathbf{1}\boldsymbol{\mu}^t$.

However, when the measurement matrix is incomplete, the error minimization problem is modified to consider only the observed data, giving

$$min \quad \psi = \frac{1}{2}\sum_I (Y_{ij} - \mu_i - \mathbf{u}_i^t \mathbf{v}_j)^2, \tag{3.4.2}$$

where $I = \{(i,j): Y_{ij}\, is\, observed, 1 i d, 1 j n\}$ and $\mathbf{u}_i$ and $\mathbf{v}_j$ are the column vectors that satisfy the following relations:

$$\begin{bmatrix} \mathbf{u}_1^t \\ \ldots \\ \mathbf{u}_d^t \end{bmatrix} = \widetilde{\mathbf{U}}\widetilde{\mathbf{S}}^{\frac{1}{2}}, \begin{bmatrix} \mathbf{v}_1^t \\ \ldots \\ \mathbf{v}_n^t \end{bmatrix} = \widetilde{\mathbf{V}}\widetilde{\mathbf{S}}^{\frac{1}{2}} \tag{3.4.3}$$

There are at most $r(d + n - r)$ independent elements from LU decomposition of a $d \times n$ matrix of rank r. Hence, a necessary condition for obtaining a unique solution of Eq. (3.4.2) is that the number of observable elements in $\mathbf{Y}$ should be greater than $mr(d + n - r)$. To obtain a more stable solution for Eq. (3.4.2), either the left matrix $\widetilde{\mathbf{U}}$ or the right matrix $\widetilde{\mathbf{V}}$ should be normalized; the norm of column vector should be equal to 1.

If we write the measurement matrix $\mathbf{Y}$ as a *m*-dimensional vector $\mathbf{y}$ then, the minimization problem can be re-written as

$$min \quad \psi = \frac{1}{2}\mathbf{f}^t\mathbf{f}, \tag{3.4.4}$$

where

$$\mathbf{f} = \mathbf{y} - \boldsymbol{\mu} - \mathbf{B}u = \mathbf{y} - \mathbf{G}\widetilde{\mathbf{v}}, \tag{3.4.5}$$

and

$$\mathbf{u} = \begin{bmatrix} \mathbf{u}_1 \\ \dots \\ \mathbf{u}_d \end{bmatrix}, \widetilde{\mathbf{v}} = \begin{bmatrix} \widetilde{\mathbf{v}}_1 \\ \dots \\ \widetilde{\mathbf{v}}_n \end{bmatrix}, \widetilde{\mathbf{v}}_i = \begin{bmatrix} \mathbf{v}_i^t & \mu_i^t \end{bmatrix}, \tag{3.4.6}$$

where $\mathbf{B}$ and $\mathbf{G}$ are the $m \times rn$ and $m \times (r + 1)d$ matrices that are determined by $\widetilde{\mathbf{v}}$ and $\mathbf{y}$.

In order to solve the minimization problem of Eq. (3.4.4), we set the derivatives of Eq. (3.4.7) with respective to $\mathbf{u}$ and $\widetilde{\mathbf{v}}$ to zero:

$$\dot{\psi} = \begin{bmatrix} \mathbf{B}'\mathbf{B}u - \mathbf{B}'(\mathbf{y} - \boldsymbol{\mu}) \\ \mathbf{G}'\mathbf{G}\widetilde{\mathbf{v}} - \mathbf{G}'\mathbf{y} \end{bmatrix} = 0 . \tag{3.4.7}$$

Obviously, Eq. (3.4.7) is nonlinear because $\mathbf{B}$ and $\mathbf{G}$ are functions of $\widetilde{\mathbf{v}}$ and $\mathbf{u}$, respectively. Although we can solve the problem using a nonlinear optimization method that requires a huge amount of computation, we take a simple PCAMD algorithm that computes the least square solutions of $\mathbf{u}$ and $\widetilde{\mathbf{v}}$ iteratively. The overall procedure of PCAMD is given in Table 3.4.1.

3.4.2. View-Based 2D+3D AAM

As mentioned earlier, the performance of human face tracking degrades as the pose deviates from the frontal face. Also, it is not sufficient for all of the posed face images because a general face model cannot cover all possible poses. To overcome this problem, a view-based approach use multiple face models that are constructed from multiple views independently and select an appropriate face model for an input face image. In this work, we extend the 2D+3D AAM to a view-based approach. For simplicity, only the rotation around the vertical axis (yaw) is explained, but this can easily be extended to rotation around the horizontal axis (pitch).

3.4.2.1 Model Construction

To build a view-based 2D+3D model, a set of training face images is needed that consists of several hand-labeled feature points. The feature points are marked manually and all training face images are divided into three pose face image sets, Frontal, Left and Right face. For each pose training set, we apply the model construction procedure independently in order to construct 2D shape, 2D appearance, and 3D shape models for a view-based 2D+3D AAM as described below.

View-based_2D+3D AAM

- Collect the training images and mark the feature points manually.
- Divide the training images into three pose sets.

For each pose
-   Perform a 2D alignment with the marked feature points.
-   For 2D shape model
    1) Apply PCAMD to the aligned feature points and obtain the 2D mean shape $\mathbf{s}_0^v$ and the 2D shape basis vectors $\mathbf{s}_i^v$:

    $$\mathbf{s}^v = \mathbf{s}_0^v + \sum_{i=1}^{l^v} p_i^v \mathbf{s}_i^v, \qquad (3.4.8)$$

    where v denotes the v-th view and p_i^v is the i-th 2D shape parameter.
    2) Warp the training images from the shape $\mathbf{s}$ to the mean shape $\mathbf{s}_0$ using a piece-wise warping $W(x; p)$:

    $$\begin{bmatrix} x_i & x_j & x_k \\ y_i & y_j & y_k \\ 1 & 1 & 1 \end{bmatrix} = \begin{bmatrix} p_1 & p_3 & p_5 \\ p_2 & p_4 & p_6 \\ 0 & 0 & 1 \end{bmatrix} \begin{bmatrix} x_i^0 & x_j^0 & x_k^0 \\ y_i^0 & y_j^0 & y_k^0 \\ 1 & 1 & 1 \end{bmatrix}, \qquad (3.4.9)$$

    where $\mathbf{x}$ is a mesh point and $p_1, p_2, \ldots, p_6$ are the warping parameters. An original triangular mesh $\{(x_i^0, y_i^0), (x_j^0, y_j^0), (x_k^0, y_k^0)\}$ is warped to a
    destination mesh $\{(x_i, y_i), (x_j, y_j), (x_k, y_k)\}$ by the piece-wise warping.
-   For 2D appearance model
    1) Apply PCAMD to the warped images and obtain the 2D mean appearance A_0^v and the 2D appearance basis vectors A_i^v:

    $$A^v = A_0^v + \sum_{i=1}^{m^v} \alpha_i^v A_i^v, \qquad (3.4.10)$$

    where v denotes the v-th view and α_i^v is the i-th 2D appearance parameter.
    2) Perform a stereo matching on two corresponding 2D shapes and obtain a depth map from them. Then, obtain a 3D shape from the 2D shape and the depth map.
-   For 3D shape model
    1) Apply PCAMD to the aligned 3D shapes and obtain the 3D mean shape $\bar{\mathbf{s}}_0^v$ and the 3D shape vectors $\bar{\mathbf{s}}_i^v$:

Table 3.4.1. Procedure of the principal component analysis with missing data

(1) Initialize $\tilde{\mathbf{v}}$.
(2) For a given $\tilde{\mathbf{v}}$, build the matrix $\mathbf{B}$ and the mean vector μ. Then, update $\mathbf{u}$ using a least squares solution $\mathbf{u} = \mathbf{B}^+(\mathbf{y} - \mu)$, where $\mathbf{B}^+$ is the pseudo inverse of $\mathbf{B}$.
(3) For a given $\mathbf{u}$, build the matrix $\mathbf{G}$. Then update $\tilde{\mathbf{v}}$ using a least square solution
$\tilde{\mathbf{v}} = \mathbf{G}^+\mathbf{y}$, where $\mathbf{G}^+$ is the pseudo inverse of $\mathbf{G}$.
(4) Repeat the steps (2) and (3) until both $\mathbf{u}$ and $\tilde{\mathbf{v}}$ converge.

$$\overline{\mathbf{s}}^v = \overline{\mathbf{s}}_0^v + \int_{i=1}^{n^v} \overline{\mathbf{p}}_i^v \overline{\mathbf{s}}_i^v, \tag{3.4.11}$$

where v denotes the v-th view and $\overline{\mathbf{p}}_i^v$ is the i-th 3D shape parameter.

3.4.2.2 Model Selection

Since we have several face models that are built from different views, we need a method to select the appropriate model for a unknown input image. Cootes et al. (2002) suggested to estimate the pose angle of an input image, in which a regression is used to estimate the pose angle. Then, they select the face model that is the closest to the estimated pose. In this work, the pose angle is directly obtained from the input image using 2D+3D AAM. When an input image fits to 2D+3D AAM, 3D rigid transformation in the parameterized vector $q = (w_x, w_y, w_z, t_x, t_y, t_z)$ provides estimates around 3D rotation angle and 3D translation. Fig. 3.4.1 shows a pose angle distribution of three different posed face images, assuming a Gaussian distribution.

Once we obtain a distribution of the pose angles of the training face images, we can infer the cover range of the pose angle in each face model and compute the threshold pose angle to be used for selecting the face model. For example, we consider three different posed face models: Left, Frontal, and Right face model. We assume that two threshold face angles τ_1, and τ_2 are determined appropriately to change from left to frontal and from the frontal to right face model. Then, the model selection method can be written as

Current Model = Left-Model, if $\hat{\phi} < \tau_1$,
Current Model = Frontal-Model, if $\hat{\phi} >= \tau_1$ and $\hat{\phi} < \tau_2$,
Current Model = Right-Model, if $\hat{\phi} >= \tau_2$,

where $\hat{\phi}$ is the estimated pose angle of an input image.

However, this simple model selection method does not work well because there is a gap of the estimated pose angle between two adjacent models as shown in Fig. 3.4.2, where the horizontal and vertical axis denote the ground truth and the estimated pose angle by the 2D+3D AAM. Ideally, these two values should be equal as shown by the dotted line. However, the estimation characteristics of two face models are not equal to each other. The frontal face model is accurate around the frontal face image but the estimated pose angle becomes smaller than the ground truth as the true pose approaches to $\phi = T$. In contrast, the right face model is accurate around the right posed face image but the estimated pose angle becomes larger than the ground truth as the true pose approaches to $\phi = T$. Fig. 3.4.2 illustrates that the different estimation characteristics of each face model produces the gap $\Delta\hat{\phi} = \hat{\phi}_R(T) - \hat{\phi}_F(T)$ between the estimated pose angles of two face models, where $\hat{\phi}_F(T)$ and $\hat{\phi}_R(T)$ are the pose angles estimated by the frontal and right face model at $\phi = T$.

When the face model changes from frontal to right at the pose angle $\phi = T$, the right face model experiences as if it is located at the pose angle $\phi = T$, where T is determined such that $\hat{\phi}_R(T) = \hat{\phi}_T(T)$, which is far from the real pose angle T. To overcome the pose angle discrepancy between two different face models, we examined how to select an appropriate face model and determine the threshold pose angles where the face model changes. In this work, we consider the following four model selection methods.

Method I - Using Two Competitive Models

This method divides the range of pose angles into several areas: certain and ambiguous areas. Fig. 3.4.3 (a) illustrates the certain and ambiguous areas, where the estimated pose angles τ_1 and τ_2 are the threshold values that are used to change from frontal to right face model and from right to frontal face model, respectively. Usually, they are the point where the difference between the ground truth and the estimated pose angles increases abruptly. The model selection method is as follows. Within the ambiguous area, the face model which has the smallest fitting error is chosen. Within the certain area, the face model corresponding the estimated pose of input image is chosen.

Method II - Using Two Deterministic Thresholds

As shown in Fig. 3.4.3 (b), this method uses two different threshold values $\tau_1 = \hat{\phi}_F(T_{opt})$ and $\tau_2 = \hat{\phi}_R(T_{opt})$, where ϕ_{opt} is the ground truth pose angle that minimizes the gap $\Delta\phi$ between the estimated pose angles of two face models:

$$T_{opt} = \underset{\phi}{\arg\min} \Delta\hat{\phi} = \underset{\phi}{\arg\min}(\hat{\phi}_R(\phi) - \hat{\phi}_F(\phi)). \tag{3.4.12}$$

Usually, the gap is computed by the average of the differences between the estimated pose angles of two face models using a set of training samples whose ground truth pose angles are known in advance. The model selection method is as follows. When using the frontal face model, τ_1 is used as the threshold value for changing from frontal to right face model. Once the model is changed to the right face model at $\phi = T_{opt}$, the estimated pose angle is corrected by $\hat{\phi}_R(T_{opt}) = \hat{\phi}_F(T_{opt}) + \Delta\hat{\phi}(T_{opt})$. When using the right face model, τ_2 is used as the threshold value for changing from right to frontal face model. Once the model is changed to the frontal face model at $\phi = T_{opt}$, the estimated pose angle is corrected by $\hat{\phi}_F(T_{opt}) = \hat{\phi}_R(T_{opt}) - \Delta\hat{\phi}(T_{opt})$.

Method III - Using One Compensational Threshold

As shown in Fig. 3.4.3 (c), this method uses one threshold value $\tau = \frac{\tau_1 + \tau_2}{2}$, where τ_1 and τ_2 are obtained as in method II and corrects the estimated pose angle by an compensational pose term $\varepsilon(\hat{\phi})$:

$$\hat{\phi}^* = \hat{\phi} + \varepsilon(\hat{\phi}), \tag{3.4.13}$$

where $\varepsilon(\hat{\phi})$ is a function of the estimated pose angle $\hat{\phi}$. $\varepsilon(\hat{\phi})$ is computed by the average of the pose angle differences between the ground truth and the estimated pose of each face model. This computation is performed with training samples; $\varepsilon(\hat{\phi}) = Avg(\hat{\phi} - \phi)$. The model selection method is as follows. When the estimated pose angle is less than τ, we take the frontal face model. Otherwise, we take the right face model. This method does not need a correction step.

Figure 3.4.1. A distribution of pose angles

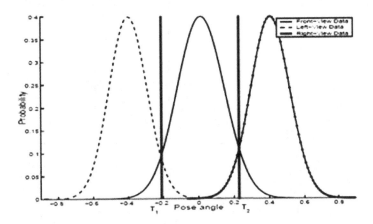

Method IV - Using Two Compensational Thresholds

As shown in Fig. 3.4.3 (d), this method is similar to method III except that we can control the degree of compensation by adding a compensational pose term:

$$\hat{\phi}^* = \hat{\phi} + \eta \varepsilon(\hat{\phi}), \tag{3.4.14}$$

where η is a proportional constant ranging from $0 < \eta < 1$. The actual value of η is determined experimentally through trial and error. In fact, method IV is equal to method II when $\eta = 0$ and is equal to method III when $\eta = 1$. For a given η, we have two thresholds T_1 and T_2 that are the shrinking version of those in method III. The model selection method is exactly like that of method II.

Figure 3.4.2. Different pose angle estimation characteristics of the frontal and right face model

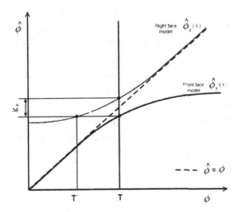

Figure 3.4.3. Four different model selection methods

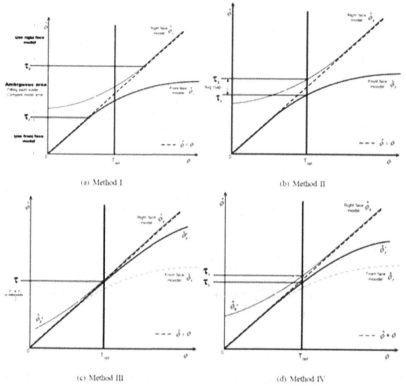

(a) Method I (b) Method II

(c) Method III (d) Method IV

Fig. 3.4.4 illustrates the algorithmic flowchart of model selection method IV, which accommodates methods II and III effectively. In this flowchart, we first initialize the current model as NONE because it has not been decided yet. In the very beginning, we fit all face models to the input image and then choose the face model that gives the smallest residual error as the current model. Once the current model is decided, we perform the 2D+3D AAM fitting. Then, we estimate the pose angle using the current model and compute the compensated pose angle $\hat{\phi}^*$ using Eq. (3.4.14). When the current model is the frontal face model, the estimated pose angle is compared to the threshold τ_1. If the estimated pose angle is less than τ_1, then the current face model keeps the frontal face model. Otherwise, the current model is changed to the right face model. When the current model is the right face model, the estimated pose angle is compared with the threshold τ_2. If the estimated pose angle is greater than τ_2, then the current face model keeps the right face model. Otherwise, the current model is changed to the frontal face model. This kind of face model selection is executed in the same way between the left and frontal face model. This procedure is repeated until no input image exists.

Considering the cost of computation, we proposed a method that requires more computation than the original method in initial state since we do not have any information on the current model. However, the required cost is equal to the original 2D+3D AAM after the second frame.

Figure 3.4.4. A flow chart of model selection algorithm

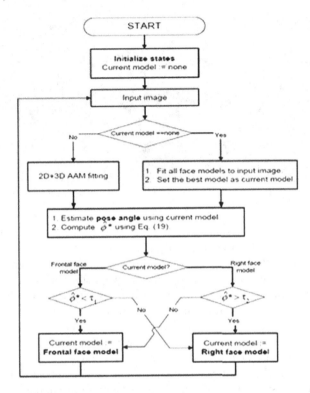

3.4.3 Experimental Results and Discussion

3.4.3.1 Test Data

To evaluation the performance of the view-based 2D+3D AAM algorithm, we gathered a set of face images. It includes a sequence of stereo images of 20 people whose facial expressions change from neutral to extreme. For each person, we consider 4 different facial expressions: neutral, happy, surprised, and angry and collect 5 different images, each having a little different degree of facial expression. Each expression consists of 3 different poses such as frontal, left, and right. As a result, the database includes 1,200 face images (20 persons × 4 expressions × 5 images × 3 views). The face images have a size of 640 × 480 gray level pixels and are captured by a Bumblebee stereo camera at a rate of 20 frame/sec. The average distance was about 700mm. Fig. 3.4.5 shows a typical example of face images of three different people in the facial expression database, where each row and column display different expressions and poses.

3.4.3.2 Constructing 2D+3D View-Based AAM

In order to obtain the shape and appearance data for the AAMs, 70 feature points in each face image were marked. Although some researchers have proposed some automatic landmark

Figure 3.4.5. A typical examples in facial expression database

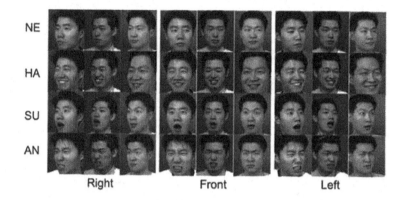

methods to remove this cumbersome process (Brett and Taylor, 1998; Hill et al., 1997), we performed this landmark process manually. Fortunately, we can perform the landmark process semi-automatically by using the AAM fitting algorithm. Once a model has been constructed with a sufficient number of face images, we first performed the AAM fitting and then accurate landmark points are manually obtained with fitting results.

After obtaining the landmark face images, we aligned the face images in order to remove the scale, translation, and rotation among face images. Then, we obtained the shape vector and the appearance data using the mean shape. Based on a pair of shape vectors, we can obtain the 3D shape mesh using a stereo image matching technique for the disparity map. Disparity refers to the difference in images from the left camera and right camera. Two cameras that are displaced by a certain distance take pictures of the same object. The disparity of the object close to the camera is larger than disparity of the object far from the camera.

Thus, we can easily compute the depth of the landmark points (Schmidt et al., 2002). Then, we applied the PCA to the shape vector and the appearance data and obtained the orthogonal basis modes for the shape vectors and appearance data. Fig. 3.4.6 shows 2D shape and appearance variation modes, where the three rows correspond to the frontal, left, and right face model. Here, Fig. 3.4.6 (a) shows the first five 2D shape basis images, where each arrow represents the movement direction of each landmark point, and Fig. 3.4.6 (b) shows the first five appearance basis images, which correspond to the basis coefficient $(\lambda_1 - \lambda_5)$. Fig. 3.4.7 shows the first five 3D shape basis meshes that are obtained by applying the PCAMD to the 3D shape meshes of all different poses. Fig. 3.4.8 shows 3D shape meshes that are recovered by the PCAMD, where the top, middle, and bottom rows represent the landmark images, the 3D shape meshes by PCA, and the 3D shape meshes by PCAMD, respectively. As mentioned before, the 3D shape meshes recovered by PCA are not complete because the PCA cannot handle the missing points that occur due to the pose. We also find that the points near lips are obtained with poor precision because the lips are too distorted by pose. However, the 3D shape meshes recovered by PCAMD are almost perfect because the PCAMD handles the missing points effectively.

Figure 3.4.6. 2D shape and appearance variation for view-based 2D+3D AAM - Frontal model (top), right model (middle) and left model (bottom)

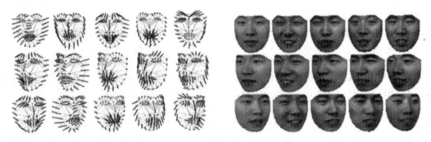

(a) The linear shape variation modes.   (b) The linear appearance variation modes.

Figure 3.4.7. The linear 3D shape variation modes

Figure 3.4.8. The reconstruction of 3D shape meshes using the PCAMD. Top) landmark points, middle row) the obtained 3D shapes, bottom) the reconstructed 3D shapes

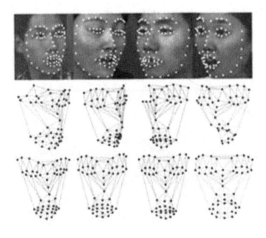

3.4.3.3 Evaluation of Model Selection Performance

To evaluate the pose robustness of the view-based 2D+3D AAM in face tracking, we investigated how well the proposed model selection algorithm works. Fig. 3.4.9 shows the ground truth pose angle and the estimated pose angles by the view-based 2D+3D AAM. 320 frontal, 360 left, and 360 right posed face images were used to construct the corresponding frontal, left, and right face model, and the estimated pose angles of 1,040 face images were determined by the three different view-based 2D+3D AAMs. Fig. 3.4.9 (a) shows that the frontal face model has the smallest pose error for frontal images, and the left and right face models also were the best models for left and right face images, respectively.

Our model selection schemes (Method II, III, and IV) require the determination of the optimal threshold pose angle ϕ_{opt} for good model selection. Fig. 3.4.9 (b) shows the estimated pose angle gap $(\hat{\phi}_R(\phi) - \hat{\phi}_F(\phi))$ between the right and frontal face model, which is equal to the difference between the estimated pose angle error of the right face model $(\hat{\phi}_R(\phi) - \phi)$ and the estimated pose angle error of the front face model $(\hat{\phi}_F(\phi) - \phi)$. This figure shows that the estimated pose angle error of the right (and frontal) face model tends to gradually decrease (and increase) as the pose angle becomes larger. As we know, the optimal threshold pose angle is determined by the pose angle that minimizes the difference of two estimated pose angle errors. We discover that the optimal threshold pose angle for changing from the frontal to right face model (or vice versa) is at 0.220 radian (12.61°). Similarly, we also discover that the optimal threshold pose angle for changing from the frontal to left face model (or vice versa) is at -0.190 radian (10.89°).

After discovering the optimal threshold pose angles, we obtain the compensational pose term $\varepsilon(\hat{\phi})$ by the average of the pose angle differences between the ground truth and the estimated pose angle of each face model using a total of 1,040 face images. Then, the estimated pose angle is adjusted by Eq. (3.4.14) Fig. 3.4.10 (a) and (b) show the compensated pose angle and the additive compensational pose term when $\eta = 0.7$. The pose angle error of each face model becomes smaller except for the area where the pose angle deviates from the normal region of each face model.

We compared the accuracy of the four different model selection methods by measuring how well each method can select the correct face model for 960 test image frames whose

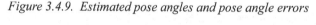

Figure 3.4.9. Estimated pose angles and pose angle errors

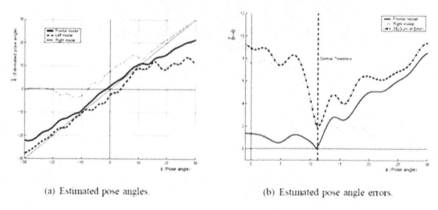

(a) Estimated pose angles.

(b) Estimated pose angle errors.

Figure 3.4.10. Compensated pose angle and additive compensational pose term

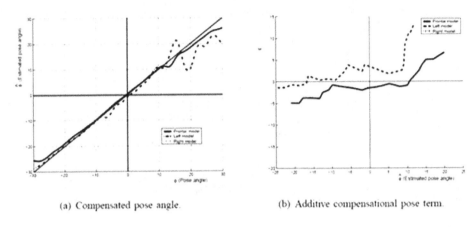

(a) Compensated pose angle.

(b) Additive compensational pose term.

Table 3.4.2. The rate of selecting wrong face model

	Method I	Method II	Method III	Method IV
F $\mapsto$ L	22	8	16	11
F $\mapsto$ R	65	32	6	7
L $\mapsto$ F	32	10	9	9
R $\mapsto$ F	83	31	28	28
Total	202	81	59	55

poses are known in advance. Table 3.4.2 summarizes the error rate for each model selection method, where each row represents the type of missed selection. For example, F $\mapsto$ L denotes that the true face pose is the frontal face but it is designated as the left face by a given face model. Method IV outperforms the other selection methods; method I has the poorest performance because the AAM fitting error, which is used as the model selection criterion, is sensitive to the initial states of the model.

Fig. 3.4.11 shows how the error rate in Method IV varies with η. When η is 0 or 1, Method IV is the same as Method II or Method III. The error rate decreases as the value of η increases, reaching its minimum value around $\eta = 0.7$; after 0.7 it starts to increase. In this work, we set $\eta = 0.7$ for all other experiments.

We tested the effectiveness of the proposed model selection method for face tracking. We used a novel face image sequence of 184 frames whose pose has changed from frontal to left, frontal, right, and frontal (F-L-F-R-F). In fact, the image sequence was recorded in a usual indoor environment, where no special constraints were imposed on lighting condition

Figure 3.4.11. The miss rate of model selection with η

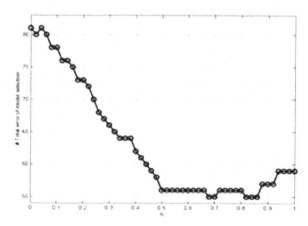

and background as shown in Fig. 3.4.12. Hence, the image sequence has a very cluttered background when compared to the database images. Fig. 3.4.12 shows the result of face tracking when the view-based 2D+3D AAM is used with the model selection Method IV. The symbols over each image denote the different face models, the black symbol denotes the selected model at the given image frame, and each fitting result is overlayed on the face image. As mentioned before, the model selection worked well as the pose changed gradually.

Since the proposed algorithm has learned the compensational pose term $\varepsilon(\phi)$ from training data, an estimated pose angle can be different from the true pose angle at the time, which can result in incorrect model selection. In our experiment, such situation usu-

Figure 3.4.12. A face tracking using the model selection IV

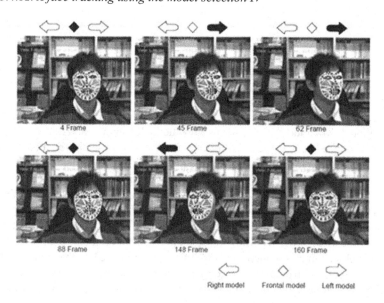

ally occurred in the intermediate pose angles where the pose coverage of two neighboring view models overlaps. However, the proposed model selection algorithm eventually found a correct face model as the true pose became closer to a specific view direction. As the aforementioned model selection errors are temporary in the cases of 'too early change' and 'too late change', they did not cause serious problems in the face tracking. On the other hand, totally incorrect model selection errors such as choosing left-view model instead of right-view model may cause the failure of face tracking; we cannot trust the fitting result of the left-view model on a right-view face image. However, such errors may occur when the fitting of the 2D+3D AAM is failed, which cannot be overcome by a model section algorithm. Fortunately, the totally incorrect model selection seldom occurs.

Finally, we tested how well the view-based 2D+3D AAM can track and recover the face successfully when its pose is not frontal. Fig. 3.4.13 compares the fitting results and the warped appearances of the frontal-view 2D+3D AAM and the view-based 2D+3D AAM. The top and bottom rows are fitted by the frontal-view 2D+3D AAM and the view-based 2D+3D AAM, and the warped appearances are displayed below of each fitted face image. The appearances fitted by the frontal-view 2D+3D AAM had some distortions due to the background but the appearance fitted by the view-based 2D+3D AAM was almost perfect.

3.5 A UNIFIED GRADIENT-BASED APPROACH FOR COMBINING ASM INTO AAM

The AAM is a very useful method that can fit the shape and appearance model to the input image. However, it often fails to accurately converge to the landmark points of the input

Figure 3.4.13. Comparison of appearances by two different 2D+3D AAMs

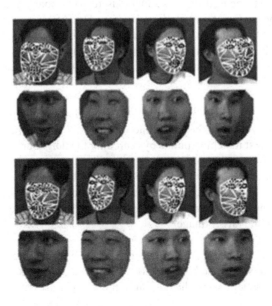

image because the goal of the AAM fitting algorithm is just to minimize the residual error between the model appearance and the input image. We overcome this weakness by combining the active shape models (ASMs) into the AAMs, called AAM+ASM, where the ASMs try to find the correct landmark points using the local profile model (Sung and Kim, 2006f; Sung and Kim, 2006g).

One simple and direct combination of ASM and AAM is to take the two methods alternatively. In this case, the parameters may not converge to a stable solution because they use the different optimization goals and techniques. To guarantee a stable and precise convergence, we change the profile search step of the ASM to a gradient-based search and combine the error terms of the AAM and ASM into a single objective function in a gradient-based optimization framework. The gradient-based ASM search method can be seen as a simplified version of the active contour model (ACM) (Kass et al., 1998) except for that the ACM uses all boundary points while the gradient-based ASM uses only the specified model points.

Fig. 3.5.1 shows how the AAM+ASM fitting method works. The AAM+ASM algorithm pre-computes the linear shape, appearance, and profile model independently from a set of the landmarked training images and uses these models simultaneously to find the optimal model parameters for an input image. By integrating the AAM and ASM error terms and optimizing them simultaneously, we can obtain more accurate fitting than using only the AAM error term. This improvement is due to the fact that the ASM error term enforces to move the shape points to nearby edge-like points. If we only take the AAM error term, then the AAM fitting often fails to converge to the ground truth points because there are no distinctive texture patterns in the cheek area of the face. The detailed explanation on the AAM+ASM fitting method is given by the following.

3.5.1 Active Appearance Model and Active Shape Model

Since ASM (Cootes, et al., 1995) and AAM (Cootes, et al., 2001d) have been introduced, many researchers have focused on these methods to solve many image interpretation problems, especially for facial and medical images. The ASMs and AAMs have some similarities. They use the same underlying statistical model of the shape of target objects, represent the shape by a set of landmark points and learn the ranges of shape variation from training images. However, the two methods have several differences as well (Cootes et al., 1999a):

- ASM only models the image texture in the neighboring region of each landmark point, whereas AAM uses the appearance of the whole image region.
- ASM finds the best matching points by searching the neighboring region of the current shape positions, whereas AAM compares its current model appearance to the appearance sampled at the current shape positions in the image.
- ASM seeks to minimize the distance between the model points and the identified match points, whereas AAM minimizes the difference between the synthesized model appearance and the target image.

Cootes et al. (1999a) found that ASM is faster and has a broader search range than AAM, whereas AAM gives a better match to the texture. However, AAM is sensitive to the illumination condition especially when the lighting condition in the test images is significantly

Figure 3.5.1. The fitting method in AAM+ASM

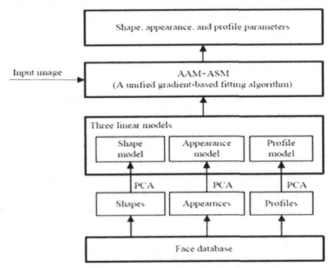

different from that in the training images. It often fails to locate boundary points correctly if the texture of the object around the boundary area is similar to the background image (Yan et. al, 2002). Until now, ASM and AAM have been treated as two independent methods in most cases even though they share some basic concepts such as the same linear shape model and linear appearance model (here, the term *appearance* is used with a somewhat broad meaning; it can represent the whole texture or the local texture).

As pointed out by Cootes et al. (2001b) and Scott et al. (2003) , the existing intensity-based AAM has some drawbacks: It is sensitive to the changes in lighting conditions and it fails to discriminate noisy flat textured area and real structure, and thus may not lead to an accurate fitting in AAM search. To alleviate this problem, Stegmann and Larsen (2002) proposed a few methods: Augmenting the appearance model using extra *feature band* that includes color and gradient channels. Scott et al. (2003) proposed to use some nonlinear transforms such as cornerness, edgeness, and gradient directions for the *feature band*. Experimental results showed that the nonlinear descriptions of local structure for the texture model improved the fitting accuracy of the AAMs. Ginneken et al. (2006) pointed out the problem of AAM formulation where only the object's interior is included into the appearance model, which means that the cost function can have a minimum value when the model is completely inside the actual object. To avoid this, they simply concatenated the appearance vector with the texture scanned along *whiskers* that are outgoing normal direction at each landmark points.

Another approach to improve the fitting performance is to combine the ideas of the AAM and ASM. Yan et al. (2002) proposed the texture constrained ASM (TC-ASM) that inherited the ASM's local appearance model due to its robustness to varying light conditions. They also borrowed the AAM's global texture, to act as a constraint over the shape providing an optimization criterion for determining the shape parameters. In TC-ASM, the conditional distribution of the shape parameters given its associated texture parameters was modeled as a Gaussian distribution. There was a linear mapping $\mathbf{s}_t = \mathbf{R}a$ between the texture $\mathbf{a}$ and its corresponding shape $\mathbf{s}_t$, where $\mathbf{R}$ is a projection matrix that can be pre-computed from the training pairs $\{(\mathbf{s}_i, \mathbf{a}_i)\}$. The search stage computes the next shape parameters by interpolating the shape from a traditional ASM search and the texture-constrained shape. Using the texture constrained shape enabled the search method to escape from the local minima of the ASM search, resulting in improved fitting results.

3.5.2 Local Profile Model of ASM

ASM and AAM use different appearance models: the ASM uses a *local profile model* and the AAM uses a whole appearance model, which is explained in Chapter 5.2 We introduce the local profile model of the ASM in this section.

ASM represents the local appearance at each model point by the intensity or gradient profile (Cootes et al., 1995). For each landmark point in the training image, the intensity profile **I** is obtained by sampling the intensity along the direction that is normal to the line that connects two neighboring landmarks of a given landmark point. Then, the gradient profile **g** is obtained, which is a derivative of the intensity profile **I**. Fig. 3.5.2 illustrates an example: (a) landmarks and a normal vector direction at a specific landmark point, (b) the intensity profile, and (c) the gradient profile. In this work, we consider the gradient profile because it is not sensitive to global intensity variations.

The gradient profile $\mathbf{g}^j$ of the j-th model point is also represented as a linear combination of a mean gradient profile $\mathbf{g}_0^j$ and l orthonormal gradient profile basis vectors $\mathbf{g}_i^j$ as

$$\mathbf{g}^j = \sum_{i=0}^{l} \beta_i \mathbf{g}_i^j,$$

(3.5.1)

where β_i is the i-th gradient profile parameter and $\beta_0 = 1$. The gradient profile basis vectors are obtained by collecting a set of gradient profile vectors, and applying the PCA. Fig. 3.5.3 shows the mean and the first three gradient profile basis vectors. In this figure, the first and second bases appear as a quadrature pair, which implies inaccurate positioning of landmarks on intensity contours. When we collect the gradient profile data, we landmark the position of the feature points manually. Hence, they cannot be aligned precisely. This may produce the quadrant pairs in the basis vectors of the gradient profile. However, this misalignment does not affect the fitting performance much.

3.5.3 A Unified Approach

Our goal is to find the model parameters that minimize the residual error of the whole and local appearance model simultaneously in a unified gradient-based framework. This required the definition of an integrated objective function that combines the objective functions of AAM and ASM in an appropriate manner.

The objective function of the AAM+ASM fitting method consists of three error terms: the error of whole appearance E_{aam}, the error of local appearance E_{asm}, and a regularization error E_{reg}. The last error term is introduced to prevent the shape parameters from deviating too widely. We explain each error term and introduce the overall objective function that consists of the three error terms.

First, we define the error of the whole appearance model for AAM as

$$E_{aam}(\boldsymbol{\alpha}, \mathbf{p}) = \frac{1}{N} \sum_{\mathbf{x} \in \mathbf{s}_0} \left[\sum_{i=0}^{m} \alpha_i A_i(\mathbf{x}) - I(W(\mathbf{x}; \mathbf{p})) \right]^2,$$

(3.5.2)

where N is the number of the pixels $\mathbf{x} \in \mathbf{s}_0$, and α, and $\mathbf{p}$ are the appearance, and shape parameters.

Second, we define the error of local appearance model for ASM as

$$
\begin{aligned}
E_{asm}(\boldsymbol{\beta}, \mathbf{p}) &= \frac{K}{v \cdot N_{pf}} \sum_{j=1}^{v} \sum_{z} E_{asm}^{j}(z)^2 \alpha^{j} \\
&= \frac{K}{v \cdot N_{pf}} \sum_{j=1}^{v} \sum_{z} \left\{ \sum_{i=0}^{t} \beta_i^{j} \mathbf{g}_i^{j}(z) - \mathbf{g}(W^{j}(z; \mathbf{p})) \right\}^2 \gamma^{j},
\end{aligned}
\tag{3.5.3}
$$

where N_{pf} is the length of the gradient profile vector, K is a scaling factor to balance the magnitude of E_{asm} with that of the E_{aam}, β_i^{j} is the i-th gradient profile model parameter corresponding to the j-th model point, $W^{j}(z; p)$ represents a warping function that transforms a scalar coordinate z of the 1-D gradient profile vector into a 2D image coordinate of the image to be used for reading the image gradient profile $\mathbf{g}$ at each j-th model point, and γ^{j} is adaptive weight control term that will be explained in the section 3.5.3.2 The warping function can be represented as

$$
W^{j}(z; \mathbf{p}) = \mathbf{s}^{j}(\mathbf{p}) + z\mathbf{n}^{j},
\tag{3.5.4}
$$

where $\mathbf{s}^j(\mathbf{p})$ and $\mathbf{n}^j$ are the j-th model point of the current shape corresponding to current shape parameters $\mathbf{p}$, and the normal vector of the j-th model point.

Third, we define a regularization error term E_{reg}, which constrains the range of the shape parameters p_i, as

$$
E_{reg}(\mathbf{p}) = R \cdot \sum_{i=1}^{n} \frac{p_i^2}{\sqrt{\lambda_i}^2},
\tag{3.5.5}
$$

where λ_i is the eigenvalue corresponding to the i-th shape basis $\mathbf{s}_i$ and R is a constant that controls the effect of regularization term. If the value of R is set to a large value, the fitting result tends to be close to the mean shape. While the shape parameters are directly limited in order not to exceed $3\sqrt{\lambda_i}$ after each iteration in ASM (Cootes et al., 1995) and AAM (Cootes et al., 2001d; Matthews, and Baker, 2004a), we add E_{reg} into the objective function to obtain a similar effect.

Figure 3.5.2. Typical examples: (a) a landmarked face image, (b) intensity profile, and (c) gradient profile

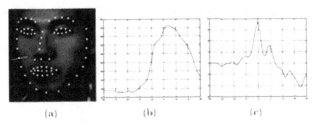

(a) (b) (c)

Figure 3.5.3. A mean and the first three gradient profile basis vectors

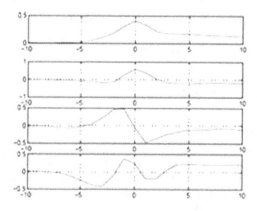

By combining Eq. (3.5.2), Eq. (3.5.3), and Eq. (3.5.5), we define an integrated objective function E as

$$E = (1-\omega)(E_{aam} + E_{reg}) + \omega E_{asm},$$
(3.5.6)

where $\omega \in [0,1]$ determines how significant the E_{asm} term will be in the overall objective function E. Thus, the AAM+ASM algorithm operates like AAM when $\omega = 0$, and like ASM when $\omega = 1$.

3.5.3.1 Derivation of Updating Parameters

The integrated objective function is optimized using the Gauss-Newton gradient descent method. To derive the formula for updating parameters, we need to compute the steepest descent vector of the parameters. Once the steepest descent vector of each term is obtained, its corresponding Hessian matrix can be easily computed. In the following, we describe the detailed derivation of the steepest descent vectors of the three error terms. During the derivation, we omit the constants $1/N$ in E_{aam} term and $K/(v \cdot N_{pf})$ in E_{asm}.

The whole appearance error term E_{aam} is almost the same as that of the traditional AAM. The difference is that E_{aam} is divided by the number of pixels to effectively balance the error function with E_{asm}. Various gradient based fitting methods for this type of error function have been proposed ((Matthews, and Baker, 2004a; Gross et. al, 2003), which are extended from the Lucas-Kanade image matching method (Kanade and Lucas, 1981).

When we take the traditional Gauss-Newton nonlinear optimization method to minimize the first term E_{aam} of Eq. (3.5.2), the increments $\Delta\boldsymbol{\alpha}$, and $\Delta\mathbf{p}$ are determined to satisfy the following condition:

$$E_{aam}(\boldsymbol{\alpha} + \Delta\boldsymbol{\alpha}, \mathbf{p} + \Delta\mathbf{p}) < E_{aam}(\boldsymbol{\alpha}, \mathbf{p}),$$
(3.5.7)

where

$$E_{aam}(\boldsymbol{\alpha} + \Delta\boldsymbol{\alpha}, \mathbf{p} + \Delta\mathbf{p}) =$$
$$\sum_{\mathbf{x} \in s_0} \left[\sum_{i=0}^{m} (\alpha_i + \Delta\alpha_i) A_i(\mathbf{x}) - I(\mathbf{W}(\mathbf{x}; ; \mathbf{p} + \Delta\mathbf{p})) \right]^2 \qquad (3.5.8)$$

and

$$E_{aam}(\boldsymbol{\alpha}, \mathbf{p}) = \sum_{\mathbf{x} \in s_0} \left[\sum_{i=0}^{m} \alpha_i A_i(\mathbf{x}) - I(\mathbf{W}(\mathbf{x}; \mathbf{p})) \right]^2. \qquad (3.5.9)$$

After obtaining the increment vectors $\Delta\boldsymbol{\alpha}$, $\Delta\mathbf{p}$, the additive update formula modifies the appearance parameter α and the warping parameters $\mathbf{p}$ as

$$\boldsymbol{\alpha} \leftarrow \boldsymbol{\alpha} + \Delta\boldsymbol{\alpha}, \mathbf{W}(\mathbf{x}; \mathbf{p}) \leftarrow \mathbf{W}(\mathbf{x}; \mathbf{p} + \Delta\mathbf{p}). \qquad (3.5.10)$$

We can simply rewrite Eq. (3.5.8) as

$$E_{aam} = \sum_{\mathbf{x} \in s_0} \left\{ E_{aam}(\mathbf{x}) + \mathbf{SD}_{aam}(\mathbf{x}) \begin{bmatrix} \Delta\boldsymbol{\alpha} \\ \Delta\mathbf{p} \end{bmatrix} \right\}^2, \qquad (3.5.11)$$

where

$$E_{aam}(\mathbf{x}) = \sum_{i=0}^{m} \alpha_i A_i(\mathbf{x}) - I(\mathbf{W}(\mathbf{x}; \mathbf{p})), \qquad (3.5.12)$$

and

$$\mathbf{SD}_{aam}(\mathbf{x}) = \left[A_1(\mathbf{x}), \quad \dots, \quad A_m(\mathbf{x}), \quad -\nabla I^T (\frac{\partial \mathbf{W}}{\partial \mathbf{p}}) \right] \qquad (3.5.13)$$

by applying the first order Taylor series expansion to Eq. (3.5.8) and simplifying it. Note that the steepest descent vector SD_{aam} must be re-computed at every iteration because the gradient of the image

$$\nabla I = (\frac{\partial I}{\partial x}, \frac{\partial I}{\partial y})^t$$

and the Jacobian of the warping function $(\frac{\partial \mathbf{W}}{\partial \mathbf{p}})$ depend on the warping parameters $\mathbf{p}$ that are updated at every iteration, i.e., ∇I is computed at $W(\mathbf{x}; \mathbf{p})$ and the warping function $\mathbf{W}$ is differentiated at current $\mathbf{p}$. Therefore, the Hessian matrix is also re-computed in each iteration.

As in the case of E_{aam}, we apply the additive Gauss-Newton update to the E_{reg} of Eq. (3.5.5), which can be reformulated as

$$E_{reg} = \left\| \Lambda^{-1} (\mathbf{p} + \Delta\mathbf{p}) \right\|^2, \qquad (3.5.14)$$

where Λ is a square diagonal matrix ($\Lambda_{i,i} = \sqrt{\lambda_i}$, and λ_i is the *i*-th eigenvalue), and is minimized with respect to $\Delta \mathbf{p}$. After obtaining the increment vector $\Delta \mathbf{p}$, the modified additive update formula modifies the shape parameter $\mathbf{p}$ as $\mathbf{p} \leftarrow \mathbf{p} + \Delta \mathbf{p}$.

When we apply the Taylor series expansion to Eq. (3.5.14), we can rewrite it as

$$E_{reg} = P\Lambda^{-1}\mathbf{p} + \Lambda^{-1}\Delta \mathbf{p} P^2 = PE_{reg,\mathbf{p}} + \mathbf{SD}_{reg}\Delta \mathbf{p} P^2, \qquad (3.5.15)$$

where

$$\mathbf{SD}_{reg} = \Lambda^{-1}, \quad E_{reg,\mathbf{p}} = \Lambda^{-1}\mathbf{p}. \qquad (3.5.16)$$

Similarly, we apply the additive Gauss-Newton gradient descent method to the local profile error E_{asm}, i.e., we want to minimize

$$E_{asm} = \sum_{j=1}^{v} \sum_{z} \left\{ \sum_{i=0}^{l} \mathbf{g}_i^j(z)(\beta_i^j + \Delta \beta_i^j) - \mathbf{g}(W^j(z;\mathbf{p}+\Delta \mathbf{p})) \right\}^2, \qquad (3.5.17)$$

with respect to $\Delta \boldsymbol{\beta}$, and $\Delta \mathbf{p}$. After obtaining the increment vectors $\Delta \boldsymbol{\beta}$, and $\Delta \mathbf{p}$, the parameters are updated:

$$\boldsymbol{\beta}^j \leftarrow \boldsymbol{\beta}^j + \Delta \boldsymbol{\beta}^j, W^j(z;\mathbf{p}) \leftarrow W^j(z;\mathbf{p}+\Delta \mathbf{p}). \qquad (3.5.18)$$

When we apply the Taylor series expansion to Eq. (3.5.17) and ignore the second and higher order terms, we can rewrite Eq. (3.5.17) as

$$E_{asm} = \sum_{j=1}^{v} \sum_{z} \left\{ E_{asm}^j(z) + \mathbf{SD}_{asm}^j(z) \begin{bmatrix} \Delta \boldsymbol{\beta} \\ \Delta \mathbf{p} \end{bmatrix} \right\}^2, \qquad (3.5.19)$$

where

$$E_{asm}^j(z) = \sum_{i=0}^{l} \mathbf{g}_i^j(z)\beta_i^j - \mathbf{g}(W^j(z;\mathbf{p})), \qquad (3.5.20)$$

and

$$\mathbf{SD}_{asm}^j(z) = \left[\mathbf{g}_1^j(z), \quad \dots, \quad \mathbf{g}_l^j(z), \quad -\nabla \mathbf{g}(z)\left(\frac{\partial W^j}{\partial \mathbf{p}}\right) \right]. \qquad (3.5.21)$$

The differentiation of the W^j with respect to the warping parameters $\mathbf{p}$ in Eq. (3.5.21) can be computed as

$$\frac{\partial W^j}{\partial \mathbf{p}} = \left(\frac{\partial W^j}{\partial z}\right)^T \frac{\partial z}{\partial \mathbf{p}}, \qquad (3.5.22)$$

where the first term $\dfrac{\partial W^j}{\partial z}$ can be computed from Eq. (3.5.24), and the second term $\dfrac{\partial z}{\partial \mathbf{p}}$ is required to represent z as a function of parameters $\mathbf{p}$. When the j-th model point $\mathbf{s}^j$ moves to $\mathbf{s}^j$ along the normal vector $\mathbf{n}^j$, the z coordinate of the $\mathbf{s}^j$ can be computed as

$$z = \left(\mathbf{n}^j\right)^T \left(\mathbf{s}^j - \mathbf{s}^j\right). \tag{3.5.23}$$

Since the overall objective function is a summation of multiple objective functions and each objective function consists of a sum of squares, the Hessian matrix of the overall objective function is the sum of the Hessian matrix of each objective function (Xiao et. al, 2004b) as

$$\begin{aligned}
\mathbf{H}_{overall} &= (1-\omega)\left\{\sum_{\mathbf{x}} \mathbf{SD}_{aam}(\mathbf{x})^T \mathbf{SD}_{aam}(\mathbf{x}) + \mathbf{SD}_{reg}^T \mathbf{SD}_{reg}\right\} \\
&+ \omega \sum_{j=1}^{v}\sum_{y} \mathbf{SD}_{asm}^j(y)^T \mathbf{SD}_{asm}^j(y).
\end{aligned} \tag{3.5.24}$$

Similarly, the steepest descent update of the overall objective function is also the sum of the steepest descent updates of the objective functions:

$$\begin{aligned}
\mathbf{SD}_{overall} &= (1-\omega)\left\{\sum_{\mathbf{x}} \mathbf{SD}_{aam}(\mathbf{x})^T E_{aam}(\mathbf{x}) + \mathbf{SD}_{reg}^T E_{reg,\mathbf{p}}\right\} \\
&+ \omega \sum_{j=1}^{v}\sum_{z} \mathbf{SD}_{asm}^j(z)^T E_{asm}^j(z).
\end{aligned} \tag{3.5.25}$$

If we define the overall parameter vector as $\boldsymbol{\theta} = \left[\Delta\boldsymbol{\alpha}^T \boldsymbol{\beta}^T \mathbf{p}^T\right]^t$, then we can compute the overall increment vector $\Delta\boldsymbol{\theta} = \left[\Delta\boldsymbol{\alpha}^T \Delta\boldsymbol{\beta}^T \Delta\mathbf{p}^T\right]^t$ as

$$\Delta\boldsymbol{\theta} = -\mathbf{H}_{overall}^{-1}\mathbf{SD}_{overall}. \tag{3.5.26}$$

Once the overall increment vector $\Delta\boldsymbol{\theta}$ is obtained, the appearance parameter $\boldsymbol{\alpha}$, the gradient profile parameter $\boldsymbol{\beta}$, and the warping parameters $\mathbf{p}$ are updated as

$$\boldsymbol{\alpha} = \boldsymbol{\alpha} + \Delta\boldsymbol{\alpha}, \boldsymbol{\beta} = \boldsymbol{\beta} + \Delta\boldsymbol{\beta}, \mathbf{p} = \mathbf{p} + \Delta\mathbf{p}. \tag{3.5.27}$$

In Eq. (3.5.26), the sizes of the three matrices are different because the parameter set of the three individual objective functions E_{aam}, E_{reg}, and E_{asm} are different. We can deal with this by thinking that they are the functions of all the entire parameter set and setting all elements in both the Hessian and the steepest descent parameter updates to zero that do not have corresponding entries in the individual functions.

3.5.3.2 Adaptive Weight Control of E_{asm}

First, we consider the effect of convergence on E_{asm}. As mentioned earlier, the local profile model for the ASM has only learned the local profile variations that are near the landmark points of the training data. Thus, the weight on E_{asm} term must be controlled appropriately for a proper model fitting in the following manner. During an early iteration, the E_{asm} term should have little influence because the synthesized shape is typically far from the landmark points. In the later iterations, as the synthesized shape becomes closer to the landmark points, the effect of E_{asm} should become stronger.

To reflect this idea, we need a measure to indicate how accurately the model shape is converged to the landmark points, and the E_{aam} term meets this requirement well. The degree of convergence is then represented by a bell-shaped function (Jang et al., 1997) of the E_{aam} term:

$$Bell(a,b,c;E_{aam}) = \frac{1}{1+\left|\dfrac{\sqrt{E_{aam}}-c}{a}\right|^{2b}},$$

(3.5.28)

where a, b, and c parameters determine the width of the bell, the steepness of downhill curve, and the center of the bell, respectively. In this work, we set $c = 0$ to use the right side of the bell-shape. Fig. 3.5.4 illustrates a typical bell-shape, where the values of a and b are 15 and 5, respectively, which were determined experimentally.

Second, we consider how well each model point has converged to its landmark point. Although the synthesized shape is converged to the landmark points on average, some points are close to their landmark points but other points are still far from them. To accommodate this situation, we consider a Normal-like function

$$exp\left(-\frac{E_{asm}^j}{2\sigma^j}\right),$$

where $E_{asm}^j (j = 1, \ldots, v)$ is the local profile error at j-th model point, and $\sigma^j > 0$ controls the sensitivity of the normal function, i.e., σ^j determines how much weight will be imposed on the j-th shape point using the current gradient profile error E_{asm}^j. The reason we use different sensitivity control parameter σ^j for each shape point is that the statistics of the gradient profile error are different from point to point. Therefore, we measured the mean value of the gradient profile errors E_{asm}^j at each landmark points from the training data and set the σ^j values as the consistently scaled values of the measured statistics. By considering these two effects, the adaptive weight γ^j in Eq. (3.5.3) is controlled as

Figure 3.5.4. A bell-shaped weight function

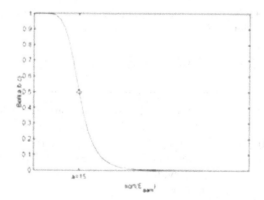

$$\gamma^j = Bell(E_{aam}) \cdot exp\left(-\frac{E_{asm}^j}{2\sigma^j}\right).$$ (3.5.29)

3.5.4 Experimental Results and Discussion

We evaluated the performance AAM+ASM fitting algorithm in terms of fitting error.

3.5.4.1 Data Sets

We used our own face database that consists of 80 face images, collected from 20 people with each person having 4 different expressions (neutral, happy, surprised and angry). All 80 images were manually landmarked. The shape, appearance, and gradient profile basis vectors were constructed from the images using the methods explained that are in Section 2. Fig. 3.5.5 shows some typical images in the face database.

3.5.4.2 Fitting Performance

First, we determined the optimal number of the linear gradient profile basis vectors. For this, we built a linear gradient model using 40 images of 10 randomly selected people, fitted the generated model to them, and measured the average fitting error of 70 landmark points, where the fitting error was defined by the distance between a landmark point and its converged vertex.

Fig. 3.5.6 shows the average fitting error, where * denotes the mean value of average fitting error when the AAM was used, the ° denotes the mean value of the average fitting error at each different number of linear gradient profile basis vectors when gradient-based ASM was used, and the bar denotes the standard deviation of the average fitting error in both methods. This figure shows that (1) the average fitting error of gradient-based ASM is smaller than that of AAM, (2) the optimal number of the linear gradient profile basis vectors is 7, and (3) the minimum average fitting error corresponds to approximately 0.5 pixel. Thus, the number of linear gradient profile basis vectors was 7 in our experiments.

Second, we investigated the effect of the E_{asm} term on the fitting performance, by setting the value of ω to 0, 0.05, 0.1, 0.2, 0.3, 0.4, 0.5, 0.6, 0.7, 0.8, 0.9, 0.95, and 1.0. The scale

Figure 3.5.5. A set of face images

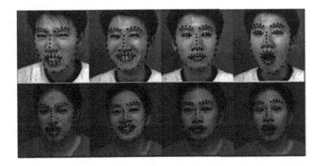

Figure 3.5.6. Mean and standard deviation of average fitting errors

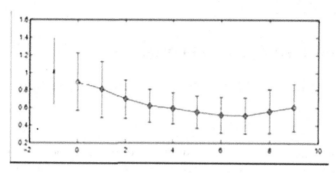

factor K was set to 10,000 to make the magnitude of the E_{asm} term similar to that of the E_{aam} term (the order of E_{aam} was 10 and the order of E_{asm} was 10^{-3}). For the 40 training images used in the first experiment, the optimal similarity transform parameters were computed from the landmark points, and then the position of the initial shape was moved 3 pixels in a random direction. The initial shape parameters are set to zero.

Fig. 3.5.7 shows the average fitting error at each ω, where the case of $\omega = 0$ corresponds to the AAM and the case of $\omega = 1.0$ corresponds to the gradient-based ASM. This figure shows that (1) the average fitting error of the AAM could be minimized further by choosing an optimal value of the ω that incorporates the effect of gradient-based ASM and (2) the smallest average fitting error was achieved when ω was set to about 0.5.

The amount of the decrease in the average fitting error in this experiment is about 0.45 pixel per each model point. Although the improvement seems to be very small, note that the improvement of 0.45 pixel per model point was difficult to achieve because the AAMs worked reasonably under the same conditions in this experiment. The average fitting error of the AAM was about 1.0, which means that every point converged to the ground truth landmark points reasonably. The improvement of 0.45 pixel per model point must be understood as follows: When comparing the average fitting error of the AAM+ASM

Figure 3.5.7. The effect of ω on the average fitting error

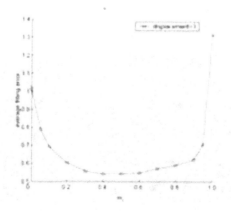

algorithm to that of the AAM algorithm, the AAM+ASM algorithm reduced the average fitting error to 55%.

In addition, the amount of 0.45 pixel is the average value. Thus, some model points move a lot while other points do not move when the fitting result is compared to that of the AAM algorithm. Usually, the moving points belong to facial features such as mouth, and eye brows. In case of facial expression recognition, extracting the exact location of such points are important because the facial expression can be changed by their small movement. The effect of the accurate fitting result is shown in the facial expression recognition experiment.

Fig. 3.5.8 illustrates a typical example of fitted results when the AAM and the AAM+ASM ($\omega = 0.5$) were used. In this figure, the white and black dots correspond to the fitted results of AAM and AAM+ASM, respectively. The AAM+ASM converged more accurately to the landmark points than the AAM, particularly near the mouth and chin.

Third, we investigated the effect of the *a* parameter of the Bell-shaped weight control function, where it determines the width of the Bell-shape function. We measured the average fitting error at different values of a = 5,10,15 and 20. For each value, we performed 8 trials of this experiment using different initial positions, where the displacement is 7 from 8 directions. Fig. 3.5.9 shows the change of average fitting error with respect to the iteration numbers, where each curve is the mean of 8 trials. This figure shows that (1) if the parameter *a* is too small (i.e., $a = 5$), the E_{asm} term is not always effective over the range of E_{aam}. This results in only the AAM error term being used, (2) if the parameter *a* is too large (i.e., $a = 20$), the E_{asm} term is always effective over the range of E_{aam}. This causes the fitting to stick to an incorrect local minima, and (3) the minimum average fitting error is obtained when α is 15.

Fourth, we compared the fitting performance of AAM+ASM to existing methods such as the traditional AAM and TC-ASM, another approach combining AAM and ASM. We set $\omega = 0$ for AAM and $\omega = 0.5$ for AAM+ASM. We built three linear models (appearance, shape, and profile) using the 40 training images that were used in previous experiments and measured the fitting performance using the remaining 40 test images. For one test image, we tried 40 different initial positions, as shown in Fig. 3.5.10, where they correspond to 5 different distances (3, 5, 7, 9, and 11) and 8 different directions. The initialization was completed as follows: the shape and appearance parameters were set to zero, and the scale and position parameters were computed from the landmark points.

Figure 3.5.8. A typical example of fitted results

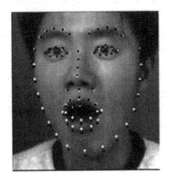

Figure 3.5.9. Change of average fitting errors for different a values

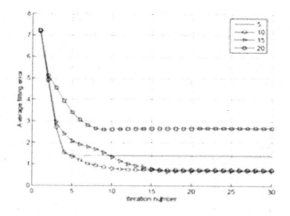

Figure 3.5.10. The configuration of 40 initial displacements

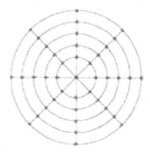

Fig. 3.5.11 shows a histogram of fitting error for 112,000 cases: 40 images × 40 initial positions × 70 vertices. It shows that the AAM+ASM produced the smallest mean and standard deviation of fitting error.

Table 3.5.1 shows the mean value of the fitting error of three different methods, which shows that the AAM+ASM method has the smallest mean value of fitting error.

Fig. 3.5.12 shows the convergence rates with respect to initial displacements of three different methods, where each plot has the threshold value of 1.5, 2.0, and 2.5, respectively. Here, we assume that the fitting result converges when the average fitting error is less than the given threshold value. In this work, the convergence rate is defined by the rate of the number of converged cases over the number of the all the trials. This figure shows that (1) the convergence rate increases as the threshold value increases for all methods, (2) the convergence rate decreases as the initial displacement increases in the AAM+ASM and the AAM methods, (3) the convergence rate is almost constant as initial displacement increases in the TC-ASM method because this method employs a search-based ASM, and (4) the convergence rate of the AAM+ASM is the highest among three methods in almost all cases.

Figure 3.5.11. A histogram of fitting errors

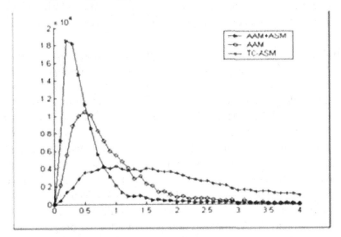

Figure 3.5.12. Convergence rate of the three fitting methods

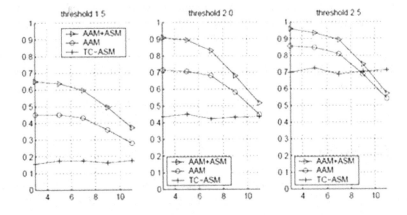

Table 3.5.1. Mean value of the fitting error

	AAM+ASM	AAM	TC-ASM
Mean	0.5	0.8	1.7

3.6 CONCLUSION

In this chapter, we explained three face modeling and fitting algorithms based on the AAM. The STAAM is a fitting algorithm that fits the 2D+3D AAM to multiple view images using the calibration algorithm. The use of calibration information removes redundunt rigid motion parameters and inconsistency between different view images in the MVAAM algorithm, which result the improved fitting performance. The idea of using the calibration information can be applied to without regard to the camera projection model. Although the STAAM fitting algorithm used the perspective projection model, Koterba et al. (2005) showed the improved fitting performance using weak perspective projection model.

The view-based 2D+3D AAM is the extension of the view-based 2D AAM (Cootes et al., 2002) for the 2D+3D AAM. Because the 2D+3D AAMs use sparse mesh model, it is difficult to represent the curvature of the face structure (especially the curvature of the cheek) and explain the deformation of the face shape in the image due to large pose change. Thus, the view-based 2D+3D AAM divided the range of view angles into three intervals: left, front, and right. Because there are three candidate 2D+3D AAMs for the three view intervals, selecting an appropriate one model during the face tracking stage is important. The view-based 2D+3D AAM algorithm compared some model selection methods and found a best model selection algorithm that uses two compensational threshold.

The AAM+ASM algorithm combines the ASM into the AAM using an adaptive weight control strategy, which determines when the ASM term should work. Basically, AAM+ASM method works similarly to AAM method and had an additive property that guarantes more precise convergence to the landmark points by reducing the fitting error due to the incorporated profile error term of the ASM. AAM+ASM is similar to TC-ASM (Yan et al., 2002) from the viewpoint of using both the whole appearance and local profile. While the TC-ASM used the whole appearance to estimate the texture-constrained shape, and its next estimated shape was obtained by interpolating the texture-constrained shape and the shape estimated by a traditional ASM search, AAM+ASM used the whole appearance and the profile information simultaneously within a gradient-based optimization framework. Extensive experimental results validated the usefulness of the AAM+ASM method because it reduced the fitting error and improved the facial expression recognition significantly.

3.7 REFERENCES

Bartlett, M. S., Movellan, J. R., & Sejnowski, T. J. (2002). Face recognition by independent component analysis. *IEEE Trans. on Neural Networks, 13*(6), 1450-1464.

Blanz, V., & Vetter, T. (1999). A morphable model for the synthesis of 3d faces. *Computer Graphics, Annual Conference Series (SIGGRAPH)* (pp. 187-194).

Brett, A., & Taylor, C. (1998). A method of automated landmark generation for automated 3D PDM construction. *British Machine Vision Conference* (pp. 914-923).

Cootes, T., Taylor, C., Cooper, D., & Graham, J. (1995). Active shape models - their training and application. *Computer Vision and Image Understanding, 61*(1), 38-59.

Cootes, T., Edwards, G., & Taylor, C. (1999a). Comparing active shape models with active appearance models. *In Proceedings of British Machine Vision Conference.*

Cootes, T., & Taylor, C. (2001a). Constrained active appearance models. *In Proceedings of IEEE International Conference on Computer Vision.*

Cootes, T., & Taylor, C. (2001b). On representing edge structure for model matching. *In Proceedings of Computer Vision and Pattern Recognition.*

Cootes, T., Wheeler, G., Walker, K., & Taylor, C. (2001c). Coupled-view active appearance models. *IEEE Transactions on Pattern Recognition and Machine Intelligence, 23*(6), 681-685.

Cootes, T., Edwards, G., & Taylor, C. (2001d). Active appearance models. *IEEE Trans. on Pattern Recognition and Machine Intelligence, 23*(6), 681-685.

Cootes, T., Wheeler, G., Walker, K., & Taylor, C. (2002). View-based active appearance models. *Image and Vision Computing, 20,* 657-664.

Duda, R. O., Hart, P. E., & Stork, D. H. (2000). *Pattern classification*. Willey Interscience, 2nd edition.

Dodge, Y. (1985). *Analysis of expreiments with missing data.* Wiley.

Edwards, G., Cootes, T., & Taylor, C. (1998a). Face recognition using active appearance models. *In Proceedings of European Conference on Computer Vision.*

Edwards, G., Taylor, C., & Cootes, T. (1998b). Interpreting face images using active appearance models. *In Proceedings of International Conference on Automatic Face and Gesture Recognition.*

Edwards, G., Taylor, C., & Cootes, T. (1998c). Learning to identify and track faces in image sequences. In Proceedings of International Conference on Face and Gesture Recognition, (pp. 260-265).

Gross, R., Matthews, I., & Baker, S. (2003). *Lucas-kanade 20 years on: A unifying framework: Part 3*. Cmu-ri-tr-03-05, CMU.

Gross, R., Matthews, I., & Baker, S. (2004b). Generic vs. person specific active appearance models. *In Proceedings of British Machine Vision Conference.*

Gross. R., Matthews. I., & Baker. S. (2004a). Constructing and fitting active appearance models with occlusion. *In Proceedings of IEEE Workshop on Face Processing in Video.*

Grull, I. (2005). *Conga: A conducting gesture analysis framework*. ULM University.

Ginneken, B. V., Stegmann, M. B., & Loog, M. (2006). Segmentation of anatomical structures in chest radiographs using supersvised methods: A comparative study on a public database. *Medical Image Analysis, 10*(1), 19-40.

Hu, C., Xiao, J., Matthews, I., Baker, S., Cohn, J., & Kanade, T. (2004). Fitting a single active appearance model simultaneously to multiple images. *In Proceedings of British Machine Vision Conference.*

Hill, A., Brett, A., & Taylor, C. (1997). Automatic landmark identification using a new method of non-rigid correspondence. *In Proceedings of The 15th International Conference on Information Processing in Medical Imaging* (pp. 483-488).

Jang, J., Sun, C., & Mizutani, E. (1997). Neuro-Fuzzy and Soft Computing. Prentice Hall.

Kanade, T., & Lucas, B. D. (1981). An iterative image registration technique with an application to stereo vision. *In Proceedings of International Joint Conference on Artificial Intelligence.*

Kass, M., Witkin, A., & Terzopoulos, D. (1988). Snakes: active conour models. *In Proceedings of the International Journal of Computer Vision,* (pp. 321-331).

Koterba, S., Baker, S., & Matthews, I. (2005). Multi-View AAM fitting and camera calibration,. *International Conference on Computer Vision.*

Matthews, I., & Baker, S. (2004a). Active appearance models revisited. *International Journal of Computer Vision, 60*(2), 135-164.

Moghaddam, B., & Pentland, A. (1997). Probablistic visual learning for object representation. *IEEE Transaction on Pattern Analysis and Machine Intelligence, 19*(7), 696-710.

Romdhani, S., Gong, S., & Psarrou, A. (1999). A multi-view non-linear active shape model using kernel PCA. *In Proceedings of British Machine Vison Conference,* (pp. 483-492).

Sung, J., & Kim, D. (2004). Extension of aam with 3d shape model for facial shape tracking. *In Proceedings of IEEE International Conference on Image Processing.*

Sung, J., & Kim, D. (2006d). Estimating 3d facial shape and motion from stereo image using active appearance models with stereo constraints. *In Proceedings of International Conference on Image Analysis and Recognition.*

Sung, J., & Kim, D. (2006e). Staam: Fitting 2d+3d aam to stereo images. *In Proceedings of International Conference on Image Processing.*

Shum, H., Ikeuchi, K., & Reddy, R. (1995). Principal component analysis with missing data and its application to polyhedral object modeling. *IEEE Transactions on Pattern Analysis and Machine Intelligence, 17*(9), 854-867.

Schmidt, J., Niemann, H., & Vogt, S. (2002). Dense disparity maps in real-time with an application to augmented reality. *In Proceedings of IEEE Workshop on Applications of Computer Vision,* (pp. 225-230).

Sung, J., & Kim, D. (2006f). A unified approach for combining asm into aam. *In Proceedings of Pacific-Rim Symposium on Image and Video Technology.*

Sung, J., & Kim, D. (2006g). A unified approach for combining asm into aam. *International Journal of Computer Vision, 75*(2), 297-309.

Scott, I., Cootes, T., & Taylor, C. (2003). Improving appearance model matching using local image structure. *Information Processing in Medical Imaging, 2732,* 258-269.

Turk, M., & Pentland, A. (1991b). Face recognition using eigenfaces. *In Proceedings of IEEE Conference on Computer Vision and Pattern Recognition,* (pp. 586-591).

Turk, M., & Pentland, A. (1991a). Eigenfaces for recognition. *Journal of Cognitive Neuroscience, 3*(1), 71-86.

Üzümcü, M., Frangi, A. F., Reiber, J. H. C., & Lelieveldt, B. P. F. (2003). Independent Component Analysis in Statistical Shape Models. *In Proceedings of Medical Imaging.*

Wiskott, L., Fellous, J. M., Krüger, N., & Malsburg, C. (1997). Face recognition by elastic bunch graph matching. *IEEE Transaction on Pattern Analysis and Machine Intelligence, 19*(7), 775-780.

Wolstenholme, C., & Taylor, C. J. (1999). Wavelet compression of active appearance models. *Proceedings of MICCAI,* (pp. 544-554).

Xiao, J., Baker, S., Matthews, I., & Kanade, T. (2004b). Real-time combined 2d+3d active appearance models. *In Proceedings of IEEE Conference on Computer Vision and Pattern Recognition.*

Xiao, J., & Kanade, T. (2002). Robust full-motion recovery of head by dynamic templates and registration techniques. *In Proceedings of Automatic Face and Gesture Recognition.*

Yuille. A., Cohen. D., & Hallinan. P. (1989). Feature extraction from faces using deformable template. *IEEE Conference on Computer Vision and Pattern Recognition,* (pp. 104-109).

Yan, S., Liu, C., Li, S., Zhang, H., Shum, H., & Cheng, Q. (2002). Texture-constrained active shape models. *In Proceedings of European Conference on Computer Vision.*

Chapter IV
Face Tracking

When we want to analyze the continuous change of the face in an image sequence, applying *face tracking* methods is a better choice than applying the face detection methods to each image frame. Usually, the face tracking methods are more efficient than the ordinary face detection methods because they can utilize the trajectory of the face in the previous image frames with an assumption that the shape, texture, or motion of the face change smoothly. There have been many approaches to face tracking. We divide the face tracking methods into several categories according to the cues that are extracted for tracking.

The first category is feature-based approaches. Maurer and Malsburg (1996) and McKenna et al., (1997) used the features extracted by Gabor filters as the cues for face tracking. This approach is usually insensitive to global intensity changes and illumination changes. However, it is computationally expensive, and accordingly hard to implement for a real-time application.

The second category is skin color-based approaches. It uses the property that human facial colors of different people are clustered in a certain transformed 2-D color space (Yang and Waibel, 1996). Raja et al., (1998), Qian et al., (1998), Jang and Kweon (2000), Schwerdt and Crowley (2000), and Stern and Efros (2005) used this approach for face tracking. It is easy to implement, fast, and has a low computational cost. However, when the illumination condition changes drastically and the background image has a skin-like color, it easily fails to track the face. Color adaptation methods have been proposed to compensate for this problem. Raja et al., (1998) used a Gaussian mixture model to represent the skin color model and updated the parameters over time as the illumination condition changed. Qian et al., (1998) collected pixel samples whose filtering scores based on the general color model exceed a prescribed threshold and updated the color model. Jang and Kweon (2000) proposed an adaptive color model which used the basic structure of condensation. Stern and Efros (2005) used a number of different color models and switched the models during the tracking sequence. However these approaches, which used only skin color as the tracking cue, inevitably misidentify skin-colored objects in the background, mistaking them for faces.

The third category is shape-based approaches which track the elliptical contour of the face (Birchfield, 1997, Pardàs and Sayrol, 2000, Bing et al., 2004). They are not influenced by background color and illumination changes, but a highly cluttered background prevents tracking. To compensate for this, Birchfield (1998) used gradient intensity to measure an object's boundary shape and a color histogram to measure color of an object's interior, but he did not integrate the two measurement scores properly. Lee et al., (2007) proposed a robust face tracking method which used skin color and facial shape tracker separately.

The fourth category is parametric model-based approaches which includes ASMs (Cootes et al., 1995), AAMs (Cootes et al., 2001d, Matthews and Baker, 2004a), and 3D MMs (Blanz and Vetters, 1999). AAMs are the generative, parametric models of certain visual objects that show both shape and appearance variations. These variations are represented by linear models such as Principal Component Analysis (PCA), which finds a subspace reserving the maximum variance of a given data. A face model can be constructed from training data using the AAM, and the face tracking is achieved by fitting the learned model to an input sequence.

The last category is geometric head model-based approaches. A cylinder (Cascia et al., 2000, Xiao and Kanade, 2002), an ellipsoid (Basu et al., 1996), or a head-like 3D shape (Malciu and Preteux, 2000) are used to recover the global head motion. They assume that the shape of the head model does not change during tracking, which means that it does not have shape parameters. The global head motion can be represented by a rigid motion, which can be parameterized by three 3D rotation and three 3D translation parameters. The low dimensionality of the parameter space results in robust tracking performance when compared to the high dimensionality of the AAMs (Stegmann et al., 2004, Matthews and Basker, 2004a). In addition, 3D model-based head tracking methods do not require any learning stages, which means that they are person independent.

The status of the face in the next frame can be estimated from the history of the past trajectory of the face. This paradigm has been persuied by many researchers in the visual object tracking problem using many dynamics modeling techniques such as Kalman filter (Kalman, 1960, Welch and Bishop, 2001), CONDENSATION (Isard and Blake, 1998). The Kalman filter has been widely used for face tracking (Storm et al., 1999, DeCarlo and Metaxas, 2000), car tracking (Dellaert and Thorpe, 1997), hand tracking (Stenger et al., 2001; Blake and Isard, 1998), and so on. The CONDENSATION algorithm is different from the Kalman filter in that it is a non-linear dynamics model based on a sampling method that means it can handle multi-modal probability distribution of the status vector whereas the Kalman filter is a linear dynamics model that assumes a uni-modal probability distribution of the status vector. Since the CONDENSATION was introduced, it has become very popular in visual object tracking such as the hand tracking (Blake and Isard, 1998), and face tracking (Hamlaoui and Davoine, 2005; Sung and Kim, 2006a).

The requirements of the face tracking algorithms may be different from applications to applications according to their goals. However, the requirements of an ideal face tracking algorithm can be identified as follows. The ideal face tracking algorithm must be robust, fast, and detailed. The algorithm must be robust to the rotation of the face that cause the distortion of the texture and shape of the face, and the change of the environment such as illumination that make the face look different although the face does not move. The algorithm must be fast enough to be applied to real-time purpose applications. The algorithm must provide detailed information about the change of shape and texture not only the motion, these are useful for face recognition, facial expression recognition, lip reading, gaze tracking and so on.

Developing a face tracking algorithm that satisfies all the three requirements are very difficult because the improvement of the performance for one specific reqirement can be obtained by decreasing other requirements. For example, we have to use a dense and flexible 3D face model if we want to obtain detailed shape information. Such face models usually have a larger number of parameters, which makes the fitting algorithm complex and decreases the speed of fitting due to increased computations.

This chapter is organized by two parts. The first part reviews some preliminary backgrounds such as the particle filter framework, the geometric head models, and the incremental principal component analysis (IPCA). The particle filter, which is called CONDENSATION or *Bayesian filter*, is a general framework that can be applied to various tracking problems. When we are interested in only the rigid motion (rotation and translation) of the face, we often model the face as the goemetric head model such as a cylinder or ellipsoid. The incremental principal component analysis (IPCA) is used to update the linear appearance models of the AAMs to adapt the model to the untrained lighting condition of the environment.

The seond part explains several approaches to make face tracking successful. The first approach is a detection-based tracking algorithm, which initializes the AAM using the face and eye detection results at every frame, the second and third approaches try to estimate the global motion of the face efficiently using the ACM and CHM, respectively, where the estimated global motion of the face is used to compute good initial motion parameters of the AAMs before the AAMs' fitting algorithm begins. The fourth approach adapts the linear apperance model of the AAMs to the gradually changing illumination condition of the environment for stable face traking results. The fifth approach combines the AAM and particle filter and uses the motion prediction method for robust face tracking under a very fast moving head.

4.1 PARTICLE FILTERS

For visual object tracking problem, the Kalman filter have been widely used. However, the movement of the visual object does not follow constant velocity or constant acceleration dynamics model. Sometimes, the 2D trajectory of the visual object in an image sequence can change rapidly although the object moves at constant acceleration in the real 3D space. The particle filter is a generic framework that can alleviate this problem. Although the particle filter has been successfully applied to many difficult object tracking problems, the optimal number of partlcles, observation model, and dynamics model should be carefully designed to obtain good results.

The *particle filter* is a probabilistic approximation algorithm that implements the Bayesian filter, where they try to estimate the state of a dynamic system from a noisy observation probabilistically. Fig. 4.1.1 illustrates a graphical model of the Bayesian filters, where xt and yt are the hidden variable and the observed variable, respectively.

Bayesian filters take three important assumptions such as (i) the conditional independence, (ii) probabilistic relationship like Gaussian model, and (iii) the first order Markov process. Also, they include the motion model $p(x_y \mid x_{t-1})$ that is used to update the temporal change of the motion state x_t and the sensor likelihood model $p(y_t \mid x_t)$ that is used to update the measurement weights.

When we denote an observation sequence from time index 1 to t as $Y_{1:t}=(y1,y1,\ldots,yt)$, the operating process of the Bayesian filters can be described by the following two equations as

$$p\left(x_t \mid Y_{1:t-1}\right) = \sum p\left(x_t \mid x_{t-1}\right) p\left(x_{t-1} \mid Y_{1:t-1}\right) dx_{t-1} \qquad (4.1.1)$$

$$p\left(x_t \mid Y_{1:t}\right) = \frac{p\left(y_t \mid x_t\right) p(x_t \mid Y_{1:t-1})}{p(y_t \mid Y_{1:t-1})}$$

$$p\left(y_t \mid Y_{1:t-1}\right) = \sum p\left(y_t \mid x_t\right) p\left(x_t \mid Y_{1:t-1}\right) dx_t \qquad (4.1.2)$$

Here, Eq. (4.1.1) and (4.1.2) represent the time update that predicts the next state by the motion model $p(x_t \mid x_{t-1})$, and the measurement update that predicts the next observation by the sensor likelihood model $p(y_t \mid x_t)$, respectively. According to Bayes rule, the posterior distribution $p\left(x_t \mid Y_{1:t}\right)$ can be computed by the product of the prior distribution $p\left(x_t \mid Y_{1:t-1}\right)$ and the sensor likelihood model $p(y_t \mid x_t)$, where the evidence $p(y_t \mid Y_{1:t-1})$ is used as a normalization factor.

Among several Bayesian filter, the Kalman filter and the particle filter are generally used for the location tracking. The Kalman filter is an optimal estimator, where it assumes that the random variable is the Gaussian model and both the motion model and the sensor likelihood model are linear functions of the states. However, the particle filter can represent arbitrary probability densities. It can converge to the true posterior even in the non-Gaussian model and nonlinear dynamic systems

Particle filter is often called as SMC (Sequential Monte Carlo) or SIR (Sequential Importance sampling with Resampling). Fig. 4.1.2 illustrates the working principle of par-

Figure 4.1.1. A graphical model of Bayesian filters

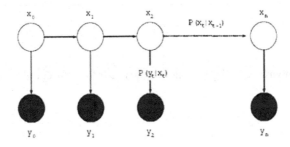

Figure 4.1.2. An operating process of particle filter

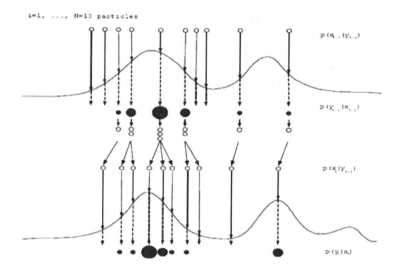

ticle filter, which can be summarized by the following. First, we create N initial samples. Second, we compute the weights of samples in the importance sampling process using the likelihood of the observed distribution. Third, we perform the resampling process to solve the degeneracy problem which samples are centralized in a specific region. Fourth, we perform the time update process. This process will be repeated until no more observation is founded.

In the practical implementation of *particle filter*, we take the sampling method to reduce the computational cost. According to the central limit theorem, the summation can approximate the integration when the number of samples N approaches to infinity as

$$I_N(f) = \frac{1}{N}\sum_{i=1}^{N} f(x^{(i)}) \overset{N\to\infty}{\Rightarrow} I(f) = \int_x f(x)p(x)dx.$$

(4.1.3)

So, if we substitute the integration for an approximation sampling, the time update process will be replaced by

$$p(x_t|Y_{1:t-1}) \approx \sum_{m=1}^{M} w_{t-1}^{(m)} p(x_t|x_{t-1}^{(m)})$$

$$w_{t-1}^{(m)} = \frac{p(y_{t-1}|x_{t-1}^{(m)})}{\sum_{m=1}^{M} p(y_{t-1}|x_{t-1}^{(m)})}$$

(4.1.4)

where $w_{t-1}^{(m)}$ is an importance weight of the mth sample of the observed distribution in the time t.

4.2 GEOMETRIC HEAD MODELS

The rigid motion of the head/face can be estimated by model-based 3D face tracking algorithms. When we are interested in the global head motion (Hereafter, we will use global motion to represent the rigid motion of the head/face and local motion to represent the local deformation of the face due to facial expression, speech, eye blinking, and so on.), using a simple *geometric head models* such as such as a cylinder (Cascia et al. (2000); Xiao and Kanade (2002)), an ellipsoid (Basuet et al. (1996)), or a head-like 3D shape Malciu and Preteux (2000) is a better choice than using the flexible face models such as the AAMs and MMs. The geometrical head models recover the global motion by minimizing the difference of texture or optical flow between observation and their model. Vacchetti et al. (2004) used multiple key frames and feature point matching to estimate the motion of their model under large pose variation. These approaches assume that the 3D shape of the object does not change during tracking, which means that they do not have shape parameters.

On the other hand, some researchers tried to track the deforming shape and global motion at the same time. Storm et al. (1999) used feature point tracking result with structure from motion in Kalman filter framework. Decarlo and Metaxas (1996) used a deforming face model whose fitting algorithm integrated optical flow and edge information. However, these algorithms are not adequate for tracking of large head pose change and the quality of the estimated 3D shapes cannot be guaranteed. The global head motion can be represented by a rigid motion, which can be parameterized by 6 parameters; three for 3D rotation and three for 3D translation. Therefore, the number of all the model parameters are only 6. The low dimensionality of the parameter space results in robust tracking performance when compared to the high dimensionality of the AAMs.

The geometric head models have shown good tracking results. In addition, these methods do not require any learning stage, which means that they are person independent. Moreover, they are robust to a large pose change because they use the whole area of the head in the image instead of a specific part. Among the various geometric head models, the cylinder head model seems the most generally applicable because the shape is very simple. If the shape become more detailed, then the fitting performance become more sensitive to initialization.

Among the various geometric head models, we will review the cylinder head model because it is the generally applicable and simplest method. The *cylinder head model* (CHM) s assume that the head is shaped as a cylinder and the face is approximated by the cylinder surface. Since the global motion of the cylinder is a kind of rigid motion, the global motion can be parameterized by a rigid motion vector μ, which includes the 3D rotation angles (w_x, w_y, w_z) and the 3D translations (t_x, t_y, t_z). When the 3D coordinate of a point on the cylinder surface is $\mathbf{x} = (x, y, z)^t$ in the camera-centered 3D coordinate system, the new location of $\mathbf{x}$ transformed by the rigid motion vector μ is

$$\mathbf{M}(\mathbf{x};\mu) = R\mathbf{x} + T, \qquad (4.2.1)$$

where M is a rigid transformation function that is represented by a 3D rotation matrix $R \in \mathbb{R}^{3\times3}$ corresponding to (w_x, w_y, w_z) and a 3D translation vector $T \in \mathbb{R}^{3\times1} = (t_x, t_y, t_z)^t$. Fig. 4.2.1 shows a cylinder surface point $\mathbf{x}_t = (x, y, z)$ in the camera-centered 3D coordinate system and its projection point $\mathbf{u}_t = (u, v)$ in the image plane at time t.

Figure 4.2.1. A cylinder model in the camera-centered 3D coordinate system

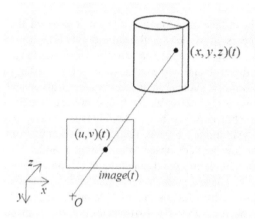

When the rigid head motion between the time t and $t + 1$ is represented by the rigid motion vector $\Delta\mu$, the new location of $\mathbf{u}_t$ at time $t + 1$ can be represented as

$$\mathbf{u}_{t+1} = \mathbf{F}(\mathbf{u}_t; \Delta\mu), \tag{4.2.2}$$

where $\mathbf{F}$ is the 2D parametric motion function of $\mathbf{u}_t$. If we assume that the illumination condition does not change between two image frames, then the intensity of the pixel $I_t(\mathbf{u}_t)$ must be consistent with that of the corresponding pixel in the next frame image as

$$I_{t+1}\big(\mathbf{F}(\mathbf{u}_t; \Delta\mu)\big) = I_t(\mathbf{u}_t). \tag{4.2.3}$$

The rigid motion vector $\Delta\mu$ can be obtained by minimizing the image difference between two image frames as

$$\min E(\Delta\mu) = \sum_{\mathbf{u}\in\Omega} \{I_{t+1}(\mathbf{F}(\mathbf{u}_t; \Delta\mu)) - I_t(\mathbf{u}_t))\}^2, \tag{4.2.4}$$

where Ω is the region of the template I_t whose corresponding pixel at the time $t + 1$ is also visible. The minimization problem can be solved by the *Lucas-Kanade* method (Kanade and Lucas, 1981) as

$$\Delta\mu = -\left(\sum_{\Omega}\big(I_u\mathbf{F}_\mu\big)\big(I_u\mathbf{F}_\mu\big)\right)^{-1}\sum_{\Omega}\big(I^t\big(I_u\mathbf{F}_\mu\big)\big), \tag{4.2.5}$$

where I_u and I_t are the spatial and temporal image gradient, and $\mathbf{F}_\mu = \dfrac{\partial \mathbf{F}}{\partial \mu}\big|_{\Delta\mu=0}$ denotes the partial derivative of $\mathbf{F}$ with respect to the rigid motion vector.

The new location $\mathbf{u}_{t+1}$ is the perspective projection of a 3D point that is the rigid transformation M of $\mathbf{x}_t$ by the rigid motion vector $\Delta\mu = (w_x, w_y, w_z, t_x, t_y, t_z)'$ as

$$\mathbf{u}_{t+1} = \mathbf{p}(\mathbf{M}(\mathbf{x}_t; \Delta\mu)), \tag{4.2.6}$$

where **p** represents the perspective projection function. When the rotation is small, the rotation matrix can be approximated as

$$R = \begin{bmatrix} 1 & -\omega_z & \omega_y \\ \omega_z & 1 & -\omega_x \\ -\omega_y & \omega_y & 1 \end{bmatrix} \tag{4.2.7}$$

using the exponential map (Bregler and Malik, 1998). Then, the perspective projection function **p** in (4.2.6) can be represented as

$$\mathbf{p}(\mathbf{M}(\mathbf{x}_t; \Delta\boldsymbol{\mu})) = \begin{bmatrix} x - y\omega_z + z\omega_y + t_x \\ x\omega_z + y - z\omega_x + t_y \end{bmatrix} \cdot \frac{f}{-x\omega_y + y\omega_x + z + t_z}, \tag{4.2.8}$$

where f is the camera focal length.

By comparing (4.2.2) and (4.2.8), we know that the perspective projection function **p** is merely a parametric motion function $\mathbf{F}(\mathbf{u}_t; \Delta\boldsymbol{\mu})$. Thus, the Jacobian of the parametric motion function $\mathbf{F}_{\boldsymbol{\mu}}|_{\Delta\boldsymbol{\mu}=0}$ can be computed by the derivative of the perspective projection function **p** as

$$\mathbf{F}_{\boldsymbol{\mu}}|_{\Delta\boldsymbol{\mu}=0} = \begin{bmatrix} -xy & x^2 + z^2 & -yz & z & 0 & -x \\ -(y^2 + z^2) & xy & xz & 0 & z & -y \end{bmatrix} \frac{f}{z^2}. \tag{4.2.9}$$

By plugging the computed Jacobian of the parametric motion function into (4.2.5), we can obtain the rigid head motion vector $\Delta\boldsymbol{\mu}$.

If we want to obtain the exact distance of head from the camera, we need to know the exact size of head and the focal length of camera. However, we fix the size of the cylinder model to be constant in this work. Hence, the estimated translation t_z does not give the exact distance of head from the camera. In addition, we do not know the exact focal length f when we do not calibrate the camera. However, it is known that the effect of f is usually small (Azarbayejani and Pentland, 1995).

4.3 INCREMENTAL PRINCIPAL COMPONENT ANALYSIS

PCA is a useful method to compress large amount of image data and keep the data in a compact size. Representative example is the eigenface in the face recognition research, where lots of high dimensional training face images are encoded into low dimensional coefficients vectors using the eigenface. However, the weakness of the traditional PCA is that we have to keep all the training data to update the eigenfaces using a new face image is to be added to the training data. The incremental PCA algorithms alleviate the problem because they can update the eigenfaces with the compactly represented coefficient vectors and the new image data. Thus, the incremental PCA has can be used for visual object tracking problems, where the PCA is used to learn the appearance variation of a target object (Artac et al., 2002, Li, 2004).

Many researchers have proposed incremental subspace learning algorithm (Artac et al., 2002; Hall et al., 1998; Li, 2004). Among them, we use the method proposed by Hall et al.(Hall et al., 1998). Suppose that a set of m-dimensional data vectors is $D = \{\mathbf{d}_1,...,\mathbf{d}_n\}$. The eigenspace of the data set can be obtained by solving the singular value decomposition (SVD) of the covariance matrix

$$\mathbf{C} = \frac{1}{n}\sum_{i=1}^{n}(\mathbf{d}_i - \mathbf{d})(\mathbf{d}_i - \mathbf{d})^T,$$ (4.3.1)

where

$$\mathbf{d} = \frac{1}{n}\sum_{i=1}^{n}\mathbf{d}_i$$

is the sample mean. Then, the given data set can be represented by $k(<m)$-dimensional coefficient vectors $\mathbf{a}_i$ by projecting the data vector $\mathbf{d}_i$ to a subspace spanned by k eigenvectors corresponding to k largest eigenvalues.

In the incremental PCA, it is assumed that the k eigenvectors $\{\mathbf{u}_1,...,\mathbf{u}_k\}$ that correspond to the k largest eigenvalues $\{\lambda_1,...,\lambda_k\}$ are already obtained. For the ease of the explanation, we will use a matrix $\mathbf{U} = [\mathbf{u}_1 \cdots \mathbf{u}_k] \in \mathbb{R}^{m \times k}$ that contains the k eigenvectors and a diagonal matrix $\boldsymbol{\Lambda} \in \mathbb{R}^{k \times k}$ that contains k large eigenvalues as the diagonal elements in the descending order.

When a new data vector $\mathbf{d}_{n+1}$ is given, the incremental PCA updates the mean and the basis vector as follows. Since the total amount of the data is changed, we should update the mean and the basis vector to represent the data including a new data. The mean is updated as

$$\overline{\mathbf{d}}' = \frac{1}{n+1}(n\overline{\mathbf{d}} + \mathbf{d}_{n+1}).$$ (4.3.2)

Then, the orthogonal residual vector $\mathbf{b}_{n+1}$ is computed as

$$\mathbf{b}_{n+1} = (\mathbf{U}\mathbf{a}_{n+1} + \overline{\mathbf{d}}) - \mathbf{d}_{n+1}.$$ (4.3.3)

Then, the orthogonal residual vector is normalized as

$$\hat{\mathbf{b}}_{n+1} = \frac{\mathbf{b}_{n+1}}{\|\mathbf{b}_{n+1}\|_2}.$$ (4.3.4)

We acquire the new basis set $\mathbf{U}'$ by rotating the basis set $[\mathbf{U} \quad \hat{\mathbf{b}}_{n+1}]$ so that the i-th basis of the new basis represents the i-th largest maximal variance as the

$$\mathbf{U}' = [\mathbf{U} \quad \hat{\mathbf{b}}_{n+1}]\ \mathbf{R}$$ (4.3.5)

The rotation matrix can be obtained by solving SVD for $\mathbf{D}$ matrix:

$$\mathbf{D}\ \mathbf{R} = \mathbf{R}\ \boldsymbol{\Lambda}'.$$ (4.3.6)

Then, we compose $\mathbf{D} \in \mathbb{R}^{(k+1)x(k+1)}$ as

$$\mathbf{D} = \frac{n}{n+1}\begin{bmatrix} \mathbf{\Lambda} & \mathbf{0} \\ \mathbf{0}^T & 0 \end{bmatrix} + \frac{n}{(n+1)^2}\begin{bmatrix} \mathbf{a}\mathbf{a}^T & \beta\mathbf{a} \\ \beta\mathbf{a}^T & \beta^2 \end{bmatrix} \qquad (4.3.7)$$

where $\beta = \hat{\mathbf{b}}_{n+1}^T(\mathbf{d}_{n+1} - \overline{\mathbf{d}})$ and $\mathbf{a} = \mathbf{U}^T(\mathbf{d}_{n+1} - \overline{\mathbf{d}})$, Among the several methods for constructing $\mathbf{D}$, we use the method proposed by Hall et al. (Hall et al., 1998).

4.4 A NAIVE APPROACH

When we try to apply the AAM for a practical application such as a face tracking, we need to consider some drawbacks of the AAM fitting method. First, the fitting result of an AAM is so sensitive to the initialization that the unconstrained AAM fitting algorithms may not converge to the correct solution (Cootes and Taylor, 2001a). To alleviate this problem, we proposed to use a face and eye detector that can provide a suitable initialization for a given input image by finding the face location and initializing the model parameters so that model's eyes match the detected eyes. Second, the fitting result of the AAM largely depend upon the stability of camera characteristics. Usually, the capturing characteristics of the stereo camera changes largely from time to time due to the instability of the electronic circuits and this makes a random fluctuation of captured images.

To alleviate this problem, we proposed to use a motion detector that can compensate the instability of camera characteristics by holding the current AAM parameters with the previous AAM parameters when the face is not moving. Third, the lighting conditions in the model construction may not be compatible with that in the test phase and this incompatibility of lighting conditions degrades the fitting performance of the AAM very much (Cootes and Taylor, 2001b). To alleviate this problem, we proposed to use a histogram matching technique (Gonzalez, 1993) that can match the image characteristics of the model image with those of the input image. Fig. 4.4.1 illustrates the result of histogram matching, where the left, middle, and right images are the model image, the transformed model image using the histogram matching, and the input image, respectively. As you can see, the transformed model image using the histogram matching, looks more similar to the input image.

Fig. 4.4.2 shows a face tracking system using the face detection (Jun and Kim, 2007). It works alternating two different modes: DETECTION and TRACKING mode. In DETECTION mode, we perform a face detection that locates the upright face and its two eyes in the left and right images, respectively. Because the face detector is based on the cascaded AdaBoost algorithm (Viola and Jones, 2002), it detects a face very fast. Then, the input image is matched to the model image by a histogram matching technique to alleviate the lighting incompatibility problem. Then, AAM parameters are initialized as $\mathbf{p}(t) = 0$, $\mathbf{a}(t) = 0$ and $\mathbf{q}(t) = \mathbf{q}_{eye}(t)$, where $\mathbf{q}_{eye}(t)$ denotes the similar transform parameters that is computed from the detected eye positions at the current frame t. Then, change current mode into TRACKING mode and go to the STAAM fitting algorithm.

In TRACKING mode, we perform a motion detection that checks a face motion in the current frame. If there is no motion, we take the previous AAM parameters as the current frame AAM parameters like $\mathbf{p}(t) = \mathbf{p}(t-1)$, $\mathbf{a}(t) = \mathbf{a}(t-1)$ and $\mathbf{q}(t) = \mathbf{q}(t-1)$ and go to the STAAM fitting algorithm. Else, we perform another face detection. If the face is not

Figure 4.4.1. An illustrative example of a histogram matching

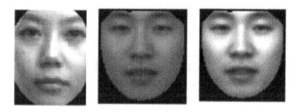

Figure 4.4.2. A block diagram of the face tracking using the face detection

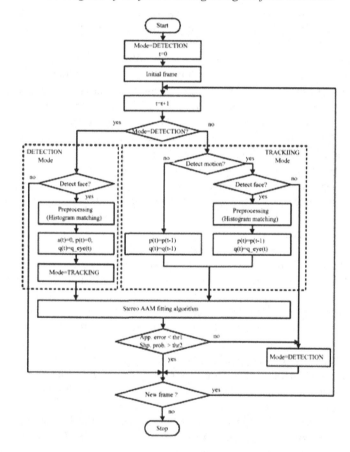

detected, change current mode into DETECTION mode and go to the next frame. Else, we perform the histogram matching similarly with the DETECTION mode and set the AAM model parameters as $\mathbf{p}(t) = \mathbf{p}(t{-}1)$, $\mathbf{a}(t) = \mathbf{a}(t{-}1)$ and $\mathbf{q}(t) = \mathbf{q}_{eye}(t)$, then go to the STAAM fitting algorithm.

After executing the STAAM fitting, we check whether the fitting result is normal or not, where we define the fitting result to be normal if the appearance error is smaller than a given threshold value and the 2D shape parameters are not far from their mean value. If the fitting result is normal, increase time index as $t = t + 1$ and go to the next frame. Else, change current mode into DETECTION mode and go to the next frame. The above operation will be stopped when there is no more frame.

Face tracking module recovers the 3D shape and rigid transformation parameters using the proposed STAAM and the modified ICSU algorithm. After fitting on the input stereo images, the module verifies whether the fitting is successful or not. We assume that the fitted 2D shape parameters are distributed in a Gaussian manner $G(\mathbf{p}, \sigma_p^2)$. If the fitted 2D shape parameter is deviated from the normality, we treats the current fitting to be failed and returns to the *detection mode* that tries to detect a new face in the next stereo image frame. Otherwise, we treat the current fitting to be successful and advance to the facial expression classification.

4.5 BACKGROUND-ROBUST FACE TRACKING USING AAM AND ACM

The fitting result of an AAM is very sensitive to the initialization. Since the existing AAM fitting algorithms try to find the solution in the AAM parameter space with dozens of dimensions, they are apt to be trapped in the local minima which is not the best solution. In many practical applications, an appropriate initialization is required for a good solution because the unconstrained AAM fitting algorithms may not always converge to the correct solution (Cootes et al., 2001b). Generally, the initialization is executed by using the external methods such as face detector and/or feature detectors that provide the information on the location of the object or important feature points (Cristinacce et al., 2004).

These information can be used to make a good initial estimation of the parameters so that AAMs can begin the search from nearby points of the best solution. If the information on the location of some feature points are reliable, then such information can be used to impose some constraints to the fitting algorithm (Cootes et al., 2001a). However, these approaches usually require a heavy computation to detect face or locate the feature points at every frames. In addition, if we take these approaches, then we need a pose invariant face and feature detector because we are targeting an on-line face tracking system, where unfortunately the face changes its pose freely. The pose invariant face and feature detection are very difficult problems.

The AAMs inherently model the foreground of the object and do not consider the background image. We have found that the AAMs often fail to converge accurately when the estimated object area in the target image includes the image background due to the misalignment that occurs frequently when we are tracking an object. The inclusion of the background image makes the backward warped image inconsistent with the original appearance, which causes the algorithm to update the parameters incorrectly and diverge eventually. This non-convergence of AAMs is salient when there are very bright backgrounds and/or textured backgrounds adjacent to the target object. One way to alleviate this image background problem is the *robust* AAM methods (Gross et al., 2003; Gross et al., 2004a) that use the weighted least square formulation to minimize the sum of weighted squared errors between the AAM synthesized instance and the input image.

Namely, the error between the synthesize appearance with currently estimated appearance parameters and the backward warped input image is weighted by an appropriate weight function, and then the weight values of some parts whose error are relatively large are set to small values and ignored in the parameter estimation process. In general, this approach requires more iterations than the original AAM fitting method because its update step size is smaller due to the ignorance of some part of object in the matching. In addition, this approach cannot handle the large motion of the object because the convergence depends on the local information.

To overcome these drawbacks, novel face tracking algorithm was proposed, called *AAM+ACM* method, that is robust to the large motion of the face and the image background (Sung and Kim, 2006a; Sung and Kim, 2006b; Sung and Kim, 2006c). The proposed algorithm estimates the motion of the face efficiently and separates the object foreground from the image background using the *active contour model*s (ACMs) and involves only the selected foreground part of the object in the process of AAM fitting. Although active contour was first introduced by Kass et al. (Kass et al., 1988) (their active contour is also known as SNAKE), many researchers have used this term to call the similar methods that model the shape of the non-rigid objects such as the deformable template (Yuille et al., 1989), the dynamic contour (Blake an Isard, 1998), and CONDENSATION (Isard and Blake, 1998).

4.5.1 Active Contour Technique

In this section, we explain how to locate the position of the face using a CONDENSATION-like contour-tracking technique, which is based on probabilistic sampling.

A contour $\mathbf{c}_0$ of an object can be extracted from the fitting result of the AAM at the previous frame by collecting the boundary points which is represented by a vector: $\mathbf{c}_0 = (x_1, y_1, ..., x_v, y_v)^T$, where we assume that the shape of the object does not change much in the consecutive frames, and the motion of the object we want to recover can be represented by a similarity transformation function that allows the scaling, the rotation, and the translation. A similarity transformation function can be parameterized by four parameters as

$$\begin{bmatrix} x' \\ y' \end{bmatrix} = \begin{bmatrix} 1+h_1 & h_2 \\ -h_2 & 1+h_1 \end{bmatrix} \begin{bmatrix} x \\ y \end{bmatrix} + \begin{bmatrix} h_3 \\ h_4 \end{bmatrix}, \tag{4.5.1}$$

where $h_1, ... h_4$ describe the scale, rotation, and translation of a point (x,y), respectively.

Using Eq. (4.5.1), we can represent all the possible contours $\mathbf{c}$ at the next frame by a linear equation as

$$\mathbf{c} = \mathbf{c}_0 + S\mathbf{h}, \tag{4.5.2}$$

where $\mathbf{h}$ is a motion parameter vector and S is

$$S = \begin{bmatrix} \mathbf{c}_{0x} & \mathbf{c}_{0y} & 1 & 0 \\ \mathbf{c}_{0y} & -\mathbf{c}_{0x} & 0 & 1 \end{bmatrix} \in R^{2v \times 4}, \tag{4.5.3}$$

where $\mathbf{c}_{0x}$ and $\mathbf{c}_{0y}$ are the $v \times 1$ column vectors that correspond to the x and y coordinate of the contour $\mathbf{c}_0$, respectively, and 1 and 0 are the $v \times 1$ unit and zero vectors.

The CONDENSATION method (Blake and Isard, 1998) aims to estimate the posterior probability distribution $p(\mathbf{h} \mid \mathbf{z})$, where $\mathbf{h}$ is a parameter vector in the contour space $S_\mathbf{h}$ using a factored sampling and $\mathbf{z}$ denotes the observations from a sample set. The output of a factored sampling step in the CONDENSATION method is a set of samples with the weights denoted as $\{(\mathbf{s}_1, \pi_1), (\mathbf{s}_2, \pi_2), ..., (\mathbf{s}_N, \pi_N)\}$, which approximates the conditional observation density $p(\mathbf{h} \mid \mathbf{z})$. In the factored sampling, a sample set $\{\mathbf{s}_1, \mathbf{s}_2, ..., \mathbf{s}_N\}$ is randomly generated from the prior density $p(\mathbf{h})$ and the weights π_i of the N generated samples are computed by

$$\pi_i = \frac{p_z(\mathbf{s}_i)}{\sum_{j=1}^{N} p_z(\mathbf{s}_j)}, \tag{4.5.4}$$

where $p_z(\mathbf{s}) = p(\mathbf{z} \mid \mathbf{h} = \mathbf{s})$ is the conditional observation density.

The relative weight of the conditional observation density $p(\mathbf{z} \mid \mathbf{h})$ represents the fitness of a sample, where the higher fitted sample is better matched to the boundary contour of the object. Usually, the boundary contour is represented by the salient edge features and the generated contour sample consists of a set of boundary points. Thus, we need to compute the distance at every boundary point individually, and the individual distances are summed to obtain the distance between the generated contour sample and the edge features of the object in the image. The distance at a boundary point is defined by the distance between the boundary point and the nearest edge point which is found along the normal direction of the contour. In this work, the weight of the sample is measured within a probabilistic framework assuming that the difference ε between the boundary point and the searched edge point is Gaussian distributed as $\varepsilon N(0, \sigma)$. We consider three different ways of computing the conditional observation density by the following.

1) Method I: based on the distance without prior knowledge

The conditional observation density $p(\mathbf{z} \mid \mathbf{h})$ of a given sample is computed by

$$p(\mathbf{z} \mid \mathbf{h}) \propto exp\left(-\frac{1}{2N\sigma^2} \sum_j d_j^2 \right), \tag{4.5.5}$$

where d_j is the distance measured at the jth boundary point of the ith contour sample. The searching of edge features near a boundary point on a contour sample is performed along the normal direction of the contour at the boundary point. Edge features are searched only within a predetermined range. When no edge feature is found within the range, the distance is set to the maximum value which is equal to the search range.

2) Method II: based on the distance with prior knowledge

Method I does not consider the prior knowledge $p(\mathbf{h})$ on the contour samples. If we employ the prior knowledge on the parameter vector, then we can restrict the generation of current contour samples to a range around the previous contour. This removes the outliers of the generated contour samples and accelerates convergence. We adopt the prior knowledge information to compute the conditional observation density $p(\mathbf{z} \mid \mathbf{h})$ of a given contour sample by the following.

$$p(\mathbf{z} \mid \mathbf{h}) \propto exp\left(-\frac{1}{2N\sigma^2}\sum_i d_i^2\right)exp\left(\mathbf{h}^T\Sigma^{-1}\mathbf{t}\right),$$ (4.5.6)

where the second term is a probabilistic representation of the dynamics of the parameters $\mathbf{h}$ that obeys $p(\mathbf{h}): N(0,\Sigma)$. Here, $\mathbf{h}$ is the contour parameter of the current image frame, and Σ is the covariance of the parameters $\mathbf{h}$. This term reflects the higher values of conditional observation density of the contour samples near the previous parameter.

3) Method III: Based on the Strength and Length

Methods I and II do not consider the quality of the image edge features found in the image but only the distance between the contour sample and the image edge features. We define the quality of image edge features in terms of the strength and/or the length. Thus, when two contour samples have the same fitness values in terms of the distance, the contour sample with the stronger and longer edge feature is chosen as a good contour sample. To cope with this idea, we define the conditional observation density as

$$p(\mathbf{z} \mid \mathbf{h}) \propto n_f \frac{\overline{s}_f}{\sigma_s \overline{d}_f},$$ (4.5.7)

where n_f is the number of boundary points on the contour sample within a given search range, $\overline{s}_f$ and $\overline{d}_f$ are the mean magnitude of edge gradient and the mean distance of the n_f image edge features, and σ_s is used to compensate the different scales of the edge gradient and the distance. When n_f is less than a given threshold value, the conditional observation density sets to zero.

4.5.2 Combining AAM and ACM

As mentioned before, a sampling-based active contour technique can be used to estimate the location of the moved face and separate the foreground area (face image area) from the image background area. Here, we propose to estimate the global motion of the face (similar transform) and eliminate the effect of the image background on AAM fitting by combining the active contour technique into the AAM fitting as follows.

Initially, we apply a face detection algorithm to find the area of the face image. Then, we apply the AAM fitting algorithm to the detected face image. The parameters of the fitted AAM are denoted as $\{\mathbf{p}^0, \mathbf{q}^0, \alpha^0\}$. Then, we apply an edge detection algorithm to the detected face image and find the initial contour $\mathbf{c}^0$ that fits the detected edge well. Then, we apply the following two stages alternatively in order to track the face image.

During stage I, we perform the active contour technique to find the contour sample that best fits the face image as follows.

Stage I: Active Contour Fitting

• Compute the contour $\mathbf{c}$ using Eq. (4.5.2), where the base shape $\mathbf{c}_0$ and the shape matrix S are obtained from the fitted contour parameters $\mathbf{s}^{t-1}$ at the $(t-1)$th image frame.

- Generate N random samples $\{\mathbf{s}_1 \ldots \mathbf{s}_N\}$ that are located near the contour $\mathbf{c}$.
- Evaluate the fitness of all generated samples using the conditional observation density function $p(\mathbf{z} \mid \mathbf{h})$.
- Choose the best sample $\mathbf{s}_{best}$ with the highest fitness value among N samples. We estimate the motion parameter $\hat{\mathbf{q}}^t$ at the next image frame t by composing two similar transformations $\mathbf{q}^{t-1}$ and $\Delta\hat{\mathbf{q}}^t$, where $\Delta\hat{\mathbf{q}}^t = \mathbf{s}_{best}$.

During stage II, we perform the active appearance model fitting algorithm over the best selected contour $\mathbf{s}_{best}$ as follows.

Stage II: Active Appearance Model Fitting

- Run the AAM fitting algorithm using the shape parameter $\mathbf{p}^{t-1}$, the appearance parameter α^{t-1}, and the estimated motion parameter, $\hat{\mathbf{q}}^t$.
- Obtain the optimal AAM model parameters $\mathbf{p}^t$, $\mathbf{q}^t$, and α^t.
- Perform the edge detection algorithm over the fitted face image and find the optimal contour $\mathbf{s}^t$ for the detected face edge.
- Set the image frame index $t = t - 1$, and return to stage I until reaching the final frame.

The proposed AAM+ACM face tracking algorithm is effective because we consider the following facts in the algorithm design. First, the base shape $\mathbf{c}_0$ in Eq. (4.5.2) is initialized using the boundary points of the fitted shape of the AAM from the previous image frame. Second, the initial global motion parameters of the AAM from the previous image frame are used to estimate the similar transformation parameters $\mathbf{h}$ of the generated contours. Third, the motion parameters in the selected contour are used to estimate the motion parameters of the AAM All these should expedite the convergence of the proposed algorithm.

Fig. 4.5.1 illustrates the proposed algorithm. The top left figure shows the shape $\mathbf{s}^{t-1}$ is overlaid on the image at the time t. The top right figure shows the N generated contour samples. The right bottom figure shows the motion vector $\Delta\mathbf{q}^t$ that is estimated from the selected best sample $\mathbf{s}_{best}$ as $\mathbf{q}^t = \Delta\mathbf{q}^t \circ \mathbf{q}^{t-1}$. Finally, the left bottom figure shows the result of AAM fitting from $\mathbf{p}^t$, $\mathbf{q}^t$, and α^{t-1}.

4.5.3 Experimental Results and Discussion

We performed several different experiments to evaluate the fitting performances of the proposed active contour-based AAM. First, we compared the performances of three different fitness functions in order to determine the appropriate fitness function. Then, we compared the performances of various AAM fitting methods.

4.5.3.1 Finding Edge Features of Contour Sample

For a given input image, we computed an edge map and a gradient map using a Canny edge detector. The Canny edge detector provided the directional edge features where four directions are defined as depicted in Fig. 4.5.2. We determined the threshold values for the Canny edge detector to produce few spurious edges and used the same threshold values

Figure 4.5.1. The proposed AAM+ACM tracking algorithm

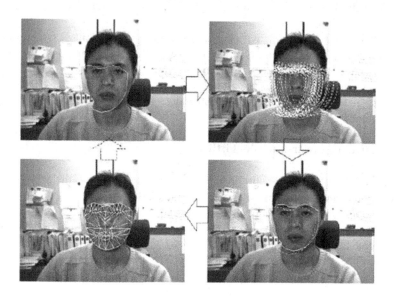

during all the experiments. Fig. 4.5.3 illustrates the input image and its corresponding directional edge map from the Canny edge detector.

For a boundary point of a given contour sample, we computed a normal vector direction at the boundary point and searched for edge features along the normal vector direction as depicted in Fig. 4.5.4. Our searching strategy was very simple in that it began from the first pixel to the left of the boundary point and then the first pixel to the right, then the second left pixel, then, the second right pixel, etc., until the nearest edge feature was detected. When the direction of the detected edge feature matched the direction of searching normal vector, we stopped the searching procedure of the boundary point and stored the value of the gradient at this point as the strength of the edge feature. Then, we continued edge feature searching from the next boundary point of the contour sample. However, if the two directions did not match each other, then we continued the searching for the edge features.

Figure 4.5.2. Four different directions in the Canny edge detector

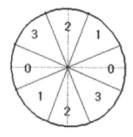

Figure 4.5.3. An input image and its directional edge map

Figure 4.5.4. An illustration of searching along the normal direction

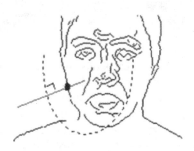

4.5.3.2 Comparison of Different Fitness Functions

First, we compared the fitting performances of the three different fitness functions to determine which one gave the best fit. Here, we generated 50 contour samples randomly near the boundary of the face image and applied three different fitness functions. Fig. 4.5.5 shows the 50 contour samples used in the top left. The top right, bottom left, and the bottom right of Fig. 4.5.5 show the active contour fitting results when methods I, II, and III were used as the fitness functions, respectively. From the figure, we can see that (1) Method II shows a better fitting result than Method I due to the use of prior information on the contours in the previous frame and (2) Method III shows the best fitting result among three different fitness functions due to the use of edge attributes strength and length.

Next, we compared the convergence performance of active contour fitting methods in terms of convergence rate, which was defined by the ratio of convergence cases to all trials. In this work, convergence means that each boundary point of the selected best contour sample is so close to the ground truth contour points that the average distance of all matching points is smaller than a specific threshold value. In this work, we set the convergence threshold value to 4 pixels, which is greater than the convergence threshold value for the AAM fitting.

We considered two kinds of face contour models. One contour model consists of only the boundary points at cheeks and chin (NOEYE type) and the other contour model includes the upper boundary points of the two eye brows (EYE type). We also consider three kinds

Figure 4.5.5. Comparison of fitting results among three different fitness functions

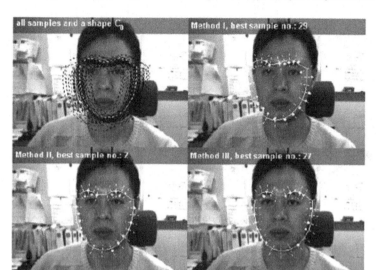

of sampling methods: one with 27 boundary points, another (51 points) which incorporated an additional point extrapolated between each adjacent pair, and the last one (75 points) incorporated two additional points between each pair.

Fig. 4.5.6 shows the convergence performances of three different fitness functions in the case of six different conditions, where the top three figures represent the NOEYE and the bottom three are the EYE cases. The three figures in each row represent the case of 27, 51, and 75 points, respectively. In each picture, the vertical axis denote the convergence rate of 100 trials and the horizontal axis denote the displacement σ in pixel size. The ground truth AAM parameters were perturbed to generate test contour samples with various values of the spatial displacement variable. In this work, the test sample contour was randomly perturbed from the ground truth contour by a white noise $N(0,\sigma^2)$.

From Fig. 4.5.6, we can see that (1) the EYE type of edge features results in a better convergence rate than the NOEYE type of edge features, (2) the convergence rate becomes larger as the number of boundary points increases, (3) Method III had the best convergence rate in all situations, and (4) the superiority of Method III is more salient as the number of points in the contour becomes smaller. From the above two experiments, we choose the Method III as the fitness function for the following experiments.

4.5.3.3 Comparison of Different AAM Fitting Methods

To measure and compare the performance of the proposed algorithm with other algorithms, we used the face image database that were gathered from 20 people in our lab. For each person, 20 images are registered in the database which contain four facial expression variations (neutral, happy, surprised, and angry) at frontal view and modest horizontal pose variations as shown in Fig. 4.5.7. Therefore, there are 400 images which we manually landmarked. We divided 20 people into 10 training sets and remaining 10 test sets. Thus, the AAM model is constructed using 200 training images and the number of shape and

Figure 4.5.6. Comparison of different fitness functions

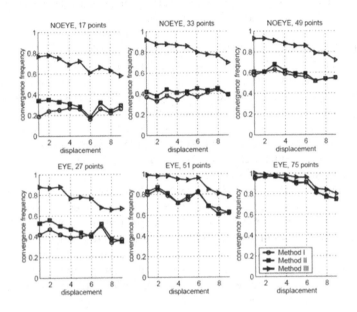

Figure 4.5.7. A set of face images for a specific person

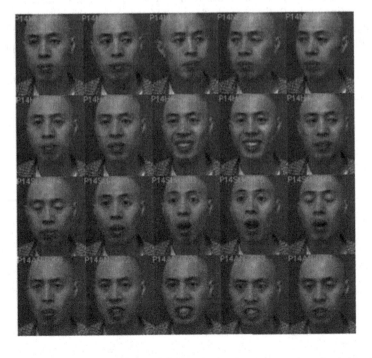

appearance bases are determined to keep 95% of the total shape and appearance variations respectively. The performance of the proposed algorithm is measured against 40 test images, i.e., 4 expression images are selected for 10 peoples in the test set.

First, we compared the general convergent characteristics between the robust AAM (Gross et al., 2003; Gross et al., 2004a) and the proposed AAM+ACM. We compared the accuracy of three different AAM fitting methods. They are the existing robust AAM (R-AAM), the proposed active contour based AAM (AAM+ACM), and a combination of the existing robust AAM and the proposed active contour based AAM (R-AAM+ACM), which utilizes the active contour technique as the face area detector and the existing robust method as the AAM fitting algorithm. For each method, we used two different types of parameter updates such as the normalization method (NO-update) and the simultaneous update method (SI-update), where the former uses the fixed Hessian matrix during the whole iterations and the latter updates the Hessian matrix every iteration (Gross et al., 2003).

Fig. 4.5.8 shows the RMS error of test images as the fitting algorithm is iterated, where the RMS error is defined as the mean distance between the 70 mesh points of the ground truth shape and the corresponding points of the current fitted shape. The left and right figures show the RMS error of the NO-update and SI-update, respectively. In each picture, the horizontal and vertical axis denotes the iteration index and the RMS error, respectively. Two curves are represented for each AAM method, corresponding to two differently perturbed AAM shapes that are generated from $N(0,3\sigma^2)$ and $N(0,6\sigma^2)$, respectively. Each point over the curve is the average value of the RMS errors of 800 independent trials (10 people * 4 images * 20 repeats).

From Fig. 4.5.8, we can see that (1) the RMS error of the proposed active contour based method rapidly drops to a certain level while the RMS error of the robust algorithms decrease smoothly, (2) the RMS error of the SI-update is smaller than that of the NO-update due to its update of every iteration, (3) the AAM fitting is converged within 5 iterations in most cases, (4) the fitting of the R-AAM method is not effective when the initial displacement is great, and (5) the proposed AAM+ACM has a good convergence accuracy even if there is a great initial displacement between the ground truth shape and the fitted shape.

Figure 4.5.8. Comparison of RMS errors among three different background robust AAM fitting methods

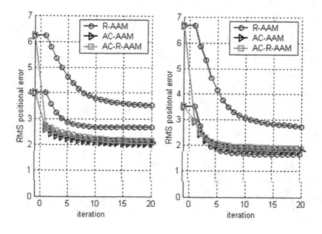

Second, we also compared the convergence rate of the three different AAM fitting methods, where the convergence rate is defined by the ratio of converged cases to all trials. If the fitted RMS error value is lower than a certain threshold value, then it is classified as a converged case. In this experiment, we used 2.0 as the threshold value. Fig. 4.5.9 shows the convergence rate where each point of the figure is the average convergence rate of 800 trials and again, the left and right figures correspond to NO-update and SI-update, respectively.

From 4.5.9, we know that (1) the convergence rate of the SI-update is higher than that of the NO-update due to its update of every iteration, (2) the difference of convergence rate between R-AAM and AAM+ACM becomes larger as the initial displacement error increases, which implies that the proposed AAM+ACM is more effective when the AAM shape is placed far from the target face, and (3) the R-AAM+ACM shows the best convergence performance, although even the difference of convergence rate between R-AAM and R-AAM+ACM is not large.

Third, we performed the same convergence experiments using another data set that are gathered under a very different imaging condition from the previous experiment. In this work, we call the previous face database as DATA-I and the current set of images as DATA-II. The face images in the data set DATA-I have relatively dark and clear background, but those in the data set DATA-II have more textured and bright background. Noisy edges from cluttered background can hamper the contour search algorithm and the bright background near the face can make the algorithm divergent. The ground truth data of these images are obtained using refitting technique (I. Matthews et al., 2004), where we used SI-update algorithm in the refitting procedure. Fig. 4.5.10 shows the convergent results when we are using the DATA-II, where the upper and bottom rows show the RMS errors and the convergence frequency, respectively, and in each row, the left and right figure are the convergent results of NO-update and SI-update, respectively.

From 4.5.10, we know that (1) the RMS error of the test results are very small when successfully converged to the target especially when SI-update algorithm is used because the ground truth of DATA-II data set are generated by refitting technique, where SI-update algorithm is used, (2) the RMS errors of the proposed active contour based method

Figure 4.5.9. Comparison of convergence rate among three different background robust AAM fitting methods on DATA-I

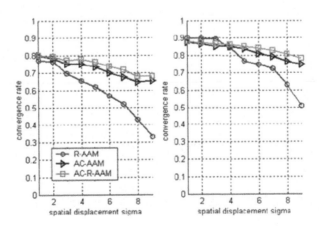

rapidly drop in contour search stage, which means that the proposed method works also in the image with cluttered background, (3) the proposed AAM+ACM method converged within 5 iterations in most cases, (4) the fitting of the R-AAM method is not effective when the initial displacement is great while the proposed AAM+ACM has a good convergence accuracy even if there is a great initial displacement error, (5) the convergence rate of the SI-update is higher than that of the NO-update due to its update of every iteration, (6) the difference of convergence rate between R-AAM and AAM+ACM becomes larger as the initial displacement error increases, which implies that the proposed AAM+ACM is more effective when the AAM shape is placed far from the target face even in the image with complex background, and (7) the R-AAM+ACM shows the best convergence performance, although even the difference of convergence rate between R-AAM and R-AAM+ACM is not large when SI-update is used.

Finally, we compared the execution time of the three different AAM methods in terms of the number of iterations. We only considered the converged cases among all trials and we stopped the iteration procedure when the difference of the average displacement of all vertices between two consequent iterations became smaller than 0.5 pixel. Fig. 4.5.11 shows the average number of iterations of the different methods, where the horizontal and the vertical axes denote the average number of iterations and the displacement σ, respec-

Figure 4.5.10. Comparison of RMS errors among three different background robust AAM fitting methods on DATA-II

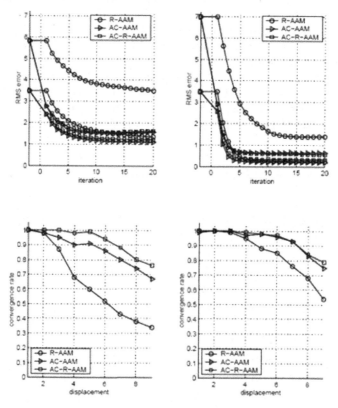

Figure 4.5.11. Comparison of number of iterations of three different AAM methods on DATA-II

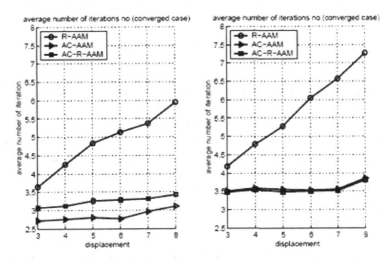

tively. Each point represents the average number of iterations of successfully converged trails that are independent.

From the Fig. 4.5.11, we note that 1) the NO-update was faster than the SI-update because the former uses the fixed Hessian matrix during the convergence but the latter updates the Hessian matrix every iteration, 2) while the average number of iterations of R-AAM increased as the displacement σ increased, those of AAM+ACM and R-AAM+ACM were almost constant even as the displacement σ increased, 3) AAM+ACM had the smallest average number of iterations. Two reasons can be found to explain this effect. The first one is that active contour technique rapidly pre-estimates the motion of the object. As we can see in Table 4.5.1, the cost of contour processing amounts to one iteration at most, which may cost more than one iteration in robust algorithms. The second reason is that this algorithm uses the entire error values that the algorithm can utilize because the active contour technique has already separated the object area from the background image.

We measured the execution time of the different methods in our C implementation, which took about 5 msec for the active contour fitting when 50 samples, 51 contour points, and 10 pixels of search range were considered. Also, it took about 8 msec and 26 msec for the NO-update and SI-update, respectively, in the robust AAM and it takes about 4 msec and 23 msec for the the NO-update and SI-update, respectively, in the the proposed AAM+ACM. Table 4.5.1 summarizes the execution time of the three different AAM methods, where N is the average number of iterations. From this table, we can see that the proposed AAM+ACM is the fastest method because the number of iterations for both AAM+ACM and R-AAM+ACM are almost the same but the execution time for each iteration of AAM+ACM is less than that of R-AAM+ACM.

The fitting result of the proposed AAM+ACM algorithm depends on the result of the ACM fitting stage that can fail to find correct face boundary when the background image has many noisy edges or when there are too little edges due to insufficient image contrast. The noisy edge problem can be alleviated by applying some preprocessing algorithms before the ACM fitting stage; We use the edges in the moving area (where the image dif-

Table 4.5.1. Comparison of the execution times (N represents the number of iterations)

Algorithm	NO-update	SI-update
R-AAM	N × 8 msec	N × 26 msec
AC-AAM	5 + N × 4 msec	5 + N × 23 msec
AC-R-AAM	5 + N × 8 msec	5 + N × 26 msec

ference is large) and in the area where the face was found in the previous frame (to detect the face boundary when the face is not moving) and remove the remaining edges in the static image background. However, the insufficient image contrast problem is difficult to overcome and the AAM+ACM algorithm cannot work when the edge information is not sufficient. A simple but not perfect solution is to measure the amount of the edge information by counting the number of edge pixels and skip the ACM fitting stage when the edge information is judged to be not sufficient for the ACM fitting.

4.5.3.4 Benefits of AAM+ACM Face Tracking Method

The proposed AAM+ACM can be understood as a combination of existing AAM fitting algorithm with more general search algorithm: active contour technique. The benefits of the algorithm can be summarized in three aspects as follows.

First, the proposed method is robust to a variety of background environments than the traditional AAM fitting algorithms and converges more fast. Fig. 4.5.12 shows the convergence procedure of the two AAM methods, where they start from the same situation with a bright and cluttered background and a modest displacement between the AAM model and the real face area. Although both algorithms have converged in this figure, the number of the robust algorithm requires more iterations than the proposed AAM+ACM algorithm on average. In this specific situation, the number of iterations of the robust AAM and AAM+ACM are 12 and 4, respectively.

Second, when the AAMs are used in tracking problems, the AAM+ACM can handle a large motion of the object more efficiently than the robust AAM. This property comes from the broad search property of the active contour technique. Although the number of samples and the assumed probability distribution must be handled carefully to generate appropriate contour sample set, active contour based algorithm searches a far more broader area in parameter space than traditional gradient based fitting algorithms. Li et al. (Li et al., 2001) suggested a similar idea that they used genetic algorithm to find the 3D shape model parameters and texture parameters in a sequence of face images. However, their formulation requires heavy computation when compared to active contour technique. Fig. 4.5.13 shows an example of a large motion where the robust algorithm cannot follow up while the proposed method can follow the motion of the face effectively.

4.6 POSE-ROBUST FACE TRACKING USING AAM AND CHM

The face tracking using only the AAMs cannot be successful when the face moves fast and changes its pose freely. Although the AAM+ACM face tracking algorithms can solve the large motion problem, they cannot handle the problems due to the pose change of the face.

Figure 4.5.12. Comparison of two different background robust tracking algorithms in terms of number of iterations

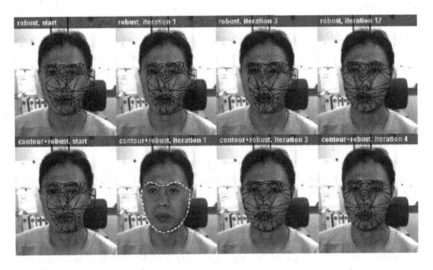

Figure 4.5.13. Comparison of two different background robust tracking algorithms in terms of tracking performance

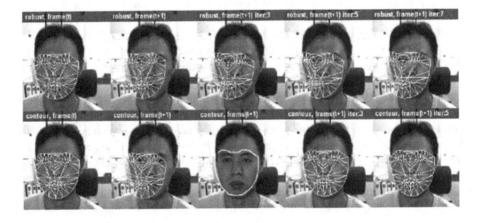

When the head pose is deviated from the front view too much, the AAMs fail to converge correctly because most part of the face image becomes invisible. Once the AAMs fail to track the face, they cannot work until it is re-initialized. Since the re-initialization can be usually done by the face detector at the font view, the AAMs cannot operate until the face pose returns to near frontal view.

For the head tracking problem, many researchers have used several simple geometric head models such as a cylinder (Cascia et al., 2000; Xiao et al., 2002) , an ellipsoid (Basu et al., 1996), or a head-like 3D shape (Malciu et al., 2000) to recover the global head motion. They assume that the shape of the head model does not change during tracking, which means that they do not have shape parameters. The global head motion can be represented by a rigid motion, which can be parameterized by 6 parameters; three for 3D rotation and three for 3D translation. Therefore, the number of all the model parameters are only 6. The low dimensionality of the parameter space results in robust tracking performance when compared to the high dimensionality of the AAMs. In addition, these methods do not require any learning stage, which means that they are person independent.

Moreover, they are robust to a large pose change because they use the whole area of the head in the image instead of a specific part. However, the rigid head model cannot provide detailed information such as the local movement of the facial features; opening mouth, closing eyes, raising eye brows, and so on. Among three different geometric head models, we take the cylinder head model because it is the generally applicable and simplest method. The *CHM* is more appropriate for approximating the 3D shape of the generic faces than the ellipsoid model. Also, the head-like 3D shape model requires a large number of parameters and its fitting performance is very sensitive to their initialization.

Fig. 4.6.1 compares the working range of pose angles, in which an AAM and a CHM are tracking a face that is moving horizontally, where the horizontal and vertical axes represent the time and the yaw angle of the head, respectively. We assume that the CHM can follow the head motion within the range of 90 degree and the AAM can fit within a limited range of pose angle from the frontal view. The two lines in the bottom represent the time-interval of successful face tracking of the CHM (solid line) and the AMM (dotted line), respectively. As it is shown, the AAM can track the face within the very limited time interval while the CHM can track the face through the whole range of pose angles.

To solve the large motion and pose problems simultaneously, a new face tracking algorithm was proposed which combining the AAMs and the CHMs together. They are tightly coupled with each other in the following manner. In the very beginning of face tracking, the AAM local motion parameters provide the initial cues of the global motion parameters of the CHMs[1]. During the face tracking, the global motion parameters of CHMs provide the initial cues of the facial feature parameters of the AAMs. The proposed face tracker have many advantages by the following. From the viewpoint of AAMs, the global motion parameters obtained from the CHMs can be used to estimate a good candidate of initial parameters for the AAM fitting, and to re-initialize the face tracking when AAMs fail to fit the current face image. This makes the face tracking robust to the change of face pose and extends the range of face tracking effectively. From the view point of CHMs, the detailed information of the local movements of the facial features obtained from the AAMs enables the CHMs to recognize the facial expressions, gazes, and several facial gestures such as nodding/disapproval by head motion, blinking eyes, and opening/closing mouth, and so on.

The detailed explanation on the AAM+CHM face tracking method is given by the following.

4.6.1 Local Motion Tracking Using the AAMs

When the AAMs are used for the face tracking problems, the AAM parameters obtained in the previous frame are usually used as the initial parameters for the fitting in the current frame. The AAM fitting fails frequently when the head movement is large or the pose deviation from the frontal face is great. Eventually, this results in the failure of the local

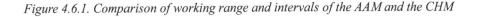

Figure 4.6.1. Comparison of working range and intervals of the AAM and the CHM

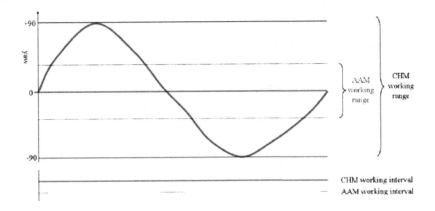

motion tracking. When the local motion tracking fails, we usually find the face area via face detector and eyes via eye detector to restart the AAM fitting from the initial AAM parameters estimated from these initial cues.

Table 4.6.1 shows a typical face tracking algorithm using the 2D+3D AAMs. It alternates two operating modes: detection and tracking, where they are different in obtaining the initial AAM parameters for fitting. In the beginning, the algorithm starts in the detection mode (step 1) and reads an input image (step 2). Then, it tries to find a face in the image. If a face is detected, then it computes the 2D similarity transform vector $\mathbf{q}$ so that the two eye points of the mean shape $\mathbf{s}_0$ match to the detected two eye points and sets the 2D shape parameters $(p_1,\dots,p_n)$ to zero (step 3). Next, it synthesizes a 2D shape $\mathbf{s}$ and computes the 3D shape parameters $\mathbf{p}$ and projection parameters $\mathbf{q}$ (the parameters of the affine projection model: 3D rotation, scale and 2D translation) from $\mathbf{s}$ by using the algorithm proposed by Romdhani et al. (Romdhani et al., 2003) (step 4). Then, it changes the operating mode to the tracking mode (step 5). In the tracking mode, it takes the previous 2D+3D AAM parameters as the initial 2D+3D AAM parameters (step 6), and fits the 2D+3D AAM to the current image to obtain optimal 2D+3D AAM parameters (step 7). If it fails to converge to the current image correctly, then it changes the operating mode to detection mode and goes back to step (2) (step 9). Although it is difficult to determine whether the AAM's fitting is successful or not, we use the amount of difference between the model synthesized image and the current image as a measure of successful fitting in this work.

However, the AAM parameters in the previous frame are not always a good estimate for the current frame when the face is moving fast. The AAM's sensitivity to initial parameters becomes more critical when the face pose is deviated from the frontal view. As the face pose is approaching to the profile view, the larger area of the face becomes invisible, which means that only a small part of the texture information is available and the fitting on the little textured image is apt to fail. Fig. 4.6.2 (a) shows how sensitive the 2D+3D AAM fitting is to the initial model parameters at five different pose angles (0°, 10°, 20°, 30°, and 40°) that are shown in Fig. 4.6.2 (b). The fitting performance is measured by the convergence rate that is defined by the ration of the number of successful AAM fitting over the number of trials of AAM fitting (= 100). The initial model parameters for each trial of AAM fitting

Table 4.6.1. Face tracking algorithm using the 2D+3D AAMs

	Procedure Local_motion_tracking_using_AAMs
(1)	Set *mode = detection* and $t = 1$.
(2)	Obtain an input image I_t.
	If *mode = detection*
	If a face is detected
(3)	Compute 2D similarity transform parameters $q_{t-1} = (p_{n+1}, \ldots, p_{n+4})^t$ using the detected two eye points, and set $(p_1, \ldots, p_n)_{t-1} = 0$.
(4)	Synthesize a 2D shape $\hat{s}$ using estimated AAM parameters in step (3), compute $\bar{p}_{t-1}$ and $\bar{q}_{t-1}$ from $\hat{s}$, and set $\alpha_{t-1} = 0$.
(5)	Set *mode = tracking*.
	End
	End
	If *mode = tracking*
(6)	Set $\alpha_t = \alpha_{t-1}$, $p_t = p_{t-1}$, $\bar{p}_t = \bar{p}_{t-1}$, and $\bar{q}_t = \bar{q}_{t-1}$.
(7)	Obtain optimal 2D+3D AAM parameters α_t, p_t, $\bar{p}_t$, and $\bar{q}_t$ by fitting the 2D+3D AAM to I_t.
	If failed to converge correctly
(8)	Set *mode = detection*.
	End
	End
(9)	Set $t = t + 1$ and goto (2).

Figure 4.6.2. The sensitivity of AAM fitting to difference initial displacements

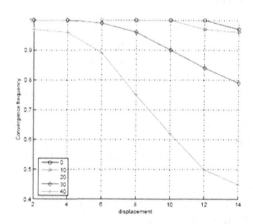

(a) Convergence rate vs. initial displacements

(b) 0°   (c) 10°   (d) 20°   (e) 30°   (f) 40°

are computed by translating the ground truth landmark points by the amount of displacement value to a random direction. This figure shows that (1) the convergence rate decreases as the initial displacement increases for a given pose angle and (2) the convergence rate decreases abruptly as the face pose is deviated from the frontal view for a given initial displacement due to the lack of texture information; The area of the left half side of the face becomes small (15,675, 11,803, 9,387, 8,044, and 5,423) as the pose angle is deviated from the frontal view.

Another problem occurs when the most part of the face becomes invisible. In this situation, the AAMs fail to fitting and the algorithm loses its tracing of the face (step 10). The problem is that the AAMs cannot work until they are re-initialized even though they possess the fitting capability to the images that arrive before the re-initialization.

4.6.2 Global Motion Tracking

Although the AAMs and the CHMs use the same gradient-based iterative optimization techniques for their fitting algorithms, fitting of the CHMs is easier than that of the AAMs because the CHMs have only 6 global motion parameters. Therefore, it is better to use the CHMs for global motion of the face. Among the various face tracking methods that use the CHMs, we take the tracking method that was proposed by Xiao and Kanade (2002) due to its robustness to the occlusion, the local motion in the face, and the gradual lighting change.

Table 4.6.2 shows the face tracking algorithm using the CHM. Initially, the algorithm operates in the detection mode (step 1) and reads an image (step 2). Then, it tries to find a face in the current image. If a face is detected, it initializes the global motion parameters μ_t using the face detection results (step 3), and changes the operating mode into the tracking mode and proceeds to the next input image (step 10).

When it is operating in tracking mode, it takes the previous global motion parameters μ_{t-1} as the initial values of the current global motion parameters μ_t (step 5). Then, it estimates the global motion parameters μ_t using the fitting algorithm given in the section 4.2 (step 6). Next, it performs the re-registration procedure that is given in Table 4.6.3 (step 7). Finally, it performs the dynamic template update in order to adapt the template image with the gradually changing current input image (step 8). When it fails to converge to the current image, it change the operating mode into the detection mode and goes back to step (2).

4.6.3 Combining AAM and CHM

As mentioned before, the AAMs and CHMs are appropriate for the local motion tracking of facial feature movements and global motion tracking of head movements, respectively. Hence, the face tracking using the AAMs works only when the face pose is deviated not too much from the fontal view. To overcome this limitation, we propose to combine the *AAMs* and the *CHMs*, where the global motion parameters of the CHMs provide the cues of the initial parameters that are appropriate for the AAM fitting. By combining these two models, we expect that we can obtain advantages by the following. First, the duration of successful face tracking increases because the CHMs re-initialize the AAMs effectively. Second, the pose angle of successful face tracking extends because the CHMs can provide accurate initial parameters for the AAM fitting. Third, the pose angle of the CHMs can be used to determine whether to run the AAM fitting or not. Last, the result of the AAM fitting is used to initialize the CHMs.

Table 4.6.2. Global motion tracking algorithm using the CHMs

	Procedure Global_motion_tracking_using_CHMs
(1)	Set *mode* = *detection* and $t = 1$.
(2)	Obtain an input image I_t.
	If *mode* = *detection*
	If a face is detected
(3)	Initialize the global motion parameters μ of CHMs using the face Detection result.
(4)	Set *mode* = *tracking* and go to step (10).
	End
	Else
(5)	Set μ_{t-1} as the initial global motion parameters of μ_t.
(6)	Estimate the current global motion parameters μ_t using the fitting algorithm given in Section 3.1.
(7)	Perform *re-registration* given in Table 3.
(8)	Perform *dynamic template update* that takes the current input image I_t as the template image T for the next time.
	If failed to converge correctly
(9)	Set *mode* = *detection*.
	End
	End
(10)	Set $t = t + 1$ and goto step (2).

Although the global motion parameters of the CHMs can be initialized using the face detection result, sometimes, its location and size do not exactly match the face in the image, which results in incorrect initialization of the CHMs. Hence, the AAMs provide precise locations of the landmark points such as face boundaries and eyes. The initial global motion parameters of the CHM are computed in two steps. First, the AAMs are initialized using the face detection result and fitted to the image. Second, the fitted 2D shape of the AAMs is used to compute the 3D rotation angles and 3D translation parameters as follows. The roll (rotation about z axis) angle is computed by measuring the angle between the line passing through the two eye centers and the horizontal axis in the image (u axis); the roll angle will be zero if the face is upright. The yaw (rotation about y axis) angle is computed by looking into the location of the center of the two eyes; it will be located at the center

Table 4.6.3. Re-registration procedure

	Procedure Re-registration
(7.1)	Find a reference image I_r whose global motion parameters μ_r are the most closest to μ_t among the registered reference images.
	If $\|\mu_r - \mu_t\| < \delta_1$
(7.2)	Estimate the global motion parameters μ_t' using the selected reference image I_r.
	If $error(I_r, T) < error(I_t, T)$
(7.3)	Set $\mu_t = \mu_t'$
	End
	End

of the left and right boundary of the face if the yaw angle is zero. The t_z is computed by comparing the ratio of the width of the cylinder model, which is predefined as a constant, to the width of the face in the image. The t_y is computed so that the bottom line of the face (jaw) matches the bottom of the projected cylinder model and the t_x is computed so that the left and right boundaries of the face match to the boundary of the projected cylinder model whose distance is t_z. The only one parameter that cannot be computed is tilt (rotation about x axis) because it is difficult to estimate how much the face is tilted from the 2D locations of the landmark points. Thus, we set the tilt angle to zero.

Table 4.6.4 shows the detailed procedure to compute the initial 2D+3D AAM parameters using the global motion parameters $\Delta\boldsymbol{\mu}$ estimated by the CHM fitting. In the procedure, the initial shape and motion parameters ($\mathbf{p}$, $\mathbf{p}$ and $\mathbf{q}$) are estimated using $\Delta\boldsymbol{\mu}$ and the appearance parameters are copied from previous appearance parameters.

Sometimes, it is impossible to compute the inverse projection when the locations of the shape points do not belong to the area that is the projection of the CHM. In that case, we used the previously computed surface coordinates corresponding to such shape points, instead of computing the surface coordinates of them in the step (step 1) of the Table 4.6.4. The points on the cylinder surface may become invisible as the face rotates. Thus, only the visible surface points are projected to image and used to compute the model parameters of the 2D+3D AAM in the step (3) of Table 4.6.4.

Table 4.6.5 shows the proposed face tracking algorithm using the combination of the AAMs and the CHMs. Initially, the algorithm operates in the detection mode (step 1) and reads an input image (step 2). Then, it tries to find a face in the current image. If a face is detected, then it computes the initial 2D+3D AAM parameters using the face detection result and fits the 2D+3D AAM to the current image Then, it initializes the global motion parameters $\boldsymbol{\mu}_t$ using the 2D+3D AAM fitting result (step 3), changes the operating mode into the tracking mode, and proceeds to the next input image (step 4). When it is operating in the tracking mode, it estimates the global motion parameters $\boldsymbol{\mu}_t$ as in the face tracking

Table 4.6.4. A procedure of estimating the initial AAM parameters from the CHM fitting result $\Delta\boldsymbol{\mu}$

	Procedure Estimation_of_initial_AAM_parameters
(1)	Each point of the 2D shape s_{t-1} that is obtained in the previous time is inversely projected to the cylinder surface to compute corresponding 3D coordinates $\{x_{t-1}^j\}_{j=1}^v$ as $$x_{t-1}^j = p^{-1}(s_{t-1}^j; \mu_{t-1}),$$ where μ_{t-1} is the previous global motion parameters.
(2)	The 3D surface points $\{x_{t-1}^j\}_{j=1}^v$ are transformed by the global motion $\Delta\mu$ that is estimated by the CHM fitting: $$\hat{x}_t^j = M(x_{t-1}^j; \Delta\mu).$$
(3)	Project the transformed 3D surface points to image plane to obtain the estimate of the current 2D shape $\hat{s}_t$: $$\hat{s}_t^j = p(\hat{x}_t^j).$$
(4)	Compute the 2D and 3D shape parameters of the 2D+3D AAM from $\hat{s}_t$, and set the previous appearance parameters as the initial appearance parameters: $\alpha_t = \alpha_{t-1}$.

algorithm given in Section 3.2 (step 5). Next, it performs the re-registration procedure that is given in Table 4.6.4 (step 6). Then, it performs the dynamic template update in order to adapt the template image with the gradually changing current input image (step 7). If it fails to converge to the current image, then it changes the operating mode into the detection mode and proceeds to the next input image (step 8), else it performs the *estimation of initial AAM parameters* procedure, whose details are given in Table 4.6.5, (step 9). Then, it fits the 2D+3D AAM to the current image (step 10).

4.6.4 Experimental Results and Discussion

4.6.4.1 Dataset

We used two image sequences, where the first image sequence consists of 409 images with freely yawing and tilting head movements and the second image sequence consists of 839 images with freely yawing head movements. The head moved from left to right and then from right to left repeatedly in an increasing yawing angles.

The first image sequence was used to construct the 2D+3D AAM, i.e., the sequence was manually landmarked, and gathered to build a 2D+3D AAM. The 3D shape model was also built from the landmarked shapes using the *structure from motion* algorithm (Xiao et al., 2004a). The number of bases in each model was determined to keep 95% of

Table 4.6.5. The proposed face tracking algorithm using the AAMs and CHMs

Procedure Face_tracking_using_AAMs_and_CHMs
(1) Set *mode* = *detection* and $t = 1$.
(2) Obtain an input image I_t.
If *mode* = *detection*
If a face is detected
(3)   Initialize the global motion parameters μ_t of the CHM using the result of 2D+3D AAM fitting.
(4)   Set *mode* = *tracking* and go to step (9).
End
Else
(5)   Estimate the global motion parameters μ_t using the global motion tracking algorithm.
(6)   Perform *re-registration* given in Table 3.4.
(7)   Perform *dynamic template update* that takes the current input image I_t as the template image T for the next time.
If failed to converge correctly
(8)   Set *mode* = *detection* and go to step (11).
End
If pose angle is within the AAM working range
(9)   Perform the procedure *Estimation of initial AAM parameters* given in Table 3.2.
(10)   Obtain the optimal model parameters α_t, p_t, $\bar{p}_t$, and $\bar{q}_t$ by fitting the 2D+3D AAM on I_t.
End
End
(11) Set $t = t + 1$ and goto step (2).

variations. Fig. 4.6.3 shows some examples of the appearance model, the 2D shape model, and 3D shape model.

4.6.4.2 Evaluation Methods

We compared two face tracking methods: AAM and AAM+CHM, where AAM denotes the face tracking method using only the 2D+3D AAM and AAM+CHM denotes the face tracking method that combines the 2D+3D AAM and the CHM together. In this work, we evaluated the face tracking performance in terms of two measures: *tracking rate* and *pose coverage*.

The tracking rate measures how many image frames are successfully tracked as

$$tracking\ rate = \frac{the\ number\ of\ successfully\ tracked\ image\ frames}{the\ number\ of\ total\ iamge\ frames}, \qquad (4.6.1)$$

where the face is successfully tracked when the RMS error between the fitted shape points and the ground truth landmark points is smaller than a given threshold.

Figure 4.6.3. The appearance, the 2D shape, and the 3D shape model of the 2D+3D AAM

(a) Appearance model: A_0, $A_0 + 3\sigma A_1$, and $A_0 - 3\sigma A_1$

(b) 2D shape model: s_1, s_2, and s_3

(c) 3D shape model: $\bar{s}_1$, $\bar{s}_2$, and $\bar{s}_3$

The pose coverage measures the range of pose angles where the face is successfully tracked as

$$pose\ coverage = (min(\{\widetilde{\theta}_k\}), max(\{\widetilde{\theta}_k\})), k \in \mathcal{B}, \tag{4.6.2}$$

where $\widetilde{\theta}_k$ and $\mathcal{B}$ represent the pose angles of the kth frames and a set of frame numbers in which the face is tracked successfully, respectively.

4.6.4.3 Face Tracking Using a Training Image Sequence

In this experiment, we took the first image sequence to build the 2D+3D AAMs and took the same image sequence for evaluating the tracking performances of two different face tracking algorithms: AAM and AAM+CHM. The training sequence contains the moderate yawing and tilting head motions. Fig. 4.6.4 shows the measured RMS errors, where the horizontal and vertical axes represent the frame number and the RMS error value, respectively, and the thin and thick solids line denote the RMS errors of the AAM and AAM+CHM tracking method, respectively. This figure shows that the AAM+CHM tracking method tracked the whole image sequence successfully, while the AAM tracking method failed to track the faces in many frames, especially at the end of the image sequence even though the AAM was built from the training image sequence.

Fig. 4.6.5 compares the tracking results of the two different tracking algorithms at some specific image frames (from left to right, 310, 320, 330, 340, and 350th frame), where the face turned from the upper left side (310th frame), through the front (330th frame), to the upper right side (350th frame). The top and bottom rows in the figure correspond to the tracking result of the AAM and AAM+CHM tracking method, respectively. In the case of the AAM tracking method, the face tracking began to fail near the 320th frame because there was a large head motion between the 310th and 320th frame. Then, it continued to fail because the model parameters at the previous frame were not appropriate for the initial parameters for the face image at the current frame. The success of face tracking at the 350th frame occurred unexpectedly because the fitting result at the 340th frame was as good as

Figure 4.6.4. Face tracking results in a training image sequence

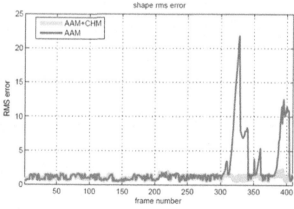

Figure 4.6.5. Some tracking results of two different tracking methods

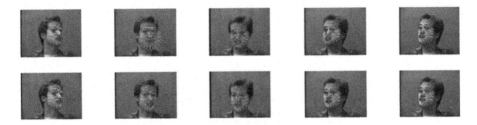

the initial parameters for the face image at the 340th frame. In the case of the AAM+CHM tracking method, it tracked the face successfully during all image frames.

Table 4.6.5 compares two different tracking methods in terms of the tracking rate and the pose coverage, where the second and third column correspond to the AAM+CHM and AAM tracking method, respectively. This table shows that (1) the pose coverages of two tracking methods are almost the same because we tested the tracking performance of two tracking methods by using the training image sequence, (2) the maximum angles of yawing and tilting were about 40°, and (3) the AAM+CHM tracking method greatly improves the face tracking performance; the tracking rate increased from 0.87 to 1.0. Since the head motion in the training image sequence is within the range of the AAM fitting, the re-initialization did not occur. Therefore, the improvement of the tracking rate of the AAM+CHM tracking method was obtained by the proposed initialization method of combining the AAMs and the CHMs.

4.6.4.4 Face Tracking Using a Test Image Sequence

In this experiment, we used the first image sequence to build the 2D+3D AAMs and took the second image sequence, which contains a large amount of the yawing head motions, to evaluate the tracking performances of two face tracking algorithms. When we employed the AAM+CHM tracking method, we used the tracking result of the CHMs for the AAM re-initialization. As mentioned before, the AAM+CHM tracking method can designate the working range of the AAMs. In this work, we took the working range 40° of yawing angles because the previous experiment showed that the yawing angle coverage was (-34.2,40.4)). When we employed the AAM tracking method, we used the front view face detector for the AAM re-initialization. For this experiment, we used the fitted face shapes obtained from by the AAM+CHM tracking method as the ground truths. This implies that the tracking rate of the AAM+CHM tracking method is 1.0. Then, in the case of AAM tracking method, an image frame was judged to be successfully tracked if the RMS error between the fitted shape and the ground truth is less than 2.5.

Fig. 4.6.6 compares the estimated yawing angles among three different tracking methods: AAM, AAM+CHM, and CHM, where the horizontal and vertical axes represent the frame number and the estimated yawing angles, respectively, and the thin solid line, the thick solid line, and the dotted line represent the estimated yawing angles obtained by the AAM, AAM+CHM, and CHM tracking method, respectively. This figure shows that (1) the CHM tracking method successfully tracked the faces when they were rotated much up

Table 4.6.5. Comparison of the tracking performances in the training image sequence

	AAM	AAM + CHM
Tracking rate	0.87	1.00
Pose coverage(yaw) Pose coverage(tilt) Pose coverage(roll)	(-37.2, 40.4)° (-31.9, 10.9)° (- 4.9, 13.2)°	(-37.2, 40.4)° (-31.9, 10.9)° (- 6.0, 13.8)°

Figure 4.6.6. Face tracking result in a test image sequence

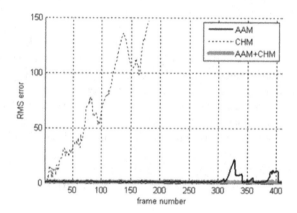

to 80° yawing angle, and (2) the AAM+CHM tracking method outperformed the AAM tracking method in terms of the tracking rate and the pose coverage.

Table 4.6.6 compares two different tracking methods in terms of the tracking rate and the pose coverage, where the second and third columns correspond to the AAM+CHM and AAM tracking method, respectively. This table shows that (1) the tracking rates of the AAM+CHM and AAM tracking method were 0.63, and 0.37, respectively, which implies the improvement of tracking rate by 170%, and (2) the pose coverage of the AAM+CHM and AAM tracking method were (-39.8,40.0) and (-34.4,34.8), respectively, which implies the improvement of pose coverage by 115%.

The improvement of tracking performance in the AAM+CHM tracking method is due to the following facts. First, the improved tracking rate was obtained by the proper re-initialization of the AAM by the estimated global motion parameters of the CHM when the head pose moves inside from the outside of the the AAM's working range. Second, the improved pose coverage was obtained by the good initialization of the AAM by the estimated global motion parameters of the CHM near the boundary between the working and non-working area of the AAM fitting.

The proposed AAM+CHM algorithm assumes that the face tracking algorithm using the CHM can track the face always, which is not true for the simple CHM fitting algorithm introduced in this chapter. In fact, the illumination condition affects the fitting quality of the

Table 4.6.6. Comparison of the tracking performances in the test image sequence

	AAM	AAM + CHM
Tracking rate	0.37	0.63
Angle coverage(yaw)	(-34.4, 34.8)°	(-39.8, 40.0)°
Angle coverage(tilt)	(-17.2, 3.3)°	(-17.2, 4.6)°
Angle coverage(roll)	(- 7.4, 5.0)°	(- 7.4, 5.2)°

CHM, which can be alleviated by the illumination robust CHM fitting algorithms proposed by Cascia et al. (Cascia et al., 2000), and Ryu and Kim (Ryu and Kim, 2007).

4.7 ILLUMINATION-ROBUST FACE TRACKING USING AAM AND IPCA

The AAMs are very sensitive to the illumination changes. The fitting performance of AAMs are degraded when the lighting condition of input image is significantly different from that of training images. This can be solved by collecting a large number of training images that contain every possible illumination conditions. However, collecting such large number of training images is impossible. Instead, we proposed an adaptive *AAM* that updates its appearance bases by the IPCA.

However, an unconditional update of the appearance bases using the fitting result can worse their fitting performance of the AAMs than that of the original AAMs. Hence, we need a measure to determine whether to update the appearance bases or not when a new fitting result is given. Unfortunately, the fitting error of the AAMs, E (See Eq. 3.2.5), is not a good measure for this purpose because a small fitting error can be observed even when the fitting fails. Instead, we measured the percentage of the outlier pixels using a modified *Adaptive Observation Model* (AOM) (Zhou et al., 2004), which is an appearance modeling technique that has been used for a stable on-line object tracking, where the varying appearance of an object is represented by Gaussian mixture models[2].

Using the AOM, we proposed a conditional update of the appearance bases as follows. First, we measured the goodness of AAM fitting, that is defined by the percentage of outliers, using AOM update it uses the mixture of Gaussian models only when the current appearance bases produced a good AAM fitting. Second, we computed the goodness of the appearance bases defined by the magnitude of AAM error and updated the appearance bases by the incremental PCA only when the current appearance bases produced a large AAM error. This conditional update of the appearance bases stabilized the AAM fitting by the AOM and improved the face tracking performance over the change of illumination by the adaptive appearance bases.

The detailed explanation on the adpative AAM is given by the following.

4.7.1 Adaptive Observation Model

The *AOM* is defined by the mixture of Gaussians at each pixel of the template to represent the varying observation values. It assumes that the varying appearance can be explained by three causes and the probability of an observed appearance can be explained by the mixture density of three components that correspond to the three causes. The three components $\Omega = \{S, W, F\}$ are defined as follows. The S component depicts the stable structure within all past observations (though it is slowly-varying), the W component characterizes the two-frame variations, and the F component accounts for the fixed template.

The stable component S captures the temporally stable and slowly changing image observation from the past frames by weighting their contributions such that the more recent frame has more weight. The wandering component W is introduced to cope with the sudden changes of image appearance. When the appearance changes abruptly, it makes sense to use the model which adapts to a short time change, as in a two-frame tracker[3]. In effect, the wandering component permits the tracker to gracefully change into a two-frame motion tracker when the appearance model does not account for the past data observations. The fixed component F is used to stabilize the tracker, i.e., this component prevents the drifting template problem of the two-frame tracker. This component is a fixed template that is expected to be observed most often.

The OAM assumed that each component obeys the Gaussian distribution and the d pixels consisting of the OAM are independent of each other. At time t, the OAM $\Omega_t = \{S_t, W_t, F_t\}$ is defined with the mixture centers $\{\mu_{i,t}; i = s, w, f\}$, their corresponding variances $\{\sigma^2_{i,t}; i = s, w, f\}$, and the mixing probabilities $\{m_{i,t}; i = s, w, f\}$.. Once the OAM $\Omega_t = \{S_t, W_t, F_t\}$ is given, an image patch $\hat{Z}_t$ that best matches to this model and the model parameters are updated to $\{m_{i,t+1}, \mu_{i,t+1}, \sigma^2_{i,t+1}; i = s, w, f\}$ for the next frame. To update the model parameters, the posterior responsibility probability $\omega_{i,t}(j)$ for the jth pixel $(j = 1, \ldots, d)$ should be computed:

$$\omega_{i,t}(j) \propto m_{i,t}(j)\ N(\hat{Z};; \mu_{i,t}(j), \sigma^2_{i,t}(j)), \quad i = w, s, f, \tag{4.7.1}$$

where $\omega_{i,t}$ is normalized such that $\int_{=s,w,f} \omega_{i,t} = 1$ and N is a normal distribution as

$$N(x; \mu, \sigma^2) = \frac{1}{\sqrt{(2\pi\sigma^2)}}\ exp\left\{-\frac{1}{2}\left(\frac{x-\mu}{\sigma}\right)^2\right\} \tag{4.7.2}$$

Second, the new mixing probabilities are obtained as

$$m_{i,t+1}(j) = \alpha\,\omega_{i,t}(j) + (1-\alpha)m_{i,t}(j); \quad i = w, s, f, \tag{4.7.3}$$

where α is used to make sure that the past images are exponentially forgotten with respect to their contributions to the current appearance and is defined as

$$\alpha = 1 - exp(-n_h/log2^{-1}) \tag{4.7.4}$$

where n_h is a half life of the frames. Third, the first- and second-moment $\{M^p_{t+1}; p = 1, 2\}$ are evaluated as

$$M_{t+1}^p(j) = \alpha \hat{Z}_t^p(j)\omega_{s,t}(j) + (1-\alpha)M_t^p(j); \quad p=1,2. \tag{4.7.5}$$

Once $\omega_{i,t}, m_{i,t+1}$, and M_{t+1}^p are computed, the mixture centers and the variances are simply updated with following equations as

$$W_{t+1}(j) = m_{w,t+1}(j) = \hat{Z}_t(j),$$
$$\sigma_{w,t+1}^2(j) = \sigma_{w,1}^2(j), \tag{4.7.6}$$

$$S_{t+1}(j) = \mu_{s,t+1}(j) = \frac{M_{t+1}^1(j)}{m_{s,t+1}(j)},$$
$$\sigma_{s,t+1}^2(j) = \frac{M_{t+1}^2(j)}{m_{s,t+1}(j)} - \mu_{s,t+1}^2(j), \tag{4.7.7}$$

$$F_{t+1}(j) = \mu_{f,t+1}(j) = F_1(j),$$
$$\sigma_{f,t+1}^2(j) = \sigma_{f,1}^2(j) \tag{4.7.8}$$

As shown in Eq. (4.7.6), (4.7.7) and (4.7.8), the variances of W and F component are not updated but also merely assigned as the initial values. Moreover, W component is simply updated as the image patch of the previous frame.

4.7.2 Adaptive Active Appearance Model

The AAM cannot fit to a new image that has significantly different characteristics from the training images. Fig. 4.7.1 shows an example, where the left image of a pair is the input image, which is warped to the shape template, and the right image is the reconstructed image of the left image by an AAM's appearance bases. The AAM is trained using a set of images that are captured at normal illumination condition. Fig. 4.7.1 (a) shows a case where an input image is captured at normal illumination condition; the input image (left) and its reconstructed image (right) are very similar. Fig. 4.7.1 (b) shows a case when the input image is captured at the untrained illumination condition (front illumination in this example); the input image and its reconstructed image are quite different. The face in the input image is looking at the left side and has a closed mouth but the face in the reconstructed image is looking at the upper front side with a slightly open mouth. The difference between the model image (reconstructed image) and the input image may cause the AAM to change the shape parameters to minimize the difference further and may result in the bad[4] fitting result. For these reasons, the AAM is sensitive to the illumination changes that frequently occur in the real environment.

4.7.2.1 Active Appearance Model with the Incremental PCA

This problem can be solved by updating the appearance bases of the AAM to adapt to the unforeseen images using the incremental PCA in the online manner. Once the appearance bases are updated appropriately, the adapted AAM will reconstruct the unforeseen image well and fit correctly.

Figure 4.7.1. Input images and synthesized appearances

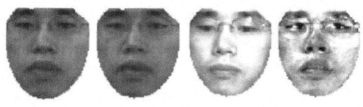

(a) The trained illumination   (b) The untrained illumination

However, we need a measure for the goodness of the fitting results to determine whether the fitting result is used for updating the appearance bases because the update of the appearance bases with bad fitting result can rather degrade the fitting performance. Fig. 4.7.2 shows the effects of the incremental learning with a bad fitting result; (a) a bad fitting result, and (b) the fitting result for a new image using an incrementally updated AAM and (c) the fitting result for a new image using non-updated AAM. This figure shows that the updated AAM failed to converge correctly while the non updated AAM fitted well.

4.7.2.2 Active Appearance Model with Adaptive Update

To measure the goodness of a fitting result, we used the percentage of outlier pixels in the fitting result, where the outlier pixels are identified using the robust statistics as follows. After fitting the AAM to the input image, we can synthesize the model appearance image

$$A_{model}(\mathbf{x}) = \sum_{i=0}^{m} \alpha_i A_i(\mathbf{x}),, \qquad (4.7.9)$$

where $\alpha_0 = 1$ and measure the reconstruction error that is the difference between the pixel x in the model synthesized appearance image and its corresponding image pixel.

Then, the pixels that have the large difference values are regarded as the outlier pixels as

$$\mathbf{x} := outlier, \qquad if \quad \left| \frac{A_{model}(\mathbf{x}) - I(W(\mathbf{x};\mathbf{p}))}{\sigma} \right| > c_1, \qquad (4.7.10)$$

where σ and c_1 are the variance for the reconstruction error and a threshold value, respectively. Once we identify the outlier pixels, the percentage of outlier pixels $r = n_{outlier}/n_{total}$ is computed and the goodness indicator ξ for the fitting is decided as

$$\xi = \begin{cases} 1, & if \ r < c_2 \\ 0, & if \ r > c_2 \end{cases}, \qquad (4.7.11)$$

where c_2 is a threshold for a decision of good fitting.

However, we still can not know whether the outliers are caused by the bad fitting or the illumination change. Fig. 4.7.3 shows two fitting results where the fitted shape is overlayed over the input image in the left picture and the outlier decision results are illustrated in the right picture, where the white and gray pixels represent the outlier and the normal pixels,

Figure 4.7.2. Effects of the incremental learning with a bad fitting result

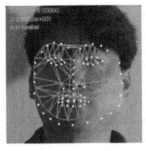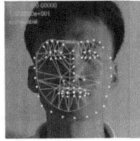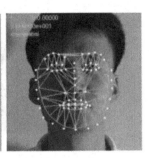

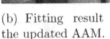

(a) Bad fitting result. (b) Fitting result with the updated AAM. (c) Fitting result with the non-updated AAM.

respectively. Fig. 4.7.3 (a) and (b) are the example of the bad fitting and the good fitting, respectively. These two fitting results have the same percentage of outliers but the outliers are caused by the different reasons.

To solve this problem, we adopted the AOM that is used to identify the type of outlier pixels. In this work, the *AOM* models the varying appearance of the object due to the environment change such as the illumination condition. We assume that the appearance variation due to the change of shape and the pose of the object is already learned in the linear appearance bases of the AAMs. Among the three components of the AOM, the *F* component is inappropriate for this work because the appearance of the face changes severely due to person-to-person variation, pose change, illumination change and so on.

In this work, we use the modified AOM, in which the *F* component is replaced with *R* component. The *R* component also has mean and variance where the mean is always set to the synthesize image A_{model} and the variance is set to the σ of the *S* component as

$$\mu_{r,t+1}(j) = A_{model}(j), \tag{4.7.12}$$

and

$$\sigma_{r,t+1} = \sigma^2_{s,t+1}(j). \tag{4.7.13}$$

The *R* component helps the AOM to adapt to the appearance variation of the face more flexibly than the *F* component. For example, suppose that a new input image with a facial expression is given. *R* component reflects the difference of the synthesized image and the input image, where the appearance variation due to the facial expression is removed by the AAM's appearance bases while the *F* component considers these variation due to the facial expression as an error.

Once we determine the success of fitting ξ, we should decide whether to update the appearance bases of the AAM and AOM parameters or not. If the fitting result is good ($\xi=1$), then we update both. Otherwise, we do not update the appearance bases of the AAM but we have two policies for the update of AOM as

Figure 4.7.3. Two causes of the outlier pixels

(a) Outliers are caused by the bad fitting.

(b) Outliers are caused by the illumination change.

- Policy 1: update the AOM that corresponds to inlier pixels,
- Policy 2: do not update AOM.

When we take the policy 1, the parameters of the AOM are updated although the AAM fitting is failed as in the case of Fig. 4.7.3 (a); some pixels are regarded as inliers while they are the background pixels and the AOM starts to diverge from the correct observation model. To prevent this erroneous update, we decided to choose the policy 2 in this work.

The proposed adaptive AAM (adpative AAM) fitting algorithm is summarized in Fig.4.7.4. For a new image, the AAM is initialized using a face and eye detector and fitted to the input image. Next, the goodness of the fitting result is determined. If the fitting result is good, the AOM parameters are updated and the new appearance bases of the AAM are computed using the incremental PCA algorithm. Then, the updated AOM and AAM are used for the next input image.

4.7.3 Experiment Results

To prove the effectiveness of the proposed adaptive AAM algorithm, we conducted following experiments to compare the fitting quality, tracking performance of the conventional AAM, and adaptive AAM.

4.7.3.1 Dataset

We recorded two image sequences under different lighting conditions. The first image sequence is recorded under normal lighting condition as shown in Fig. 4.7.5. The second

Figure 4.7.4. A procedure of the adaptive AAM fitting algorithm

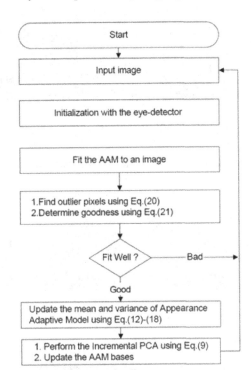

image sequence is recorded under the varying lighting conditions, where the lighting direction changes from front, left, right and upper-side as shown in Fig. 4.7.6. Two sets of images are extracted from the first and second image sequence: 100 images from the first sequence and 250 images from the second sequences, used as training and test set, respectively, and manually landmarked. From the landmarked training images, a 2D AAM has been built.

4.7.3.2 Fitting Quality Measurement Using the Modified AOM

To determine whether to update the appearance bases of the AAM or not, we measured the goodness of the AAM fitting by counting the number of outlier pixels using the modified AOM. We performed tests to see the outlier detection capability of the modified AOM. In this work, the initial parameters of the modified AOM: the mean, variance, and mixing probabilities, are set as follows: $\mu_{s,1}(j) = \mu_{w,1}(j) = \mu_{r,1}(j) = A_0(j)$, $\sigma_{s,1}(j) = \sigma_{w,1}(j) = \sigma_{r,1}(j) = 0.1\pi$ and $\{m_{s,1}, m_{w,1}, m_{r,1}\} = 0.4, 0.25, 0.35$.

Fig. 4.7.7 shows two examples of the AAM fitting and outlier detection results by the modified AOM, where the three pictures in a row are the AAM fitting result, the input image backward warped to the shape template, and outlier detection result (white pixels represent the outlier pixels), respectively, from left to right. Fig. 4.7.7 (a) shows the result for a training image, where the pixels corresponding to background image are classified to outlier pixels. Fig. 4.7.7 (b) shows the result for a test image, where the AAM fitting is

Figure 4.7.5. The face sequence with expression under the normal illumination

Figure 4.7.6. The face sequence under the various illumination such as front, left, right and upper-side

Figure 4.7.7 The measurements for goodness

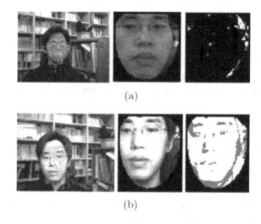

failed due to the significantly different lighting condition and most of the pixels are classified to the outlier pixels.

Fig. 4.7.8 shows the AAM fitting result and outlier detection results using AOM and proposed modified AOM, where the four pictures, from left to right, are the AAM fitting result, the input image backward warped to the shape template, outlier detection results using F component of AOM (white pixels represent the outlier pixels), and R component of the proposed modified AOM. respectively. In this example, where the appearance of the face image is changed to happy expression from the first neutral expression, the F component

Figure 4.7.8. Comparison of the original AOM with the proposed modified AOM

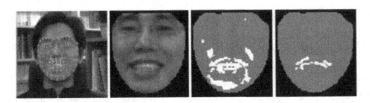

regarded the varying appearance due to the facial expression as outlier pixels because F component is a fixed template. On the other hand, the R component detected only a few pixels as outliers because the R component measures the reconstruction error, where the learned appearance variations are not accounted.

4.7.3.3 Comparison of PCA and IPCA

Fig. 4.7.9 shows the fitting results of the original AAM in the top row, and proposed adaptive AAM in the bottom row on face images recorded under strong directional light source. In this figure, the dots are ground truth landmark points and the mesh are the fitting results. The AAM fitting results of the original AAM using traditional PCA were far from the ground-truth while the fitting results of the adaptive AAM using incremental PCA were close to the ground-truth. Using the incremental PCA, the AAM was able to adapt to unforeseen lighting conditions of the input image.

4.7.3.4 Comparison of Face Tracking Result Using the Adaptive AAM and the Original AAM

We compared the face tracking performance of the original AAM and the adaptive AAM using the test image sequence, in which the lighting condition is dynamically changes. At the first frame, the original AAM and the adaptive AAM are initialized using the landmarked ground truth so that the both AAMs began from the good initial conditions. In the remaining frames, the adaptive AAM dynamically updated the appearance bases and AOM parameters as explained in the section 4.7.2.

Fig. 4.7.10 shows the change of AAM fitting errors that are measured by the sums of squared errors of the two methods: the original AAM and the adaptive AAM. This figure shows that the fitting error of the original AAM began to increase drastically after the 25th frame where the lighting condition began to change, while the fitting error of the adaptive AAM was retained at small values. We can see that the fitting error of the adaptive AAM occasionally dropped at some frames, where the appearance bases of the adaptive AAM were incrementally updated.

To compare the tracking performance of the two methods quantitatively, the fitting are classified as one of three error types: small-error, medium-error, large-error according to the magnitude of fitting error and counted the number of fitting results belonging to each error types. Table 4.7.1 summarizes the relative percentages of the error types. This table shows that the fitting of the adpative AAM was successful at most of the frames; small fitting errors were measured at 87.5% of the frames and medium fitting errors at 12.4%

Figure 4.7.9. The comparison of AAM fitting with PCA and the incremental PCA

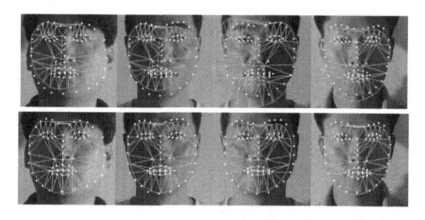

Figrue 4.7.10. A comparison of the sums of squared errors

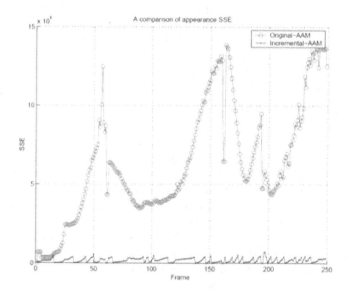

Table 4.7.1. A comparison of the tracking errors

	Small-error	Medium-error	Large-error
AAM	53.4 %	20.9%	25.7%
Adaptive AAM	87.6 %	12.4%	0%

while the fitting of the original AAM was unsuccessful at many frames; small fitting errors were measured at 53.4% of the frames, medium fitting errors at 20.9%, and large fitting errors at 24.7%.

Fig. 4.7.11 shows some fitting results of the original AAM in the first column and the adpative AAM in the second column. The third and fourth columns show the backward warped input image and outlier detection result of the adpative AAM algorithm. The test sequence began from normal lighting condition as shown in the first row and both algorithms fitted well. As the lighting condition began to change, the fitting of the original AAM began to wander around the face, while the fitting of the adpative AAM were very stable throughout the whole sequence as shown in the remaining rows.

4.8 ROBUST FACE TRACKING USING AAM IN PARTICLE FILTER FRAMEWORK

Many research groups in the computer vision society have been interested in the topics related to the human face such as face detection, face recognition, face tracking, facial expression recognition, facial gesture recognition, gaze tracking, etc. Among them, face tracking is an important work that can be applied to several applications such as human-

Figure 4.7.11. A comparison of tracking results of (a) the original AAM and (b) the proposed incremental AAM

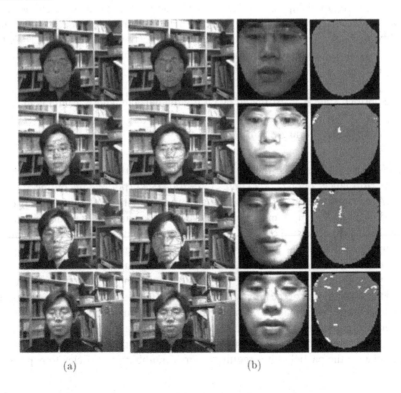

(a)   (b)

computer interaction, facial expression recognition, and robotics, etc. Face tracking is still a difficult problem and its tracking performance is largely dependent on several factors such as pose, illumination, and facial expression.

Several works related with the face tracking have been performed as follows. The face tracking based on the optical flow showed the robust tracking performance, but it required a huge amount of computational load (Horn and Schunck, 1981). Hence, it is not appropriate for the real-time application. Lucas and Kanade (Lucas and Kanade, 1981) introduced a gradient-based approach for the face tracking, but it was often trapped into the local minimum. Bayesian filters such as Kalman filter (Azarbayejani and Pentland, 1995) and particle filter (Doucet et al., 2000; Arulampalam et al., 2002; Okuma, et al., 2004) are the most popular techniques for the face tracking. The Kalman filter assumed that the state transition model obeyed the Gaussian function. Thus, it does not work well when the state transition model obeys the non-linear/non-Gaussian function, which is common when the face moves very fast.

We take the particle filter because its stochastic tracking property is appropriate when the face moves fast. The particle filter tries to estimate the state θ_t from a series of noisy observations $\{I_1,...,I_t\}$. It consists of the state transition model and the observation model as

$$\begin{aligned} StateTransitionModel \quad &: \quad \boldsymbol{\theta}_t = F_t(\boldsymbol{\theta}_{t-1}, U_t), \\ ObservationModel \quad &: \quad I_t = G_t(\boldsymbol{\theta}_t, V_t). \end{aligned} \tag{4.8.1}$$

where the *state transition* function F_t approximates the dynamics of the object being tracked using the previous state θ_{t-1} and the system noise U_t, and the measurement function G_t models a relationship between the observation I_t and the state θ_t given the observation noise V_t. We usually characterize the *state transition* model with the state transition probability $p(\boldsymbol{\theta}_t \mid \boldsymbol{\theta}_{t-1})$ and the observation model with the likelihood $p(I_t \mid \boldsymbol{\theta}_t)$. Often, the *particle filter* approximates the posterior distribution $p(\boldsymbol{\theta}_t \mid I_{1:t})$ by a set of weighted particles $\{\boldsymbol{\theta}_t^{(p)}, \omega_t^{(p)}\}_{p=1}^P$.

Then, the optimal state $\hat{\boldsymbol{\theta}}_t$ is estimated by taking the particle whose weight is maximal as

$$\hat{\boldsymbol{\theta}}_t = \underset{\boldsymbol{\theta}_t}{\operatorname{argmax}}\, p(\boldsymbol{\theta}_t \mid I_{1:t}) \approx \underset{\boldsymbol{\theta}_t}{\operatorname{argmax}}\, \omega_t^{(p)}. \tag{4.8.2}$$

Several works showed that the face tracking using particle filter provided the robust tracking performance. Zhou *et al.* (Zhou, et al., 2004) incorporated the online appearance model (OAM) (Jepson et al., 2003) and the adaptive velocity model into the observation model and the state transition model, respectively, of the particle filter for the robust face tracking. The OAM consisted of three components that obeyed the mixture of Gaussians. Each component updated the appearance information using the current face image in order to cover both short-term and long-term appearance changes. This method allowed the observation model to cope with moderate illumination changes. Adaptive velocity model predicted the shift amount of the moving face using the least-square estimation. This model used the appearance information from all particles to estimate the velocity and compute the pseudo-inverse of Jacobian matrix J^+, which required a high amount of computation time. Therefore, the adaptive velocity model was not appropriate for tracking the fast moving face because the particle filter required a great number of particles to cope with the fast moving face and the computational cost of the pseudo-inverse operation with many particles prohibited the real-time tracking.

Hamlaoui *et al.* (Hamlaoui et al., 2005) used the AAM (Cootes et al., 2001d) for the observation model and the predicted shift in the global 2D pose and the local appearance parameter for the state transition model, respectively. AAM is a linear model that can handle both shape variation and appearance variation in terms of the subspaces of shape and appearance of human face. When the AAM is employed for representing the face image, the state vector is compact because it contains a small number of global and local motion parameters. However, their observation model would fail to track the face image when the illumination condition changed because they did not provide any method to update their observation model. Also, their state transition model would fail to predict the global 2D pose and local appearance parameters accurately because the AAM often failed to fit when the particle is far from the input face image. To guarantee robust AAM fitting, it is necessary to generate a sufficient number of particles to cover the wide range of sample space. However, this complicates the real-time face tracking.

We propose two novel approaches such that the conventional particle filter can robustly track the fast moving faces under the illumination change. To track the faces under the illumination change, we update the basis vectors of the AAM adaptively using the IPCA (Hall et al., 1998; Artac et al., 2002; Ross et al., 2004) when the illumination condition changes. This injects the current face image into the appearance basis vectors and makes the face tracking robust to the illumination change. To track the fast moving faces in the real-time, we estimate the most plausible position of the face at the next time using the motion prediction method based on the history of motion trajectory and generate a moderate number of particles near the predict position. The reduced number of generated particles makes the real-time face tracking possible although the face moves fast.

4.8.1 Adaptive Observation Model

As mentioned earlier, the AAM is taken to define the observation model for the input face image due to its simplicity and flexibility. The observation model image $A_t(\mathbf{x})$ at the time t is only the appearance image $A_{t-1}^*(\mathbf{x})$ that was obtained by the following way. First, we take the best particle whose observation likelihood is maximal at the time $t-1$ and denote its state vector as $\hat{\boldsymbol{\theta}}_{t-1} = \{\hat{\mathbf{p}}_{t-1}, \hat{\boldsymbol{\alpha}}_{t-1}, \hat{\mathbf{q}}_{t-1}\}$, where the observation likelihood will be explained later. Second, we perform the AAM fitting by minimizing the difference between the warped patch image $\hat{Z}_{t-1}(\mathbf{x}) = I_t(W(\mathbf{x}; \hat{\mathbf{p}}_{t-1}, \hat{\mathbf{q}}_{t-1}))$ using the best particle's shape and 2D pose parameter, where W is a warping function, and the appearance image

$$\hat{A}_{t-1}(\mathbf{x}) = A_0(\mathbf{x}) + \sum_{i=1}^{m} \hat{\alpha}_{t-1,i} A_i(\mathbf{x})$$

using the best particle's appearance parameter. After the AAM fitting, we obtain a new state vector of fitted parameters, $\boldsymbol{\theta}_{t-1}^* = \{\mathbf{p}_{t-1}^*, \boldsymbol{\alpha}_{t-1}^*, \mathbf{q}_{t-1}^*\}$. Finally, we compute the appearance image using the new state vector as

$$A_{t-1}^*(\mathbf{x}) = A_0(\mathbf{x}) + \sum_{i=1}^{m} \alpha_{t-1,i}^* A_i(\mathbf{x})$$

and set the appearance image $A_{t-1}^{*}(\mathbf{x})$ at the time t − 1 to the observation model image $A_t(\mathbf{x})$ at the time t as

$$A_t(\mathbf{x}) = A_{t-1}^{*}(\mathbf{x}) = A_0(\mathbf{x}) + \sum_{i=1}^{m} \alpha_{t-1,i}^{*} A_i(\mathbf{x}). \qquad (4.8.3)$$

4.8.1.1 Observation Likelihood

The observation likelihood $p(I_t \mid \boldsymbol{\theta}_t^{(p)})$ measures the similarity between the warped patch image

$$Z_t^{(p)}(\mathbf{x}) = I_t(W(\mathbf{x}; \mathbf{p}_t^{(p)}, \mathbf{q}_t^{(p)})),$$

and the observation model image $A_t(\mathbf{x})$ as

$$p(I_t \mid \boldsymbol{\theta}_t^{(p)}) = p(Z_t^{(p)} \mid \boldsymbol{\theta}_t^{(p)}) \propto exp\left\{ -\frac{1}{2} \sum_{\mathbf{x}} \left(\frac{Z_t^{(p)}(\mathbf{x}) - A_t(\mathbf{x})}{\sigma_0(\mathbf{x})} \right)^2 \right\}, \qquad (4.8.4)$$

where $\sigma_0(\mathbf{x})$ is the standard deviation of the pixel value at the position $\mathbf{x}$ which can be obtained from the training face images in advance. Since we do not want the observation likelihood of the good pixels to be spoiled by a few outlier pixels, we use the robust statistics (Huber, 1981) to decrease the weight of outliers as

$$p(I_t \mid \boldsymbol{\theta}_t^{(p)}) = p(Z_t^{(p)} \mid \boldsymbol{\theta}_t^{(p)}) \propto exp\left\{ -\sum_{\mathbf{x}} \rho\left(\frac{Z_t^{(p)}(\mathbf{x}) - A_t(\mathbf{x})}{\sigma_0(\mathbf{x})} \right) \right\}, \qquad (4.8.5)$$

where

$$\rho(x) = \begin{cases} \dfrac{1}{2}x^2, & if \mid x \mid < \xi, \\ \xi \mid x \mid -\dfrac{1}{2}\xi^2, & if \mid x \mid \geq \xi, \end{cases} \qquad (4.8.6)$$

where ξ is a threshold that determines whether a pixel is an outlier or not.

4.8.1.2 Adaptive Observation Model Using IPCA

The observation model image is the appearance image that was obtained from the AAM fitting of the best patch image corresponding to the best particle. However, the current basis vectors of the appearance image are not appropriate for representing the face image when the illumination condition is changed. To solve this problem, we propose to use the *IPCA* that can adjust the basis vectors of the appearance image with the current face image incrementally. However, it is undesirable that we adjust the current appearance basis vectors with the wrongly AAM fitted patch image because it decreases the further AAM fitting performance. To reflect this idea, we take the following adaptive observation model when the illumination change is greater than a certain amount of threshold value.

$$\begin{cases} \text{Appearance basis vectors are updated} & \text{when the AAM fitting is good,} \\ \text{Appearance basis vectors are not updated} & \text{when the AAM fitting is bad.} \end{cases} \quad (4.8.7)$$

For the adaptive observation model, we need to determine whether the current AAM fitting is good or not. We often use the AAM reconstruction error, which is defined by the difference between the warped patch image and the appearance image, to determine whether the AAM fitting is good or not. However, it is not appropriate for measuring the AAM fitting quality because we do not know that a high value of the AAM reconstruction error comes from the ill-fitted result or the illumination change. To solve this problem, we take the OAM approach because it can measure the AAM fitting quality accurately irrespective of the illumination change.

The original version of OAM is mainly based on the work by Zhou *et al.* (Zhou et al., 2004), where they proposed three mixture components that consisted of the stable structure component (S component) for the long-term appearance changes, the two-frame variations component (W component) for the short-term appearance changes, and the fixed template component (F component). One problem of the original OAM is that the F component is fixed even if there exists an illumination change. In this work, we propose to use the modified version of OAM that replaces the F component by the R component, where the R component absorbs the illumination change by the adaptive observation model. Therefore, the modified version of OAM is irrespective of the illumination change.

The modified version of OAM can be explained briefly. It consists of three components: S, W, and R components. They are described by the mixture means $\{\mu_{t,c}; c = s, w, r\}$, the mixture variances $\{\sigma_{t,c}^2; c = s, w, r\}$, and the mixing probabilities $\{m_{t,c}; c = s, w, r\}$. Their parameters are updated as follows. First, we compute the posterior responsibility probabilities $\{o_{t,c}; c = s, w, r\}$ as :

$$o_{t,c}(\mathbf{x}) = \frac{1}{T} m_{t,c}(\mathbf{x}) N\left(Z_t^*(\mathbf{x}); \mu_{t,c}(\mathbf{x}), \sigma_{t,c}^2(\mathbf{x})\right), c = s, w, r, \quad (4.8.8)$$

$$T = \sum_{c=s,w,r} m_{t,c}(\mathbf{x}) N\left(Z_t^*(\mathbf{x}); \mu_{t,c}(\mathbf{x}), \sigma_{t,c}^2(\mathbf{x})\right), \quad (4.8.9)$$

$$N\left(x; \mu, \sigma^2\right) = \frac{1}{\sqrt{2\pi\sigma^2}} exp\left\{-\frac{1}{2}\left(\frac{x-\mu}{\sigma}\right)^2\right\}, \quad (4.8.10)$$

where $Z_t^*(\mathbf{x}) = I_t(W(\mathbf{x}; \mathbf{p}_t^*, \mathbf{q}_t^*))$ is the warped patch image of the AAM fitting of the best particle. Second, update the mixing probabilities as :

$$m_{t+1,c}(\mathbf{x}) = \alpha o_{t,c}(\mathbf{x}) + (1-\alpha) m_{t,c}(\mathbf{x}), \quad (4.8.11)$$

$$\alpha = 1 - exp\left\{-log 2/n_h\right\}, \quad (4.8.12)$$

where n_h is the half life of the frames.

Third, first moment M^{t+1} and second moment M^{t+1} are calculated to update the S component as :

$$M_{t+1}^{(i)}(\mathbf{x}) = \alpha (Z_t^*(\mathbf{x}))^i o_{t,s}(\mathbf{x}) + (1-\alpha) M_t^{(i)}(\mathbf{x}), \quad i = 1,2. \tag{4.8.13}$$

Fourth, we can update the mixture means and variances as :

$$
\begin{aligned}
\mu_{t+1,s}(\mathbf{x}) &= \frac{M_{t+1}^{(1)}(\mathbf{x})}{m_{t+1,s}(\mathbf{x})}, & \sigma_{t+1,s}^2(\mathbf{x}) &= \frac{M_{t+1}^{(2)}(\mathbf{x})}{m_{t+1,s}(\mathbf{x})} - \mu_{t+1,s}^2(\mathbf{x}), \\
\mu_{t+1,w}(\mathbf{x}) &= Z_t^*(\mathbf{x}), & \sigma_{t+1,w}^2(\mathbf{x}) &= \sigma_{0,w}^2(\mathbf{x}), \\
\mu_{t+1,r}(\mathbf{x}) &= A_t^*(\mathbf{x}), & \sigma_{t+1,r}^2(\mathbf{x}) &= \sigma_{0,r}^2(\mathbf{x}).
\end{aligned}
\tag{4.8.14}
$$

To measure the AAM fitting quality, we need to define the outlier of each pixel in the component as

$$
outlier(\mathbf{x},c) = \begin{cases} 0, & if \left| \dfrac{Z_t^*(\mathbf{x}) - \mu_{t,s}(\mathbf{x})}{\sigma_{t,s}(\mathbf{x})} \right| < \xi \\[3mm] 1, & if \left| \dfrac{Z_t^*(\mathbf{x}) - \mu_{t,s}(\mathbf{x})}{\sigma_{t,s}(\mathbf{x})} \right| > \xi \end{cases}
\tag{4.8.15}
$$

where ξ is a threshold that classifies whether a pixel is an inlier or an outlier. Then, we define the average number of outliers of three components as

$$N_{outlier} = \frac{\sum_{c=s,w,r} \sum_{\mathbf{x}} outlier(\mathbf{x},c)}{3}. \tag{4.8.16}$$

Finally, we measure the AAM fitting quality by the average number of outliers as

$$
\begin{cases} AAM fitting\,is\,good & if N_{outlier} \le N_0, \\ AAM fitting\,is\,bad & if N_{outlier} > N_0, \end{cases}
\tag{4.8.17}
$$

where N_0 is a threshold that determines whether the AAM fitting is good or not. Fig. 4.8.1 summarizes how we update the observation model.

4.8.2 Adaptive State Transition Model

The *state transition* model describes the dynamics of the moving objects between two frames. There are two ways to approximate the motion model: using a trained motion model by learning from video examples and using a fixed constant-velocity model. However, these approaches do not work well when the objects are moving very fast. To overcome this problem, Zhou *et al.* (2004) introduced an adaptive velocity model, where the adaptive motion velocity is predicted using a first order linear approximation based on the appearance difference between the incoming observation and the previous particle configuration.

Figure 4.8.1. An overall process for updating the observation model

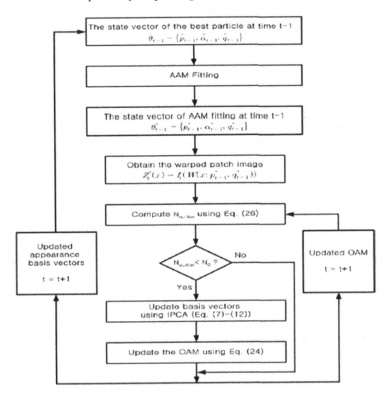

However, their approach cannot be used for real-time face tracking when the face moves very fast because the adaptive motion velocity requires to compute the matrix inversion whose computational load is proportional to the number of particles and performs several iterations when the objects move very fast.

We implement their tracking algorithm and evaluate the tracking performance and operating speed. Fig. 4.8.2 (a) shows the tracking performance when 20 particles are used to track the fast moving face, where the vertical axis denotes the pixel displacement between two consecutive frames and the circles denote the cases of failed tracking. From this figure, we know that their tracking algorithm often fails to track the very fastly moving face whose pixel displacement between two consecutive frames is greater than 20. Fig. 4.8.2 (b) shows the average operating speed when the number of particles is changed. From this figure, we know that the number of particles should be less than 30 for the real-time face tracking operating at the speed of 15 frames per second. To realize the real-time face tracking, we propose the adaptive state transition model using the motion prediction based on the motion history model.

4.8.2.1 Motion History Model

Here, we assume that the dynamics of moving face obey the constant acceleration model. Then, the velocity $\mathbf{v}_{t-1}$ and the acceleration $\mathbf{a}_{t-1}$ at the time $t-1$ can be computed by

Figure 4.8.2 Tracking experimentation results of Zhou et al. (Zhou et al., 2004) algorithm

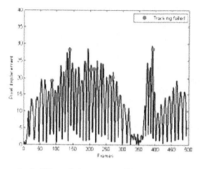

(a) Tracking performance.

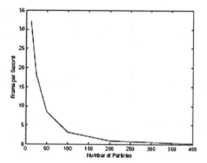

(b) Operating speed.

$$\mathbf{v}_{t-1} = \boldsymbol{\theta}^*_{t-1} - \boldsymbol{\theta}^*_{t-2}, \tag{4.8.18}$$

$$\mathbf{a}_{t-1} = \mathbf{v}_{t-1} - \mathbf{v}_{t-2}, \tag{4.8.19}$$

where θ_{t-1} is the motion state that is only the global 2D pose parameter $\mathbf{q}$ of the AAM fitted image at the time $t-1$ in this section.

In the *motion history model*, the motion velocity at the current time is predicted by the motion velocity and the acceleration at the previous time. Then, the velocity of moving face at the time t can be estimated by

$$\widetilde{\mathbf{v}}_t = \mathbf{v}_{t-1} + \mathbf{a}_{t-1}. \tag{4.8.20}$$

Fig. 4.8.3 shows how to compute the moving distance between time $t-1$ and t from the constant acceleration model. The actual moving distance between time $t-1$ and t is the sketched area of the trapezoid. This area is equivalent to the area of the rectangle that is obtained by the multiplication of the time duration and the average of two velocities, $\mathbf{v}_{t-1}$ and $\widetilde{\mathbf{v}}_t$. From this fact, we can treat that the face moves by the effective velocity $\overline{\mathbf{v}}$ as

$$\overline{\mathbf{v}}_t = \frac{\mathbf{v}_{t-1} + \widetilde{\mathbf{v}}_t}{2}. \tag{4.8.21}$$

4.8.2.2 Motion Prediction Model

In the real situation, the actual motion of moving face cannot follow the assumption that the dynamics of moving face obey the constant acceleration model. Hence, the effective velocity obtained from the motion history model may be overestimated or underestimated. To overcome this problem, we suggest to use the motion prediction model that performs the motion estimation technique (Bhaskaran and Konstantinides, 1997) around the estimated motion state $\overline{\boldsymbol{\theta}}_t = \boldsymbol{\theta}^*_{t-1} + \overline{\mathbf{v}}_t$, which is computed by the effective velocity obtained from the motion history model.

In the motion estimation technique, each macroblock in the current frame is compared to a macroblock in the reference frame to find the best matching macroblock. To achieve

Figure 4.8.3. Moving distance under the constant acceleration model

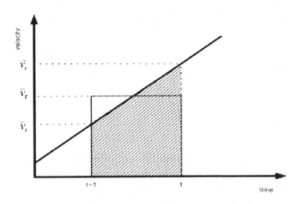

this goal, block matching criterion such as the mean absolute error (MAE) or the mean squared error (MSE) is usually used. These errors are obtained by summarizing all pixel differences between two macroblocks. Thus, the computational load of finding the best matching macroblock is proportional to the size of macroblock.

It takes much time to apply these block matching criteria to the face tracking problem, because the macroblock of face image is usually very large. Therefore, rather than using MAE or MSE, we use the face detector based on AdaBoost (Fröba and Ernst, 2004) to reduce the computational load. We can obtain the predicted motion state of the face $\boldsymbol{\theta'}_t$ by applying motion estimation technique around $\overline{\boldsymbol{\theta}}_t$. However, the face detector sometimes fails to detect the face. Hence, when face detector fails, we use $\overline{\boldsymbol{\theta}}_t$ as the predicted motion state of the face. Therefore, the predicted motion state of the face $\tilde{\boldsymbol{\theta}}_t$ can be obtained as :

$$\tilde{\boldsymbol{\theta}}_t = \begin{cases} \overline{\boldsymbol{\theta}}_t, & \text{if the face is not detected,} \\ \boldsymbol{\theta'}_t, & \text{if the face is detected.} \end{cases} \qquad (4.8.22)$$

The particles are distributed around the predicted motion state of the face $\tilde{\boldsymbol{\theta}}_t$ as in the following state transition model :

$$\boldsymbol{\theta}_t^{(p)} = \tilde{\boldsymbol{\theta}}_t + U_t^{(p)}, \qquad (4.8.23)$$

where U_t is the system noise that follows Gaussian distribution $N(0, \sigma_t^2)$.

As an option, we can include the adaptive velocity model into our state transition model. Since we can obtain the predicted motion state of the face by using the motion estimation technique, only a small number of particles is required, hence, we can apply the adaptive velocity model without suffering from the heavy computational load. The particles are generated as :

$$\boldsymbol{\theta}_t^{(p)} = \tilde{\boldsymbol{\theta}}_t + V_{LS}\{I_t; \tilde{\boldsymbol{\theta}}_t\} + U_t^{(p)}. \qquad (4.8.24)$$

4.8.2.3 Adaptive Noise Variance and Number of Particles

To save the computational load and increase the flexibility of the system, we take adaptive noise variance σ_t^2. To measure the quality of tracking, we take the Mahalanobis distance D_t between the warped image from the fitting result at the time $t-1$, Z_{t-1}^*, and the appearance image from the fitting result at the time $t-1$, A_{t-1}^*.

$$D_t = \sqrt{\sum_{\mathbf{x}} \left(\frac{Z_{t-1}^*(\mathbf{x}) - A_{t-1}^*(\mathbf{x})}{\sigma_R(\mathbf{x})} \right)^2}, \tag{4.8.25}$$

where σ_R is the standard deviation of the appearance image which is learned during the training phase. We update the system noise variance, σ_t^2, as :

$$\sigma_t = max\left(min\left(\sigma_0 \times \frac{D_t}{D_0}, \sigma_{max} \right), \sigma_{min} \right), \tag{4.8.26}$$

where σ_{min}^2 is the lower bound of the noise variance to guarantee the stable tracking performance, and σ_{max}^2 is the upper bound of the noise variance to restrict the computational load. The number of particles, P_t, is updated as :

$$P_t = P_0 \times \frac{\sigma_t}{\sigma_0}. \tag{4.8.27}$$

4.8.3 Experimenal Results and Discussion

Table 4.8.1 summarizes the overall process of the proposed face tracking method. Basically, this table is similar to the particle filter framework except that the prediction of the state transition model and the update of the observation model update are added.

Fig. 4.8.4 shows the detailed process of the proposed face tracking method that has occurred during one time interval. The step index within the block in the figure denotes the corresponding step in the Table 4.8.2.

4.8.3.1 Face Tracking Speed

When we performed the proposed face tracking over a sequence of 1,000 face images, it took about 56.4 seconds without any tracking error when 20 particles were used. This implies that the tracking time for an face image frame was about 56.4 milliseconds on the average. Hence, we guarantee that the proposed face tracking method is executed in the speed of 17 frames per second.

4.8.3.2 Face Tracking Performance

We performed six different experiments to prove the robustness of the proposed face tracking system. The first three experiments have been performed to show the robustness and effectiveness of the proposed face tracking method in terms of the speed of moving faces,

Table 4.8.1. The proposed face tracking algorithm

1. **Initialization** : set the system noise variance, and the number of particles, to σ_0^2 and P_0, respectively, generate a particle set $S_0 = \{\theta_0^{(p)}, 1/P_0\}_{p=0}^{P_0}$ according to prior distribution $p(\theta_0)$, and obtain the observation model and the state θ_t using the face detector and the AAM fitting.

Loop : t = 1, 2, ...
   2. **Predict state transition model** : predict the effective velocity $\tilde{v}$, compute the system noise variance σ_t^2, and compute the number of particles P_t using Eq. (31), (36), and (37), respectively.

   Loop : p = 1, 2, ..., P_t
      3. **Resample** $\{\theta_{t-1}^{(p)}, \omega_{t-1}^{(p)}\}$ to obtain a new particle $\{\theta_{t-1}'^{(p)}, 1\}$.
      4. **Predict** the motion state of the face $\tilde{\theta}_t$ using Eq. (32).
      5. **Generate** particles around the predicted location using Eq. (33) or (34).
      6. **Update** the weight according to the observation likelihood using Eq. (15).
   End
   7. **Normalize** the weight of each particle.
   8. **Select** the best particle that has the largest observation likelihood.
   9. **Update** the observation model according to the Fig. 1.
   10. **Break** the loop if no more image is given.
End

Figure 4.8.4. An overall process of the proposed face tracking system

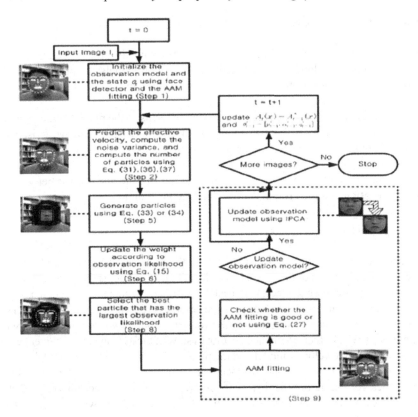

Table 4.8.2. Parameters for experiments

Categories	Parameters	Values
Camera	Frame rate Frame size	30 fps 320 × 240
AAM	Size of warped image Number of fitting iterations Number of shape vectors Number of appearance vectors	45 × 47 5 5 5
OAM	n_h N_0	15 0.18 × 45 × 47
Outlier	ξ	1.7

the required number of particles, and the failed tracking rate. The fourth and fifth experiments have been conducted to show the robustness of the proposed face tracking method under the illumination changes and occlusions. The last experiment has been performed to illustrate that the proposed face tracking method can be extended to the multiple face tracking.

1) The speed of moving faces

We captured three types of the face image sequences with different speed of moving faces: fast, medium, and slow. We took two different motion models: the proposed motion prediction model and the existing adaptive velocity model and used 20 particles for all experimentation.

Fig. 4.8.5 shows how much the faces are moving in terms of the pixel displacement between two consecutive frames. The maximum pixel displacement between two consecutive frames were about 37, 23, and 8 in the image sequence with the high/medium/low speed of moving faces, respectively.

To measure the tracking accuracy, we compute the displacement error between the tracked face location and the ground truth of the face location as

$$E = \sqrt{\left(q_x - g_x\right)^2 + \left(q_y - g_y\right)^2}, \qquad (4.8.28)$$

where q_x and q_y are the horizontal/vertical location of the tracked face and g_x and g_y are the horizontal/vertical location of the ground truth face. Fig. 4.8.6 shows the error curves E of three different face image sequences, where each face image sequence was tested using the existing adaptive velocity model and the proposed motion prediction model. As we can see, there is no big difference of the displacement error between the two velocity models when the face moves slowly. In fact, when the face moves slowly, the average displacement errors of the existing adaptive velocity model and the proposed motion prediction model are 1.50 and 1.17, respectively. However, the displacement error of the existing adaptive velocity model becomes very large but the displacement error of the proposed motion prediction model is very low when the face moves fast. In fact, when the face moves slowly, the aver-

Figure 4.8.5. The pixel displacement of moving faces in the face image sequences with the high/medium/low speed of moving faces

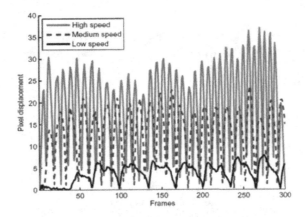

Figure 4.8.6. Tracking accuracy in terms of the displacement error

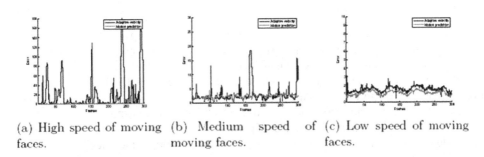

(a) High speed of moving (b) Medium speed of (c) Low speed of moving
faces.   moving faces.   faces.

age displacement errors of the existing adaptive velocity model and the proposed motion prediction model are 19.86 and 0.68, respectively. Hence, the proposed motion prediction model is effective especially when the face moves fast.

Fig. 4.8.7 shows the result of the face tracking using the face image sequence with the high speed of moving faces using two different motion models, where the upper, middle, and lower rows correspond to the original face image sequence, the tracking result using the existing adaptive velocity model, and the tracking result using the proposed motion prediction model, respectively, and the 1-5 columns correspond to the frame 155, 158, 161, 164, and 167, respectively. The existing adaptive velocity model fails to track the fast moving face at 161th frame, while the proposed motion prediction model successfully tracks the face for all frames.

2) The required number of particles

We compared the required number of particles for a successful face tracking when two different motion models are used. To guarantee successful tracking and restrict the computational load, we limited the range of particles from 10 to 60. We set the initial number

Figure 4.8.7. Tracking results using two different motion models

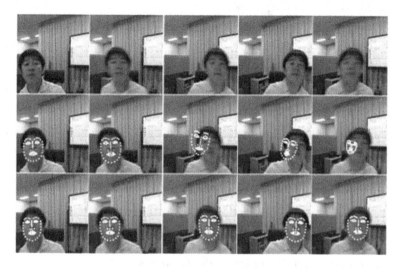

of particles to 20 and used the face image sequence with the high speed of moving faces. Fig. 4.8.8 shows the required number of particles and the AAM reconstruction error of the two different velocity models. As shown in the Fig. 4.8.8 (a), the existing adaptive velocity model needs more particles than the proposed motion prediction model by 18.74 particles on average. Further, as shown in the Fig. 4.8.8 (b), the existing adaptive velocity model shows larger AAM reconstruction error than the proposed motion prediction model by 8.73 on the average. Hence, we need a smaller number of particles with the proposed motion prediction model due to its better tracking result to save computation time for the tracking.

Figure 4.8.8. Comparison of the required number of particles and the AAM reconstruction error

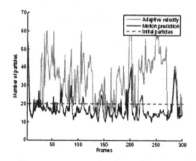 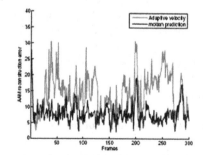

(a) The required number of particles.

(b) AAM reconstruction errors.

3) The failed tracking rate

We compared the tracking performance of the two velocity models in terms of the failed tracking rate that is defined by the ratio of the number of frames having the failed tracking over the total number of frames for the face tracking (=500). Fig. 4.8.9 shows the failed tracking rate when the number of particles changes. As we can see, the tracking performance of the existing adaptive velocity model is stable when we take more than 200 particles, while the tracking performance of the proposed motion prediction model is stable with less than 20 particles. Hence, the proposed face tracking system shows robust face tracking performance with only small number of particles even though the face is moving fast.

4) Adaptive observation model

We compared the face tracking performances between the fixed observation model and the proposed adaptive observation model. We performed these experiments with the face image sequences whose illumination change is gradual. We restricted the number of particles within the range from 10 to 30, and set the initial number of particles to 20. Fig. 4.8.10 compares the AAM reconstruction errors of the different observation models. As we can see, the AAM reconstruction error of the fixed observation model is larger than that of the proposed adaptive observation model. This implies that the updated basis vectors provide a better representation ability than the fixed basis vectors when the illumination changes.

Fig. 4.8.11 compares the representation ability between the fixed and adaptive observation model, where the three rows correspond to the mean face image, the warped patch image, and the appearance obtained from the AAM fitting. As shown in the Fig. 4.8.11 (a) and Fig. 4.8.11 (b), the warped patch image and the appearance image look very similar in the case of the adaptive observation model while they look much different in the case of the fixed observation model.

Fig. 4.8.12 shows the typical tracking results using two different observation models, where the upper and lower rows correspond to the adaptive and fixed observation model, respectively, and the 1-3 columns correspond to the frame 251, 368, and 378, respectively.

Figure 4.8.9. Comparison of the failed tracking rates

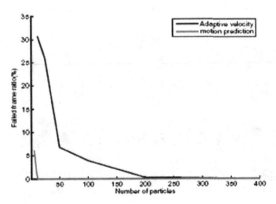

Figure 4.8.10. Comparison of the AAM reconstruction errors between the fixed and adaptive observation model

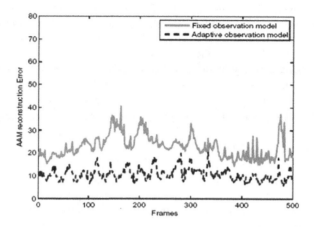

Figure 4.8.11. Comparison of the representation ability between the fixed and adaptive observation model

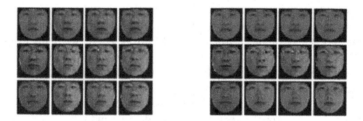

(a) The adaptive observation model.

(b) The fixed observation model.

Figure 4.8.12. Typical tracking results of two different observation models

As we can see, the adaptive observation model produces a successful tracking result while the fixed observation model fails to track after an elapse of time.

5) Occlusion handling

We evaluated the proposed face tracking system when the face is occluded. We restricted the number of particles in the range from 10 to 30, and set the initial number of particles to 20. We declared that the face was occluded when the number of outliers $N_{outlier}$ is larger than N_0. When the face is declared to be occluded, using of the proposed motion prediction model deteriorates rather the tracking performance because it fails to detect the face. Hence, we should stop using the proposed motion prediction model and use the effective velocity with the maximum number of particles and the maximum noise variance as

$$\sigma_t = \sigma_{max},$$
$$P_t = P_0 \cdot \sigma_{max}/\sigma_0,$$
$$\theta_t^{(p)} = \bar{\theta}_t + U_t^{(p)}.$$

As shown in the Fig. 4.8.13, the proposed face tracking method can track the occluded face properly even though it is heavily occluded, where the upper, middle, and lower rows contain the frames 43, 56, 65, the frames 277, 281, 285, and the frames 461, 463, 465, respectively, and the small patch window at the upper right corner in each image shows the outlier pixels.

6) Multiple face tracking

We extended the proposed face tracking method to handle multiple faces. We restricted the number of particles within the range from 10 to 30 and set the initial number of particles to 20 for each tracker. To handle the multiple face tracking problem, we invoked the face detector periodically to find a newly incoming face. If a new face was detected, then we

Figure 4.8.13. Tracking results of the occluded face

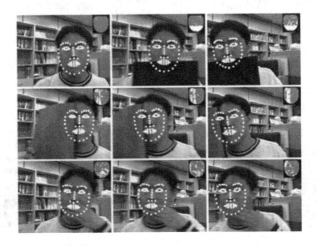

allocated the corresponding tracker, initialized it using the AAM fitting, and applied the proposed face tracking method to the new face. Fig. 4.8.14 shows one typical example of multiple face tracking, where the first and second rows correspond to the frames 190, 200, 210, and the frames 230, 330, 430, respectively. Our system tracks two faces initially. At the 210th frame, a new face comes into the image and a new tracker is allocated to the new face. At the 430th frame, one existing face is disappeared and the corresponding face tracker is deallocated. We can see that the scale, rotation, and translation of three faces are different from each other, but our system can track multiple faces successfully.

To handle the overlapped face problem in multiple face tracking, we had to check whether the faces were overlapped or not. When the faces were overlapped, the smaller face was assumed to be far from the camera, and it was declared to be occluded. We inactivated the tracker of the occluded face, and waited until we found it again. Fig. 4.8.15 shows the multiple face tracking result when two faces are overlapped with each other, where each column correspond to the frame 53, 70, and 90, respectively. At the 90th frame, we can see that the hidden face is reappeared and a new tracker is reallocated.

4.9 CONCLUSION

The naïve face tracking approach is very inefficient because it calls the face detector too frequently when the face is moving. Also, the system merely waits until the user looks at

Figure 4.8.14. One typical example of multiple face tracking

Figure 4.8.15. Occlusion handling in the case of multiple face tracking

the front view because a front-view face detector is used. The problems can be alleviated by using the face tracking algorithms introduced after the naïve face tracking approach in this chapter.

The AAM+ACM face tracking algorithm employed active contour technique to find the face boundary effectively and the detected face area is used to fit the AAM model. Therefore, the method was robust to the cluttered background and large motion because the active contour technique guarantees selection of the object foreground reliably even in the case of large movement of the foreground due to its random generation of a variety of foreground candidates. The proposed AAM fitting method was also fast because all pixels in the selected foreground area participated in the AAM fitting and the motion information obtained during the determination of the active contour of the image foreground was used as a pre-estimate for the motion parameters of AAM, which made AAM fitting fast.

The AAM+CHM face tracking algorithm uses two face models internally; the AAM and CHM, which focus on the rigid and non-rigid natures, separately. The proposed `AAM+CHM' tracking method increased the tracking rate and pose coverage by 170% and 115%, respectively, when compared to those of the `AAM' tracking method when we used the database DATA-I and a person specific AAM. The improvements of the tracking rate and pose coverage were 112%, and 111%, respectively, when we used the database DATA-II and a generic AAM. The improvements were obtained by combining the CHM and AAM, where the CHM re-initialized the AAM effectively during the tracking process by providing a good estimate of the initial AAM parameters, and the AAM initialized the CHM precisely by providing estimated 3D rotation angles and the positions of facial feature points.

The AAM+IPCA face tracking algorithm is employed an adaptive AAM that updates the appearance bases incrementally to adapt itself to the time-varying appearance using IPCA technique. Because the proposed algorithm uses the AAM fitting result as a new appearance data, the wrong update of the appearance basis vector by the badly fitted image can degrade the further AAM fitting performance. Therefore, it is necessary to measure the quality of the AAM fitting result. We proposed to used an adaptive observation model that used the modified OAM to count the number of outlier pixels. The experiment results show that the proposed adaptive observation model accurately detects the outlier pixels irrespective of the appearance variation and provide a good guide to judge the goodness of the AAM fitting result. The experiment results showed that the tracking performance of the proposed adaptive AAM was more robust and stable than that of the conventional AAM in that the adaptive AAM successfully tracked the faces throughout the all test image sequence while the conventional AAM soon failed to track the faces as the illumination condition was changed.

The AAM and particle filter-based face tracking algorithm tracks the fast moving face under the illumination change by using an adaptive observation model and the adaptive state transition model in the existing particle filter framework. The adaptive state transition model (called the motion prediction model) is based on the motion history to compute the effective velocity and the motion estimation to predict the state vector of the moving faces when the faces move fast. We could reduce the required number of particles when we used the adaptive state transition model because we could generate the particles only near the predicted state vector. This resulted in the reduction of the computational load for the face tracking. In the experiments, the face tracking was executed in the speed of 17 frames per second on the average and the face tracking performance of the motion prediction model outperformed that of the existing adaptive velocity model in terms of the speed of moving faces, the required number of particles, and the failed tracking rate. Moreover, the adaptive observation model showed better tracking performance than the fixed observation model when the illumination condition was changed.

4.10 REFERENCES

Artac, M., Jogan, M., & Leonardis, A. (2002). Incremental pca for on-line visual learning and recognition. *In Proceedings of International Conference on Pattern Recognition.*

Arulampalam, S., Maskell, S., Gordon, N., & Clapp, T. (2002). A tutorial on particle filters for online nonlinear/non-Gaussian Bayesian tracking. *IEEE Transactions on Signal Processing, 50*(2), 174-189.

Azarbayejani, A., & Pentland, A. (1995). Recursive estimation of motion, structure and focal length. *IEEE Transactions on Pattern Analysis and Machine Intelligence, 17*, 562-575.

Basu, S., Essa, I., & Pentland, A. (1996). Motion regularization for model-based head tracking. *In Proceedings of International Conference on Pattern Recognition*, (pp. 611-615).

Bhaskaran, V., & Konstantinides, K. (1997). *Image and Video Compression Standards.* Kluwer Academic Publishers.

Bing, X., Wei, Y., & Charoensak, C. (2004). Face contour tracking in video using active contour model. *In Proceedings of European Conference on Computer Vision*, (pp. 1021-1024).

Birchfield, S. (1997). An Elliptical Head Tracker. *In Proceedings of 31st Asilomar Conference*, (pp. 1710-1714).

Birchfield, S. (1998). Elliptical Head Tracking Using Intensity Gradients and Color Histograms. *In Proceedings of Computer Vision and Pattern Recognition*, (pp. 232-237).

Blake, A., & Isard, M. (1998). *Active Contours.* Springer.

Bregler, C., & Malik, J. (1998). Tracking people with twists and exponential maps. *Proceedings of IEEE Computer Vision and Pattern Recognition.*

Cascia, M., Sclaroff, S., & Athitsos, V. (2000). Fast, reliable head tracking under varying illumination: an approach vased on registration of texture-mapped 3d models. *IEEE Transaction on Pattern analysis and Machine Intelligence, 22*(4).

Cootes, T., & Taylor, C. (2001a). Constrained active appearance models. *In Proceedings of IEEE International Conference on Computer Vision.*

Cootes, T., & Taylor, C. (2001b). On representing edge structure for model matching. *In Proceedings of Computer Vision and Pattern Recognition.*

Cootes, T., Edwards, G., & Taylor, C. (2001d). Active appearance models. *IEEE Trans. on Pattern Recognition and Machine Intelligence, 23(*6), 681-685.

Cootes, T., Taylor, C., Cooper, D., & Graham, J. (1995). Active shape models - their training and application. *Computer Vision and Image Understanding, 61*(1), 38-59.

Cowell, J. R. & Ayesh, A. (2004). Extracting subtle facial expression for emotional analysis. *In Proceedings of IEEE International Conference on Systems Man and Cybernetics*, (pp. 677–681).

Craw, I., Costen, N., Kato, T., & Akamatsu, S. (1999). How should we represenfaces for automatic recognition? *IEEE Transactions on Pattern Analysis and Machine Intelligence, 21*(8), 725-736.

Cristinacce, C., Cootes, T. F., & Scott, I. M. (2004). A multi-stage vector machines. *In Proceedings of British Machine Vision Conference.*

DeCarlo, D., & Metaxas, D. (1996). The Integration of Optical Flow and Deformable Models with Applications to Human Face Shape and Motion Estimation. *In Proceedings of IEEE Computer Vision and Pattern Recognition*, (pp. 231-238).

DeCarlo, D. & Metaxas, D. (2000). Optical flow constraints on deformable models with applications to face tracking. *International Journal of Computer Vision, 38*(2), 99-127.

Dellaert, F., & Thorpe, C. (1997). Robust car tracking using Kalman filtering and Bayesian templates. *Proceeding of Conference on Intelligent Transportation Systems.*

Doucet, A., Godsill, J., & Andrieu, C. (2000). On sequential Monte Carlo sampling methods for Bayesian filtering. *Statistics and Computing, 10*(3), 197-209.

Fröba, B., & Ernst, A. (2004). Face detection with the modified census transform. *In Proceedings of IEEE International Conference on Automatic Face and Gesture Recognition*, (pp. 91-96).

Gonzalez, R. C., & Woods, R. E. (1993). *Digital Image Processing.* Addison-Wesley.

Gross, R., Matthews, I., & Baker, S. (2003). *Lucas-kanade 20 years on: A unifying framework: Part 3.* Cmu-ri-tr-03-05, CMU.

Gross. R., Matthews. I., & Baker. S. (2004a). Constructing and fitting active appearance models with occlusion. *In Proceedings of IEEE Workshop on Face Processing in Video.*

Hall, P. M., Marshall, D., & Martin, R. R. (1998). Incremental eigenanalysis for classification. *In Proceedings of British Machine Vision Conference.*

Hamlaoui, S., & Davoine, F. (2005). Facial action tracking using particle filters and active appearance models. *In Proceedings of Joint Soc-Eusai Conference*, (pp. 165-169).

Horn, B., & Schunck, B. (1981). Determining optical flow. *Journal of Artificial Intelligence, 17*, 85-203.

Isard, M., & Blake, A. (1998). Condensation-conditional density propagation for visual tracking. *International Journal of Computer Vision, 29*, 5-28.

Jang, G., & Kweon, I. (2000). Robust Real-time Face Tracking Using Adaptive Color Model. *In Proceedings of International* Symposium on Mechatronics and Intelligent Mechanical System for 21 Century.

Jepson, A., Fleet, D., & El-Maraghi, T. (2003). Robust online appearance model for visual tracking. *IEEE Transactions on Pattern Analysis and Machine Intelligence, 25*(10), 1296-1311.

Jun, B., & Kim, D. (2007). Robust real-time face detection using face certainty map. *In Proceedings of International Conference on Biometrics,* (pp. 29-38).

Kalman, R. E. (1960). A new approach to linear filtering and prediction problems. *Journal of Basic Engineering, 82*(Series D), 35-45.

Kanade, T., & Lucas, B. D. (1981). An iterative image registration technique with an application to stereo vision. *In Proceedings of International Joint Conference on Artificial Intelligence.*

Kass, M., Witkin, A., & Terzopoulos, D. (1988). Snakes: active ontour models. *In Proceedings of the International Journal of Computer Vision,* (pp. 321-331).

Kawaguchi, T., & Rizon, M. (2003). *Iris detection using intensity and edge information.*

Lee, H.-S., & Kim, D. (2007). Robust face tracking by integration of two separate trackers: Skin color and facial shape. *Pattern Recognition, 40,* 3225-3235.

Li, Y., Gong, S., & Liddell, H. (2001). *Modelling faces dynamically across views and over time.* Computer Vision.

Li, Y. (2004). On incremental and robust subspace learning. *Pattern recognition, 37,* 1509–1518.

Matthews, I., & Baker, S. (2004a). Active appearance models revisited. *International Journal of Computer Vision, 60*(2), 135-164.

Maurer, T., & Malsburg, C. (1996). Tracking and learning graphs and pose on image sequences of faces. *In Proceedings of International Conference on Automatic Face and Gesture Recognition,* (pp. 176-181).

McKenna, S., Gong, S., Würtz, R., Tanner, J., & Banin, D. (1997). Tracking facial feature points with Gabor wavelets and shape models. *In Proceedings of International conference on audio and video-based biometric person authentication,* (pp. 35-42).

Okuma, K., Taleghani, A., de Freitas, N., Little, J., & Lowe, D. (2004). A boosted particle filter: multitarget detection and tracking. *In Proceedings of European Conference on Computer Vision,* (pp. 28-39).

Pardàs, M., & Sayrol, E. (2000). A New Approach to Tracking with Active Contours. *In Proceedings of International Conference on Image Processing,* (pp. 259-262).

Qian, R., Sezan, M., & Matthews, K. (1998). A Robust Real-Time Face Tracking Algorithm. *In Proceedings of International Conference on Image Processing,* (pp. 131-135).

Raja, Y., McKenna, S., & Gong, S. (1998). Colour Model Selection and Adaptation in Dynamic Scenes. *In Proceedings of European Conference on Computer Vision,* (pp. 460-474).

Romdhani, S., & Vetter, T. (2003). Efficient, robust and accurate fitting of a 3D morphable model. *In Proceedings of IEEE International Conference on Computer Vision*, (pp. 59-66).

Ross, D., Lim, J., & Yang, M. (2004). Adaptive probabilistic visual tracking with incremental subspace update. *In Proceedings of 8th European Conference on Computer Vision*, (pp. 470-482).

Ryu, W., & Kim, D. (2007). Real-time 3d head tracking under rapidly changing pose, head movement and illumination. *In Proceedings of International Conference on Image Analysis and Recognition*.

Schwerdt, K., & Crowley, J. (2000). Robust face tracking using color. *In Proceedings of International Conference on Automatic Face and Gesture Recognition*, (pp. 90-95).

Stegmann, M., Fisker, R., Ersboll, B., Thodberg, H., & Hyldstrup, L. (2004). Active appearance models: Theory and Cases. *In Proceedings of 9th Danish Conference on Pattern Recognition and Image Analysis*, (pp. 49-57).

Stenger, B., Mendonca, P., & Cipolla, R. (2001). Model-based hand tracking using an unscented Kalman filter. *Proceedings of the Britisch Machine Vision Conference*.

Stern, H., & Efros, B. (2005). Adaptive color space switching for tracking under varying illumination. *Image and Vision Computing, 23*(3), 353-364.

Strom, J., Jebara, T., Basu, S., & Pentland, A. (1999). Real time tracking and modeling of faces: An ekf-based analysis by synthesis approach. *Proceedings of International Conference on Computer Vision*: Workshop onModelling People.

Sung, J., & Kim. D. (2006a). A background robust active appearance models using the active contour technique. *Pattern Recognition, 40*, 108-120.

Sung. J., & Kim. D. (2006b). Background robust face tracking usinf active contour technique combined active appearance model. *In Proceedings of International Conference Biometrics*.

Sung. J., & Kim. D. (2006c). Large motion object tracking using active contoure combined active appearance model. *In Proceedings of International Congerence on Computer Vision Systems*.

Vacchetti, L., Lepetit, V., & Fua, P. (2004). Stable real-time 3D tracking using online and offline information. *IEEE Transactions on Pattern Analysis and Machine Intelligence, 26*(10), 1385-1391.

Viola, P., & Jones, M. (2002). Fast and robust classification using asymmetric adaboost and a detector cascade. *Advances in Neural Information Processing System, 14*. Cambridge: MIT Press

Welch, G., & Bishop, G. (2001). *An introduction to the Kalman filter*. Presented at SIGGRAPH.

Xiao, J., & Kanade, T. (2002). Robust full-motion recovery of head by dynamic templates and registration techniques. In *Proceedings of Automatic Face and Gesture Recognition*.

Yang, J., & Waibel, A. (1996). A real-time face tracker. In *Proceedings of Workshop on Application of Computer Vision*, (pp. 142-147).

Yuille. A., Cohen. D., & Hallinan. P. (1989). Feature extraction from faces using deformable template. *IEEE Conference on Computer Vision and Pattern Recognition*, (pp. 104-109).

Zhou, S., Chellappa, R. & Moghaddam, B. (2004). Visual tracking and recognition using appearance-adaptive model in particle filter. *IEEE Transactions on Image Processing, 13*(11), 1491–1506.

4.11 ENDNOTES

[1]   In this section, we separate the facial motion into two types of motions: local motion and global motion. The local motion represents the local movements of facial features such as eyebrows, eyes, nose, mouths, and so on within a face. The global motion represents global head movements that can be explained by 3D rotation and 3D translation of the whole face such as shaking, nodding, and so on.

[2]   Note that these kind of appearance models including AOM are quite different from the linear appearance model of the AAMs. Usually, they aim to model the unpredictably varying appearance in the on-line tracking phase, while the AAMs aim to learn a set of manually verified legal variation of the appearance in the training phase.

[3]   In a two-frame tracker, the fitting result at the previous frame is used as the reference appearance for the next frame.

[4]   Here, we say that a fitting result is bad, when the fitted shape points do not coincide with the expected ground truth landmarks.

Chapter V
Face Recognition

In the modern life, the need for personal security and access control is becoming an important issue. Biometrics is the technology which is expected to replace traditional authentication methods that are easily stolen, forgotten and duplicated. Fingerprints, face, iris, and voiceprints are commonly used biometric features. Among these features, face provides a more direct, friendly and convenient identification method and is more acceptable compared with the individual identification methods of other biometrics features. Thus, face recognition is one of the most important parts in biometrics.

Since Kanade (1973) attempted automatic face recognition 30 years ago, many researchers have investigated face recognition. Research into face recognition can be categorized into three approaches. The first approach is the appearance-based method which represents the face image as a one-dimensional vector and applies algebraic or statistical tools for extracting the characteristics of the face image. The face images are represented as a vector and the pattern of these vectors are analyzed by pattern analysis methods such as principal component analysis (PCA) (Turk and Pentland, 1991a, Turk and Pentland, 1991b), linear discriminant analysis (LDA) (Belhumeur et. al., 1997), and independent component analysis (ICA) (Bartlett et. al., 2002). The second approach is the feature-based method which extracts the facial local features such as the eyes, nose, and mouth and analyzes the geometry of the extracted local features. Most early research which was proposed by Kelly (1970) and Kanade (1973) belonged to this category. The third approach is the-model based method which first constructs a model of the human face, then fits the model to the given face image and finally uses the parameters of the fitted model as the feature vector. An explicit modeling of face variations, such as pose, illumination and expression, can handle these variabilities in practice. However, the model construction is complicated and laborious, and facial feature points are difficult to extract automatically with robustness. Bunch graph (Wiskott et. al., 1997), active appearance models (AAM) (Cootes et. al., 2001d), and 3D mophable model (3D MM) (Blanz and Vetters, 1999) belong to this category.

Among various face recognition methods, the holistic appearance-based approach is most prevalent. However, this approach often fails when the input face has internal and/or external variations. To tackle this problem, there are many examples of previous work presented in this chapter.

First, we review several approaches to cope with the pose variation in face recognition, which are divided into two categories: single-view based approaches and multi-view based approaches. The single-view based approach uses the single-view gallery, in which each probe image is transformed to a fixed, canonical head pose prior to nearest neighbor identification. There are two methods in the single-view based approach: the geometric method and the statistical approach. (1) The geometric method takes a single probe image at one pose and creates a full 3D face model for the subject based on just one image. Then, the 3D face model is used to re-render the face at a canonical pose (Blanz et. al., 2005). Although the geometric method is the state-of-the-art in the pose-invariant face recognition, it takes a lot of time to create a 3D face model from an image due to the iterative optimization. (2) The statistical approach treats the relationship between the frontal and the non-frontal images as a statistical learning problem. Beymer and Poggio (1993), Wallhoff et al., (2001), and Lee and Kim (2005) used this approach. The multi-view based approach uses the multi-view gallery, which consists of the multiple views of various poses for each known person. Pose-invariance is achieved by assuming that, for each probe face, there exists an image with the same face pose as the probe image for each known person in the gallery. Beymer (1994), Biuk and Loncaric (2001), Huang et. al., (2000), and Pentland et. al., (1994) divided the face images into several subsets according to the facial angles and represented each view in a different subspace, estimated the pose angle of each input facial image and projected the image onto the corresponding subspace, and then classified the face image in the projected subspace. The multi-view based approach is preferred because it avoids establishing the 3D face model from each pose image, which often tends to be a more complicated problem.

Second, we review several approaches to cope with the illumination variation in face recognition, which are divided into three categories: the invariant feature, the statistical, and the canonical form approach. The invariant feature approach seeks the features of the face which remains invariant under the illumination variation. 2D Gabor-like filters (Adini et. al., 1997), the retinex algorithm (Land, 1986), and the quotient image (Riklin-Raviv and Shashua, 2001) belong to this approach. The statistical approach learns the extent of the variation in some suitable subspace or manifold and performs the face recognition by choosing the subspace or manifold closest to the input image. Belhumeur and Kriegman (1998) and Georghiades et. al., (1998, 2001) introduced a generative appearance-based method for recognizing the human face under the illumination and viewpoint variation and argued that the images under all possible illumination conditions built a convex cone in the space of images and the reconstructed shape and albedo of the face from a small number of samples served as a generative model for rendering or synthesizing images of the face under the novel pose and illumination conditions. The canonical form approach attempts to normalize the illumination variation by transforming the input image into a normal condition and performs the face recognition using the transformed images. The illumination ratio image (Zhao et. al., 2003) and illumination transformation (Lui et. al., 2005; Lee and Kim, 2006) belong to this category.

On the other hand, other conditions such as age, gender, and race are considered. Lantis et. al., (1999, 2002) proposed a parametersized statistical model for age transformation which is learned to control the effects of aging on the facial appearance. Gandhi (2004) proposed the support vector regression machine to derive age prediction function. Suo et. al., (2007) proposed the dynamic Markov process to model the face aging and hair features. To classify gender, Golomb et. al., (1991) first tried to use neural network. Moghaddam et. al., proposed gender classification using SVM with RBF kernel (Moghaddam et. al., 2002). The performance of SVM is shown to be superior to the traditional classifiers such as the SVM with linear and quadratic kernel, Fisher linear discriminant, and nearest-neighbor. Adaboost is also used to classify gender (Verschae et. at., 2006). Adaboost algorithm is 1000 times faster than the algorithm proposed by Moghaddam et. al., (2002). Race classification is the other exploratory research. Yongsheng et. al., (2005) proposed a real time race classification system. They used PCA for feature generation, ICA for feature extraction, and SVM to classify a frontal face into Asian or non-Asian.

For the last few years, numerous novel face recognition algorithms have been proposed. The developed algorithms include face recognition from three-dimensional (3D) scans, high resolution still images, multiple still image, and these techniques are evaluated by The Face Recognition Grand Challenge (FRGC) (Phillips et. al., 2005). The FRGC is designed to achieve an increase in performance by presenting to researchers with challenging problems. The results of FRGC may have the potential to cause a rethinking and re-engineering of how face recognition is deployed in real-world applications.

This chapter is organized into two parts. The first part reivews some feature extraction methods of the recent face recognition algorithms, which are the mixture model, embedded hidden Markove model, local feature analysis, tensor analysis, and 3D morphable models. The face recognition performance is largely affected by the feature extraction method of the algorithm. A feature vector obtained by the feature extraction method should be compact while not losing the inherient characteristics of the input face to privde a good recognition performance. The second part introduces five different face recognition methods, each method belongs to one of the face recognition approaches explained earlier, as follows. The face recognition using mixture model belongs to the appearance-based approach, the face recognition using embedded HMM belongs to the feature-based approach, the face recognition using LFA and adaboost belongs to the combination of the appearance-based and feature-based approaches, and the face recognition using tensor-based AAM and the face recognition using 3D MM belong to the model-based approach.

5.1 MIXTURE MODELS

In a mixture model (Jacobs et. al., 1991; Jordan and Jacobs, 1994), a class is partitioned into a number of clusters and its density function of n-dimensional observed data $\mathbf{x} = \{x_1, \cdots, x_n\}$ is represented by a linear combination of componet densities of the partitioned clusters as

$$P(\mathbf{x}) = \sum_{k=1}^{K} P(\mathbf{x} \mid k, \theta_k) P(k), \qquad (5.1.1)$$

where $P(\mathbf{x} \mid k, \theta_k)$ and $P(k)$ represent the conditional density and the prior probability of the kth cluster, respectively, and θ_k is the unknown model parameter of the kth cluster.

The prior probabilities are chosen to satisfy the condition $\sum_{k=1}^{K} P(k) = 1$. The conditional density function $P(\mathbf{x} \mid k, \theta_k)$ is often modeled by a Gaussian function as

$$P(\mathbf{x} \mid k, \theta_k) = \frac{1}{(2\pi)^{\frac{n}{2}} |\Sigma_k|^{\frac{1}{2}}} exp\{-\frac{1}{2}(\mathbf{x} - \mu_k)^T \Sigma_k^{-1}(\mathbf{x} - \mu_k)\}, \qquad (5.1.2)$$

where μ_k and Σ_k are the sample mean and covariance of the kth cluster, respectively. The parameters in the mixture model can be estimated from a data set using an Expectation-Maximization (EM) algorithm (Dempster et. al., 1977).

Given a data set data $\mathbf{X} = \{\mathbf{x}_1, \cdots, \mathbf{x}_N\}$, the EM algorithm aims to find parameter values that minimize the negative log-likelihood function

$$\begin{aligned} \mathcal{L}(\mathbf{X}\Theta) &= -\sum_{p=1}^{N} ln P(\mathbf{x}_p) \\ &= -\sum_{p=1}^{N} ln\{\sum_{k=1}^{K} P(\mathbf{s}_p \mid k, \theta_k) P(k)\}. \end{aligned} \qquad (5.1.3)$$

The EM algorithm is an iterative algorithm, where each iteration consists of two steps: an expectation step (E-step) followed by a maximization step (M-step) as given in the following.

(1) E-step: Evaluate the posterior distribution $P(z \mid \mathbf{x}, \Theta^{(t)})$ using

$$P(z \mid \mathbf{x}, \Theta^{(t)}) = \frac{P(\mathbf{x} \mid z, \Theta^{(t)}) P(z)}{\sum_{k=1}^{K} P(\mathbf{x} \mid k, \Theta^{(t)}) P(k)}, \qquad (5.1.4)$$

where $P(\mathbf{x} \mid z, \Theta^{(t)})$ is calculated by Eq. (5.1.1) and (5.1.2).

(2) M-step: Estimate the new model parameters $\Theta^{(t+)}$ by maximizing the expectation of log-likelihood as

$$\Theta^{(t+)} = \arg\max_{\Theta} \mathcal{E}[\mathcal{L}(\mathbf{Y} \mid \Theta)]. \qquad (5.1.5)$$

The new prior probabilities of the ith cluster $P(k)$ are updated by

$$P(k) = \frac{1}{N} \sum_{p=1}^{N} P(k \mid \mathbf{x}_p, \Theta^{(t)}) \qquad (5.1.6)$$

and the new mean parameters $\mu_k^{X(t+1)}$ of the ith cluster are obtained by

$$\mu_k^{X(t+1)} = \frac{\sum_{p=1}^{N} P(k \mid \mathbf{x}_p, \Theta^{(t)}) \mathbf{x}_p}{\sum_{p=1}^{N} P(k \mid \mathbf{x}_p, \Theta^{(t)})}, \qquad (5.1.7)$$

and the new covariance matrix $\Sigma_k^{X(t+)}$ is computed by

$$\Sigma_k^{X^{(t+1)}} = \frac{\sum_{p=1}^{N} P(k \mid \mathbf{x}_p, \Theta^{(t)})(\mathbf{x}_p - \mu_k^{X^{(t+1)}})^T (\mathbf{x}_p - \mu_k^{X^{(t+1)}})}{\sum_{p=1}^{N} P(\mathbf{x}_p \mid \Theta^{(t)})}. \tag{5.1.8}$$

5.2 EMBEDDED HIDDEN MARKOV MODEL

An embedded hidden Markov model (EHMM) is an extension of the previous 1-D HMM in order to deal with two-dimensional data such as images and videos. The EHMM was previously used for character recognition by Kuo and Agazzi (Kuo and Agazzi, 1994). In fact, a fully connected 2-D HMM would be desirable for modelling a 2-D face image. However, the computational complexity for a fully connected 2-D HMM increases explosively as the number of states grows. In this work, we adopt the Samaria's Pseudo 2-D HMM (P2D-HMM) obtained by linking 1-D left-right HMMs to form super states. The structure includes one internal 1-D HMM in each state in the outer 1-D HMM. While transitions in a vertical direction are allowed between two adjacent super states which include the super state itself, transitions in a horizontal direction are only allowed between two adjacent states in a super state including the state itself. From this structure, we know that the sequence of super states are used to model a horizontal slice of face image along the vertical direction and that the sequence of states in a super state are used to model a block image along the horizontal direction. We call this model an *embedded HMM*. It differs from a 2-D HMM since a transition between the states in different states are allowed. Fig. 5.2.1 illustrates a 5-super states EHMM for face modelling, where each super state represents vertical facial features, such as forehead, eyes, nose, mouth, and chin in the face and each state in the super state represents horizontal local block features in the corresponding facial feature.

The EHMM is defined by specifying the following parameters (Samaria and Young, 1994):

Figure 5.2.1. An illustration of 2-D EHMM with 5 super states for face modeling

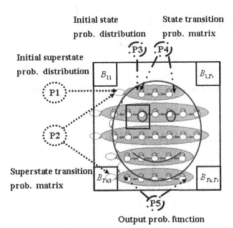

- N_0 is the number of super states in the vertical direction of EHMM.
- $\Pi_0 = \{\pi_{0,i} : 1 \le i \le N_0\}$ is the initial super state distribution, where $\pi_{0,i}$ is the probability of observation sequence $O_{1,1}, \cdots, O_{1,T_1}$ being in the ith super state.
- $A_0 = \{a_{0_{ij}} : 1 \le i, j \le N_0\}$ is the super state transition probability matrix, where $a_{0_{ij}}$ is the probability of transition from the ith to the jth super state.

- $\Lambda_0 = \{\lambda^i : 1 \le i \le N_0\}$ is the set of left-right 1-D HMMs in each super state. Each λ^i is specified by the standard 1-D HMM parameters as follows.
  - N_1^k is the number of states in the kth super state.
  - $\Pi_1^k = \{\pi_{1,i}^k : 1 \le i \le N_1^k\}$ is the initial state distribution, where $\pi_{1,i}^k$ is the probability of observation $O_{t_0,1} 1 \le t_0 \le T_0$ being in the ith state of the kth super state.
  - $A_1^k = \{a_{1,ij}^k : 1 \le i, j \le N_1^k\}$ is the state transition probability matrix, where $a_{1,ij}^k$ is the probability of transition from the ith to the jth state of the kth super state.
  - $B_1^k = \{b_i^k(O_{t_0,t_1}) : 1 \le i \le N_1^k\}$ is the output probability function, where $b_i^k(O_{t_0,t_1})$ represents the probability of the observation vector at the t_0-th row and the t_1-th column in the ith state of the kth super state. In a continuous density HMM, the states are characterized by continuous observation density function that is typically represented in terms of a mixture of Gaussian funtions $b_i^k(O_{t_0,t_1}) = \sum_{m=1}^{M} c_{i,m}^k G(O_{t_0,t_1}, \mu_{i,m}^k, \Sigma_{i,m}^k)$, where $1 \le i \le N_i^k$, $c_{i,m}^k$ is the mixing coefficient for the kth mixture component in the ith state of the kth super state, and $G(O_{t_0,t_1}, \mu_{i,m}^k, \Sigma_{i,m}^k)$ ia s Gaussian probability density function with mean vector $\mu_{i,m}^k$ and covariance matrix $\Sigma_{i,m}^k$ (Tipping and Bishop, 1999).

In summary, the EHMM is defined by the set of parameters for super states as $\Lambda = \{\Pi_0, A_0, \Lambda_0\}$, where $\Lambda_0 = \{\lambda^i : 1 \le i \le N_0\}$, and each super state is defined by the set of parameters as $\lambda^k = \{\Pi_1^k, A_1^k, B_1^k\}$. Let the number of super state, the number of states in the kth super state, and the number of mixture components of the output in the ith state of the kth super state be N_0, N_1^k, and M_i^k, respectively. Then, the required number of parameters to define a EHMM can be computed as follows. For super states, we need to determine N_0 and $N_0 \times N_0$ parameters for Π_0 and A_0, respectively. For states, we need to determine $\sum_{k=1}^{N_0} N_1^k$, $\sum_{k=1}^{N_0} N_1^k \times N_1^k$, and $\sum_{k=1}^{N_0} \sum_{i=1}^{N_1^k} (1 + K + K^2) \times M_i^k$ for Π_1, A_1, and B_1, respectively, where K is the dimension of the observation output.

5.3 LOCAL FEATURE ANALYSIS

In feature extraction, there are two approaches, a global and a local method. Among the global methods, eigenface (Turk and Pentland, 1991b) and fisherface (Belhumeur, et. al.,

1997) are the two most representative methods, which use Principal Component Analysis (PCA) and Fisher Linear Discriminant (FLD) respectively. Both methods construct bases and they are named as *eigenfaces* and *fisherfaces*, and they are considered as models for faces, where the features are extracted by linearly projecting a face image onto the bases. The eigenfaces and fisherfaces describe the whole shape of a face rather than local structures of a face such as nose, eye, jaw-line, and cheekbone. While eigenfaces are constructed from the covariance matrix of face images, fisherfaces are obtained from between-class scatter matrix and within-class scatter matrix. In other words, eigenface is an unsupervised method and fisherface is a supervised method. Previous experiments show that fisherface performs better than eigenface, and it is robuster to the variations of illumination and poses than eigenface. However, fisherface is known to be prone to overfit to the classes whose data are used in basis construction (Bartlette, 2001). Global methods is global methods are said that they are weak to such variations.

On the contrary, it is known that local methods are robust to the variations. Local Feature Analysis (LFA) (Penev and Atick, 1996) is referred to as a local method since it constructs a set of kernels that detects local structures; e.g., nose, eye, jaw-line, and cheekbone, and the kernels are used as bases for feature extraction as in eigenface and fisherface. However, LFA requires feature selection step since the number of the constructed kernels is as same as the dimension of input images, and it does not use any class information as in eigenface.

Local Feature Analysis constructs kernels, which are basis vectors for feature extraction. Kernels are constructed using the eigenvectors of the covariance matrix of face images as in eigenface. However, unlike eigenface, kernels describe local structures of a face(see Fig. 5.8.3) rather than a whole face structure, and they are *topographic* since the kernels are indexed by spatial location (Bartlette, 2001; Penev and Atick, 1996). Let's suppose that there is a set of n d-dimensional sample images $x_1, \ldots, x_n$. Hence, the covariance matrix, C, of the images is computed as

$$C = \frac{1}{n} \sum_{t=1}^{n} (x_t - m)(x_t - m)^T \tag{5.3.1}$$

where $m = \frac{1}{n} \sum_{t=1}^{n} x_t$. When there are N largest eigenvalues of C, λ_r, and the corresponding eigenvectors, W_r, a set of kernels, K, is derived by enforcing topology into the eigenvectors. In addition, the outputs of kernels, O, and the covariance of the outputs, P, are written in a matrix form,

$$K = W\Lambda W^T \tag{5.3.2}$$

$$O = K^T X \tag{5.3.3}$$

$$P = WW^T \tag{5.3.4}$$

where $W = [W_1 \cdots W_N]$, $\Lambda = diag(1/\sqrt{\lambda_r})$, and $X = [x_1 \cdots x_n]$. Since K is symmetric, we only consider the columns of K as the bases. Note that the number of kernels constructed by LFA is as same as the dimension of input images, V. Hence, the dimension of the outputs is reduced by choosing a subset of kernels, M. M is constructed by iteratively adding a kernel whose output produces the biggest reconstruction error. At each step, the point added to M is chosen as the kernel corresponding to location, x,

$$\arg\max_{\mathbf{x}} \; <| O_t(\mathbf{x}) - O_t^{re}(\mathbf{x})\|^2> \tag{5.3.5}$$

where subscript t and x in a parenthesis denote tth input image and index of elements of vectors, respectively. That is, $O_t(x)$ represents the output of xth kernel for tth input image. And $O_t^{re}(x)$ is the reconstruction of the output. The reconstruction of tth output is

$$O_t^{re}(\mathbf{x}) = \sum_{m=1}^{|M|} Z(m, x) O_t(y_m) \tag{5.3.6}$$

where $Z(m; x)$ is the reconstruction coefficient and $y_m \in M$.

For all images, the reconstruction is written in a matrix form as follows

$$O^{re} = Z^{T} O(M, :) \tag{5.3.7}$$

$O(M; :)$ denotes the subset of O corresponding to the points in M for all n images. And, Z is calculated from

$$Z = P(M, M)^{-1} P(M, :) \tag{5.3.8}$$

5.4 TENSOR ANALYSIS

A tensor is a generalization of vectors and matrices. For example, a vector is a first-order tensor and a matrix is a second-order tensor. The multilinear algebra, which is the algebra of higher-order tensors, is a generalization of the linear algebra. This tensor concept allows us to manipulate the quantities of higher-order data.

In the sequel, we denote scalars by lower-case letters ($a, b, \dots$), vectors by bold lower-case letters ($a, b, \dots$), matrices by bold upper-case letter ($\mathbf{A}, \mathbf{B}, \dots$), and higher-order tensors by italic letters ($\mathcal{A}, \mathcal{B}, \dots$).

A tensor of order N is given by $\mathcal{A} \in R^{I_1 \times I_2 \cdots \times I_N}$, where N is the order. We can unfold the tensor $\mathcal{A}$ by stacking the mode-n vectors of it as columns in a matrix as $\mathbf{A}_{(n)} \in R^{I_n \times (I_1 I_2 \cdots I_{n-1} I_{n+1} \cdots I_N)}$. This tensor unfolding allows easy manipulation of the tensor.

The multiplication of higher-order tensor $\mathcal{A} \in R^{I_1 \times I_2 \cdots \times I_N}$ by a matrix $\mathbf{M} \in R^{J_n \times I_n}$ is represented as $\mathcal{B} = \mathcal{A} \times_n \mathbf{M}$, where $\mathcal{B} \in R^{I_1 \times I_2 \cdots \times I_{n-1} \times J_n \times I_{n+1} \cdots \times I_N}$, and its entries are given by

$$(\mathcal{A} \times_n \mathbf{M})_{i_1 i_2 \dots i_{n-1} j_n i_{n+1} \dots i_N} = \sum_{i_n} a_{i_1 \dots i_{n-1} i_n i_{n+1} \dots i_N} m_{j_n i_n}. \tag{5.4.1}$$

This mode-n product of tensor and matrix can be expressed in unfolded form:

$$\mathbf{B}_{(n)} = \mathbf{MA}_{(n)}, \tag{5.4.2}$$

where $\mathbf{A}_{(n)}$ and $\mathbf{B}_{(n)}$ are mode-n matrix unfolding of tensor $\mathcal{A}$ and $\mathcal{B}$, respectively.

Using the higher order singular value decomposition (HOSVD) (Lathauwer et. al., 2000), the tensor $\mathcal{A} \in R^{I_1 \times I_2 \cdots \times I_N}$ can be decomposed as the mode-n product between N orthogonal mode matrices $\mathbf{U}_1 \cdots \mathbf{U}_N$ and a core tensor $\mathcal{Z} \in R^{I_1 \times I_2 \cdots \times I_N}$:

$$\mathcal{A} = \mathcal{Z} \times_1 \mathbf{U}_1 \cdots \times_N \mathbf{U}_N. \tag{5.4.3}$$

The core tensor $\mathcal{Z}$ is analogous to the diagonal singular value matrix of conventional SVD, but it is a full rank tensor. In addition, it governs the interaction between the mode matrices $\mathbf{U}_n$, where $n = 1, \cdots, N$. The mode matrix $\mathbf{U}_n$ contains the orthonormal vectors spanning the column space of the matrix $\mathbf{A}_{(n)}$. The HOSVD of a tensor $\mathcal{A}$ can be computed as follows:

- Set the mode-n matrix $\mathbf{U}_n$ by the left singular matrix of the mode-n matrix unfolding of $\mathbf{A}_{(n)}$ for $n = 1, \cdots, N$.
- Compute the core tensor by
$$\mathcal{Z} = \mathcal{A} \times_1 \mathbf{U}_1^T \cdots \times_N \mathbf{U}_N^T. \tag{5.4.4}$$

5.5 3D MORPHABLE MODELS

3DMMs are the generative and parametric models of certain visual phenomena with the shape and texture variations that are appropriate for representing the linear object classes (Vetter and Poggio, 1997). They represent a 3D face image in terms of a shape vector of the n vertices $\mathbf{S} = (X_1, Y_1, Z_1, \ldots, X_n, Y_n, Z_n)^T \in \mathbf{R}^{3n}$ and a texture image of the R, G, B color values at the n corresponding vertices $\mathbf{T} = (R_1, G_1, B_1, \ldots, R_n, G_n, B_n)^T \in \mathbf{R}^{3n}$. The detailed explanation about the model construction for the 3D MMs is given as follows.

First, we collect a training set of m 3D face images $\{\mathbf{S}^i, \mathbf{T}^i\}_{i=1,\ldots,m}$, where $\mathbf{S}^i$ and $\mathbf{T}^i$ are the shape and the texture of the ith 3D face image, respectively. Second, we perform the shape alignment of all training 3D face images using *Procrustes Analysis* (Cootes et. al, 2001) to obtain the full correspondence among them. Third, we apply the PCA to the training set and obtain the 3D shape basis vector $\mathbf{S}_k$ and the 3D texture basis image $\mathbf{T}_k$ through the eigenvalue analysis. Then, the shape $\mathbf{S}$ and the texture $\mathbf{T}$ of a given 3D face are expressed as a linear combination of a mean 3D shape $\mathbf{S}_0$ and the N_s 3D shape basis vector $\mathbf{S}_k$ and a linear combination of the mean 3D texture $\mathbf{T}_0$ and the N_t 3D texture basis image $\mathbf{T}_k$, respectively, as

$$\mathbf{S} = \mathbf{S}_0 + \sum_{k=1}^{N_s} \alpha_k \mathbf{S}_k, \mathbf{T} = \mathbf{T}_0 + \sum_{k=1}^{N_t} \beta_k \mathbf{T}_k. \tag{5.5.1}$$

Fig. 5.5.1 illustrates some examples of the 3D shape basis vectors, where the three shape basis vectors from $\mathbf{S}_1$ to $\mathbf{S}_3$ are displayed. The first, second, and third rows show the variations of the first, second, and third 3D shape basis vector from $-3\sigma^2$ to $+3\sigma 2$, respectively, and the center column is the mean shape vector $\mathbf{S}_0$ of the 3D MMs.

Fig. 5.5.2 illustrates some examples of the 3D texture basis images, where the first four 3D texture basis images $\mathbf{T}_0(\mathbf{x})$ to $\mathbf{T}_3(\mathbf{x})$ are shown. These 3D texture basis images are shape-normalized face images because they are warped to the same 3D mean shape vector $\mathbf{S}_0$.

5.6 FACE RECOGNITION USING MIXTURE MODELS

Face recognition is an active research area spanning several research fields such as image processing, pattern recognition, computer vision, and neural networks (Chellappa et. al., 1995). Face recognition has many applications, such as the biometrics system, the surveillance

Figure 5.5.1. Some examples of the 3D shape basis vectors

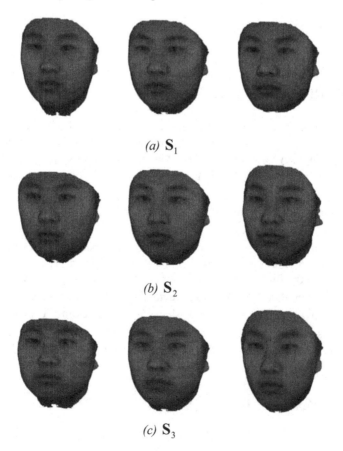

(a) $\mathbf{S}_1$

(b) $\mathbf{S}_2$

(c) $\mathbf{S}_3$

Figure 5.5.2. Some examples of the first four 3D texture basis images

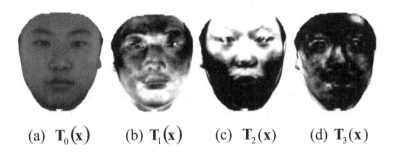

(a) $\mathbf{T}_0(\mathbf{x})$ (b) $\mathbf{T}_1(\mathbf{x})$ (c) $\mathbf{T}_2(\mathbf{x})$ (d) $\mathbf{T}_3(\mathbf{x})$

system, and the content-based video processing system. However, there are still many open problems, such as the recognition under illumination and/or pose variations.

There are two main approaches for face recognition (Chellappa et. al.,1995; Samal and Iyengar, 1992; Brunelli and Poggio, 1993). The first approach is the feature-based matching approach using the relationship between facial features such as eyes, mouth and nose (Brunelli and Poggio, 1993; Wiskott et. al., 1997). The second approach is the template matching approach using the holistic features of face image (Brunelli and Poggio, 1993; Turk and Pentland, 1991a, 1991b; Belhumeur and Kriegman, 1997; Etemad and Chellappa, 1997; Moghaddam and Pentland, 1997). The approach to combine the feature-based matching approach and the template matching approach has been also proposed (Edwards et. al., 1998b; Craw et. al., 1999)

The eigneface method is a well-known template matching approach (Turk and Pentland, 1991a, 1991b; Moghaddam and Pentland, 1997). Face recognition using the eigenface method is performed using the feature values transformed by the PCA. In addition, the eigenface method can be used for the face coding (face reconstruction), which is the technology of extracting a small face code so as to reconstruct face images well, because the eigenface method uses the PCA having the property of the mean squared error (MSE)-sense optimal reconstruction (Moghaddam and Pentland, 1997).

We propose the mixture-of-eigenfaces method, which is an extension of the existing eigenface method. While the eigenface method uses one set of features by PCA, the mixture-of-eigenfaces method uses more than one set of features by the PCA mixture model. Since PCA is a linear method, it is not effective for analyzing a nonlinear structure. The PCA mixture model overcome this limitation in PCA by using a combination of PCAs (Kim et. al., 2001c). Therefore, the mixture-of-eigenfaces method is expected to represent face images more effectively and show a better recognition performance than the existing eigenface method.

There are some researches using the mixture model for face recognition. Mckenna et. al. (1998) modeled the face of one person by one Gaussian mixture model. Lawrence et. al. (1997a) used mixture model to model faces of all people and used a mixture-distance which is similar to our recognition method. However, they used Gaussian mixture model and did not show a result for face coding. Moghaddam and Pentland proposed the Gaussian-like mixture models, where its density was estimated in the principal space (Moghaddam and

Pentland, 1997). However, they used the mixture models only for face detection and used the eigenface method for face coding and recognition.

5.6.1 Eigenface Method

Principal component analysis (PCA) (Jolliffe, 1986) is a well-known technique in multivariate linear data analysis. The central idea of PCA is to reduce the dimensionality of a data set while retaining as much variation as possible in the data set. In PCA (Hotelling, 1933), a set of observed l-dimensional data vector $\mathbf{X} = \{\mathbf{x}_p\}$, $p \in \{1, \cdots, N\}$ is reduced to a set of m-dimensional feature vector $\mathbf{S} = \{\mathbf{s}_p\}$, $p \in \{1, \cdots, N\}$ by a transformation matrix $\mathbf{W}$ as

$$\mathbf{s}_p = \mathbf{W}^T(\mathbf{x}_p - \mathbf{m}),\tag{5.6.1}$$

where $\mathrm{m} \leq 1$, $\mathbf{m} = \dfrac{1}{N}\sum_{p=1}^{N}\mathbf{x}_p$, $\mathbf{W} = (\mathbf{w}_1, \cdots, \mathbf{w}_m)$ and the vector $\mathbf{w}_j$ is the eigenvector corresponding to the j th largest eigenvalue of the sample covariance matrix

$$\mathbf{C} = \frac{1}{N}\sum_{p=1}^{N}(\mathbf{x}_p - \mathrm{m})(\mathbf{x}_p - \mathrm{m})^T$$

such that $\mathbf{C}\mathbf{w}_k = \lambda_k\mathbf{w}_k$. The m principal axes in $\mathbf{W}$ are orthonormal axes onto which the retained variance under projection is maximal. When PCA is applied to face images, eigenvectors are designated to as eigenfaces in (Turkand Pentland, 1991a).

A distance measure for face recognition can be defined. This distance measure is defined between a template image in a training set and a given image in the test set. Distance measure $\delta_{PCA}(\mathbf{x}, \mathbf{x}')$ between a template image $\mathbf{x}$ and a given face image $\mathbf{x}'$ is defined as

$$\delta_{PCA}(\mathbf{x}, \mathbf{x}') = \left\|\mathbf{s} - \mathbf{s}'\right\|,\tag{5.6.2}$$

where $\mathbf{s}$ and $\mathbf{s}$ are feature values of face image $\mathbf{x}$ and $\mathbf{x}'$, respectively.

According to the central idea mentioned above, an image $\mathbf{x}_p$ can be reconstructed by $\mathbf{s}_p$. We can reconstruct face images in the eigenface method as follows.

$$\hat{\mathbf{x}}_p = \mathbf{W}^T\mathbf{s}_p + \mathbf{m},\tag{5.6.3}$$

where $\hat{\mathbf{x}}_p$ is a reconstruction of $\mathbf{x}_p$.

5.6.2 Mixture-of-Eigenfaces Method using PCA Mixture Model

The eigenface method uses only one set of features. One set of features may be insufficient to represent face images with the large variations. We propose a mixture-of-eigenfaces method using more than one set of features. To accomplish this, we explain the PCA mixture model first.

5.6.2.1 PCA Mixture Model

The PCA mixture model is used to estimate a density function. Basically, its central idea comes from the combination of mixture models and PCA. The PCA mixture model to be explained here is a simplified version of Tipping and Bishop's model (Tipping and Bishop, 1999). The PCA mixture model has several PCAs, where each PCA corresponds to a set of eigenfeatures.

In the mixture model (Jacobs et. al., 1991; Jordan and Jacobs, 1994), a class is partitioned into a number of clusters and its density function of the n-dimensional observed data $\mathbf{x} = \{x_1, \cdots, x_n\}$ is represented by a linear combination of component densities of the partitioned clusters as

$$P(\mathbf{x}) = \sum_{k=1}^{K} P(\mathbf{x} \mid k, \theta_k) P(k), \tag{5.6.4}$$

where $P(\mathbf{x} \mid k, \theta_k)$ and $P(k)$ represent the conditional density and the prior probability of the k th cluster, respectively, and θ_k is the unknown model parameter of the k th cluster. The prior probabilities are chosen to satisfy the condition $\sum_{k=1}^{K} P(k) = 1$. The conditional density function $P(\mathbf{x} \mid k, \theta_k)$ is often modeled by a Gaussian function as

$$P(\mathbf{x} \mid k, \theta_k) = \frac{1}{(2\pi)^{\frac{n}{2}} |\Sigma_k|^{\frac{1}{2}}} exp\{-\frac{1}{2}(\mathbf{x} - \mu_k)^T \Sigma_k^{-1} (\mathbf{x} - \mu_k)\}, \tag{5.6.5}$$

where μ_k and Σ_k are the sample mean and covariance of the k th cluster, respectively.

We consider a PCA mixture model of the data $\mathbf{x}$ by combining the mixture model (Eq. (5.6.4)) and PCA (Eq. (5.6.1)) in a way that the component density of the mixture model can be estimated onto the PCA transformed space as

$$\begin{aligned} P(\mathbf{x}) &= \sum_{k=1}^{K} P(\mathbf{x} \mid k, \theta_k) P(k) \\ P(\mathbf{x} \mid k, \theta_k) &= (\mathbf{s}_k \mid k, \theta_k), \end{aligned} \tag{5.6.6}$$

where $\mathbf{s}_k = \mathbf{W}_k^T (\mathbf{x} - \mu_k)$. The PCA feature vectors $\mathbf{s}_k$ are decorrelated due to the orthogonality of the transform matrix $\mathbf{W}_k$. Thus, its covariance matrix $\Sigma_k^S = \mathcal{E}[\mathbf{s}_k \mathbf{s}_k^T]$ is a diagonal matrix whose diagonal elements are corresponding to the principal eigenvalues.

Next, the conditional density function $P(\mathbf{s}_k \mid k, \theta_k)$ of the PCA feature vectors in the kth cluster can be simplified as

$$\begin{aligned} P(\mathbf{s}_k \mid k, \theta_k) &= \frac{1}{(2\pi)^{\frac{m}{2}} |\Sigma_k^S|^{\frac{1}{2}}} exp\{-\frac{1}{2} \mathbf{s}_k^T \Sigma_k^{S^{-1}} \mathbf{s}_k\} \\ &= \prod_{j=1}^{m} \frac{1}{(2\pi)^{\frac{1}{2}} \lambda_{k,j}^{\frac{1}{2}}} exp\{-\frac{s_j^2}{2\lambda_{k,j}}\}, \end{aligned} \tag{5.6.7}$$

where $\mathbf{s} = \{s_1, \cdots, s_m\}$, and $\{\lambda_{k,1}, \cdots, \lambda_{k,m}\}$ are the m dominant eigenvalues of the feature covariance matrix Σ_k^S in the k th cluster.

Fig. 5.6.1 illustrates the PCA mixture model where the number of mixture components K is 2, the dimension of feature vectors m is 2, the line segments in each cluster represent the two column vectors $\mathbf{w}_1$ and $\mathbf{w}_2$, and the intersection of two line segments represents a mean vector $\mathbf{m}_1, \mathbf{m}_2$.

To use the PCA mixture model for estimating the distribution of data, we need to perform both the appropriate partitioning of the class and the estimation of model parameters of the partitioned clusters. We can perform this task successfully due to an important property of the mixture model: for many choices of component density function, they can approximate any continuous density to arbitrary accuracy if the model has a sufficient large number of components and the parameters of the model are well chosen. Since the transformation matrix $\mathbf{W}$ is linear, the log-likelihood function with respect to data $\mathbf{X} = \{\mathbf{x}_1, \cdots, \mathbf{x}_N\}$ can be represented as

$$\begin{aligned}
\mathcal{L}(\mathbf{X}\,|\,\Theta) &= \sum_{p=1}^{N} ln P(\mathbf{x}_p) \\
&= \sum_{p=1}^{N} ln\{\sum_{k=1}^{K} P(\mathbf{s}_p\,|\,k,\theta_k)P(k)\}.
\end{aligned} \tag{5.6.8}$$

This formulation will allow to determine both the appropriate partitioning of the data and the estimation of the model parameters simultaneously when the log-likelihood is maximized. We solve the likelihood maximization problem using the EM (Expectation Maximization) iterative learning algorithm (Dempster et. al., 1977).

For log-likelihood maximization, the observed data vector $\mathbf{x}_p$ is treated as incomplete because its cluster membership is not known before learning. We consider a hypothetical complete data $\mathbf{y} = (\mathbf{x}, z)$ in which a PCA feature vector is labeled with the component which generated it. Thus, for each data vector $\mathbf{x}$, we assign an indicator variable z, which is an integer in the range of $(1\ K)$ specifying which component of the mixture generates the data point.

Figure 5.6.1. An illustration of PCA mixture model

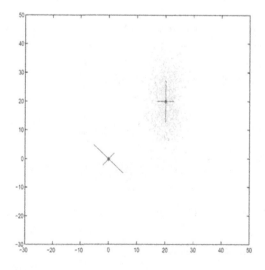

Then, the log-likelihood for the complete data $\mathbf{Y} = \{\mathbf{y}_1, \cdots, \mathbf{y}_N\}$ is given by

$$
\begin{aligned}
\mathcal{L}(\mathbf{Y}\,|\,\Theta) &= \sum_{p=1}^{N} ln\{P(\mathbf{x}_p, z_p\,|\,\Theta)\} \\
&= \sum_{p=1}^{N} ln\{P(z_p)P(\mathbf{x}_p\,|\,z_p,\Theta)\}.
\end{aligned}
\tag{5.6.9}
$$

Since we do not know which component is responsible for each data point, we cannot know the distribution of the $P(z)$. Therefore, we adopt an iterative EM learning strategy to maximize the log-likelihood function. Each iteration consists of two steps: an expectation step (E-step) followed by a maximization step (M-step).

(1) E-step

Given the feature data set $\mathbf{X}$ and the parameters $\Theta^{(t)}$ of the mixture model at the t th iteration, we estimate the posterior distribution $P(z\,|\,\mathbf{x},\Theta^{(t)})$ using

$$
P(z\,|\,\mathbf{x},\Theta^{(t)}) = \frac{P(\mathbf{x}\,|\,z,\Theta^{(t)})P(z)}{\sum_{k=1}^{K} P(\mathbf{x}\,|\,k,\Theta^{(t)})P(k)},
\tag{5.6.10}
$$

where $P(\mathbf{x}\,|\,z,\Theta^{(t)})$ is calculated by Eq. (5.6.6) and (5.6.7). Next, we compute the expectation of the log-likelihood $\mathcal{L}(\mathbf{Y}\,|\,\Theta)$ using the posterior distribution $P(z\,|\,\mathbf{x},\Theta^{(t)})$ at the t th iteration as

$$
\begin{aligned}
\mathcal{E}[\mathcal{L}(\mathbf{Y}\,|\,\Theta)] &= \sum_{z_1=1}^{K} \cdots \sum_{z_N=1}^{K} \mathcal{L}(\mathbf{Y}\,|\,\Theta) \\
&\quad \times \prod_{p=1}^{N} P(z_p\,|\,\mathbf{x}_p,\Theta^{(t)}) \\
&= \sum_{p=1}^{N}\sum_{k=1}^{K} P(k\,|\,\mathbf{x}_p,\Theta^{(t)}) \\
&\quad \times ln\{P(k)P(\mathbf{x}_p\,|\,k,\Theta^{(t)})\} \\
&= \sum_{p=1}^{K}\sum_{k=1}^{K} P(k\,|\,\mathbf{x}_p,\Theta^{(t)}) \\
&\quad \times ln\{P(k)P(\mathbf{s}_p\,|\,k,\Theta^{(t)})\}.
\end{aligned}
\tag{5.6.11}
$$

When the conditional density function is modeled by the Gaussian function as in Eq. (5.6.7), the expectation of the log-likelihood can be represented as

$$
\mathcal{E}[\mathcal{L}(\mathbf{Y}\,|\,\Theta)] = \sum_{p=1}^{N}\sum_{k=1}^{K} P(k\,|\,\mathbf{x}_p,\Theta^{(t)})\{lnP(k) - \sum_{j=1}^{m}(\frac{1}{2}ln\lambda_{k,j} - \frac{s_j^2}{2\lambda_{k,j}})\} + const.
\tag{5.6.12}
$$

(2) M-step

Next, the new model parameters $\Theta^{(t+)}$ is estimated by maximizing the expectation of log-likelihood as

$$\Theta^{(t+1)} = \arg\max_{\Theta} \mathcal{E}[\mathcal{L}(\mathbf{Y}\,|\,\Theta)]..$$ (5.6.13)

The mixing parameters $P(z_p)$ can be estimated by introducing a Lagrange multiplier γ and minimizing the function

$$\mathcal{E}[\mathcal{L}(\mathbf{Y}\,|\,\Theta)] + \gamma\,(\sum_{k=1}^{K} P(k) - 1).$$ (5.6.14)

Setting the derivatives of Eq. (5.6.14) with respect to $P(k)$ to zero, we obtain

$$0 = -\sum_{p=1}^{N} \frac{P(k\,|\,\mathbf{x}_p)}{P(k)} + \gamma\,,$$ (5.6.15)

where the value of γ can be found by multiplying both sides of Eq. (5.6.15) by $P(k)$ and summing over k. Using $\sum_{k=1}^{K} P(k) = 1$ and $\sum_{k=1}^{K} P(k\,|\,\mathbf{x}_p) = 1$ we obtain $\gamma = N$. Next, the update rule for $P(k)$ is obtained as

$$P(k) = \frac{1}{N} \sum_{p=1}^{N} P(k\,|\,\mathbf{x}_p,\Theta^{(t)}).$$ (5.6.16)

Other parameters for maximizing the expectation of log-likelihood are obtained in a straightforward manner as follows. The new mean parameters $\mu_k^{X(t+1)}$ of the kth cluster are obtained using the following update formula.

$$\mu_k^{X(t+1)} = \frac{\sum_{p=1}^{N} P(k\,|\,\mathbf{x}_p,\Theta^{(t)})\mathbf{x}_p}{\sum_{p=1}^{N} P(k\,|\,\mathbf{x}_p,\Theta^{(t)})}.$$ (5.6.17)

The new eigenvalue parameters $\lambda_{k,j}^{(t+1)}$ and the new eigenvetor (PCA basis) parameters $\mathbf{w}_{k,j}$ are obtained by selecting the largest m eigenvalues in the eigenvector computation (PCA computation) as

$$\Sigma_k^{X(t+1)}\mathbf{w}_{k,j} = \lambda_{k,j}^{(t+1)}\mathbf{w}_{k,j},$$ (5.6.18)

where the new covariance matrix $\Sigma_k^{X(t+1)}$ is computed by

$$\Sigma_k^{X(t+1)}$$
$$\stackrel{\pm}{=} \frac{\sum_{p=1}^{N} P(k\,|\,\mathbf{x}_p,\Theta^{(t)})(\mathbf{x}_p - \mu_k^{X(t+1)})^T(\mathbf{x}_p - \mu_k^{X(t+1)})}{\sum_{p=1}^{N} P(\mathbf{x}_p\,|\,\Theta^{(t)})}.$$ (5.6.19)

PCA transformation matrixes $\mathbf{W}_k$ is obtained as $\mathbf{W}_k = [\mathbf{w}_{k,1}\mathbf{w}_{k,2}\dots\mathbf{w}_{k,m}]$. The above two steps will be repeated until a stopping condition is satisfied, where the three parameters will not be changed any further.

5.6.2.2 Mixture-of-Eigenfaces Method

As mentioned previously, the eigenface method uses only one set of features. Sometimes, it may not be enough to represent face images with large variations. When we deal with many face images, we prefer to use more than one set of features. Dividing all face images into more than one cluster and receiving one set of features for each cluster, we can use the most appropriate set of features for a given face image. Usually, we select one set of features among them that represents the given face image best.

In the eigenface method, we can obtain only one set of eigenfaces by applying PCA to the face images. However, in the mixture-of-eigenfaces method, we can obtain several sets of eigenfaces by applying the PCA mixture model to the face images. The PCA mixture model has several mixture components and each mixture component provides one set of PCA bases (eigenfaces). So, we can obtain the same number of sets of eigenfaces as the number of mixture components.

We learn the PCA mixture model by the EM learning algorithm where some face images are used for training data. After learning, we obtain the means $\mathbf{m}_k$, the variances $\mathbf{V}_k$, and the transformation matrices $\mathbf{W}_k$, for the k th mixture component. Here, $\mathbf{V}_k$ is a diagonal matrix whose diagonal elements are eigenvalues λ_{k_i} ($i = 1, 2, \cdots, m$). Although we have only one matrix $\mathbf{W}$ in the eigenface method, we have several matrices $\mathbf{W}_k$ in the PCA mixture model. The column vectors $\mathbf{w}_{k_j}$ corresponds to the jth eigenface of the kth set), and a set of column vectors $\mathbf{w}_{k_j}$ of $\mathbf{W}_k^j$ corresponds to the k th set of features. In this way, we obtain the same number of sets of eigenfaces as the number of mixture components ($= K$).

A given face image $\mathbf{x}$ is represented by the best set of features that produces the smallest Mahalanobis distance. Among the K sets of eigenfaces, we take the matrix $\mathbf{W}_j$ as the best set of eigenfaces, which produces the smallest Mahalanobis distance as $j = \arg\min_k \left\| (\mathbf{x} - \mathbf{m}_k) \mathbf{W}_k \mathbf{V}_k \mathbf{W}_k^T (\mathbf{x} - \mathbf{m}_k) \right\|$. The feature value vector $\mathbf{s}_j$ corresponding to the best component is obtained by a simple matrix computation as $\mathbf{s}_j = \mathbf{W}_j (\mathbf{x} - \mathbf{m}_j)$.

We define a distance measure for face recognition. The distance $\delta_{PM}(\mathbf{x}, \mathbf{x'})$ is defined by the norm between a template image $\mathbf{x}$ in the training set and a given image $\mathbf{x'}$ in the test set as

$$\delta_{PM}(\mathbf{x}, \mathbf{x'}) = \| \mathbf{s}_j - \mathbf{s'}_j \|, \tag{5.6.20}$$

where $\mathbf{s}_j$ and $\mathbf{s'}_j$ are the feature values of the face images $\mathbf{x}$ and $\mathbf{x'}$, and j is the selected index of the best eigenface set for the template image $\mathbf{x}$, as

$$j = \arg\min_k | (\mathbf{x} - \mathbf{m}_k) \mathbf{W}_k \mathbf{V}_k \mathbf{W}_k^T (\mathbf{x} - \mathbf{m}_k) \|.$$

As in the eigenface method, a face image x can be reconstructed in the mixture-of-eigenfaces method. We can reconstruct a face image using each set of eigenfaces which corresponds to each mixture component. Among several images reconstructed from several sets of eigenfaces, we select the reconstructed image whose reconstruction error is the smallest. Therefore, the reconstruction x for an image x can be obtained as follows.

$$\hat{\mathbf{x}} = \mathbf{W}_q^T \mathbf{s}_q + \mathbf{m}_q,$$

$$\text{where } q = \arg\min_k | \mathbf{x} - \mathbf{W}_k^T \mathbf{s}_k + \mathbf{m}_k \|.$$

(5.6.21)

5.6.3 Experimental Results and Discussion

5.6.3.1 Dataset

We took two partial sets of PSL database that were obtained from the MPEG7 community (Wang and Tan, 2000b). The PSL database consists of the normalized images of 271 persons, where some images have lighting variations and other images have pose variations. Among all images, we selected images of 133 persons with lighting variations and images of 123 persons with pose variations, where they are noted as F_{light} and F_{pose}, respectively. In the set of F_{light}, there are images of normal, smiling, angry expressions and images of left and right lightings for each person. In the set of F_{pose}, there are images of a normal pose and 4 different poses for each person. Fig. 5.6.2 and 5.6.3 illustrate some typical images used in the simulation.

   We performed two kinds of simulations: face reconstruction (face coding) and face recognition. The former was performed to show usefulness of the mixture-of-eigenfaces method for the reconstruction of face images, and the latter was performed to validate excellence of the mixture-of-eigenfaces method for the face recognition problem. For all the simulations, we used 5-fold cross-validation.

5.6.3.2 Face Reconstruction (Face Coding)

We applied the eigenface method and the mixture-of-eigenfaces method to reconstruction of a face image set F_{pose}. For the mixture-of-eigenfaces method, EM learning in the PCA mixture model was applied to the face data sets, independently. Since the number of data is deficient compared with the dimension of data, we reduced the dimensionality of the data by PCA. The reduced dimensionality of pose-variant data was 100. To learn PCA mixture model better, we modified the density function given by Eq. (5.6.7) into

$$P(\mathbf{s}_k \mid k, \theta_k) = \prod_{j=1}^{m} \frac{1}{(2\pi)^{\frac{1}{2}} \lambda_{k,j}^{\frac{1}{4}}} exp\{-\frac{s_j^2}{2\lambda_{k,j}}\},$$

(5.6.22)

where the exponent of $\lambda_{k,j}$ is changed from 1/2 to 1/4. This modification helps PCA mixture model to be learned in spite of small magnitudes of eigenvalues $\lambda_{k,j}$. We do not use the method of setting a hard lower bound on the eigenvalues because it give a smaller number of features. The use of 1/4 as the exponent is also related to the fact that non-Gaussian features are good for recognition (Bartlett et. al., 1998).

   Using the strategy as described in Section 2 and 3.2, we performed the reconstruction process for the data set F_{pose}. We used all images in each set to train PCA and PCA mixture

Figure 5.6.2. Some face images in the set F_{light}

Figrue 5.6.3 Some face images in the set F_{pose}

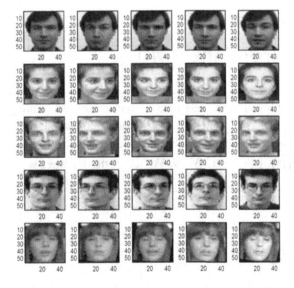

model and computed the reconstruction errors. Since the number of images for each person is too small, we used the 5-fold cross-validation method to evaluate the performance of face recognition. We partitioned the set of all images into 5 segments each of which has one image per person for all people. Each segment contains 123 images. We used 4 segments for EM-learning and evaluated the performance for the remaining segment. This process is repeated for each of the 5 possible choices. The resultant performance is an average of all the performances in all repeated processes.

Fig. 5.6.4 shows reconstruction errors corresponding to different number of features. They contain the results of the eigenface method and the mixture-of-eigenfaces method with 10 mixture components (K=10). From this figure, we note that the mixture-of-eigenfaces method outperforms the eigenface method for face reconstruction in case of using a relatively small number of features, and that the eigenface method outperform the mixture-of-eigenfaces method in case of using a relatively large number of features.

5.6.3.3 Face Recognition

We applied the eigenface method and the mixture-of-eigenfaces method to the recognition of face images F_{light} and F_{pose}. For the mixture-of-eigenfaces method, EM learning for the PCA mixture model was applied to means of each person's face images in a training set. Since the number of data is deficient compared with the dimension of data, we reduced the dimensionality of the data by PCA. The reduced dimensionality of light-variant data and pose-variant data were 135 and 120, respectively. When we learned PCA mixture model better, we also took the density function in Eq. (5.6.22).

Our recognition strategy is as follows. For the eigenface method, we transform a labelled training data (a template data) $\mathbf{x}_r$ and a test data (a given input data) $\mathbf{x}$ by a transformation matrix $\mathbf{W}$. Next, we assign the test data x to the class C_{PCA} whose transformed training data is nearest to the transformed test data as

$$
\begin{aligned}
C_{PCA} &= L(\arg\min_{\mathbf{x}_r} \delta_{PCA}(\mathbf{x},\mathbf{x}_r)) \\
&= L(\arg\min_{\mathbf{x}_r} \|(\mathbf{x}-\mathbf{x}_r)W\|),
\end{aligned}
\tag{5.6.23}
$$

where $L(\mathbf{x}_r)$ indicates the class label of the sample $\mathbf{x}_r$. For the mixture-of-eigenfaces method, we transform the test data x and a labelled training data x_r by the transformation matrix $\mathbf{W}_{I(\mathbf{x}_r)}$, where $I(\mathbf{x}_r)$ indicates the index of the mixture component that produces the smallest Mahalanobis distance for the training data $\mathbf{x}_r$, as $I(\mathbf{x}_r)=\arg\min_k |(\mathbf{x}_r - \mathbf{m}_k)\mathbf{W}_k\mathbf{V}_k\mathbf{W}_k^T(\mathbf{x}_r - \mathbf{m}_k)\|$. Next, we assign the test data $\mathbf{x}$ to the class C_M whose transformed training data is nearest to the transformed test data as

$$
\begin{aligned}
C_{PM} &= L(\arg\min_{\mathbf{x}_r} \delta_{PM}(\mathbf{x},\mathbf{x}_r)) \\
&= L(\arg\min_{\mathbf{x}_r} \| (\mathbf{x}-\mathbf{x}_r)\mathbf{W}_{I(\mathbf{x}_r)} \|),
\end{aligned}
\tag{5.6.24}
$$

where $L(\mathbf{x}_r)$ indicates the class label of a sample $\mathbf{x}_r$.

Since the number of images for each person is too small, we used the 5-fold cross-validation method to evaluate the performance of face recognition, like in face coding. We

Figure 5.6.4. Reconstruction errors according to different number of features

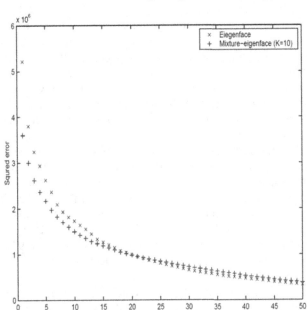

partitioned the set of all images into 5 segments each of which has one image per person for all people. In case of light-variant data, each segment contains 133 images, and in case of pose-variant data, each segment contains 123 images. We used 4 segments for EM-learning and evaluated the performance for the remaining segment. This process is repeated for each of the 5 possible choices. The resultant performance is an average of all the performances in all repeated processes. Even though more than 2 mixture components have been taken, they do not show any significant improvement in classification performance. So we used only two mixture components for learning the PCA mixture model.

Fig. 5.6.5 and 5.6.6 show the classification errors according to a different number of features when the eigenface method and the mixture-of-eigenfaces method are applied to the data sets F_{light} and F_{pose}, respectively. While the number of features increases, the performance does not always increase. This seems to be due to overfitting. The number of features and classification errors for the best case in the case of the data sets F_{light} and F_{pose} are shown in Table 5.6.1 and 5.6.2, respectively. For two data sets, the best performance of the mixture-of-eigenfaces method outperforms the best performance of the eigenface method. From Fig. 5.6.5 and 5.6.6, we note that the mixture-of-eigenfaces method outperforms eigenface method in the case of using any number of features in both cases of data sets F_{light} and F_{pose}. From Table 5.6.1 and 5.6.2, we note that the mixture-of-eigenfaces method with a smaller number of features outperforms the eigenface method with a larger number of features.

5.7 FACE RECOGNITION USING EMBEDDED HMM

Face recognition is an active research area spanning several research fields such as image processing, pattern recognition, computer vision, neural network, and MPEG-7 video (Chellappa et. al., 1995). Face recognition has many applications, such as biometrics systems, surveillance systems, and content-based video retrieval systems. A robust face recognition system must operate under a variety of conditions, such as varying illuminations, poses, and backgrounds, and it must be able to handle non-frontal facial images of males and females of different ages and races. However, state-of-the-art in face recognition is far from complete. There are two main approaches to face recognition (Chellappa et. al., 1995; Samal and Iyengar, 1992; Brunelli and Poggio, 1993). The first approach is the feature-based matching approach using the relationship between facial features, such as eyes, mouth and nose (Brunelli and Poggio, 1993; Wiskott et. al., 1997). This approach requires a segmentation of facial features which has proven to be difficult. The second approach is the template matching approach using the holistic features of face image (Brunelli and Poggio, 1993; Turk and Pentland, 1991a; Turk and Pentland, 1991b; Belhumeur and Kriegman, 1997; Etemad and Chellappa, 1997; Moghaddam and Pentland, 1997). This approach is simple but does not reflect the details of facial local features.

To overcome these disadvantages, Samaria et. al. proposed a model-based approach using the HMM (Samaria and Young, 1994). According to this model, a face image was divided into a number of regions, such as the forehead, eyes, nose, mouth, and chin and the face image was modelled using a 1D HMM by assigning each of these regions to a state. Since the 1D HMM is used to model two-dimensional data, this method could achieve a

Figure 5.6.5. Classification errors according to different number of features in the case of the data set F_{light}

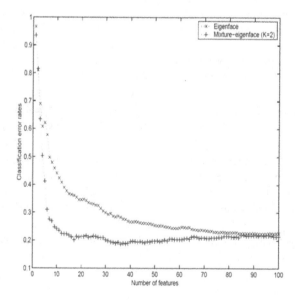

Figure 5.6.6. Classification errors according to different number of features in the case of the data set F_{pose}.

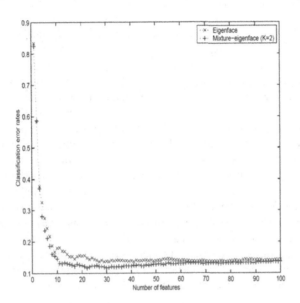

Table 5.6.1. The best performance and the corresponding number of features in the case of the data set F_{light}.

Methods	Number of features	Classification error
Eigenface method	92	22.41%
Mixture-of-eigenfaces method	36	18.65%

Table 5.6.2. The best performance and the corresponding number of features for the data set F_{pose}

Methods	Number of features	Classification error
Eigenface method	27	14.80%
Mixture-of-eigenfaces method	22	12.68%

recognition rate of about 85% (Samaria and Young, 1994). They also extended the 1D HMM model to a 2D structure called a pseudo 2D HMM (P2D HMM) by adding a marker block at the end of each line in the face image, and introducing an additional end-of-line state at the end of each horizontal HMM. They reported a recognition rate of about 90-95% for the P2D HMM. However, this result was obtained from the ORL database that consists of relatively simple images for recognition due to limited side movements and tilts.

Nefian and Hayes (Nefian and Hayes, 1998) proposed a new approach to face recognition using the EHMM as introduced by Kuo and Agazzi for character recognition (Kuo and Agazzi, 1994). The EHMM was used to model each face image in a hierarchical manner as follows. Some super-states are used to model vertical facial features, such as the forehead, the eyes, the nose, the mouth, the chin, and the cheeks, where each super-state is matched to several blocks of one horizontal line. Each state in the super-state is used to model a localized feature and is matched to a specific block in the face image. Recognition has been performed by identifying the person of the model that provides the maximum observation probability. They used the 2D DCT (Discrete Cosine Transform) coefficients as observation vector, where the coefficients were obtained by applying the same basis vectors to all blocks in the face image. However, each block in the face image has different a spatial property depending on its position in the face image. So, instead of using the same basis vector over all constituent blocks in the face image, it is necessary for all blocks to be represented by their own distinct basis vectors appropriate to their local spatial properties.

To meet the requirement, we propose to use the 2nd-order block-specific basis vector that is adaptive to the local spatial property of each block. The idea of the 2nd-order block-specific basis vector comes from the original work of Wang and Tan (Wang and Tan, 2000b), who proposed the *2nd-order eigenface* method using a couple of feature sets from the MPEG-7 community. As they discussed in (Wang and Tan, 2000b), the 1st-order eigenfaces are effective to describe low-passed face images and the 2nd-order eigenfaces are effective to describe high-passed face images. They applied the 2nd-order eigenface method to the lighting-invariant and view-angle-invariant face descriptions. In the case of view-angle-invariant case, the 1st-order eigenfaces are useful since they reveal the characteristics of low-passed face images. Therefore, the faces with many different poses are described with both the 1st-order and 2nd-order eigenfaces. On the other hand, under different lighting conditions, the 1st-order eigenfaces are not effective since the low-passed face images are very different in this situation. Thus, face images with many different lightings are effectively described with only 2nd-order eigenfaces.

We adopt the 2nd-order eigenface method in order to represent the constituent blocks of the face image. We assume that a face image consists of many (possibly overlapping) blocks and each block can be represented by the 2nd-order block-specific basis vectors that are obtained by consecutively applying the PCA to the original and residual block images. After obtaining the 2nd-order block-specific basis vector for every block, each block is represented by the 2nd-order feature vector obtained from a projection of the original and residual block image onto the 1st- and 2nd-order basis vector, respectively. The 2nd-order block-specific feature vector is used as an observation vector to train EHMM. This simple modification that replaces one fixed DCT basis vector by many 2nd-order block-specific basis vectors improves the recognition performance considerably.

5.7.1 The 2nd-Order Block-Specific Observations

In this work, we represent a face image in a hierarchical manner as follows. Each face image consists of several vertical facial feature blocks, such as forehead, eyes, nose, mouth, and chin, and each facial feature block consists of several horizontal local blocks. Fig. 5.7.1 illustrates how to divide a face image with a size of $X \times Y$ into several blocks, where a $W_0 \times W_1$ sampling window scans the image from left to right, and from top to bottom. As the sampling windows moves from left to right on a line, each observation has W_1' columns of overlap with the preceding observation block. When the right edge on the current line is reached, the sampling window moves back to the beginning of the line and shifts down with W_0' rows of overlap between successive lines. So, each image can be represent by a sequence of observations $O = O_{1,1}, \cdots, O_{1,T_0}, \cdots, O_{T_0,1}, \cdots, O_{T_0,T_1}$, where T_1 and T_0 represent the number of horizontal blocks

$$ (T_1 = \left\lceil \frac{X - W_1}{W_1 - W_1'} \right\rceil) $$

in X and the number of vertical blocks

$$ (T_0 = \left\lceil \frac{Y - W_0}{W_0 - W_0'} \right\rceil) $$

in Y, respectively. In EHMM, an observation vector generated from all blocks along a horizontal direction corresponds to one specific super state and an observation generated from one block in the designated horizontal blocks corresponds to a specific state in the designated super state.

The existing EHMMs used the pixel values (Samaria and Young, 1994) or DCT coefficients (Nefian and Hayes, 1998) as an observation vector to represent the constituent blocks of the face image. However, these methods had some disadvantages. First, the use

Figure 5.7.1. A selection of blocks in a face image

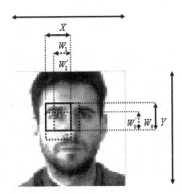

of pixel values as observation vectors in the first method were not adequate because 1) pixel values did not represent robust features due to the high sensitivity to image noise as well as image rotations or shifts and illumination changes and 2) a lengthy observation vector required high computational complexity in the training and recognition of EHMM. Second, the use of DCT coefficients as observation vectors in the second method were not adequate because they used the same basis vector for all constituent blocks even though the spatial property of each block is very different depending on its position in the face image. To overcome these disadvantages, we propose to use the 2nd-order block-specific feature vectors for representing the constituent blocks in the face image, where a couple of block-specific feature vectors are obtained by applying the PCA to the original and residual block images consecutively. This simple modification replaces one fixed DCT basis vector by many 2nd-order block-specific basis vectors and improves the recognition performance considerably.

The idea of the 2nd-order eigenface method was proposed by Wang and Tan (Wang and Tan, 2000b) to overcome the limitation of the conventional eigenface method. For example, in the various lighting conditions, the first some principal components in the set of eigenfaces are mainly used to reflect the lighting factors in the face image. In this situation, only using the set of eigenfaces is not effective for representing the face images. They argued that it was desirable to use not only the set of eigenfaces for the original face image but also the set of the 2nd-order eigenfaces of the residual face images that are defined by the differences between the original face images and the reconstructed images obtained from the set of eigenfaces.

The eigenface method is based on the PCA, a well-known technique of multivariate linear data analysis (Jolliffe, 1986). The central idea of PCA is to reduce the dimensionality of a data set while retaining the variations in the data set as much as possible. In PCA (Hostelling, 1993), a set of the N-dimensional observation vector $X = \{x_1, x_2, \cdots, x_M\}$ is reduced to a set of the N_1-dimensional feature vector $Y = \{y_1, y_2, \cdots, y_M\}$ by a transformation matrix U as

$$y_i = U^T(x_i - m), \tag{5.7.1}$$

where the superscript T means a matrix transpose, m is the mean vector of X as $m = \mathcal{E}[X]$, $U = (u_1, \cdots, u_{N_1})$, and $N_1 \leq N$. The vector u_j is the eigenvector corresponding to the jth largest eigenvalue of the sample covariance matrix

$$C = \frac{1}{M} \sum_{i=1}^{M} (x_i - m)(x_i - m)^T$$

such that $Cu_j = \lambda_j u_j$. The N_1 principal components in U are the orthonormal axes onto which the retained variance under projection is the maximal. When PCA is applied to face images, eigenvectors are referred to as eigenfaces in (Turk and Pentland, 1991a; Turk and Pentland, 1991b) and it is often called as the eigenface method when we perform the face recognition using the eigenfaces.

The set of the 2nd-order eigenfaces are obtained by applying the PCA to a set of the N-dimensional residual vector $X' = \{x'_1, x'_2, \cdots, x'_M\}$, where $x'_i = x_i - \hat{x}_i$, and the x_i and the $\hat{x}_i$ are the original face image and the reconstructed image, respectively (Kim et. al., 2001c). The reconstructed image is obtained by $x_i = \hat{U}y_i + m$, where $y_i = U^T(x_i - m)$ and $m = \mathcal{E}[X]$. A set of the N-dimensional residual observation vector $X' = \{x'_1, x'_2, \cdots, x'_M\}$ is reduced to a set of the N_2-dimensional residual feature vector $Y' = \{y'_1, y'_2, \cdots, y'_M\}$ by a transformation matrix V as

$$y'_i = V^T(x'_i - m'),$$ (5.7.2)

where the superscript T means a matrix transpose, m' is the mean vector of X' as $m' = \mathcal{E}[X']$, $V = (v_1, \cdots, v_{N_2})$, and $N_2 \leq N$. The vector v_j is the eigenvector corresponding to the jth largest eigenvalue of the residual sample covariance matrix

$$C' = \frac{1}{M} \sum_{i=1}^{M} (x'_i - m')(x'_i - m')^T$$

such that $C'v_j = \lambda'_j v_j$. The N_2 principal axes in V are the orthonormal axes onto which the retained variance under projection is the maximal. Considering both an approximate eigenface set U and a residual eigenface set V at the same time, the observed face image x_i is approximated by the 2nd-order reconstructed image x_i as

$$\begin{aligned} x_i &\cong x_i = Uy_i + m + Vy'_i, \\ y_i &= U^T(x_i - m) \\ y'_i &= V^T(x_i - Uy_i - m). \end{aligned}$$ (5.7.3)

Fig. 5.7.2 illustrates a procedure how to obtain a reconstructed image using a couple of approximate and residual eigenface feature vectors in the 2nd-order eigenface method. Refer the text for a detailed explanation about all symbol notations.

We obtain the 2nd-order block-specific feature vector by simply applying the 2nd-order eigenface method to each block independently as follows. First, we obtain a set of the 1st-order block-specific basis vectors $U_{i,j}$ by applying a PCA technique to the (i,j)th block images $(B_{i,j}^k, k = 1, \cdots, M)$ that are selected from M training face images, and then obtain another set of the 2nd-order block-specific basis vectors $V_{i,j}$ by applying another PCA technique to the (i,j)th residual block images ($B_{i,j}^{'k} = (B_{i,j}^{k,j} - \hat{B}_{i,j}^k), k = 1, \cdots, M$) that are obtained by subtracting the reconstructed block image from the original block image, where the reconstruction is performed based on the 1st-order basis vectors. Then, the 1st and 2nd-order observation vectors $O_{i,j}^1$ and $O_{i,j}^2$ are obtained by projecting the (i,j)th block image $B_{i,j}$ and the (i,j)th residual block image $B_{i,j}'$ onto the 1st-order block-specific basis vectors $U_{i,j}$ and the 2nd-order block-specific basis vectors $V_{i,j}$, respectively. Fig. 5.7.3 shows how to obtain the 2nd-order block-specific feature vectors of a face image.

Fig. 5.7.4 illustrates four different block images corresponding to a specific block, such as the original block image (upper-left), the reconstructed block image using both the 1st-order and the 2nd-order basis vectors (upper-right), the reconstructed block image using the 1st-order basis vector (lower-left), and the residual block image (lower-right). From the images, we know that the reconstructed block image using both the 1st-order and the

Figure 5.7.2. A procedure of processing face images in the 2nd-order eigenface method

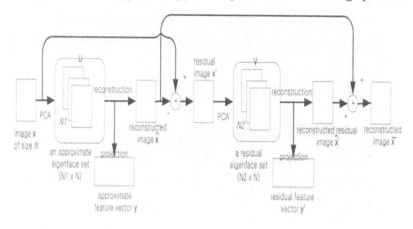

Figure 5.7.3. A procedure of obtaining the 2nd-order block-specific feature vectors

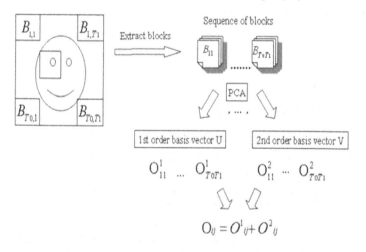

Figure 5.7.4. Four different block images corresponding to a specific block

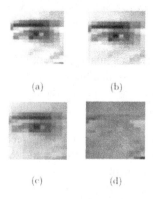

2nd-order basis vectors is more similar to the original block image than the reconstructed image which uses only the 1st-order basis vector.

5.7.2 Training and Recognition

5.7.2.1 Training EHMM

Each person in the face database is modelled by an EHMM. Several images of the same person under different poses and/or illuminations are used for training the person. The 2nd-order block-specific feature vectors that were extracted from a couple of the 1st-order and 2nd-order block-specific basis vectors were used as an observation vector for each block. Fig. 5.7.5 illustrates a training procedure of the EHMM for a person, which consists of the following three steps.

(1)   Step 1: Initialization
   (a)   Initialize model structure.
         Set the number of super state N_0 and the number of states in each super state N_1^k and determine the block size (W_0 and W_1) and block overlap size ($W_0^{'}$ and $W_1^{'}$).
   (b)   Obtain the observation vectors.
         Extract the 2nd-order block-specific observation vectors using the predetermined 2nd-order block-specific basis vectors.
   (c)   Perform uniform segmentation.
         According to the predetermined N_0 and N_1^k, the observation data is uniformly segmented to obtain the initial estimates of the model parameters. First, the observations of the overall top-to-bottom HMM are segmented in N_0 vertical super states, then the data corresponding to each super state is uniformly segmented from left to right into N_1^k states.
   (d)   Initialize model parameters.
         Determine initial model parameters randomly in the case of Π_0, A_0, Π_1^k, and A_1^k or average the segmented observations in the case of B_1^k.
(2)   Step 2: Iteration
   (a)   Perform a doubly embedded Viterbi segmentation.
         The set of training observation vectors is segmented into states via a doubly embedded Viterbi segmentation (See Fig. 5.7.6) which consists of two stages as follows. First, the Viterbi segmentation is applied to an observation vector $O_{t_0,1}, \cdots, O_{t_0,T_1}$ of each row of image blocks and the horizontal state probabilities $P(q_{1,\{t_0,1\}}, \cdots, q_{1,\{t_0,T_1\}} \mid O_{t_0,1}, \cdots, O_{t_0,T_1}, \mathbb{1}^k), (\mathbb{1} \leq k \leq N_0)$ are computed, where $q_{1,\{t_0,t_1\}}, (\mathbb{1} \leq t_1 \leq T_1)$ represents the state of a super state corresponding to the observation O_{t_0,t_1}. Then, the horizontal state probabilities with the initial parameter values such as Π_0 and A_0 are used to perform the Viterbi segmentation from the top to the bottom of the face image and the vertical super state probabilities $P(q_{0,1}, \cdots, q_{0T_0} \mid O_{1,1}, \cdots, O_{1,T_1}, \cdots, O_{T_0,1}, \cdots, O_{T_0,T_1}, \Lambda)$

Figure 5.7.5. A training procedure of the EHMM

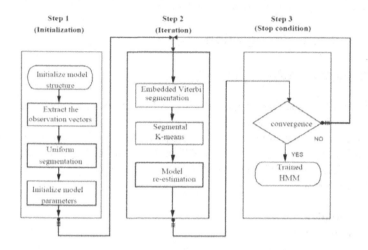

are computed, where $q_{0\,t_0}, (1 \le t_0 \le T_0)$ are the super states corresponding to the t_0-th observation sequence, $O_{t_0,1}, \cdots, O_{t_0,T_1}$.

(b)   Re-estimate HMM model parameters.

The model parameters are re-estimated using a 2-D segmental K-means algorithm (Rabiner, 1989). The model parameters are adjusted as follows.

$$\mu_{i,m}^k = \frac{\sum\limits_{t_0,t_1} O_{t_0,t_1} \delta 1_{i,m}^k(t_0,t_1)}{\delta 1_{i,m}^k(t_0,t_1)},$$

$$\Sigma_{i,m}^k = \frac{\sum\limits_{t_0,t_1} (O_{t_0,t_1} - \mu_{i,m}^k)(O_{t_0,t_1} - \mu_{i,m}^k)^T \delta 1_{i,m}^k(t_0,t_1)}{\delta 1_{i,m}^k(t_0,t_1)},$$

$$c_{i,m}^k = \frac{\sum\limits_{t_0,t_1} \delta 1_{i,m}^k(t_0,t_1)}{\sum\limits_{t_0,t_1} \sum\limits_{m} \delta 1_{i,m}^k(t_0,t_1)},$$

$$a_{1,ij}^k = \frac{\sum\limits_{t_0,t_1} \delta 2_{1,ij}^k(t_0,t_1)}{\sum\limits_{t_0,t_1} \sum\limits_{j} \delta 2_{i,ij}^k(t_0,t_1)},$$

$$a_{0,ij}^k = \frac{\sum\limits_{t_0} \delta 3_{0,ij}^k(t_0)}{\sum\limits_{t_0} \sum\limits_{j} \delta 3_{0,ij}^k(t_0)},$$

$$\tag{5.7.4}$$

where $\delta 1_{i,m}^{k}(t_0, t_1)$ equals 1 if the observation O_{t_0,t_1} is assigned to the kth state and the mth mixture component in the kth super state, and 0 otherwise. $\delta 2_{1,ij}^{k}(t_0, t_1)$ equals 1 if the observation O_{t_0,t_1} transits from the ith state to the jth state in the kth super state, and 0 otherwise. $\delta 3_{0,ij}^{k}(t_0)$ equals 1 if the observation sequence $O_{t_0,1}, \cdots, O_{t_0,T_1}$ transits from the ith super state to the jth super state, and 0 otherwise.

(3)   Step 3: Stop condition

    (a)   Check the stop condition.

        Check the convergence of model parameters. If the stop condition is satisfied, stop the training and obtain a trained EHMM with adjusted model parameters. Otherwise, go to step 2.

5.7.2.2 Recognition

Recognition is accomplished by matching a test face image against all trained EHMMs ($\Lambda_i (i = 1 \cdots, P)$, where P is the number of persons in the face database (Rabiner, 1989). The matching procedure consists of the following steps, as illustrated in Fig. 5.7.7.

(1)   Generate a 2nd-order observation sequence $O = O_{1,T_1}, \cdots, O_{T_0,1}, \cdots, O_{T_0,T}$.

(2)   Find the optimal state sequence $Q_i^* (i = 1 \cdots, P)$ for all EHMMs using a doubly embedded Viterbi algorithm, i.e.,

$$Q_i^* = \arg \min_{Q} P(Q \mid O, \Lambda_i).$$

(5.7.5)

(3)   Compute the state-optimized likelihood function $P(O, Q_i^* \mid \Lambda_i)$ for all stored EHMMs.

(4)   Decide the identity of the test face image as the person who has the highest value of state-optimized likelihood function.

5.7.3 Experiment Results and Discussion

5.7.3.1 Dataset

Even we can execute the experiments using a new face database, we used the old face database shown in Table 5.7.1 in order to compare the previous experimental results. Some previous experimental results did not provide the experimental results using the new face database. The old database consisted of only 1,355 face images of 271 persons, which is categorized into two disjoint data sets for lighting-invariant and pose-invariant experiments. The lighting-invariant data set contains 745 face images of 149 persons and the view-angle-invariant data set contains 410 face images of 102 persons. Each person has 5 images in both data sets. The images were selected from AR (Purdue), ATandT, Yale, UMIST, University of Berne, and some face images were obtained from the MPEG-7 news videos (MPEG, 2000). Fig. 5.7.8 shows some examples of face images in the MPEG-7 face database, where (a) and (b) correspond to the face images in the lighting-invariant and pose-invariant data sets, respectively.

Figure 5.7.6. A doubly embedded Viterbi segmentation algorithm.

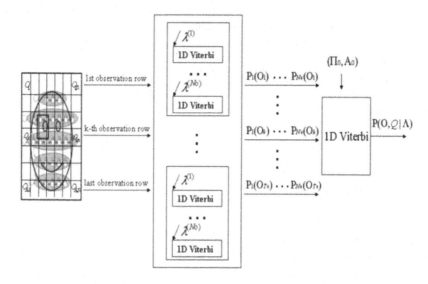

Our proposed method requires two different types of training. One is the block training to determine a couple of block-specific basis vectors appropriate for a given block of the face image and another is the EHMM training to determine the model parameters used for identifying each person. For the block training, we apply two independent PCA techniques to a training set of block images and another training set of residual block images corresponding to a specific block, consequently, and obtain the 1st-order and the 2nd-order basis vectors for the specific block. We used 200 images of 40 persons from the face database (face_0066_01--face_0085_05 and face_0181_01--face_0200_05) for training the 1st- and 2nd-order block-specific vectors for a given block of face image. For the EHMM training, each EHMM was trained independently using the face images of each person, one HMM by one person. Among five images of each person, four images are chosen for training and one remaining image for testing. To increase the number of training samples, we mirrored the four images in the training set to double the size of training images. Thus far, 8 images of the person have been used for training. To avoid data tweak problem, We used 5-fold cross validation technique such that all the images in the database were included in the testing set.

5.7.3.2 Accuracy Measure

We evaluated the recognition performances of four different face recognition methods in terms of the retrieval performances such as ANMRR (Average of the Normalized Modified Retrieval Rank) and FIR (False Identification Rate) which has been widely used in the MPEG-7 society. ANMRR was designed to measure image retrieval accuracy in (MPEG, 2000). See Section 5.7.4 for a detailed explanation about ANMRR. For our experiments, we took the number of ground truth as four, i.e. $NG(q) = 1$ and $K = 2$. In identification, a face image is identified as one person in the face database. FIR is the error rate of identifi-

Figure 5.7.7. A recognition procedure using the trained EHMM

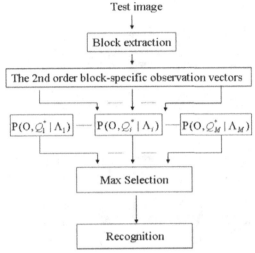

Table 5.7.1. Training and test data set

	Training set	Test set	
		Light varying set	Pose varying set
Exp. 1 (M6001)	200 images: 40 persons x 5 images/person face_0066_01--face_0085_05 face_0181_01--face_0200_05	745 images: 149 persons x 5 images/person face_0001_01--face_0065_05 face_0086_01--face_0169_05	410 images: 82 persons x 5 images/person face_0170_01--face_0180_05 face_0201_01--face_0271_05
Exp. 2 (M7689)			
Exp. 3 (M7251)	1335 images: 271 persons x 5 images/person all of MPEG7 face data set		
Proposed			

cation, $FIR = 1 - (topranksuccessfulrecognitionrate)$. FIR is an effective measure to evaluate identification accuracy and is often used in biometric identification evaluation (Blackburn et. al., 2001).

5.7.3.3 Face Image Identification: 4-image Registration Case

After extracting the block-specific optimal observation vectors corresponding to the test face images, the probability of the observation sequence given embedded HMM face model is computed via a doubly embedded Viterbi recognizer. The model with the highest likelihood is selected and this model reveals the identity of the unknown face. The software used in these experiments was a modified version of the HMM source code in the Intel's Open Source Computer Vision Library (OpenCV)[1].

Figure 5.7.8. Examples of face images: (a) in the lighting-varying condition and (b) in the pose-varying condition

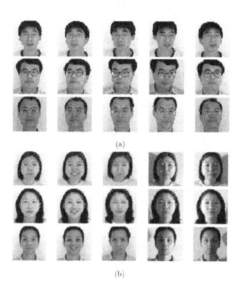

(a)

(b)

We compared four different techniques, such as the 2nd-order eigenface method (m6001) (Wang and Tan, 2000b), the EHMM method with DCT observations (m7632) (Nefian and Davies, 2001), the 2nd-order eigenface method using a confidence factor (m7689) (Kamei and Yamada, 2001), and our proposed method. For a clear comparison, we re-wrote the experimental conditions as follows. In the case of the 2nd-order eigenface method, the 1st-order eigenface features were 10 and the 1st-order eigenface features were 30, i.e, 40 eigenface features were used in total. In the case of the embedded HMM method, 9 DCT coefficients for each block was used as an observation vector. In the case of the 2nd-order eigenface method using a confidence factor, the numbers of the 1st-order and the 2nd-order eigenface features were not specified. So we assumed that they also used the same combination of the 2nd-order eigenface method. With our proposed method, we used a combined feature selection scheme (4;12), where 4 and 12 denotes the number of the 1st and 2nd-order block-specific eigenvectors for each block, respectively. For all experiments, four images for a person is registered by training the corresponding embedded HMM and one remaining image of the person is applied to the trained embedded for testing the recognition performance.

Table 5.7.2 shows the experimental results of person identification among different recognition methods in terms of the ANMRR (NG(q)=1 and K=2 in our experiment) and the FIR = 1-(top rank success recognition rate). Here, Ex *i* means that the *i*th image of each person is used for testing of person identification and all remaining images are used for training the EHMM of the person, and Avg. means the average performance of all five different experiments. From the table, we note that the recognition performance of our proposed method is superior to all previous methods, such as the 2nd-order eigenface method, the embedded HMM method, the 2nd-order eigenface method using a confidence factor, in terms of the ANMRR and the FIR.

We also compare our proposed method with the existing EHMM method with DCT observations (m7251) (Nefian and Davies, 2001) under different feature selection schemes. However, we keep the number of features to be 16 features for all feature selection schemes as follows. In the case of our proposed method, we consider two kinds of feature selection schemes such as, a combined feature selection scheme of (4;12) (Proposed I) and the 1st-order block-specific eigenvectors only of (16;0) (Proposed II). In the case of the existing EHMM method, we also consider two kinds of feature selection schemes, such as 16 2-D DCT coefficients without DC component (EHMM I) and 16 2-DCT coefficients with DC component (EHMM II). For all experiments, the structures of the EHMMs are identical, such that the number of super-states is 5 and the number of states per each super-state is configured as 3, 7, 7, 7, and 3.

Table 5.7.3 shows the experimental results of person identification among different feature selection schemes of our proposed method and the embedded HMM method in terms of the ANMRR (NG(q)=1 and K=2 in our experiment) and the FIR = 1-(top rank success recognition rate). From the table, we note that (1) our proposed method using a combined feature selection scheme of (4; 12) is superior to the EHMM using 16 2-D DCT coefficients in terms of the ANMRR and the FIR. This is because our proposed method uses the different block-specific eigenvectors for each block while the existing EHMM uses the same kinds of DCT over all blocks in the face image, and (2) the elimination of DC component improves the recognition performance in the case of existing EHMM.

We also performed two different types of experiments such as the lighting-invariant face image retrieval and the pose-invariant face image retrieval. Here, we used a variety of different feature selection schemes such as 1) a combined feature selection scheme of (4; 12) (Proposed I) for lighting invariant retrieval and (8;8) (Proposed I) for the pose-invariant retrieval, 2) the 1st-order block-specific eigenvectors only of (16; 0) (Proposed II), 3) the 2nd-order block-specific eigenvectors only of (0; 16) (Proposed III), and 16 2-D DCT coefficients (HMM I). For all experiments, the structure of the embedded HMM is exactly same such that the number of super-states is 5 and the number of states per each super-state is configured as 3, 7, 7, 7, and 3.

Table 5.7.4 shows the experimental results of the lighting-invariant and pose-invariant person identification among different feature selection schemes of our proposed method and the embedded HMM method in terms of the ANMRR ($NG(q) = 1$ and $K = 2$ in our

Table 5.7.2. The experimental results of person identification using different recognition methods (ANMRR and FIR)

	ANMRR				FIR			
	Proposed	M6001	M7251	M7689	Proposed	M6001	M7251	M7689
Ex1	**0.015**	0.125	0.024	0.072	**0.015**	0.140	0.026	0.089
Ex2	**0.057**	0.114	0.046	0.079	**0.074**	0.129	0.063	0.089
Ex3	**0.006**	0.139	0.072	0.076	**0.011**	0.173	0.092	0.103
Ex4	**0.096**	0.151	0.100	0.090	**0.114**	0.177	0.118	0.111
Ex5	**0.166**	0.153	0.258	0.114	**0.210**	0.173	0.314	0.129
Avg.	**0.068**	0.137	0.100	0.086	**0.085**	0.159	0.123	0.104

experiment). Here, for block training, all face images for all persons have been used. From the table, we note that 1) our proposed method using a combined feature scheme of the 1st and 2nd-order eigenvectors outperformed all other feature selection schemes in the lighting-invariant and pose-invariant retrievals in terms of ANMRR, 2) our proposed method using a combined feature scheme of 1st and 2nd-order eigenvectors or the 1st-order block-specific eigenvectors only is superior to the embedded HMM using 16 2-D DCT coefficients in terms of ANMRR, and (3) our proposed method using the 2nd-order block-specific eigenvectors only is not effective for person identification in both lighting-invariant and pose-invariant retrievals.

5.7.4 ANMRR

Let the number of ground truth images for a query q be $NG(q)$ ($NG(q) =1$ in our experiment)

- Compute $NR(q)$, number of found items in first K retrievals (the top ranked K retrievals($K =2$ in our experiment)),
- Compute $MR(q) = NG(q) - NR(q)$, number of missed items
- Compute from the ranks $Rank(k)$ of the found items counting the rank of the first retrieved item as one.
- A rank of ($K+1$) is assigned to each of the ground truth images which are not in the first K retrievals.
- Compute $AVR(q)$ for query q as follows:
- Compute the modified retrieval rank as follows:

$$AVR(q) = \sum_{k=1}^{NG(q)} \frac{Rank(k)}{NG(q)} \qquad (5.7.6)$$

- Compute the normalized modified retrieval rank as follows:

$$MRR(q) = AVR(q) - 0.5 - \frac{NG(q)}{2} \qquad (5.7.7)$$

Table 5.7.3. The experimental results of lighting-invariant and pose-invariant person identification using different feature selection scheme (ANMRR)

	ANMRR				FIR			
	Prop. I	Prop. II	EHMM I	EHMM II	Prop. I	Prop. II	EHMM I	EHMM II
Ex1	**0.015**	0.020	0.031	0.035	**0.015**	0.026	0.037	0.041
Ex2	**0.057**	0.063	0.042	0.081	**0.074**	0.077	0.055	0.100
Ex3	**0.006**	0.022	0.046	0.057	**0.011**	0.030	0.059	0.077
Ex4	**0.096**	0.124	0.111	0.157	**0.114**	0.144	0.133	0.196
Ex5	**0.166**	0.239	0.188	0.256	**0.210**	0.277	0.229	0.288
Avg.	**0.068**	0.090	0.084	0.117	**0.085**	0.111	0.103	0.140

Table 5.7.4. The experimental results of person identification using different feature selection scheme (ANMRR and FIR)

	Light-invariant retrieval				Pose-invariant retrieval			
	Prop. I	Prop. II	Prop. III	EHMM I	Prop. I	Prop. II	Prop. III	EHMM I
Ex1	**0.006**	0.006	0.012	0.012	**0.059**	0.078	0.108	0.078
Ex2	**0.029**	0.027	0.115	0.071	**0.078**	0.123	0.201	0.123
Ex3	**0.006**	0.012	0.092	0.036	**0.040**	0.054	0.132	0.108
Ex4	**0.050**	0.104	0.234	0.133	**0.147**	0.172	0.225	0.167
Ex5	**0.180**	0.325	0.379	0.234	**0.093**	0.147	0.221	0.127
Avg.	**0.054**	0.094	0.166	0.097	**0.083**	0.115	0.177	0.121

Note that the $NMRR(q)$ will always be in the range of $[0.0,1.0]$.

- Compute average of $NMRR$ over all queries

$$ANMRR = \frac{1}{Q}\sum_{q=1}^{Q}NMRR(q) \tag{5.7.8}$$

- Compute the retrieval rate as follows:

$$RR(q) = \frac{NR(q)}{NG(q)} \tag{5.7.9}$$

- Compute average of R over all queries

$$ARR = \frac{1}{Q}\sum_{q=1}^{Q}R\ (q) \tag{5.7.10}$$

- Provide numbers $NR(q), MR(q), RR(q), AVR(q), MRR(q), NMRR(q)$ for each query, the average of RR, and the average of $ANMRR$ over whole set of queries

5.8 FACE RECOGNITION USING LFA

In this section, we address the problems of the local feature analysis (LFA) for recognition and propose a new feature extraction method based on the LFA. Our method consists of three steps: construction, selection, and combination of the local structures. In Eq. (5.3.2), we can see that the kernels of LFA whiten the coefficients of the eigenvectors using the square root of the eigenvalues.

The covariance matrix C of the difference vectors is written as

$$C = \frac{1}{2n^2}\sum_{t=1}^{n}\sum_{s=1}^{n}(x_t - x_s)(x_t - x_s)^T, \tag{5.8.1}$$

where the mean of difference vectors is zero. In other words, it can be also considered that kernels whiten the coefficients of the eigenvectors for difference vectors. This means that kernels from LFA diminish the variations between two images, even if they come from different classes. For the efficient recognition, feature extractors (i.e., bases) have to either maximize the variations from different people or minimize them from the same person. Differently from the orignal LFA, our proposed method constructs the kernels from intra-class covariance matrix to minimize the variations from the same person. For c classes, assume that there is a set of n_i samples in the subset X_i labelled c_i. Then, the intra-class covariance matrix C_I is defined as

$$C_I = \frac{1}{\sum_{i=1}^{c} n_i^2} \sum_{i=1}^{c} \sum_{x_t \in X_i} \sum_{x_s \in X_i} (x_t - x_s)(x_t - x_s)^T,$$

(5.8.2)

where C_I is the covariance matrix of intra-difference vectors. Hence, the proposed new kernels are defined as

$$K_I = VUV^T,$$

(5.8.3)

where $V = [v_1 \cdots v_N]$, $U = diag(1/\sqrt{u_r})$, and u_r and v_r denote the rth largest eigenvalue and the corresponding eigenvector of C_I, respectively. Therefore, the new kernels K_I reduce the variations between images from the same person by whitening the coefficients of the eigenvectors for the intra-difference vectors. The more rigorous discussion related to the eigenvectors of C and C_I can be found in the paper (Wang and Tang, 2003). Fig. 5.8.3 shows that our new kernels show the local properties similar to those of LFA. The output matrix Q of the proposed kernels and the correlation matrix R are written as

$$Q = K_I^T X,$$

(5.8.4)

$$R = K_I C K_I^T,$$

(5.8.5)

where $Q = [q_1 \cdots q_t \cdots q_n]$ and $q_t = K_I^T x_t$.

Another shortcoming of LFA is in its feature selection method. As mentioned in previous section, LFA chooses a set of kernels whose outputs produce the biggest reconstruction error. Although mean reconstruction error is a useful criterion for representing data, there is no reason to assume that it must be useful for discriminating between data in different classes. This problem can be easily verified through an experiment with face images which include some background as shown in Fig. 5.8.1. In this experiment, we used the first 200 eigenvectors to construct a set of kernels and selected 200 kernels which produced the biggest reconstruction errors. Dots in Fig. 5.8.1 (a) are placed in the selected kernel's locations on the mean image of input images, and the first 20 kernel's order in M are written in Fig. 5.8.1 (b). In Fig. 5.8.1 (a), it can be seen that kernels which belong to the outside of the face are also selected, which means that the kernel selection process aims at reducing reconstruction error on a whole picture not just on a face. Note that it is difficult to select kernels more than the number of eigenvectors used for kernel construction since the algorithm involves the matrix inversion and may cause rank defficiency.

Therefore, to overcome such inefficiencies of LFA, we use the class information to select the useful kernels for recognition. After constructing kernels from C_I, we calculate their Fisher scores using the outputs of kernels Q. Fisher score is a measure of discriminant power which estimates how well classes are separated from each other by the ratio of the *between-class scatter* S_B and the *within-class scatter* S_W as

$$J(x) = \frac{S_B(x)}{S_W(x)} = \frac{\sum_{i=1}^{c} n_i (m_i(x) - m(x))^2}{\sum_{i=1}^{c} \sum_{q \in X_i} (q(x) - m_i(x))^2}, \quad (5.8.6)$$

where $m(x) = \frac{1}{n} \sum_{i=1}^{c} n_i m_i(x)$ and $m_i(x) = \frac{1}{n_i} \sum_{q \in X_i} q(x)$.

In Fig. 5.8.2 (a), the score values are displayed on the location of the corresponding kernels. It shows that kernels belonging to the meaningful areas for recognition such as eyebrow, nose, cheekbone, and jaw-line received the higher scores than the others, hence such areas are brighter than the others. This verifies the usefulness of Fisher score for the kernel selection. The locations of the first 1,300 kernels selected according to Fisher score are represented in Fig. 5.8.2 (b). However, kernel selection by Fisher score does not regard the redundancy between the outputs of kernels. To cover the meaningful area of a face, a large number of kernels are required, which can be a serious burden for computation and storage. This problem can be solved by overlaying the set of local structures onto a single sheet. We call the derived bases as the composite template, since the bases of our method consist of a set of local structures.

Suppose that we choose a subset H of column vectors (i.e., kernels) from the matrix K_I (Eq. (5.3.3)) using Fisher score (Eq. (5.8.6)) and their elements are denoted by $K_I(:, x_i)$. Hence, a composite template g is composed by linear combination of local structures as

$$g = \sum_{i=1}^{|H|} \omega_i K_I(:, x_i), \quad (5.8.7)$$

where w_i is a linear combination weight and $x_i \in H$. However, we do not want to lose information by combining the local structures. Hence, we select the combination weights to maximize the entropy of the outputs of g. For simplicity, we assume the Gaussian density for

Figure 5.8.1. (a) The locations of 200 kernels selected according to the minimum reconstruction error and (b) The locations of the first 20 kernels and their orders of selection

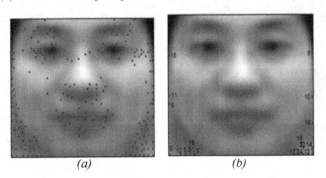

(a)   (b)

the outputs. Other criterions and density assumptions can be used for different combination strategies. Let a_t be the final output for the tth input x_t.

$$a_t = g^T x_t = \sum_{i=1}^{|H|} \omega_i q_t(x_i)$$ (5.8.8)

Without loss of generality, we assume that a has a normal distirbution as

$$p(a) = \frac{1}{\sqrt{2\pi}\sigma} exp\ [-\frac{a^2}{2\sigma^2}],$$ (5.8.9)

where σ^2 is the variance of a. Maximization of the entropy of Eq. (5.8.9) is equivalent to the maximization of σ^2, which can be rewritten as

$$\sigma^2 = \frac{1}{n}\sum_{t=1}^{n} a_t^2 = \sum_{i=1}^{|H|}\sum_{j=1}^{|H|}\omega_i R(x_i, x_j)\omega_i = \omega^T R(H, H)\omega,,$$ (5.8.10)

where $\omega^T = [\ \omega_1 \cdots \omega_{|H|}]$. Since $R(H, H)$ is symmetric, the linear combination weights, ω, which maximizes Eq. (5.8.10) can be easily estimated if we constrain $\omega^T \omega = 1$. In this case, it is equivalent to carry out PCA for the outputs from H. This makes it clear how many composite templates, g, should be constructed. The maximum number of composite templates is N since a set of kernels K_I, the outputs Q and the covariance matrix $R(H;H)$ are all based on the N eigenvectors, i.e., their ranks are N.

Fig. 5.8.3 shows (a) eigenfaces, (b) kernels of LFA, (c) fisherfaces (Belhumeur, et. al., 1997), (d) the proposed kernels, and (e) the composite templates. Similar to kernels of LFA, the proposed new kernels also show local properties. Eigenfaces and kernels of LFA are at the extreme cases, one is global and the other is local. Our composite templates, which are constructed by combining kernels, show intermediate aspects between kernels(local) and eigenfaces(global). Fisherfaces, which also use Fisher score, are somehow similar to

Figure 5.8.2. (a) The Fisher scores of the kernels, where white color corresponds to larger magnitude and (b) The locations of the first 1,300 kernels selected according to Fisher score

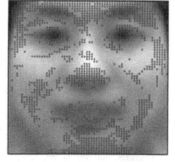

composite templates, however, it can be thought that fisherfaces are constructed by combining the global structures(i.e., eigenfaces) since Fisher Liner Discriminant(FLD) is applied after the dimension of the images is reduced using PCA.

To verify the efficiency of our suggested method through face recognition experiments, we used images from a group of 55 people and a few images are shown in Fig. 5.8.4. For each person, 20 facial images were taken. To construct bases for feature extraction, the images of 20 randomly selected people from the group were used. Among the images that were not used in base construction, 10 images for each person were used for training (gallery), and the rest were used for testing (probe). The size of image is 64x64, and the experiments were conducted using Euclidean distance.

Throughout the experiments, we have compared the results from the following feature extraction methods: (a) eigenface, (b) LFA, (c) fisherface, and (d) composite template. For LFA, 200 eigenvectors of C (Eq. (5.3.1)) were used to construct a set of kernels and 200 kernels were chosen among them (Fig. 5.8.1). For composite template, 250 eigenvectors of CI (Eq. (5.8.2)) were used to construct a set of kernels and 1,300 kernels were selected (Fig. 5.8.2). For fisherface, the dimension of the images was reduced into 120 using PCA, and the FLD was applied to the reduced dimension images. The bases constructed by each method are shown in Fig. 5.8.3.

Table 5.8.1 shows the best recognition rates of eigenface, LFA, fisherface, and composite template are 60.57%, 71.71%, 82.29%, and 94.29%, respectively, for the rank 1. To achieve the best recognition rate in each method, 178, 199, 17, and 158 features were needed. In LFA and fisherface, we increased the number of the eigenvectors, however, it did not show any improvements. Note that the number of fisherfaces is bounded on the number of classes, which are used in the basis construction. By fixing the shortcomings of LFA, our proposed method showed the best performance among the tested methods. It can be also seen that the size of kernels chosen by Fisher score was reduced effectively.

Fig. 5.8.5 shows the face recognition rates of eigenface, LFA, fisherface, and the proposed composite template method, as the number of feature increases. As you can see in this figure, the proposed composite template method outperforms all other methods in terms of the recognition accuracy over all range of the numbers of the feautes.

5.9 FACE RECOGNITION USING TENSOR-BASED AAM

The AAM has been widely used for the face and medical image modeling (Beichel et. al., 2001, Bosch et. al., 2002, Stegmann et. al., 2003, Edwards et. al., 1998a, 1998b) and the extracted model parameters have been used for the classification problems such as the pose estimation (Cootes et. al., 2002, Yan et. al. 2003), the expression recognition (Sung et. al., 2006h, About and Davoine, 2004b) and the face recognition (Edwards et. al., 1998a, Lee and Kim, 2006). However, the fitting results of the AAM are often unsatisfactory, especially when the facial pose, expression and illumination conditions of the input image are much deviated from those of the training images. There have been many approaches to improve the AAM fitting performance given below.

The first category is to modify the AAM fitting algorithm by proposing a novel AAM fitting algorithm or improving the existing fitting algorithm. The original AAM, proposed by Cootes et. al. (1998), obtained the model parameters by a linear regression between the image difference and the model parameter difference. Later, they modified the regression

Figure 5.8.3. (a) The first 12 eigenfaces, (b) The kernels of LFA selected manually, (c) The first 12 fisherfaces, (d) The proposed kernels, and (e) The first 12 composite templates

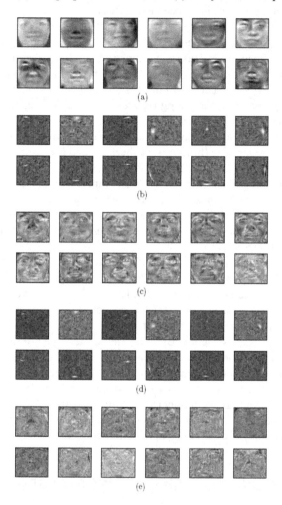

Table 5.8.1. Face recognition rates of eigenface, LFA, fisherface and composite tempate methods

Rank	(a): 178	(b): 199	(c): 17	(d): 158
1	60.57	71.71	82.29	94.29
2	70.00	79.14	88.29	96.57
3	75.43	81.14	92.00	98.00
4	77.43	83.43	93.43	98.57
5	77.71	84.57	94.00	98.86

Figure 5.8.4. Example faces in our database

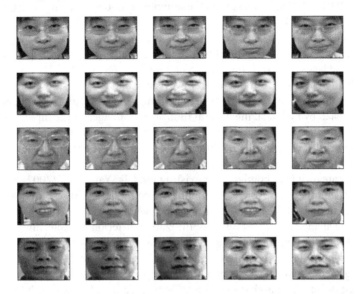

based-approach to a simplified Gauss-Newton approach (Cootes et. al., 2001d). Donner et. al. (2006) proposed a fast AAM using the canonical correlation analysis (CCA) that modeled the relation between the image difference and the model parameter difference to improve the convergence speed of fitting algorithm. Matthews and Baker (2004a) proposed an efficient AAM fitting algorithm that did not require the linear relationship between the image difference and the model parameter difference. It performs better than the original AAM (Cootes et. al., 1998) in terms of the convergence speed and the fitting accuracy. Sung and Kim (2006e) proposed a new fitting algorithm of 2D + 3D AAMs for the mul-

Figure 5.8.5. Face recontion rates vs. the number of features

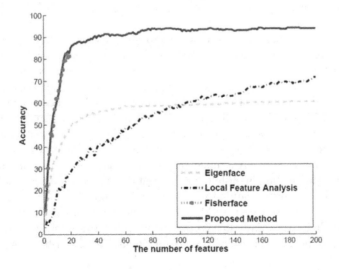

tiple calibrated camera system, called stereo AAM (STAAM), to increase the stability of the fitting of 2D + 3D AAMs. It reduces the number of model parameters, and resultantly improves the fitting stability.

The second category is to make the AAM bais appearance images adaptive to the external variations. Lee et. al. (2007a) proposed to use adaptive linear appearance model that updated the basis appearance images using the incremental PCA. It worked well under the gradually changing illumination. However the update of basis appearance images using ill-fitted images degraded the fitting performance. Lee et. al. (2007b) extended the previous approach by synthesizing several illumination images of the input face and then updating the basis appearance images by the synthesized illumination images only when a new face appears. It works well under the rapidly changing illumination and is free from the influence of the ill-fitted images.

The third category is to combine the existing models. Yan et. al. (2002) proposed the TC-ASM that inherited the ASM's local appearance model because of its robustness to varying light conditions. They also borrowed the AAM's global texture, to act as a constraint over the shape and providing an optimization criterion for determining the shape parameters. Using the texture constrained shape enabled the search method to escape from the local minima of the ASM search, resulting the improved fitting results. Sung et. al. (2006g) integrated AAM and ASM in a unified gradient-based optimization framework. They changed the profile search step of the ASM to a gradient-based search like the AAM and combined the error terms of the AAM and ASM into a single objective function. By integrating the AAM and ASM error terms and optimizing them simultaneously, they obtained accurate fitting results.

The fourth category is to use the specific AAM model that is appropriate for the different people and external variations. Gross et. al. (2004b) showed that the fitting performance of the AAM learned from the data set of a single person across pose, illumination and expression was better than that of the AAM learned from the data set of many persons. Lucey et. al. (2006) used the person-specific AAM model to track the subject and used generic AAM model to compute the subject-independent features. Cootes et. al. (2002) proposed to use multiple face models to fit an input image, where the pose of an input face image was estimated by regression technique and then the face model close to the estimated pose was fitted to the input image. However, it required several face models that should be learned for different poses and persons.

Tensor-based AAM belongs to the fourth approach because it generates a specific AAM model that is specific to the subject, pose, expression and illumination of the input image in the tensor algebra framework (Lathauwer et. al., 2000). Tensor algebra is a generalization of linear algebra, which offers a powerful mathematical framework to model the interaction of multiple factors. Vasilescu et. al. (2002a, 2002b) introduced the concept of tensor algebra to the face modelling, which is called TensorFace, where, each face image was explicitly formulated as the compound effect of multiple factors in an elegant mathematical form. The tensor-based AAM is different from the other methods in the last category in that the former generate the specific AAM model that is appropriate for the current subject, pose, expression and illumination in on-line manner, but the latter train the a variety of AAM models for different subjects, poses, expressions and illuminations in off-line manner.

The goal of the tensor-based AAM is to generate the variation-specific AAM basis vectors from a single basis tensor that is constructed from the training face images with all possible subjects, poses, expressions, and illuminations. The tensor-based AAM consists of two kinds of tensors: image tensor and model tensor. The image tensor is constructed using face images with eyes alignment and used to estimate the image variations such as the pose, the expression and the illumination by finding the basis subtensor whose reconstruction error is the minimal. On the other hand, the model tensor is constructed using the aligned shape points and shape normalized appearance images and used to generate the specific AAM basis vectors by indexing into the model tensor in terms of the estimated image variations.

Fig. 5.9.1 summarizes the overall procedure of the tensor-based AAM. When a new input image is given, it is detected and normalized by the face detector (Jun and Kim, 2007). Then, the pose, expression, and illumination of the input face image is estimated using the image tensor. Then, the specific AAM basis vectors are generated from the model tensor using the estimated pose, expression, and illumination. Finally, AAM fitting is performed on the input face image using the generated specific AAM basis vectors.

5.9.1 Tensor-Based AAM

5.9.1.1 Image Tensor

In order to estimate the pose, expression and illumination of the input face image, we propose the image tensor which is constructed from the normalized training face images with all possible subjects, poses, expressions, and illuminations. We construct a fifth-order image tensor $\mathcal{D}_i \in R^{I \times J \times K \times L \times M_i}$ to represent the face images by stacking normalized training face images, where I, J, K, L, and M_i are the number of peoples, poses, facial expressions, illuminations and face image pixels, respectively. The image tensor $\mathcal{D}_{img}$ can be decomposed into five factors by applying the HOSVD as

$$\mathcal{D}_i = \mathcal{Z}_i \times_1 \mathbf{U}_{peop} \times_2 \mathbf{U}_{pose} \times_3 \mathbf{U}_{exp} \times_4 \mathbf{U}_{ill} \times_5 \mathbf{U}_{pixel}, \tag{5.9.1}$$

where $\mathcal{Z}_i$ is the core image tensor which governs the interaction among the five mode matrices ($\mathbf{U}_{peop}$, $\mathbf{U}_{pose}$, $\mathbf{U}_{exp}$, $\mathbf{U}_{ill}$ and $\mathbf{U}_{pixel}$) which represent the people subspace, pose subspace, facial expression subspace, illumination subspace and face image pixel subspace, respectively. Based on the concept of the TensorFace which is proposed by Vasilescu and Terzopoulos (2002a), we can define a basis image tensor about people as

$$\mathcal{B}_i = \mathcal{Z}_i \times_2 \mathbf{U}_{pose} \times_3 \mathbf{U}_{exp} \times_4 \mathbf{U}_{ill} \times_5 \mathbf{U}_{pixel}. \tag{5.9.2}$$

We can make a basis image subtensor $\mathcal{B}_i(j,k,l)$ by indexing the basis image tensor $\mathcal{B}_i$ with a specific pose, expression, and illumination as

$$\mathcal{B}_i(j,k,l) = \mathcal{Z}_i \times_2 \mathbf{U}_{pose}(j) \times_3 \mathbf{U}_{exp}(k) \times_4 \mathbf{U}_{ill}(l) \times_5 \mathbf{U}_{pixel}. \tag{5.9.3}$$

where $\mathbf{U}_{pose}(j)$, $\mathbf{U}_{exp}(k)$ and $\mathbf{U}_{ill}(l)$ represent the jth, kth and lth row vectors of the subspace $\mathbf{U}_{pose}$, $\mathbf{U}_{exp}$ and $\mathbf{U}_{ill}$, respectively. The basis image subtensor spans all the face images of different peoples with a specific pose j, expression k and illumination l. In this case, the basis image tensor has $J \times K \times L$ different basis image subtensors, for each

Figure 5.9.1. Overview of the tensor-based AAM

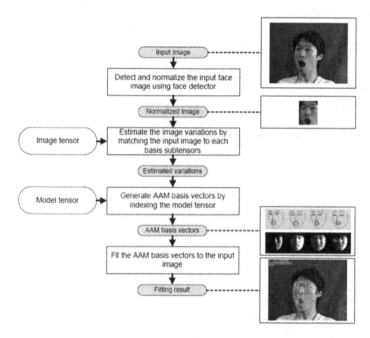

combination of pose, expression and illumination, and these basis have I eigenvectors. For the simplicity of notation and readability, the basis image subtensor $\mathcal{B}_i(j,k,l)$ is usually represented by the $M \times I$ basis image matrix $\mathbf{B}_{i(pixel)}(j,k,l)$ by unfolding it along the image pixel mode.

In order to estimate the pose, expression and illumination of the $M \times 1$ input face image $\mathbf{I}$, we need to compute $J \times K \times L$ parameter vectors, where one specific parameter vector $p_i(j,k,l)$ is obtained by projecting $\mathbf{I}$ to each basis image matrix $\mathbf{B}_{i(pixel)}(j,k,l)$ as

$$p_i(j,k,l) = \mathbf{B}_{i(pixel)}^{-1}(j,k,l)\mathbf{I}. \tag{5.9.4}$$

Then, we determine the pose, expression, and illumination $(\hat{j},\hat{k},\hat{l})$ of the input face image by finding the basis image matrix $\mathbf{B}_{i(pixel)}(j,k,l)$ which has the minimum reconstruction error as

$$(\hat{j},\hat{k},\hat{l}) = \underset{i,j,k}{\arg\min} \left\| \mathbf{I} - \mathbf{B}_{i(pixel)}(j,k,l)p_i(j,k,l) \right\|. \tag{5.9.5}$$

5.9.1.2 Model Tensor

In order to generate the specific AAM basis vector, we propose to use the model tensor that consists of the shape and appearance tensor which are constructed from the aligned shape vectors and the normalized appearance images, respectively. The shape model tensor is constructed as follows. First, the training face images are manually landmarked for obtaining the shape vectors. Second, the shape vectors are aligned using Procrustes analysis (Cootes et. al., 2001d) and the mean shape subtraction. Third, the fifth order shape model tensor $\mathcal{D}_s \in R^{I \times J \times K \times L \times M_s}$ is constructed to represent the shape vectors by stacking the aligned shape vectors, where I, J, K, L, and M_s are the number of subjects, poses, facial expressions, illuminations and shape vectors, respectively. The shape model tensor $\mathcal{D}_s$ can be decomposed into five factors by applying the HOSVD as

$$\mathcal{D}_s = \mathcal{Z}_s \times_1 \mathbf{V}_{peop} \times_2 \mathbf{V}_{pose} \times_3 \mathbf{V}_{exp} \times_4 \mathbf{V}_{ill} \times_5 \mathbf{V}_{point}, \tag{5.9.6}$$

where $\mathcal{Z}_s$ is the core tensor which governs the interaction among the five mode matrices ($\mathbf{V}_{peop}$, $\mathbf{V}_{pose}$, $\mathbf{V}_{exp}$, $\mathbf{V}_{ill}$ and $\mathbf{V}_{point}$) which represent the people subspace, pose subspace, facial expression subspace, illumination subspace and shape subspace, respectively.

Similarly, the appearance model tensor is constructed as follows. First, the training face images are warped to the mean shape s_0 using the piece-wise affine warping. Second, the warped face images are normalized by subtracting the mean appearance a_0 from them. Third, the fifth order appearance model tensor $\mathcal{D}_a \in R^{I \times J \times K \times L \times M_a}$ is constructed to represent the appearance image by stacking the normalized appearance images, where I, J, K, L, and M_a are the number of peoples, poses, facial expressions, illuminations and appearance image pixels, respectively. The appearance model tensor $\mathcal{D}_a$ can be decomposed into five factors by applying the HOSVD as

$$\mathcal{D}_a = \mathcal{Z}_a \times_1 \mathbf{W}_{people} \times_2 \mathbf{W}_{pose} \times_3 \mathbf{W}_{exp} \times_4 \mathbf{W}_{ill} \times_5 \mathbf{W}_{pixel}, \tag{5.9.7}$$

where $\mathcal{Z}_a$ is the core tensor which governs the interaction between the five mode matrices ($\mathbf{W}_{peop}$, $\mathbf{W}_{pose}$, $\mathbf{W}_{exp}$, $\mathbf{W}_{ill}$ and $\mathbf{W}_{pixel}$) which represent the people subspace, pose subspace, facial expression subspace, illumination subspace and appearance subspace, respectively.

Fig. 5.9.2 shows that different types of training data are used for constructing the image and model tensor. As we can see, the image tensor, the shape model tensor and the appearance model tensor are using the clipped and normalized face images, the aligned landmark shape vectors, and the normalized appearance images by the mean shape, respectively.

Next, we define the basis shape tensor as follows. Since the shape vector of the face image is not influenced by the change of illumination, we consider the pose and expression variations for the basis shape tensor as

$$\mathcal{B}_s = \mathcal{Z}_s \times_2 \mathbf{V}_{pose} \times_3 \mathbf{V}_{exp} \times_5 \mathbf{V}_{point} \tag{5.9.8}$$

We can make a basis shape subtensor by indexing the basis shape tensor $\mathcal{B}_s$ with the estimated pose and expression as

$$\mathcal{B}_s(\hat{j}, \hat{k}) = \mathcal{Z}_s \times_2 \mathbf{V}_{pose}(\hat{j}) \times_3 \mathbf{V}_{exp}(\hat{k}) \times_5 \mathbf{V}_{point}, \tag{5.9.9}$$

where $\mathbf{V}_{pose}(\hat{j})$ and $\mathbf{V}_{exp}(\hat{k})$ represent the row vectors of the subspace $\mathbf{V}_{pose}$ and $\mathbf{V}_{exp}$ for specific pose $\hat{j}$ and expression $\hat{k}$, respectively. This basis shape subtensor spans all the shape vectors of face images of different peoples under different illuminations with a specific pose $\hat{j}$ and expression $\hat{k}$.

For the simplicity of notation and readability, the basis shape subtensor $\mathcal{B}_s(\hat{j},\hat{k})$ is usually represented by the $M_s \times L$ basis shape matrix $\mathbf{B}_{s(point)}(\hat{j},\hat{k})$ by unfolding it along the shape vector mode, which is denoted by $\mathbf{S}(\hat{j},\hat{k})$. Then, the AAM shape model (Eq. (4.2.2)) is re-written as

$$s = s_0 + s_0(\hat{j},\hat{k}) + \sum_{t=1}^{p} p_t s_t(\hat{j},\hat{k}), \qquad (5.9.10)$$

where $s_t(\hat{j},\hat{k})$ means the t th column vector of the basis shape matrix $\mathbf{S}(\hat{j},\hat{k})$. Since the first shape eigenvector $s_0(\hat{j},\hat{k})$ is the mean shape vector over all peoples and illuminations for a specific pose $\hat{j}$ and expression $\hat{k}$, the mean shape for the AAM shape model is $s_0 + s_0(\hat{j},\hat{k})$.

Next, we define the basis appearance tensor as follows. Since the appearance of the face image is influenced by the change of illumination rather than the change of pose and expression, we consider the illumination variation for the basis appearance tensor as

$$\mathcal{B}_a = \mathcal{Z}_a \times_4 \mathbf{W}_{ill} \times_5 \mathbf{W}_{pixel}. \qquad (5.9.11)$$

We can make a basis appearance subtensor by indexing the basis appearance tensor $\mathcal{B}_a$ with the estimated illumination $\hat{l}$ as

Figure 5.9.2. Different types of training data for constructing image and model tensor

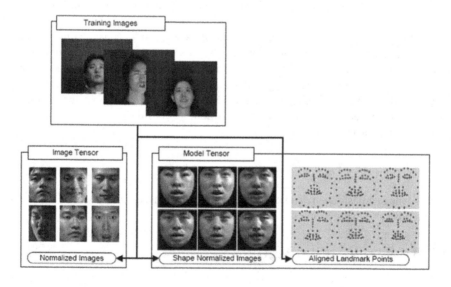

$$\mathcal{B}_a(\hat{l}) = \mathcal{Z}_a \times_4 \mathbf{W}_{ill}(\hat{l}) \times_5 \mathbf{W}_{pixel},$$ (5.9.12)

where $\mathbf{W}_{ill}(\hat{l})$ represent the row vector of the subspace $\mathbf{W}_{ill}$ for specific illumination $\hat{l}$. This basis appearance subtensor spans all the appearances of face images of different peoples with different expressions and poses under illumination $\hat{l}$.

For the simplicity of notation and readability, the basis appearance subtensor $\mathcal{B}_a(\hat{l})$ is usually represented by the $M_a \times IJK$ basis appearance matrix $\mathbf{B}_{a(pixel)}(\hat{l})$ by unfolding it along the pixel mode, which is denoted by $\mathbf{A}(\hat{l})$. Then, the AAM appearance model (Eq. (4.2.3)) is re-written as

$$\mathbf{A} = \mathbf{A}_0 + \mathbf{A}_0(\hat{l}) + \sum_{t=1}^{q} \alpha_t \mathbf{A}_t(\hat{l}),$$ (5.9.13)

where $\mathbf{A}_t(\hat{l})$ means the tth eigenface image of the basis appearance matrix $\mathbf{A}(\hat{l})$. Since the first appearance eigenface image $\mathbf{A}_0(\hat{l})$ is the mean appearance over all the face images, the mean appearance for the AAM appearance model which is specific to the particular illumination $\hat{l}$ is $\mathbf{A}_0 + \mathbf{A}_0(\hat{l})$.

Fig. 5.9.3 illustrates some examples of the basis shape vectors of the conventional AAM and the tensor-based AAM, where Fig. 5.9.3-(a) represents the first five basis shape vectors over the mean shape and three rows in the Fig. 5.9.3-(b) represent the basis shape vectors that correspond to the happy, surprise, and angry expression, respectively, at the left pose. As you can see in Fig. 5.9.3, the conventional AAM has a single shape model that covers all the pose and expression variations, but the tensor-based AAM has several shape models, where each shape model covers a specific pose and expression.

Fig. 5.9.4 illustrates some examples of basis appearance images of the conventional AAM and the tensor-based AAM, where Fig. 5.9.4-(a) represents the first five basis appearance images over the mean appearance and three rows in the Fig. 5.9.4-(b) represent the basis appearance images that correspond to the 5th, 6th, and 10th illumination condition, respectively. As you can see in Fig. 5.9.4, the conventional AAM has a single appearance model that covers all the illumination variations, but the tensor-based AAM has several appearance models, where each appearance model covers a specific illumination.

5.9.2 Tensor-Based AAM Fitting

The procedure of the tensor-based AAM can be explained as follows. First, when a new input image $\mathbf{I}$ is given, the face detector (Jun and Kim, 2007) locates the face and normalizes it by two eye positions. Second, the image tensor estimates the pose, expression, and illumination $(\hat{j}, \hat{k}, \hat{l})$ of the normalized face image by finding the basis image matrix $\mathbf{B}_{i(pixel)}(j,k,l)$ which has the minimum reconstruction error (See Eq. (5.5.10)). Third, the model tensor generates the pose/expression-specific basis shape vectors $\{s_t(\hat{j},\hat{k})\}_{t=1}^{p}$ and the illumination-specific basis appearance images $\{\mathbf{A}_t(\hat{l})\}_{t=1}^{q}$. Finally, AAM fitting is performed on the input face image using the generated AAM basis shape vectors and the generated AAM basis appearance images.

The problem of fitting the AAM to a given input image $\mathbf{I}$ can be formulated as a search for the appearance and shape parameters of the AAM that minimizes the following error

$$E = \sum_{x \in s_0} \left[\mathbf{A}(\alpha) - \mathbf{I}(W(x;p,q)) \right]^2, \qquad (5.9.14)$$

where $\mathbf{A}$ is the shape normalized appearance image over the pixels x that belongs to the inside of s_0 (Eq. (5.9.13)) and $W(\mathbf{x};\mathbf{p},\mathbf{q})$ transforms the coordinate x in the base shape s_0 into the corresponding location in the target image. After the AAM fitting, we obtain the fitted shape vector s_{aaam} and the fitted appearance image $\mathbf{A}_{aam}$.

Among the various gradient descent fitting algorithms of the AAM (Matthews and Baker, 2004a, Gross et. al., 2003), we used the inverse compositional simultaneous update (ICSU) algorithm. Since the tensor-based AAM only replaces the shape and appearance model from the conventional AAM, the fitting process is the same with the conventional AAM.

5.9.3 Image Transformation for Face Recognition

In the previous section, we estimated the pose, expression and illumination ($\hat{j}, \hat{k}, \hat{l}$) of the input face image using the image tensor, obtained the shape basis vectors that are specific to the estimated pose and expression and the appearance basis images that are specific to the estimated illumination using the model tensor, and also obtained the fitted shape vector s_{aam} and the fitted appearance image $\mathbf{A}_{aam}$ of the input face image using the tensor-based AAM.

In order to validate the usefulness of the proposed tensor-based AAM, we perform the face recognition using those results of the tensor-based AAM. Since we assume that the

Figure 5.9.3. Comparison of the basis shape vectors between (a) the conventional AAM and (b) the tensor-based AAM

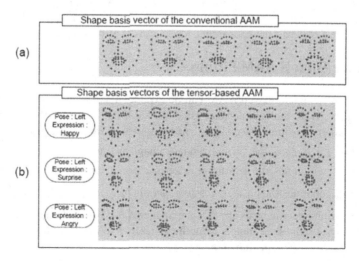

Figure 5.9.4. Comparison of the basis appearance images between (a) the conventional AAM and (b) the tensor-based AAM

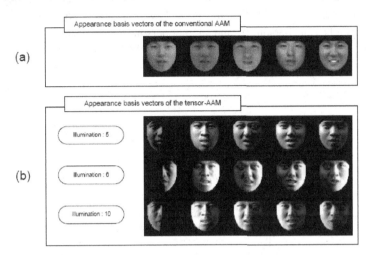

gallery consists of face images with the specific condition such as the frontal pose j_n, the neutral expression k_n, and the normal illumination l_n, we need to transform the input face image with an arbitrary pose, expression and illumination into the normalized face image with the frontal pose, the neutral expression, and the normal illumination. Fig. 5.9.5 shows an overall procedure of the face image transformation that consists of the shape transformation and the appearance transformation, where the former uses the fitted shape vector $s_{aam}(\hat{j},\hat{k})$ corresponding to the estimated pose $\hat{j}$ and expression $\hat{k}$, and the latter uses the appearance image $\mathbf{A}_{aam}(\hat{l})$ corresponding to the estimated illumination $\hat{l}$.

5.9.3.1 Shape Transformation

Since the illumination change does not make a large effect on the shape vector of the face image, we consider the expression and pose variations in the shape transformation. So, the shape transformation converts the fitted shape vector $s_{aam}(\hat{j},\hat{k})$ of the input face image with the pose $\hat{j}$ and the expression $\hat{k}$ into the normalized fitted shape vector $s_{aam}(j_n,k_n)$ of the input face image with the frontal pose j_n and the neutral expression k_n. However, the model tensor itself can not express well the new person who is not contained in the training set. To solve this problem, we propose the indirect transformation that does obtain the shape difference using the model translation and transform the fitted shape vector into the normalized fitted shape vector using the shape difference.

In general, the shape difference Δs_1 of one person p_1 that is computed by subtracting the shape vector $s_1(j_1,k_1)$ at the pose j_1 from the expression k_1 and the shape vector $s_1(j_2,k_2)$ at the pose j_2 and the expression k_2 is assumed to be similar as the shape difference the shape difference Δs_2 of another person p_2 that is computed by subtracting the shape vector $s_2(j_1, k_1)$ at the pose j_1 from the expression k_1 and the shape vector $s_2(j_2, k_2)$ at the pose j_2 and the expression k_2. In this work, the reference shape vector that is obtained from the training face images and the fitted shape vector of the input face image correspond to one person p_1 and another person p_2, respectively.

The detailed explanation of the overall procedure of the shape transformation is given below.

Figure 5.9.5. The overall procedure of image transformation

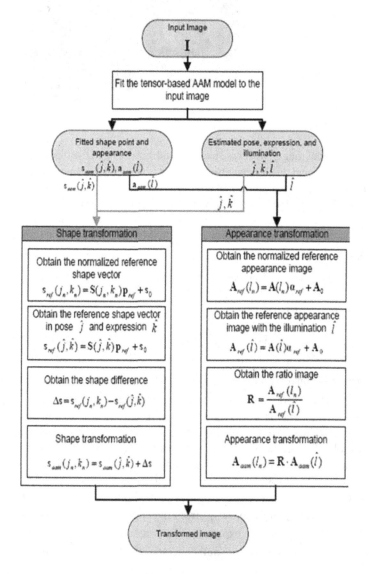

- Make the reference shape vector s_{ref} which is often taken as the mean of the shape vectors of the training images and the reference shape parameter p_{ref} which is the mean of the shape parameters of the training shape vectors.

- Obtain the normalized reference shape vector $s_{ref}(j_n, k_n)$ with the frontal pose j_n and the neutral expression k_n using the reference shape parameter p_{ref} and the basis shape matrix $\mathbf{S}(j_n, k_n)$ as $s_{ref}(j_n, k_n) = \mathbf{S}(j_n, k_n) p_{ref}$.

- Estimate the pose $\hat{j}$ and the expression $\hat{k}$ of the input face image using the image tensor.

- Obtain the reference shape vector $s_{ref}(\hat{j}, \hat{k})$ with the estimated pose $\hat{j}$ and the estimated expression $\hat{k}$ using the reference shape parameter p_{ref} and the basis shape matrix $\mathbf{S}(\hat{j}, \hat{k})$ as $s_{ref}(\hat{j}, \hat{k}) = \mathbf{S}(\hat{j}, \hat{k}) p_{ref}$.

- Obtain the shape difference Δs between $s_{ref}(j_n, k_n)$ and $s_{ref}(\hat{j}, \hat{k})$ as $\Delta s = s_{ref}(j_n, k_n) - s_{ref}(\hat{j}, \hat{k})$.

- Obtain the the normalized fitted shape vector $s_{aam}(j_n, k_n)$ from the fitted shape vector $s_{aam}(\hat{j}, \hat{k})$ as $s_{aam}(j_n, k_n) = s_{aam}(\hat{j}, \hat{k}) + \Delta(s)$.

Fig. 5.9.6 shows one result of the shape transformation, where the five input face images are given along the first row. We can see that the transformed images given along the second row have almost identical shape with the target image in the third row while keeping the same identity. Therefore, we expect that the shape transformation will improve the face recognition performance even though the input face image has the different poses and expressions.

5.9.3.2 Appearance Transformation

Since the illumination change makes a larger effect on the appearance image than the pose and expression variation, we consider the illumination variation in the appearance transformation. So, the appearance transformation converts the fitted appearance image $\mathbf{A}_{aam}(\hat{l})$ of the input face image with the illumination $\hat{l}$ into the normalized fitted appearance image $\mathbf{A}_{aam}(l_n)$ of the input face image with the normalized illumination l_n. However, the model tensor itself can not express well the new person who is not contained in the training set. To solve this problem, we propose the indirect transformation that does obtain the ratio image using the model translation and transform the fitted appearance into the normalized fitted appearance image using the ratio image.

In general, the ratio image $\mathbf{R}_1$ of one person p_1 that is computed by dividing the appearance image $\mathbf{A}_1(l_1)$ under the illumination l_1 over the appearance image $\mathbf{A}_1(l_2)$ under the illumination l_2 is assumed to be similar as the ratio image $\mathbf{R}_1$ of another person p_2 that is computed by dividing the appearance image $\mathbf{A}_2(l_1)$ under the illumination l_1 over the appearance image $\mathbf{A}_2(l_2)$ under the illumination l_2. In this work, the reference appearance image that is obtained from the training face images and the fitted appearance image of the input face image correspond to one person p_1 and another person p_2, respectively.

The detailed explanation of the overall procedure of the appearance transformation is given below.

- Make the reference appearance image $\mathbf{A}_{ref}$ which is often taken as the mean of the appearance images of the training images and the reference appearance parameter α_{ref} which is the mean of the appearance parameters of the training appearance images.

- Obtain the normalized reference appearance image $\mathbf{A}_{ref}(l_n)$ with the normal illumination l_n using the reference illumination parameter α_{ref} and the basis appearance matrix $\mathbf{A}(l_n)$ as $\mathbf{A}_{ref}(l_n) = \mathbf{A}(l_n)\alpha_{ref}$.

- Estimate the illumination $\hat{l}$ of the input face image using the image tensor.

- Obtain the reference appearance image $\mathbf{A}_{ref}(\hat{l})$ with the estimated illumination $\hat{l}$ using the reference appearance parameter α_{ref} and the basis appearance matrix $\mathbf{A}(\hat{l})$ as $\mathbf{A}_{ref}(\hat{l}) = \mathbf{A}(\hat{l})\alpha_{ref}$.

- Obtain the ratio image $\mathbf{R}$ between $\mathbf{A}_{ref}(l_n)$ and $\mathbf{A}_{ref}(\hat{l})$ as $\mathbf{R} = \dfrac{\mathbf{A}_{ref}(l_n)}{\mathbf{A}_{ref}(\hat{l})}$.

- Obtain the the normalized fitted appearance image $\mathbf{A}_{aam}(l_n)$ from the fitted appearance image $\mathbf{A}_{aam}(\hat{l})$ as $\mathbf{A}_{aam}(l_n) = \mathbf{R} \times \mathbf{A}_{aam}(\hat{l})$.

Fig. 5.9.7 shows one result of the appearance transformation, where the five input face images are given along the first row. We can see that the transformed images given along the second row have almost identical illumination with the target image in the third row while keeping the same identity. Therefore, we expect that the appearance transformation will improve the face recognition performance even though the input face image has the different illuminations.

Figure 5.9.6. The result of shape transformation

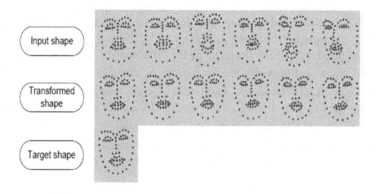

Input shape

Transformed shape

Target shape

5.9.4 Experimental Results and Discussion

5.9.4.1 Database

We used the database PF07 (Postech Faces 2007) (Lee et. al., 2007c), which included 100 male and 100 female subjects and the face images of each subject were captured with 5 different poses, 4 different expressions, and 16 different illuminations, where the 5 different poses are front, left, right, upper, and down, and the angle between the frontal pose and other poses is 22.5°, the 4 different expressions are neutral, happy, surprise, and angry, and the 16 different illuminations consist of no light condition and 15 different light conditions. One specific light condition corresponds to the turn-on of one specific light on the 15 different locations that are the intersection points of three vertical positions (high, middle, and low) and five horizontal positions (-90°, -45°, 0°, 45°, 90°). Therefore, the database contains a total of 64,000 face images as $200 \times 5 \times 4 \times 16 = 640,000$. Fig. 5.9.8 shows 16 face images of a subject in frontal pose with happy expression under 16 different illumination conditions from I1 to I16. Fig. 5.9.9 shows the full image set of a subject, four image groups represent the different expressions, the five columns in each image group represent the different poses, and five rows in each image group represent some of 16 different illuminations due to the limitation of page space.

5.9.4.2 Tensor-Based AAM

Among the 64,000 face images in the database, 32,000 ($= 100 \times 5 \times 4 \times 16$) face images of 100 subjects are used for following experiments. We divided 32,000 face images into two disjoint sets: the training set and the test set. The training set consisting of the randomly chosen 50 subjects was used to construct the image and model tensor for the tensor-based AAM including the AAM model for the comparison study with the conventional AAM. and the remaining 50 subjects as the test set, where the training set was used to construct the AAM and the image/model tensors, while the test set was used to evaluate the fitting performance of the proposed method.

We manually landmarked the location of two eye points of the face images for constructing the image tensor, then the face images in the database are normalized to the size

Figure 5.9.7. The result of the appearance transformation

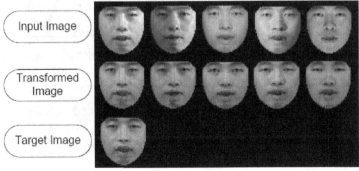

of 40 × 50. First, we constructed the image tensor $\mathcal{D}_i$ of which the size is 50 × 5 × 4 × 16 × 2000. Next, we applied HOSVD to decompose the image tensor and then obtained the 2000 × 50 basis matrices $\mathbf{B}_{s(pixel)}(j,k,l)$ for all combination of j, k and l. In this experiment, we have 320 basis matrices (5 × 4 × 16).

We also manually landmarked the 70 shape points of the face images for constructing the AAM and the model tensor. The AAM model was built using 15 shape bases and 137 appearance bases which can explain the 95% shape and appearance variations. Then we constructed the shape model tensor $\mathcal{D}_s$ and the appearance model tensor $\mathcal{D}_a$ using the shape vectors and warped appearances obtained from the AAM, where the size of shape and appearance model tensors are 50 × 5 × 4 × 16 × 140 and 50 × 5 × 4 × 16 × 1726, respectively. Next, we applied HOSVD to decompose the model tensors.

First, we evaluated the estimation performance of the image tensor using the 16,000 images of the 50 subjects in the test set. For the test input image $\mathbf{I}$, we find the basis matrix which has the minimum reconstruction error (Eq. (5.9.5)) and determine $\hat{j}$, $\hat{k}$, and $\hat{l}$ as the estimated pose, expression, and illumination of the input image. Table 5.9.1 shows correct estimation rate of the pose, expression and illumination of the input face image using image tensor. The estimation rate of the expression is lower than that of other variations. This is because the neutral facial expression is similar with the angry facial expression, and

Figure 5.9.8. Some illumination images of PF07 database

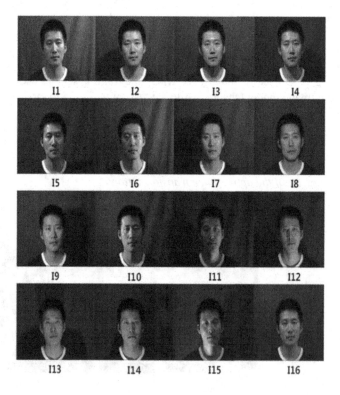

Figure 5.9.9. Example images of PF07 database

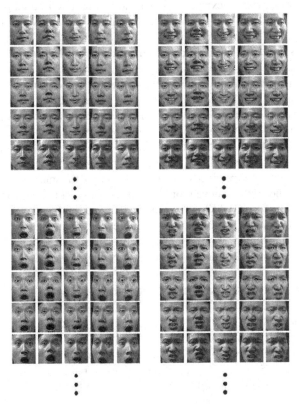

the algorithm confuses these two expressions. This means that the shape points of neutral expression and angry expression are also similar. Therefore, the low estimation rate of facial expression is not critical for the AAM fitting performance.

We compared the fitting performance of the conventional AAM and the tensor-based AAM. The fitting error is measured as the sum of squared error between the fitted shape points and the ground-truth shape points as

$$Error = \sqrt{\frac{1}{N}\sum_{i=1}^{N}\{(x_i^{fit} - x_i^g)^2 + (y_i^{fit} - y_i^g)^2\}},$$ (5.9.15)

where (x_i^{fit}, y_i^{fit}) is the i-th fitted shape point, (x_i^g, y_i^g) is the i-th ground-truth shape point, and N is the number of shape points.

Fig. 5.9.10 shows the fitting error of the conventional AAM and the tensor-based AAM. The fitting error of tensor-based AAM is lower than that of the conventional AAM for all five poses. Moreover, the fitting errors of conventional AAM for the upper, the down, the left, and the right poses are much higher than the tensor-based AAM. This explains that the single model of the conventional AAM can not cover all the pose variations.

Fig. 5.9.11 compares the fitting error of the conventional AAM and the tensor-based AAM with respect to different expressions. The horizontal line in each graph represents the mean fitting error of each algorithm. From this figure, we can see that the fitting error of the conventional AAM is higher than that of the tensor-based AAM, irrespective of the input facial expression. This means that the tensor-based AAM can fit the model to the input image well, even when the pose and expression of the input image are changed.

We also investigated the fitting convergence speed of the conventional AAM and the tensor-based AAM. Fig. 5.9.12 shows the change of average fitting error with respect to the iteration numbers. This figure shows that (1) the tensor-based AAM converges faster than the conventional AAM, (2) average fitting error of the tensor-based AAM is lower than conventional AAM.

Fig. 5.9.13 shows the histogram of the fitting errors of all face images in the test set, where the tensor-based AAM produces the smaller mean and the smaller standard deviation of fitting errors than those of the conventional AAM. This implies that the convergence characteristic of the tensor-based AAM is more stable than that of the conventional AAM.

Fig. 5.9.14 illustrates a typical example of fitted results. The subject is in left pose with anger facial expression under illumination I11. From this figure, we know that the tensor-based AAM converges more accurately than the conventional AAM.

5.9.4.3 Illumination-Robust Face Recognition

In this work, we prove the validity of the proposed tensor-based AAM by performing the illumination-robust face recognition, which requires only the appearance transformation. Since we only consider the illumination variation for the face recognition, we selected 800 training face images (= 50 subjects × 16 illuminations) at the frontal pose and the neutral expression to train the LDA and 800 test face images (= 50 subjects × 16 illuminations) to evaluate the face recognition performance, where the dimension of LDA subspace was selected such that it showed the best recognition rate over the test set for each recognition method. 800 test face images were divided into the gallery set and the probe set, where the gallery set consisted of 50 face images under no light condition (= 50 subjects × 1 illumination) and the probe set consisted of 750 face images under all other different illuminations (= 50 subjects × 15 illuminations). The face images were fitted by the conventional AAM or the tensor-based AAM, the AAM fitted face images were warped into the mean shape of the AAM, and the illuminations of the warped face images were transformed into the normal illumination (no light) which was the same as the illumination of gallery images.

We transformed the illuminated face images in the probe set into the face images without light. Fig. 5.9.15-(a) and Fig. 5.9.15-(b) show the examples of six different illumination transformations using the conventional AAM and the tensor-based AAM, respectively, where the first and second rows of each figure represent the original face images and its

Table 5.9.1. Estimation performance of image tensor

	Pose	Expression	Illumination
Recognition Rate	96.95	90.37	97.96

Figure 5.9.10. Fitting error of the conventional AAM and the tensor-based AAM

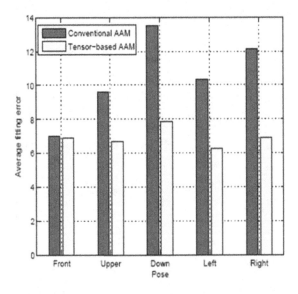

Figure 5.9.11. Fitting error of (a) the tensor-based AAM and (b) the conventional AAM

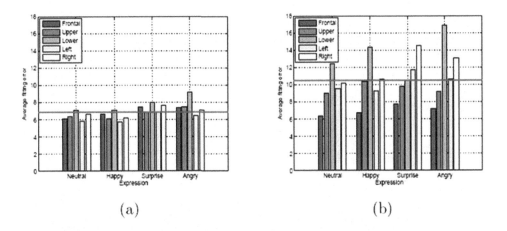

corresponding transformed face images, respectively. As shown in Fig. 5.9.15-(a) and (b), the transformed face images look similar from each other although the original face images have different illuminations, and the transformed images of using the tensor-based AAM are more natural and realistic than those of using the conventional AAM because the former produces the smaller residual errors than the latter due to their accurate fitting results.

Figure 5.9.12. The convergence speed of fitting errors

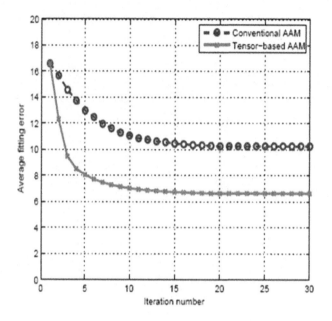

Figure 5.9.13. A histogram of fitting errors

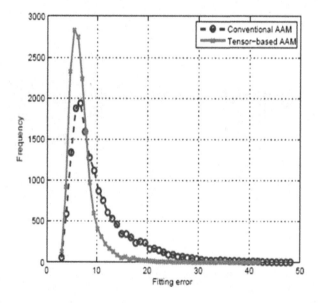

Figure 5.9.14. A typical example of fitted result

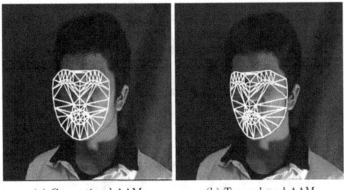

      (a) Conventional AAM   (b) Tensor-based AAM

5.9.4.4. Face Recognition Performance

We evaluated how the proposed tensor-based AAM affects the face recognition performance. For doing this, we performed many face recognition experiments with several different criteria: (1) two different fitting algorithms (the conventional AAM (CAAM) and the tensor-based AAM (TAAM)), (2) three different face recognition methods (the face recognition without the illumination transformation (NOTRANS), the face recognition with the illumination transformation (TRANS), and the face recognition using TensorFaces (TF) (Vasilescu, 2002b)), and (3) two different classification methods (the nearest neighbor method (NN) and the linear discriminant analysis followed by the neural networks (LDA+NN)).

The face recognition using the TensorFaces (TF) had been performed as follows. First, we stored the identity factors of all gallery images with the frontal pose, the neutral expression, and the normal illumination. Then, we defined the appearance basis subtensor from the appearance model tensor (Eq. (5.9.7)) as

$$\mathcal{B}_a(1,1,l) = \mathcal{Z}_a \times_2 \mathbf{W}_{pose}(1) \times_3 \mathbf{W}_{exp}(1) \times_4 \mathbf{W}_{ill}(l) \times_5 \mathbf{W}_{pixel}, \qquad (5.9.16)$$

where we set the pose and expression index to 1 and 1, respectively, because we only used the face images with the frontal pose and the neutral facial expression in this experiment. Then, we flattened $\mathcal{B}_a(1,1,l)$ along the pixel mode and obtained the appearance basis images $\mathbf{B}_{a(pixel)}(1,1,l)$. Next, we projected a probe image to the appearance basis images for every illumination index $l = 1,...,15$. Finally, we determined the identity of the probe image as the subject label of the identity factor that provides the smallest Euclidean distance between the identity factors of the probe image and the identity factors of the gallery images.

Table 5.9.2 shows the face recognition results of 12 possible recognition methods. From this table, we know that (1) the recognition results of using the TAAM outperforms those of using the CAAM because the TAAM has the smaller fitting error that results in more accurate face image alignment, (2) the recognition rates with the illumination transformations are the highest among three different face recognition methods, irrespective of

Figure 5.9.15. Examples of illumination transformations

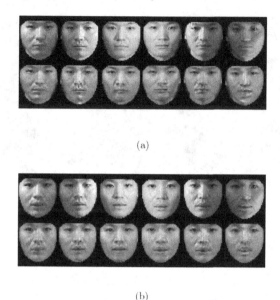

(a)

(b)

the fitting methods, (3) the face recognition results using TensorFaces show a very low recognition rate because we take the test face images that are not included in the training face image in this experiment, (4) the LDA+NN classification method outperforms the NN classification method in most cases, and (5) the recognition rate is the best when we use the TAAM as the fitting method, the TRANS as the recognition method, and the LDA+NN as the classification method.

Fig. 5.9.16 shows the recognition rates of three different face recognition methods with the tensor-based AAM fitting and the LDA+NN classification method, with respect to the illumination variation, where the horizontal axis represents the 15 different illumination conditions and the vertical axis represents the average recognition rate for the probe images. From this figure, we know that (1) the face recognition rates without the illumination transformation (NOTRANS) are higher than 70% when the probe images are illuminated by the upper or middle lights (I1 to I10), but they are dropped to 20% when the probe images are illuminated by the lower lights (I11 to I15), (2) the face recognition rates with the illumination transformation (TRANS) are always higher than the recognition rates without the illumination transformation (NOTRAN) and they are not changed much with respect to the illumination conditions, and (3) the recognition rates using TensorFaces are the lowest among three different face recognition methods irrespective of the illumination conditions.

Fig. 5.9.17 shows the face recognition rates in terms of the cumulative match characteristic (CMC) curve. From this figure, we know that the face recognition rate of the proposed tensor-based AAM outperforms that of using the conventional AAM, irrespective of the face recognition methods and the classification methods.

In the previous experimental results, the face recognition rate using TF is very low compared to other face recognition methods. Thus, for fair comparison, we changed the

Table 5.9.2. Face recognition results

Fitting Methods	Face Recognition Methods	Classification Methods	Recognition Rate
CAAM	No Transformation	NN	33
		LDA+NN	71.38
	Transformation	NN	64.5
		LDA+NN	80.88
	Tensor Face	NN	16.75
		LDA+NN	15.88
TAAM	No Transformation	NN	35.63
		LDA+NN	73.25
	Transformation	NN	68.75
		LDA+NN	86.62
	Tensor Face	NN	15.25
		LDA+NN	14.55

experimental setting to the similar way with M. Vasilescu and D. Terzopoulos (Vasilescu, 2002b). We used the face images of all the subjects in the test set under illumination I2, I4, I6, I8, I10, I12, I14, and I16 as the gallery image set and the remaining images as the probe image set. The 400 gallery images (= 50 subjects × 8 illuminations) are used to construct the tensor for TF. The face recognition results using this data setting is shown in table 5.9.3. From this table, we know that (1) although the recognition rate using TF is increased, the recognition rate for all other face recognition methods are also increased and (2) the face recognition rate is still the best when we use the TAAM as the fitting method, the TRANS as the recognition method, and the LDA+NN as the classification method. Consequently, we can say that our proposed method always outperforms the TF, irrespective of the data setting.

5.10 FACE RECOGNITION USING 3D MM

Recently, many researchers have been interested in the human face analysis such as face detection, face recognition and facial expression recognition. To conduct the researched in these topics, we need to perform the face modeling and the fitting method of the model to the input image. There are two kinds of face modelings: the 2D face modeling and the 3D face modeling.

There are many approaches such as the active contour models (ACMs), the active shape models (ASMs) and the active appearance models (AAMs) in the 2D face modeling. ACMs are usually defined by the energy-minimizing spline guided by the external constraint forces and influenced by the image forces that pull it toward the features such as lines and edges (Kass et. al., 1987a; Kass et. al., 1987b). However, the ACMs are only used to extract the facial contour of frontal-view faces and the performance crucially de-

Figure 5.9.16. Comparison of the face recognition rates with respect to the illumination variation

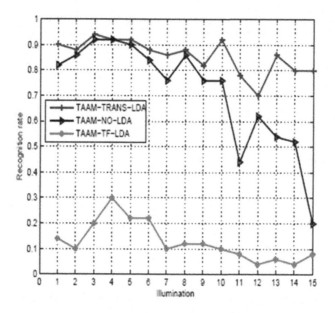

Figure 5.9.17. Cumulative recognition rates of each recognition method

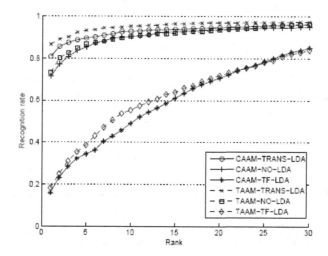

pends on the weight in the energy function, for which manual parameters tuning may be inevitable in many applications. To overcome these problems, ASMs have been developed to characterize a class of objects by learning a training set of correctly annotated images and the new shapes of objects can be represented by a weighted sum of a small number of significant 3D shape basis vectors (Cootes et. al., 1994; Cootes and Edwards, 1995). This allows the main facial features to be located and a set of shape and gray-level appearance parameters to be recovered.

However, the linear characteristics of ASMs limit their application to the small range of shape variations. AAMs contain the shape and texture model, where the shape model is a moderate level of complexity and easy to control when compared to the anatomical model where shape is controlled by the activation level of attached muscles. AAMs have the efficient fitting methods that are suitable for the real-time applications as the inverse compositional simultaneous update (ICSU) (Gross et. al., 2003) and the inverse compositional project out (ICPO) (Matthews and Baker, 2004). They do not fulfill the two requirements such as the stability and the operating speed at the same time because the ICSU is stable but slow and the ICPO is fast but unsTable The above 2D-based face modeling and their fitting methods still have the limitations that the face modelings are not robust to the pose and illumination variations and the fitting methods are unstable and inaccurate for representing the input facial images.

To reduce these limitations, many researchers have proposed the 3D face models whose shape or texture can be controlled by a compact set of parameters, where the shape of the face controlled by the linear models (Ahlberg, 2001; Gokturk et. al., 2002; Gong and Liddell, 2001) or the activation of the face muscles attached to the face models (Essa and Pentland, 1997; Terzopoulos and Waters, 1990). In general, the 3D face models enable us to model the physical imaging process in the real world, which require a huge amount of computation time due to the large number of vertices of 3D mesh for describing the texture model and several factors related to imaging process such as the direction and the brightness of light sources. For example, the 3D Morphable Models (MMs) use the most detailed 3D shape consisting of thousands of vertices and linear texture.

In the 3D MMs, there are two famous fitting methods such as a stochastic Newton optimization (SNO) (Blanz and Vetter, 1999) and an inverse compositional image alignment (ICIA) (Romdhani and Vetter, 2003). The SNO is based on the forward additive method

Table 5.9.3. Face recognition results for another data setting

Fitting Methods	Face Recognition Methods	Classification Methods	Recognition Rate
CAAM	No Transformation	NN	42
		LDA+NN	84
	Transformation	NN	86
		LDA+NN	92.25
	Tensor Face	NN	71.75
		LDA+NN	81.13
TAAM	No Transformation	NN	56.5
		LDA+NN	86.5
	Transformation	NN	92
		LDA+NN	94.37
	Tensor Face	NN	83
		LDA+NN	86.75

of the Lucas-Kanade image registration method (Lucas and Kanade, 1981; Baker and Matthews, 2002) that aligns the template image to an image warped back onto the coordinate frame of the template by minimizing the error function. It requires a huge amount of computation time because it is necessary to compute the Jacobian and Hessian matrices of the warping function

$$\frac{\partial \mathbf{W}(\mathbf{x};\mathbf{p})}{\partial \mathbf{p}}$$

at the pixel coordinate $\mathbf{x} = (x, y)^T$ every iteration. On the other hand, the ICIA is based on the inverse composition method of the LK image registration (Baker and Matthews, 2002; Baker and Matthews, 2001, Baker eta al, 2004). It is a time-efficient method because the Jacobian and the Hessian matrices of the warping function are pre-computed once for all iterations by switching the role of the input image and the template. Despite this time-efficiency, the ICIA took about 30 seconds (Romdhani and Vetter, 2003), which makes the real-time applications impossible.

To reduce the computation time of the existing ICIA fitting method, we propose a fast hierarchical ICIA fitting method for 3D MMs that guarantees the more efficient and accurate fitting performance. It requires a set of multi-resolution 3D face models and the Gaussian image pyramid of the input face image and the fitting has been performed hierarchically from the low resolution fitting to the high resolution fitting. To obtain the more accurate fitting, we take the two-stage parameter update where the motion and texture parameters are updated at the first stage and all parameters including the shape parameters are updated after the convergence of the first stage. We also use the revised modified census transform (RMCT)-based face detector (Jun and Kim, 2007) to obtain the initial position of the faces in the input image automatically.

Fig. 5.10.1 shows an overall process of the proposed fast hierarchical ICIA fitting method, which consists of two processes: the 3D face model construction and the the hierarchical ICIA fitting method. The 3D face model construction consists of 5 steps: (1) Align 3D face data in the training set using the ICP (Iterative Closest Point) algorithm (Besl and McKay, 1992), (2) Find the correspondences among the aligned 3D face data using the Gaussian pyramid-based optical flows (Horn and Schunck, 1981), (3) Align the shapes of the 3D face data using the Procrustes Analysis (Cootes et. al., 2001), (4) Construct the 3D shape basis vectors and the 3D texture basis images using the PCA, and (5) Construct the multi-resolution 3D face models (3D shape and 3D texture models) by sub-sampling.

The hierarchical ICIA fitting method consists of 5 steps: (1) generate the Gaussian face image pyramid by the smoothing and the sub-sampling, (2) perform the first layer fitting of the level-1 3D face model to the level-1 face image using the initial parameters $\boldsymbol{\alpha}^0 = \mathbf{0}$, $\boldsymbol{\beta}^0 = \mathbf{0}$, and $\boldsymbol{\rho}^0$ obtained from the face detection result, (3) perform the second layer fitting of the level-2 3D face model to the level-2 face image using the parameters obtained from the 1st layer fitting result as $\boldsymbol{\alpha}^0 = \boldsymbol{\alpha}^*_{level-1}$, $\boldsymbol{\beta}^0 = \boldsymbol{\beta}^*_{level-1}$, and $\boldsymbol{\rho}^0 = \boldsymbol{\rho}^*_{level-1}$, (4) perform the third layer fitting of the level-3 3D face model to the level-3 face image using the parameters obtained from the second layer fitting result as $\boldsymbol{\alpha}^0 = \boldsymbol{\alpha}^*_{level-2}$, $\boldsymbol{\beta}^0 = \boldsymbol{\beta}^*_{level-2}$, and $\boldsymbol{\rho}^0 = \boldsymbol{\rho}^*_{level-2}$, and (5) obtain the 3D synthesized face image using the fitted parameters.

5.10.1 Fitting Methods

The fitting method performs the matching of the 3DMM to a 2D face image and seeks the parameters of the 3DMM that expresses the mean texture image in the reference frame as close to the input image as possible. It can be formulated by searching the shape and texture parameters of the 3DMM that minimizes the error function as

$$E_I = \sum_{x,y} \left\| \mathbf{I}_{input}(x, y) - \mathbf{I}_{model}(x, y) \right\|^2. \tag{5.10.1}$$

There are two well-known fitting methods for 3D MMs : *Stochastic Newton Optimization (SNO)* (Blanze and Vetter, 1999) and *Inverse Compositional Image Alignment (ICIA)* (Romdhani and Vetter, 2003). They aim to find the model parameters **α, ρ** and **β** that explain an input face image by a *Maximum a Posteriori (MAP)* estimator which maximizes $p(\mathbf{\alpha}, \mathbf{\rho}, \mathbf{\beta} \mid \mathbf{I}_{input})$. Thanks to the Bayes rule, the posterior probability can be represented as

$$p(\mathbf{\alpha}, \mathbf{\rho}, \mathbf{\beta} \mid \mathbf{I}_{input}) \sim p(\mathbf{I}_{input} \mid \mathbf{\alpha}, \mathbf{\rho}, \mathbf{\beta}) \cdot p(\mathbf{\alpha}) \cdot p(\mathbf{\rho}) \cdot p(\mathbf{\beta}), \tag{5.10.2}$$

Figure 5.10.1. An overall process of the proposed hierarchical ICIA fitting algorithm

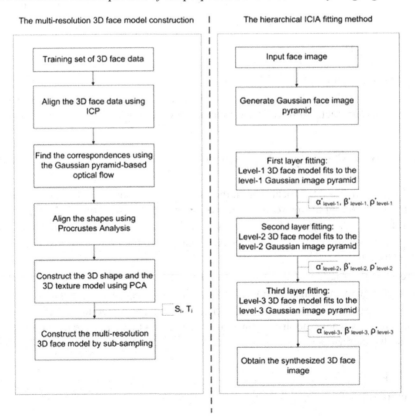

where $p(\mathbf{I}_{input}\mid\boldsymbol{\alpha},\boldsymbol{\rho},\boldsymbol{\beta})$ is the likelihood, and $p(\boldsymbol{\alpha})$, $p(\boldsymbol{\rho})$, and $p(\boldsymbol{\beta})$ are the prior probabilities of the shape, texture, and rigid parameter, respectively. The prior probabilities of $p(\boldsymbol{\alpha})$ and $p(\boldsymbol{\beta})$ are given by the process of the building 3D face model by PCA, and the prior probability of $p(\boldsymbol{\rho})$ is assumed to be a Gaussian distribution.

The SNO fitting method provides a more accurate fitting result but takes a huge amount of computation time because the Jacobian and the Hessian matrices should be re-computed every iteration and a subset of the vertices is randomly chosen to avoid to being trapped into the local minimum. According to the experiment results by V. Blanz and T. Vetter, the fitting procedure in the SNO fitting method required 10^5 iterations and took about 50 minutes (Blanz and Vetter, 1999). The ICIA fitting method is more computationally efficient than the SNO fitting method because the Jacobian and the Hessian matrices are pre-computed once (Gross et. al., 2003; Matthews andBaker, 2004; Baker and Matthews, 2002; Baker et. al., 2004) and the necessary portion corresponding to the visible vertices is selected at each iteration (Romdhani and Vetter, 2003). A detailed derivation of the ICIA fitting method for the 3DMM is given in (Romdahni and Vetter, 2003; Romdhnai et. al., 2002).

5.10.1.1 3D Shape Model and its Inverse

In the 3D MMs, the 3D shape of an object is defined by a mapping function $s(u,v)$ that maps the (u,v) coordinate system into the three-dimensional (x,y,z) coordinate system and is modeled by a linear combination of modes of variations $\mathbf{S}_k$ that are obtained by applying PCA on a set of training shapes as

$$\mathbf{S}_{3\times N_v} = \mathbf{S}_0 + \sum_{i=k}^{N_s}\alpha_k\cdot\mathbf{S}_k,\qquad(5.10.3)$$

where N_s is the number of shape dimensions.

Then, the projection of the vertices of a 3D shape $\mathbf{S}_{3\times N_v}$ to the 2D image frame (x,y) using the weak-perspective projection is computed as

$$\mathbf{P}_{2\times N_v} = f\cdot\mathbf{R}_{2\times3}\cdot(\mathbf{S}_0 + \sum_{i=k}^{N_s}\alpha_k\cdot\mathbf{S}_k) + \mathbf{t}_{2\times1}\cdot\mathbf{1}_{1\times N_v},\qquad(5.10.4)$$

where f, $\mathbf{R}$ and $\mathbf{t}$ are the focal length, the rotation matrix, and the translation, respectively. In the remaining of this section, the weak-perspective projection is denoted by the function $\mathbf{P}=\mathbf{p}(u,v;;\boldsymbol{\alpha},\boldsymbol{\rho})$. After projecting the 3D shape to the 2D image coordinate, only N_w vertices among the N_v vertices are visible and the domain of visible vertices is denoted by $\Omega(\boldsymbol{\alpha},\boldsymbol{\rho})$.

To recover the shape and the projection parameters from $\mathbf{P}_{2\times N_v}$, the inverse shape projection that maps an image point (x,y) on the 2D image frame to an vertex point (u,v) on the reference frame is needed. The inverse shape projection is defined as the following property where the shape projection composed with its inverse projection shape is equal to the identity as

$$\mathbf{p}(u,v;;\boldsymbol{\alpha},\boldsymbol{\rho})\circ\mathbf{p}^{-1}(x,y;;\boldsymbol{\alpha},\boldsymbol{\rho}) = (x,y),$$
$$\mathbf{p}^{-1}(x,y;;\boldsymbol{\alpha},\boldsymbol{\rho})\circ\mathbf{p}(u,v;;\boldsymbol{\alpha},\boldsymbol{\rho}) = (u,v)\qquad(5.10.5)$$

It is difficult to express $\mathbf{p}^{-1}$ as a function of $\mathbf{p}$ because the shape is discrete. But it can be computed using the triangle list: the 2D image point (x, y) lies in a single triangle under the projection $p(u, v, \boldsymbol{\alpha}, \boldsymbol{\rho})$. Thus, the vertex point (u, v) under the inverse projection $\mathbf{p}^{-1}(x, y; ; \boldsymbol{\alpha}, \boldsymbol{\rho})$ has the same relative position in this triangle on the reference frame. Fig. 5.10.2 shows how the inverse projection recovers the vertex point (u, v) on the reference frame that corresponds a 2D image point (x, y) on the image frame.

The shape and projection parameters are recovered from $\mathbf{P}_{2 \times N_v}$ using a novel Kernel-based selective method (Romdhani et. al., 2002), where the projection parameters $\boldsymbol{\rho}$ are estimated first by the least square estimator and then the shape parameters $\boldsymbol{\alpha}$ are obtained by inverting Eq. (5.10.5) using the estimated projection parameters.

5.10.1.2 3D Texture Model and its Inverse

In the 3D MMs, the texture of an object is defined by a mapping function $t(u, v)$ that maps the (u, v) coordinate system into the RGB color space and is modeled by a linear combination of modes of variations $\mathbf{T}_k$ that are obtained by applying PCA on a set of training textures as

$$\mathbf{t}(u, v; ; \boldsymbol{\beta}) = \mathbf{T}_{3 \times N_v} = \mathbf{T}_0 + \sum_{i=k}^{N_t} \beta_k \cdot \mathbf{T}_k, \tag{5.10.6}$$

where N_t is the number of texture dimensions.

Similarly, the inverse texture is defined is defined as the following property where the texture mapping composed with its inverse texture under the same texture parameters $\boldsymbol{\beta}$ is equal to the mean texture as

$$\mathbf{t}^{-1}(\mathbf{t}(u, v); ; \boldsymbol{\beta}) = \mathbf{t}(u, v; ; \boldsymbol{\beta}) - \sum_{k=1}^{N_t} \beta_k \mathbf{T}_k, \tag{5.10.7}$$

The image of an object is synthesized by warping a texture from the reference frame to the image frame using a shape projection as

Figure 5.10.2. The inverse shape projection

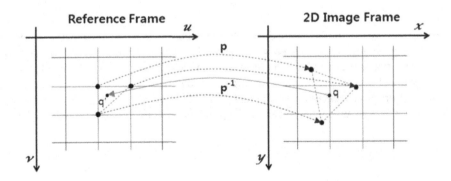

$$\mathbf{I}(x,y;;\boldsymbol{\alpha},\boldsymbol{\rho},\boldsymbol{\beta}) = \mathbf{t}(u,v;;\boldsymbol{\beta}) \circ \mathbf{p}^{-1}(x,y;;\boldsymbol{\alpha},\boldsymbol{\rho}).$$

(5.10.8)

5.10.1.3 3D ICIA Fitting Method

In the 3D ICIA fitting method, the cost function E_I is an iteratively minimized log-likelihood that is the sum of the squares of the difference between the model texture and the image texture defined in the reference frame (u,v) as

(5.10.9)

$$
\begin{aligned}
E_I(\Delta\boldsymbol{\alpha},\Delta\boldsymbol{\rho},\Delta\boldsymbol{\beta},\boldsymbol{\alpha}^d,\boldsymbol{\rho}^d,\boldsymbol{\alpha}^t,\boldsymbol{\rho}^t,\boldsymbol{\beta}^t,\mathbf{I}) &= -2logp(\mathbf{I}\mid\boldsymbol{\alpha}^t,\boldsymbol{\rho}^t,\boldsymbol{\beta}^t) \\
&= \frac{1}{2\sigma_I^2}\cdot\sum_{u_i,v_i}[\mathbf{t}(u,v;\Delta\boldsymbol{\beta})\circ\mathbf{p}^{-1}(x,y;;\boldsymbol{\alpha}^d,\boldsymbol{\rho}^d)\circ\mathbf{p}(u_i,v_i;;\boldsymbol{\alpha}^d+\Delta\boldsymbol{\alpha},\boldsymbol{\rho}^d+\Delta\boldsymbol{\rho}) \\
&\qquad\qquad\qquad -\mathbf{t}^{-1}(\mathbf{I}(x,y)\circ\mathbf{p}(u_i,v_i;;\boldsymbol{\alpha}^t,\boldsymbol{\rho}^t);;\boldsymbol{\beta}^t)]^2,
\end{aligned}
$$

where the superscripted parameters by d refer to the parameters at which the derivatives are computed, the parameters $\boldsymbol{\alpha}^t$, $\boldsymbol{\rho}^t$, and $\boldsymbol{\beta}^t$ are the current shape, motion, and texture parameters, respectively, and $\Omega(\boldsymbol{\alpha}^d,\boldsymbol{\rho}^d)$ is a set of the visible vertices. Here, the first and second terms in the summation are the model texture that is the result of a texture update with respect to the parameters $\Delta\boldsymbol{\beta}$ composed with a shape projection update with respect to the parameters $\Delta\boldsymbol{\alpha}$ and $\Delta\boldsymbol{\rho}$ and the image mean texture that removes the modes of texture variations by the inverse texture using the current texture parameters $\boldsymbol{\beta}^t$, respectively.

To obtain the updates of the model parameters, we need to compute the derivatives of the ICIA cost function with respect to the shape parameters $\Delta\boldsymbol{\alpha}$, the projection parameters $\Delta\boldsymbol{\rho}$, and the texture parameters $\Delta\boldsymbol{\beta}$ at the condition $(0,0,0,\boldsymbol{\alpha}^d,\boldsymbol{\rho}^d,\boldsymbol{\alpha}^t,\boldsymbol{\rho}^t,\boldsymbol{\beta}^t)$.

First, the derivative with respect to the shape parameters $\Delta\dot{\mathbf{a}}$ is computed as

$$
\frac{\partial E_I}{\partial\Delta\rho_k} = \sum_i \frac{\partial\big(\mathbf{t}(u,v;0)\circ\mathbf{p}^{-1}(x,y;\boldsymbol{\alpha}^d,\boldsymbol{\rho}^d)\circ\mathbf{p}(u_i,v_i;\boldsymbol{\alpha}^d+\Delta\boldsymbol{\alpha},\boldsymbol{\rho}^d)\big)}{\partial\Delta\alpha_k}\bigg|_{\Delta\boldsymbol{\alpha}=0}^{T}
$$

$$
\begin{aligned}
&\cdot[\mathbf{t}(u,v;0)\circ\mathbf{p}^{-1}(x,y;\boldsymbol{\alpha}^d,\boldsymbol{\rho}^d)\circ\mathbf{p}(u_i,v_i;\boldsymbol{\alpha}^d,\boldsymbol{\rho}^d) \\
&\qquad\qquad -\mathbf{t}^{-1}(\mathbf{I}(x,y)\circ\mathbf{p}(u_i,v_i;\boldsymbol{\alpha}^t,\boldsymbol{\rho}^t);\boldsymbol{\beta}^t)],
\end{aligned}
$$

(5.10.10)

where the first term is the Jacobian $\mathbf{J}^s$ of the shape parameters that are constant at every iteration because it depends only on $\boldsymbol{\alpha}^d$ and $\boldsymbol{\rho}^d$. The second term is the texture error at the ith vertex that is the difference between the mean texture of the 3D face model and the image texture obtained by the inverse texture mapped with the current texture parameters. This texture error term becomes zero at its optimum.

Second, the derivative with respect to the projection parameters $\Delta\boldsymbol{\rho}$ is computed as

$$\frac{\partial E_I}{\partial \Delta \rho_k} = \sum_i \frac{\partial \left(\mathbf{t}(u,v;0) \circ \mathbf{p}^{-1}\left(x,y;\boldsymbol{\alpha}^d,\boldsymbol{\rho}^d\right) \circ \mathbf{p}\left(u_i,v_i;\boldsymbol{\alpha}^d,\boldsymbol{\rho}^d+\Delta\boldsymbol{\rho}\right)\right)}{\partial \Delta \rho_k} \Big|_{\Delta \boldsymbol{\rho}=0}^{T}$$

$$\cdot [\mathbf{t}(u,v;0) \circ \mathbf{p}^{-1}(x,y;\boldsymbol{\alpha}^d,\boldsymbol{\rho}^d) \circ \mathbf{p}(u_i,v_i;\boldsymbol{\alpha}^d,\boldsymbol{\rho}^d)$$
$$- \mathbf{t}^{-1}(\mathbf{I}(x,y) \circ \mathbf{p}(u_i,v_i;\boldsymbol{\alpha}^t,\boldsymbol{\rho}^t);\boldsymbol{\beta}^t)],$$

(5.10.11)

where the first term is the Jacobian $\mathbf{J}^r$ of the projection parameters that are constant at every iteration because it depends only on $\boldsymbol{\rho}^d$.

Third, the derivative with respect to the texture parameters $\Delta\boldsymbol{\beta}$ is computed as

$$\frac{\partial E_I}{\partial \Delta \beta_k} = \sum_i \frac{\partial (\mathbf{t}(u,v;\Delta\boldsymbol{\beta}) \circ \mathbf{p}^{-1}(x,y;\boldsymbol{\alpha}^d,\boldsymbol{\rho}^d) \circ \mathbf{p}(u_i,v_i;\boldsymbol{\alpha}^d,\boldsymbol{\rho}^d))}{\partial \Delta \beta_k} \Big|_{\Delta\boldsymbol{\beta}=0}^{T}$$

$$\cdot [\mathbf{t}(u,v;0) \circ \mathbf{p}^{-1}(x,y;\boldsymbol{\alpha}^d,\boldsymbol{\rho}^d) \circ \mathbf{p}(u_i,v_i;\boldsymbol{\alpha}^d,\boldsymbol{\rho}^d)$$
$$- \mathbf{t}^{-1}(\mathbf{I}(x,y) \circ \mathbf{p}(u_i,v_i;\boldsymbol{\alpha}^t,\boldsymbol{\rho}^t);\boldsymbol{\beta}^t)],$$

(5.10.12)

where the first term is the Jacobian $\mathbf{J}^t$ of the texture parameters that are equal to the basis texture images of the texture model: $\mathbf{J}^t_{,k} = vec(\mathbf{T}_k)$.

The Jacobian matrices of the shape, motion, and texture parameters are combined and denoted as $\mathbf{J} = [\mathbf{J}^s \mathbf{J}^r \mathbf{J}^t]$. Then, the increments of the model parameters are computed by the Gauss-Newton formula as

$$\begin{pmatrix} \Delta\boldsymbol{\alpha} \\ \Delta\boldsymbol{\rho} \\ \Delta\boldsymbol{\beta} \end{pmatrix} = -\mathbf{H}^{-1} \cdot \mathbf{J}^T \cdot \mathbf{E},$$

(5.10.13)

where $\mathbf{H}$ is the Hessian matrix that is defined by $\mathbf{H} = \mathbf{J}^T \cdot \mathbf{J}$. After obtaining the increments of the model parameters, they are updated by the following procedures. First, the shape projection is updated using the increments of the shape and projection parameters as

$$\mathbf{p}^{t+1}(u_i,v_i) = \mathbf{p}(u,v;\boldsymbol{\alpha}^t,\boldsymbol{\rho}^t) \circ \mathbf{p}^{-1}(x,y;\boldsymbol{\alpha}^d,\boldsymbol{\rho}^d) \circ \mathbf{p}(u_i,v_i;\boldsymbol{\alpha}^d+\Delta\boldsymbol{\alpha},\boldsymbol{\rho}^d+\Delta\boldsymbol{\rho})$$

(5.10.14)

Second, the updated shape parameters $\boldsymbol{\alpha}^{t+1}$ and the updated projection parameters $\boldsymbol{\rho}^{t+1}$ are obtained from the Kernel-based selective method (Romdhan et. al., 2002). Third, the texture parameters are updated by the additive manner as $\boldsymbol{\beta}^{t+1} = \boldsymbol{\beta}^t + \Delta\boldsymbol{\beta}$. Table 5.10.1 summarizes the overall procedure of the ICIA fitting method.

5.10.2 The Proposed Hierarchial ICIA Fitting Method

Although the ICIA fitting method is time-efficient due to the pre-computation of the derivatives such as the Jacobian and the Hessian matrices in the initial step, it still requires
a lot of computation time ($\approx$ 30 seconds) for the 3DMM fitting by the following reasons
(Romdhani et. al., 2003) (1) we handle thousands of vertices in the 3D MMs, (2) we need
to select the visible vertices at each iteration, and (3) we need to change the Jacobian
matrix by adding the new vertices and discarding the invisible vertices accordingly and
re-compute the Hessian matrices at each iteration. Although we pre-compute the Jacobian
and Hessian matrices corresponding to all possible vertices due to the immutability of the
3D MMs, we need to select the visible vertices among all possible vertices at each iteration, and modify the Jacobian matrix and re-compute the Hessian matrix according to the
selected visible vertices.

The computation time complexity for the 3DMM fitting of the existing ICIA fitting
method is $O((N_s + N_t) \cdot N_v + N_v \log N_v + (N_s + N_t)^2 \cdot N_v)$, where N_s, N_t, and
N_v are the dimension of the shape model, the dimension of the texture model and the
number of the visible vertices, respectively, and the first terms are due to the update of the
shape and texture parameters, the second term is due to the computation of the median of
absolute deviations (MAD) which is necessary for sorting the residuals to designate the
outliers, and the third term is due to the re-computation of the Hessian matrix. As you can
see the time complexity of the ICIA fitting algorithm, we need to reduce the number of
visible vertices as many as possible to reduce the overall fitting time. To meet this requirement, we propose the hierarchical ICIA fitting method that uses a set of multi-resolution
3D face models and the Gaussian image pyramid of the input face image, where each 3D
face model has the different number of vertices.

5.10.2.1 Multi-Resolution 3D Face Models

The multi-resolution 3D face models are constructed by sub-sampling the model shape $\mathbf{S}$
that is formed by the mean shape $\mathbf{S}_0$ and the shape basis vectors $\{\mathbf{S}_k, k = 1,2,\cdots,N_s\}$,
as well as the model texture $\mathbf{T}$ that is formed by the mean texture $\mathbf{T}_0$ and the texture basis
images $\{\mathbf{T}_k, k = 1,2,\cdots,N_t\}$. The model shape $\mathbf{S}_{level-3}$ and the model texture $\mathbf{T}_{level-3}$
at the level-3 are merely the model shape $\mathbf{S}$ and the model texture $\mathbf{T}$, respectively, that
consists of 7,238 vertices with a size of 20 × 20. Then, the model shape and the model
texture at the layer-3 are sub-sampled at the 2:1 sampling rate to construct the model shape
$\mathbf{S}_{level-2}$ and the model texture $\mathbf{T}_{level-2}$, that consist of 1,807 vertices with a size of 10 ×
10. Next, the model shape and the model texture at the layer-2 are sub-sampled at the 2:1
sampling rate to construct the model shape $\mathbf{S}_{level-1}$ and the model texture $\mathbf{T}_{level-1}$, that
consist of 452 vertices with a size of 50 × 50. Table 5.10.2 summarizes the overall procedure
of constructing the proposed multi-resolution 3D face models.

Fig. 5.10.3 illustrates how the three level 3D face models are constructed, where the
first, second, and third columns represent the 3D mean faces, the mean shapes, and the
mean textures, respectively.

Table 5.10.1. The overall process of ICIA fitting algorithm

Procedure$ICIA\_fitting($**I**, **S**, **T**, $\boldsymbol{\alpha}^0, \boldsymbol{\rho}^0, \boldsymbol{\beta}^0$)

$t = 0$

Set the initial parameters:
$\boldsymbol{\alpha}^t = \boldsymbol{\alpha}^0, \boldsymbol{\rho}^t = \boldsymbol{\rho}^0, \boldsymbol{\beta}^t = \boldsymbol{\beta}^0, \mathbf{e}^{old} = \infty$.

Iterate:
Compute the current shape projection $\mathbf{I}(x, y) \circ \mathbf{p}(u, v; \boldsymbol{\alpha}^t, \boldsymbol{\rho}^t)$.
Compute the texture error $\mathbf{E}^t = \mathbf{t}(u, v; \mathbf{0}) - \mathbf{t}^{-1}(\mathbf{I}(x, y) \circ \mathbf{p}(u, v; \boldsymbol{\alpha}^t, \boldsymbol{\rho}^t); \boldsymbol{\beta}^t)$.
  Check stop condition:

  If($(t > max\_iter)$ or $(|\mathbf{E}^{old} - \mathbf{E}^t| < E_h)$), Stop.
Compute the combined Jacobian matrix $\mathbf{J} = [\mathbf{J}^s \mathbf{J}^r \mathbf{J}^t]$.
Compute the Hessian matrix $\mathbf{H} = \mathbf{J}^T \cdot \mathbf{J}$.
Compute $\Delta\boldsymbol{\alpha}, \Delta\boldsymbol{\rho}, \Delta\boldsymbol{\beta}$ using Eq. (5.10.12).
Update $\boldsymbol{\alpha}^{t+1}, \boldsymbol{\rho}^{t+1}$ using the kernel-based selective method
                                        (Romdhani et. al., 2002).
Update $\boldsymbol{\beta}^{t+1} = \boldsymbol{\beta}^t + \Delta\boldsymbol{\beta}$.
$\mathbf{E}^{old} = \mathbf{E}^t$.
Set $t = t + 1$ and go to Iterate.
End

5.10.2.2 Gaussian Image Pyramid

We also generate the Gaussian image pyramid, which is a hierarchy of the low-pass filtered versions of the original image such that the successive level corresponds to the lower frequency image, where the low-pass filtering is conducted using the convolution with a Gaussian filter kernel. Fig. 5.10.4 illustrates a Gaussian pyramid image, where the base image $\mathbf{I}_{level-3}$ is the original input face image, the next level image $\mathbf{I}_{level-2}$ is formed by smoothing the base image, sub-sampling is conducted to obtain the image with a half of the number of pixels in each dimension, and the subsequent level image $\mathbf{I}_{level-1}$ is formed by further smoothing and sub-sampling.

Fig. 5.10.5 shows the example of the Gaussian image pyramid of an input face image, where Fig. 5.10.5 (a) is the original face image (level-3), Fig. 5.10.5 (b) is the sub-sampled image with a half of the number of pixels at the level-3, and Fig. 5.10.5 (c) is the sub-sampled image with a half of the number of pixels at the level-2.

5.10.2.3 Hierarchical ICIA Fitting Method

After generating the multi-resolution 3D face models and the Gaussian image pyramid of the input face image, we apply the proposed hierarchical ICIA fitting method. At the initialization, the ICIA fitting method requires the correspondences between some of the model vertices (typically 8) and the input face image (Romdhani and Vetter, 2003), which

Table 5.10.2. The overall procedure of constructing the multi-resolution 3D face models

---

(1) **Construct the level-3 3D face model.**

(2) **Construct the level-2 3D face model:**

  (a) **Subsample the mean face of the level-3 3D face model** by 2.

  (b) **Subsample the shape basis vectors and the texture basis images**
  using the indices that are obtained in the above mean face sub-sampling.

  (c) **Make a triangle list** for the level-2 face model.

  (d) **Compute the Jacobian matrices** of the shape and texture model parameters
  of the level-2 face model.

(3) **Construct the level-1 3D face model:**

  (a) **Subsample the mean face of the level-2 3D face model** by 2.

  (b) **Subsample the shape basis vectors and the texture basis images**
  using the indices that are obtained in the above mean face sub-sampling.

  (c) **Make a triangle list** for the level-1 face model.

  (d) **Compute the Jacobian matrices** of the shape and texture model parameters
  of the level-1 face model.

---

is provided manually. But the proposed fitting method tries an automatic initialization by aligning between the pre-designated eye's positions in the face model and the detected eye's positions by the RMCT-based face detector (Jun and Kim, 2007), where they are also used to compute the initial model parameters $\boldsymbol{\rho}^0$. Experimental results show that the fitting accuracy of using the automatic initialization is more accurate than that of using the manual initialization.

Table 5.10.3 shows the overall procedure of the proposed hierarchical ICIA fitting method: (1) we generate the Gaussian image pyramid $\mathbf{I}_{level-1}$, $\mathbf{I}_{level-2}$, and $\mathbf{I}_{level-3}$ from the input face image, (2) we detect the face and eyes using the RMCT-based face detector, (3) we obtain the initial model parameters $\boldsymbol{\rho}^0$ by using the pre-designated eye positions of the face model and the detected eye positions, (4) we set the initial shape and texture parameters as $\boldsymbol{\alpha}^0 = \mathbf{0}$ and $\boldsymbol{\beta}^0 = \mathbf{0}$, (5) we perform the first layer ICIA fitting process using the face image $\mathbf{I}_{level-1}$, the model texture $\mathbf{T}_{level-1}$, and the model parameters $\boldsymbol{\alpha}^0$, $\boldsymbol{\rho}^0$, and $\boldsymbol{\beta}^0$, (6) we set the model parameters obtained from the first layer ICIA fitting results as the initial model parameters for the second layer ICIA fitting as $\boldsymbol{\alpha}^0 = \boldsymbol{\alpha}^*_{level-1}, \boldsymbol{\rho}^0 = \boldsymbol{\rho}^*_{level-1}$, and $\boldsymbol{\beta}^0 = \boldsymbol{\beta}^*_{level-1}$, where the superscript * implies the parameter value after the ICIA fitting, (7) we perform the second layer ICIA fitting process using the face image $\mathbf{I}_{level-2}$, the model texture $\mathbf{T}_{level-2}$, and the re-computed model parameters $\boldsymbol{\alpha}^0$, $\boldsymbol{\rho}^0$, and $\boldsymbol{\beta}^0$, (8) we set the model parameters obtained from the second layer ICIA fitting results as the initial model parameters for the third layer ICIA fitting as $\boldsymbol{\alpha}^0 = \boldsymbol{\alpha}^*_{level-2}, \boldsymbol{\rho}^0 = \boldsymbol{\rho}^*_{level-2}$, and $\boldsymbol{\beta}^0 = \boldsymbol{\beta}^*_{level-2}$, (9) we perform the third layer ICIA fitting process using the face image $\mathbf{I}_{level-3}$, the model texture $\mathbf{T}_{level-3}$, and the model parameters $\boldsymbol{\alpha}^0$, $\boldsymbol{\rho}^0$, and $\boldsymbol{\beta}^0$, and (10) we obtain the synthesized face image using the obtained model parameters $\boldsymbol{\alpha}^*_{level-3}, \boldsymbol{\rho}^*_{level-3}$, and $\boldsymbol{\beta}^*_{level-3}$ as $\mathbf{S} = \mathbf{S}_0 + \sum_{i=1}^{i=N_s} \boldsymbol{\alpha}^*_{level-3,i} \cdot \mathbf{S}_i$ and $\mathbf{T} = \mathbf{T}_0 + \sum_{i=1}^{i=N_t} \boldsymbol{\beta}^*_{level-3,i} \cdot \mathbf{T}_i$.

Figure 5.10.3. Construction of the multi-resolution 3D face models

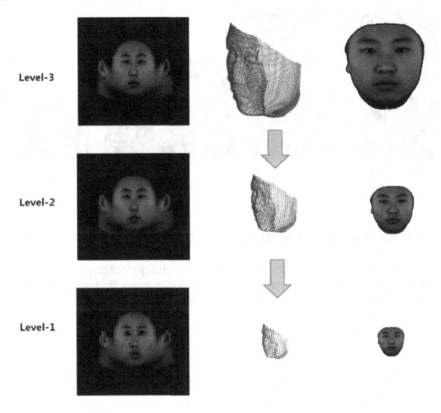

Level-3

Level-2

Level-1

Figure 5.10.4. An example of Gaussian pyramid image

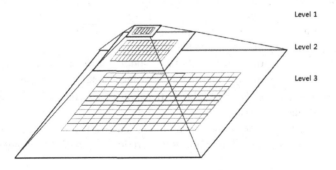

Level 1

Level 2

Level 3

Figure 5.10.5. An Gaussian image pyramid of the input face image

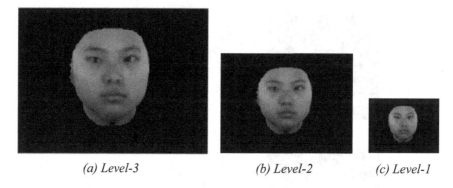

| (a) Level-3 | (b) Level-2 | (c) Level-1 |

5.10.3 Experimental Results and Discussion

We have performed several experiments that showed the validity of the proposed hierarchical fitting method. We define some performance measures to evaluate the fitting performance such as the normalized correlation and the root mean squared error (RMSE). First, we define the normalized correlation as

$$C = \frac{\boldsymbol{\alpha}^T \cdot \widetilde{\boldsymbol{\alpha}}}{\|\boldsymbol{\alpha}\| \cdot \|\widetilde{\boldsymbol{\alpha}}\|} ,$$

(5.10.15)

where $\acute{\mathbf{a}}$ and $\widetilde{\mathbf{a}}$ are are the ground truth model parameters and the recovered model parameters after the 3DMM fitting, respectively. Second, we define the root mean squared error (RMSE) as the average distance between the ground truth shape (or texture) and the fitted shape (or texture).

All experiments have been conducted on the desktop PC that consists of a Pentium IV CPU with a clock speed of 3GHZ, a 4GB RAM, Window XP professional x64 Edition, and C++ and OpenCV development tools.

5.10.3.1 Database

We used the BJUT-3D Face Database (BJUT-3D DB, 2005), which included 500 Chinese people (250 males and 250 females whose ages are between 16 and 49) and their facial expression is natural without the glasses or other accessories. Fig. 5.10.6 shows some typical 3D face images in the BJUT-3D Face Database.

We constructed the multi-resolution 3D face models for the proposed hierarchical fitting method using the 50 manually landmarked 3D face images and mapped the 3D face models to the reference frame (u, v). Table 5.10.4 shows the structural information of the multi-resolution 3D face models.

For conducting the experiments, we need the ground-truth facial images whose model parameters are known. To meet this requirement, we took 50 3D facial images that were

Table 5.10.3. The overall procedure of the hierarchical ICIA fitting method

---

ProcedureHierarchical_**ICIA_fitting**($\mathbf{I}$)

(1) Generate the Gaussian image pyramid from the input image $\mathbf{I}$:

$\mathbf{I}_{level-1}$, $\mathbf{I}_{level-2}$, $\mathbf{I}_{level-3}$.

(2) Detect a face and eyes using the face detector.

(3) Compute the initial parameter $\boldsymbol{\rho}^0$ using the detected two eye positions.

(4) Set the initial parameters for the first layer ICIA fitting:

$\boldsymbol{\alpha}^0 = \mathbf{0}, \boldsymbol{\beta}^0 = \mathbf{0}.$

(5) Perform the first layer ICIA fitting:

$ICIA\_fitting(\mathbf{I}_{level-1}, \mathbf{S}_{level-1}, \mathbf{T}_{level-1}, \boldsymbol{\alpha}^0, \boldsymbol{\rho}^0, \boldsymbol{\beta}^0).$

(6) Set the initial parameters for the second layer ICIA fitting:

$\boldsymbol{\alpha}^0 = \boldsymbol{\alpha}^*_{level-1}, \boldsymbol{\rho}^0 = \boldsymbol{\rho}^*_{level-1}, \boldsymbol{\beta}^0 = \boldsymbol{\beta}^*_{level-1}.$

(7) Perform the second layer ICIA fitting:

$ICIA\_fitting(\mathbf{I}_{level-2}, \mathbf{S}_{level-2}, \mathbf{T}_{level-2}, \boldsymbol{\alpha}^0, \boldsymbol{\rho}^0, \boldsymbol{\beta}^0).$

(8) Set the initial parameters for the third layer ICIA fitting:

$\boldsymbol{\alpha}^0 = \boldsymbol{\alpha}^*_{level-2}, \boldsymbol{\rho}^0 = \boldsymbol{\rho}^*_{level-2}, \boldsymbol{\beta}^0 = \boldsymbol{\beta}^*_{level-2}$

(9) Perform the third layer ICIA fitting:

$ICIA\_fitting(\mathbf{I}_{level-3}, \mathbf{S}_{level-3}, \mathbf{T}_{level-3}, \boldsymbol{\alpha}^0, \boldsymbol{\rho}^0, \boldsymbol{\beta}^0).$

(10) Obtain the 3D synthesized face image using the fitted parameters.

$$\mathbf{S} = \mathbf{S}_0 + \sum_{i=1}^{i=N_s} \alpha^*_{level-3,i} \cdot \mathbf{S}_i.$$

$$\mathbf{T} = \mathbf{T}_0 + \sum_{i=1}^{i=N_t} \beta^*_{level-3,i} \cdot \mathbf{T}_i.$$

---

synthesized from the known model parameters whose variances were ranged $[-3\sigma^2, +3\sigma^2]$ as the test 3D face images. Fig. 5.10.7 shows some synthesized 3D face images with the known model parameters.

5.10.3.2 Correlation of the Model Parameters Among Different Layers

First, we evaluated the correlation of the shape and the texture parameters among two different levels. Since we take the model parameters obtained from the fitting result at the lower layer as the initial model parameters for the ICIA fitting at the upper layer, there should be a strong correlation between the model parameters of two adjacent levels. The correlation of the shape or texture parameters is evaluated by fitting the 3D face model to the face image at each level, starting from $\boldsymbol{\alpha}^0 = \mathbf{0}, \boldsymbol{\rho}^0 = \boldsymbol{\rho}_{Ground-Truth}$, and $\boldsymbol{\beta}^0 = \mathbf{0}$, where *Ground – Truth* means that the motion parameter values are the ground-truth values,

Figure 5.10.6. Some 3D face images in the BJUT-3D Face Database

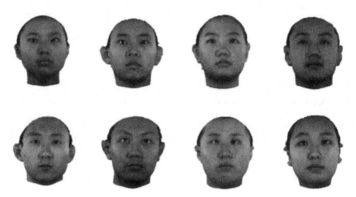

and computation of the normalized correlation of the shape or texture parameters between two levels.

Table 5.10.5 shows the normalized correlation of the fitted shape parameters between two levels, where they are 1 in all cases. This means that we can use the fitted shape parameters at the lower layer as the initial shape parameters of the next upper layer completely.

Table 5.10.6 shows the normalized correlation of the fitted texture parameters between two levels, where they are different from each other. The normalized correlation between level-1 and level-2 is the highest one (0.9475), the normalized correlation between level-2 and level-3 is the next highest one (0.8476), and the the normalized correlation between level-1 and level-3 is the smallest but is still strong (0.7932). This also indicates that we can also use the fitted texture parameters at the lower layer as the initial texture parameters of the next upper layer sufficiently.

5.10.3.3. Comparison of the Fitting Performance using Different Types of Image Pyramids

Second, we compared the fitting performance with respect to two different types of image pyramid constructions: the sub-sampling image pyramid (SIP) and the Gaussian image pyramid (GIP) when the proposed hierarchical ICIA fitting method was used with the two-stage parameter updates (TSPU), starting from $\alpha^0 = 0$, $\rho^0 = \rho_{Face-Detector}$, and $\beta^0 = 0$,

Table 5.10.4. The structural information of the multi-resolution 3D face models

Structure	Level-3 model	Level-2 model	Level-1 model
Resolution	200x200	100x100	50x50
Number of vertices	7,238	1,807	452
Dimension of shape basis vectors	(7,238*3)x50	(1,807*3)x50	(452*3)x50
Dimension of texture basis images	7,238x50	1,807x50	452x50
Number of the triangle lists	14,187	3,474	832
Dimensionality of Jacobian	7,238x106	1,807x106	452x106

Figure 5.10.7. Examples of synthetic 3D face images

where $Face - Detector$ means that the motion parameter values are obtained from the results of detecting the face and the eyes.

Table 5.10.7 compares the fitting performance of two different types of image pyramids: SIP and GIP. From this table, we know that the fitting performance of using GIP outperforms that of using SIP in all performance measures such as $C(shape)$, $C(texture)$, $RMSE(shape)$, and $RMSE(texture)$.

Fig. 5.10.8 shows a histogram of the shape errors between the ground truths and the fitted shapes using SIP and GIP. It shows that GIP has the smaller mean and the smaller standard deviation of the shape errors than SIP.

5.10.3.4 Comparison of the Fitting Performance Using Different Types of Parameter Updates

Third, we compared the fitting performance with respect to two different types of parameter updates: the single-stage parameter update (SSPU) and the two-stage parameter update (TSPU), where the former updates all model parameters in all layer ICIA fittings and the latter updates the motion and texture parameters in the first layer ICIA fitting and then updates all model parameters in the second and third layer ICIA fitting, when the proposed hierarchical ICIA fitting method was used with the GIP construction, starting from $\alpha^0 = 0$, $\rho^0 = \rho_{Face-Detector}$, and $\beta^0 = 0$, where $Face - Detector$ means that the parameter values are obtained from the results of detecting the face and the eyes.

Table 5.10.8 compares the fitting performance of two different types of parameter updates: SSPU and TSPU. From this table, we know that the fitting performance of using

Table 5.10.5. The correlation of the shape parameters among different levels

$C(\alpha^*_{level-i}, \alpha^*_{level-j})$	$\alpha^*_{level-1}$	$\alpha^*_{level-2}$	$\alpha^*_{level-3}$
$\alpha^*_{level-1}$	1	1	1
$\alpha^*_{level-2}$	1	1	1
$\alpha^*_{level-3}$	1	1	1

Table 5.10.6. The correlation of the texture parameters among different levels

$C(\beta^*_{level-i},\ \beta^*_{level-j})$	$\beta^*_{level-1}$	$\beta^*_{level-2}$	$\beta^*_{level-3}$
$\beta^*_{level-1}$	1	0.9475	0.7932
$\beta^*_{level-2}$	0.9475	1	0.8476
$\beta^*_{level-3}$	0.7932	0.8476	1

TSPU outperforms that of using TSPU in all performance measures such as $C(shape)$, $C(texture)$, $RMSE(shape)$, and $RMSE(texture)$.

Fig. 5.10.9 shows a histogram of the shape errors between the ground truths and the fitted shapes using SSPU and TSPU. It shows that TSPU has the smaller mean and the smaller standard deviation of the shape errors than SSPU.

5.10.3.5 Comparison of the Fitting Performance with Different Types of Fitting Methods

Finally, we compared the fitting performance with respect to two different types of fitting methods: the conventional ICIA fitting method (CICIA)and the proposed hierarchical ICIA fitting method (HICIA), when GIP is used to generate the image pyramid and TSPU is used for the parameter updates, stating from $\alpha^0 = 0$, $\rho^0 = \rho_{Face-Detector}$, and $\beta^0 = 0$, where $Face-Detector$ means that the parameter values are obtained from the results of detecting the face and the eyes.

Table 5.10.9 summarizes the fitting performances of two fitting methods in terms of the average number of iterations (N_{iter}), the average computation time for ICIA fitting ($T_{fitting}$), the normalized correlation of the fitted shape parameters (C_{shape}), the normalized correlation of the fitted texture parameters ($C_{texture}$), the RMSE of the shape errors (R_{shape}), and the RMSE of the texture errors ($R_{texture}$). This table indicates that (1) the proposed hierarchical ICIA fitting method is faster than the conventional ICIA fitting method by a speed up of 3, (2) the correlations of shape and texture parameters of using HICIA are much higher than those of using CICIA, and (3) the RMSEs of the shape and texture errors of using HICIA are reduced by 3-4 times than those of using CICIA.

Fig. 5.10.10 shows a histogram of the shape errors between the ground truths and the

Table 5.10.7. Comparison of the fitting performance between SIP and GIP

	C(shape)	C(texture)	RMSE(shape)	RMSE(texture)
SIP	0.5623	0.9682	4.0623	3.0681
GIP	0.8200	0.9934	2.1677	1.6054

Figure 5.10.8. A histogram of the shape errors using SIP and GIP

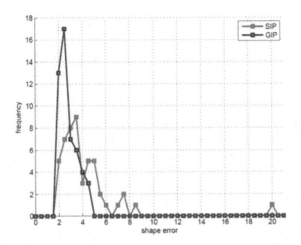

Table 5.10.8. Comparison of the fitting performance between SSPU and TSPU

	C(shape)	C(texture)	RMSE(shape)	RMSE(texture)
SSPU	0.5623	0.9682	4.0623	3.0681
TSPU	0.8200	0.9934	2.1677	1.6054

Figure 5.10.9. A histogram of the shape errors using SSPU and TSPU

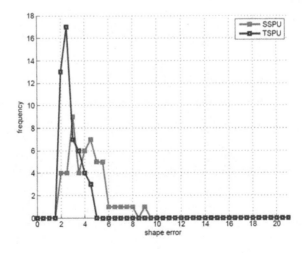

Table 5.10.9. Comparison of fitting performance between CICIA and HICIA

	N_{iter}	$T_{fitting}$	C_{shape}	$C_{texture}$	R_{shape}	$R_{texture}$
CICIA	71.02	16.3	0.3754	0.8550	6.4540	6.0410
HICIA	57.52	5.7936	0.8200	0.9934	2.1667	1.6054

fitted shapes using CICIA and HICIA. It shows that HICIA has the smaller mean and the smaller standard deviation of the shape errors than CICIA.

Fig. 5.10.11 compares the convergence rates of five different fitting methods: TYPE1 (CICIA), TYPE2 (HICIA+SIP+SSPU), TYPE3 (HICIA+SIP+TSPU), TYPE4 (HICIA+GIP+SSPU), and TYPE5 (HICIA+GIP+TSPU), stating from $\alpha^0 = 0$, $\rho^0 = \rho_{Face-Detector}$, and $\beta^0 = 0$, where $Face - Detector$ means that the parameter values are obtained from the results of detecting the face and the eyes. In this experiment, the input face image is successfully converged when the shape error of the fitting face image is smaller than a given threshold value and the convergence rate is defined by the ratio of the number of successfully converged face images over the total number of face images. This table indicates that the convergence rate of the proposed hierarchical ICIA fitting method with GIP construction and TSPU update outperforms those of other fitting methods.

Fig. 5.10.12 shows some fitting results of the proposed hierarchical ICIA fitting method, where the first, second, third, and fourth columns represent the input face images, the fitted shapes, the synthesized face images using the fitted model parameters, and the different views of the synthesized images of four different people, respectively. From this figure, we know that the proposed hierarchical ICIA fitting method provides good fitting performances, thus it can be used for fitting a new subject that is not included in the training set.

Figure 5.10.10. A histogram of the shape errors using CICIA and HICIA

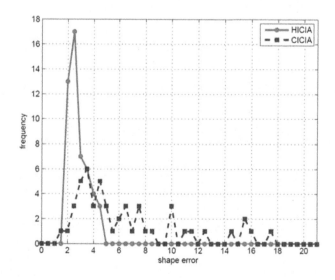

In summary, we performed several experiments that validate the efficiency and accuracy of the proposed hierarchical ICIA fitting algorithm. From the experiment results, we know that (1) it completed the fitting within about 57 iterations ($\approx$ 5 seconds), (2) its speed-up ratio is about 3, (3) the performance of the shape and the texture recovery of the proposed fitting method outperformed that of the existing fitting method, (4) the two-stage parameter update showed better fitting performance than single-stage parameter update in terms of the fitting time and fitting error.

5.11 CONCLUSION

The face recogntion is difficult because there are lots of factors that distort the face images of a person such as illumination, pose, facial expression, camera distortion, and so on. Therefore, good feature extraction method must be robust to these variations, i.e., the extracted feature vectors must be consistent without respect to the variations. Until now, no method has developed that satisfies the requirement of the ideal feature extractor and there exists many feature extraction methods. In this chapter, we introduced some recently developed feature extraction methods, which are the mixture model, embedded hidden markov models, local feature analysis, and tensor analysis. The morphable model is a dense and sophisticated face modeling technique that requires large amout of comuptation. Although the morphable model cannot be applied to real-time application due to the computational complexity, many researcher are focusing on the morphable model because it can simulate the pose, illumination, and facial expression factors

While the traditional eigenface method uses only one set of features, the mixture-of-eigenfaces method uses more than one set. This improves the ability of facial representation greatly. In terms of recognition accuracy, the mixture-of-eigenfaces method outperforms the traditional eigenface method for both the light-variant face image set and the pose-

Figure 5.10.11. Convergence rates of the different fitting methods

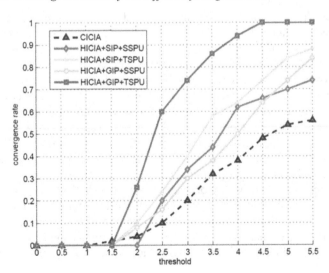

Figure 5.10.12. Some fitting results of the proposed HICIA fitting method

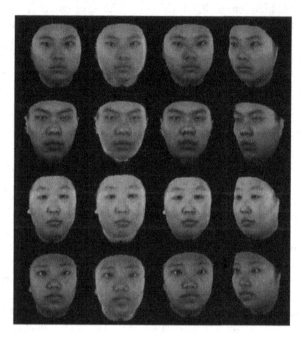

variant face image set. For face coding, the mixture-of-eigenfaces method can be used as an alternative of the eigenface method, when we should use a relatively small size of code. The performance improvement is expected to increase by using more sets of features which involve more persons or larger variations. In particular, the mixture-of-eigenfaces method will be useful for the identification system under conditions of large people or large variations. The framework of using more than one set of features can be used to extend other recognition or coding methods.

The face description method based on the embedded HMM with 2nd-order block-specific observations uses a couple of optimal block-specific feature vectors as an observation for a block, where two sets of feature vectors for a specific block were obtained by projecting the original and residual block image of the specific block onto the 1st-order and the 2nd-order block-specific basis vectors, respectively. Two sets of basis vectors were obtained by applying two independent PCA techniques to a training set of original block images and another training set of residual block images consecutively. A couple of the 1st- and 2nd-order block-specific feature vectors comprised of an observation vector and a sequence of all observation vectors for a given face was applied to train the embedded HMM for the specific person. The experiment results showed the face descriptor using the embedded HMM with the 2nd-order block-specific eigenvectors outperformed all other compared recognition methods, such as the 2nd-order eigenface method, the HMM method with the DCT observations, and the 2nd-order eigenface method using a confidence factor in terms of accuracy measures such as ANMRR and FIR. This method outperformed some approaches based on holistic features such as the 2nd-order eigenface method (m6001) (Wang and Tan, 2000b) and the 2nd-order eigenface method using a confidence factor (m7689) (Kamei and

Yamada, 2001) because our approach is using many block-specific component features while their approaches are based on the holistic features. Also, this method outperformed the EHMM method with DCT observation (m7632) (Nefian and Davies, 2001) because our block features are block-optimal due to its block-specific learning. The improvement of face recognition performance results from the following two facts: (1) a face image was represented by many (possibly overlapping) constituent blocks, not by a holistic feature, (2) each block represented a combined observation of 1st-order and 2nd-order feature vectors, and (3) the feature vectors of all constituent blocks were obtained individually to reflect their different spatial properties, which depended on their positions in the face image, not using the same basis vectors for all constituent blocks.

The LFA-based feature extraction method for face recognition consists of three steps. First, local features are extracted using the LFA. Second, a subset of the features are selected, which is efficient for recognition. Finally, the local structures are combined into composite templates. The composite templates represent data in a more compact form and show compromised aspects between kernels of LFA and eigenfaces. Although LFA is originally problematic for recognition, the composite template method showed better recognition performance than existing eigenface, LFA, and fisherface.

The tensor-based AAM generates a variation specific AAM from a tensor structure. We first estimate the pose, expression and illumination of the input face image from the image tensor, then generate the appropriate AAM bases from the model tensors. For validating the usefulness of the tensor-based AAM, we applied the fitted result to the face recognition. For the illumination-robust face recognition, we also proposed a novel illumination image transformation method which adopts the ratio image concept into the multilinear model framework. Extensive experimental results validated the usefulness of the tensor-based AAM because it reduced the fitting error and improved the face recognition performance significantly.

The fast and accurate hierarchical ICIA fitting method is more efficient and provides better fitting performance than the existing ICIA fitting method for 3D MMs. The proposed fitting method is fast because it generates the multi-resolution 3D face models and constructs the Gaussian image pyramid. Further, the fitting is conducted hierarchically from the lower layer to the higher layer. As a side effect, this also improves the fitting performance because the fitted model parameters at the lower layer are used as the initial model parameters for the upper layer fitting. The proposed two-stage parameter update method updates the motion parameter and the texture parameters only at the first layer fitting, and updates all parameters at the succeeding upper layer fitting. This update method reduces the computation time for fitting and improves the stability of fitting because it is very difficult to discriminate the movement of vertex positions due to the shape parameter changes and the motion parameter changes in the very beginning of fitting, In addition, we only update the motion parameters and the texture parameters in the first layer fitting.

5.12 REFERENCES

Abboud, B., and Davoine, F. (2004b). Face appearance factorization for expression analysis and synthesis. In Proceedings of Workshop on Image Analysis for Multimedia Interactive Services.

Adini, Y., Moses, Y., and Ullman, S. (1997). Face Recognition: The Problem of Compensating for Changes in Illumination Direction. IEEE Transactions on Pattern Analysis and Machine Intelligence, 19(7), 721-732.

Ahlberg, J. (2001). Using the Active appearance algorithm for face and facial feature tracking of faces and gestures in real-time system, RATFG-RTS'01

Baker, S., and Matthews, I. (2001). Equivalence and efficiency of image alignment algorithms, In Proceedings of IEEE Conference on Computer Vision and Pattern Recognition, (pp. 1090-1097).

Baker, S., and Matthews, I. (2002). Lucas-Kanade 20 years on: A unifying framework: Part I. CMU Technical Report CMU-RI-TR-02-16.

Baker, S., Gross, R., and Matthews, I. (2004). Lucas-Kanade 20 years on: A unifying framework: Part 4, CMU Technical Report CMU-RI-TR-04-14.

Bartlett, M. (2001). Face Image Analysis by Unsupervised Learning. Kluwer Academic Publisher.

Bartlett, M. S., Lades, H. M., and Sejnowski, T. J. (1998). Independent component representations for face recognition, In Proceedings of Conference on Human Vision and Electronic Imaging III, (pp. 528-539).

Bartlett, M. S., Movellan, J. R., and Sejnowski, T. J. (2002). Face recognition by independent component analysis. IEEE Trans. on Neural Networks, 13(6), 1450-1464.

Beichel, R., Mitchell, S., Sorantin, E., Leberl, F., Goshtasby, A., and Sonka, M. (2001). Shape and appearance-based segmentation of volumetric medical images, In Proceeding of the International Conference on Image Processing, (pp. 589-592).

Belhumeur, P., and Kriegman, D. (1998). What is the set of images of an object under all possible illumination conditions. International Journal of Computer Vision, 28(3), 245-260.

Belhumeur, P., Hespanha, J., and Kriegman, D. (1997). Eigenfaces vs.fisherfaces: class specific linear projection. IEEE Transactions on Pattern Analysis and Machine Intelligence, 19(7), 711-720.

Besl, P. J., and MacKay, N. (1992). A method for registration of 3-d shapes. IEEE Transantions on Pattern Analysis and Machine Intelligence, 14(2), 239-256.

Beymer, D. (1994). Face recognition under varying pose. In Proceedings of IEEE International Conference on Computer Vision and Pattern Recognition, (pp. 756-761).

Beymer, D., and Poggio, T. (1993). Face recognition from one example view. AI Laboratory, Massachussetts Institute of Technology.

Biuk, Z., and Loncaric, S. (2001). Face recognition from multi-pose image sequence. In Proceedings of International Symposium on Image and Signal Processing and Analysis, (pp. 319-324).

Blanz, V., and Vetter, T. (1999). A morphable model for the synthesis of 3d faces. Computer Graphics, Annual Conference Series (SIGGRAPH) (pp. 187-194).

Blanz, V., Grother, P., Phillips, P., and Vetter, T. (2005). Face recognition based on frontal views generated from non-frontal images. In Proceedings of IEEE International Conference on Computer Vision and Pattern Recognition, (pp. 454-461).

Bosch, J. G., Mitchell, S. C., Lelieveldt, B. P. F., Nijland, F., Kamp, O., Sonka, M., and Reiber, J. H. C. (2002). Automatic segmentation of echocardiographic sequences by active appearance models, IEEE Transactions on Medical Imaging, 21(11), 1374-1383.

Brunelli, R., and Poggio, T. (1993). Face recognition: features versus templates. IEEE Transactions on Pattern Analysis and Machine Intelligence, 15(10), 1042-1052.

Chellappa, R., Wilson, C. L., and Sirohey, S. (1995). Human and machine recognition of faces: a survey, Proceedings of the IEEE, 83(5), 705-740.

Cootes, T., and Taylor, C. (2001a). Constrained active appearance models. In Proceedings of IEEE International Conference on Computer Vision.

Cootes, T., and Taylor, C. (2001b). On representing edge structure for model matching. In Proceedings of Computer Vision and Pattern Recognition.

Cootes, T., Edwards, G., and Taylor, C. (1998). Active appearance models. In Proceedings of European Conference on Computer Vision, (pp. 484-498).

Cootes, T., Edwards, G., and Taylor, C. (2001d). Active appearance models. IEEE Trans. on Pattern Recognition and Machine Intelligence, 23(6), 681-685.

Cootes, T., Taylor, C., and Lanitis, A. (1994). Active shape models: evaluation of a multi-resolution method for improving image search. In British Machine Vision Conference, (pp.38-59).

Cootes, T., Taylor, C., Cooper, D., and Graham, J. (1995). Active shape models - their training and application. Computer Vision and Image Understanding, 61(1), 38-59.

Cootes, T., Wheeler, G., Walker, K., and Taylor, C. (2001c). Coupled-view active appearance models. IEEE Transactions on Pattern Recognition and Machine Intelligence, 23(6), 681-685.

Cootes, T., Wheeler, G., Walker, K., and Taylor, C. (2002). View-based active appearance models. Image and Vision Computing, 20, 657-664.

Craw, I., Costen, N., Kato, T., and Akamatsu, S. (1999). How should we represenfaces for automatic recognition? IEEE Transactions on Pattern Analysis and Machine Intelligence, 21(8), 725-736.

Dempster, P., Laird, N., and Rubin, D. (1977). Maximum likelihood from incomplete data via the EM algorithm, Journal of the Royal Statistical Society: series-B, 39(4), 1-38.

Donner, R., Reiter, M., Langs, G., Peloschek, P., and Bischof, H. (2006). Fast active appearance model search using canonical correlation analysis, IEEE Transactions on Pattern Analysis and Machine Intelligence, 28(10), 1690-1694.

Edwards, G., Cootes, T., and Taylor, C. (1998a). Face recognition using active appearance models. In Proceedings of European Conference on Computer Vision.

Edwards, G., Taylor, C., and Cootes, T. (1998b). Interpreting face images using active appearance models. In Proceedings of International Conference on Automatic Face and Gesture Recognition.

Essa, I., and Pentland, A. (1997a) Coding, analysis, interpretation and recognition of facial expressions, IEEE Trans. on Pattern Analysis and Machine Intelligence, 19(7), 757-763.

Essa, I., and Pentland, A. (1997b). Facial expression recognition using image motion.

Gandhi, M. (2004). A Method for Automatic Synthesis of Aged Human Facial Images. M.S. Thesis, McGill Univ., Montreal, QC, Canada.

Georghiades, A., Kriegman, D., and Belhumeur, P. (1998). Illumination cones for recognition under variable lighting: Faces. In Proceedings of IEEE Conference on Computer Vision and Pattern Recognition. (pp. 52-58).

Georghiades, A., Kriegman, D., and Belhumeur, P. (2001). From few to many: Illumination cone models for face recognition under variable lighting and pose. IEEE Transaction on Pattern Analysis and Machine Intelligence, 23(6), 643-660.

Gokturk, S., Bouguet, J., Tomasi, C., and Girod, B. (2002). Model-based face tracking for view-independent facial expression recognition, Proceedings of IEEE International Conference on Automatic Face and Gesture Recognition.

Golomb, B.A., Lawrence, D.T., and Sejnowski, T.j. (1991). Sexnet: A neural network identifies sex from human faces. In the Proceedings of the 1990 conference on Advances in nueral information processing systems 3. (pp. 572–577)

Gong, S., McKenna, S. J., and Psarrou, A. (2000) Dynamic Vision, Imperial College Press.

Gross, R., Matthews, I., and Baker, S. (2003). Lucas-kanade 20 years on : A unifying framework : Part 3. Cmu-ri-tr-03-05, CMU.

Gross, R., Matthews, I., and Baker, S. (2004b). Generic vs. person specific active appearance models. In Proceedings of British Machine Vision Conference.

Horn, B., and Schunck, B. (1981). Determining optical flow. Journal of Artificial Intelligence, 17, 85-203.

Hotelling, H. (1993). Analysis of a complex statistical variables into principal components. Journal of Educational Psychology, 24, 417-441.

Huang, F., Zhou, Z., Zhang, H., and Xhen, T. (2000). Pose invariant face recognition. In Proceedings of International Conference on Automatic Face and Gesture Recognition, (pp. 245-250).

Jacobs, R., Jordan, M., Nowlan, S., and Hinton, G. (1991). Adaptive mixtures of local experts, Neural Computation, 3, 79-87.

Jolliffe, I. T. (1986). Principal component analysis. New York : Springer-Verlag.

Jordan, M., and Jacobs, R. (1994). Hierarchical mixtures of experts and the EM algorithm. Neural Computation, 6(5), 181-214.

Jun, B., and Kim, D. (2007). Robust real-time face detection using face certainty map, In Proceedings of International Conference on Biometrics, (pp. 29-38).

Kamei, T. and Yamada, A. (2001). Extension of the face recognition descriptor using a confidence factor. ISO/IEC/JTC1/SC21/WG11/m7689, Pattaya, December.

Kanade, T. (1973). Picture processing by computer complex and recognition of human faces. Ph.D. thesis, Kyoto University.

Kass, M., Witkin, A., and Terzopoulos, D. (1987). Snakes: Active Contour Models, IEEE International Conference on Computer Vision, (pp.259-268).

Kelly, M. D. (1970). Visual identification of people by computer. Technical Report. AI-130, Stanford AI Project, Stanford, CA.

Kim, H., Kim, D., and Bang, S. (2001c). A pca mixture model with an efficient model selection method, Proceedings of International Joint Conference on Neural Networks, (pp. 430-435).

Kuo, S., and Agazzi, O. (1994). Keyword spotting in poorly printed documents using sseudo 2-d hidden markov models. IEEE Transactions on Pattern Analysis and Machine Intelligence, 16(8), 842-848.

Land, E. (1986). An alternative technique for the computation of the designator in the Retinex theory of color vision. National Academical Science, 83, 3078-3080.

Lanitis, A., Taylor, C.J., and Cootes., T.F. (2002). Modeling the process of ageing in face images. In Proceedings of IEEE International Conference on Computer Vision. (pp. 131-136).

Lanitis, A., Taylor, C.J., and Cootes., T.F. (2002). Toward Automatic Simulation of Aging Effects on Face Images. IEEE Transactions on Pattern Analysis and Machine Intelligence, 24(4), 442-455.

Lathauwer, L. D., Moor, B. D., and Vandewalle, J. (2000). A multilinear singular value decomposition, SIAM Journal on Matrix Analysis and Applications, 21(4), 1253-1278.

Lawrence, S., Yianilos, P., and Cox, I. (1997a). Face recognition using mixtured-distance and raw images. IEEE International Conference on Systems, Man, and Cybernetics, 2016-2021.

Lee, H.-S. and Kim, D. (2006). Generating frontal view face image for pose invariant face recognition. Pattern Recognition Letters, 27, 747-754.

Lee, H.-S., and Kim, D. (2007). Robust face tracking by integration of two separate trackers: Skin color and facial shape, 40, 3225-3235.

Lee, H. S., and Kim, D. (2006). Facial expression transformations for expression-invariant face recognition. In Proceedings of International Symposium on Visual Computing (pp. 323-333).

Lee, H. S., Park, S., Kang, B., Shin, J., Lee, J. Y., Je, H. M., Jun, B., and Kim, D. (2007c). Asian face image database PF07, Technical report, Intelligen Media Lab. Department of CSE, POETECH.

Lee, H. S., Sung, J., and Kim, D. (2007b). Incremental aam using synthesized illumination images, In Proceedings of the Pacific-Rim Conferene on Multimedia.

Li, Stan. Z, and Jain, Anil. K. (2005). Handbook of Face Recognition. Springer.

Lucas, B., and Kanade, T. (1981). An iterative image registration technique with an application to stereo vision, In proceedings of International Joint Conference on Artificail Intelligence, (pp. 674-679).

Lucey, S., Matthews, I., Hu, C., Ambadar, Z., la Torre Frade, F. D., and Cohn, J. (2006). Aam derived face representations for robust facial action recognition, In Proceedings of the Seventh IEEE International Conference on Automatic Face and Gesture Recognition, (pp. 155-160).

Matthews, I., and Baker, S. (2004a). Active appearance models revisited. International Journal of Computer Vision, 60(2), 135-164.

Matthews, I., Baker, S., and Gross, R. (2004b). Genetic vs. person specific active appearance models. In Proceedings of British Machine Vision Conference.

Moghaddam, B., and Pentland, A. (1997). Probablistic visual learning for object representation. IEEE Transaction on Pattern Analysis and Machine Intelligence, 19(7), 696-710.

Moghaddam, B., and Yang, M.H. (2002). Learning Gender with Support Faces. IEEE Trasactions on Pattern Analysis and Machine Intelligence, 24(5), 707-711.

Nefian, A. V., and Hayes, M. (1998). A Hidden Markov Model for Face Recognition. In Proceedings of International Conference on Acoustic Speech and Signal Processing, (pp. 2721-2724).

Nefian, A., and Davies, B. (2001). Results of the core experiments for standard support for automatic face recognition, ISO/IEC JTC1/SC21/WG11/m7632, Pattaya, Dec.

Penev, P., and Atick, J. (1996). Local feature analysis: A general statistical theory for object representation. Network: Computation in Neural Systems, 7, 477-500.

Pentland, A., Moghaddam, B., and Starner, T. (1994). View-based and modular eigenspaces for face recognition. In Proceedings of IEEE International Conference on Computer Vision and Pattern Recognition, (pp. 84-91).

Phillips, P. J., Flynn, P. J., Scruggs, T., Bowyer, K. W., Chang, J., Hoffman, K., Marques, J., Min, J., and Worek, W. (2005). Overview of the Face Recognition Grand Challenge. In Proceeding of the IEEE International Conference on Computer Vision and Pattern Recognition, (pp. 947-954).

Rabiner, L. (1989). A tutorial on hidden markov models and selected applications in speech recognition. Procedddings of IEEE, 77(2), 257-285.

Riklin-Raviv, T., and Shashua, A. (2001). The quotient image: class-based rerendering and recognition with varying illuminations. IEEE Transaction on Pattern Analysis and Machine Intelligence, 23(2), 129-139.

Romdhani, S., and Vetter, T. (2003). Efficient, robust and accurate fitting of a 3D morphable model, In Proceedings of IEEE International Conference on Computer Vision, (pp. 59-66).

Romdhani, S., Canterakis, N., and Vetter, T. (2003). Selective vs. global recovery of rigid and non-rigid motion. Technical report, CS Dept, University of Basel.

Samal, A., and Iyengar, P. A. (1992). Automatic recognition and analysis of human faces and facial expressions: a survey. Pattern Recognition, 25(1), 65-77.

Samaria, F., and Young, S. (1994). HMM-based architecture for face identification. Image and Computer Vision, 12, 537-543.

Stegmann, M. B., Ersbøll, B. K., and Larsen, R. (2003). Fame - a flexible appearance modeling environment, IEEE Transactions on Medical Imaging, 22(10), 1319-1331.

Sung, J., and Kim, D. (2006e). Staam: Fitting 2d+3d aam to stereo images. In Proceedings of International Conference on Image Processing.

Sung, J., and Kim, D. (2006g). A unified approach for combining asm into aam. International Journal of Computer Vision, 75(2), 297-309.

Sung, J., Lee, S., and Kim, D. (2006h). A real-time facial expression recognition using the STAAM. In Proceedings of IEEE International Conference on Pattern Recognition.

Suo, J., Min, F., Zhu, S.C., Shan, S.G., and Chen, X.L. (2007). A Multi-Resolution Dynamic Model for Face Aging Simulation. In Proceedings of IEEE Conference on Computer Vision and Pattern Recognition. (pp. 1-8).

Terzopoulos, D., and Waters, K. (1990). Analysis of facial images using physical and anatomical models, IEEE International Conference on Computer Vision, (pp. 727-732).

Tipping, M., and Bishop, C. (1999). Mixtures of probabilistic principal component analyzers. Neural Computation, 11, 443-482.

Turk, M., and Pentland, A. (1991b). Face recognition using eigenfaces. In Proceedings of IEEE Conference on Computer Vision and Pattern Recognition, (pp. 586-591).

Turk, M., and Pentland, A. (1991a). Eigenfaces for recognition. Journal of Cognitive Neuroscience, 3(1), 71-86.

Vasilescu, M., and Terzopoulos, D. (2002a). Multilinear analysis of image ensembles: tensorfaces. Proceedings of European Conference on Computer Vision, (pp. 447-460).

Vasilescu, M., and Terzopoulos, D. (2002b). Multilinear analysis for facial image recognition. Proceedings of International Conference on Pattern Recognition, 2002.

Verschae, R., Ruiz-del-Solar, J., and Correa, M. (2006). Gender classification of Faces Using Adaboost. In the Proceedings of Iberoamerican Congress in Pattern Recognition, (pp. 68-78).

Vetter, T., and Poggio, T. (1997). Linear object classes and image synthesis from a single example image, IEEE Transaction on Pattern Analysis and Machine Intelligence, 19(7), 773-742.

Wallhoff, F., Muller, S., and Rigoll, G. (2001). Hybrid face recognition systems for profile views using the mugshot database. In Proceedings of IEEE ICCV Workshop Recognition, Analysis and Tracking of Faces and Gestures in Real-Time Systems, (pp. 149-156).

Wang, L., and Tan T. K. (2000b). Experimental results of face description based on the 2nd-order Eigenface Method. ISO/IEC JTC1/SC29/WG11/m6001, Geneva, May.

Wang, L., Hu, W., and Tan, T. (2003). Recent developments in human motion analysis, 36(3), 585-601.

Wechsler, H. (2007). Reliable Face Recognition Methods: system design, implementation and evaluation. Springer.

Wiskott, L., Fellous, J. M., Krüger, N., and Malsburg, C. (1997). Face recognition by elastic bunch graph matching, IEEE Transaction on Pattern Analysis and Machine Intelligence, 19(7), 775-780.

Yan, S., Hou, X., Li, S., Zhang, H., Cheng, Q. (2003). Face alignment using view-based direct appearance models, International Journal of Imaging Systems and Technology, 13(1), 106-112.

Yan, S., Liu, C., Li, S., Zhang, H., Shum, H., and Cheng, Q. (2002). Texture-constrained active shape models. In Proceedings of European Conference on Computer Vision.

Yongsheng, O., Xinyu, W., Huihuan, Q., and Yangsheng, X. (2005). A Real Time Race Classification System, In the Proceedings of IEEE International Conference on Information Acquisition. (pp. 6).

Zhao, J., Su, Y.,Wang, D., and Luo, S. (2003). Illumination ratio image:synthesizing and recognition with varying illuminations. Pattern Recognition Letters, 23(15), 2703-2710.

Zhao, W., Chellappa, R., Philips, P., and Rosenfeld, A. (2003). Face recognition: A literature survey. ACM Computing Surveys, 35(4), 399-458.

Chapter VI
Facial Expression Recognition

The facial expression has long been an interest for psychology, since Darwin published *The expression of Emotions in Man and Animals* (Darwin, C., 1899). Psychologists have studied to reveal the role and mechanism of the facial expression. One of the great discoveries of Darwin is that there exist prototypical facial expressions across multiple cultures on the earth, which provided the theoretical backgrounds for the vision researchers who tried to classify categories of the prototypical facial expressions from images. The representative 6 facial expressions are afraid, happy, sad, surprised, angry, and disgust (Mase, 1991; Yacoob and Davis, 1994). On the other hand, real facial expressions that we frequently meet in daily life consist of lots of distinct signals, which are subtly different. Further research on facial expressions required an object method to describe and measure the distinct activity of facial muscles. The *facial action coding system* (FACS), proposed by Hager and Ekman (1978), defines 46 distinct *action units* (AUs), each of which explains the activity of each distinct muscle or muscle group. The development of the objective description method also affected the vision researchers, who tried to detect the emergence of each AU (Tian et. al., 2001).

The general automated facial expression analysis system consists of three components: face acquisition, facial feature extraction, and facial expression classification (Fasel and Luettin, 2003). The facial expression acquisition includes face detection and facial image normalization to remove the effect of translation, scaling, and rotation. The facial feature extraction component extracts appropriate features for the facial expression recognition, where numerous techniques such as holistic image feature, geometric shape feature, optical flow, and wavelets are used. The recent trend is to adapt a model-based approach because the face acquisition and facial feature extraction can be done relatively easy once the model is fitted to the input image successfully. The facial expression classification component classifies the extracted facial features into the one of the prototypical facial expressions or facial action units, where lots of classification algorithms are used such as neural network, support vector machines and Bayesian classifiers.

The model-based approaches can be divided along the face models into two groups: 2D face model group and 3D face model group. Among the two groups, many researchers have used 3D face models (Essa and Pentland, 1997a; Blanz and Vetter, 1999; Gokturk et. al., 2002). In general, using a 3D face model requires more computation time than traditional 2D based methods (Lyons et. al., 1999); however, it has several advantages. First, the problem of image distortion in the face image due to head pose change can be alleviated by using texture map (Blanz and Vetter, 1999). Second, a pose invariant 3D shape can be obtained, which is more adequate for natural facial expression recognition system than a 2D shape (Blanz and Vetter, 1999; Gokturk et. al., 2002). The approaches using a 2D shape (Zheng et. al., 2004, Michel and Kaliouby, 2003) always assume frontal view face images. Third, lighting problems can be alleviated by integrating the lighting model into a 3D face model fitting algorithm (Blanz and Vetter, 1999).

Although we can remove the effect of pose change or lighting conditions using the 3D face model, there exist many kinds of variations due to inter-person, facial expressions, verbal movements, and so on. These variations make the distributions of the facial expressions complicated and difficult to distinguish them. Some researchers have tried to separate these variations explicitly using bilinear model (Chuang et. al., 2002) or singular value decomposition (SVD) (Wang and Ahuja, 2003). Hence, such algorithms are inappropriate for explicit separation of the variations in on-line manner. Instead, other researchers used non-linear classification algorithms such as NN, or kernel methods to recognize facial expressions (Zheng et. al., 2004; Michel and Kaliouby, 2003). These approaches learn the complex manifolds itself. Another issue in facial expression recognition is to use dynamic features (Cohen et. al., 2003) rather than static features (Zheng et. al., 2004; Michel and Kaliouby, 2003). These approaches usually assume that they already know the neutral state and then compute the displacement of feature points or change of the parameters with respect to the neutral state. If it is possible to specify the image frame corresponding to neutral expression such information can be used to remove inter-person variation. However, specifying the exact neutral state of an unknown person is difficult.

This chapter is organized into two parts. The first part reviews some preliminary background such as the generalized discriminant analysis (GDA) (Baudat and Anouar, 2000), the bilinear models (BM) (Chuang et. al., 2002), and the relative expression image (REI) (Zhou and Lin, 2005). The GDA is an extension of the traditional discriminant analysis (Duda et. al., 2000) that are useful feature extraction algorithms for classification problems. The difference between two algorihms, LDA and GDA, is that the LDA is designed for linearly separable cases whereas the GDA is extended to handle nonlinearly separable cases. Because the facial expression features have complex distributions in the feature space, the GDA is a good choice for the facial expression classification problems. The BM is a kind of image analysis technique especially useful when the images have two factors. For example, assume that we collected a set of face images for a specific person by changing the illumination direction and head pose. The collected face images have two factors that are illumination direction and head pose. When the collected face images are given, the BM can extract two parameter vectors corresponding to the illumination direction and head pose. This technique can be used for the synthesis of facial expression images when one of the factors is facial expressions. The REI is introduced for robust facial expression image synthesis, where the REI is defined by the ratio of image intensity values of two expression images.

The second part introduces three different facial expression recognition methods. The first two methods are the facial expression recognition algorithms using the 2D+3D AAM as the face model. The difference between them is that the former uses a facial expression classifier using static features and the latter uses a facial expressioin classifier using dynamic features, that is, the former's classifier accepts the facial features at a given image frame and the latter's classifier accepts a sequence of facial features to analyze the change of facial features. The third method recognizes the subtle facial expressions using motion magnification by extracting the subtle motion vector of the predefined feature points and magnifying them by an appropriate motion magnification vector for facial expression recognition. Also, this part introduces a facial expression synthesis algorithm using the AAM and bilinear model.

6.1 GENERALIZED DISCRIMINATE ANALYSIS

Generalized discriminant analysis (GDA) (Baudat and Anouar, 2000) generalizes the linear discriminant analysis (LDA) (Duda et. al., 2000) for the linearly inseparable data using the kernel technique (Cristianini and Taylor, 2000). The main idea of kernel technique is to use the non-linear mapping function that maps the linearly inseparable input data into a high dimensional feature space where the mapped feature vectors can be linearly separable.

A nonlinear mapping function Φ maps an input data $\mathbf{x}$ in the data space $\mathcal{X}$ into the high dimensional feature space F as $\Phi : \mathcal{X} \mapsto \mathcal{F}$. Then, the covariance matrix in the feature space $\mathcal{F}$ can be written as

$$V = \frac{1}{N}\sum_{l=1}^{N}\sum_{k=1}^{n_l} \Phi(\mathbf{x}_k)\Phi(\mathbf{x}_k)'. \tag{6.1.1}$$

We assume that the observations are centered in feature space $\mathcal{F}$. Then, the between class scatter matrix in the feature space is represented as

$$V = \frac{1}{N}\sum_{l=1}^{N} n_l \overline{\Phi}_l \overline{\Phi}_l', \tag{6.1.2}$$

where $\overline{\Phi}_l = (1/n_l)\sum_{k=1}^{n_l} \Phi(\mathbf{x}_k)$ is the mean vector of the l-th class in the feature space.

The goal of GDA is to maximize the between-class scatter and minimize the within-class scatter in the feature space. The solution can be found by solving the following generalized eigenvalue problem as

$$\lambda V \mathbf{v} = B\mathbf{v}, \tag{6.1.3}$$

where λ and $\mathbf{v}$ are the corresponding eigenvalue and eigenvector. The largest eigenvalue gives the maximum of the following discrimination measure as

$$J(\mathbf{v}) = \frac{|\mathbf{v}^t B \mathbf{v}|}{|\mathbf{v}^t V \mathbf{v}|}. \qquad (6.1.4)$$

For a more compact formulation in the matrix form, the original eigenvalue resolution can be rewritten by multiplying $\Phi(\mathbf{x}_{i,j})$ as (Baudat and Anouar, 2000),

$$\lambda \Phi^t(\mathbf{x}_{ij}) V \mathbf{v} = \Phi^t(\mathbf{x}_{ij}) B \mathbf{v} \qquad (6.1.5)$$

For more derivation, we consider the following facts. First, the eigenvectors are expressed by a span of all observations in the feature space $\mathcal{F}$ as

$$\mathbf{v} = \sum_{p=1}^{N} \sum_{q=1}^{n_l} \alpha_{pq} \Phi(\mathbf{x}_{pq}). \qquad (6.1.6)$$

Second, the inner product in the feature space $\mathcal{F}$ can be expressed in a compact form by the help of a kernel function

$$k(\mathbf{x}_i, \mathbf{x}_j) = k_j = \Phi^t(\mathbf{x}_i) \Phi(\mathbf{x}_i). \qquad (6.1.7)$$

For a condense notation, we define a coefficient matrix

$$\alpha = (\alpha_{pq})_{p=1,\dots,N;;q=1,\dots,n_p} \qquad (6.1.8)$$

and a $M \times M$ kernel matrix

$$K = (K_{pq})_{p=1\dots,n;;q=1\dots,n}, \qquad (6.1.9)$$

where $(K)_{pq}$ is a $n_p \times n_p$ matrix that is composed of the inner product in the feature space $\mathcal{F}$ by $(k_j)_{i=1\dots,n_p;j=1,\dots,n_q}$, and a $M \times M$ block diagonal matrix by $(W_l)_{l=1\dots,N}$, where W_l is a $n_l \times n_l$ matrix with all terms equal to $1/n_l$.

By combining Eq. (6.1.6) and Eq. (6.1.7), the discrimination measure $J(\mathbf{x})$ is modified into a new form $J(\alpha)$ as

$$J(\alpha) = \frac{\alpha^t K W K \alpha}{\alpha^t K K \alpha}. \qquad (6.1.10)$$

More detailed derivation can be found in the paper written by Baudat et. al. (Baudat and Anouar, 2000). This expression has a simple form due to the powerful idea that the inner product between the two mapped feature vector is computed by the kernel matrix K without carrying out the nonlinear mapping.

The solution of Eq. (6.1.10) can be computed more easily by decomposing K. Because the kernel matrix K is symmetric, it can be decomposed as

$$K = P\Gamma P^{t},$$

(6.1.11)

where Γ is the diagonal matrix with the non-zero eigenvalues and P is the matrix of normalized eigenvectors associated to Γ that satisfies $\boldsymbol{P}^{t} = I$.

Using Eq. (6.1.11), Eq. (6.1.10) can be rewritten as

$$J(\alpha) = \frac{(\Gamma P^{t}\alpha)^{t} P^{t} WP(\Gamma P^{t}\alpha)}{(\Gamma P^{t}\alpha)^{t} P^{t} P(\Gamma P^{t}\alpha)},$$

(6.1.12)

and the corresponding generalized eigenvalue problem can be rewritten as

$$\lambda P^{t} P\beta = \lambda \ \beta = P^{t} WP\beta,$$

(6.1.13)

where $\beta = \Gamma P^{t}\alpha$, and $\alpha = P\Gamma^{-1}\beta$. Thus, we can compute α by finding β in Eq. (6.1.13). After obtaining β, we can compute α as $\alpha = P\Gamma^{-1}\beta$.

Once we know the coefficient matrix α, we can compute the projection result of a sample data $\mathbf{z}$ in the data space as

$$\mathbf{v}^{t}\Phi(\mathbf{z}) = \sum_{p=1}^{N}\sum_{q=1}^{n_{l}}\alpha_{pq}k(\mathbf{x}_{pq},\mathbf{z}).$$

(6.1.14)

6.2 BILINEAR MODELS

Bilinear models (Tenenbaum and Freeman, 2000) are two-factor models that separate the observations into two factors as style and content. Bilinear models reduce to the linear model when one factor is fixed. Bilinear models are categorized as symmetric and asymmetric. For example, when we see a character, we separate it into a font and a meaning. The font and the meaning are independent factors that represent the character. This work considers the identity as a content factor and the illumination as a style factor.

In a symmetric model, the bilinear model interacts with style and content using an interaction matrix that is independent of the two factors. In an asymmetric model, we assume that one of two factors is known and the bilinear model acts as the linear model. Bilinear models can be used in a variety of applications such as classification, extrapolation and translation. Fig. 6.2.1 illustrates the bilinear model that represents the observations as the interaction of style and content. In this figure, the style factor **a** represents the illumination change and the content factor **b** represents the identity change. The five vectors of style factor contain illumination coefficients for each row of observation images and the four vectors of content factor contain identity coefficients for each column of observation image. An observation vector with specific illumination and identity can be rendered by the bilinear combination of the interaction matrix and corresponding style and content factor.

6.2.1 Bilinear Model Learning

In this section, we describe the learning algorithms for a symmetric model and an asymmetric model. The derivations shown here follow that of Tenenbaum and Freeman (2000). A symmetric bilinear model represents the observation vector $\mathbf{y}$ as

$$\mathbf{y} = \sum_{i=1}^{I} \sum_{j=1}^{J} \mathbf{w}_{ij} a_i b_j,$$
(6.2.1)

where $\mathbf{w}$ is an interaction matrix which interacts with style factor a and content factor b, and I and J are the dimensions of style factor a and content vector b, respectively.

Using the symmetric bilinear model requires learning the interaction matrix $\mathbf{w}$. We use the singular vector decomposition (SVD) to estimate the interaction matrix because SVD tends to obtain the global and non-localized features (Grimes and Rao, 2003). Assume that we have $S \times C$ training samples and have built the observation matrix $\mathbf{Y}$ by stacking them:

$$\mathbf{Y} = \begin{pmatrix} \mathbf{y}_{11} & \cdots & \mathbf{y}_{1C} \\ \vdots & \ddots & \vdots \\ \mathbf{y}_{S1} & \cdots & \mathbf{y}_{SC} \end{pmatrix}, \mathbf{Y}^{\mathbf{r}} = \begin{pmatrix} \mathbf{y}_{11} & \cdots & \mathbf{y}_{1S} \\ \vdots & \ddots & \vdots \\ \mathbf{y}_{C1} & \cdots & \mathbf{y}_{SC} \end{pmatrix},$$
(6.2.2)

Figure 6.2.1. An illustration of bilinear model

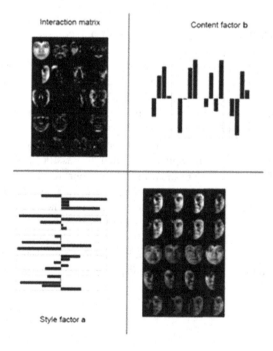

where the superscript VT means vector transpose, each element $\mathbf{y}_j$ is a K-dimensional observation vector, and S and C represent the number of style and content factors, respectively. The observation matrix $\mathbf{Y}$ has a size of $SK \times C$. Fig. 6.2.2 illustrates how to build the $SK \times C$ observation matrix from the $S \times C$ training images, where each image has a size of $K = N \times M$ pixels. In this figure, we have (S×C) face images which have (N×M) dimension. We vectorized each face image to (NM×1) vectors and stacked each vectors into a single (SK×C) observation matrix where $K = N \times M$.

Then, the symmetric model can be represented in a compact form as

$$\mathbf{Y} = (\mathbf{W}^{VT}\mathbf{A})^{VT}\mathbf{B} \ or \ \mathbf{Y}^{VT} = (\mathbf{WB})^{VT}\mathbf{A}, \tag{6.2.3}$$

where A and B represent the stacked style and content factor matrices whose size are $I \times S$ and $J \times C$, respectively:

$$\mathbf{A} = (\mathbf{a}_1, \cdots, \mathbf{a}_S), \mathbf{B} = (\mathbf{b}_1, \cdots, \mathbf{b}_C), \tag{6.2.4}$$

and $\mathbf{W}$ is the stacked interaction matrix:

$$\mathbf{W} = \begin{pmatrix} \mathbf{w}_{11} & \cdots & \mathbf{w}_{1J} \\ \vdots & \ddots & \vdots \\ \mathbf{w}_{I1} & \cdots & \mathbf{w}_{IJ} \end{pmatrix}. \tag{6.2.5}$$

Usually, the optimal style and content matrices **A** and **B** are estimated by an iterative computation of the singular value decomposition. The overall procedure for obtaining the model parameters **A, B** and the interaction matrix **W** is given below.

Figure 6.2.2. An illustration of building the observation matrix $\mathbf{Y}$

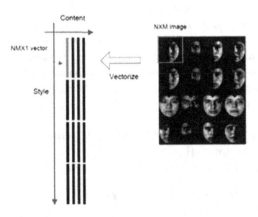

Algorithm I: compute_model_parameter(input: **Y**; output: **A, B, W**)

Decompose the stacked observation matrix **Y** into $\mathbf{Y} = \mathbf{U}S\mathbf{V}^T$ using SVD and initialize **B** as the first J rows of $\mathbf{V}^T$. Then, $\mathbf{YB}^T = \left(\mathbf{W}^{VT}\mathbf{A}\right)^T$ from Eq. (6.2.3).

Perform the SVD of $\left(\mathbf{YB}^T\right)^T = \mathbf{U}S\mathbf{V}^T$ and set **A** to the first I rows of $\mathbf{V}^T$. Then, $\mathbf{Y}^{VT}\mathbf{A}^T = \left(\mathbf{W}B\right)^{YT}$ from Eq. (6.2.3).

Perform the SVD of $\left(\mathbf{Y}^{VT}\mathbf{A}^T\right)^T = \mathbf{U}S\mathbf{V}^T$ and set **B** to the first J rows of $\mathbf{V}^T$.

Repeat steps 2) and 3) until **A** and **B** converge.

Finally, compute $\mathbf{W} = \left(\!\left(\mathbf{YB}^T\right)^T\mathbf{A}^T\right)^T$ from the obtained **A** and **B**.

An asymmetric bilinear model can be expressed by

$$
\begin{aligned}
\mathbf{y} &= \sum_{j=1}^{J}\left(\sum_{i=1}^{S}\mathbf{w}_{ij}a_i\right)b_j, \\
&= \mathbf{W}^s\mathbf{b},
\end{aligned}
\tag{6.2.6}
$$

where $\mathbf{W}^s$ and **b** are the style specific linear mapping with a known style s and a content parameter vector.

Assume that the observation matrix **Y** is given in Eq. (6.2.2). Then, the asymmetric model can be rewritten in a compact form as

$$
\mathbf{Y} = \mathbf{W}^s\mathbf{B},
\tag{6.2.7}
$$

where $\mathbf{W}^s$ and **B** have the sizes of $SK \times J$ and $J \times C$, respectively.

Usually, the optimal content matrix **B** and the interaction matrix **W** are estimated by applying the singular value decomposition of the observation matrix **Y**. From the SVD of **Y**, we obtain the decomposition result $\mathbf{Y} = \mathbf{U}S\mathbf{V}^T$. Then, $\mathbf{W}^s$ and **B** are obtained from the first J columns of **US** and the first J rows of $\mathbf{V}^T$, respectively.

6.1.2 Bilinear Model Translation

The bilinear model allows an unknown face with an unknown illumination to be translated to face with the known illuminations and the known faces to be translated to the unknown illumination. After training the symmetric bilinear model, we obtain the interaction matrix **W**. We obtain the estimates of the style (illumination) factor **a** and the content (identity) factor **b** of a test face image **y** with an unknown identity and an unknown lighting condition by an iterative application of the pseudo inverse operation, where the † symbol denotes the pseudo inverse operation. The overall procedure for obtaining the style and content factors **a** and **b** for a test face image **y** is given below.

Algorithm II: compute_style_content_BM(input: **W, y**; output: **a, b**)

Initialize **b** as the mean vector of **B**.

Update the style factor **a** using $\mathbf{a} = \left(\left(\mathbf{W}b\right)^{YT}\right)^{\dagger}\mathbf{y}$.

Update the content factor **b** using $\mathbf{b} = \left(\left(\mathbf{W}^{VT}\mathbf{a}\right)^{VT}\right)^{\dagger}\mathbf{y}$.

Repeat steps 2) and 3) until **a** and **b** converge.

In the case of the asymmetric bilinear model, we do not use an iterative approach because a style specific basis of the observation **y** is known in advance. If the style specific basis of the observation is $\mathbf{W}_i$, then the content vector can be computed by a single pseudo inverse operation as

$$\mathbf{b} = \left(\mathbf{W}_i\right)^{\dagger} \mathbf{y},$$
(6.2.8)

where the symbol $\dagger$ denotes the pseudo inverse operation.

After obtaining the style and content factor **a** and **b**, we can reconstruct the face images of a unknown person under known lighting conditions or the face images of known persons under a new light condition in the following ways. In the case of the symmetric bilinear model,

$$\tilde{\mathbf{y}} = \left(\mathbf{W}^{VT}\mathbf{a}\right)^{T} \mathbf{b} \; or \; \tilde{\mathbf{y}} = \left(\mathbf{W}b\right)^{VT} \mathbf{a}.$$
(6.2.9)

In the case of asymmetric bilinear model,

$$\tilde{\mathbf{y}} = \mathbf{W}^s \mathbf{b}.$$
(6.2.10)

Fig. 6.2.3 illustrates some typical examples that translate a person $\mathbf{b}_1$ with a lighting condition $\mathbf{a}_1$ to three different lighting conditions $\mathbf{a}_2$, $\mathbf{a}_3$, and $\mathbf{a}_4$ of another person $\mathbf{b}_2$. We extract a set of the style and content factors $\mathbf{a}_1$, $\mathbf{b}_1$ from a test input image and extract three different sets of the style and content factors $(\mathbf{a}_2, \mathbf{b}_2)$, $(\mathbf{a}_3, \mathbf{b}_2)$, and $(\mathbf{a}_4, \mathbf{b}_2)$ from three training samples of a person under different light conditions. Then, we translate the person $\mathbf{b}_1$ to the three different lighting conditions $\mathbf{a}_2$, $\mathbf{a}_3$, and $\mathbf{a}_4$, respectively. As shown in Fig. 6.2.3, the synthesized images look similar with the original images for all different lighting conditions. Test image with content factor $\mathbf{b}_1$ and style factor $\mathbf{a}_1$ is translated into the three different lighting conditions $\mathbf{a}_2, \mathbf{a}_3$ and $\mathbf{a}_4$. The translated images look similar with the original images.

6.3 RELATIVE EXPRESSION IMAGE

Zhou and Lin (Zhou and Lin, 2005) proposed the relative expression parameters for robust facial expression image synthesis. The basic idea of their approach is as follows. When two persons with the same facial expressions are in the same pose and lighting condition, the shape difference Δs and the appearance ratio $R(u,v)$ between two different expressions which are defined as

$$\Delta s = s_n - s_s, \qquad R(u, v) = \frac{A_n(u, v)}{A_s(u, v)}$$
(6.3.1)

Figure 6.2.3. Typical examples of bilinear model translation

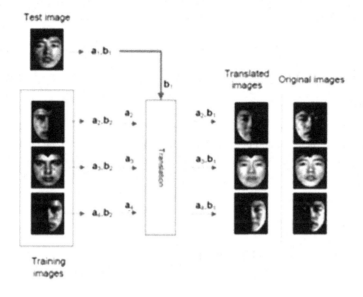

are almost identical for both people. Here s_n and s_s are the shape vectors of the neutral and s expression state, A_n and A_s are the appearance images of the neutral and s expression state, and (u, v) are the 2D coordinates of a pixel in the appearance image.

Thus, $\Delta s \cong \Delta s'$, where $\Delta s = s_n - s_s$ and $\Delta s' = s_n' - s_s'$ are the shape differences between two different expressions of two persons, and the subscripts n and s denote the neutral and s facial expression state, respectively. Similarly, we also know that

$$R(u,v) \cong R'(u,v)$$.

We can obtain the neutral shape vector s_n' of a new person from the new person's shape vector s_s' with the facial expression s and the shape difference Δs of a given person by the following:

$$s_n' = s_s' + \Delta s' \cong s_s' + \Delta s. \qquad (6.3.2)$$

Similarly, we can obtain the neutral appearance image $A_n'(u, v)$ of a new person from the new person's appearance image $A_s'(u, v)$ with the facial expression s and the appearance ratio $R(u,v)$ of a given person by the following:

$$A_n'(u, v) = R'(u, v)A_s'(u, v) \cong R(u, v)A_s'(u, v). \qquad (6.3.3)$$

6.4 FACIAL EXPRESSION RECOGNITION USING AAM FEATURES AND GDA

The 2D+3D AAM is an appropriate face modeling tool for facial expression recognition because it provides the 3D shape and appearance of the face, which changes as the facial expression changes. The difficulty of the person independent facial expression recognition comes from the inter person variation and the subtlety of facial expression itself, i.e., the neutral face of a person can be understood as a smiling or sad face to others. Although 3D shape and appearance feature of the 2D+3D AAM explain the status of face well, classifying them to a specific facial expression class is difficult because their distributions in the feature space is very complicated. Therefore, we used the generalized discriminant analysis (GDA) (Baudat and Anouar, 2000) algorithm to build a facial expression clasifier, which consists of two layers. The layered structure provides the ability to efficiently combine the 3D shape and appearance features and enhance the classification performance for non-linearly distributed complex manifolds.

Fig. 6.4.1 shows the overall structure of the facial expression recognition system that consists of on-line real-time facial expression recognition system and off-line model building process. The on-line system tracks a face in the input stereo image stream using the STAAM algorithm and classifies the estimated 3D shape and 2D appearance into one of four facial expressions (neutral, happy, surprised, and angry) using the layered GDA classifier. The off-line process constructs a 2D+3D AAM model and learn the model parameters for the layered GDA classifier.

6.4.1 A Layered GDA Classifier

Generalized Discriminant Analysis (GDA) (Baudat and Anouar, 2000) is an extension of Linear Discriminant Analysis (LDA) to deal with linearly inseparable data using a kernel method. The proposed facial expression recognition system is based on a GDA algorithm because the distributions of the appearance and shape parameters are greatly intermingled. Although GDA provides a better discrimination ability than the linear discrimination technique, the discrimination performance can be improved by constructing a layered GDA discriminator using the multiple GDAs. The idea of combining multiple discriminators can be found in the fuzzy classifier ensemble (Kim et. al., 2003), the SVM ensemble (Chinnasamy et. al., 2004), the and NN ensemble (Tan et. al., 2003).

We combined the 3D shape and appearance information, which provide complementary information for facial expression classification. The proposed layered classifier (GDA-L) consists of two layers, as shown in Fig. 6.4.2. The first layer consists of two GDAs (GDA-S and GDA-A) that transform the 3D shape and appearance coefficients into the 3D shape feature and appearance feature vectors, respectively. These transformations map the 3D shape and appearance coefficients into their own feature spaces such that they are rouped together along their class labels, and then they are classified easily. The 3D shape and the appearance feature vectors are simply concatenated into one feature vector that is fed for further processing. The second layer consists of one GDA (GDA-L) that transforms the concatenated feature vector into an integrated facial expression feature vector that is more suitable and discriminating for facial expression recognition. After obtaining the integrated feature from the the GDA-L, the integrated feature vector is classified into one of the four

Figure 6.4.1. Structure of the facial expression recognition system

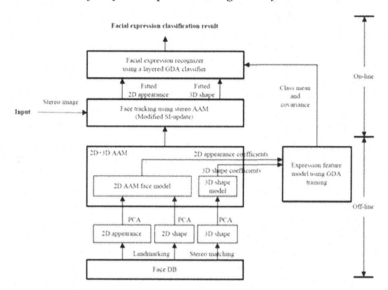

facial expressions: neutral, happy, surprised, and angry. Since the GDA-L provides a rich and well-discriminant feature, we use a simple Mahalanobis distance based classification in this work.

Each facial expression class is assumed to have Gaussian distribution in the integrated feature space. The parameters of a Gaussian distribution function, mean vector $\mathbf{ì}$ and the covariance matrix Σ, are learned from the training data. We classify the input data into a class whose Mahalanobis distance d to the input data is the minimum as

$$\arg \min_i d_i = (\mathbf{y} - \boldsymbol{\mu}_i)' \Sigma_i^{-1} (\mathbf{y} - \boldsymbol{\mu}_i), i = 1, \ldots, 4, \tag{6.4.1}$$

where $\mathbf{ì}_i$ and Σ_i are the mean vector and covariance matrix of the i-th class, and $\mathbf{y}$ is a integrated feature vector that is obtained from the GDA-L.

6.4.2 Experiment Results and Discussion

A face image database is used, which consists of 800 face images (= 100 people × 4 expressions × 2 views). The database was used to evaluate the performance of facial expression recognition of the several layered GDA classifiers. These images were manually landmarked, and the landmark data were used as the ground truth data. A BumbleBee stereo camera was used, which captures a video sequence at 20 frames/sec. Each image was saved as a 640x480 256 gray level image. Fig. 6.4.3 shows some face images in the face database, where the first, second, third, and fourth rows represent the stereo images with neural, happy, surprised, and angry expressions, respectively.

Because the layered GDA facial expressioin classifier uses the 3D shape and appearance parameters of the 2D+3D AAM as the input features, a 2D+3D AAM is constructed from the landmarked face database as follows. 400 3D shapes were collected from the 400

Figure 6.4.2. Combining the shape and appearance using a layered structured GDAs

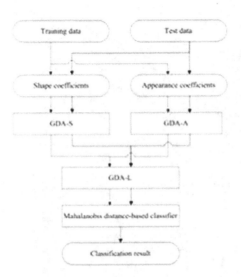

stereo image pairs to build the 3D shape model and 400 right view images were used to build the 2D shape and appearance model. To obtain a 3D shape from a stereo image, we computed a disparity map using a stereo matching algorithm (Chen and Medioni, 2001) and reconstructed the 3D shape using the disparity map and the landmarks in the right view image. Then, a 3D shape model was built from a set of 3D shape data collected from training stereo images. In the experiments, the number of bases was determined to keep 95\% of variation of training data. In Fig. 6.4.4, examples of three linear models are illustrated: (a) the first five 2D shape bases from s_1 to s_5 overlayed on the mean shape s_0, (b) the mean appearance and the first four appearance variation modes from $A_1(\mathbf{x})$ to $A_4(\mathbf{x})$, and (c) the first five 3D shape bases from $\bar{s}_1$ to $\bar{s}_5$ overlayed on the mean shape $\bar{s}_0$.

Fig. 6.4.5 shows the distributions of the 3D shape and appearance features in principal component analysis (PCA) space, respectively. The features in the PCA space are so intermingled that they cannot be discriminated effectively using linear classification methods. Fig. 6.4.6 shows the distributions of 3D shape, appearance, and integrated feature vectors that are obtained from GDA-S, GDA-A, and GDA-L, respectively. This figure shows that (1) the output feature vectors of the GDA-S and GDA-A are more discriminating than those in the PCA space, and (2) the output feature vectors of the GDA-L provide the best discrimination ability.

The test of facial expression classification was performed using a four-fold cross validation method, where the first 75 people (300 3D shape and appearance features) were chosen for training and the remaining 25 people (100 3D shape and appearance features) were tested for facial expression classification. We learned the distributions of four classes in the output feature space using the training data and each test data was classified using Mahalanobis distance. The classification performance was measured using five different types of facial expression features to examine which information among the 3D shape and appearance is useful and how the classification performance can be improved by combining the different

Figure 6.4.3. Some face images in the face database

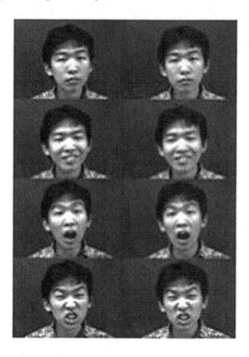

Figure 6.4.4. (a) 2D shape model, (b) appearance model, (c) 3D shape model

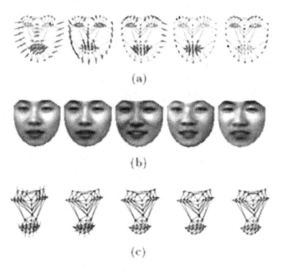

(a)

(b)

(c)

Figure 6.4.5. Distributions of 3D shape (left) and appearance features (right) in the PCA space

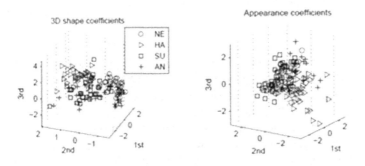

Figure 6.4.6. Distributions of feature vectors obtained from three different GDAs

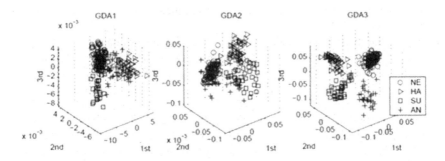

types of information. We repeated this experiment 10 times after randomly permutating the sequence of 100 people. Thus, there are total 40 experiment sets (= 10 repeats × 4 folds), in which differently divided training and test sets were used. The results were obtained by averaging the results of 40 experiments and summarized in Table 6.4.1. In this table, the features PCA-S and PCA-A are the output vectors that were obtained by applying the PCA to 3D shape and appearance, respectively. To show the effectiveness of the proposed layered GDA classifier, we summarized the classification rate of a single layer GDA in the fifth row as GDA-C, where the shape and appearance coefficient are concatenated to create the input vector of this single layer GDA.

Table 6.4.1 shows that (1) the average classification rates in the linear feature spaces (PCA-S and PCA-A) were increased after non-linear transformations using GDA-S and GDA-A, respectively, which means that the distributions in this space are mingled, (2) the 3D shape and appearance provide different information for the classification of facial expressions because they were good at classifying different facial expressions; the 3D shape features (PCA-S) were better to classify the angry (AN) expression than the appearance features (PCA-A) while the appearance features were better to classify the neutral (NE), happy (HA), and surprised (SU) expressions than the 3D shape features in the linear feature space, which implies that we might achieve better classification performance using the 3D shape and appearance information simultaneously, (3) the combination of the 3D shape and appearance information using the layered GDA (GDA-L) showed the highest average classification rate 98.2% and the smallest standard deviation 1.1, which implies that the classification performance of the layered GDA were less affected by the change of training and test data, (4) the average classification rate of the single layer GDA (GDA-C), 96.7%, was lower than that of the layered GDA, although it was higher than those of GDA-S and GDA-A.

The statistical significance of the improved classification rates with respect to the classification rate of a base classification algorithm was also measured and summarized in Table 6.4.2, where the titles of 2nd, 3rd, 4th, 5th, and 6th columns are the base classification algorithm, and the statistical significance is represented by p -values ($-log_{10}p$ in the table). We computed the p -values using the *paired comparison* technique because we compared two algorithms at a time, where the pair of algorithms measured the classification rates against same experiment sets. We set the hypothesis as H_0: $\mu_1 = \mu_2$, where μ_1 and μ_2 were the means of two sets of observed classification rates (40 pairs of classification rates). Thus, the p -values in the Table 6.4.2 represent the probability that the two comparing algorithms have same classification performance. This table shows that the statistical significance of the improvement by the GDA-L with respect to the GDA-C was 0.0013 ($\approx -log_{10}2.9$), which means that the GDA-L was significant over GDA-C algorithms at a significance level $\alpha = 0.05$.

We applied the layered GDA facial expression classifier to long image sequences to show real-time recognition performance. Fig. 6.4.7 shows a typical example of the facial expression classification results for a long image sequence, where the horizontal axis represent the the image frame number. The vertical axes of Fig. 6.4.7 (a) and 6.4.7 (b) are similarity scores to four facial expressions in the GDA-S feature space and the final classification outputs of the layered GDA classifier (GDA-L), respectively. In the long image sequence, the facial expression changes between neutral and happy expressions several times. At some image frames, the similarity scores to angry (AN) expression were the highest score when the expression transits between the neutral (NE) and happy (HA) expressions, but the classifier outputs correct classification results because the layered classifier produces the output considering the shape (GDA-S) and appearance (GDA-A) information simultaneously. Although the classifier is trained using only the peak expressions, this result shows that the classifier work successfully for intermediate expression data.

Table 6.4.1. Comparison of facial expression classification rates (%)

Feature	Classification rate				
type	NE	HA	SU	AN	Avg. / Std.
PCA-S	81.3	96.8	91.5	97.3	91.7 / 3.0
PCA-A	86.4	97.8	97.6	95.6	94.4 / 1.7
GDA-S	97.0	95.5	93.9	90.3	94.2 / 1.5
GDA-A	96.3	97.2	98.4	90.0	95.5 / 1.8
GDA-C	97.3	95.6	98.1	95.9	96.7 / 2.0
GDA-L	99.1	98.3	100.0	95.2	98.2 / 1.1

Table 6.4.2. Statistical significance measures

Feature	$-log_{10}p$ -value given base classification result				
type	PCA-S	PCA-A	GDA-S	GDA-A	GDA-C
PCA-A	6.1				
GDA-S	7.0	0.2			
GDA-A	13.3	2.6	3.2		
GDA-C	15.4	9.2	8.6	2.5	
GDA-L	39.3	23.5	29.3	19.3	2.9

6.5 NATURAL FACIAL EXPRESSION RECOGNITION USING DIFFERENTIAL-AAM AND MANIFOLD LEARNING

A facial expression recognition is applied in many areas such as human computer interaction, multimedia information retrieval, medicine, and commercial products such as digital cameras, due to its one of the most important ways of displaying the emotions. Hence, many researchers have had a growing interest in the facial expression analysis (Fasel and Luettin, 2003). However, it is still difficult to develop a facial expression recognition system that is real-time implementable, person-independent, camera and illumination robust, and more

Figure 6.4.7. Facial expression recognition result for a long time image sequence

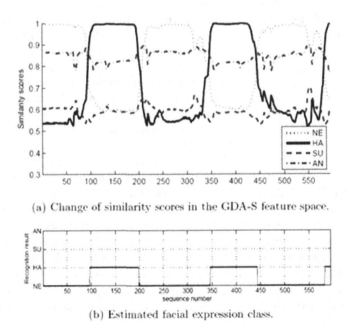

(a) Change of similarity scores in the GDA-S feature space.

(b) Estimated facial expression class.

stably recognizable because the person, camera, and illumination variations complicate the distribution of the facial expressions.

Given input face images, we need to represent them and reduce their dimensions to analyze the facial expressions effectively. There are two representation methods using the linear and non-linear models. Linear models such as PCA (Yang et. al., 2004), bilinear (Tenenbaum and Freeman, 2000), and tensor model (Wang and Ahuja, 2003) are simple and efficient (Chanang et. al., 2002). However, they are not suitable for representing the dynamically changing facial expressions due to their inherent non-linearity. To overcome this problem, many researchers have analyzed the facial expressions in the non-linear space.

Chang et. al. (Chang and Turk, 2003, Chang and Turk, 2004, Chang et. al., 2006) have exploited the Lipschitz manifold embedding to model and align the facial features in a low-dimension embedding space, which improved the facial expression recognition performance much. But it has two limitations : (1) they used only the shape information extracted by the active shape model (ASM) to learn the expression manifold, and (2) they learned and evaluated the facial expression recognition performance only for two subjects.

To overcome these limitations, Shan et. al. (Shan et. al., 2005a, Shan et. al., 2005b, Shan et. al., 2006) proposed appearance manifold of the facial expressions, where the appearance feature was extracted from the raw image data using the local binary patterns (LBP). They also added the method of aligning the expression manifolds for different subjects and supervised locality preserving projections (SLPP). Their works to represent facial images on the non-linear space were very impressive, but their approach had a critical problem that the expression manifold for each subject should be learned individually. It implies that their approach requires training samples containing all facial expressions in off-line and should align the expression manifolds. Also, their approach does not provide the robustness in the change of illuminations due to the difference of illuminations between the training images and the test input image sequence.

To solve the above mentioned problems, we propose the differential-AAM features (DAFs) and the unified expression manifolds. The DAFs are computed from the difference of the AAM parameters between an input face image and a reference face image, which is the neutral expression image that is extracted from the image sequences of the target person. We can develop the person independent facial expression recognition system using DAFs because the differences from a neutral expression to a specific expression (angry, happy, surprised) or vice versa are almost similar among different peoples. This also causes the manifold learning to use all training samples in the unified expression space.

After extracting the DAFs, there are two approaches to recognize the facial expressions : static and temporal approaches. The static classifiers such as the neural networks (NN) (Zhang et. al., 1998, Tian et. al., 2002), the support vector machines (SVM) (Ford, 2002), the linear discriminant analysis (LDA) (Cohn et. al., 1999), and the k nearest neighbors (k-NN) attempt the facial expression recognition using one frame image. The temporal classifiers such as the Hidden Markov model (HMM) (Cohen et. al., 2003), and the recurrent neural networks (RNN) (Rosenblum et. al., 1996) attempt the facial expression recognition using a sequence of images. Sebe et. al. (Sebe et. al., 2007) compared the recognition performances of the several facial expression classifier such as SVM, Naive-Bayes classifier (NB), the tree-augmented naive-Bayes classifier (TAN), and k-NN. According to their experimental results, k-NN classifier shows the best classification result among their static classifier methods. However, the sequence-based classifiers have better recognition performances than the frame-based classifiers. Although the HMM is one of the well known sequence-based classifiers, it fails to estimate the model parameters effectively given a small number of training sequences in a high-dimensional space.

To overcome these limitations, we propose to use the k-nearest neighbor sequences (k-NNS) classifier (Jiangsheng, 2002) that is a sequence-based temporal classifier where it searches the k-NN sequences based on the directed Hausdorff distance (DHD), and then classifies the facial expression as the class of most NNs using the majority voting.

Fig. 6.5.1 shows the overall procedure of the proposed facial expression recognition system, which consists of 3 modules: the differential-AAM features extraction, the manifold embedding, and the expression recognition. In the first module, DAFs extraction has been conducted by the AAM fitting and the neutral expression detection, which is implemented for computing the probability that an input image is a neutral facial expression using the differential facial expression density model (DFEDM). In the second module, we perform the manifold learning that maps the high-dimensional DAFs into the low-dimensional expression space. In the last module, we recognize the facial expressions using k-NNS classifier based on directed Hausdorff distance (DHD) and majority voting.

6.5.1 Differential-AAM Features (DAFs)

For face images, there are many latent variables such as the identity, facial expression, pose, camera, and illumination, etc. Each person has his/her own facial expression, and therefore the variations of facial expressions among peoples are very dispersed, which complicates developing a robust and person-independent facial expression recognition system. To solve this problem, we propose the differential-AAM feature (DAFs) using the property that the differences from the neutral expression to a specific expression (angry, happy, surprised) or vice versa are almost similar among different people.

DAFs are computed using two steps as follows. First, the AAMs is taken to represent the input face images as a compact set of parameters due to its simplicity and flexibility. After the AAM fitting, we obtain the AAM parameters $\theta = \{p, \alpha, q\}$, where p, α, and q are the shape parameter vector, the appearance parameter vector, and the global 2D pose parameter vector including the scale, rotation, and horizontal/vertical translation,

Figure 6.5.1. Diagram of the proposed facial expression recognition system

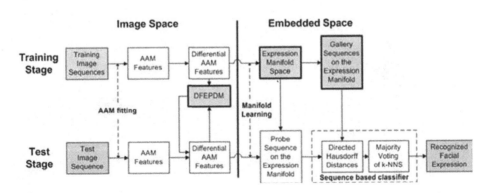

respectively. Often, the shape and appearance parameter vectors are simply concatenated into a integrated feature vector, $\mathbf{y} = \left[\mathbf{p}^T, \boldsymbol{\alpha}^T\right]^T$. Second, we compute the different-AAM features (DAFs) as the difference of the AAM features between the input face image and the reference face image as

$$\Delta\mathbf{y}(t) = \mathbf{y}(t) - \mathbf{y}_{ref}, \tag{6.5.1}$$

where $\Delta\mathbf{y}(t)$ is the differential-AAM feature of the input face image at time t, $\mathbf{y}(t)$ is the AAM feature at time t, and $\mathbf{y}_{ref}$ is the AAM feature of the reference image.

Fig. 6.5.2 shows the distribution of the shape and appearance parameters of the AAMs and the DAFs, respectively, in the PCA space. From this figure, we know that the shape and the appearance parameters in the DAFs are more discriminable than those in the AAMs.

Figure 6.5.2. Distributions of shape and appearance parameters of AAMs (top) and DAFs (bottom)

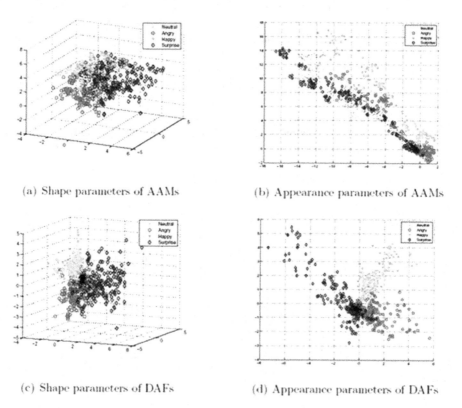

(a) Shape parameters of AAMs   (b) Appearance parameters of AAMs

(c) Shape parameters of DAFs   (d) Appearance parameters of DAFs

6.5.2 Differential Facial Expression Probability Density Model (DFEPDM)

The proposed DAFs need an efficient method of finding the neutral facial expression that is used as the reference image to compute them. We model the similarity of facial expression domain and position of neutral expression using probability models.

To discriminate the positively directional DAFs and the negatively directional DAFs, the differential AAM features are redefined as

$$\Delta \mathbf{y}(t) = \mathbf{y}(t) - \mathbf{y}_{ref} = \mathbf{y}(t) - \mathbf{y}(0), \tag{6.5.2}$$

where $\mathbf{y}(0)$ is the AAM feature at time 0 that is used as the reference, which is often the neutral expression image in the case of the positively directional DAFs and a specific facial expression (angry, happy, or surprised) in the case of the negatively directional DAFs.

The positively and negatively directional DAF's distributions are approximated by the Gaussian kernel estimates $G_p(\mathbf{x}, \boldsymbol{\sigma}_p^2)$ and $G_n(\mathbf{x}, \boldsymbol{\sigma}_n^2)$, respectively, where $\boldsymbol{\sigma}_p^2$ and $\boldsymbol{\sigma}_p^2$ are the variances of the positively and negatively directional DAFs, respectively. Then, we define the differential facial expression probability density model (DFEPDM) by the difference between $G_p(\mathbf{x}, \boldsymbol{\sigma}_p^2)$ and $G_n(\mathbf{x}, \boldsymbol{\sigma}_n^2)$ as

$$P_{DFEPDM}(\mathbf{x}) = G_p(\mathbf{x}, \boldsymbol{\sigma}_p^2) - G_n(\mathbf{x}, \boldsymbol{\sigma}_n^2). \tag{6.5.3}$$

When we take the positively directional input image sequence changing from the neutral facial expression to a specific facial expression, the probability values of $P_{DFEPDM}(\mathbf{x})$ are positively increasing. On the other hand, when we take the negatively directional input image sequence changing from a specific facial expression to the neutral facial expression, the probability values of $P_{DFEPDM}(\mathbf{x})$ are negatively decreasing.

Fig. 6.5.3 shows several figures where the positively directional DAF's distribution and its corresponding Gaussian kernel approximation are represented in Fig. 6.5.3 (a), the negatively directional DAF's distribution and its corresponding Gaussian kernel approximation are represented in Fig. 6.5.3 (b), and the differential facial expression probability density model (DFEPDM) is represented in Fig. 6.5.3 (c).

We consider the AAM feature of the neutral expression as the reference feature for the DAFs. A detailed explanation of obtaining the reference feature is given by the following. First, we obtain the AAM features $\{\mathbf{y}(t+i-1)\}_{i=1}^{W_s}$ of the face images $\{I(t+i-1)\}_{i=1}^{W_s}$ within the sampling window whose size is W_s. Second, we compute the DAFs $\{\Delta \mathbf{y}(t+i-1)\}_{i=1}^{W_s}$ of the face images using the first AAM feature $\mathbf{y}(t)$ as the reference feature (See the Fig. 6.5.4). Third, we compute the probabilities of the DAFs using the pre-computed DFEPDM $P_{DFEPDM}(\mathbf{x})$. Fourth, we compute the cumulative probability $C_{DFEPDM}(t)$ that is the summation of probabilities $P_{DFEPDM}(\Delta \mathbf{y})$ within the sampling window as

$$C_{DFEPDM}(t) = \sum_{i=1}^{W_s} P_{DFEPDM}(\Delta \mathbf{y}(t+i-1))$$, when the first image feature $\mathbf{y}(t)$ within the sampling window is used as the reference feature. Finally, we apply an average filter (Gonzalez and Woods, 2002) to the cumulative probabilities $C_{DFEPDM}(t)$ in order to make the probabilities more smooth. We take the AAM feature of the input image whose probability of $C_{DFEPDM}(t)$ is maximal as the reference feature.

Figure 6.5.3. Differential facial expression probability density model (DFEPDM)

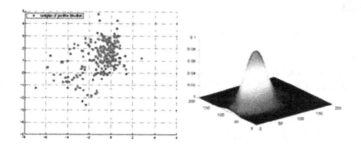

(a) Positively directional DAFs, and it's kernel density approximation.

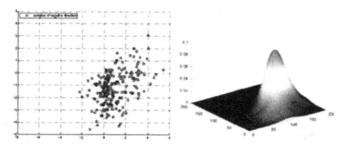

(b) Negatively directional DAFs, and it's kernel density approximation.

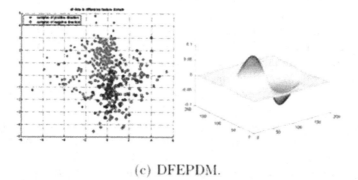

(c) DFEPDM.

Fig. 6.5.5 shows an overall procedure of determining the reference feature: Fig. 6.5.5 (a) shows a test input image sequence, Fig. 6.5.5 (b) shows the cumulative probabilities of $C_{DFEPDM}(t)$ with respect to the test input image sequence, and Fig. 6.5.5 (c) shows the smoothing results using the average filter of size W_{gi} , where the reference features are marked as the field circle.

Figure 6.5.4. An illustration of computing the DAFs using the sampling window

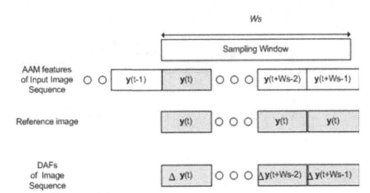

6.5.3 Manifold Learning

The classical linear methods such as the PCA and the classical MDS are simple and efficient because they are linear. However, they are not suitable for representing the dynamically changing facial expressions due to their inherent non-linearity. To overcome this limitation, many nonlinear dimensionality reduction techniques have been exploited to model the manifold structures in the facial expression analysis. Typically, the manifold embedding is trained for the specific person's facial expression because the embedded manifolds are much different among different peoples. To make the manifold embedding person-independent, Chang et. al. (Chang and Turk, 2004) proposed a Lipschitz embedding which was an aligned manifold embedding of different subjects and Elgammal et. al. (Elgammal and Lee, 2004) warped the person-specific manifold to the mean manifold to obtain a unified imbedding. These methods to align the different manifolds cannot be used to implement the real-time facial expression system because they need many training samples with all facial expressions.

Fortunately, the DAFs do not require the alignment process for the unified manifold embedding because we assume that all person's patterns of facial expressions changing from the neutral expression to a specific expression (angry, happy, or surprised), or vice versa, are similar. This enables to represent the DAFs for all persons in the one manifold embedding space.

In this work, we adapt the k -Isomap framework (Tenenbaum et. al., 2000) for manifold embedding, which is explained in detail as follows.

- Compute the pairwise distance matrix D_{DAF}, where the element $d_{DAF}(i, j)$ is the distance between all i th and j th pairs of DAFs.
- Construct the neighborhood graph G, where the element $g(i, j)$ is 1 if the j th DAF is one of the k nearest neighbors of the j th DAF, and otherwise, it is 0.
- Compute the shortest path distances in the geodesic distance matrix $D_{manifold}$, where the element $d_{manifold}(i, j)$ is initialized as $d_{DAF}(i, j)$ if the i th DAF and the j th DAF are linked by an edge, otherwise it is initialized as ∞, and then $d_{manifold}(i, j)$ is

Figure 6.5.5. An overall procedure of determining the reference feature

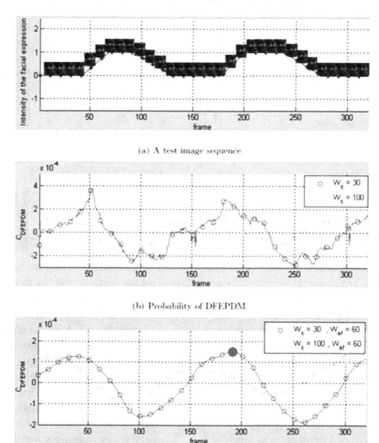

(a) A test image sequence.

(b) Probability of DFEPDM.

(c) The smoothing result using the average filter.

updated by the shortest path distance in the graph G using the Dijkstra's algorithm.

•   Construct the expression manifold embedding by applying the classical multidimensional scaling (MDS) (Mardia et. al., 1979) to the geodesic distance matrix $D_{manifold}$

6.5.4 k -Nearest Neighbor Sequences Classifier (k -NNS)-NNS)"

The k -nearest neighbors (k -NN) classifier is very easy and efficient, but it considers only a static image. To overcome this limitation of k -NN classifier, we propose to use the k -nearest neighbor sequences (k -NNS) classifier. The training procedure for the k -NNS classifier is to construct the gallery as

$$Gallery = \{(\mathbf{S}_1, y_1), (\mathbf{S}_2, y_2), \cdots, (\mathbf{S}_{N_G}, y_{N_G})\},$$

(6.5.4)

where each sequence consists of the N_S DAFs $\mathbf{S} = \mathbf{s}_1, \mathbf{s}_2, \cdots, \mathbf{s}_{N_S}$, y_i is the facial expression class of the i th sequence in the gallery, and N_G is the number of the sequences in the gallery.

The test procedure for the k-NNS classifier is performed as follows. First, we compute the distances between the test image sequence and the gallery image sequences. In this work, we take the directed Hausdorff distance (DHD) that measures the distance between a test image sequence $\mathbf{X} = \mathbf{x}_1, \mathbf{x}_2, \cdots, \mathbf{x}_{N_X}$ and a reference sequence $\mathbf{Y} = \mathbf{y}_1, \mathbf{y}_2, \cdots, \mathbf{y}_{N_Y}$, where the N_X and N_Y are the length of the X and Y, respectively, as

$$D_{DHD}(\mathbf{X}, \mathbf{Y}) = \sum_{i=1}^{N_X} w_i \cdot \left\| \mathbf{x}_i - \mathbf{y}_j \right\|, \tag{6.5.5}$$

where w_i is the weight factor that emphasizes the recent input image as

$$w_i = \frac{1 + \alpha \cdot i}{\sum_{k=1}^{N_X}(1 + \alpha \cdot k)}, \tag{6.5.6}$$

where α is a magnification constant (when α is zero, all face images in the test image sequence have the same weights.), and the index j is the relative index in the reference sequence that corresponds to the ith index in the test image sequence as

$$j = Round(1 + \frac{N_Y - 1}{N_X - 1} \cdot (i - 1)). \tag{6.5.7}$$

Second, we gather the k nearest neighbor sequences among the N_G gallery sequences according to the directed Hausdorff distances and decide the facial expression of the input image sequence by a majority voting.

6.5.5 Experiment Results and Discussion

We have performed several experiments that show the validity of the proposed facial expression recognition method. We have implemented the proposed facial expression recognition system in the Visual C++ environment on the PC platform with a Pentium-4 Duo CPU with a clock speed of 2.8GHz, a 2GB RAM, and the Window XP professional.

6.5.5.1 Database

We used the POSTECH Facial Expression Database FED06, which included 16 Korean peoples (12 males and 4 females whose ages are between 20 and 35, and 8 peoples of them wear the glasses) and had four image sequences changing from the neutral expression to the neutral (angry, happy, surprised) facial expression, or vice versa, and repeated these image sequences 4 times. Therefore, there are 256 positively directional face image sequences (16 peoples × 4 expressions × 4 times) and 256 negatively directional face image sequences (16 peoples × 4 expressions × 4 times). The BumbleBee stereo camera used to capture a video sequence at the speed of 30 frames/sec and each face image was saved as a 640x480 256 gray level image. Fig. 6.5.6 shows some face images of 6 participants, where each column from the left to the right represents the neutral, angry, happy, and surprised facial expression and each row from the top to the bottom corresponds to the different people.

We partitioned the 512 face image sequences of 16 people into the training and test sets, where the first half of the FED06 consisting of 128 positively directional face image sequences and 128 negatively directional face image sequences is the training set and the remaining half of the FED06 consisting of the remaining 128 positively directional face image sequences and the remaining 128 negatively directional face image sequences is the test set. We have landmarked all the face images in all face image sequences and evaluated the facial expression recognition performance using the 2-fold cross validation technique, which is repeated 5 times.

6.5.5.2 Different Types of Features

We compared the facial expression recognition performances when two different types of features (the AAM feature and the DAF feature) and three different modes of features (the 3D shape feature, the appearance feature, and the integrated feature combining the 3D shape and the appearance) are used. Fig. 6.5.7 shows the facial expression recognition rates of 6 different feature combinations using the 5-NN classifier when the number of the basis vectors of each component is varying from 1 to 30. From this figure, we know that (1) the facial expression recognition performances vary much with respective to the number

Figure 6.5.6. Some face images of the database FED06

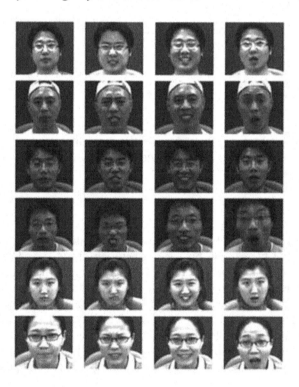

of the basis vectors, (2) the DAF feature provides better recognition performance than the AAM feature in all feature types, and (3) the facial expression recognition rate is the best when the combination of the DAF and the integrated feature is used.

Table 6.5.1 summarizes the best facial expression recognition rates of 6 different feature combinations with respective to the different facial expressions in the case of using the 5-NN classifier, where the combination of the DAF and the integrated feature of the 3 largest 3D shape features and the 3 largest appearance features gives the best facial expression recognition performance of 91.52%.

6.5.5.3 Neutral Expression Detection

We evaluated the detection accuracy of the proposed neutral facial expression detection method when the window size W_s varies from 10, 30, 100, to 300, and the average filter size W_{af} varies from 0 to 300. In this experiment, it is assumed that the neutral expression is correctly detected when the expression class obtained from the proposed method is equal to the ground-truth facial expression class given manually and both are the neutral facial expressions. Fig. 6.5.8 shows the neutral expression detection rates when the window size W_s and the average filter size W_{af} vary. From this figure, we know that (1) the detection rates increase as the window size W_s increases, (2) the detection rates increase initially, reach to their peaks, and decrease gradually after peaks as the average filter size W_{af} increases, and (3) the best detection rate occurs when $W_s = 100$ and $W_{af} = 60$.

Figure 6.5.7. Comparison of the facial expression recognition rates of 6 different feature combinations

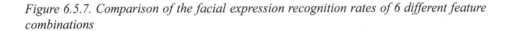

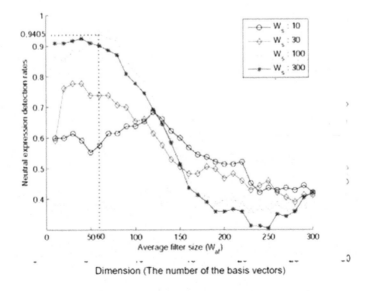

Table 6.5.1. Comparison of the best facial expression recognition performances (%)

	Overall	Neutral	Angry	Happy	Surprised
shape+AAM (3 dim.)	66.24	62.86	54.89	76.37	70.21
appearance+AAM (3 dim.)	64.52	50.82	70.00	80.25	61.00
integrated+AAM (5 dim.)	71.72	70.38	74.44	79.62	81.00
shape+DAF (3 dim.)	79.16	89.99	59.61	86.75	77.00
appearance+DAF (5 dim.)	89.71	94.18	78.06	88.81	97.79
integrated+DAF (6 dim.)	**91.52**	92.50	82.11	93.69	96.29

6.5.5.4 Manifold Learning

We compared the facial expression recognition performances using the frame-based 5-NN classifier when the number of nearest neighbors k in the Isomap manifold embedding varies. Fig. 6.5.9 shows the facial expression recognition rates with respect to different values of k. From this figure, we know that (1) the facial expression recognition rates are not changed much with respective to the different values of k, and (2) the best facial expression recognition rate is 92.53% when $k = 9$.

6.5.5.5 Facial Expression Recognition Using the *k*-NNS Classifier

We compared the facial expression recognition performances using the k-NNS classifier when the number of the nearest neighboring sequences k varies. Fig. 6.5.10 shows the facial

Figure 6.5.8. The neutral expression detection rates

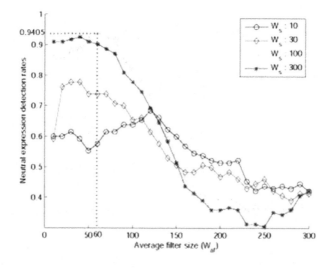

Figure 6.5.9. Recognition rates with different values of k in the Isomap

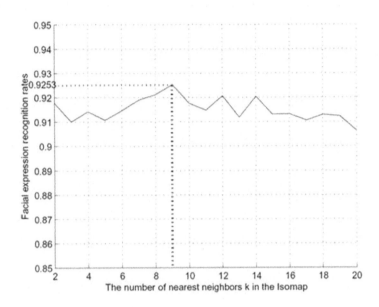

expression recognition rates when the values of k vary. From this figure, we know that (1) the recognition rates becomes smaller after a peak value, and (2) the best facial expression recognition rate is 96.09% when $k = 3$.

Table 6.5.2 shows the confusion matrix of the facial expression recognition when the 3-NNS classifier is used. From this table, we know that most of the neutral, happy, surprised expression sequences are classified almost perfectly but some of the angry expression sequences are classified as the neutral expression due to their similarity.

Table 6.5.3 compares the facial expression recognition performances using different types of classifiers: the k-NN and the rbf-SVM (Ma et. al., 2002) classifiers are the frame-based classifier while the HMM and the k-NNS classifiers are the sequence-based classifier. From this table, we know that (1) although the HMM is known as one of the best temporal classifiers, it shows poor recognition performance, especially in the neutral image sequences, and (2) the k-NNS classifier outperforms all other classifiers in terms of the highest recognition rate of 96.09%.

Table 6.5.2. Confusion matrix of the recognition results using the 3-NNS classifier

	Neutral	Angry	Happy	Surprised
Neutral	320	0	0	0
Angry	31	289	0	0
Happy	0	10	310	0
Surprise	0	9	0	311

Figure 6.5.10. Recognition rates with different values of k in the k-NNS classifier

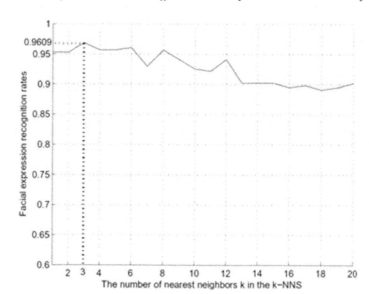

6.5.5.6 Robustness of DAFs

We validated that DAFs were appropriate for the facial expression recognition because they were robust to not only the inter-person variations but also the camera and illumination variations due to the differential property of the DAFs. Table 6.5.4 shows three different environmental configurations, where three different types of cameras (the BumbleBee stereo camera, the CCD camera, and the Webcam camera) are used and three different locations (room, office, and outdoor) are taken.

Table 6.5.5 summarizes the facial expression recognition rates with respective to three different environmental configurations. From this table, we know that the proposed facial expression recognition method works well under the different types of cameras and the different types of illuminations.

Table 6.5.3. Comparison of facial expression recognition performances (%)

	Overall	Neutral	Angry	Happy	Surprised
k -NN(k=5)	92.53	93.30	84.78	94.25	96.79
rbf-SVM(Gamma = 0.07)	93.37	94.45	88.50	93.04	95.79
HMM	83.59	67.19	87.50	93.75	85.94
k -NNS (k=3)	96.09	100.00	90.31	96.88	97.17

6.5.5.7 Practical implementation

We have implemented the proposed facial expression recognition system in the Visual C++ environment on the PC platform with a Pentium-4 Duo CPU with a clock speed of 2.8GHz, a 2GB RAM, and the Window XP professional. The implemented system works for the real people in the rate of 5-7 frames. You can see how the system is working at the video clip that is linked at http://imlab.postech.ac.kr/ dkim/new_imlab/video/facial_expression1. wmv. The video clip includes several facial expression recognitions at the extreme cases, the mild cases, under the changing illuminations, and at the long distance.

6.6 SUBTLE FACIAL EXPRESSION RECOGNITION USING MOTION MAGNIFICATION

Recently, facial expression analysis has attracted a plenty of interest in the area of computer vision because it plays an important role in the human-machine communication (Fasel and Luettin, 2003). Facial expressions are generated by contractions of facial muscles, which results in temporally deformed facial features such as eye lids, eye brows, nose, lips, and skin texture. They are measured by three characteristics: the location of facial actions, the intensity of facial actions, and the dynamics of facial actions.

There are two main methodological approaches on measuring these three characteristics of facial expressions: sign-based approaches and judge-based approaches (Ekman, 1982). The sign-based approaches represent the facial actions in a coded way, where the facial actions are abstracted and described by their location and intensity in the facial action coding systems (FACS) developed by Ekman and Friesen (1978). In the FACS, local deformations of the face7 are defined as 44 action units (AUs) such as raising eye brows, turning eyes, checking nose wrinkle, pulling down lip corners, and so on. Many researchers have tried to recognize human emotion by classifying action units (Donalto et. al., 1999; Pantic and Rothkrantz, 2000; Tian et. al., 2001). However, it is difficult to interpret AUs by the common peoples because of the inter-person variations. That is the reason why the emotion interpretations were only provided by several experts such as the psychologists. The judge-based approaches directly associate specific facial patterns with the mental activities, where the facial actions are classified into one of the six basic emotion classes introduced by Ekman and Friesen (1978). Many researchers have adopted this approaches for the automatic facial expression recognition (Mase and Pentland, 1991; Liu et. al., 20011 Essa and Pentland, 1997). We also adopt the latter approach because it is difficult to define the subtle facial expressions by the FACS.

Table 6.5.4. Three different environmental configurations

	Camera	light source	location	# of subjects
Environment 1	BumbleBee stereo camera	fluorescent light	room	16
Environment 2	CCD Camera	fluorescent light	office	10
Environment 3	Logitech Web Camera	natural light	outdoor	10

Table 6.5.5. Comparison of facial expression recognition performances with respective to different cameras and illuminations (%)

	Overall	Neutral	Angry	Happy	Surprised
Environment 1	**96.09**	100.00	90.31	96.88	97.19
Environment 2	**94.17**	100.00	86.67	100	90.00
Environment 3	**92.50**	96.67	86.67	100	86.67

Automatic facial expression analysis is a complicated task because the human faces vary from one individual to another quite considerably due to different age, ethnicity, gender, facial hair, cosmetic products, occluding objects such as glasses and hair, poses and lighting changes. The generic facial expression analysis framework consists of three components: face acquisition, facial feature extraction, and facial expression classification. We mainly focus on the facial feature extraction and facial expression classification problem.

Most of existing facial expression analysis methods attempt to recognize the extreme facial expressions. However, in the real situation, people do not always express the facial expression extremely. To tackle this problem, several researchers have been tried to recognize the subtle and spontaneous facial expressions (Song et. al., 2006; Cowell and Ayesh, 2004), but there are no effective or novel methods yet to recognize the subtle and spontaneous facial expressions. We propose an effective and novel method of recognizing the subtle facial expressions using the motion magnification which transforms the subtle facial expressions to the corresponding exaggerated facial expressions by magnifying the motion vectors of the feature points.

We extract the motion features using the feature point tracking. But, the motion features of the subtle facial expressions of different expression classes are intermingled in the facial expression feature space, which makes the facial expression classification difficult. To overcome this problem, we apply the motion magnification technique that transforms the subtle facial expressions to the corresponding exaggerated facial expressions which makes the discrimination of facial expression features easier, improving the facial expression recognition performance greatly.

The facial expression classification methods must handle the nonlinear characteristics among the exaggerated facial expression features of different expression classes. Generally, there are two nonlinear classification approaches: the spatio-temporal classifications and the spatial classifications. In the spatio-temporal approaches, the hidden Markov Models (HMMs) (Otsuka and Ohya, 1998) or the recurrent neural networks (RNNs) (Kobayahsi and Hara, 1997) were commonly used to model the dynamics of facial actions and classify them into their classes. In the spatial approaches, neural networks were often used for facial expression classifications (Zheng et. al., 2004) and were applied directly on face images or combined with facial feature extraction and representation method such as the principal component analysis (PCA), the independent analysis (ICA) or Gabor wavelet filters. We take another nonlinear spatial classification using the support vector machine (SVM) due to its superiority of classification performance.

Fig. 6.6.1 shows an overall process of the proposed subtle facial expression recognition method. It consists of two main parts: (1) motion magnificaiton and (2) facial expression recognition.

6.6.1 Motion Magnification

To effectively classify subtle facial expressions, we transform them into exaggerated facial expressions using the motion magnification. The motion magnification is performed by the subsequent four steps: (1) we extract the feature points using the AAM, (2) we align the face image using the extracted feature points, (3) we estimate motion vectors using the feature points tracking, and (4) obtain the exaggerated facial expression images by magnifying the motion vectors. A detailed explanation of the subsequent procedures is given below.

6.6.1.1 Feature Point Extraction

To process the face images, we first need to extract the good facial feature points. Some other facial expression recognition methods usually extract the feature points manually, but we automatically extract the feature points using the AAM, which is a suitable method to extract the important facial shape points by fitting the model on the face images. In this work, we extract 70 shape feature points by applying the AAM fitting on the first image frame, as shown in Fig. 6.6.2. We use 3 static shape feature points for the image alignment and 27 dynamic shape feature points for the motion estimation.

6.6.1.2 Image Alignment

Due to inevitable small motions that are caused by the camera and/or human motions, some static feature points may have unnecessary movements, which cause them to be dynamic feature points. To compensate these unnecessary movements, we align the face images by fixing the movement of the static feature points that are not moved much when the facial

Figure 6.6.1. Overall process of the proposed subtle facial expression recognition method

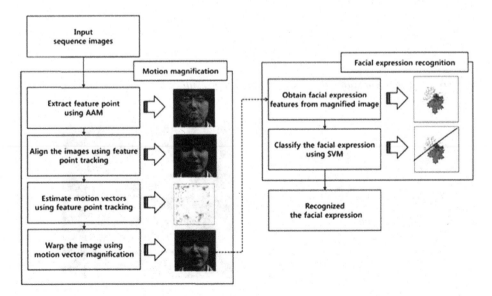

expression is changed. In this work, we select three feature points (inner points of both eyes, and the middle point of both nostrils as the static feature points for the image alignment, as shown in Fig. 6.6.3.

The three static feature points maintain the ratio of the distance between two feature points and the shape of positions although the facial expression is changed. Each of these points forms the center of a 15 x 15 window, and they are automatically tracked in the remaining frames using the feature point tracking.

Here, we use the feature point tracking method developed by Lien (1998) based on the Lucas (1984) registration method, where the feature tracking is obtained by finding the closest corresponding matching feature points between two consecutive frames, which minimizes the sum of the weighted squared differences between the $N \times N$ window R of one feature point $I_t(\mathbf{x})$ and that of another feature point $I_{t+1}(\mathbf{x}')$ in the iterative manner. Fig. 6.6.4 illustrates one example of the feature tracking.

A detailed explanation on the feature point tracking is given below. The goal of feature point tracking is to find the best matching positions between an $N \times N$ window R in the image at time t and that of the following image at time $t+1$ that minimizes a cost function E of the weighted sum of squared differences (SSD) as

$$E(\mathbf{d}(\mathbf{x})) = \sum_{\mathbf{x} \in R} w(\mathbf{x}) \cdot [I_t(\mathbf{x}) - I_{t+1}(\mathbf{x} - \mathbf{d}(\mathbf{x}))]^2, \qquad (6.6.1)$$

where $I_t(\mathbf{x})$ denotes the gray value of the pixel position $\mathbf{x}$ in R at time t, $\mathbf{d}(\mathbf{x})$ is the motion vector of $\mathbf{x}$ of region R between two consecutive image frames and $w(\mathbf{x})$ is the window function for weighting the squared differences in E, which is defined by several ways such as the Lucas-Kanade based weight (Lucas, 1984), the spline-based weight (Szeliski and Coughlan, 1997), and the wavelet-based weight (Wu et. al., 1998).

In this work, we update the motion vector $\mathbf{d}(\mathbf{x})$ iteratively as

$$\mathbf{d}_{i+1}(\mathbf{x}) = \mathbf{d}_i(\mathbf{x}) + \Delta \mathbf{d}_i(\mathbf{x}), \qquad (6.6.2)$$

Figure 6.6.2. The mean shape of AAM and the fitting result of the AAM

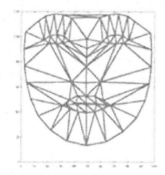 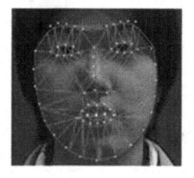

Figure 6.6.3. An illustration of image alignment

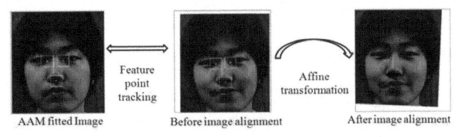

AAM fitted Image   ⟷ Feature point tracking   Before image alignment   ⌢ Affine transformation   After image alignment

where $\Delta \mathbf{d}_i(\mathbf{x})$ is the incremental motion vector at the th iteration and the value of the motion vector is initialized as $\Delta \mathbf{d}_0(\mathbf{x}) = [0,0]^T$. The incremental motion vector $\Delta \mathbf{d}_i(\mathbf{x})$ is obtained by minimizing $E(\Delta \mathbf{d}(\mathbf{x}))$, which is approximated as

$$
\begin{aligned}
E\big(\Delta \mathbf{d}_i(\mathbf{x})\big) &\approx E\big(\mathbf{d}_i(\mathbf{x}) + \Delta \mathbf{d}_i(\mathbf{x})\big) - E\big(\mathbf{d}_i(\mathbf{x})\big) \\
&= \sum_{\mathbf{x} \in R} w(\mathbf{x})[I_t(\mathbf{x}) - I_{t+1}(\mathbf{x} - \mathbf{d}_i(\mathbf{x}) - \Delta \mathbf{d}_i(\mathbf{x}))]^2 \\
&\quad - \sum_{\mathbf{x} \in R} w(\mathbf{x})[I_t(\mathbf{x}) - I_{t+1}(\mathbf{x} - \mathbf{d}_i(\mathbf{x}))]^2.
\end{aligned}
\tag{6.6.3}
$$

By the first order Taylor series expansion, Eq. (6.6.3) is approximated as

$$
\begin{aligned}
E(\Delta \mathbf{d}_i(\mathbf{x})) &\approx \sum_{\mathbf{x} \in R} w(\mathbf{x})[I_t(\mathbf{x}) - I_{t+1}(\mathbf{x} - \mathbf{d}_i(\mathbf{x})) + I'_{t+1}(\mathbf{x} - \mathbf{d}_i(\mathbf{x}))\Delta \mathbf{d}_i(\mathbf{x})]^2 \\
&\quad - \sum_{\mathbf{x} \in R} w(\mathbf{x})[I_t(\mathbf{x}) - I_{t+1}(\mathbf{x} - \mathbf{d}_i(\mathbf{x}))]^2 \\
&= \Delta \mathbf{d}^{\mathrm{T}}_i(\mathbf{x}) G_i(\mathbf{x}) \Delta \mathbf{d}_i(\mathbf{x}) - 2\mathbf{e}^{\mathrm{T}}_i(\mathbf{x}) \Delta \mathbf{d}_i(\mathbf{x}).
\end{aligned}
\tag{6.6.4}
$$

Figure 6.6.4. An illustration of feature point tracking using motion estimation

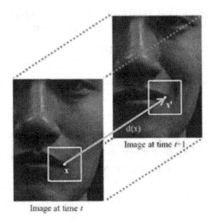

d(x)

Image at time $t+1$

Image at time t

where

$$G_i(\mathbf{x}) = \sum_{\mathbf{x} \in R} w(\mathbf{x}) [I'_{t+1}(\mathbf{x} - \mathbf{d}_i(\mathbf{x})) I_{t+1}'(\mathbf{x} - \mathbf{d}_i(\mathbf{x}))^T],$$ (6.6.5)

is the Hessian matrix of the gradients of $I_t(\mathbf{x})$ with a window function $w(\mathbf{x})$ and

$$e_i(\mathbf{x}) = \sum_{\mathbf{x} \in R} w(\mathbf{x}) [I_t(\mathbf{x}) - I_{t+1}(\mathbf{x} - \mathbf{d}_i(\mathbf{x}))] [I'_{t+1}(\mathbf{x} - \mathbf{d}_i(\mathbf{x}))^T],$$ (6.6.6)

is a difference-gradient row vector which is the product of the difference (or error) between the regions in the two sequence images and the gradient of the gray-value $I_t(\mathbf{x})$ together with a weighting window function $w(\mathbf{x})$. The maximum decrement of $E(\Delta \mathbf{d}_i(\mathbf{x}))$ occurs when its gradient with respect to $\Delta \mathbf{d}_i(\mathbf{x})$ is zero as

$$\frac{\partial E(\Delta \mathbf{d}_i(\mathbf{x}))}{\partial(\Delta \mathbf{d}_i(\mathbf{x}))} \quad = \quad G_i(\mathbf{x})\Delta \mathbf{d}_i(\mathbf{x}) + (\Delta \mathbf{d}_i^T(\mathbf{x}) G_i(\mathbf{x}))^T - 2e_i(\mathbf{x})$$
$$= \quad 2(G_i(\mathbf{x})\Delta \mathbf{d}_i(\mathbf{x}) - e_i(\mathbf{x})) = 0.$$ (6.6.7)

Hence,

$$\Delta \mathbf{d}_i(\mathbf{x}) = G_i(\mathbf{x})^{-1} e_i(\mathbf{x}).$$ (6.6.8)

The motion vector $\mathbf{d}_i(\mathbf{x})$ can be iteratively estimated using Eq. (6.6.2) combined by Eq. (6.6.5), (6.6.6), and (6.6.8).

The positions of three tracked facial feature points (two eyes and nose tip) are normalized by the affine transformation as

$$\mathbf{X}' = \begin{bmatrix} cos\theta & -sin\theta \\ sin\theta & cos\theta \end{bmatrix} \begin{bmatrix} S_x & 0 \\ 0 & S_y \end{bmatrix} \mathbf{X} + \begin{bmatrix} t_x \\ t_y \end{bmatrix},$$ (6.6.9)

where the parameters S_x, S_y, t_x, t_y and θ are the horizontal/vertical scaling, the horizontal/vertical translations and rotation factors. Here, $\mathbf{X}$ and $\mathbf{X}$ are a pair of three corresponding static feature points between two consecutive image frames by the computed feature point tracking method. Then, these parameters can be computed by the least square method. Finally, we obtain the feature point position $\mathbf{X}_{aligned}$ in the aligned face image by applying the affine transformation as

$$\mathbf{X}_{aligned} = \mathbf{W}_{norm} \mathbf{x}',$$ (6.6.10)

where $\mathbf{W}_{norm}$ is a normalizing warping matrix which consists of the above parameters and $\mathbf{x}'$ is the position of feature point in the non-aligned face image. The position of feature points in the non-aligned face image has integer values, but it obtains real values after the image alignment. To adjust this problem, we use bilinear interpolation based on four nearest neighbor pixels.

6.6.1.3 Motion Estimation

Once the face images have been aligned, we choose the 27 representative feature points and apply the feature point tracking method to estimate the motion vectors of each feature point as follows.

First, we obtain 70 feature points by applying the AAM fitting to the aligned face image and select 27 dynamic feature points among them, which are 4 points around the left and the right eyebrow contour, 4 points around the left and the right eye contour, and 11 points around the mouth contour, as shown in Fig. 6.6.5 (a). We only obtain the motion vectors of these 27 dynamic feature points $(\mathbf{x}_1, \mathbf{x}_2, \cdots, \mathbf{x}_{27})$ because they effectively represent facial motions when the facial expression is changed.

Second, we obtain the motion vectors of feature points using the feature point tracking method explained above. Fig. 6.6.5 shows an example of obtaining the motion vectors, where Fig. 6.6.5 (a) and (b) show the neutral expression image and the subtle surprised expression image while Fig. 6.6.5 (c) shows the result of obtaining the motion vectors of feature vectors. The tracked 27 feature points in the subtle surprised expression image $(\mathbf{x}_1', \mathbf{x}_2', \cdots, \mathbf{x}_{27}')$ are estimated as

$$\mathbf{x}_i' = \mathbf{x}_i + \mathbf{d}(\mathbf{x}_i)i = 1,2,\cdots,27, \tag{6.6.11}$$

where $(\mathbf{d}(\mathbf{x}_i) : i = 1,2,\cdots,27)$ represents the motion vector of of each feature point.

6.6.1.4 Motion Magnificaiton

We transform subtle facial expression into exaggerated facial expressions by multiplying the motion vectors of feature points by the wanted magnification vector, which may have different values with respect to the facial regions such as eyebrow regions, eyes regions, and mouth region. We relocate the AAM fitted feature points by adding the magnified motion vectors to them as

Figure 6.6.5. The result of motion estimation

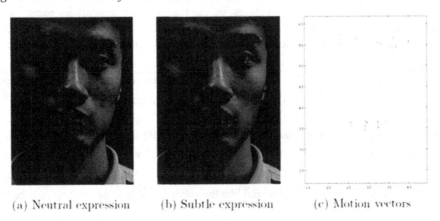

(a) Neutral expression   (b) Subtle expression   (c) Motion vectors

$$\mathbf{x}_i'' = \mathbf{x}_i + \beta_i \mathbf{d}(\mathbf{x}_i), \qquad (6.6.12)$$

where $(\beta_i : i = 1,2,\cdots,27)$ is the magnification vector.

Since the fitted feature points are changed by adding the magnified motion vectors, the magnified facial expression image is recovered by the piece-wise affine warping as follows. The three feature points of the original face image determine a triangle mesh $(\mathbf{x}_1,\mathbf{x}_2,\mathbf{x}_3)$ and warp the triangle mesh to the destination triangle $(\mathbf{x}_1'',\mathbf{x}_2'',\mathbf{x}_3'')$ determined by the magnified motion vectors. One image point $\mathbf{x}$ in a triangle mesh $(\mathbf{x}_1,\mathbf{x}_2,\mathbf{x}_3)$ is represented as

$$\mathbf{x} = \mathbf{x}_1 + a(\mathbf{x}_2 - \mathbf{x}_1) + b(\mathbf{x}_3 - \mathbf{x}_1), \qquad (6.6.13)$$

where a and b are the coefficients determining the position $\mathbf{x}$ in the triangle, which are determined by the mesh points $(\mathbf{x}_1,\mathbf{x}_2,\mathbf{x}_3)$. After obtaining the coefficients a and b, point $\mathbf{x}''$ in the warped triangle mesh $(\mathbf{x}_1'',\mathbf{x}_2'',\mathbf{x}_3'')$ is computed by

$$\mathbf{x}'' = \mathbf{x}_1'' + a(\mathbf{x}_2'' - \mathbf{x}_1'') + b(\mathbf{x}_3'' - \mathbf{x}_1''). \qquad (6.6.14)$$

Fig. 6.6.6 shows the facial expression transformation using motion magnification, where Fig. 6.6.6 (a) and (b) represent the original subtle facial expressions and their corresponding exaggerated facial expressions, respectively.

6.6.2 Subtle Facial Expression Recognition

The magnified facial expressions have the nonlinear distribution in the facial feature space, thus we need a nonlinear classifier such as the SVM classifier to classify them. The facial expression recognition system consists of two steps. First, we extract the facial expression features to achieve a good classification. Then, we classify these features into their corresponding facial expressions.

6.6.2.1 Facial Expression Feature Extraction

For extracting the facial expression features, we use the shape and appearance parameters that are obtained from the AAM fitting. Fig. 6.6.7 shows the overall process of obtaining the facial expression features as follows. First, we obtain a neutral expression shape vector $\mathbf{s}$ from the AAM fitting. Second, we obtain a subtle facial expression shape vector $\mathbf{s}'$ by adding the motion vector $\Delta\mathbf{s}$ obtained from the feature point tracking, to the shape vector $\mathbf{s}$. From the shape vector $\mathbf{s}'$, we extract the shape parameter vector $\mathbf{p}'$ by projecting the shape vector $\mathbf{s}'$ to the l shape basis vectors $\mathbf{s}_i$. The appearance image $A'(\mathbf{x})$ is obtained by warping the subtle facial expression image with the shape parameter vector $\mathbf{p}'$, where the appearance parameter vector $\boldsymbol{\alpha}'$ is extracted by projecting the appearance image $A'(\mathbf{x})$ to the m appearance basis images $A_i(\mathbf{x})$. Third, the magnified facial expression shape vector $\mathbf{s}''$ is also computed like the subtle facial expression shape vector $\mathbf{s}'$

Figure 6.6.6. Facial expression transformation using the motion magnification

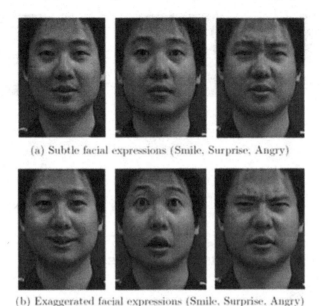

(a) Subtle facial expressions (Smile, Surprise, Angry)

(b) Exaggerated facial expressions (Smile, Surprise, Angry)

by adding the magnified motion vector $\boldsymbol{\beta}\Delta\mathbf{s}$ to the shape vector $\mathbf{s}$. The magnified facial expression appearance image $A''(\mathbf{x})$ is equal to the subtle facial expression appearance image $A'(\mathbf{x})$, because the magnified facial expression image is warped from the subtle facial expression image.

After obtaining the shape and appearance parameters of the magnified facial expression image, we obtain a combined AAM shape and appearance parameter vector by combining them as

$$\mathbf{c} = \begin{bmatrix} \mathbf{p}' \\ \boldsymbol{\Gamma} \cdot \boldsymbol{\alpha}' \end{bmatrix}, \tag{6.6.15}$$

where $\tilde{\mathbf{A}}$ is a scaled diagonal matrix to balance the different dynamic ranges of the shape and appearance feature vectors. In this work, we take the combined AAM shape and appearance parameter vector $\mathbf{c}$ as the facial expression feature.

6.6.2.2 Facial Expression Classificaiton

To classify the extracted facial expression features, we take the SVM classifier, as shown in Fig. 6.6.8. It consists of 4 facial expression SVM classifiers which are the neutral, smile, surprise and angry classifiers, then we determine the facial expression of the input facial feature as the label of the classifier whose output value is the maximal.

Figure 6.6.7. Overall process of obtaining the facial expression features

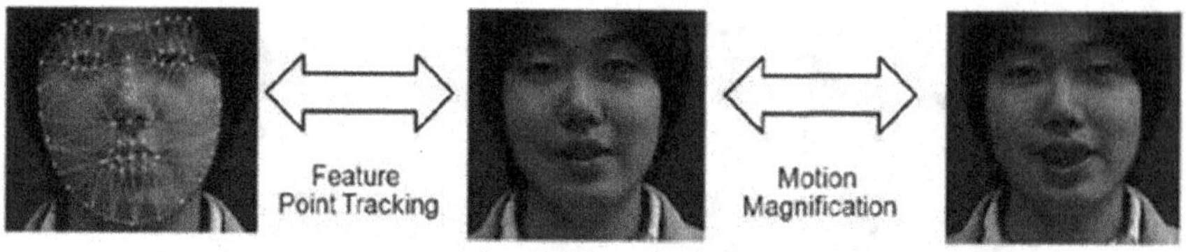

Feature
Point Tracking

Motion
Magnification

$$s = s_0 + \sum_{i=1}^{l} p_i s_i$$

$$s' = s + \Delta s$$
$$= s_0 + \sum_{i=1}^{l} p'_i s_i$$

$$s'' = s + \beta \Delta s$$
$$= s_0 + \sum_{i=1}^{l} p''_i s_i$$

$$A'(\mathbf{x}) = I(W(\mathbf{x}; \mathbf{p}'))$$
$$= A_0(\mathbf{x}) + \sum_{i=1}^{m} \alpha'_i A_i(\mathbf{x})$$

$$A''(\mathbf{x}) = A'(\mathbf{x})$$
$$= A_0(\mathbf{x}) + \sum_{i=1}^{m} \alpha'_i A_i(\mathbf{x})$$

6.6.3 Experimental Results and Discussion

6.6.3.1 Database

The database used for the experiments was the POSTECH SFED07 DB (Park, 2007) which included 20 persons with 4 facial expressions (neutral, subtle smile, subtle surprise, and subtle angry). Fig. 6.6.9 shows some examples of the subtle facial expression images in POSTECH SEFD07 DB. All of the people in the database are Asians, and the image resolution is 640×480. For evaluating the subtle facial expression recognition performance, we used the half of the subjects as the training set, and the remaining subjects as the test set for the 2-fold cross validation.

6.6.3.2 Motion Estimation

Motion estimation is one of the essential parts for recognizing subtle facial expressions due to the difficulty of obtaining precise motion vectors in the subtle motions. Generally, the optical flow algorithm is the most popular method for estimating motions. However, the optical flow algorithm does not provide precise motion vectors because the face images do not have enough texture information around the cheek or the skin, as shown in Fig. 6.6.10 (c) that is obtained from the result of applying the optical flow algorithm to Fig. 6.6.10 (a) and (b). To overcome this problem, we select the features that provide high texture gray values and apply the feature point tracking method which is based on Lucas-Kanade registration to the selected feature points. This method uses the feature point region (15×15 window) to find one position to another most similar position between two sequence images. Fig. 6.6.10 (f) represents the result of applying the feature point tracking (motion vector at one of mouth point) to Fig. 6.6.10 (d) and (e), which provides more accurate motion vectors than the optical flow algorithm in the case of subtle facial expressions.

Figure 6.6.8. The facial expression classification based on the SVM classifiers

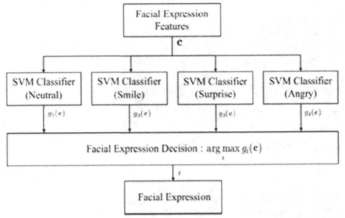

6.6.3.3 Motion Magnificaiton

Motion magnification plays an important role to improve the subtle facial expression recognition performance. In the subtle facial expression recognition, it is difficult to discriminate one subtle facial expression feature from the others because they are intermingled with each other, as shown in Fig. 6.6.11 (a). However, it is easier to discriminate them by using motion magnification, as shown in Fig. 6.6.11 (b).

By applying motion magnification to subtle facial expressions, we can transform them into more discriminable facial expressions. After obtaining the motion vector from the feature point tracking method, we magnify the motion vector by an appropriate magnification vector, which consists of several independent magnification parameters of the eyebrows, upper eyes, lower eyes, and the mouth along the horizontal and vertical directions. Fig.

Figure 6.6.9. The facial expression classification based on the SVM classifiers

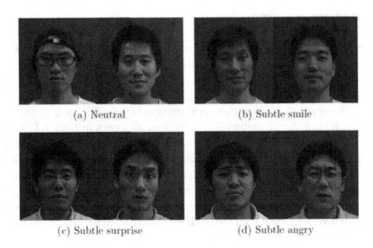

Figure 6.6.10. Comparison of motion estimation results between the optical flow method and the feature point tracking method

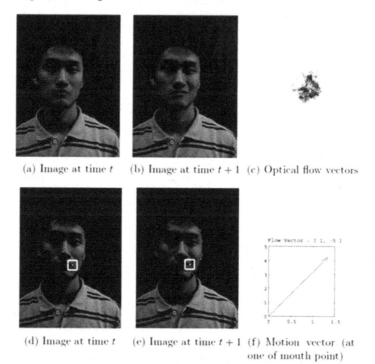

(a) Image at time t (b) Image at time $t + 1$ (c) Optical flow vectors

(d) Image at time t (e) Image at time $t + 1$ (f) Motion vector (at one of mouth point)

6.6.12 illustrates the transformed facial expressions using the motion magnification with respect to the different magnification vectors corresponding to the weak, medium, and strong exaggerated facial expressions, as shown in Table 6.6.1.

6.6.3.4 Facial Expression Recogntion

1) The effect of motion magnification

First, we performed an experiment to observe how the performance of the facial expression recognition is changed with respect to the degree of motion magnification including no motion magnification. To conduct this experiment, we consider the SVM as the facial expression classifier.

Table 6.6.2 compares the recognition performances of the subtle facial expression recognition with respect to different motion magnifications, as shown in Table 1. From this table, we know that (1) the recognition rates in the case of the weak and medium magnifications are improved continuously compared to those in the case of non-magnification, (2) the recognition rate in the case of the strong magnification is rather degraded compared with that in the case of medium magnification. We increased the magnification vector parameters like in the medium case to obtain better performance than the weak case. However, we increased motion vectors more than the medium case (like in the strong case), oppositely

Figure 6.6.11. Distributions of facial expression features in feature space

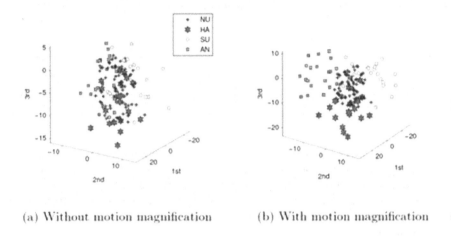

(a) Without motion magnification   (b) With motion magnification

Figure 6.6.12. Motion magnification results with the different magnification vectors

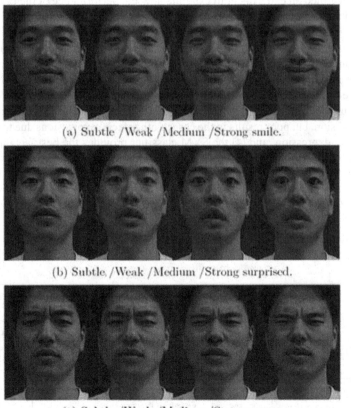

(a) Subtle /Weak /Medium /Strong smile.

(b) Subtle /Weak /Medium /Strong surprised.

(c) Subtle /Weak /Medium /Strong angry.

Table 6.6.1. Magnitude of magnification vector parameters

Degree of Magnitude	Eyebrow points	Upper eye points	Lower eye points	Mouth points (Y-direction)	Mouth points (X-direction)
Weak	2	1.5	1	2.4	1.8
Medium	3	2	1.2	3.6	2.7
Strong	4	2.5	1.5	4.8	3.6

the performance rate was decreased. According to the experiment, large magnification destroyed the angry expression features, causing incorrect classification results. Thus, we choose the medium motion magnification for the later experiments.

Fig. 6.6.13 compares the recognition results with different motion magnifications. Experimental results indicate that the proposed method is extremely suitable for recognizing the subtle facial expressions.

2) The effect of classifier

Next, we performed an experiment to examine how the performance of the facial expression recognition is changed according to different classifiers. To conduct this experiment, we used the facial expression images with the medium motion magnification.

Table 6.6.3 compares the recognition performances of different classification methods. From this table, we know that (1) the nearest neighbor method is not suitable to apply the facial expressions recognition because it is a simple linear-based method, (2) the linear discriminate analysis (LDA) provides low recognition rate because it also deals with linear classification, (3) the probability neural network (PNN) provides good results in case of neutral expression, but poor results in the case of other facial expressions due to its overfitting to neutral expression, and (4) the SVM classifier provides the best facial expression recognition performance because it can handle the nonlinearly distributed feature points effectively.

Table 6.6.2. Comparison of the recognition rates with different motion magnifications

	Neutral	Smile	Surprise	Angry	Overall
Non agnification	65.0%	45.0%	67.5%	50.0%	56.875%
Weak agnification	77.5%	57.5%	77.5%	62.5%	68.750%
Medium magnification	92.5%	87.5%	82.5%	90.0%	88.125%
Strong magnification	82.5%	85.0%	85.0%	60.0%	79.375%

Figure 6.6.13. Comparison of the recognition rates with different motion magnifications

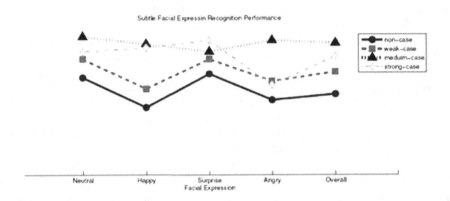

6.7 FACIAL EXPRESSION SYNTHESIS USING AAM AND BILINEAR MODEL

Recently, face recognition has become one of the most active research areas in the field of biometrics. Since the related research started in 1970, a number of problems have been solved and the recognition performance improved. However, illumination-robust face recognition is still a challenging problem. Usually inter-person variances are used to recognize the identity. But, the intra-person variations made by illumination change can be much bigger than the intra-person variations. Many different approaches have been introduced to solve this problem as follows:

Riklin-Raviv and Shashua (2001) introduced the quotient image that uses class-based re-rendering and recognition with varying illuminations. They defined an illumination invariant signature image that enables an analytic generation of images with varying illuminations. The experiment of quotient image showed that the recognition rate of the quotient images outperformed that of the eigenface images. However, their approach might fail in obtaining the illumination invariant feature when the input image has a shadow. Zhou and Chellappa (2003) imposed the constraints on albedo and surface normal to remove the restriction of the quotient image. Zhao and Chellappa (2003) introduced an illumination ratio image that uses the reference image for synthesizing a new image which has a similar illumination effect to the reference image. Lui et. al. (2005) transformed an image with an arbitrary il-

Table 6.6.3. Comparison of the recognition rates among different classification methods

Classifier	Neutral	Smile	Surprise	Angry	**Overall**
Nearest neighbor	92.50%	65.00%	70.00%	60.00%	71.875%
PNN	100.0%	65.00%	72.50%	60.00%	74.375%
LDA	77.50%	77.50%	82.50%	80.00%	79.375%
SVM	**92.50%**	**87.50%**	**82.50%**	**90.00%**	**88.125%**

lumination into the image with a frontal illumination by blurring a single frontal image by Gaussian filter in accordance with the reference images. Shan et. al. (2003) introduced an algorithm that combines histogram equalization, gamma intensity correction and quotient image with a region-based strategy to eliminate the side-lighting effect.

Belhumeur and Kriegman (1998); Georghiades et. al. (1998, 2001) introduced a generative appearance-based method for recognizing human faces under variation in lighting and viewpoint. They argued that the images under all possible illumination conditions built a convex cone in the space of images and the reconstructed shape and albedo of the face from a small number of samples served as a generative model for rendering or synthesizing images of the face under novel poses and illumination conditions. However, their approach is an iterative method that requires a lot of time to recognize the identity of a test input image. Basri and Jacobs (2003, 2001) defined all sets of Lambertian reflectance functions that could be characterized as 9 dimensional linear subspaces. This implied that the images of the convex Lambertian object could be approximated by a low-dimensional linear subspace and a faster face recognition performed. Wang et. al. (2003a) proposed a method based on Ronen and Jacobs' theory for modeling a 3D face shape. This method is based on the photometric stereo algorithm, which required three images of an object to construct the 3D face shape and albedo. Fortuna and Capson (2004) used ICA (Independent Component Analysis) and SVM (Support Vector Machine) for illumination invariant face recognition. They used the ICA for constructing the filters to obtain the illumination invariant feature.

All the above methods are based on the technique of analysis by synthesis for an illumination invariant face recognition and use the illumination model like a Lambertian function. Hence, it is very difficult to apply these approaches in real time, and their recognition performance can be degraded when the illumination conditions deviate from the model. To overcome these drawbacks, we propose a bilinear model to separate the identity factor and the illumination factor.

Tenenbaum and Freeman (2000) introduced bilinear models that could separate the observations into two independent factors such as style and content. They presented a general framework for learning to solve two-factor tasks using the bilinear models, which sufficiently provided expressive representations of factor interactions and could be fit to data using an efficient algorithm based on singular value decomposition and expectation-maximization. They reported promising results on three different tasks: spoken vowel classification, extrapolation of fonts to unseen letters, and translation of faces to novel illuminations. Abboud and Davoine (2004) proposed the bilinear model to decompose the appearance parameters of facial expression factor and the identity factor. They performed facial expression synthesis on unseen faces showing any undetermined facial expression, as well as facial expression recognition. Du and Lin (2004) presented a sample based method for synthesizing face images in a wide range of view. They extended the original bilinear factorization model to a nonlinear case so that the global optimum solution could be found in solving the translation task. Lee and Kim (2006) proposed expression invariant face recognition by synthesizing neutral facial expressional images using a bilinear model.

When we attempt to recognize the identity factor with the novel illumination, we need to translate the new face to the known illumination or translate the known face to the new illumination. This translation procedure requires a repetitive computation of matrix inverse operations to reach the identity and illumination factors. This computation may result in a nonconvergent case when the observation has noisy information or the model is overfitted.

To alleviate this situation, we suggest a ridge regressive bilinear model that combines the ridge regression technique into the bilinear model. Ridge regression technique (Naes and Mevik, 2001; Hastie et. al., 2001; Høy et. al., 2002) impose a penalty to reduce the variance of a certain model. This combination provides a number of advantages: it stabilize the bilinear model by shrinking the range of identity and illumination factors appropriately and improves the recognition performance.

6.7.1 Regression Model

Regression analysis is a traditional technique which investigates the relationship between independent variables and a dependent variable. A regression model represents the dependent variable in terms of a linear combination of independent variables and is widely used for data description, inference, and prediction.

6.7.1.1 Regression Using the Least Square Method

A regression model can be written as

$$\mathbf{y} = \mathbf{X}b + \mathbf{e}, \tag{6.7.1}$$

where $\mathbf{y}$, $\mathbf{X}$, $\mathbf{b}$, and $\mathbf{e}$ are an observation vector, a dependent variable matrix, the model parameter vector, and an error vector that is assumed to be an independent identically distributed random variable with mean 0 and variance o^2. The goal of regression is to find the model parameter vector $\hat{\mathbf{b}}$, which minimizes the residual error as

$$\hat{\mathbf{b}} = arg \min_{\mathbf{b}} \left(\sum_{i=1}^{I} (y_i - b_0 - \sum_{j=1}^{J} x_{ij} b_j)^2 \right). \tag{6.7.2}$$

When the dependent variable matrix $\mathbf{X}$ has a full rank, we can obtain the estimate of the model parameter vector $\mathbf{b}$ using the least square estimation as

$$\hat{\mathbf{b}} = (\mathbf{X}^T \mathbf{X})^{-1} \mathbf{X}^T \mathbf{y}. \tag{6.7.3}$$

The variance of the model parameter vector $\hat{\mathbf{b}}$ in the regression model is represented as

$$
\begin{aligned}
\mathrm{Var}(\hat{\mathbf{b}}) &= \mathbf{E}\left[(\hat{\mathbf{b}} - \mathbf{b})(\hat{\mathbf{b}} - \mathbf{b})^T \right] \\
&= \mathbf{E}\left[(\mathbf{X}^T \mathbf{X})^{-1} \mathbf{X}^T \mathbf{e} \mathbf{e}^T \mathbf{X} (\mathbf{X}^T \mathbf{X})^{-1} \right] \\
&= \sigma^2 (\mathbf{X}^T \mathbf{X})^{-1} \\
&= \sigma^2 (\mathbf{V} D \mathbf{U}^T \mathbf{U} D \mathbf{V}^T)^{-1} \\
&= \sigma^2 \sum_{j=1}^{J} \mathbf{v}_j \frac{1}{d_j} \mathbf{v}_j^T,
\end{aligned} \tag{6.7.4}
$$

where $\mathbf{X} = \mathbf{U}D\mathbf{V}^T$, $\mathbf{v}_j$ is an eigenvector that is the jth column of $\mathbf{V}$ and d_j is an eigenvalue that is corresponding to $\mathbf{v}_j$

When data are strongly correlated, we experience a collinearity among the variables that makes most of the eigenvalues of $\mathbf{V}$ except some principal components very small.

This destabilizes the regression model because the variance of $\hat{\mathbf{b}}$ becomes relatively large as the eigenvalue is very small. To alleviate this instability problem, a variety of unbiased methods such as ridge regression, partial least square, and principal component regression, etc. have been introduced to trade the bias for the imprecision (Abboud and Davoine, 2004). In this work, we use the ridge regression technique due to its simplicity.

6.7.1.2 Ridge Regression

The goal of ridge regression is to find the optimal model parameter vector $\hat{\mathbf{b}}$ to minimize the modified residual error as

$$\hat{\mathbf{b}} = arg \min_{\mathbf{b}}\left(\sum_{i=1}^{I}(y_i - b_0 - \sum_{j=1}^{J} x_{ij} b_j)^2 + \lambda \sum_{j=1}^{J} b_j^2\right), \tag{6.7.5}$$

where the last term imposes a penalty to the regression model in order to reduce the variances of the model.

The above ridge regression can be written in the matrix form as

$$\mathbf{RSS}(\lambda) = (\mathbf{y} - \mathbf{Xb})^T(\mathbf{y} - \mathbf{Xb}) + \lambda \mathbf{b}^T\mathbf{b}, \tag{6.7.6}$$

and the optimal estimate of the parameter vector $\hat{\mathbf{b}}$ can be computed by

$$\hat{\mathbf{b}} = (\mathbf{X}^T\mathbf{X} + \mathbf{I} \, \mathbf{I})^{-1} \mathbf{X}^T\mathbf{y}. \tag{6.7.7}$$

The variance of the parameter vector $\hat{\mathbf{b}}$ in the ridge regression model can be computed as

$$\begin{aligned}
\mathrm{V}ar(\hat{\mathbf{b}}) &= \mathbf{E}\left[\hat{\mathbf{b}} - \mathbf{E}(\hat{\mathbf{b}}))(\hat{\mathbf{b}} - \mathbf{E}(\hat{\mathbf{b}}))^T\right] \\
&= \mathbf{E}\left[(\mathbf{X}^T\mathbf{X} + \lambda\mathbf{I})^{-1}\mathbf{X}^T\mathbf{e}\mathbf{e}^T\mathbf{X}(\mathbf{X}^T\mathbf{X} + \lambda\mathbf{I})^{-1}\right] \\
&= \sigma^2 \sum_{j=1}^{J} \mathbf{v}_j \left(\frac{d_j}{(d_j + \lambda)^2}\right) \mathbf{v}_j^T.
\end{aligned} \tag{6.7.8}$$

From the above equation, we determine that the ridge regression adds a small amount of constant value λ to the diagonal term of $\mathbf{X}^T\mathbf{X}$. This addition reduces the variance of the parameter vector $\hat{\mathbf{b}}$ and stabilizes the regression model.

6.7.2 Ridge Regressive Bilinear Model

We introduce the ridge regressive bilinear model that combine the ridge regression technique into the bilinear model. To give the properties of ridge regression to the bilinear model, we modify the object function of the bilinear model as

$$E(\mathbf{a}, \mathbf{b}) = \sum_{k=1}^{K} \left(y_k - \sum_{i=1}^{I} \sum_{j=1}^{J} w_{ijk} a_i b_j \right)^2 + \lambda \sum_{i=1}^{I} \sum_{j=1}^{J} (a_i b_j)^2. \tag{6.7.9}$$

The above equation can be represented in a compact matrix form as

$$E(\mathbf{a}, \mathbf{b}) = (\mathbf{y} - (\mathbf{W}b)^{VT} \mathbf{a})^T (\mathbf{y} - (\mathbf{W}b)^{VT} \mathbf{a}) + \lambda \mathbf{a}^T \mathbf{a} \mathbf{b}^T \mathbf{b}. \tag{6.7.10}$$

In order to obtain the minimum value of $\mathbf{E}$, we differentiate the objective function $\mathbf{E}$ with the model parameter vectors $\mathbf{a}$ and $\mathbf{b}$ and set the differentiations to zero as

$$\frac{\partial \mathbf{E}}{\partial \mathbf{a}} = 0$$

and

$$\frac{\partial \mathbf{E}}{\partial \mathbf{b}} = 0$$

.

By solving these conditions, we obtain the optimal style and content parameter vectors $\mathbf{a}$ and $\mathbf{b}$ as

$$\mathbf{a} = \left(\left((\mathbf{W}b)^{VT} \right)^T \left((\mathbf{W}b)^{VT} \right) + \lambda \mathbf{b}^T \mathbf{b} \right)^{-1} \left((\mathbf{W}b)^{VT} \right)^T \mathbf{y}, \tag{6.7.11}$$

$$\mathbf{b} = \left(\left(\mathbf{W}^{VT} \mathbf{a} \right)^T \left(\mathbf{W}^{VT} \mathbf{a} \right) + \lambda \mathbf{a}^T \mathbf{a} \right)^{-1} \left(\mathbf{W}^{VT} \mathbf{a} \right)^T \mathbf{y}. \tag{6.7.12}$$

In the ridge regressive bilinear model, the overall procedure for obtaining the style and content model parameter vectors $\mathbf{a}$ and $\mathbf{b}$ for a given test face image $\mathbf{y}$ is given below.

Algorithm: compute_style_content_RRBM(input: **W, y**; output: **a, b**)
Initialize **b** as the mean vector of $\mathbf{B}$.
Update the style factor **a**
  using $\mathbf{a} = \left(\left((\mathbf{W}b)^{VT} \right)^T \left((\mathbf{W}b)^{VT} \right) + \lambda \mathbf{b}^T \mathbf{b} \right)^{-1} \left((\mathbf{W}b)^{VT} \right)^T \mathbf{y}.$
Update the content factor **b**
  using $\mathbf{b} = \left(\left(\mathbf{W}^{VT} \mathbf{a} \right)^T \left(\mathbf{W}^{VT} \mathbf{a} \right) + \lambda \mathbf{a}^T \mathbf{a} \right)^{-1} \left(\mathbf{W}^{VT} \mathbf{a} \right)^T \mathbf{y}.$
Repeat steps 2) and 3) until **a** and **b** converge.

In the case of an asymmetric bilinear model, we do not use the iterative approach because a style specific basis of the observation **y** is known in advance. If the style specific basis of the observation is $\mathbf{W}_i$, then the content vector can be computed by a single pseudo inverse operation as

$$\mathbf{b} = \left(\mathbf{W}_i^T \mathbf{W}_i + \lambda \mathbf{I}\right)^{-1} \mathbf{W}_i^T \mathbf{y}. \qquad (6.7.13)$$

In a real implementation, we control the eigenvalues in the following strategy. For the dominant eigenvectors whose eigenvalues are greater than λ, we keep the eigenvalues. For the nonsignificant eigenvectors whose eigenvalues are smaller than λ, we change their eigenvalues to λ.

6.7.3 Experiment Results and Discussion

The CMU PIE database (Sim et al. ,2003) was used for the experiment; it includes images of 68 people, each of whom has 13 different poses, 43 different illuminations, and 3 different facial expressions. Among the entire DB, we use some images with 43 illuminations. The 43 different illumination conditions are obtained by the following. There are two light sources: 21 direct light sources that are located circularly around the subject and one room light source. Thus, one can capture 21 different illuminated images by turning on the direct light source one by one with the room light turned on, 21 different illuminated images by turning on the direct light source one by one with the room light turned off, and one image with only the room light turned on. Fig. 6.7.1 illustrates a set of the images used for our experiments, where each row shows the face images under 21 different illumination conditions of a specific person and each column shows the face images with 7 different identities under a specific illumination condition. We cropped the face region manually, using the location of two eyes and the ratio of the distance between two eyes. After cropping the images, we resized the images to 56×46 and applied a mask to remove noisy information such as hair style, image background and clothes.

Figure 6.7.1. Some face images from the CMU PIE database. Each row shows the face images under 21 different illumination conditions of a specific person and each column shows the face images with 7 different identities under a specific illumination condition

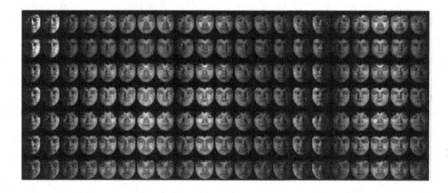

For the experiments, we divided the PIE database images into three disjoint sets: training set, evaluation set, and test set. Among 68 people, we randomly and exclusively took 25 people, 15 people, and 28 people as training set, evaluation set, and test set, respectively. The training set was used to train the bilinear model, while the evaluation set was used to determine the optimal value of λ. The test set was divided into two independent sets: a probe set and a gallery set. The frontally illuminated images were used for the gallery set and all remaining images were used for the probe set.

The experiment consists of training, λ-tuning, and test phases, where the test phase consists of two tasks: registration and recognition. During the training phase, we obtain the interaction matrix **W**. During the λ-tuning phase, we determine the optimal value of λ. During the test phase, we perform two tasks. First, in the registration task, we store the content factors that are obtained from all images in the gallery set using Algorithm II or III. Second, in the recognition task, we determine the identity by computing the Euclidean distances between content factor of probe image and all content factors of the gallery set and taking the identity whose Euclidean distance is minimal. Fig. 6.7.2 summarizes the overall procedure of the illumination-robust face recognition.

6.7.3.1 Separability

We compared the separability of the bilinear model and the ridge regressive bilinear model. Fig. 6.7.3 shows the distribution of style and content factors for the bilinear model. Here,

Figure 6.7.2. Overall procedure of the experiments. The procedure consists of training, λ-tuning, and test phases, where the test phase consists of two tasks: registration and recognition

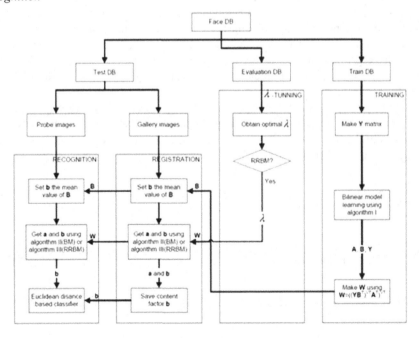

Figure 6.7.3. The style and content factor distributions for the bilinear model

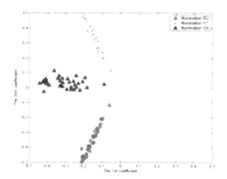
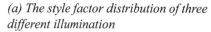

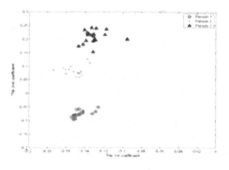

(a) The style factor distribution of three different illumination

(b) The content factor distribution of three different person

Fig. 6.7.3-(a) represents the style factor distribution of three different illuminations: f02(the left-side lighting), f20(the front-side lighting) and f17(the right-side lighting), where each illumination class consists of 34 different persons, and Fig. 6.7.3-(b) represents the content factor distribution of three different persons: p1, p2 and p3, where identity class consists of 21 different light conditions. For clarity, only the first two components are chosen for the display. This figure shows that (1) the content factor is more discriminant than the style factor and (2) the variance of the content factor is much bigger than that of the style factor.

Fig. 6.7.4 compares the content factor distributions that are obtained from the bilinear model and the ridge regressive bilinear model. For clarity, we represent the content factors of two persons in terms of the first two components. This figure shows that (1) the intra-person variation of content factors from the ridge regressive bilinear model is smaller than that from the bilinear model variation and (2) the inter-person distance of content factors from the ridge regressive bilinear model is larger than that from the bilinear model. This implies that the ridge regressive bilinear model should be more effective for face recognition than the bilinear model.

To support our argument that the content factor distribution of ridge regressive bilinear model is more suitable for discrimination than that of the bilinear model, we compared the scatter matrix of the two models. The within-class scatter matrix $\mathbf{S}_W$ is computed by the following Duda et. al. (2001):

$$\mathbf{S}_W = \sum_{i=1}^{c} \mathbf{S}_i, \tag{6.7.14}$$

where

$$\mathbf{S}_i = \sum_{\mathbf{x} \in D_i} (\mathbf{x} - \mathbf{m}_i)(\mathbf{x} - \mathbf{m}_i)', \tag{6.7.15}$$

Figure 6.7.4. Comparison of content factor distributions of two bilinear models

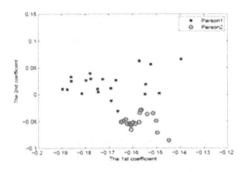
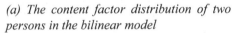
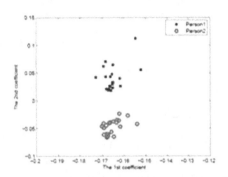

(a) The content factor distribution of two
persons in the bilinear model

(b) The content factor distribution of two
persons in the ridge regressive bilinear
model

$$\mathbf{m}_i = \frac{1}{n_i} \sum\nolimits_{\mathbf{x} \in D_i} \mathbf{x}, \tag{6.7.16}$$

and c is the number of classes and n_i is the number of data in class D_i. In this experiment, we set $c = 34$ and $n_i = 21$. In addition, the between-class scatter matrix $\mathbf{S}_B$ is computed by the following:

$$\mathbf{S}_B = \sum\nolimits_{i=1}^{c} n_i (\mathbf{m}_i - \mathbf{m})(\mathbf{m}_i - \mathbf{m})^t, \tag{6.7.17}$$

where

$$\mathbf{m} = \frac{1}{n} \sum\nolimits_{\mathbf{x}} \mathbf{x}, \tag{6.7.18}$$

and $n = \sum\nolimits_{i=1}^{c} n_i$ is the total number of data. It is obvious that a data set which has a greater scatter matrix ratio

$$\mathbf{S} = \frac{\mathbf{S}_B}{\mathbf{S}_W}$$

is easier to discriminate. We randomly constructed five different data sets from the database and computed the scatter matrix ratio for the bilinear model and the ridge regressive bilinear model. Table 6.7.1, the norms of the scatter matrix ratio, shows that the scatter matrix ratio of the ridge regressive bilinear model is greater than that of the bilinear model. This result supports our argument that the content factor distribution of the ridge regressive bilinear model is more suitable for discrimination.

Table 6.7.1. The comparison of the scatter matrix ratio of bilinear model(BM) and ridge regressive bilinear model(RRBM)

Methods	Data set 1	Data set 2	Data set 3	Data set 4	Data set 5
BM	2.200080	1.659176	2.286809	1.348738	1.880055
RRBM	3.430023	2.472958	2.501905	1.901105	2.013569

6.7.3.2 Stability

We investigated the stability of the two different bilinear models by comparing the variances of the content factors. Fig. 6.7.5 shows the distribution of the content factors of bilinear models with different values of λ, where $\lambda = 0$ corresponds to the bilinear model. Here, we compare the 10th and 20th components of the content factor since the model parameter λ has a more serious effect on the insignificant components. This figure shows that the content factor shrinks and its variance decreases as the value of λ increases. This is a graphical explanation why the ridge regressive bilinear model is more stable than the bilinear model.

6.7.3.3 Illumination-Robust Face Recognition

We compared the recognition performances of the bilinear model and the ridge regressive bilinear model. To the end, we performed four different set of experiments as follows. First, we determined the optimal value of λ. For this, 25 of the 40 people were selected for the training set and remaining 15 people for the evaluation set. The training set was used to obtain the interaction matrix $\mathbf{W}$ and the evaluation set was used to evaluate the recognition performance with different values of λ. Fig. 6.7.6 shows the recognition performances with different values of λ when the numbers of the content factors are 15, 20 and 25, respectively. This figure shows that we have the lowest error rate when $\lambda = 14.666$. If the value of λ exceeds a certain value, the content factor shrinks too much and loses useful information, which is why the error rate increases again as the value of λ increases over a certain value.

Figure 6.7.5. A content factor distribution with respective to different values of λ

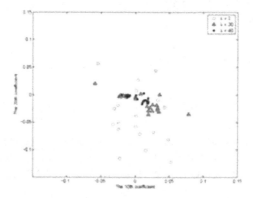

Figure 6.7.6. Error rate with respect to different values of λ

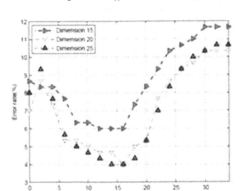

Second, we compared the recognition performance of the two models with respect to different numbers of people for training. We took λ = 14.666 according to the result of previous experiment. For a fixed value of λ, we trained the BM and the RRMM with different numbers of people, which were changed from 25 to 40. Then, we evaluated the recognition performance using test set for each interaction matrix **W**. Fig. 6.7.7 shows the error rate of the experiment of the two models when the first 20 components of the content factor are taken. From this figure, we determine that (1) the error rates of the two models decrease as the number of training face images increase, and (2) the ridge regressive model has a lower error rate than the bilinear model.

Third, we compared the recognition performance of the two models with different numbers of content factor. Fig. 6.7.8 shows the error rate when the numbers of content factor are changed from 12 to 40, where λ = 14.666 and the number of training people is 40. This figure shows that the error rate of the ridge regressive bilinear model decreases continuously as the number of components of content factor increases, while the error rate of the bilinear model reaches a minimum value at a specific number of components and starts to increase as the number of components increases further. This implies that the

Figure 6.7.7. Error rate of the bilinear model and the ridge regressive bilinear model with different numbers of training people

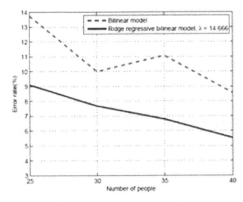

Figure 6.7.8. Error rate of the bilinear model and the ridge regressive bilinear model with different numbers of components of content factor

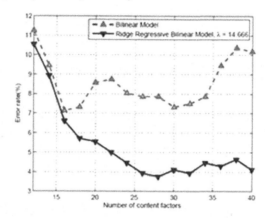

bilinear model is unstable when the number of components of the content factor is chosen inappropriately.

Fourth, we compared the recognition performance of the bilinear models with other approaches such as the eigenface method and the quotient image method (Riklin-Raviv and Shashua, 2001). For a fair comparison, we used the number of components of content factor of each approach such that it produces the best recognition rate except for the quotient image method which uses the raw image directly. We repeated all approaches 10 times using different combinations of training, evaluation and test set. In addition, the optimal values of λ for ridge regressive bilinear model for 10 trials are determined as 12.666, 10.666, 10, 8, 12, 8.666, 9.333, 15.333, 23.333, and 14.666, respectively. Fig. 6.7.9 shows the average recognition rate of the four different approaches in a bar chart, where the center tick of each bar denotes the average error rate and the intervals correspond to the minimum and maximum values of error rates. This figure shows that (1) the quotient image has a very poor recognition rate because it is modeled on only the non-shadow images, (2) the ridge regressive bilinear model outperforms the other methods and (3) the ridge regressive bi-

Figure 6.7.9. Recognition results of four different methods: BM (Bilinear Model), RRBM (Ridge Regressive Bilinear Model), Eigenface, and Quotient Image

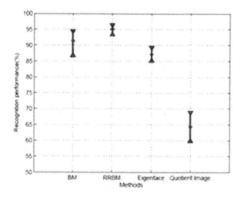

linear model has the smallest variance of recognition rate over the 10 runs. This implies that the proposed ridge regressive bilinear model performs a very robust and stable face recognition irrespective of the change of lighting conditions. Table 6.7.1 summarizes the face recognition results in terms of the number of components, recognition rate, variance of recognition rate, and runtime. Although the recognition rate of ridge regressive bilinear model is the best, its runtime is the slowest among four different methods due to its iterative fitting procedure. However, the runtime of the ridge regressive bilinear model and the bilinear model are similar when the number of components is equal.

6.8 CONCLUSION

In this chapter, we presented the facial expression recognition method using the 3D shape and the 2D appearance of the face that was obtained from the 2D+3D AAM and the GDA classifier. Although the 3D shape and the 2D appearance feature of the 2D+3D AAM explained the status of face well, classifying them to a specific facial expression class was difficult because their distributions in the feature space was very complicated. Therefore, we used the generalized discriminant analysis (GDA) (Baudat and Anouar, 2000) that consisted of two layers. The layered structure provided the ability to efficiently combine the 3D shape and appearance features and enhanced the classification performance for non-linearly distributed complex manifolds.

We presented the facial expression recognition method using the dynamic differential-AAM features and the manifold learning. It was composed of the proposed 3 modules: differential-AAM feature extraction, manifold embedding, and the classification using k-nearest neighbor sequences (k-NNS). The differential-AAM features (DAFs) were defined by the difference between the AAM feature of the input face image and that of the reference image. Thus, they are person-independent because the differences among people are almost similar even though a specific expression among peoples may be largely different from each other. This subtraction property also makes the DAFs robust to the camera and illumination variations. The automatic neutral expression detection was introduced to find the reference feature for the DAFs in the on-line manner, which makes the proposed facial expression recognition applicable for the real-time application. The manifold embedding using the Isomap was used to map the high dimensional DAFs onto the smooth and continuous feature space, which reduces the overall computation time for the facial expression recognition much. The temporal k-nearest neighbor sequences (k-NNS) classifier was introduced to

Table 6.7.2. Comparison of recognition performances of four different methods

Methods	No. of components	Average Recognition rate (%)	Variance	runtime (Sec.)
BM	30	91.38	6.28	0.4934
RRBM	40	95.14	1.32	0.8679
Eigenface	100	87.196	2.424	0.015
Quotient image	56 × 46	64.4	9.14	0.2055

be considered the directed Hausdorff distance (DHD) that measured the distance between two face image sequences, and the majority voting scheme, which provided the best facial expression recognition rate of 95% among many other classifiers

We developed a novel approach to recognize the subtle facial expressions using motion magnification. The proposed method transformed the subtle facial expressions into the corresponding exaggerated facial expressions by extracting the subtle motion vector of the predefined feature points and magnifying them by an appropriate motion magnification vector for facial expression recognition. After the motion magnification, we obtained the combined AAM shape and appearance facial expression features from the exaggerated facial expression image and applied them to the SVM classifier. The experimental results showed that (1) the medium motion magnification provided the best facial expression recognition performance, (2) the SVM classifier provided the best classification performance among many other classifiers, and (3) the subtle facial expression recognition rate in the case of medium motion magnification is better than that in the case of no motion magnification by 32% when the experiments are conducted on the POSTECH SFED2007 DB.

We proposed the bilinear model for the illumination robust face recognition. Bilinear model itself provided a good discrimination power of the content factor, irrespective of changing the lighting conditions. However, it could fail to provide a stable recognition since the convergence of bilinear model was subject to observation and bilinear model can use small portion of information due to overfitting. To alleviate this problem, we proposed a ridge regressive bilinear model that combined the ridge regression technique into the bilinear model. This combination provides a number of advantages: it stabilized the bilinear model by shrinking the range of identity and illumination factors appropriately and improves the recognition performance.

6.9 REFERENCES

Abboud, B., and Davoine, F. (2004a). Appearance factorization based facial expression recognition and synthesis. In Proceedings of International Conference on Pattern Recognition. (pp. 163-166).

Abboud, B., and Davoine, F. (2004b). Face appearance factorization for expression analysis and synthesis. In Proceedings of Workshop on Image Analysis for Multimedia Interactive Services.

Basri, R., and Jacobs, D. (2001). Photometric stereo with general, unknown lighting. In Proceedings of IEEE Conference on Computer Vision andP Pattern Recognition. (pp. 374-381).

Basri, R., and Jacobs, D. (2003). Lambertian reflectance and linear subspace. IEEE Transaction on Pattern Analysis and Machine Intelligence, 25(2), 218-233.

Baudat, G., and Anouar, F. (2000). Generalized discriminant analysis using a kernel approach. Neural Computation, 12, 2385-2404.

Belhumeur, P., and Kriegman, D. (1998). What is the set of images of an object under all possible illumination conditions. International Journal of Computer Vision, 28(3), 245-260.

Blanz, V., and Vetter, T. (1999). A morphable model for the synthesis of 3d faces. Computer Graphics, Annual Conference Series (SIGGRAPH) (pp. 187-194).

Chang, Y., Hu, C., and Turk, M. (2003). Manifold of facial expression. In Proceedings of IEEE international Workshop on Analysis and Modeling of Faces and Gestures.

Chang, Y., Hu, C., and Turk, M. (2004). Probabilistic expression analysis on manifolds. In Proceedings of IEEE Conference on Computer Vision and Pattern Recognition.

Chang, Y., Hu, C., Feris, R., and Turk, M. (2006). Manifold based analysis of facial expression. Image and Vision Computing, 24, 605-614.

Chen, Q., and Medioni, G. (2001). Building 3-D humn face models from two photographs, Journal of VLSI Signal Processing Systems, 27, 127-140.

Chinnasamy, A., Sung, W. K., and Mittal, A. (2004). Protein structure and fold prediction using tree-augmented naïve bayesian classifier. Pacific Symposium on Biocomputing.

Chuang, E., Deshpande, H., and Bregler, C. (2002). Facial expression space learning. In Proceedings of Pacific Conference on Computer Graphics and Applications, (pp. 68-76).

Cohen, I., Sebe, N., Chen, L., Garg, A., and Huang, T. (2003). Facial expression recognition from video sequences: temporal and static modeling. Computer Vision and Image Understanding, 91 (1), 160-187.

Cohn, J., Zlochower, A., Lien, J., and Kanade, T. (1999). Automated face analysis by feature point tracking has high concurrent validity with manual FACS coding, Psychophysiology 36, 35-43.

Cowell, J. R. and Ayesh, A. (2004). Extracting subtle facial expression for emotional analysis. In Proceedings of IEEE International Conference on Systems Man and Cybernetics, (pp. 677–681).

Cristianini, N., and Taylor, J. S. (2000). An introduction to support vector machine. Cambridge university press.

Darwin, C. (1899). The Expression of the Emotions in Man and Animals, Newyork D. Appleton and Company.

Donalto, G., Bartlett, M. S., Hager, J. C., Ekman, P., and Sejnowski, T. (1999). Classifying facial actions. IEEE Transactions on Pattern Analysis and Machine Intelligence, 21(10), 974–999.

Du, Y., and Lin, X. (2004). Multi-view face image synthesis using factorization model. International Workshop on Human-Computer Interaction(HCI/ECCV). (pp. 200-201).

Duda, R. O., Hart, P. E., and Stork, D. H. (2000). Pattern classification. Willey Interscience, 2nd edition.

Duda, R., Hart, P., and Stork, D. (2001). Pattern classification, Wiely-Interscience

Ekman, P. (1982). Emotions in the human face. Cambridge University Press.

Ekman, P. and Friesen, W. (1978). A mathematical introduction to robotic manipulation, Consulting Psychologists Press.

Elgammal, A., and Lee, C. (2004). Separating Style and Content on a Nonlinear Manifold. In Proceedings IEEE Conference on Computer Vision and Pattern Recognition, (pp. 520-527).

Essa, I., and Pentland, A. (1997a) Coding, analysis, interpretation and recognition of facial expressions, IEEE Trans. on Pattern Analysis and Machine Intelligence, 19(7), 757-763.

Essa, I., and Pentland, A. (1997b). Facial expression recognition using image motion.

Fasel, B., and Luettin, J. (2003). Automatic facial expression analysis: a survey, Pattern Recognition, 36, 259-275.

Ford, G. (2002). Fully automatic coding of basic expressions from video, Technical Report INC-MPLab. TR-2002.03, University of California, San Diego.

Fortuna, J., and Capson, D. (2004). Ica filters for lighting invariant face recognition. In Proceedings of International Conference on Pattern Recognition. (pp. 334-337).

Georghiades, A., Kriegman, D., and Belhumeur, P. (1998). Illumination cones for recognition under variable lighting: Faces. In Proceedings of IEEE Conference on Computer Vision and Pattern Recognition. (pp. 52-58).

Georghiades, A., Kriegman, D., and Belhumeur, P. (2001). From few to many: Illumination cone models for face recognition under variable lighting and pose. IEEE Transaction on Pattern Analysis and Machine Intelligence, 23(6), 643-660.

Gokturk, S., Bouguet, J., Tomasi, C., and Girod, B. (2002). Model-based face tracking for view-independent facial expression recognition, Proceedings of IEEE International Conference on Automatic Face and Gesture Recognition.

Grimes, D., and Rao, R. (2003). A bilinear model for sparse coding, neural information processing systems. Neural Information Processing Systems 15, 1287-1294.

Hastie, T., Tibshirani, R., and Friedman, J. (2001). The Elements of Statistical Learning: Data Mining, Inference and Prediction, Springer.

Høy, M., Westad, F., and Martens, H. (2002). Combining bilinear modelling and ridge regression. Journal of Chemometrics, 16(6), 313-318.

Jiangsheng, Y. (2002). Method of k-Nearest Neighbors, Institute of Computational Linguistics, Peking University, China, 100871, Sep.

Kim, H., Pang, S., Je, H., Kim, D. and Bang. S. (2003). Constructing support vector machine ensemble. Pattern Recognition, 36, 2257–2767.

Kobayahsi, K. and Hara, F. (1997). Dynamic recognition of bias facial expressions by discrete-time recurrent neural networks. In Proceedings of the International Conference on Systems, Man, and Cybernetics. pp. 3732–3737.

Lee, H.-S. and Kim, D. (2006). Generating frontal view face image for pose invariant face recognition. Pattern Recognition Letters, 27, 747-754.

Lien, J. (1998). Automatic recognition of facial expressions using hidden markov models and estimation of expression intensity. Ph.D. thesis, Carnegie Mellon University.

Liu, Z., Shan, Y., and Zhang, Z. (2001). Expressive expression mapping with ratio images. In Proceedings of SIGGRAPH.

Lucas, B. D. (1984). Generalized image matching by the method of differences. Ph.D. thesis, Carnegie Mellon University.

Lui, D., Lam, K., and Shen, L. (2005). Illumination invariant face recognition. Pattern Recognition, 38, 1705-1716.

Lyons, M., Budynek, J., and Akamatsu, S. (1999). Automatic classification of single facial images, IEEE Trans. on Pattern Analysis and Machine Intelligence, 21(12), 1357-1362.

Ma, J., Zhao, Y., and Ahalt, S. (2002) OSU SVM classifier matlab toolbox (version 3.00), Ohio State University, Columbus, USA.

Mase, K. (1991). Recognition of facial expression from optical flow. IEICE Transactions E, 74(10), 3474-3483.

Michel, P., and Kaliouby, R. (2003). Real time facial expression recognition in video using support vector machines. Proceedings of International Conference on Multimodal Interfaces.

Naes, T., and Mevik, B. (2001). Understanding the collinearity problem in regression and discriminant analysis. Journal of Chemometrics 15(4), 413-426.

Otsuka, T., and Ohya, J. (1998). Spotting segments displaying facial expression from image sequences using hmm. In Proceedings of IEEE Proceedings of the Second International Conference on Automatic Face and Gesture Recognition, (pp. 442–447).

Pantic, M. and Rothkrantz, L. (2000). Expert system for automatic analysis of facial expressions. Image and Vision Computing Journal, 18(11), 881–905.

Park, S. (2007). Subtle facial expression database 2007, Technical Report Intelligent Media Lab. Department of CSE, POSTECH.

Riklin-Raviv, T., and Shashua, A. (2001). The quotient image: class-based rerendering and recognition with varying illuminations. IEEE Transaction on Pattern Analysis and Machine Intelligence, 23(2), 129-139.

Rosenblum , M., Yacoob, Y., and Davis, L. (1996). Human expression recognition from motion using a radial basis function network architecture, IEEE Transaction on Neural Network 7(5), 1121-1138.

Sebe, N., Lew, M., Sun, Y., Cohen, I., Gevers, T., and Huang, T. (2007). Authentic facial expression analysis, Image and Vision Computing 25, 1856-1863.

Shan, C., Gong, S., and McOwan, P. W. (2005a). Robust Facial Expression Recognition Using Local Binary Patterns. In Proceedings of IEEE International Conference on Image Processing.

Shan, C., Gong, S., and McOwan, P. W. (2005b). Appearance Manifold of Facial Expression. In IEEE International Workshop on Human-Computer Interaction , 2005.

Shan, C., Gong, S., and McOwan, P. W. (2006). Dynamic facial expression recognition using a Bayesian temporal manifold model. In Proceedings British Machine Vision Conference.

Shan, S., Gao, W., Cao, B., and Zhao, D. (2003). Illumination normalization for robust face recognition against varying lighting conditions. In Proceedings of IEEE International Workshop on Analysis and Modeling of Faces and Gestures, (pp. 157-164).

Sim, T., Baker, S., and Bsat, M. (2003). The cmu pose, illumination, and expression (pie) database. IEEE Transaction on Pattern Analysis and Machine Intelligence 25(12), 1615-1618.

Song, J., and Kim, D. (2006). Simultaneous gesture segmentation and recognition based on forward spotting accumulative hmms. In Proceedings of International Conference on Pattern Recognition, (pp.1231-1235).

Szeliski, R. and Coughlan, J. (1997). Spline-based image registration, International Journal of Computer Vision, 22(3), 199–218.

Tan, A. C., Gilbert, D., and Deville, Y. (2003). Integrative machine learning approach for multi-class scope protein fold classification. In Proceedings of German Conference on Bioinformatics.

Tenenbaum, J. B., Silva, V., and Langford, J. C. (2000). A Global Geometric Framework for Nonlinear Dimensionality Reduction, Science, 290 (5500), 2319-2323.

Tenenbaum, J., and Freeman, W. (2000). Separating style and content with bilinear models. Neural Computation 12, 1247-1283.

Tian, Y., Kanade, T., and Cohn, J. (2002). Evaluation of Gabor-wavelet-based facial action unit recognition in image sequences of increasing complexity, In Proceedings of the Fifth IEEE International Conference on Automatic Face and Gesture Recognition, (pp. 229-234).

Tian, Y., Kanade, T., and Cohn, J. F. (2001). Recognizing Action Units for Facial Expression Analysis, IEEE Transcations on Pattern Analysis and Machine Intelligence, 23(2), 32-66.

Wang, H. and Ahuja, N. (2003). Facial expression decomposition, In Proceedings of the Ninth IEEE International Confefence on Computer Vision, (pp. 958-965).

Wu, Y. T., Kanade, T., and Cohn, J. F., Li, C. (1998). Optical flow estimation using wavelet motion model. In Proceedings of IEEE International Conference on Computer Vision. (pp. 992–998)

Yang, J., Zhang, D., Frangi, A., and Yang, J. (2004). Two-dimentional pca: a new approach to appearance-based face representation and recognition. IEEE Transaction on Pattern Analysis and Machine Intelligence, 26(1), 131-137.

Zhang, Z., Lyons, M., Schuster, M., and Akamatsu, S. (1998) Comparison between geometry-based and gabor-wavelets-based facial expression recognition using multi-layer perceptron, In Proceedings of the Third IEEE Conference on Face and Gesture Recognition, (pp. 454-459).

Zheng, W., Zhou, X., Zou, C., and Zhao, L. (2004). Facial expression recognition using kernel discriminant plane. Proceedings of International Symposium on Neural Networks, (pp. 947-952).

Zhou, C., Lin, X. (2005). Facial expression image synthesis controlled by emotional parameters. Pattern Recognition Letters, 26(16), 2611-2627.

Zhou, S., and Chellappa, R. (2003). Rank constrained recognition under unknown illuminations. In Proceedings of IEEE International Workshop on Analysis and Modeling of Faces and Gestures, (pp. 11-18).

Chapter VII
Facial Gesture Recognition

From facial gestures, we can extract many kinds of messages in human communication: they represent visible speech signals and clarify whether our current focus of attention is important, funny or unpleasant for us. They are direct, naturally preeminent means for humans to communicate their emotions (Russell and Fernandez-Dols, 1997).

Automatic analyzers of subtle facial changes, therefore, seem to have a natural place in various vision systems including automated tools for psychological research, lip reading, bimodal speech analysis, affective computing, face and visual-speech synthesis, and perceptual user interfaces.

Most approaches to automatic facial gesture analysis in face image sequences attempt to recognize a set of prototypic emotional facial expressions, such as happiness, sadness, fear, surprise, anger and disgust (Pantic and Rothkrantz, 2000). From several methods for recognition of facial gestures based on visually observable facial muscular activity, the FACS system (Ekman and Friesen, 1978) is the most commonly used in psychological research. Following this trend, all of the existing methods for automatic facial gesture analysis, including the method proposed here, interpret the facial display information in terms of the facial action units (AUs) (Tian et al., 2001) of the FACS system. Yet no automatic system is capable of encoding the full range of facial mimics, i.e., none are capable of recognizing all 44 AUs that account for the changes in facial display. From the previous works on automatic facial gesture recognition from face image sequences, the method Pentland (2000) presented performs the best in this aspect: it encodes 16 AUs occurring alone or in a combination in frontal-view face image sequences (Pantic and Rothkrantz, 2002).

Another approach for recognition of facial gestures is to observe the human head or face movements (Darrel and Pentland, 1995). The movements allow us to infer the intentions of other people who are nearby and to comprehend important nonverbal forms of communication. For example, if the human head moves left to right, that is understood to say 'No'.

This chapter is organized into two parts. The first part reviews the hidden Markov model which has been frequently used for sequential data analysis such as speech signal processing (Rabiner, 1989). The second part introduces two application systems that contain the vision-based facial gesture recognition algorithm in the main component. The first application is a facial gesture recognition system that recognizes some pre-defined facial gestures such as nodding, shaking, and blinking. The second application is a TV remote control system using the facial gesture recognition technique, where the channel and volume of the TV are controlled.

7.1 HIDDEN MARKOV MODEL

An HMM is a statistical modeling tool which is applicable to analyzing time-series with spatial and temporal variability (Lee et al., 1999; Jordan, 2003; Duda et al, 2000). It is a graphical model that can be viewed as a dynamic mixture model whose mixture components are treated as states. It has been applied in classification and modeling problems such as speech or gesture recognition. Fig. 7.1.1 illustrates a simple HMM structure.

The hidden Markov model (HMM) is extension of a Markov model, where each state generates an observation. We can extend the concept of Markov models to include the case where the observation is a probabilistic function of the state. The resulting model, called a hidden Markov model, is a doubly embedded stochastic process with an underlying stochastic process that is not observable, but can only be observed through another set of stochastic processes that produce the sequence of observations. The HMM model is usually exploited to investigate the time varying sequence of observations and is regarded as a special case of a Bayesian belief network because it can be used for a probabilistic model of causal dependencies between different states (Gong et al., 2000). Fig. 7.1.2 illustrates a 5-state (1-D) HMM used for face modelling.

The HMM is defined by specifying the following parameters (Rabiner, 1989):

- N: The number of states in the model. The individual states are denoted as $S = \{S_1, S_2, \cdots, S_N\}$ and the state of the model at time t is q_t, $q_t \in S$ and $1 \leq t \leq T$, where T is the length of the output observable symbol sequence.

Figure 7.1.1. HMM structure

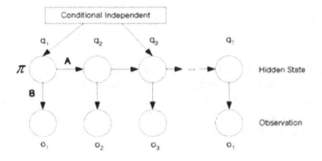

Figure 7.1.2. An illustration of 1-D HMM with 5 states for face modeling

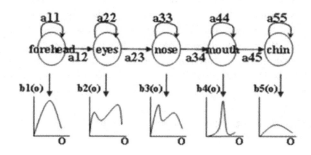

- *M*: The number of distinct observable symbols. The individual symbols are denoted as $V = \{v_1, v_2, \cdots, v_M\}$.
- $A_{N \times N}$: An $N \times N$ matrix specifies the state-transition probability that the state will transit from state S_i to state S_j. $A_{N \times N} = [a_{ij}]_{1 \le i,j \le N}$, where $a_{ij} = P(q_{t+1} = S_j | q_t = S_i)$.
- $B_{N \times M}$: An $N \times M$ matrix specifies that the the system will generate the observable symbol v_k at state S_j and at time t. $B_{N \times M} = [b_j(k)]_{1 \le j \le N, 1 \le k \le M}$, where $b_j(k) = P(v_k \, att | q_t = S_j)$.
- π_N: An N-element vector that indicates the initial state probabilities. $\pi_N = [\pi_i]_{1 \le i \le N}$, where $\pi_i = P(q_1 = S_i)$.

The complete specification of an HMM requires to determine two model parameters (N and M), the observation symbols, and the three probability measures A, B, and π. For convenience, the compact notation $\lambda(\pi, A, B)$ is used to represent an HMM. Given appropriate values of N, M, A, B and π, the HMM can be used as a generator to give an observation sequence $O = O_1 \, O_2 ... O_T$, where each observation O_t is one of the symbols from V and T is the number of observations in the sequence. The observation sequence $O = O_1 \, O_2 ... O_T$ is made in the following manner.

- Choose an initial state $q_1 = S_i$ according to the initial state distribution π.
- Set $t = 1$.
- Choose $O_t = V_k$ according to the symbol probability distribution in state S_i, i.e., $b_i(k)$.
- Transit to a new state $q_{t+1} = S_j$ according to the state transition probability distribution for state S_i, i.e., a_{ij}.
- Set $t = t + 1$: If $t < T$, return to step 3. Otherwise, terminate the procedure.

An HMM can perform a number of tasks based on sequences of observations as follows.

- *Prediction*: An HMM model λ can predict observation sequences in which the probabilistic characteristics of the model are inherently reflected.
- *Sequence classification*: For an observation sequence $O = O_1 \, O_2 ... O_T$ and by computing $P(O|\lambda_i)$ for a set of known model λ_i, the sequence can be classified as belonging to class i for which $P(O|\lambda_i)$ is maximized.

- *Sequence interpretation*: Given an observation sequence $O = O_1\, O_2 ... O_T$ and an HMM model λ, we estimate an optimal state sequence $Q = \{q_1\, q_2, ..., q_T\}$ that explains the observation best.
- *Learning*: Given an observation sequence $O = O_1\, O_2 ... O_T$ and an HMM model λ, the model parameter set (π, A, B) can be adjusted to maximize the output probability $P(O|\lambda_i)$.

For prediction and sequence classification, the forward-backward procedure has been used to compute $P(O|\lambda_i)$ efficiently. For sequence interpretation, the Viterbi algorithm has been used to estimate the best state sequence. For learning, the Baum-Welch re-estimation method has been used to adjust the model parameters effectively. All detailed explanations about the forward-backward procedure, the Viterbi algorithm, and the Baum-Welch re-estimation method were found in (Rabiner, 1989).

In an HMM, the Left-Right (LR) model can represent an order-constrained, temporal characteristic, does not have backward paths, and uses increasing states or keeps the same state. Therefore, it can model a sequentially variant time-series of voices or gestures (Lee et al., 1999; Huang et al., 1990). Fig. 7.1.3 illustrates an example of the LR model of HMM.

7.2 FACIAL GESTURE RECOGNITION USING CHM AND HMM

First, we consider two head gesture such as nodding and shaking, where they mean "Yes" and "No", respectively. To recognize these head gestures, we use the accumulative hidden Markov models (accumulative HMMs) (Song and Kim, 2006) as the recognizer and define six indices of head motions as the inputs of the accumulative HMMs as follows. Index 1 is defined when the head pose is near the front and keep this pose for a little time. Index 2, 3, 4, and 5 are defined when the head movement is changed from leftward to rightward, from rightward to leftward, from upward to downward, and from downward to upward, respectively. Fig. 7.2.1 shows how to determine the index of each head motion. We define other motions which do not belong to the above five cases as index 0. While tracking the head, the estimated head pose are converted to the these six indices and then applied to the accumulative HMMs. The index sequence is classified as "yes" or "no" action by selecting the accumulative HMMs which gives the higher score.

Second, we consider the eye blinking. We use the active appearance model (AAM) to track eye movement. The shape is defined with 32 2D points and has 45 triangle meshes. The eye state is classified to the two classes "open" and "closed" by using the eye width e_w and

Figure 7.1.3. An example of the LR model

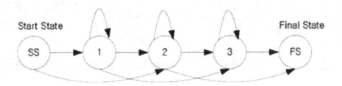

Figure 7.2.1. The index definition of the head motion for the head gesture recognition

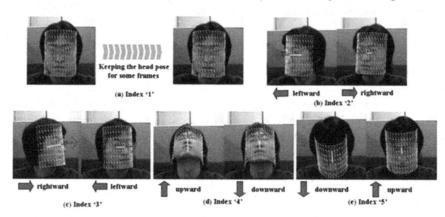

If $\dfrac{e_h}{e_w} > \delta_e$　Eye is open,

Else　eye is closed,

where δ_e is a threshold value. Then, we can recognize the eye blinking to monitor the change of eye state. The eye blinking recognition can be executed when the head pose is the front because we define the AAM in the front face image. Fig. 7.2.2 shows the AAM definition of the eye, and the different fitting results when the eyes are open and closed, respectively.

7.3 FACIAL GESTURE-BASED TV REMOTE CONTROLLER

We developed the face remote controller (FRC) for real world application. The FRC is the remote controller which is controlled by the head gesture instead of the hand. The head gestures are used for moving the current cursor to the left, right, up, and down side, where the cursor is designated to move discretely between buttons. And, the eye blinking is used for generating the button click event. We apply the FRC to a TV remote controller system using the CCD camera that can zoom in/out and is located on the top of the TV. The TV watcher sits in the chair which is approximately 5 meters far from the TV. Fig. 7.3.1 shows

Fig. 7.2.2 The AAM definition and fitting results

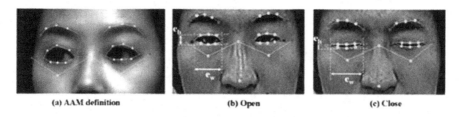

Figure 7.3.1. Cursor movement and click using the head gesture and the eye blinking

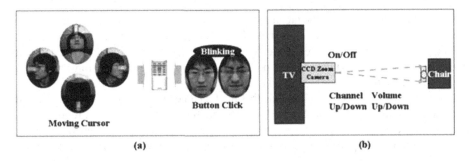

(a)   (b)

Figure 7.3.2. The face remote controller

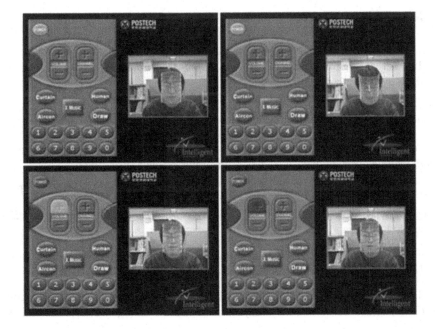

how to perform the cursor movement and button click with the head gesture and the eye blinking, and how the FRC is applied to the TV remote controller system.

Fig. 7.3.2 shows how to execute the FRC system. In the system, the TV is turned on by pointing the TV screen by hand, When the TV is turned on, the virtual remote controller and the head tracking result are appeared on the TV screen. Initially, the cursor is located at the TV on/off button. This figures illustrates that the cursor is moved to volume-up button by moving the head downward. Then, we click the volume-up button by blinking the eye and the TV volume is turned up.

7.4 CONCLUSION

In this chapter, we introduced the facial gesture recognition algorithm and a facial gesture-based TV remote controller system to show the usefulness of the facial gesture recognition technique. The systems use a real-time face tracking algorithm using the cylinder head model to monitor the head motion, an upper face AAM to monitor the openning and closing of the eyes, and a behavor classification algorithm using the hidden Markov model.

There are many kinds of applications that the facial gesture recognition technique can be used. Assistant systems for the disabled who cannot speech may be an representavie example. Moreover, various human machine interaction (HMI) can be devised also. An intelligent robot equipped with gaze tracking ability can understand the context of the conversation by knowing where the other is looking at. An intelligent car will alarm the driver when he dozes.

7.5 REFERENCES

Darrel, T., & Pentland, A. P. (1995) Attention-driven Expression and Gesture Analysis in an Interactive Environment. *Proceedings of the International Workshop on Automatic Face and Gesture Recognition* (pp. 135-140).

Duda, R. O., Hart, P. E., & Stork, D. H. (2000). *Pattern classification.* Willey Interscience, 2nd edition.

Ekman, P., & Friesen, W. (1978). *Facial Action coding system: A technique for the measurement of facial movement.* Palo Alto, CA: Consulting Psychologists Press.

Gong, S., McKenna, S. J., & Psarrou, A. (2000) *Dynamic Vision.* Imperial College Press.

Huang, X., Ariki, Y., & Jack, M. A. (1990). *Hidden markov models for speech recognition.* Edinburgh: Edinburgh Univ. Press.

Jordan, M. (2003). An introduction to probabilistic graphical models. *Hidden markov models.* University of California Berkeley.

Lee, H., & Kim, J. (1999). An HMM-based threshold model approach for gesture recognition. *IEEE Transaction on Pattern Analysis and Machine Intelligence, 21*(10), 961-973.

Pantic, M., & Rothkrantz, L. (2000). Expert system for automatic analysis of facial expressions. *Image and Vision Computing Journal, 18*(11), 881–905.

Pantic, M., & Rothkrantz, L. J. M. (2002). Facial gesture recognition in face image sequences: a study on facial gestures typical for speech articulation. *In Proceedings of IEEE International Conference on System, Man and Cybernetics.*

Pentland, A. (2000). Looking at people. *IEEE Transaction on Pattern Analysis and Machine Intelligence, 22*(1), 107-119.

Rabiner, L. (1989). A tutorial on hidden markov models and selected applications in speech recognition. *Proceddings of IEEE, 77*(2), 257-285.

Russell, J., & Fernandez-Dols, J. (1997). *The psychology of facial expression.* Cambridge University Press.

Song, J., & Kim, D. (2006). Simultaneous gesture segmentation and recognition based on forward spotting accumulative hmms. *In Proceedings of International Conference on Pattern Recognition* (pp. 1231-1235).

Tian, Y., Kanade, T., & Cohn, J. F. (2001). Recognizing Action Units for Facial Expression Analysis. *IEEE Transcations on Pattern Analysis and Machine Intelligence 23*(2), 32-66.

Chapter VIII
Human Motion Analysis

Human motion analysis (Moeslund et. al., 2006; Wang et. al., 2003) is currently one of the most active research areas in computer vision due both to the number of potential applications and its inherent complexity. This high interest is driven by many applications in many areas such as surveillance, virtual reality, perceptual, control applications or analysis of human behaviors. However, the research area contains a number of difficult, such as ill-posed problem. So, many researchers have investigated these problems. Human motion analysis is generally composed of three major parts: human detection, tracking and the behavior understandings.

Human detection finds the segmentation regions corresponding to human and people in an image sequence. It is a very important part in human motion analysis because it greatly affects the subsequent processes such as the tracking and behavior understandings. There are many approaches for finding the human including: background subtraction (Kristensen et. al., 2006; Piccardi, 2004), motion-based segmentation (Sidenbladh, 2004; Gonzalez et. al., 2003; Sangi et. al., 2001), appearance-based segmentation (Mohan et. al., 2001; Utsumi and Tetsutani, 2002: Kang et. al., 2005), shaped-based segmentation (Zhao and Thorpe, 2002; Haritaoglu et. al., 1998), depth-based segmentation (Haritaoglu et. al., 2002; Hayashi et. al., 2004; Li et. al, 2004). Currently many researchers focuse on segmenting human or people in only a still image(Tuzel et. al., 2008, Navneet et.al., 2005, Zhu et. al., 2006). It is quite a difficult problem because we do not know prior information such as motion cues and background cues. The key framework of their method is that a certain feature extractor such as covariance descriptor, histogram of gradient is used for representing each human and then train classifier such as SVM or applying boosting method. And efficient detection method with variously scaled image is crutial to detect humans.

Human tracking involves matching objects between consecutive frames with respect to position, velocity, shape, texture and color using features such as points, lines or blobs.

The tracking methods in essence assume temporal relations among continuous frames. This issue is also important as a means for the pose estimation and gesture recognition. In most of the approaches for tracking, some mathematical techniques are used: Kalman filter (Kalman, 1960; Welch and Bishop, 2001), Condensation algorithm (Isard and Blake, 1998) or Particle filter and Dynamic Bayesian Network (Pavlovic, 1999). Even though these alrogithms give optimal estimation, there may be no way to track a human or humans in the case of partially occuled situations. In order to solve this problem, many researchers currently study tracking a human or humans in partial occlusion. Part based human representation with edgelet (Wu and Nevatia, 2005) give a chance to avoid partial occluision, because we do not track the whole body of a human but only a limb such as an arm, head, or leg. The part based representation is not a state of the art idea: however, a combination of both part detector and priorily known articulated human structure can solve the problem. By using these ideas, we can boost up not only detection but also tracking performance.

Understanding human behavior is to analyze and recognize human motion patterns. In this area, there are many investigations reflected by a large number of different ideas and approaches. The approaches relay on the goal of applications or researchers. But generally, because the behavior understanding problems handles the time-varying data, the general methods for handling time-varying data are proposed: dynamic time warping (Myers and Rabinier, 1980; Bobick and Wilson, 1995; Takahashi and Seki, 1994), hidden Markov models (Poritz, 1988; Brand et. al., 1997; Galata et. al., 2001), neural network (Guo et. al., 1994; Rosenblum et. al., 1994).

This chapter is organized into two parts. The first part reivews some preliminary background, which are the scale adaptive filters, the self-organizing feature map (SOM), and the iterative closest point (ICP) algorithm. The scale adaptive filters (SAF) are specially designed 3D shape filters for human detection using disparity map data. Because the disparity map contains geometric range data, applying the SAF to the disparity map is more robust than applying similar shape filters to image data. Self organizing maps (SOM), also known as Kohonen feature maps or topology-preserving maps, uses a competition-based network paradigm for data clustering (Jang et. al., 1997; Kohohen, 1990; Fausett, 1999). The ICP is a kind of registration algorithm that finds an optimal tranformation that maps given two sets of point data.

The second part introduces five recently developed human motion analysis algorithms. The first algorithm is a pose-robust human detection algorithm based on the SAFs. The second is a hand gesture recognition algorithm and its application to smart home environment systems, where the electronic devices in the smart home are controlled by hand gestures. The third is another example of the hand gesture recognition algorithm that recognizes musical conducting actions. The fourth is a human body gesture recognition algorithm using multiple cameras and silhouette analysis technique. The fifth is another approach to human body gesture recognition using a 3D articulated human body model.

8.1 SCALE ADAPTIVE FILTERS

Human detection is an essential task for many applications such as human robot interaction, video surveillance, human motion tracking, gesture recognition, human behavior analysis, etc. Among many applications, we are interested in the human detection in the field of human robot interaction (HRI). Due to the need for intelligent robots to co-exist with humans in a human-friendly environment, it is essential to be aware of human around.

Often, a single static camera is used for human detection due to its inexpensive cost and the easy handling (Hussein et. al., 2006; Ghidary et. al., 2000; Zhou and Hoang, 2005). However, in the case of mobile robots, human detection is difficult because the robot (camera) and the human are moving around each other, the illumination conditions are changing, and the backgrounds are changing over time. In this situation, it is effective to use the depth cues from a stereo camera to detect the humans (Xu and Fujimura, 2003; Beymer and Konolige,1999; Salinas et. al., 2005; Li et. al., 2004a, 2004b). In this work, we also use stereo-based vision to detect the humans..

There are a variety of human detection methods. Beymer et. al. (1999) used the background subtraction in disparity map obtained from the stereo camera and the template matching in disparity to detect the humans. Their method was not appropriate for the mobile stereo camera. Salinas et. al. (2005) created a map of static background information and segmented the moving objects in the map. They used face detection for human verification. However, they assumed that the humans were posed frontally. Li et. al. (2004a, 2004b) designed the object-oriented scale-adaptive filter (OOSAF) and segmented the human candidates by applying the OOSAF whose filter parameter was changed in accordance with the distance between the camera and the human. They verified the human candidates using the template matching of the human head-shoulder. Their approach showed a good human detection rate and was suitable for a mobile robot platform because it did not use the background subtraction. However, it showed a poor human detection rate when the humans were not faced frontal.

We propose a pose robust human detection method from a sequence of stereo images in the cluttered environment in which the camera and the human are moving around and the illumination conditions are changed. It consists of two modules: human candidate detection, human verification. To detect humans, we apply the MO2DEFs of four specific orientations to the 2D spatial-depth histogram, and segment the human candidates by taking the thresholds over the filtered histograms. After that, we aggregate the segmented human candidates to improve the evidence of human existence and determine the human pose by taking the orientation of the 2D elliptical filter whose convolution is maximal among the MO2DEFs. Human verification has been conducted by either detecting the face or matching head-shoulder shapes over the segmented human candidates of the selected rotation.

8.1.1 Object Oriented Scale Adaptive Filters

Li et. al. (2004a, 2004b) introduced the object-oriented scale-adaptive filter (OOSAF) that extracts humans by using the scale-adaptive filter whose adequate scale varies according to the distance between the human and the camera. It executes the convolution with the scale adaptive filter over the 2D spatial-disparity histogram $H(x_d, d)$ which is obtained by projecting the 3D disparity map $D(x, y)$ along the Y axis of human height.

One problem of the existing OOSAF is that it executes the convolution operation in the 2D spatial-disparity (X-D) space. This causes many problems as follows. First, two coordinates have different natures from each other because they represent the position in the scale of pixels and disparity, respectively. Second, the size parameter of the scale adaptive filters should be changed according to the distance between the human and the camera. Third, the disparity is untractable to handle because it is inversely proportional to the distance between the human and the camera. To avoid this problem, we propose to use the 2D spatial-depth histogram $H(x_z, z)$ that can be obtained by an appropriate transformation.

Let x_d be the spatial coordinate in the scale of pixels in the spatial-disparity histogram $H(x_d, d)$ and x_z be the spatial coordinate in the scale of real values in the spatial-depth histogram $H(x_z, z)$. Then, the 2D spatial-depth histogram is obtained from the 2D spatial-disparity histogram as

$$H(x_z, z) = H\left(\frac{C_F}{z} x_z + c_{x_d}, \frac{C_B C_F}{z}\right), \tag{8.1.1}$$

where c_{x_d} is the center of spatial axis of the 2D spatial-disparity histogram, C_F is a focal length of the stereo camera, and C_B is a baseline of the stereo camera. Fig. 8.1.1 shows one typical example of the transformation from the 2D spatial-disparity histogram to the 2D spatial-depth histogram.

Figure 8.1.1 The 2D spatial-disparity histogram and the 2D spatial-depth histogram

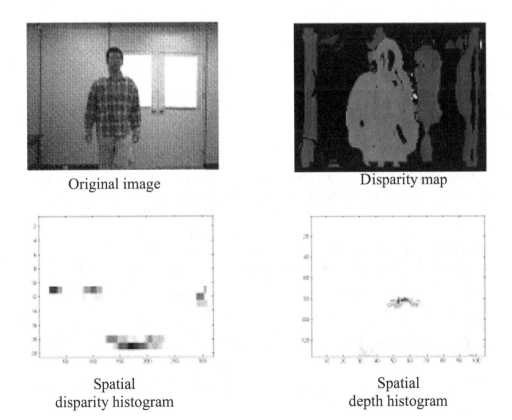

Original image	Disparity map
Spatial disparity histogram	Spatial depth histogram

Another problem of the existing OOSAF is that it does not work well when the human is rotated from the frontal direction. To overcome this problem, we propose a new pose-robust MO2DEF that executes the convolution over the 2D spatial-depth histogram. It has the following properties: (1) their shapes are the 2D ellipses that mimic the contour of human body in the 2D spatial-depth space, (2) their weights are decreased smoothly along the normal direction of body contour, and (3) they are oriented in the specific directions such as 0°, 45°, 90°, and 135°. Among four oriented 2D elliptical filters, one specific filter whose orientation is matched well with the human pose is selected to segment the human candidates. The estimated rotation of the human pose will be also used as the cue for the human verification. A detailed explanation of how to design the proposed MO2DEF is given below.

8.1.2 Multiple Oriented 2D Elliptical Filters

The proposed MO2DEF has the elliptical shape that resembles the body contour of a human and contains the oriented 2D elliptical filter to cope with the rotation of humans. The elliptical shape of the oriented 2D elliptical filter rotated by an angle θ can be represented by

$$\frac{(x\cos\theta + z\sin\theta)^2}{\left(\dfrac{W}{2}\right)^2} + \frac{(-x\sin\theta + z\cos\theta)^2}{\left(\dfrac{T}{2}\right)^2} = V_\theta,$$

(8.1.2)

where W and T are the average width and thickness of human bodies. Similarly, the 2D kernel function $F_\theta(x,z)$ of the oriented 2D elliptical filter can be represented by

$$F_\theta(x,z) = \begin{cases} V_\theta & \text{if } 0 \le V_\theta \le 1, \\ 2 - V_\theta & \text{if } 1 < V_\theta \le 2, \\ 0 & \text{otherwise.} \end{cases}$$

(8.1.3)

The filter weight is maximal (=1) on the contour of the ellipse and it decreases as the (x,z) is far from the contour of the ellipse.

Then, the designed 2D kernel function is normalized such that the sum of the 2D kernel function is 1 in order to keep up the sum of the filtering results as the same. Fig. 8.1.2. illustrates the 2D kernel functions of the multiple oriented 2D elliptical filters rotated by $0°, 45°, 90°$, and $135°$. As shown in Fig. 8.1.2., only a half of the 2D kernel functions is shown because the camera can only see the frontal side of the person.

The filtered results are obtained by the convolution of the spatial-depth histogram (Fig. 8.1.1 (d)) with four oriented 2D elliptical filters as

$$\Psi_\theta(x,z) = (H(x,z) * F_\theta)(x,z), \quad (\theta = 0, 45, 90, 135),$$

(8.1.4)

where $*$ is a convolution operator, and $F_\theta(\cdot,\cdot)$ is the 2D kernel function.

Figure 8.1.2. Multiple oriented 2D elliptical filters

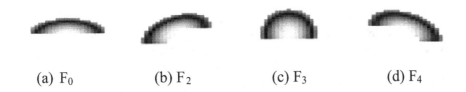

(a) F_0 (b) F_2 (c) F_3 (d) F_4

8.2 SELF ORGANIZING MAP

Self organizing maps (SOM), also known as Kohonen feature maps or topology-preserving maps, use a competition-based network paradigm for data clustering (Jang et. al., 1997; Kohohen, 1990; Fausett, 1999). It imposes a neighborhood constraint on the output units such that a certain topological property in the input data is reflected in the weights of output units. Fig. 8.2.1 (a) presents a simple Kohonen self-organizing network topology with 2 inputs and 49 outputs and Fig. 8.2.2 (b) shows that the neighboring units of a winner unit decrease with successive iterations.

The SOM learning procedure is similar to that of competitive learning networks. That is, a similarity (or dissimilarity) measure is selected and the winning unit is considered to be the one with the largest (or smallest) activation. However, the SOM updates not only the winning unit's weights but also the weights in a neighborhood around the winning units. The neighborhood's size generally decreases slowly with each iteration. A sequential description of how to train a Kohonen self-organizing network is given below.

- **Step 1:** Select the winning output unit as the one with the largest similarity measure (or smallest dissimilarity measure) between all weight vectors w_i and the input vector x. If the Euclidean distance is chosen as the dissimilarity measure, then the winning unit c satisfies the following equation:

Figure 8.2.1. An illustration of SOM

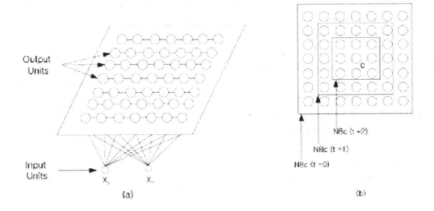

$$\|x - w_c\| = \min_i \|x - w_i\|, \tag{8.2.1}$$

where the subscript c refers to the winning unit.

- **Step 2:** Let NB_c denote a set of neighboring units around the winner unit c. The weights of the winner and its neighboring units are then updated by

$$\Delta w = \eta(x - w_i) \qquad i \in NB_c, \tag{8.2.2}$$

where η is a small positive learning rate. Instead of defining the neighborhood of a winning unit, we can use a neighborhood function $\Omega_c(i)$ around a winning unit c. For instance, the Gaussian function can be used as the neighborhood function:

$$\Omega_c(i) = exp(\frac{-\text{P}p_i - p_c\text{P}^2}{2\sigma^2}), \tag{8.2.3}$$

where p_i and p_c are the positions of the output units i and c, respectively, and σ reflects the scope of the neighborhood. By using the neighborhood function, the update formula can be rewritten as

$$\Delta w_i = \eta \Omega_c(i)(x - w_i), \tag{8.2.4}$$

where i is the subscript for all output units.

- **Step 3:** Continue the above two steps until the weights converge. To achieve better convergence, the learning rate η and the size of neighborhood (or σ) should be decreased gradually with each iteration.

8.3 ITERATIVE CLOSEST POINT ALGORITHM

The iterative closest point (*ICP*) algorithm (Besl and MacKay, 1992; Chen and Medioni, 1991) is a method for solving the fitting or registration problem between two sets. The basic concept of the algorithm finds the corresponding points and estimates the motion transformation by minimizing the error between the model point sets and the data point sets.

Besl and McKay (Besl and MacKay, 1992) proposed an algorithm of registering two sets of three-dimensional points. It always converges monotonically to the minimum of a distance metric in a few iterations. Chen and Medioni (Chen and Medioni, 1991) proposed a new approach which worked on the 3D range data directly, and registered several view data to obtain an accurate transformation between them. Some *ICP* algorithm (Feldmar and Ayache, 1996; Godin et. al., 1994) can handle various observations by using the three-dimensional points, color or orientation similarities. Currently, many variants of the *ICP* algorithm have been proposed (Rusinkiewicz and Levoy, 2001).

The registration problem between the model set $\mathbf{X} = \{\mathbf{y}_1, \cdots, \mathbf{y}_N\}$ and the data set $\mathbf{Y} = \{\mathbf{x}_1, \cdots, \mathbf{x}_N\}$, where N is the number of points, is to find the transformation parameter vector $\grave{\mathbf{e}}$ (the rotation parameter R and the translation parameter T) which minimizes a cost function in the least-squared distance metric as

$$\min_{\theta} \sum_i | \mathbf{y}_i - M(\mathbf{x}_i; \boldsymbol{\theta}) |^2, \qquad (8.3.1)$$

where $\mathbf{x}_i$ and $\mathbf{y}_i$ represent the i th model and data point, respectively, and the M is the rigid transformation function. Table 8.3.1 summarizes how the *ICP* algorithm minimizes the distance metric by iterating over the several steps.

8.4 HUMAN DETECTION USING POSE-ROBUST SAFS

We propose a pose robust *human detection* method from a sequence of stereo images in the cluttered environment in which the camera and the human are moving around and the illumination conditions are changed. It consists of two modules: human candidate detection, human verification. To detect humans, we apply the MO2DEFs of four specific orientations to the 2D spatial-depth histogram, and segment the human candidates by taking the thresholds over the filtered histograms. After that, we aggregate the segmented human candidates to improve the evidence of human existence and determine the human pose by taking the orientation of the 2D elliptical filter whose convolution is maximal among the MO2DEFs. Human verification has been conducted by either detecting the face or matching head-shoulder shapes over the segmented human candidates of the selected rotation.

Table 8.3.1 The ICP algorithm

---

(1) Initialize the transformation parameter vector $\grave{\mathbf{e}}^0$. Reset the iteration variable k to zero.

(2) Compute the closest data point set $\mathbf{Z}^k$ that correspond to the model point set $\mathbf{X}^k$ as

$$\mathbf{Z}^k = C(\mathbf{X}^k, \mathbf{Y}),$$

where C is the closest point operator, and the closest point is obtained by the distance

metric as $\mathbf{z}_i = \min_{y \in Y} | \mathbf{x}_i - \mathbf{y} |^2$.

(3) Obtain the transformation parameter vector $\grave{\mathbf{e}}^k$ using the least square registra-

tion method over a pairs of points $\{\mathbf{X}, \mathbf{Z}^k\}$ (Besl and MacKay, 1992) as

$$(\grave{\mathbf{e}}^k, e^k) = Q(\mathbf{X}, \mathbf{Z}^k)$$

where Q is the registration process and e^k is an error.

(4) Apply the registration to the model set as $\mathbf{X}^{k+1} = M(\mathbf{X}^k; \grave{\mathbf{e}}^k)$

(5) If the error change ($e^{k-1} - e^k$) falls below a threshold τ, set the local increment

$\Delta \grave{\mathbf{e}} = \grave{\mathbf{e}}^k - \grave{\mathbf{e}}^0$ and terminate the iteration. Otherwise, set $k = k+1$ and goto step 2.

8.4.1 Human Candidate Segmentation

Li et. al. (2004b) suggested the human candidate segmentation. They obtained the position of the human candidates using the average cross section area of human bodies from the filtered spatial-depth histograms $\Psi_\theta(x, z)$, and determined the area of the human candidates by the average width and the average thickness of the human body. That method uses the spatial-disparity space to find the human. However, we use the spatial-depth space to use the MO2DEFs. So, we retouch all processes of that human segmentation in the spatial-disparity space to suit to the spatial-depth space. To segment the humans regardless of the rotation, we should segment the human candidates from the each 4 results of the filtering by the MO2DEFs

8.4.2 Human Pose Angle Estimation

We can estimate the human pose approximately when we use multiple oriented 2D elliptical filters to segment the human candidates. We know that the filtered spatial-depth histogram $\Psi_\theta(x, z)$ produces a higher peak value when the filter orientation is similar with the human pose. The human pose estimation has been performed as follows.

First, we merge the corresponding bounding boxes whose positions are coincident among the filtered 2D spatial-depth histograms $\Psi_\theta(x, z)$, where $\theta = 0°, 45°, 90°$, and $135°$. The effective areas that are surrounded by the corresponding bounding boxes will be increased.

Second, we find the peak value of the filtered 2D spatial-depth histograms $\Psi_\theta(x, z)$ within the effective area of each bounding box for the segmented human candidates. This process is repeated for the oriented 2D elliptical filters with four different orientations.

Third, we set the human pose as the orientation angle of the 2D elliptical filter whose peak value is maximal among four peak values.

8.4.3 Human Verification

The segmented human candidates obtained by the human candidate detection may be real or not. To guarantee that the human candidates are the real humans, we need a human verification method. In this work, we use two verification methods: face detection and the head-shoulder shape matching.

8.4.3.1 Human Verification Using Face Detection

Before conducting the face detection, we perform the head candidate segmentation using the method by Li et. al. (2004b) within the bounding boxes of the segmented human candidates. Then, we perform the face detection using the AdaBoost-based face detector (Jun and Kim, 2007) with the region of the head candidates. When we find the face, we verify that the segmented human candidate is a real human. However, the face detector cannot find the face when the face is not frontally posed. To solve this problem, we propose to use the head-shoulder shape matching.

8.4.3.2 Human Verification Using Head-Shoulder Shape Matching

The human verification using *head-shoulder shape* matching consists of the following tasks: head-shoulder silhouette extraction, head-shoulder shape extraction, and head-shoulder shape matching.

First, we should extract the head-shoulder silhouette using the motion and the disparity information. The silhouette is extracted from a result of the double temporal differencing (Kameda and Minoh, 1996) from the input image and a result of the human candidate segmentation from the disparity map, and the holes of the silhouette are filled with the points (Kim and Hwang, 1999).

Second, the head-shoulder shape should be obtained. The shape is extracted by sampling the point at the edge of the extracted head-shoulder silhouette. The number of the sampling is always fixed and the sampling is always clockwise order to match the shapes.

Finally, the extracted head-shoulder shape is matched with the registered head-shoulder shapes. The extracted shape is not aligned, so that shape cannot be applied to the shape matching directly. As the preprocessing of shape matching (Cootes, et. al., 1995), alignment process is executed to remove the similarity transformation factors. We decide whether the aligned input shape is similar to the predefined head-shoulder shape or not. The measure of that decision is the Mahalanobis distance between the shape parameter vector $\mathbf{p}$ of the extracted head-shoulder shape and the shape parameter vector $\mathbf{p}_\theta$ of the registered head-shoulder shape, where the rotation angle θ is the human pose obtained from the human pose angle estimation. If that distance is smaller than a threshold D_{th}, that shape is human's one.

8.4.4 Experimental Results and Discussion

We used the BumbleBee stereo camera (Point Gray Research) which was installed at the height of $1.2m$ from the ground. Also, we implemented the proposed human detection system on the PC with 3.4GHz Pentium-4 CPU and RAM 2GB.

For our experiments, we took three different types of image sequences denoted as TYPE1, TYPE2, and TYPE3, respectively. TYPE1 image sequence consists of four image sequences, where each image sequence consists of one human who was moving back and forth with four different human poses. TYPE2 image sequence also consists of four image sequences whose number of frames are 430, 550, 600, and 419, respectively, where each image sequence consists of one human who was moving back and forth with arbitrary human poses. TYPE3 image sequence consists of two image sequences whose number of frames are 500 and 565, respectively, where each image sequence consists of three humans who was moving back and forth with arbitrary human poses and was allowed to be overlapped each other. There are the 5 and 7 overlapped cases between two humans in the image sequence 1 and 2 of the TYPE3 image sequence.

8.4.4.1 Pose Angle Estimation

Pose angle estimation plays an important role for achieving a good human detection. The estimated pose angle was used in which the angle of the registered head-shoulder shape was taken for the shape matching in the human verification step. We measured the accuracy of the pose angle estimation using the TYPE1 image sequence. Table 8.4.1 summarizes the accuracy of the pose angle estimation. As shown in Table 8.4.1, the pose angles of 0° and 90° are estimated perfectly, while the pose angles of 45° and 135° are estimated in the accuracy of 81% and 71%, respectively. The pose angles of 45° and 135° are sometimes estimated with the pose angles of a with 0° and 90°, respectively.

8.4.4.2 Human Detection

We measured the human detection performance using three different types of images sequences: TYPE1, TYPE2, and TYPE3. We defined the detection accuracy f_d by the ratio of the number of detected humans N_d over the total number of humans N_t as

$$f_d = \frac{N_d}{N_t}. \tag{8.4.1}$$

Table 8.4.2 compares the human detection performances of the existing OOSAF and the proposed MO2DEF using the TYPE2 image sequence. As we can see in Table 8.4.2., we know that (1) the human detection rate of the proposed MO2DEF is higher than that of the existing OOSAF by almost 20% because it provides a suitable pose robustness by using multiple 2D elliptical filters, and (2) the face detector is not effective to improve the human detection rate in the case of the TYPE2 image sequence because the image sequence does not contain the frontally posed face images

Fig. 8.4.1 shows some examples from the human detection results of the existing OOSAF method and the proposed MO2DEF method using the TYPE2 and TYPE3 image sequences. The results about the TYPE2 in Fig 8.4.1. show that (1) the existing OOSAF method cannot detect the human bodies when they are turned by the posed angles 45° (frame 215 of the first row) or 90° (frame 197 of the first row), (2) the existing OOSAF can detect the human body by the help of the face detector (frame 215 of the second row), and (3) the proposed MO2DEF can detect the human bodies regardless of the human poses by the help of the multiple pose-robust 2D elliptical filters (the third and fourth rows about TYPE2).

Table 8.4.3 compares the human detection performances of the existing OOSAF and the proposed MO2DEF using the TYPE3 image sequence, where two humans are walking around and may overlap each other. As we can see in Table 3., we know that (1) the human detection rates of using the MO2DEF are higher than those of using the OOSAF, (2) the human detection rates using the TYPE3 image sequence is decreased less than those of using the TYPE2 image sequence because there are some detection failures when two

Table 8.4.1. Accuracy of the pose angle estimation

	0°	45°	90°	135°
Sequence 1	100%	64.71%	100%	75%
Sequence 2	100%	85%	100%	66.67%
Sequence 3	100%	86.96%	100%	69.57%
Sequence 4	100%	88.68%	100%	72.09%
Total	100%	81.34%	100%	70.83%

humans overlap each other, (3) the human detection rate in the case of the image sequence 2 is poorer than that in the case of the image sequence 1 because the image sequence 2 has a higher frequency of the human overlapping, and (4) the effect of the face detector on the human detection rate in the case of TYPE3 image sequence is more apparent than that in the case of the TYPE2 image sequence because the face detector is more effective than the shape matching for the human verification when the humans are overlapped.

The results about the TYPE3 in Fig. 8.4.1. show that (1) the existing OOSAF method cannot detect the human bodies when they are turned by the posed angles 90° (frame 157 of the first row) or they are overlapped (frame 490), (2) the existing OOSAF can detect the human bodies by the help of multiple pose-robust 2D elliptical filters when they are turned by 90° (frame 157 of the third row), and (3) the face detector is effective for human verification when the detected humans are overlapped (frame 490 of the fourth row).

8.5 HAND GESTURE RECOGNITION FOR CONTROLLING THE SMART HOME

Recently, there are many interests in the hand gesture recognition as a part of human-computer interface (HCI) (Quek, 1994). For a convenient environment, it is required to make the smart home to be automatic. The present situation is manually and physically controlled using the remote controller and etc. But, we want to have a simple manner for the samrt home to be controlled by the human directly. Among many modalities, we take the hand gesture recognition because it is the most intuitive and convenient.

A *hand gesture recognition* has more been studied more than 10 years. Various techniques have been developed to recognize the hand gestures: where the hand is and what the gesture is. Shin et. al. (2006) presented the method that could adaptively obtain the hand region in the change of lighting by measuring the entropy from the color and motion information between the continuous frames. Tanibata et. al. (2002) proposed the method to get the hand features from input images by using the color information and the template matching to extract the hand and the face.

To recognize the gesture, many researchers have used the *HMM* because it can model the spatial and temporal characteristics of gestures effectively. Lee and Kim (Lee and Kim, 1999) proposed an *HMM* based threshold model that computed the likelihood threshold of

Table 8.4.2 Comparison of human detection rates between the OOSAF and the MO2DEF using the TYPE2 image sequence

	OOSAF		MO2DEFs	
	Without face detection	With face detection	Without face detection	With face detection
Sequence 1	73.25%	75.58%	96.05%	96.05%
Sequence 2	75.27%	75.27%	90.63%	90.63%
Sequence 3	75.00%	75.50%	96.50%	97.00%
Sequence 4	77.57%	79.00%	91.41%	93.08%
Average	75.27%	76.34%	93.65%	94.19%

Figure 8.4.1. Some examples of the human detection results using the TYPE2 and TYPE3 image sequences

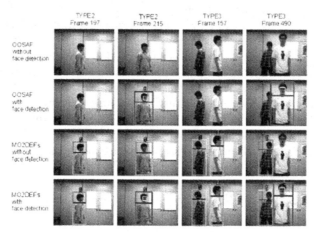

an input gesture pattern and could spot the start and end points by comparing the threshold model with the predefined gesture models. Deng and Tsui (2000) proposed an evaluation method based on *HMM* for gesture patterns that accumulated the evaluation scores along the input gesture pattern. Song and Kim (2006) proposed a *forward spotting* scheme that performs gesture segmentation and recognition at the same time.

There are several applications that the hand gesture recognition is used to control the TV set remotely. Freeman and Weissman (1995) developed the television control system by the gesture recognition of the open hands, where they used the normalized correlation of templates to analyze the hand. Bretzener and Laptev (2002) presented an algorithms and a prototype system that performed the hand tracking and the hand posture recognition, where they used hierarchies of multi-scale color image features at the different scales.

We propose an intuitive, simple and easy TV remote control system using the hand gesture recognition. Our system consists of two steps. The first step is to detect the hand using a cascade of techniques such as the skin color segmentation and the graph-cuts algorithm. The second step is to recognize a sequence of hand gestures using a forward spotting scheme. Fig. 8.5.1 shows the flow chart of our system that we are developed.

8.5.1 Hand Detection

The human hand is a non-rigid object which has five fingers. It has a variety of shape according to different views, which makes it very difficult to be found. So, most of hand detection methods are view-dependent except using the multi-cameras. Our proposed approach is also view-dependent because of using a single stereo camera. Fig. 8.5.2 shows the structure of the TV watching environment, where the people is looking at the TV stand and cotrolling it by using the hand gesture like the TV remote controller. We think that this structure is very natural for our application.

Table 8.4.3. Comparison of human detection rates between the OOSAF and the MO2DEF using the TYPE2 image sequence

	OOSAF		MO2DEFs	
	Without face detection	With face detection	Without face detection	With face detection
Sequence 1	70.70%	73.18%	92.09% False acceptance : 1	94.19% False acceptance : 1
Sequence 2	65.16%	66.04%	88.28%	89.38%
Average	67.93%	69.61%	90.19%	91.79%

8.5.1.1 Hand Candidate Region Detection

We find the hand candidate region using the human anatomy in a sequential manner. First, we observe the head of the human. Second, we observe the arm based on the position of the observed head. Third, we designate the hand candidate region. A detailed procedure of finding the hand candidate region is accomplished on the disparity map sequentially as follows.

First, we project the disparity image to the depth axis. Second, we apply the depth window mask to the projected disparity map. Third, we observe the head as follows. Because the camera is positioned at the ceiling, the maximal disparity regions are the candidates of the human head. To verify whether each maximal disparity region is the head or not, we use the observation that the head has a circlrar shape. From the eigenvalue analysis, when the rate of the first eigenvalue and the second eigenvalue is close to 1, it has a shape of circle. Otherwise, it has a shape of stick. Therefore, the candidate head region is verified as the real head if the rate is close to 1. Fourth, we observe the arm as follows. Each disparity regions that are smaller than the head disparity region are assumed as the arm candidate regions and they are veified as the real arm if the rate is not close to 1. Finally, we regard the end of the arm region as the hand candidate region. Fig. 8.5.3 shows a sequential process of detecting the hand candidate region.

8.5.1.2 Hand Detection Using Skin Color and Graph-Cut

To detect the hand region exactly, we use the skin color and graph-cut technique. Because the hand region detection using just the skin color is affected by the illuminant variation, it is advantageous to use the shape of the hand region.

We use the YCbCr color space for detecting the skin color region. The YCbCr color space is less sensitive to the illumination than the RGB space. Because the luma component is also dependent on the illumination, we just use Cb, Cr chroma components among Y, Cb and Cr. The skin color classifier is modelled by a unimodal Gaussian (Phung, et. al, 2005) for each Cb, Cr component. In the training step, the hand skin pixel values of each component are obtained manually.

$$P(X_{cb} \mid skin_{cb}) = g(X_{cb}; m_{cb}, C_{cb})$$
$$P(X_{cr} \mid skin_{cr}) = g(X_{cr}; m_{cr}, C_{cr})$$

(8.5.1)

Figure 8.5.1. TV remote control system

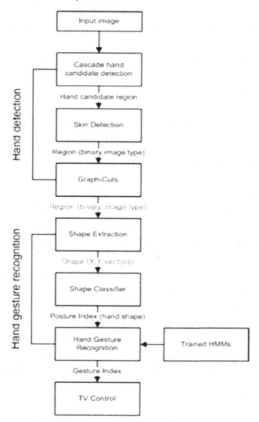

Figure 8.5.2. TV watching environment

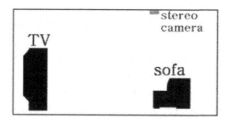

where $g(X_{cb}; m_{cb}; C_{cb})$ is the Gaussian distribution of pixel values of color component Cb with the mean m_{cb} and the covariance C_{cb}.

We apply a simple threshold to the multiplication value of the each skin component's conditional pdf as

$$P(X_{cb} \mid skin_{cb}) \times P(X_{cr} \mid skin_{cr}) \geq \tau \tag{8.5.2}$$

Figure 8.5.3. A sequential detection of the hand candidate region, 1st row: the head region, 2st row: the arm region, 3rd row: the hand candidate region

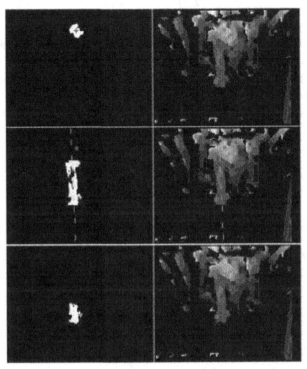

where τ is threshold. All pixels whose multiplication values are greater than τ are treated as the hand region. Intuitively, the multiplication of two pdfs will be the mean-centered pdf. So, such a distribution has more separable capabilities.

The graph-cuts algorithm (Boykov and Funka-Lea, 2006; Boykov and Kolmogorov, 2004) is used to find the globally optimal segmentation of the image. The obtained solution gives the best balance of boundary and region properties among all segmentations satisfying the color constraints. We apply the graph-cut algorithm suggested by Boykov and Funka-Lea (Boykov and Funka-Lea, 2006) to each component of YCbCr. We consider a set of pixels $\mathcal{P}$ in the input image, and all unordered pairs of the 8-neighboring pixels of that pixels $\mathcal{N}$. A vector $\mathbf{L}=\left(L_1,\cdots,L_p,\cdots,L_{|\bullet|}\right)$ describes the labels to pixels p in $|\mathcal{P}|$, where each pixel is identified as the hand region pixel or the background pixel. Each region of the hand and the background is obtained by the hand skin classifier at the previous step. The color values of the pixel p is specified by a vector $\mathbf{I}_p = \left(Y_p, B_p, R_p\right)$ which are the pixel value of the color components Y, Cb, and Cr, respectively.

Then, we try to minimize the Potts energy as

$$E(\mathbf{L}) = \lambda \cdot D(\mathbf{L}) + V(\mathbf{L}) \qquad (8.5.3)$$

where $D(\mathbf{L})$ is a regional term and $V(\mathbf{L})$ is a boundary term and they are computed by

$$D(\mathbf{L}) = \sum_{p\in\mathcal{P}} D_p(L_p)$$
$$V(\mathbf{L}) = \sum_{(p,q)\in\mathcal{N}} K_{(p,q)} \cdot T(L_p \neq L_q) \qquad (8.5.4)$$

where the coefficient λ controls the importance of the regional term $D(\mathbf{L})$ and the boundary term $V(\mathbf{L})$ in the energy function.

The regional term $D(\mathbf{L})$ notifies the assignment penalties for respective pixels P in the set $\mathcal{P}$. When we use the as 'h' and 'b' as the hand and the background, respectivley, the individual penalty of pixel P about the object is $D_p('h')$ is computed by

$$
\begin{aligned}
D_p('h') &= -lnPr(\mathbf{I}_p | 'h') \\
&= -ln\{Pr(Y_p|'h')Pr(B_p|'h')Pr(R_p|'h')\} \\
&= -lnPr(Y_p|'h') - lnPr(B_p|'h') - lnPr(R_p|'h')
\end{aligned}
\qquad (8.5.5)
$$

Similarly, the pixel about the background $D_p('b')$ is computed by

$$D_p('b') = -lnPr(Y_p|'b') - lnPr(B_p|'b') - lnPr(R_p|'b') \qquad (8.5.6)$$

$Pr(\mathbf{I}_p|\cdot)$ could be known from the previous Gaussian modeling, The boundary term $V(\mathbf{L})$ specifies the boundary penalty of labeling $\mathbf{L}$ and $V_{p,q}$ means the penalty for the discontinuity between the point p and q. When $V_{p,q}$ becomes bigger, the values of two points are more similar as

$$V_{p,q} \propto exp\left(-\frac{(\mathbf{I}_p - \mathbf{I}_q)^2}{2\sigma_{p,r}^2}\right) \cdot \frac{1}{dist(p,q)} \qquad (8.5.7)$$

where σ is estimated from the camera noise. The result of calculation of $(\mathbf{I}_p - \mathbf{I}_q)^2$ is obtained by computing a square of the Euclidean distance between the two vectors $\mathbf{I}_p$ and $\mathbf{I}_q$. Fig. 8.5.4 show the result of hand region using the skin color and the graph-cut.

8.5.2 Hand Posture Classification and Gesture Recognition

8.5.2.1 Hand Shape Extraction

We need to extract the hand shape from the segmented hand region in the previous section. First, we apply the canny edge detection technique to the segmented hand region. Second, we obtain a sequence of pixels on the edge.

We now present a simple *shape extraction* method how to arrange that pixels. First of all, we compute the centroid of the edge and take the topmost point p_1 as a reference point, which has the same horizontal position with the centroid. Then, we find the 8 nearest neighbors from p_1 and should decide a next pixel p_2 on the clockwise manner as follows: 1) The first search direction is to the bottom and search the next point on the anticlockwise direction until a point is found. 2) Search a nearest neighbor until a point is found from one more rotated direction than the opposite direction from the point found in the previous step to the current point. 3) Repeat step 2 until all pixels on the hand edge is ordered. 4) For matching between each shape, normalize it into the number of uniform points. The figure 8.5.5 shows the shape extraction process, wherer '1', '2', $\cdots$ are the extracted points, 'a', 'b', $\cdots$ are the searching direction in step by step, 't' is the direction that is found in previous step.

Since the extracted hand shapes have various scales, translations and rotation factors, we need to remove them by the shape alignment process (Cootes et. al, 1995) that is a general pre-processing step for matching between two shapes.

8.5.2.2 Hand Posture Classification

We should classify an input hand shape into one of the predefined postures. We select the nearest posture by measuring the distance between the input hand shape and each predefined hand posture, where each predefined hand shape is the mean of the hand shapes with the same class.

8.5.2.3 Hand Gesture Recognition

Main concern of gesture recognition is how to segment some meaningful gestures from a continuous sequence. Existing method uses generally the backward spotting scheme that first detects the end point, then do back-tracing to the start point. Song and Kim (2006) introduce the forward spotting accumulative *HMM*s for solving the problem about the time delay between the gesture segmentation and recognition. This method is suitable for our real-time application system.

Figure 8.5.4. Result of hand detection

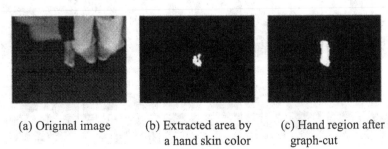

| (a) Original image | (b) Extracted area by a hand skin color | (c) Hand region after graph-cut |

Figure 8.5.5. Shape extraction method

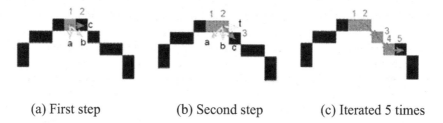

(a) First step   (b) Second step   (c) Iterated 5 times

8.5.3 Experimental Results and Discussion

8.5.3.1 Experiment Setup

We apply the TV control system to turn on/off the power, turn up/down volumes and turn up/down channels. This system is composed of one TV in the front of one user and a Bumblebee stereo camera which attached to the ceiling. In this work, five gestures were defined to control the TV set. Fig. 8.5.6 displays the five gestures which are composed of nine postures.

8.5.3.2 Hand Gesture Recognition

To perform the experiments, some modules had to be trained as follows. First, we should obtain each mean of the predefined hand shape postures. Second, we trained the six HMMs for five gesture models and one non-gesture model using a set of training posture sequences.

The extracted hand shape data has a size of 160 dimensions, we apply PCA to the shape data to represent it in a reduced from using the basis vectors that were obtained from the aligned training sample set. The size of reduced dimension is 80. Then we are able to obtain the means of each hand data shape. The number of the mean is 9.

We tested a total of 75 gesture sequences, where each 5 gesture consists of 15 gesture sequences. Table 8.5.1 summarizes the hand gesture recognition results, which shows that the recognition accuracy of the proposed system is enough to use as the TV remote control.

Figure 8.5.6. The hand gestures. 1st col: Power on/off, 2nd col: Channel up, 3rd col: Channel down, 4th col: Volume up, 5th col: Volume down

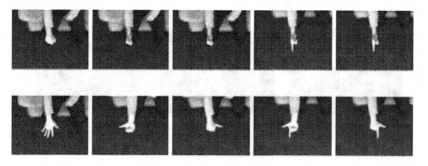

8.6 HAND GESTURE RECOGNITION FOR UNDERSTANDING MUSICAL CONDUCTION ACTION

Hand gesture recognition, as one of pattern recognition and analysis problem, is so important that the motion of human hands can provide abundant information of human intention and implicit meaning to the machines in real world. Many reports on intelligent human machine interaction using hand gesture recognition have already been presented (Wu and Huang, 2004), which can be mainly divided into "Data Glove- based" and "Vision-based" approaches.

The 'data glove-based" methods use a special input device named "hand data sensor glove" for digitizing hand and finger motions into multi-parametric data. It is possible to analyze 3D space hand motion with the sensing data. However, the device is too expensive and the users might feel uncomfortable when they communicate with a machine (Mulder,1996).

The 'vision-based' methods use only the vision sensor; camera (Quek, 1994). In general, the entire system of the vision-based hand gesture recognition must be more simple than the Data Glove-based approach, and it makes human-friendly interaction with no extra device. The vision-based hand gesture recognition is a challenging problem in the field of computer vision and pattern analysis, since it has some difficulties of algorithmic problems such as camera calibration, image segmentation, feature extraction, and so on.

Conducting a music band is a highly sophisticated art that has been matured over centuries (Grull, 2005). Recently, some researchers in the filed of human computer interaction also have been concerned about creating a machine-based music play system, which includes intelligent robots or computers, and considers the conductor's desired beat and the tempo. The first electronic orchestra with a complex performance database and Musical Instrument Digital Interface (MIDI) controllers responds to the gestures of the conductor through a sensor glove. Also, a special purpose electronic baton was introduced in (Morita et. al., 1991). It can identify 4 over 4 beat timing pattern (4/4) by following the motion of electronic baton in the right hand, while recognizing a play speed by tracking the 3D motion of the left hand wearing a sensor glove. Another method of using sensor glove had been proposed by Winker (1995). Modler (2000) used neural networks for mapping hand gestures into the music play parameter in the "virtual musical system". In addition, a research of mapping gesture into music using 3D motion data captured by a commercial 3D motion capture system (Vicon 8) has been reported (Dobrian and Bevilacqua, 2002).

Table 8.5.1. Gesture recognition accuracy of the TV remote control

Gestures	The number of test gesture sequences	Recognition rate (%)
1	15	15 (100.00%)
2	15	14 (93.33%)
3	15	15 (100.00%)
4	15	14 (93.33%)
5	15	15 (100.00%)
Total	75	73 (97.33%)

Bien and Kim (1992) have suggested a vision-based method for understanding human's conducting action for chorus with a special purpose light baton and infra-red camera. They proposed a vision system which captures the image sequences, tracks each end-point of the baton which is a stick having a distinguished color feature to be detected easily by a camera, and analyzes a conducting action by fuzzy-logic based inference. Lately, Watanabe and Yachida (1999) have proposed a real-time interactive virtual conducting system using the principle component analysis (PCA)-based gesture recognition that can identify only 3/4 time pattern.

In general, conductors perform various music using both hands and natural conducting actions may be very difficult to represent. Hence, we take the following assumptions to alleviate the problem:

- The conductor uses only one-side hand.
- The conducting action must be in the view range of the camera.
- The conductor may indicate four timing patterns (2/4, 3/4, 4/4, 6/8 see Fig. 8.6.1) with three tempos (Andante, Moderato, Allegro) by his/her hand motion.
- The conductor needs no special devices.

We propose a very simple but reliable vision-based hand gesture recognition of the music conductor with no extra devices. Unlike the previous vision-based hand gesture recognition, we use the depth information, instead of using the intensity or the color information of image, generated by a stereo vision camera to extract human hand region that is the key region of interest (ROI) in this application. Our proposed system can obtain the motion velocity and the direction by tracking the center of gravity (COG) of the hand region, which provides the speed of any conducting time pattern. We introduce two methods to recognize the musical time pattern. One is the *CFP tracking* which uses only special features like conducing feature point and another is the *motion histogram* matching which can identify the time pattern and the tempo at once, where the ``Mahalanobis distance'' is chosen as the distance metric of *motion histogram* matching.

8.6.1 Hand Segmentation

Hand segmentation is the first step of our proposed hand gesture recognition system, which separates the human hand region from the others. Most methods for the hand segmentation uses the skin color information to extract the hand region. The skin color-based hand region extraction is quiet simple, but it is sensitive to light condition change and complicated and cluttered background which has many skin-like colored objects such as wood and wall papers. We use the depth information of a stereo image instead of the 2D pixel image. The depth information might not only be insensitive in any light condition but also robust even if there is a complicated background.

Normally, the members of orchestra must concentrate their attention on the conductor's face and hands to read his/her intention and his/her hands are placed in front of conductor's body when conducting. Based on this fact, we utilize a face detector to detect the human face, which allow us to find the hand candidate region easily because we know that the depth of hand region must be closer than the face region to the stereo camera. Fig. 8.6.2 shows how the hand candidate region is changed according to the distance of human faces from the camera.

Figure 8.6.1. Four typical musical time patterns: (a) 2/4, (b) 3/4, (c) 4/4 and (d) 6/8

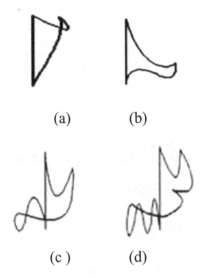

(a)   (b)

(c)   (d)

The exact hand region can be completely segmented after postprocessing on the extracted hand candidate region. Fig. 8.6.3 shows several postprocessing stages such as the morphological operator and the connected component analysis to remove the non-hand region (Bloem et. al., 2000).

To track the motion of the hand, the COG of the hand region needs to be computed. We approximate the COG by computing the mean coordinates of the segmented hand region as

$$X_{cog} = \frac{\sum_i x_i}{N}, Y_{cog} = \frac{\sum_i y_i}{N} \qquad (8.6.1)$$

where x_i, y_i are the x and y coordinates at the i th pixel position, respectively, and N is the number of pixels of the hand region.

8.6.2 The Proposed Hand Gesture Recognition

In contrast to the gesture recognition for hand sign language, the hand gesture recognition for understanding a musical time pattern and tempo does not have to be accurate. While a slight posture or movement of hands in the hand sign language represents an independent and important meaning, only salient features like beat transition point of hand motion are the most important information in the conducting gesture.

8.6.2.1 The Direction Dode of the Hand Motion

The easiest way to find the trajectory of the conducting gesture is to track the motion direction of the hand. We obtain the direction angle of the hand motion by computing the difference between the previous COG of hand region and the current COG of it as

$$\Delta X_{cog}(t) = X_{cog}(t) - X_{cog}(t-1),$$
$$\Delta Y_{cog}(t) = Y_{cog}(t) - Y_{cog}(t-1),$$
$$\theta(t) = \arctan \frac{\Delta Y_{cog}(t)}{\Delta X_{cog}(t)}, \tag{8.6.2}$$

where $\theta(t)$ is the direction of the hand movement on time t. To represent the direction-code, the real value of the hand direction should be quantized in eight directions. Fig. 8.6.4 shows three-bit codes for the eight dominant direction of hand movement.

8.6.2.2 Conducting Feature Point

Instead of analyzing all the sequences of motion directions, we simply track the salient features of conducting gestures. Fig. 8.6.6 illustrates the representative features which are called as ``Conducting Feature Point (CFP)'', of each musical time pattern. For example, a musical time pattern of 2/4 has three CFPs which are *3to6*, *6to1*, and *1to3*. Assuming that the new coming CFP is *6to1* while the previous CFP is *3to6* or the start point of the initial gesture, then the gesture recognition system expects the next CFGs *1to3* following *3to6*. Thus, the recognition system can identify the time pattern by observing the sequence of CFPs.

Figure 8.6.2. Real images vs. depth images of the hand candidate regions: (a) and (d) A human conductor stands at 1.0m from the camera, (b) and (e) at 1.5m from the camera, (c) and (f) at 2.0m from the camera

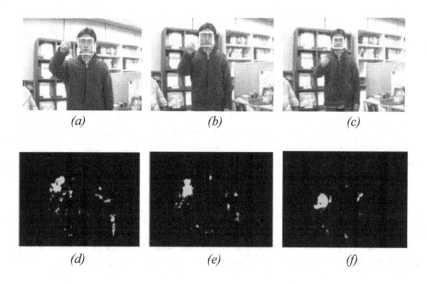

Figure 8.6.3. Post processing: (a) the extracted hand candidate region, (b) noise removal by morphological operation, and (c) component merging by connected component analysis

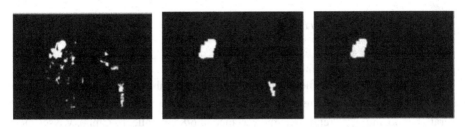

8.6.2.3 Motion Histogram Matching

Although the analysis of CFP sequences is reliable for identifying musical time patterns, it can fail when the system misses an important CFP. This can be occur for a complicated time pattern like 6/8 which has a large variation among the different human conductors. To avoid this problem, we propose a *motion histogram* matching based on the musical time pattern tempo analysis. Fig. 8.6.5 indicates the plot of the average *motion histogram* of direction codes for each musical time patterns with the moderato tempo.

We can obtain a cycle of each time pattern, where one cycle means a sequence of the direction-code from the start point of time patterns to thier end point (usually both the start point and the end point are the same). In general, most musical time patterns have ``*3to6*'' type of the CFP as the start point of thier action.

In the training stage, we collect the histogram vectors $H = [h_0, h_1, ..., h_7]$ where h_0 to h_7 are the number of each direction code for the cycle and obtain the statistics (mean, variance) of *motion histogram* for all combinations of time patterns (2/4, 3/4, 4/4, 6/8) and tempos (Andante, Moderato, Allegro). Then, the mean and variance vectors H_m and H_Σ of the histogram vectors can be computed as

Figure 8.6.4. Eight direction codes

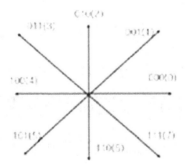

$$H_\mu = \frac{1}{N}\sum_i H_i,$$

$$H_\Sigma = \frac{1}{(N-1)}\sum_i (H_i - H_\mu)^2, \tag{8.6.3}$$

where N is the number of training data.

Thus, we have twelve profiles of *motion histogram*. Table 8.6.1 denotes the profile index for the time patterns and tempos. For example, H_m^1 represents the mean of 2/4 with moderato tempo and H_Σ^1 represents the variance of 6/8 with allegro tempo. We selected the "Mahalanobis distance" as a metric of *motion histogram* matching. By Eq. (8.6.4), the similarity scores for all profile are evaluated. The proposed musical time pattern and tempo recognition system identify the time pattern and tempo by taking the profile whose similarity score is the minimum.

$$MD^k = \sqrt{(H_c - H_\mu^k)^T H_\Sigma^{k-1} (H_c - H_\mu^k)} \tag{8.6.4}$$

$$ProfileIndex = \arg\min_k MD^k, \tag{8.6.5}$$

where H_c is the current *motion histogram* and k is the profile index given in Table 8.6.1.

8.6.3 Experimental Results and Discussion

We used the BumbleBee stereo camera which provides a depth map for each frame of stereo images. We collected the conducting gesture data for each time pattern and tempo which consists of 150 cycles respectively. We divided them into 100 cycles for training the recognition system and 50 cycles for testing the recognition system. Tables 8.5.2 and 8.6.3 summarize the recognition results in the form of confusion matrix, where the left and right table are obtained from the CFP sequence analysis and the *motion histogram* matching, respectively. As a result, the recognition rate of using the CFP sequence analysis is 78.8% and that of using the *motion histogram* matching is 86.5%.

Table 8.6.1. The profile index for the time patterns and tempos

Index	0	1	2	3	4	5	6	7	8	9	10	11
Time pattern Tempo	2/4 And.	2/4 Mod.	2/4 Alle.	3/4 And.	3/4 Mod.	3/4 Alle.	4/4 And.	4/4 Mod.	4/4 Alle.	6/8 And.	6/8 Mod.	6/8 Alle.

Figrue 8.6.5. Motion histogram of direction codes for each time pattern with the moderato tempo

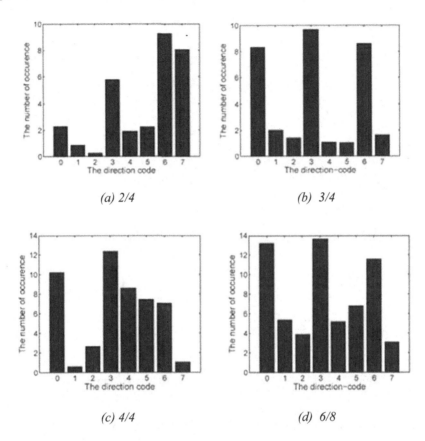

(a) 2/4   (b) 3/4

(c) 4/4   (d) 6/8

8.7 2D BODY GESTURE RECOGNITION USING FORWARD SPOTTING ACCUMULATIVE HMMS

A gesture is a movement that we make with a part of our body, face and hands as an expression of meaning or intention. Gestures are classified into two forms according to the intention: natural and artificial gestures. The natural gesture is meaningless and uncertain, and it has cultural and local diversity. However, the artificial gesture can express more detailed and various meanings using predefined motions. We focus on upper-body artificial gestures in this work.

Many existing studies (Quek, 2004; Kjeldsen and Kender, 1995; Starner and Pentland, 1995) have applied gesture recognition for Human Computer Interaction (HCI). Usually, these approaches used an *HMM* and manually segmented image sequences for gesture recognition, so they are difficult to apply to continuous gesture recognition (Park and Lee, 2005).

One main concern of gesture recognition is how to segment some meaningful gestures from a continuous sequence of motions. In other words, we need to spot the start point and

Figure 8.6.6. The real trajectories and the approximated directions of each conducting pattern. (solid line - real trajectory, dashed line - motion direction, red circle - conducting feature point).

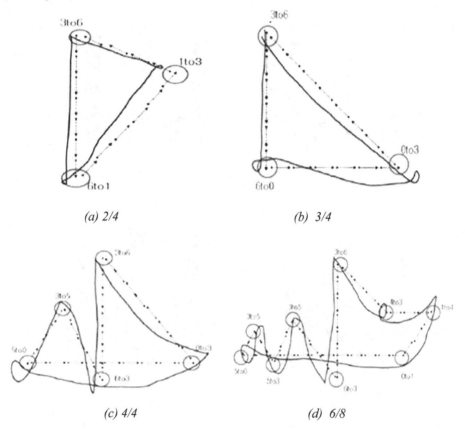

(a) 2/4   (b) 3/4

(c) 4/4   (d) 6/8

the end point of a gesture pattern. This is considered a highly difficult process because gestures have segmentation ambiguities (Takahashi et. al., 1992) and spatio-temporal variability (Baudel and Beaudouin-Lafon, 1993). The first property is caused by the fact that we do not know exactly when a gesture starts and ends in a continuous sequence of motions. The second property is caused by the fact that the same gesture varies in shape, duration, and trajectory, even for the same person.

To alleviate this problem, many researchers have used the Hidden Markov Model (*HMM*) because it can model the spatial and temporal characteristics of gestures effectively. Wilpon et. al. (1989) used an *HMM* for forword spotting and proposed a garbage or filler model to represent the extraneous speech. Lee and Kim (1999) proposed an *HMM*-based threshold model that computed the likelihood threshold of an input gesture pattern and could spot the start and end points by comparing the threshold model with the predefined gesture models. Deng and Tsui (2000) proposed an evaluation method based on an *HMM* for gesture patterns that accumulated the evaluation scores along the input gesture pattern.

Table 8.6.2. The recognition results in confusion matrix form: using CFP sequence analysis

CFP	0	1	2	3	4	5	6	7	8	9	10	11
0	41	0	1	0	2	1	1	2	0	1	0	1
1	0	42	0	0	0	1	1	0	0	2	3	1
2	0	0	40	0	0	0	3	1	1	1	2	2
3	0	1	0	0	39	0	1	3	2	1	2	0
4	0	2	0	0	0	42	1	0	1	0	1	1
5	1	0	0	2	1	39	0	4	1	0	0	2
6	3	0	1	0	1	1	38	1	0	3	1	1
7	0	2	2	0	0	0	0	40	2	3	1	0
8	0	0	0	1	2	2	3	2	39	1	0	0
9	2	0	1	0	2	2	3	1	1	36	0	2
10	0	0	1	2	1	0	2	1	1	1	39	2
11	0	1	2	0	1	0	2	0	4	0	2	38

Table 8.6.3. The recognition results in confusion matrix form: using motion histogram matching

CFP	0	1	2	3	4	5	6	7	8	9	10	11
0	45	0	1	0	1	0	0	2	0	0	0	0
1	0	44	0	0	0	0	1	0	0	2	2	1
2	1	0	45	0	0	0	0	0	2	1	0	1
3	0	1	0	47	0	1	0	0	1	0	0	0
4	0	2	0	0	43	1	0	1	0	0	1	2
5	1	0	0	2	0	44	0	3	0	0	0	0
6	3	0	1	0	1	1	43	0	0	0	1	0
7	0	2	2	0	0	0	0	41	2	3	0	0
8	0	0	0	1	2	1	2	2	42	0	0	0
9	2	0	1	0	2	0	2	0	1	40	0	2
10	0	0	1	2	1	0	1	1	1	0	42	1
11	0	1	2	0	1	0	2	0	3	0	1	40

Kang et. al. (2004) proposed a novel gesture spotting method that combined gesture spotting with gesture recognition. It recognized the meaningful movements while concurrently separating unintentional movements from a given image sequence.

Most existing methods use the backward spotting scheme, first performing the gesture segmentation and then performing the recognition. First, they usually detect the end point of gesture by comparing the observation probability of the gesture model and the non-gesture model. Second, they trace back through an optimal path via the Viterbi algorithm (Viterbi, 1967) to find the start point of the gesture. Third, they send the extracted gesture segment to the *HMM* for gesture recognition. Thus, there is an unavoidable time delay between the gesture segmentation and the gesture recognition. This time delay is not appropriate for on-line continuous gesture recognition.

To solve this problem, we propose a forward spotting scheme that performs gesture segmentation and recognition at the same time. The forward scheme computes a competitive differential observation probability (CDOP) that is defined by the difference of observation probability between the gesture and the non-gesture, and detects the zero crossing points. The start (or end) points correspond to the zero crossing points from negative to positive (or positive to negative). From the start point, we obtain the posture type of the input frame using the predetermined associative map between 2D shape and 3D articulation data and apply it to the *HMM*. Then, the *HMM* determines the gesture of each input frame until the end point.

We also propose a sliding window and accumulative *HMM* that can alleviate the problem of spatio-temporal variabilities. The sliding window technique computes the observation probability of gesture or non-gesture using a number of continuing observations within the sliding window. This reduces the undesirable effect of an abrupt change of observations within a short interval that can be caused by erroneous and incomplete feature extraction. The accumulative *HMM* decides the final gesture type by a majority vote of all recognition results that are obtained between the start and end point. This improves the classification performance of gesture recognition greatly.

To recognize the gesture, we need to extract the features from the input image. In general, two kinds of features, the 2D shape data and 3D articulation data are widely used for gesture recognition. Bobick and Davis (2001) used a 2D view-based approach to represent and recognize human movements. The temporal templates containing the motion energy image (MEI) and the motion history image (MHI) were used to represent human movements. The Hu moments of the temporal templates were used to recognize the movements. Dong et. al. (2006) presented a method for human gesture recognition based on quadratic curves, where trajectory information of the center points of skin color and 2D foreground silhouettes were used to represent the movements and six invariants from the fitted quadratic curve was used to recognize them. However, these techniques can be used for the gesture recognition within a very limited view because the obtained 2D features were very dependent on the viewing angle between the human and the cameras.

To overcome these limitations, many researchers have tried to extract 3D articulation data. Agarwal and Triggs (2006) recovered 3D body poses by the direct nonlinear regression of joint angles against shape descriptor vectors from the monocular silhouettes. Shakhnarovich et. al. (2003) introduced a new example-based algorithm for fast parameter estimation with parameter-sensitive-hashing (PSH) that could estimate the accumulated 3D human body poses. Sigal and Black (2006) proposed a general process to infer the 3D poses from the silhouettes using the hierarchical Bayesian inference framework. Sminchisescu et. al. (2004, 2005) presented a mixture density propagation framework for the 3D pose recovery.

In this work, we use the 3D articulation data as the input for the proposed gesture gesture recognition method. Since we are using multiple cameras to capture the movements, it is necessary to estimate the 3D articulation data from the captured 2D images. There are two ways to do this: (1) the direct computation from corresponding multiple 2D images and (2) the indirect estimation by fitting multiple 2D images to the 3D articulation model. Both methods are not appropriate for real-time gesture recognition because they require a large amount of computation time.

We also propose an associative mapping technique that correlates the 2D shape data to the 3D articulation data. It is built by the following manner. First, we prepare a large number of training samples with 2D shape data correlated to 3D articulation data. Second, we quantify the 2D shape and the 3D articulation data using the Self-Organizing Map (SOM) for each. Third, we find an associative mapping between the discrete 2D shape data and the discrete 3D articulation data using the learning technique by examples. This predetermined association mapping reduces the computation time for obtaining the 3D articulation data from the captured images greatly.

8.7.1 Simultaneous Gesture Segmentation and Recognition

8.7.1.1. Gesture Segmentation Using Forward Spotting

We use a sliding window technique that computes the observation probability of gesture or non-gesture using a number of continuing observations within the sliding window, not just a single observation. This reduces the undesirable effect of an abrupt change of observations within a short interval that can be caused by erroneous and incomplete feature extraction. Usually, the size of the sliding window w_s is determined empirically; here we found that 3 was the optimal value of w_s. Fig. 8.7.1 illustrates how the sliding window technique works.

Assume that the size of the sliding window W is w_s and a sequence of observations within the sliding window is $O = \{o_1, o_2, ..., o_{w_s}\}$. Then, a segment of the observation sequence is denoted as $O_t = \{o_1, o_2, ..., o_t\}$. When we consider the sliding window technique, an observation probability $P(O|\lambda_g)$ of the *HMM* for a specific gesture g is obtained by an moving average:

$$P(O|\lambda_g) = \frac{1}{w_s} \sum_{t=1}^{w_s} P(O_t|\lambda_g), \qquad (8.7.1)$$

Figure 8.7.1. An illustration of the sliding window

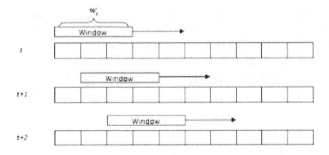

where a partial observation probability $P(O_t \mid \lambda_g)$ is computed by the induction given below, and λ_g is the model parameter set of the specific gesture model g.

Define the forward variable $\alpha_t(S_i) = P(O_t, q_t = S_j \mid \lambda_g)$ as the observation probability of the partial observation segment O_t, and the state S_j at time t, given a model λ_g. Then, we compute $\alpha_t^g(S_i)$ by induction:

- Initialization:

$$\alpha_1^g(S_i) = \pi_i^g b_i^g(o_1), 1 \leq i \leq N. \tag{8.7.2}$$

- Computation of a partial observation probability:

$$P(O_t \mid \lambda_g) = \sum_{i=1}^{N} \alpha_t^g(S_i). \tag{8.7.3}$$

- Induction:

$$\alpha_{t+1}^g(S_i) = [\sum_{j=1}^{N} \alpha_t^g(S_j) a_{ji}^g] b_i^g(o_{t+1}), 1 \leq i \leq N. \tag{8.7.4}$$

- If $t \leq w_s$, set $t = t + 1$ and go to step 2). Else, stop the computation.

For forward spotting, we define a competitive differential observation probability $\Phi(t)$ in a continuous frame of gesture images. The competitive differential observation probability is defined by the difference of observation probability between the maximal gesture and a non-gesture:

$$\Phi(t) = \max_g P(O_t \mid \lambda_g) - P(O_t \mid \lambda_{non-gesture}), \tag{8.7.5}$$

where the maximal gesture is the gesture whose observation probability is the largest among all possible gestures. Fig. 8.7.2 illustrates how to compute the competitive differential observation probability $\Phi(t)$.

When a sequence of image frames comes from the gesture g_i, the *HMM* λ_g has the maximum observation probability among all gesture and non-gesture *HMM*s if it has been trained appropriately. Similarly, when a sequence of frames comes from the non-gesture $\lambda_{\bar{g}}$, the *HMM* λ_g should have the maximum observation probability. Fig. 8.7.3 shows one typical example of the competitive differential observation probability $\Phi(t)$. In this figure, the first row shows the observation probabilities of eight gestures and one non-gesture, the second row shows the observation probabilities of a maximal gesture and one non-gesture, and the third row shows the competitive differential observation probabilities that are obtained by subtracting them.

This figures shows that the transition from non-gesture to gesture occurs approximately when the competitive differential observation probability changes from negative to positive. Similarity, the transition from gesture to non-gesture occurs around the time that this value changes from positive to negative. These observations can be used as a rule of thumb for detecting the start and end points of gestures by assuming that they are the zero crossing points of the function.

Figure 8.7.2. A block diagram for computing the competitive differential observation probability

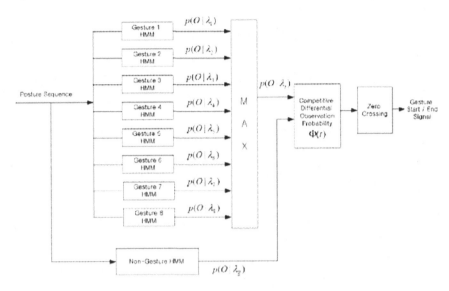

8.7.1.2 Gesture Recognition Using Accumulative HMMs

After spotting a start point in a continuous image sequence, we can obtain a segment of observations until an end point and apply the segment to all gesture *HMMs*. Let an observed gesture segment be $O = \{o_{t_s}, o_{t_s+1}, ..., o_{t_e}\}$, where t_e and t_s denote the start and end point of gesture, respectively. Then, the interval of the gesture segment becomes $w_g = t_e - w_s + 1$. For simplicity of explanation, we redefine the starting gesture o_{t_s} as o_1'. Then, the observed gesture segment can be represented as $O' = \{o_1', o_2', ..., o_{w_g}'\}$. The trained *HMM* determines the gesture type of O', g, to be that which has the highest observation probability.

$$g = \underset{k}{\operatorname{argmax}} \, P(O' | \lambda_k). \tag{8.7.6}$$

In this work, we propose an accumulative *HMM* in order to improve the the performance of gesture recognition. Fig. 8.7.4 shows how the accumulative *HMM* works. Let's define O_τ' as a partial gesture segment $\{o_1', o_2', ..., o_\tau'\}$. Then, we can represent the observed gesture segment by a union of all possible partial gesture segments: $O' = \{O_1' \cup O_2' \cup \cdots \cup O_{w_g}'\}$. The accumulated HMM accepts all possible partial gesture segments and determines that the gesture type of O_τ' is g_τ, which is the gesture type that produces the highest value of observation probability among the gesture *HMMs*:

$$g_\tau = \underset{k}{\operatorname{argmax}} \, P(O_\tau' | \lambda_k). \tag{8.7.7}$$

The observation probability is obtained by the same method as the sliding window technique, and the observed gesture segment O' will generate a gesture type set

Figure 8.7.3. An example of competitive differential observation probability

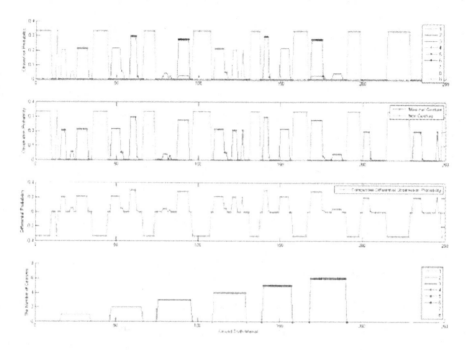

$G = \{g_1, g_2, ..., g_{w_g}\}$, one gesture type per one partial gesture segment. The final gesture type g of the observed gesture segment O' is determined by applying majority voting to the gesture type set G:

$$g = majority\_voting(g_1, g_2, ..., g_{w_g}).$$

(8.7.8)

8.7.1.3 Simultaneous Gesture Segmentation and Recognition

The proposed simultaneous gesture segmentation and recognition consists of two concurrent modules: the gesture segmentation module and gesture recognition module. First, the gesture segmentation module compute the competitive differential observation probability $\Phi(t)$ and detects the start point of a gesture. Then, it activates the gesture recognition module, which performs the recognition task until it receives the gesture end signal. At this point, the gesture recognition module decides the type of the observed gesture segment. This procedure is repeated until no more input gesture images exist. A detailed explanation of the proposed simultaneous gesture segmentation and recognition method is given in Table 8.7.1.

8.7.2 Experiment Results and Discussion

8.7.2.1 Experiment Setup

The gesture recognition method applied to open/close curtains and turn on/off lights in a smart home environment (Kim et. al., 2005). The smart home has three CNB-AN202L CCD cameras, which are attached to the ceiling at angles of 0° and 45°. Fig. 8.7.5 shows the smart home environment that was used in the experiment.

In this work, eight gestures were defined for use as control commands to open/close curtains and turn on/off lights. Fig. 8.7.6 displays the eight gestures and Table 8.7.2 explains the meaning of each gesture. This figure shows that all gestures are represented by 13 different postures and each gesture is represented by a partial set of postures.

To perform the experiments, some modules had to be trained. First, we extracted 2D shape and 3D articulation data from a set of training gesture sequences. Then, we built the 2D to 3D association map using the correspondence between the two extracted features, where the map associates the 2D shape data of input gesture images with the 3D articulation data and generates a sequence of postures. Also, we trained the nine *HMM*s for the eight different gesture models and one non-gesture model using a set of training posture sequences. Fig. 8.7.7 illustrates the overall procedure of the experiments. In this figure, the solid and dotted lines are related to the training and test phase, respectively. Below, explain how each block has been done in detail.

8.7.2.2 Feature Extraction

In this work, we used 3D articulation data to represent the gesture because 2D shape data causes gesture ambiguity. To obtain 3D articulation data, we used multiple views captured from three independent cameras. Each camera captured people with several markers at-

Figure 8.7.4. Accumulative HMM

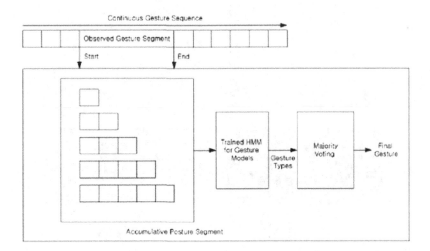

Table 8.7.1. Simultaneous gesture segmentation and recognition

---

1) Initialize of sliding window:
set t = 1;
Fill the sliding window with the first w_s observed posture images.
2) Compute a competitive differential probability $\Phi(t)$.
3) If ($\Phi(t)$!= a start point of gesture)
Shift the sliding window by one time unit;
t = t + 1 and go to step 2 .
4) Initialize accumulative HMM :
Set $\tau = 1$;
Set the partial gesture segment $O'_\tau = \{o_t\}$;
G = NULL .
5) Perform the gesture recognition task.
Determine the gesture type g_τ of O'_τ using the trained HMM;
Update $G = G \cup \{g_\tau\}$;
Shift the sliding window by one time unit;
Set t = t + 1.
6) Compute a competitive differential probability $\Phi(t)$.
7) If ($\Phi(t)$!= an end point of gesture)
$O'_\tau = O'_\tau \cup \{o_t\}$;
Set $\tau = \tau + 1$ and go to step 5.
8) Determine the gesture type g of O' by majority voting.
9) If (more gesture image)
    Shift the sliding window by one time unit;
    Set t = t + 1 and go to step 2 .
    Else stop the algorithm.

Figure 8.7.5. A smart home environment

Table 8.7.2. The definition of gestures

Gesture ID	Meaning
1	Open right curtain
2	Open left curtain
3	Open both curtains
4	Close right curtain
5	Close left curtain
6	Close both curtains
7	Turn on the lights
8	Turn off the lights

Figure 8.7.6. An illustration of eight different gestures

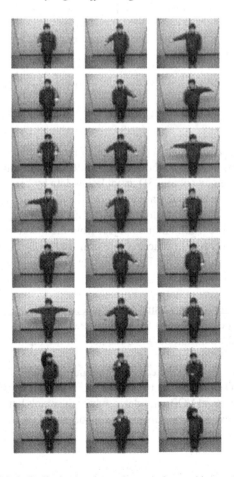

Figure 8.7.7. Overall procedure of the experiments

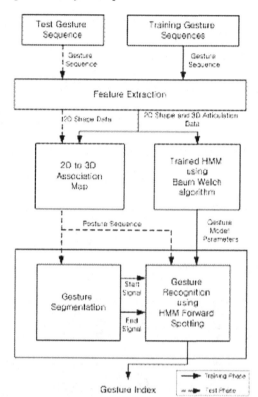

tached to their bodies. Fig. 8.7.8 shows the positions of the 8 markers: the top of the head, the junction of the neck and chest, the elbow and wrist of both arms, and both upper thighs (Pavlovic et. al., 1997). Then, we obtain 3D articulation data by correlating the calibrated 2D marker positions of the three different views.

The 2D shape data was obtained as follows. After capturing the 2D image from each camera, we separated the foreground human object from the image using the background subtraction method based on edge extraction to eliminate the direct illumination effects for controlling the curtain and lighting. Extracting the foreground object is explained in detail below. (See Fig. 8.7.9)

(1)   Get the edge of the input image using edge detection.
(2)   Perform the dilation to the edge of the background image.
(3)   Do the logical-AND operation between the edge of the input image and the dilated edge of the background image.
(4)   Subtract the result of (3) from the edge of the input image.
(5)   Do the logical-AND operation between the horizontal VOP (video object planes) candidates and the vertical VOP candidates, where the pixels between the first and the last edge points for each row (column) are the horizontal (vertical) VOP candidates (Kim and Hwang, 1999).

Figure 8.7.8. Body with attached markers

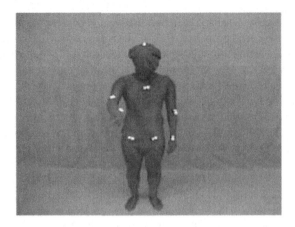

Then, we easily extracted the boundary silhouette of the foreground (Baumberg and Hogg, 1994) and normalized it into a fixed size. Finally, we extracted a fixed number of points to make a 2D shape vector $X = \{(x_1, y_1), (x_2, y_2), ..., (x_{80}, y_{80})\}$ and approximated the shape vector using the B-spline method (Blake and Isard, 1998), where the size of 2D shape vector is chosen appropriately. All these procedures were applied to each view. Then, we applied the PCA technique to the 2D shape vectors in order to reduce the data dimension, where the original size of a concatenated shape vector is $3 \times 2 \times 80$.

The 3D articulation data was obtained by correlating the 2D calibrated marker positions from the three different view images. Since the imaging characteristics of the three cameras may be different, we had to compensate for them. Fig. 8.7.10 shows three different view images, the extracted 2D shape images, and the corresponding 3D articulation data.

Figure 8.7.9. The process of extracting the foreground objects

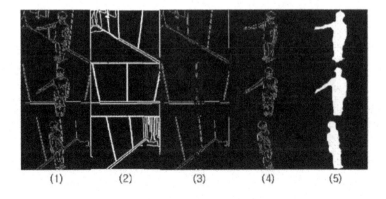

(1)   (2)   (3)   (4)   (5)

8.7.2.2 2D to 3D Association Map

Usually, we can obtain only 2D shape data because we do not wear the markers normally. Hence, we need to prepare an appropriate 2D to 3D association map that correlates the input 2D shape data to the 3D articulation data. Since the extracted 2D shape data has a size of 480 dimensions (=3 views × 80 contour points × 2 dimensional coordinates), we apply PCA to represent it in a reduced form using the basis vectors that were obtained from the training sample set. Thus, we can choose the number of 2D shape features appropriately. However, the extracted 3D articulation data has a size of 24 dimensions (= 8 markers × 3 dimensional coordinates), we do not perform a data dimension reduction. Let us denote a training set of reduced 2D shape data as $X = \{x_1, x_2,..., x_T\}$, a training set of 3D articulation data as $Z = \{z_1, z_2,..., z_T\}$, and a set of posture types corresponding to the 3D articulation data as $P = \{p_1, p_2,...., p_T\}$, where T is the number of training samples.

A simple way of correlating 2D shape data to 3D data is building a lookup table that associates the 2D shape with 3D articulation data directly. However, this simple approach requires a lot of computation time to find the 2D shape data that is the closest to an input 2D shape when the number of samples in the lookup table is large. Therefore, we propose using SOM (Fausett, 1999) to get the best match of the input 2D shape data and the corresponding 3D articulation data. A detailed procedure for building the 2D to 3D association map is given below.

(1)   Apply SOM to the training set of 2D shape data X and obtain a set of 2D shape clusters X and a set of their corresponding covariances Σ_X, where

$$X = \{X(1), X(2),..., X(M)\},$$
$$\Sigma_X = \{\Sigma_X(1), \Sigma_X(2),..., \Sigma_X(M)\},$$

(8.7.9)

and M is the number of 2D shape clusters. In this work, we set $M = 130$.

Figure 8.7.10. 2D shape and 3D articulation data

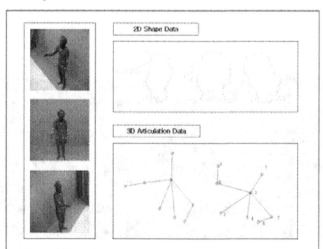

(2)   Apply SOM to the training set of 3D articulation data Z and obtain a set of 2D articulation clusters Z and a set of their corresponding covariances Σ_Z, where

$$
\begin{aligned}
Z &= \{Z(1), Z(2),..., Z(N)\}, \\
\Sigma_Z &= \{\Sigma_Z(1), \Sigma_Z(2),..., \Sigma_Z(N)\},
\end{aligned}
\tag{8.7.10}
$$

and N is the number of 3D articulation clusters. In this work, we set $N = 13$.

(3)   Decide which 2D shape cluster is the closest to a test 2D shape data x_t by

$$
I = \underset{i}{\operatorname{argmin}}(x_t - X(i))\Sigma_X^{-1}(i)(x_t - X(i))',
\tag{8.7.11}
$$

where t is a transpose.

(4)   Decide which sample in the 2D shape cluster I is the closest to a test 2D shape data x_t by

$$
x = \underset{x \in X(I)}{\operatorname{argmin}}(x - x_t)(x - x_t)'.
\tag{8.7.12}
$$

(5)   Retrieve the 3D articulation data z^t that corresponds to the nearest 2D shape data x using the 2D to 3D lookup table.

(6)   Decide which 3D articulation cluster is the closest to the 3D articulation z_t by

$$
J = \underset{j}{\operatorname{argmin}}(z_t - Z(j))\Sigma_Z^{-1}(j)(z_t - Z(j))'.
\tag{8.7.13}
$$

(7)   Decide which sample in the 3D articulation cluster J is the closest to the chosen 3D articulation data z_t by

$$
z = \underset{z \in Z(J)}{\operatorname{argmin}}(z - z_t)(z - z_t)'.
\tag{8.7.14}
$$

(8)   Set the posture type of the test 2D shape data x_t as the posture type of the chosen 3D articulation data z:

$$
posture(x_t) = posture(z).
\tag{8.7.15}
$$

After obtaining the posture sequences, the *HMMs* were learned for eight different gesture models and a non-gesture model. We used a set of 30 training sequences for each model, where each training sequence consists of 5 different image sequences with time variations for 6 different people. The *HMMs* were trained by the usual Baum-Welch method (Rabiner, 1989).

8.7.2.3 Gesture Segmentation

We considered two different gesture segmentation methods. One is a manual spotting method where the gesture start (or end) points are determined when the maximum value of the observation probability among the eight gesture models is greater (or lower) than a fixed threshold value. Another is an automatic spotting method where the gesture start (or end) points are determined by the rule of thumb.

We define the detection rate to evaluate the gesture segmentation accuracy, which is the ratio of the number of correctly detected gesture start (or end) points over the number of ground truth gesture start (or end) points. In this work, we treat the estimated gesture start (or end) points to be correctly detected if they are within 2 time units of the ground truths. Fig. 8.7.11 shows the some examples of segmentation results when different sizes of sliding window are used.

This figure shows that the gesture segmentation performance depends largely on the size of the sliding window. Thus, we need to determine the optimal size of sliding window for our experiments. To do this, we measured the gesture segmentation accuracy as we changed the window size from 1 to 7. Fig. 8.7.12 shows the gesture segmentation accuracy with respect to the different sizes of sliding window. This figure shows that the gesture segmentation accuracy is improved initially as the size of sliding window increases, but degrades as the window size increases further. This result comes from the fact that the accuracy of gesture segmentation is improved initially because the sliding window removes the effect of abrupt change of posture types in the posture sequence, but it degrades because the excessive size of the sliding window causes the start or end points to be missed eventually. From this figure, the optimal size of the sliding widow is 3. In this work, we use $w_s = 3$ for all further experiments.

We compared the gesture segmentation accuracy of the manual and automatic segmentation methods in terms of the detection rate of the gesture start or end points. We tested a total of 480 gesture sequences which include 8 different gestures × 60 image sequences. The manual spotting method was used with several threshold observation probabilities. Fig. 8.7.13 compares the two different gesture segmentation methods when the size of the sliding window is 3. This figure shows that the segmentation accuracy of automatic spotting method is 4.29% better than that of the best manual spotting method.

Table 8.7.3 compares the average segmentation time of the existing backward spotting (Lee and Kim, 1999) and the proposed forward spotting. We selected a total of 240 gesture segments, or 30 segments for each of the 8 gestures. We measured the average number of frames of each gesture, the average segmentation time of each gesture using the backward spotting method, and the average segmentation time of each gesture using the forward spotting method. This table shows that (1) the forward spotting method takes less time than the backward spotting method because the backward spotting scheme has to spend additional time tracing back to find the gesture start point, and (2) the time differential

Figure 8.7.11. An example of segmentation results

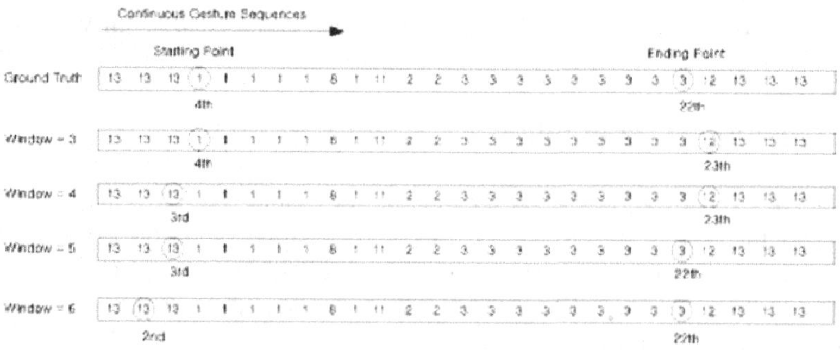

Figure 8.7.12. Segmentation accuracy with respective to different sizes of sliding window

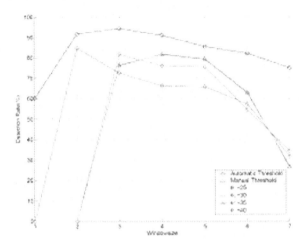

between the forward spotting and the backward spotting increases as the average number of frames of gesture increases.

8.7.2.4. Gesture Recognition

As mentioned before, the accumulative *HMM* is very effective even if there is an abrupt change of posture type in a posture sequence. Fig. 8.7.14 illustrates a typical example of simultaneous gesture segmentation and recognition. The first row shows the observation probabilities of the nine models (eight gesture models and one non-gesture model) for an input posture sequence. The second row shows the competitive differential observation

Figure 8.7.13. Gesture recognition accuracy with respect to the two different gesture segmentation methods

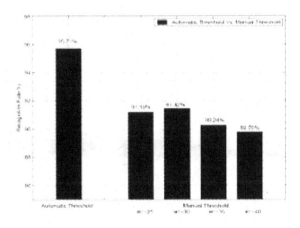

Table 8.7.3. Comparison of average segmentation time of the backward and forward spotting method

Gestures	The average number of frames of each gesture	Average segmentation time of the backward spotting method (sec.)	Average segmentation time of the forward spotting method (sec.)
1	22.9	0.397693	0.219256
2	21.8	0.374011	0.233979
3	24.0	0.427532	0.265356
4	22.3	0.387277	0.242188
5	21.5	0.360991	0.226832
6	23.3	0.408577	0.255319
7	15.9	0.270331	0.168675
8	12.5	0.207169	0.130882

probability. The third row shows the intervals between the gesture start and end points. When the interval is too narrow (< 3), we remove it because it is caused by a spike of postures due to wrong feature extraction. The fourth row shows the recognition results using the accumulative *HMM*s. As you can see, the partial recognition results in the same interval can be different. The fifth row shows the final recognition results at the gesture end points.

Fig. 8.7.15 shows a typical example that compares the gesture segmentation between the accumulative *HMM* and the standard segmentation. This figure shows why the accumulated

Figure 8.7.14. A typical example showing how the proposed gesture segmentation and recognition works

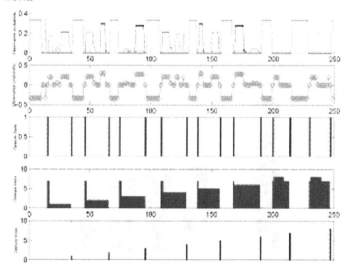

HMM gives better recognition than the standard *HMM*. Since the gesture is continuously changed, the classified posture can be wrong at any time. In this case, we know that the ground truth of the segmented gesture type is 7. When we are using the standard *HMM*, the recognized gesture index is 8. This wrong recognition is caused by the result of wrong segmentation. However, when we are using the accumulated *HMM*, the recognized gesture index is 7. Although some intermediate results may be wrong, the collective decision by the majority voting is correct in this case.

We compared the gesture recognition accuracy between the manual and the automatic gesture segmentation method. To evaluate the gesture recognition accuracy, we define the recognition rate as the ratio of the number of correctly recognized gesture sequences over the number of total test gesture sequences. We tested a total of 480 gesture sequences, or 60 sequences for each of the 8 gestures. In the manual spotting method, the threshold observation probability was fixed at -25 at the log scale. Table 8.7.4 summarizes the recognition results of the two different segmentation methods when the size of the sliding window is 3. This table shows that the recognition accuracy of the proposed method is 375% better than that of the manual threshold method. Most errors come from the failure of feature extraction, which generates erroneous posture types. As shown in Fig. 9, gesture pairs(1 and 4, 2 and 5, 3 and 6, 7 and 8) have similar postures, but opposite orders. These similarities caused gesture recognition failures.

8.8 3D BODY GESTURE RECOGNITION USING 3D ARTICULATED HUMAN MOTION BODY MODEL

Vision-based human body motion tracking has been focused on for the last couple of decades since it can be widely used for application areas such as visual surveillance, human-computer interaction (HCI), human-robot interaction (HRI), human motion analysis, and 3D character animation. The human body motion tracking still remains as a difficult problem because there is a large variation in the scale and shape of each limb among peoples and it requires a huge amount of computation time due to the high dimensionality of the

Figure 8.7.15. A comparison of gesture segmentation between the accumulative HMM and the standard HMM

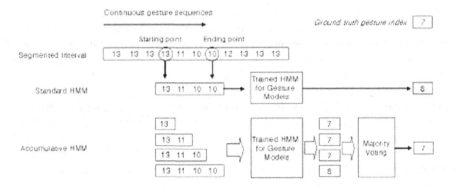

Table 8.7.4. Gesture recognition accuracy of two different segmentation methods

Gestures	The number of test gesture sequences	Recognition rate (%) of manual method	Recognition rate (%) of automatic method
1	60	60 (100.00%)	60 (100.00%)
2	60	59 (98.33%)	60 (100.00%)
3	60	57 (95.00%)	57 (95.00%)
4	60	58 (96.77%)	60 (100.00%)
5	60	52 (86.67%)	56 (93.33%)
6	60	51 (85.00%)	55 (91.67%)
7	60	52 (86.67%)	58 (96.67%)
8	60	51 (85.00%)	52 (86.67%)
Total	480	440 (91.67%)	458 (95.42%)

human body model. To solve these difficulties, many researchers have proposed a variety of approaches given below.

For the last couple of decades, vision based human body motion tracking has been focused on by many researchers because it is also closely related to visual surveillance, motion capture and human motion analysis and can be naturally extended to human-computer interaction (HCI), human-robot interaction (HRI), and human-vehicle interaction (HVI). Even though the vision-based human body motion tracking has been widely developed continuously, it still remains as a difficult problem because people have different scales and shapes of their limbs and perform many different types of complicated motions.

Among many different approaches, the model based tracking method (Liang et. al., 2003; Moeslund et. al., 2006) is most popular because it can take an advantage of prior knowledge of the model, which includes the body structures, lengths, locations and so on. It can be divided into three categories according to the geometric structure of human body: stick models, 2D contour models, and volumetric models. The stick model approximates the human body as a union of edge linked joints, the 2D contour model represents a human body as a set of 2D ribbon and blobs and the volumetric model represents a detailed human structure using 3D models such as elliptical cylinders, cones, spheres and so on.

There are some research works for the stick model based motion tracking (Karaulova et. al., 2000; Rosales and Scalroff, 2000) and the 2D contour model based tracking (Ju et. al., 1996). These approaches showed a good tracking performance but the stick model based tracking can only represent a limited motion because it generally uses the mapping trained between the input image and the generated motions and the 2D contour based motion tracking can also represent only a small rotated motion because it uses the view dependent and visually ambiguous contours. To overcome these limitations, many researchers have used the volumetric models because they can represent more detailed human structures using the 3D models. There are a variety of volumetric models: elliptical cylinder model (Rohr, 1994), cylinder model (Sidenbladh et. al., 2000; Demirdjian, 2003), hybrid model (Munkelt et. al., 1998; Delamarre and Faugeras, 1999; Deutscher et. al., 2000) and so on.

The volumetric based tracking framework projected the 3D model on the 2D image plane, and fitted the projected 2D model into the 2D image data.

Rohr (Rohr, 1994) proposed the pedestrian tracking method based on a 3D volumetric model for the first time, which consisted of 14 elliptical cylinders. However, his method showed a limited pose tracking because it found an optimal pose using just the edge similarity of the human side. Moreover, it could not track the humans under various moving velocities. Delamarre and Faugeras (Delamarre and Faugeras, 1999) proposed the 3D hybrid model-based tracking method that obtained the motion vectors by minimizing the distance between the contours of the projected 3D model and the human contours extracted from three cameras. Their approach was very efficient and also showed a good tracking performance under a fast moving condition. However, it could not track the objects accurately due to the depth ambiguity that was caused by the fact that it only used the contour information of the 3D model. Deutscher et. al. (Deutscher et. al., 2000) computed the silhouette and edge of the human through multiple cameras and then tracked their poses using the annealed particle filter which prevented the optimal pose from trapping into their local minima. Although their approach demonstrated good tracking results, it needed so much processing time. Demirdjian (Demirdjian, 2003) considered the tracking problem as a fitting of the human body model to a set of input data from stereo cameras using the iterative closest point (*ICP*) (Besl and MacKay, 1992; Chen and Medioni, 1991). They proposed a projection-based approach for enforcing the articulated constraints and guaranteed a low-cost computation so that it was possible to track the human body motion in real-time.

We take the *ICP* algorithm for tracking the human body motion because it is known as an efficient algorithm that requires low computational complexity so that it is possible to use for the real-time applications. However, it shows limited tracking performance under a rapid speed movement and large motions because the closest points may be selected mistakenly. The *ICP* algorithm is vulnerable to the outlier point sets and is often traped in a local minimum (Phillips et. al., 2007; Dalley and Flynn, 2002). To avoid this problem, some researches proposed a good initial alignment that provides global registration (Li and Guskov, 2005; Gelfand et. al., 2005).

We also employ a stochastic search process, i.e. particle filter, combined with the *ICP* to achieve robust human body motion tracking. The particle filter (Okuma et. al., 2004; Doucet et. al., 2000) is appropriate to track the fast moving object because it can track the objects in a stochastic manner. It consists of two major component models: the observation model and the state transition model. In this paper, we modify the existing models to track the fast moving human limbs as follows. First, for the observation model, we propose to use a matching function that represents the relationship between the 3D human body model and the 3D articulation data in terms of the normal vector of the 3D volume and the shape information such as the silhouette. Second, for the state transition model, we propose to use the motion prediction method based on the history of motion trajectory to track the fast moving human limbs, which enables to handle a large rotational and translational motion and reduces the iteration number of the *ICP*.

Furthermore, we consider other properties such as the hierarchically linked human structure and the initial guess of the initial 3D human pose to make the human body motion tracking more robust as follows. First, we assume that the human body movement can be represented by the hierarchical tree structure and each limb's motion is affected by only the ancestor limb's motion on this structure. Then, this hierarchically linked human structure reduces the possible search space of each limb effectively and results in the reduced fitting time. Second, we take an automatical initialization of the 3D human model parameters and 3D human motion parameters. Most existing human motion tracking methods employ a manually initialized generic model with the limb lengths and positions which approximates the individual. Only a limited number of researchers (Krahnstoever and Sharma, 2004; Song et. al., 2003) have investigated the recovery of more accurate reconstructions to automate the initialization and improve the tracking quality. We present an automatical initialization of the 3D human model parameters and the 3D human motion parameters by classifying the Hu-moment feature of the extracted human silhouette image and analyzing the horizontal and vertical histogram of the extracted human silhouette image, respectively. This allows human motion tracking although the scale and the proportion of human limbs are different.

8.8.1. 3D Human Body Model

Modeling the human body is a quite difficult task because there exists a large variation of scale, shape, and proportionality of each limb of the human body and the dynamics of the human body is too complicated to represent completely. In this paper, we take the 3D human body model that consists of 10 rigid objects, which are a head, a torso, a left upper arm, a right upper arm, a left lower arm, a right lower arm, a left upper leg, a right upper leg, a left lower leg and a right lower leg. Fig. 8.8.1 illustrates a typical example of the human body model.

The human body is not a simple object but a deformable object that consists of several organically linked limbs, where each limb's movement affects other limbs' movements or can be affected by them. To reduce the complication among limbs, the human body structure is often modeled by a hierarchical tree structure and each limb's movement of the human body is affected by the movement of only the parent limbs, where the root limb of the human body is the torso, the 1st level limbs are the left and right upper arms, and the left and right upper legs and the 2nd level limbs are the left and right lower arms, and the left and right lower legs, as shown in Fig. 8.8.2.

Each limb is modeled by a 3D cylinder or a 3D sphere that is linked by the universal joint, where each 3D cylinder is parameterized with the major radius r_{major}, minor radius r_{minor}, and height h and each 3D sphere is parameterized with only the radius r_{sphere}. The 3D points on the 3D cylinder or 3D sphere surface are represented by $X = [(x_1, y_1, z_1)^T, ..., (x_N, y_N, z_N)^T]$ in the camera-centered 3D coordinate system, where N is the number of points, the 2D

Figure 8.8.1. Human body model

Figure 8.8.2. The hierarchical human body structure

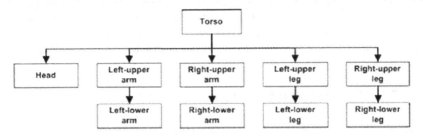

image point $\mathbf{u} = (u_x, u_y)$ corresponding to a 3D point $\mathbf{x} = (x, y, z)^T$, and pixel coordinate $\mathbf{u} = (u_x, u_y)^T$ is obtained by projecting $\mathbf{x}$ onto the 2D image coordinate under the perspective projection as

$$\mathbf{u} = p(\mathbf{x}) = \frac{f}{z}[x\ y]^T, \tag{8.8.1}$$

where f is the focal length.

The motion of each limb is represented by the 3D motion parameter vector **è** that includes three rotation parameters (w_x, w_y, w_z) and three translation parameters (t_x, t_y, t_z). When a point on the cylinder or sphere surface is represented by $\mathbf{x} = (x, y, z)^T$, the point is transformed by the motion vector **è** as

$$M(\mathbf{x}; \mathbf{è}) = R\mathbf{x} + T, \tag{8.8.2}$$

where M is a rigid transformation function that is represented by a 3D rotation matrix $R \in \mathbf{R}^{3\times3}$, which is a function of three rotation parameters (w_x, w_y, w_z), and a 3D translation vector $T \in \mathbf{R}^{3\times1} = (t_x, t_y, t_z)$.

Since it is very complicated and difficult to parameterize the 3D rotation matrix by the Euler representation, it is often approximated in the twist representation (Bregler and Malik, 1998) as

$$M(\mathbf{x}; \mathbf{è}) = \begin{pmatrix} 1 & -w_z & w_y \\ w_z & 1 & -w_x \\ -w_y & w_x & 1 \end{pmatrix} \begin{pmatrix} x \\ y \\ z \end{pmatrix} + \begin{pmatrix} t_x \\ t_y \\ t_z \end{pmatrix}. \tag{8.8.3}$$

To represent the human body motion naturally, it is required for all cylinders or spheres to comply with some constraints that prevent all cylinders and spheres from having unacceptable poses from a ego-mechanic point of view. First, all of the cylinders or spheres should be jointed under the hierarchically predefined linked structure. For example, the lower point of the head should be connected with the upper point of the torso or the upper point of the right lower arm should be connected with the lower point of the right upper arm.

Second, all human's joints have their limitations within the movable space. For example, they cannot rotate their legs to 180 degrees along the z axis. If each motion of the human limbs is out of each angle limitation, then it adjusts the angle of the cylinder to be confined within the range of allowable rotating angle. We use the statistical information of the human body published by NASA (NASA: NASA-STD-3000, 1995). Third, all of the cylinders or spheres cannot intersect each other. If one cylinder penetrates other cylinders, it should adjust the position and the angle of the cylinder to be confined within the range of allowable rotating angle.

8.8.2. 3D Motion Parameter Vector

Since we take the hierarchical 3D human body model, it is not easy to explain how to compute the increment of the motion parameter vector. For easy understanding, we take an example of Fig. 8.8.3 that shows the left upper arm (the ith limb at the time $t-1$) and the torso (its parent limb $p(i)$ at the time $t-1$), which is taken from a viewer on the ceil. Initially, two limbs are aligned horizontally in parallel (See Fig. 8.8.3-(a)). Here, assume that the torso is rotated by some degrees (See Fig. 8.8.3-(b)). Then, we can consider the following three factors to compute the total increment of the 3D motion parameter vector.

8.8.2.1. The Structural Increment

Since the human body structure is hierarchically linked, the motion increment of each limb is directly affected by the motion increment of its parent limb, which is denoted by the structural increment of the motion parameter of each limb $\Delta \grave{e}^s_{i,t}$ as

$$\Delta \grave{e}^s_{i,t} = \Delta \grave{e}_{p(i)\,t}, \qquad (8.8.4)$$

where $p(i)$ denotes the parent limb of the ith limb. When the limb is the torso, $\Delta \grave{e}^s_{torso,t} = 0$ because the parent of the torso is null. As can be seen in Fig. 3-(c), the left upper arm is also rotated by the structural increment that is caused by the rotation of its parent limb (torso).

Figure 8.8.3. Overall process of updating the 3D motion parameter vectors

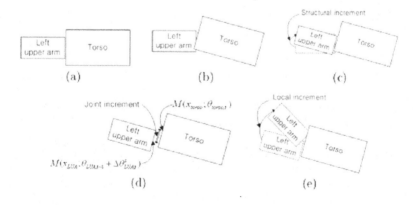

8.8.2.2. The Joint Increment

According to the articulation constraint of the 3D human body model, one limb and its parent limb are jointly connected each other. However, even after the structural increment is considered, there exists some translational difference between the joint of one limb and the joint of its parent limb, because each limb is rotated around its own central point (See Fig. 8.8.3-(d)). Thus, we need to adjust the translational difference between these adjacent joints, which is denoted by the joint increment of the motion parameter of each limb $\Delta\grave{\mathbf{e}}_{i,t}^{j}$ as

$$\Delta\grave{\mathbf{e}}_{i,t}^{j} = M(\mathbf{x}_i; \grave{\mathbf{e}}_{i,t-1} + \Delta\mathbf{q}_{i,t}^{s}) - M(\mathbf{x}_{p(i)}; \grave{\mathbf{e}}_{p(i)}) \qquad (8.8.5)$$

8.8.2.3. The Local Increment

After obtaining the structural and joint increment, the 3D human motion parameter vector is updated by

$$\grave{\mathbf{e}}_{i,t}' = \grave{\mathbf{e}}_{i,t-1} + \Delta\grave{\mathbf{e}}_{i,t}^{s} + \Delta\grave{\mathbf{e}}_{i,t}^{j}, \qquad (8.8.6)$$

where $\grave{\mathbf{e}}_{i,t}'$ is the intermediate motion parameter vector at time t that considers only the structural and joint increment. The updated 3D motion parameter vector $\grave{\mathbf{e}}_{i,t}'$ is taken as an initial value for the *ICP* registration algorithm and each limb has its own local increment of the 3D motion parameter vector $\Delta\grave{\mathbf{e}}_{i,t}^{l}$. Finally, the updated 3D motion parameter vector $\grave{\mathbf{e}}_{i,t}$ of the i-th limb at the time t is computed as

$$\begin{aligned} \grave{\mathbf{e}}_{i,t} &= \grave{\mathbf{e}}_{i,t}' + \Delta\grave{\mathbf{e}}_{i,t}^{l} \\ &= \grave{\mathbf{e}}_{i,t-1} + \Delta\grave{\mathbf{e}}_{i,t}^{s} + \Delta\grave{\mathbf{e}}_{i,t}^{j} + \Delta\grave{\mathbf{e}}_{i,t}^{l}. \end{aligned} \qquad (8.8.7)$$

Since the torso is a root node of the tree-like human body structure, it can have the rotational and translational movements. However, all limbs except for the torso have only their rotational movements based on their central points because the translational movements are already compensated by the joint increments, as shown in Fig. 8.8.3-(e). The overall procedure of updating 3D motion parameter vector between two consecutive image frames is given below.

8.8.3. The Proposed Human Body Motion Tracking

The *ICP* algorithm that was employed by Demirdjian (Demirdjian, 2003) for the human body motion tracking has two limitations for the practical application. First, it tracks the human body motion when the human body model is near the data initially. Second, it tracks the human body when the human body does not move fast. To remove these limitations, we consider two aspects: a pose initialization of the human body model and a combined model fitting using the *ICP* registration algorithm and the particle filter.

Table 8.8.1. Overall procedure of updating 3D motion parameter vector

---

For i=1,2,...,10

    (1) Compute the structural increment $\Delta \grave{\mathbf{e}}^s_{i,t}$ using Eq. (8.8.4).

    (2) Compute the joint increment $\Delta \grave{\mathbf{e}}^j_{i,t}$ using Eq. (8.8.5).

    (3) Update the 3D motion parameter vector with the structural and joint increment as

$$\grave{\mathbf{e}}'_{i,t} = \grave{\mathbf{e}}_{i,t-1} + \Delta \grave{\mathbf{e}}^s_{i,t} + \Delta \grave{\mathbf{e}}^j_{i,t} .$$

    (4) Set $\grave{\mathbf{e}}'_{i,t}$ as the initial parameter vector $\grave{\mathbf{e}}^0$.

    (5) Perform the ICP registration algorithm to the i th limb and compute the local incre-

       ment $\Delta \grave{\mathbf{e}}^l_{i,t}$.

    (6) Update the 3D motion parameter vector with the local increment as

$$\grave{\mathbf{e}}_{i,t} = \grave{\mathbf{e}}'_{i,t} + \Delta \grave{\mathbf{e}}^l_{i,t} .$$

End

8.8.3.1. The Pose Initialization

First, we detect the human candidates in the 3D articulation depth image that is obtained from the stereo image. However, the depth values are always not valid because they are obtained by using the image matching method. In particular, the feet on the floor is not easily separated from the floor in the disparity image. To overcome this problem, we extract the human silhouette using the color image as follows.

1. Apply the the object-oriented scale-adaptive filter (OOSAF) (Li et. al., 2004) to the 3D articulation depth image, which produces the human candidates.
2. Remove the floor area using the assumption that the floor color is simple and regular and modeled by a uni-modal Gaussian (Phung et. al., 2005) per each component in the YCbCr color space.
3. Apply the background subtraction method (Piccardi, 2004) to the 2D color image and extract the foreground objects.
4. Perform the AND operation between the human candidates and the extracted foreground objects, which results in the human silhouette images.

Then, we verify whether the human silhouette images are the human or not. For the human verification, we perform the face detection and/or the *head-shoulder* (omega shape) detection.

Then, we estimate the initial pose of the human body, which includes the 3D model parameters and the 3D motion parameters of the human body model. However, it is quite difficult to know the initial motion parameters of the human body because the human can have a variety of motion parameters. To overcome this problem, we assume that the human has some predefined motion parameters and classify the motion parameters of the verified human silhouette image into one of the predefined motion parameters. Also, we need to initialize the model parameters such as the major and minor radii for the cylinder or the radius for the sphere as follows.

5. Compute the Hu-moment (Bobick and Davis, 2001) feature of the verified human silhouette image.
6. Classify the Hu-moment feature into one of predefined motion parameters using the neural network that is generated by learning the training data with the predefined motion parameters.
7. Set the obtained motion parameters to the initial motion parameters of each limb.
8. Compute the horizontal and vertical histogram of the verified human silhouette image.
    A. Find the left and right position of the torso from the horizontal histogram by performing the threshold operation. Then, find the upper and lower position of the torso from the vertical histogram within the found left and right position by performing the threshold operation.
    B. Find other limbs' positions from the obtained torso size by using the statistical proportion of human body (NASA: NASA-STD-3000, 1995).
    C. Obtain the model parameters of each limb using the 3D articulation depth image and the obtained positions of each limb.

Fig. 8.8.5 shows an example of initializing the human model pose, where the left and right figures in the top row represent the horizontal and vertical histograms, respectively, and the left, middle, and right figures in the bottom row represent the original 2D image, the extracted foreground object, and the human model initialized by the estimated human pose, respectively.

Figure 8.8.4. Overall process of estimating the initial pose of the human body model

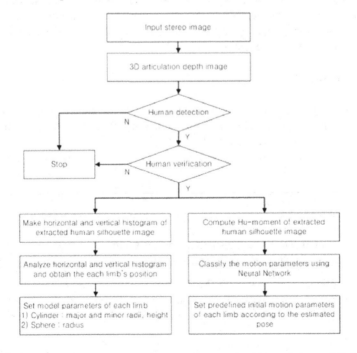

Figure 8.8.5. An example of initializing the human model pose. (See the text for a detailed explanation.)

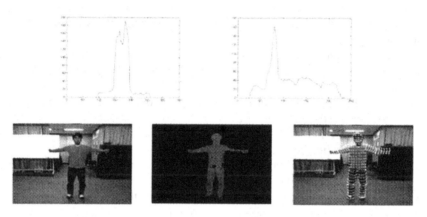

8.8.3.2. The Combined Model Fitting

To track a rapidly moving human body robustly, we propose to combine the particle filter algorithm into the *ICP* registration algorithm. The detailed explanation about the proposed combined model fitting method during two consecutive image frames is given in Table 8.8.2.

The detailed explanation on how the particle filter works is given below. The particle filter consists of two models: the observation model and the state transition model. For the observation model, we take a matching function that approximates the observation likelihood in terms of the normal vectors and the existences of the 3D articulation data at the positions projected by the model points. For the state transition model, we use the motion history information to track the fast moving limbs.

1) Observation Model

The observation model describes the relationship between the input image and the human model at the current state using the observation likelihood. Often, a matching function can be used to approximate the observation likelihood (Deutscher et. al., 2000) because it requires the minimal computational effort. In this work, we define the matching function as

$$P(I_t \mid \boldsymbol{\theta}_{i,t}^p) \propto \exp(-\frac{1}{2}(\frac{1}{N}\sum_{i=1}^{N}(1-\mathbf{n}_m(\mathbf{x}_i)\cdot\mathbf{n}_d(u_i))+\frac{1}{N}\sum_{i=1}^{N}(1-I_b(u_i)))), \qquad (8.8.8)$$

where $\mathbf{n}_m(\mathbf{x}_i)$ and $\mathbf{n}_d(u_i)$ are the surface normal vector of each limb at the position $\mathbf{x}_i$ and the surface normal vector of the 3D articulation data at the position u_i that corresponds to the projected position of the $\mathbf{x}_i$, respectively, and $I_b(u_i)$ is the binary valued function whether the 3D articulation data exists or not at the position u_i. The first term is used to represent the directional similarity of the normal vectors between the model and

Table 8.8.2. The proposed human body motion tracking

---

1. Initialize the human model motion $\mathbf{\grave{e}}_{i,0}$ using the pose initialization method in Section 8.8.3.
2. Initialize a particles set as $S_{i,0} = \{\mathbf{\grave{e}}_{i,0}^{p},1\}_{p=0}^{P(i)}$, where $P(i)$ is the number of particles of the i th limb.

For $t = 1,2,...$
    For $i = 1,2,...,10$

3. Update the 3D motion parameter vector using the structural and the joint increment as $\mathbf{\grave{e}}_{i,t}^{'} = \mathbf{\grave{e}}_{i,t-1} + \Delta\mathbf{\grave{e}}_{i,t}^{s} + \Delta\mathbf{\grave{e}}_{i,t}^{j}$.

4. Compute the local increment $\Delta\mathbf{\grave{e}}_{i,t}^{l}$ using the ICP registration algorithm with the initial condition $\mathbf{\grave{e}}^{0} = \mathbf{\grave{e}}_{i,t}^{'}$.

5. If the registration error $e_{i,t} < \tau_{i}$, then

    update the 3D motion parameter vector as $\mathbf{\grave{e}}_{i,t} = \mathbf{\grave{e}}_{i,t}^{'} + \Delta\mathbf{\grave{e}}_{i,t}^{l}$.

6. Else

    perform the particle filter tracking and set the 3D motion parameter vector of the best particle to the 3D motion parameter vector of each limb as

$$\mathbf{\grave{e}}_{i,t} = \mathbf{\hat{\grave{e}}}_{i,t}.$$
    End
  End
7. Break if no more image is given.

End

---

the data, and the second term is used to represent how much the model and the data are overlapped.

2) State Transition Model

The state transition model describes the dynamics of the moving limbs. Often, it is represented by the zero-velocity model, but it is not appreciate to track the limb like the arm because it moves fast. To solve this problem, the state transition model should be adaptive to the fast movement of the limb. In this work, we assume that the dynamics of the moving limbs obey the constant velocity model. Then, the velocity $\mathbf{v}_{t-1}$ of the i th limb at the time $t-1$ can be computed by

$$\mathbf{v}_{i,t-1} = \mathbf{\grave{e}}_{i,t-1} - \mathbf{\grave{e}}_{i,t-2}, \quad (8.8.9)$$

where $\mathbf{\grave{e}}_{i,t-1}$ and $\mathbf{\grave{e}}_{i,t-2}$ are the 3D motion parameter vectors of the i th limb at the time $t-1$ and $t-2$, respectively.

Using above motion history information, the motion velocity of the ith limb at the time t is predicted by the motion velocity of the ith limb at the time $t-1$ as

$$\overline{\mathbf{v}}_{i,t} = v_{t-1}. \quad (8.8.10)$$

Thus, we can generate a set of particles using the state transition model as

$$\grave{\mathbf{e}}_{i,t}^{p} = \grave{\mathbf{e}}_{i,t-1} + \overline{\mathbf{v}}_{i,t} + \mathsf{h}_{i,t}^{p}, \tag{8.8.11}$$

where $\mathsf{\eta}_{i,t}^{p}$ is the system noise that obeys the Gaussian distribution.

Among the set of particles, one particle whose value of the matching function is the largest is taken as the best particle as

$$\hat{\grave{\mathbf{e}}}_{i,t} = \arg\max_{\grave{\mathbf{e}}_{i,t}^{p}} \mathbf{w}_{t}^{p}, \tag{8.8.12}$$

where ω_{t}^{p} is the normalized weight.

Fig. 8.8.6 shows the overall process of the proposed human body motion tracking during two consecutive image frames.

8.8.4. Experimental Results and Discussion

The proposed human body motion tracking system was implemented on the Window PC platform with the 2.4 GHz Intel Core 2 CPU and 2GM RAM in the Visual C++ and OpenCV environment. The color stereo images were captured from the Bumblebee 2 camera and the 3D articulation data are also obtained by using the Bumblebee's SDK. All parameters used for the experiments are summarized in the Table 8.8.3.

8.8.4.1. The Pose Initialization

For the pose initialization, we defined four representative initial poses that are shown in Fig. 8.8.7, which were selected through many trials for defining easy, intuitive and natural initial poses.

To evaluate the accuracy of the pose estimation, we used the 7-50-4 fully-connected back-propagation neural network for the pose classification, where the input layer consists of 7 input nodes that correspond to 7 features (the 1st - the 7th Hu moments) from the human silhouette image, the hidden layer consists of 50 hidden nodes, and the output layer consists of 4 output nodes that correspond to 4 pose classes. We prepared 800 human silhouette images (10 peoples × 4 poses × 20 images) and used the 400 human silhouette

Table 8.8.3. Parameters for the experiments

Categories	Parameters	Values
	Frame rate	10 fps
	Image size	640 x 480
	Focal length	245.130 mm
Camera	Base line	12.0023 cm
Error threshold	τ	2.5
Particle filter	Number of particles	20 ~ 50

Figure 8.8.6. The overall process of proposed human body motion tracking

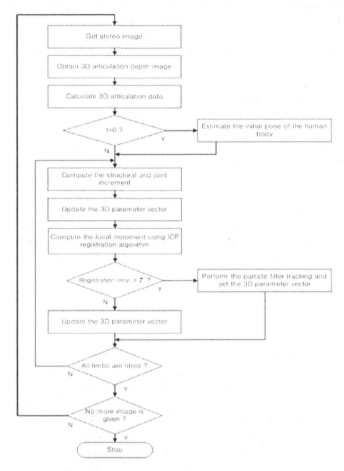

Figure 8.8.7. Four representative initial poses

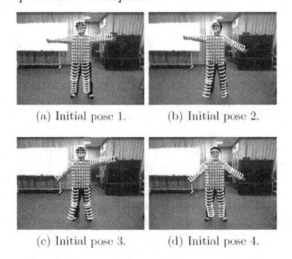

(a) Initial pose 1.   (b) Initial pose 2.

(c) Initial pose 3.   (d) Initial pose 4.

images for training the neural network and the remaining 400 human silhouette images for testing the pose classification performance.

Table 8.8.4 shows the initial pose classification result, where the 800 human silhouette images are tested because we take the 2-cross validation technique. From this table, we know that (1) the accuracy of the initial pose classification is 97.4%, which provides a good pose initialization, and (2) 15 data of the pose 2 are classified into the pose 4 because they are incorrectly segmented.

Once the pose initialization has been performed, each limb is modeled by the cylinder or the sphere with the estimated model and motion parameters. To evaluate the effectiveness of the proposed pose initialization, we measured the average mean squared error (MSE) of each limb that is the ratio of the sum of differences between the 3D human body model points and the closest 3D articulation data points over the number of data points in the limb. Table 8.8.5 shows the average MSE of each limb, where T, H, LUA, RUA, LLA, RLA, LUL, RUL, RLL, and RLL stand for the torso, the head, the left upper arm, the right upper arm, the left lower arm, the right lower arm, the left upper leg, the right upper leg, the left lower leg, and the right lower leg, respectively. From this table, we know that (1) the torso has the smallest average MSE, (2) the legs have the largest average MSEs, and (3) the average MSEs are small enough for further human body motion tracking.

8.8.4.2. Human Body Motion Tracking

1) Tracking accuracy

To compare the tracking accuracy between the *ICP* tracking method and the proposed tracking method that combines the *ICP* and particle filter, we performed the human body motion tracking using an image sequence with a rapidly swinging up and down arms whose number of image frames is 157. Fig. 8.8.8 shows the tracking results of the image sequence, where the first, second, and third rows represent the original image sequence, the tracking result using the conventional *ICP* method, and the tracking result using the proposed tracking method (*ICP* + Particle Filter), respectively, and each column represents the consecutive image frames from $t = 100$ to $t = 103$. As shown in Fig. 8.8.8, we know that the conventional *ICP* method failed to track the fast moving arms at time $t = 101$, but the proposed tracking method can track the fast moving arms continuously.

Table 8.8.4. Confusion matrix of initial pose classification results

	Pose 1	Pose 2	Pose 3	Pose 4
Pose 1	196	0	2	0
Pose 2	1	185	0	0
Pose 3	3	0	198	0
Pose 4	0	15	0	200

Table 8.8.5. Average MSE of each limb in the four initial poses

	Pose 1	Pose 2	Pose 3	Pose 4
T	4.023	4.142	3,732	3.627
H	5.715	8.005	7.965	6.571
LUA	5.776	7.487	6.907	6.869
RUA	5.766	8.315	7.895	8.033
LLA	7.666	15.924	10.889	15.014
RLA	8.766	11.847	13.852	8.138
LUL	14.303	13.202	14.328	14.523
RUL	8.250	15.451	8.263	16.086
LLL	14.033	12.264	13.110	11.979
RLL	13.446	12.974	14.081	13.380

We performed the human body motion tracking using an image sequence that consists of 157 image frames with fast swinging up and down arms at a maximally speed of $40°/frame$, and measured the MSE of each limb between the human body model points and their corresponding closest 3D articulation data points. Fig. 8.8.9 shows the MSE histogram of each limb, where the × and ○ symbols represent the MSE histograms for the *ICP* tracking method and the proposed tracking method, respectively, and the horizontal and vertical axis denote the quantized MSE value that is denoted by ceiling (for example, $\lceil 1.5 \rceil = 2$) and the number of image frames, respectively. As shown in Fig. 8.8.9, we know that (1) all other limbs except the LLA and the RLA have the similar MSE histograms in both the *ICP* tracking method and the proposed tracking method, which implies that there are no significant differences of the MSE histograms in all other limbs except for the LLA and RLA between two tracking methods and (2) the number of image frames with the smaller MSE values in the proposed tracking method is a little higher than that in the *ICP* tracking method, which implies that the tracking accuracy of the proposed tracking method is better than that of the *ICP* tracking method.

Figure 8.8.8. The tracking results using two different human motion tracking methods

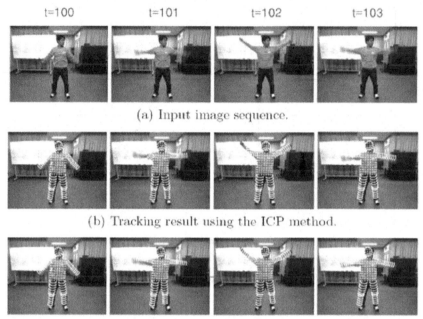

| t=100 | t=101 | t=102 | t=103 |

(a) Input image sequence.

(b) Tracking result using the ICP method.

(c) Tracking result using the proposed tracking method.

2) Tracking robustness

To compare the tracking robustness between the *ICP* tracking method and the proposed tracking method, we performed 50 trials of human body motion tracking for each image frame, where the initial pose of each trial is determined by the randomly generated motion parameter vector whose values fall on the interval of $\pm 10°$ of the the motion parameter vector that is fitted best at the previous image frame. Fig. 8.8.10 illustrates the range of allowable rotating angle of each limb for the randomly generated initial poses.

Fig. 8.8.11 shows the MSE histogram of all limbs that is obtained from the human motion tracking of the image sequence with 157 image frames and 50 different initial poses per each image frame, where the $\times$ and $\circ$ symbols represent the MSE histograms for the *ICP* tracking method and the proposed tracking method, respectively. Since we performed this fitting experiment two times, there are 157,000 fitting trials ($= 2 \times 157$ image frames $\times$ 50 initial poses $\times$ 10 limbs). From Fig. 8.8.11, we know that the proposed tracking method is more robust than the *ICP* tracking method because the number of image frames with the smaller MSE values in the proposed tracking method is a little higher than that in the *ICP* tracking method over the 50 randomly generated initial poses.

Fig. 8.8.12 shows the MSE histogram of each limb that is obtained from the human motion tracking of the the above image sequence, where the $\times$ and $\circ$ symbols represent the MSE histograms for the *ICP* tracking method and the proposed tracking method, respectively. As shown in Fig. 8.8.12, we know that (1) the average MSE of the proposed tracking method is smaller than that of the *ICP* tracking method by 0.5721, and (2) the

Figure 8.8.9. Each limb's MSE histogram when the arm is moving fast

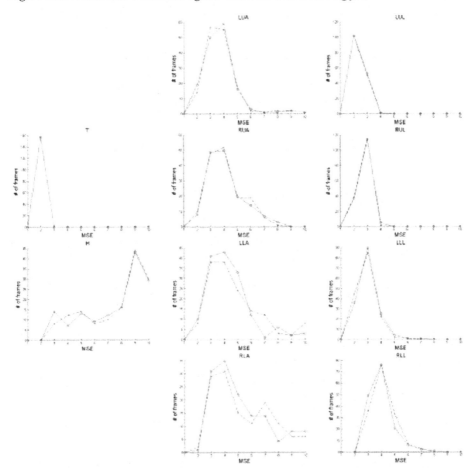

number of image frames with the smaller MSE values in the proposed tracking method is much higher than that in the *ICP* tracking method in the left and right lower arms or the left and right lower legs, which implies that the proposed tracking method is more effective to track the fast moving limbs than the *ICP* tracking method.

3) Tracking convergence

When the fitting error is smaller than a given threshold value, it is defined that the 3D input articulation data is converged to the 3D human body model. Hence, the convergence rate is the ratio of the number of the converged fitting trials over the total number of the fitting trials. When we take the above 157,000 fitting trials (= 2 × 157 image frames × 50 initial poses × 10 limbs) and take 7.0 as the MSE threshold value, the convergence rate of the proposed tracking method is 92.43% (= 145,120 converged fitting trials / a total number of 157,000 fitting trials), while the convergence rate of the *ICP* tracking method is 80.23% (= 125,960 converged fitting trials / a total number of 157,000 fitting trials).

Figure 8.8.10. The range of allowable rotating angle of each limb

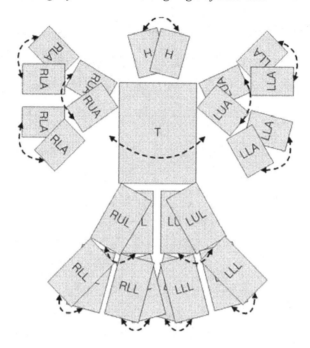

Figure 8.8.11. MSE histogram of all limbs

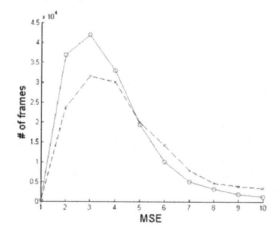

4) Tracking speed

When we performed the human body motion tracking over five sequences of 100~150 image frames using the *ICP* tracking method and the proposed tracking method, they took about 18~29 seconds and 22~34 seconds respectively, which implied 180~200 millisecond per each image frame and 200~250 milliseconds per each image frame on the average. Thus, the *ICP* tracking method is executed in the speed of 5~5.5 frames per second, while

Figure 8.8.12. Each limb's MSE histogram when 50 initial poses are randomly generated

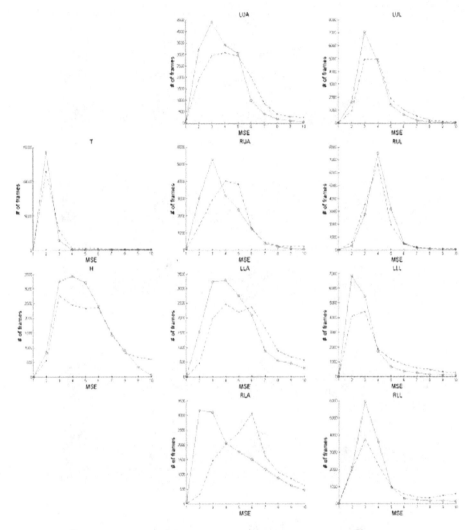

the proposed tracking method is executed about in the speed of 4~5 frames per second. As a result, we obtain the robust tracking in the proposed tracking method at the cost of 15~18% speed down.

5) Tracking examples

We performed the human body motion tracking of the proposed tracking method using four different image sequences, where the 1st, 2nd, 3rd, and 4th image sequence represent the image sequences of the swing up and down arms along the y axis, of the waving up and down arms along the x and y axis, of the swing front and up arms along the z axis, and of the swing up and down legs along the y axis, respectively. As shown in Fig. 8.8.13,

Figure 8.8.13. Human body motion tracking examples

(a) The swing up and down arms.

(b) The waiving up and down arms.

(c) The swing front and up arms.

(d) The swing up and down legs.

we know that the proposed tracking method can effectively track a variety of human body motion irrespective of the motion types and the moving speeds[1].

8.9 CONCLUSION

The pose robust human detection algorithm detects the humans regardless of their scales and poses in a sequence of stereo images using the multiple oriented 2D elliptical filters (MO2DEFs). The MO2DEFs alleviates the weakness of the existing OOSAF that cannot detect theposed humans. The MO2DEFs are pose-robust 2D elliptical filters, whose shapes are the front half of an ellipse rotated by 0°, 45°, 90° and 135°, respectively, and the size of ellipse is the average width and the average thickness of the human bodies in a real scale. We could detect the humans regardless of the rotation, because the shapes of MO2DEFs are similar to the turned humans in the spatial-depth space, where it is obtained by the transformation of the spatial-disparity space to perform the rotation of elliptical filter conveniently. The human detection algorithm segmented the human candidates and estimated the pose angle of the human candidates as one of the four angles: 0°, 45°, 90° and 135°. The estimated angle was used to verify the human candidates by the head-shoulder shape matching. Human verification decided whether the segmented human candidate is a human or not using a face detection and shape matching algorithm. The experiment results show that (1) the accuracy of the human pose angle estimation is about 88%, (2) the human detection rate using the MO2DEF is better than that of using the OOSAF by about 20% in most types of image sequences, especially it improves much when the human poses were deviated from the frontal pose, (3) the face detection and the head-shoulder shape matching are effective for the human verification when the humans are overlapped and the human poses are not frontal, respectively.

The smart home system using the hand gesture recognition algorithm provide simple, easy, and intuitive inferface to turn on and off the TV in the smart room. To detect the hand region precisely, we find the hand candidate region using human anatomy information, then apply the graph-cut algorithm to segment the hand region exactly, where the skin color feature is used for the graph-cut algorithm. To recognize several commands that are defined by different hand shapes and sequences of the pre-defined hand shapes, forward spotting accumulative *HMM*s is used. Experimental results showed that the hand gesture recognition algorithm can be used for real-time TV remote control system.

The vision-based musical conducting action recognition system is another example of the human motion analysis, where the pattern of the hand trajectory and timing analysis is important issues. To implement a fast hand tracking algorithm, we used the stereo vision camera and the depth information, where a face detector is used to limit the search area for the hands. The movement of the hand is represented by conducting feature points with the direction-codes, which encodes the trajectory and timing pattern simultaneously. To classify the conducting actions, we used a *motion histogram* matching algorithm that matches the direction-code with trained direction-code table. From the numerous experiments, the recognition accuracies were 78.8% and 86.5% using the CFP sequence analysis and the *motion histogram* matching, respectively.

The forward spotting scheme for simultaneous gesture segmentation and gesture recognition is very useful algorithm when the *HMM* is used for arbitrary gesture recognition because it tells when the recognition system must work by automatically spotting meaningful segment in the continuous input signals. In the forward spotting, the gesture segmentation module computed the competitive differential observation probability, which was defined as the difference of observation probability between the maximal gesture model and the non-gesture model, where the maximal gesture model was the model whose observation probability was the highest among all gesture models. A zero crossing point of the competitive differential observation probability from negative to positive indicated a gesture start point, and a crossing point from positive to negative indicated a gesture end point. We applied the simultaneous gesture segmentation and recognition method to recognize the upper-body gestures for controlling the curtains and lights in a smart room environment. In the experiments the method showed good recognition rate even when the continuously changing gesture signals are given and controlled the devices in the smart room in a real-time manner.

The proposed a real-time human body motion tracking method that could track the fast movement of the human body. For this purpose, we used the iterative closest point (*ICP*) algorithm because it enabled to fit the 3D human body model to the input 3D articulation data in real-time due to its computational efficiency. However, it had two limitations for the practical applications such as the pose initialization problem and the tracking problem under the rapidly moving human body motion. We estimated the initial poses of the input 3D articulation data by extracting the human silhouette using the color image, then verifying whether the human silhouette images are the human or not using the face detection and/or the head-shoulder (omega shape) detection, and classifying the motion parameters of the verified human silhouette image into one of the predefined motion parameters. We proposed to combine the modified particle filter based on the motion history model into the *ICP* to track the rapidly moving human body motion. The observation model executed the human body tracking fast because it approximated the observation likelihood by the matching function that consisted of two easily computed features such as the directional similarity between the surface normal vector of each limb and the surface normal vector of the 3D articulation data, and the binary valued function that decided whether the closest data point corresponding to the model point existed or not. The state transition model made the human body tracking possible under a rapidly moving human body motion because it took the motion history model based on the difference of the velocity to predict the motion parameter vector of the rapidly moving human body motion. We took the hierarchical 3D human body model, it was necessary to consider three types of the parameter increments such as the structural, joint, and local increments to update the 3D human motion parameter vector. Experimental results show that the proposed 3D human body motion tracking method provides the accurate fitting performance, the robustness to initial poses, the high convergence rate, and the high operating frame rate.

8.10 REFERENCES

Agarwal, A., and Triggs, B. (2006). Recovering 3D human pose from monocular images, IEEE Transaction on Pattern Analysis and Machine Intelligence, 28(1), 44-58.

Baudel, T., Beaudouin-Lafon, M. (1993). CHARADE: Remote control of objects using free-hand gestures. Communications of ACM, 36(7), 28-35.

Baumberg, A., and Hogg, D. (1994). Learning flexible models from image sequences. In Proceedings of European Conference on Computer Vision.

Besl, P. J., and MacKay, N. (1992). A method for registration of 3-d shapes. IEEE Transantions on Pattern Analysis and Machine Intelligence, 14(2), 239-256.

Beymer, D., and Konolige, K. (1999). Real-time tracking of multiple people using continuous detection. In Proceedings of International Conference on Computer Vision.

Bien, Z., and Kim, J. (1992). On-line analysis of music conductor's two-dimensional motion. International Conference on Fuzzy Systems, (pp. 1047–1053).

Blake, A., and Isard, M. (1998). Active Contours. Springer.

Bloem, R., Gabow, H. N., and Somenzi, F. (2000). An algorithm for strongly connected component analysis in n log n symbolic steps. In Proceedings of Conference on Formal Methods in Computer Aided Design, (pp. 37–54).

Bobick, A., and Davis, J. (2001). The recognition of human movement using temporal templates, IEEE Transaction on Pattern Analysis and Machine Intelligence, 23(3), 257-267.

Bobick, A., and Davis, J. (2001). The recognition of human movement using temporal templates, IEEE Transaction on Pattern Analysis and Machine Intelligence, 23(3), 257-267.

Bobick, A., and Wilson, A. (1995). A state-based technique for the summarization and recognitio of gesture, In Proceedings of International Conference on Computer Vision, (pp. 382-388).

Boykov, Y., and Funka-Lea, G. (2006). Graph cuts and efficient n-d image segmentation, International Journal of Computer Vision, 70, 109-131.

Boykov, Y., and Kolmogorov, V. (2004). An experimental comparison of min-cut/max-flow algorithm for energy minimization in vision. IEEE Transaction on Pattern Analysis and Machine Intelligence, 26, 1124-1137.

Brand, M., Oliver, N., and Pentland, A. (1997). Coupled hidden markov models for complex action recognition, In Proceedings of IEEE Conference on Computer Vision and Pattern Recognition, (pp, 994-999).

Bretzner, L., and Laptev, T. (2002). Hand gesture recognition using multi-scale color features, hierarchical models and particle filtering. In Proceedings of the fifth IEEE International Conference on Automatic Face and Gesture Recognition.

Chen, Y., and Medioni, G. (1991). Object modeling by registration of multiple range images. Image and Vision Computing, 10(3), 145-155.

Cootes, T., Taylor, C., Cooper, D., and Graham, J. (1995). Active shape models - their training and application. Computer Vision and Image Understanding, 61(1), 38-59.

Dalley, G., and Flynn, P. (2002). Pair-wise range image registration : a study of outlier classification, Computer Vision and Image Understanding, 87(1-3), 104-115.

Delamarre, Q., and Faugeras, O. (1999). 3D Articulated models and multi-view tracking with silhouettes, Proceedings of the International Conference on Computer Vision, (pp. 716-721).

Demirdjian, D. (2003). Enforcing constraints for human body tracking, Workshop on Multiple Object Tracking, (pp. 102-109).

Deng, J., and Tsui, H. (2000). An HMM-based approach for gesture segmentation and recognition. Proceedings of the 15th International Conference on Pattern Recognition, (pp. 679-682).

Deutscher, J., Davision, A., and Reid, I. (2000). Articulated body motion capture by annealed particle filtering, Computer Vision and Pattern Recognition, (pp. 126-133).

Dobrian, C., and Bevilacqua, F. (2002). Gestural control of music using the vicon 8 motion capture system.

Doucet, A., Godsill, J., and Andrieu, C. (2000). On sequential Monte Carlo sampling methods for Bayesian filtering, Statistics and Computing, 10(3), 197-209.

Fausett, L. (1999). Fundamentals of neural networks, Prentice Hall International Inc.

Feldmar, J., and Ayache, N. (1996). Affine and locally affine registration of free-form surfaces. International Journal of Computer Vision, 18(2), 99-119.

Freeman, W. T., and Weissman, C. D. (1995). Television control by hand gestures. In Proceedings of IEEE International Workshop on Automatic Face and Gesture Recognition.

Galata, A., Johnson, N., and Hogg, D. (2001). Learning variable-length markov models of behavior, Computer Vision and Image Understanding, 81 (3), 398-413.

Gelfand, N., Mitra, M., Guibas, L., and Pottmann, H. (2005). Robust global alignment, Proceedings of the 3rd Eurographics symposium on Geometry Processing.

Ghidary, S. S., Nakata, Y., Takamori, T., and Hattori, M. (2000). Localization and approaching to the human by mobile human robot. In Proceedings of 9th IEEE International Workshop on Robot and Human Interactive Communication, (pp. 63-68).

Godin, G., Rioux, M., and Baribeau, R. (1994). Three-dimensional registration using range and intensity information. In Proceedings of SPIE Videometric, Vol. 2350,(pp. 279-290).

Gonzalez, J. J., Lim, I. S., Fua, P., and Thalmann, D. (2003). Robust tracking and segmentation of human motion in an image sequence, Proceedings of International Conference on Acoustics, Speech, and Signal Processing.

Grull, I. (2005). Conga: A conducting gesture analysis framework, ULM University.

Guo, Y., Xu, G., and Tsuji, S. (1994). Understanding human motion patterns. In Proceedings of International Conference on Pattern Recognition, (pp. 325-329).

Haritaoglu, I., Flickner, M., and Beymer, D. (2002). Ghost3D: detecting body posture and parts using stereo, In Proceedings of Workshop on Motion and Video Computing.

Haritaoglu, I., Harwood, D., and Davis, L.S. (1998). W4: Who? When? Where? What? – A real time system for detecting and tracking people, In Proceedings of International Conference on Automatic Face and Gesture Recognition.

Hayashi, K., Hashimoto, M., Sumi, K., and Sasakawa, K. (2004). Multiple-person tracker with a fixed slanting stereo camera, In Proceedings of International Conference on Aumomatic Face and Gesturre Recognition.

Hussein, M., Almageed, W. A., Ran, Y., and Davis, L. (2006). A realtTime system for human detection, tracking and verification in uncontrolled camera motion environment. In Proceedings of IEEE International Conf. on Computer Vision Systems (pp. 41).

Isard, M., and Blake, A. (1998). Condensation-conditional density propagation for visual tracking. International Journal of Computer Vision, 29, 5-28.

Jang, J., Sun, C., and Mizutani, E. (1997). Neuro-Fuzzy and Soft Computing. Prentice Hall.

Ju, S., Black, M., and Yaccob, Y. (1996). Cardboard people: a parameterized model of articulated image motion, Proceedings of the IEEE International Conference on Automatic Face and Gesture Recognition, (pp. 38-44).

Jun, B., and Kim, D. (2007). Robust real-time face detection using face certainty map, In Proceedings of International Conference on Biometrics, (pp. 29-38).

Kalman, R. E. (1960). A new approach to linear filtering and prediction problems. Journal of Basic Engineering, 82 (Series D), 35-45.

Kameda, Y., and Minoh, M. (1996). A human motion estimation method using 3-successive video frames. In Proceedings of the International Conference on Virtual Systems and Multimedia.

Kang, H., Lee, H., and Jung, K. (2004). Recognition-based gesture spotting in video games. Pattern Recognition Letters, 25(15), 1701-1714.

Karaulova, I., Hall, P., and Marshall, M. (2000). A Hierarchical model of dynamics for tracking people with a single video camera, British Machine Vision Conference, (pp. 352-361).

Kim, C., and Hwang, J. N. (1999). A fast and robust moving object segmentation in video sequences. In Proceedings of International Conference on Image Processing: Vol.2. (pp. 131-134).

Kim, D., Song, J., Yun, W. and Kim, D. (2005). Smarthome control system using the multiple cameras. Technical Report, IMLAB-2004-2.

Kjeldsen, R., and Kender, J. (1995). Visual hand gesture recognition for window system control. Proceedings of International Workshop Automatic Face and Gesture Recognition, (pp. 184-188).

Krahnstoever, N., and Sharma, R. (2004). Articulated models from video, Proceedings of Computer Vision and Pattern Recognition, (pp. 894-901).

Kristensen, F., Nilsson, P., and Owall, V. (2006). Background segmentation beyond RGB, Proceedings of Asian Conference on Computer Vision, (pp. 13-16).

Lee, H., and Kim, J. (1999). An HMM-based threshold model approach for gesture recognition. IEEE Transaction on Pattern Analysis and Machine Intelligence, 21(10), 961-973.

Lee, H., and Kim, J. (1999). An HMM-based threshold model approach for gesture recognition. IEEE Transaction on Pattern Analysis and Machine Intelligence, 21(10), 961-973.

Li, L., Koh, Y. T., Ge, S. S., and Huang, W. (2004a). Stereo-based human detection for mobile service robots. In Proceedings of International Conference on Control, Automation, Robotics, and Vision, (pp. 74-79).

Li, L., Ge, S. S., Sim, T., Koh, Y. T., and Hunag, X. (2004b). Object-oriented scale-adaptive filtering for human detection from stereo images. In Proceedings of IEEE Conference on Cybernetics and Intelligent Systems, (pp. 135-140).

Li, X., and Guskov, I. (2005). Multi-scale features for approximate alignment of point-based surfaces, Proceedings of the 3rd Eurographics symposium on Geometry Processing.

Liang, W., Weiming, H., and Tieniu, T. (2003). Recent developments in human motion analysis, Pattern Recognition, 36(3), 585-601.

Moeslund, B. T., Hilton, A., and Kruger, V. (2006). A survey of advances in vision-based human motion capture and analysis, Computer Vision and Image Understandings, 104, 90-126.

Mohan, A., Papageorgiou, C., and Poggio, T. (2001). Example-based object detection in images by components. IEEE Transactions on Pattern Analysis and Machine Intelligence, 23(4) 349-361.

Morita, H., Hashimoto, S., and Ohteru, S. (1991). A computer music system that follows a human conductor, IEEE Computer Society, 24, 44–53.

Mulder, A. (1996). Hand gestures for hci, Technical Report 96-1, Simon Fraster University.

Munkelt, O., Ridder, C., Hansel, D., and Hafner, W. (1998). A model driven 3D image interpretation system applied to person detection in video images, Proceedings of the International Conference on Pattern Recognition, (pp. 70-73).

Myers, C., and Rabinier, L. (1980). Performance tradeoffs in dynamic time warping algorithms for isolated word recognition, IEEE Transactions on Accoustics, Speech, and Signal Processing, 28(6), 623-635.

NASA: NASA-STD-3000. (1995). Man-systems integration standards. NASA John Space Center.

Navneet D., and Bill T. (2005). Histograms of Oriented Gradients for Human Detection. In Proceedings of IEEE Conference on Computer Vision and Pattern Recognition, Vol:1, (pp. 886-893).

Okuma, K., Taleghani, A., de Freitas, N., Little, J., and Lowe, D. (2004). A boosted particle filter: multitarget detection and tracking. In Proceedings of European Conference on Computer Vision, (pp. 28-39).

Park, A., and Lee. S. (2005). Spotting of continuous whole body gesture using discrete hidden markov models. In Proceedings of 3rd Computer Vision Technical Workshop.

Pavlovic, V., Rehg, J. M., and Cham, T-J. (1999). A dynamic bayesian network approach to figure tracking using learned dynamic models, In Proceedings of International Conference on Comtpuer Vision, (pp. 94-101).

Pavlovic, V., Sharma, R., and Huang, T. (1997). Visual interpretation of hand gestures for human-computer interaction - A review. IEEE Transactions on Pattern Analysis and Machine Intelligence, 19(7), 677-695.

Phillips, J., Liu, R., and Tomasi, C. (2007). Outlier robust ICP for minimizing frantional RMSD, 6th International Conference on 3D Digital Imaging and Modeling, (pp. 427-434).

Phung, S., Bouzerdoum, A., and Chai, D. (2005). Skin segmentation using color pixel classfication: analysis and comparison, IEEE Transactions on Pattern Analysis and Machine Intelligence, 27(1), 148-154.

Piccardi, M. (2004). Background subtraction techniques: a review, Systems, Man and Cybernetics, 4, 3099-3104.

Poritz, A.B. (1988), Hidden markov models: a guided tour, In Proceedings of International Conference on Acoustic Speech and Signal Processing, (pp. 7-13).

Quek, F. (1994). Toward a vision-based hand gesture interface, In Proceedings of Virtual Reality Software and Technology, (pp. 17–31).

Rohr, K. (1994). Towards model-based recognition of human movements in image sequeces, CVGIP: Image Understanding, 59(1), 94-115.

Rosales, R., and Scalroff, S. (2000). Specialized mappings and the estimation of human body pose from a single image, IEEE Workshop on Human Motion, (pp. 19-24).

Rosenblum , M., Yacoob, Y., and Davis, L. (1996). Human expression recognition from motion using a radial basis function network architecture, IEEE Transaction on Neural Network 7(5), 1121-1138.

Rusinkiewicz. S., and Levoy. M. (2001). Efficient variants of the icp algorithm. In Proceedings of International Conferenece on 3D Digital Imaging and Modeling, (pp. 145-152).

Salinas, R. M., Aguirre, E., Silvente, M. G., and Gonzalez, A. (2005). People detection and tracking through stereo vision for human-robot interaction. In Proceedings of Mexican International Conference on Artificial Intelligence, (pp. 337-346).

Sangi, P., Hdikkila, J., and Silven, I. (2001). Extracting motion components from image sequences using particle filters, Proceeding of 12th Sacndinavian Conferenece on Image Analysis.

Shakhnarovich, G., Viola, P., and Darrell, T. (2003). Fast pose estimation with parameter-sensitive hashing. Proceedings of the International Conference on Computer Vision.

Shin, J., Lee, J., Kil, S., Shen, D., Ryu, J., Lee, E., Min, H., and Hong, S. (2006). Hand region extraction and gesture recognition using entropy analysis. International Journal of Computer Science and Network Security, 6(2A), 216–222.

Sidenbladh, H. (2004). Detecting human motio with support vector machines, Proceedings of International Conference on Pattern Recognition.

Sidenbladh, H., Black, M., and Fleet, D. (2000). Stochastic tracking of 3D human figures using 2D image motion, Proceedings of International Conference on Computer Vision, (pp. 702-718).

Sigal, L., and Black, M. (2006). Predicting 3D people from 2D pictures, In Proceedings of Conference on Articulated Motion and Deformable Objects, (pp. 185-195).

Sminchisescu, C., Kanaujia, A., Li, Z., and Metaxas, D. (2004). Learning to reconstruct 3d human motion from bayesian mixtures of experts. A probabilistic discrimitive approach, Technical Report CSRG-502, University of Toronto.

Song, J., and Kim, D. (2006). Simultaneous gesture segmentation and recognition based on forward spotting accumulative hmms. In Proceedings of International Conference on Pattern Recognition, (pp.1231-1235).

Song, Y., Goncalves, L., and Perona, P. (2003). Unsupervised learning of human motion, IEEE Transactions on Pattern Analysis and Machine Intelligence, 25(7), 814-827.

Starner, T., and Pentland, A. (1995). Real-time american sign language recognition from video using hidden markov models. Technical Report TR-375, MIT's Media Lab.

Takahashi, K., and Seki, S. (1994). Recognition of dexterous manipulations from time varying images, In Proceedings of IEEE Workshop on Motion of Non-Rigid and Articulated Objects, (pp. 23-28).

Takahashi, K., Seki, S., and Oka, R. (1992). Spotting recognition of human gestures from motion images, Technical Report IE92-134, The Institute of Electronics, Information, and Communication Engineers, Japan, (pp. 9-16).

Tanibata, N., Shimada, N., and Shirai, Y. (2002). Extraction of hand features for recognition of sign language words. In Proceedings of International Conference on Vision Interface, (pp. 391-398).

Tuzel. O, Porkli F. and Meer P (2007). Human Detection via Classification on Riemannian Manifolds. In Proceedings of IEEE Conference on Computer Vision and Pattern Recognition, (pp. 1-8).

Utsumi, A., and Tetsutani, N. (2002). Human detection using geometrical pixel value structures, In Proceedings of International Conference on Automatic Face and Gesture Recognition.

Viterbi, A. (1967). Error bounds for convolution codes and an asymptotically optimum decoding algorithm. IEEE Transaction on Information Theory, 13(2), 260-269.

Wang, L., Hu, W., and Tan, T. (2003). Recent developments in human motion analysis, 36(3), 585-601.

Watanabe, T., and Yachida, M. (1999). Real-time gesture recognition using eigenspace from multi-input image sequences. IEEE Computer and System in Japan, 30(13), 810–821.

Welch, G. and Bishop, G. (2001). An introduction to the Kalman filter. Presented at SIGGRAPH.

Wilpon, J., Lee, C., and Rabiner, L. (1989). Application of hidden markov models for recognition of a limited set of words in unconstrained speech. In Proceedings of IEEE International Conference on Acoustics, Speech, and Signal Processing, (pp. 254-257).

Wu B., Nevatia R. (2007) "Detection and Tracking of Multiple, Partially Occluded Humans by Bayesian Combination of Edgelet based Part Detectors, International Journal of Computer Vision, 75(2), 247-266.

Wu, Y., and Huang, T. S. (2004). Vision-based gesture recognition: a review. Gesture-Based Communication in Human-Computer Interaction: International Gesture Workshop, (pp. 103).

Xu, F., and Fujimura, K. (2003). Human detection using depth and gray images. In Proceedings of IEEE Conference on Advanced Video and Signal Based Surveillance, (pp. 115-121).

Zhao, L., and Thorpe, C.E. (2002). Stereo – and neural network-based pedestrian detection, IEEE Transactions on Pattern Analysis and Machine Intelligence, 1(3), 148-154.

Zhou, J., and Hoang, J. (2005). Real time robust human detection and tracking system. In Proceedings of IEEE Conference on Computer Vision and Pattern Recognition, Vol:3, (pp. 149).

Zhu Q., Avidari S., Yeh M.-C., Cheng K.-T. (2006). Fast Human Detection Using a Cascade of Histograms of Oriented Gradients. In proceedings of IEEE Conference on Computer Vision and Pattern Recognition.

8.11 ENDNOTE

[1]   You can see the four video clips of 3D human body tracking at the demonstration site http://imlab.postech.ac.kr/ dkim/new_imlab/video/3D_tracking/example1-4.wmv

Abbreviations and Important Symbols

ABBREVIATIONS

AAM	Active appearance model
ACM	Active contour model
ANMRR	Average of the normalized modified retrieval rank
AOM	Adaptive observation model
ASM	Active shape model
AU	Action unit
BM	Bilinear model
CAAM	Conventional AAM
CDF	Cumulative density function
CDOP	Competitive differential observation probability
CFP	Conducting feature point
CHM	Cylinder head model
COG	Center of gravity
CONDENSATION	Conditional density propagation
DAFs	Differential-AAM features
DBN	Dynamic Bayesian network
DCT	Discrete cosine transform
DFEPDM	Differential facial expression probability density model
EHMM	Embedded hidden Markov model
FACS	Facial action coding system
FAR	False acceptance rate

FIR	False identification rate
FRR	False rejection rate
GDA	Generalized discriminant analysis
GIP	Gaussian image pyramid
GMM	Gaussian mixture model
HCI	Human compter interaction
HMI	Human machine interaction
HMM	Hidden Markov model
HOSVD	High order singular valude decomposition
HRI	Human robot interaction
ICA	Independent component analysis
CICIA	Inverse compositional image aligment
ICP	Iterative closest point
IPCA	Incremental principal component analysis
KNN	K-nearest neighbor
k-NNS	k-nearest neighbor sequences
LDA	Linear discriminant analysis
LK	Lucas-Kanade
LSE	Least squares estimation
MCS	Multiple classifier system
MDS	Muldidimensional scaling
MLP	Multi layer perceptron
MM	Morphable model
MMI	Man machine interaface
MOG	Mixture of Gaussians
MVAAM	Multi-view active appearance model
NN	Nearest neighbor
NRSFM	Non-rigid structure from motion
PCA	Principal component analysis
PMF	Probability mass function
RBF	Radial basis function
ROI	Region of interest
RRBM	Ridge regressive bilinear model
SAF	Scale adaptive filter
SFM	Structure from motion
SIP	Sampling image pyramid
SMO	Sequential minimal optimization
SOM	Self organizing map
SRM	Structural risk minimization
SSPU	Single-stage parameter update
STAAM	Stereo active appearance model
SVD	Singular value decomposition
SVM	Support vector machine
TAAM	Tensor-based AAM
TF	Tensor faces
TSPU	Two-stage parameter update

IMPORTANT SYMBOLS

$\mathbf{H}$ Hessian matrix

I identity matrix

J Jacobian matrix

$\mathbf{x}^t$ Transpose of vector $\mathbf{x}$, signified by the superscript t

$\|\mathbf{x}\|$ Euclidean norm of vector $\mathbf{x}$

exp   Exponential

∇ Gradient operator

a_i The i-th appearance parameter of AAMs

p_i The i-th 2D shape parameter of AAMs

q_i The i-th 2D (similarity transform) parameter of AAMs

$\tilde{p}_i$ The i-th 3D shape parameter of 2D+3D AAMs

$\tilde{q}_i$ The i-th 3D rigid motion parameter of 2D+3D AAMs

α Shape parameters of 3D MMs

β Texture paramters of 3D MMs

ρ Motion parameters of 3D MMs

Appendix

APPENDIX A. DATABASES

1. Databases for Face Recognition

AR FACE DATABASE

1. Type: image and sequences
2. Description: This face database was created by Aleix Martinez and Robert Benavente in the Computer Vision Center (CVC) at the U.A.B. It contains over 4,000 color images corresponding to 126 people's faces (70 men and 56 women). Images feature frontal view faces with different facial expressions, illumination conditions, and occlusions (sun glasses and scarf). The pictures were taken at the CVC under strictly controlled conditions. No restrictions on wear (clothes, glasses, etc.), make-up, hair style, etc. were imposed to participants. Each person participated in two sessions, separated by two weeks (14 days) time. The same pictures were taken in both sessions.
3. Number of images : over 4,000
4. Conditions:

number of subjects	126 (70/56)
number of poses	1
number of expressions	4
number of illuminations	4
number of sessions	2
resolution	768 x 576
simultaneous	X

5.   URL: http://cobweb.ecn.purdue.edu/~aleix/aleix_face_DB.html
6.   Paper: A.M. Martinez and R. Benavente. The AR Face Database. CVC Technical Report #24, June 1998
7.   Sample images (see Fig. A.1)

BANCA FACE DATABASE

1.   Type: image and video
2.   Description: The BANCA database is a new large, realistic and challenging multi-modal database intended for training and testing multi-modal verification systems. The BANCA database was captured in four European languages in two modalities (face and voice). For recording, both high and low quality microphones and cameras were used. The subjects were recorded in three different scenarios, controlled, degraded and adverse over 12 different sessions spanning three months. In total 208 people were captured, half men and half women.
3.   Number of images: over 6,240
4.   Conditions:

number of subjects	52 (26/26)
number of poses	1
number of expressions	2
number of illuminations	-
number of sessions	12
resolution	720 x 576
simultaneous	X

Figure A.1. Example of how the images of the AR face database look like

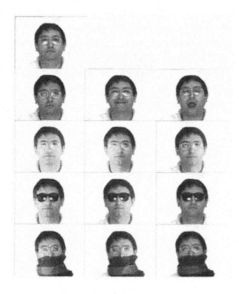

5. URL: http://www.ee.surrey.ac.uk/CVSSP/banca/
6. Paper: -

CAS-PEAL DATABASE

1. Type: image
2. Description: The CAS-PEAL face database has been constructed under the sponsors of National Hi-Tech Program and ISVISION by the Face Recognition Group of JDL, ICT, CAS. The goals to create the PEAL face database include: providing the worldwide researchers of FR community a large-scale Chinese face database for training and evaluating their algorithms; facilitating the development of FR by providing large-scale face images with different sources of variations, especially Pose, Expression, Accessories, and Lighting (PEAL); advancing the state-of-the-art face recognition technologies aiming at practical applications especially for the oriental. The CAS-PEAL face database contains 99,594 images of 1040 individuals (595 males and 445 females) with varying Pose, Expression, Accessory, and Lighting (PEAL). For each subject, 9 cameras spaced equally in a horizontal semicircular shelf are setup to simultaneously capture images across different poses in one shot. Each subject is also asked to look up and down to capture 18 images in another two shots. We also considered 5 kinds of expressions, 6 kinds accessories (3 glasses, and 3 caps), and 15 lighting directions, as well as varying backgrounds, distance from cameras, and aging variation.
3. Number of images: 99,594
4. Conditions:

number of subjects	1040 (595/445)
number of poses	27
number of expressions	6
number of illuminations	15
number of sessions	2
resolution	360 x 480
simultaneous	partially

5. URL: http://www.jdl.ac.cn/peal/index.html
6. Paper: Bo Cao, Shiguang Shan, Xiaohua Zhang, Wen Gao, Baseline Evaluations On The CAS-PEAL-R1 Face Database, Lecture Notes in Computer Science (LNCS3338), Advances in Biometric Person Authentication, pp370-378, Guangzhou, 2004.12
7. Sample images (see Fig. A.3)

CMU PIE DATABASE

1. Type: image
2. Description: Between October and December 2000, they collected a database of 41,368 images of 68 people. By extending the CMU 3D Room we were able to image each person under 13 different poses, 43 different illumination conditions, and with

4 different expressions. They call this database the CMU Pose, Illumination, and Expression (PIE) database.

3.   Number of images: 41,368
4.   Conditions:

number of subjects	68
number of poses	13
number of expressions	3
number of illuminations	43
number of sessions	1
resolution	640 x 486
simultaneous	partially

5.   URL: http://www.ri.cmu.edu/projects/project_418.html
6.   Paper: T. Sim, S. Baker, and M. Bsat, The CMU Pose, Illumination, and Expression Database, IEEE Transactions on Pattern Analysis and Machine Intelligence, Vol. 25, No. 12, December, 2003, pp. 1615 – 1618

FERET DATABASE

1.   Type: image
2.   Description: The FERET program ran from 1993 through 1997. Sponsored by the Department of Defense's Counterdrug Technology Development Program through the Defense Advanced Research Products Agency (DARPA), its primary mission was to develop automatic face recognition capabilities that could be employed to assist security, intelligence and law enforcement personnel in the performance of their duties. The FERET image corpus was assembled to support government monitored testing

Figure A.3. The 27 images of one subject under pose variation in the CAS-PEAL database. The nine cameras were spaced equally in the horizontal semicircular shelf, each about 22.5o apart. The subject was asked to look upwards, right into the camera C4 (the middle camera) and look downwards. Then, the 27 poses were named after the subject's pose (Up, Frontal, Down) and the number of the corresponding camera (from 0 to 8). The name of each pose was beneath its corresponding image

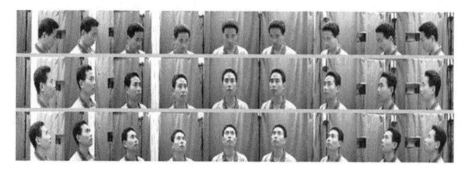

and evaluation of face recognition algorithms using standardized tests and procedures. The final corpus, presented here, consists of 14051 eight-bit grayscale images of human heads with views ranging from frontal to left and right profiles.

3. Number of images: 14,051
4. Conditions:

number of subjects	1199
number of poses	-
number of expressions	2
number of illuminations	2
number of sessions	3
resolution	256 x 384
simultaneous	X

5. URL: http://www.itl.nist.gov/iad/humanid/feret/feret_master.html
6. Paper: P. J. Phillips, H. Moon, P. J. Rauss, and S. Rizvi, "The FERET evaluation methodology for face recognition algorithms", IEEE Transactions on Pattern Analysis and Machine Intelligence, Vol. 22, No. 10, October 2000.
7. Sample images (see Fig. A.5)

KOREAN FACE DATABASE

1. Type: image
2. Description: They collected a database of 52,000 images of 1,000 people. Two colors and eight directions are considered in the illumination conditions. Five kinds of expressions - neutral, happiness, surprise, anger and blink expressions - are considered under two different illumination colors. Seven poses are considered with or without hair-band or glasses.
3. Number of images: 52,000
4. Conditions:

number of subjects	1000(500/500)
number of poses	7
number of expressions	5
number of illuminations	16
number of sessions	1
resolution	640 x 480
simultaneous	partially

5. URL: -
6. Paper: Hwang, B. W. and Byun, H. and Roh, M. C. and Lee, S. W., Performance Evaluation of Face Recognition Algorithms on the Asian Face Database, KFDB, Intl. Conf on Audio and Video Based Person Anthentication, 557-565, 2003.
7. Sample images (see Fig. A.6)

Figure A.5. Sample images of The Facial Recognition Technology (FERET) Database. pr, pl: profile left and right, hr, hl: half left and right, qr, ql: quarter left and right, fa: regular facial expression, fb: alternative facial expression, re, rd, rc,: random images

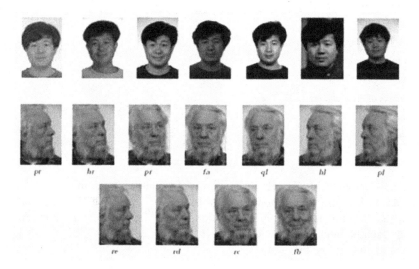

ORL DATABASE (AT&T)

1. Type: image
2. Description: The ORL Database of Faces contains a set of face images taken between April 1992 and April 1994 at the lab. The database was used in the context of a face recognition project carried out in collaboration with the Speech, Vision and Robotics Group of the Cambridge University Engineering Department. There are ten different images of each of 40 distinct subjects. For some subjects, the images were taken at different times, varying the lighting, facial expressions (open / closed eyes, smiling / not smiling) and facial details (glasses / no glasses). All the images were taken against a dark homogeneous background with the subjects in an upright, frontal position (with tolerance for some side movement). A preview image of the Database of Faces is available. The files are in PGM format, and can conveniently be viewed on UNIX (TM) systems using the 'xv' program. The size of each image is 92x112 pixels, with 256 grey levels per pixel. The images are organized in 40 directories (one for each subject), which have names of the form sX, where X indicates the subject number (between 1 and 40). In each of these directories, there are ten different images of that subject, which have names of the form Y.pgm, where Y is the image number for that subject (between 1 and 10).
3. Number of images: 400

Figure A.6. Sample images with illuminations, poses and facial expressions change of KFDB

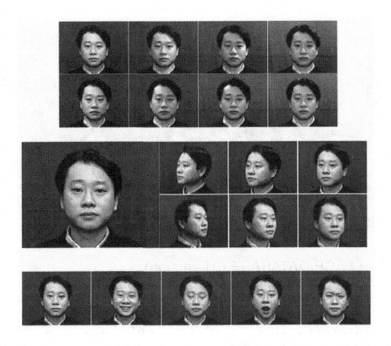

4. Conditions:

number of subjects	40
number of poses	-
number of expressions	-
number of illuminations	-
number of sessions	1
resolution	92 x 110
simultaneous	X

5. URL: http://www.cl.cam.ac.uk/research/dtg/attarchive/facedatabase.html
6. Paper: Samaria, Ferdinando and Harter, Andy, "Parameterisation of a stochastic model for human face identification", IEEE Workshop on Applications of Computer Vision, 1994.
7. Sample images (see Fig. A.7)

Figure A.7. Ten different images per person. The images were taken at different times, varying the lighting, facial expressions (open / closed eyes, smiling / not smiling) and facial details (glasses / no glasses).

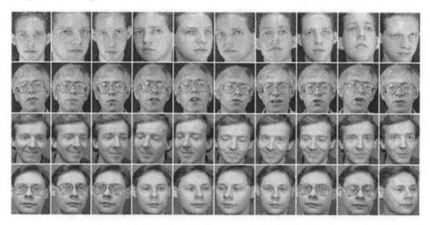

POSTECH FACE DATABASE (01 version)

1. Type: image
2. Description: We constructed a face database PF01(Postech Faces '01).PF01 contains the true-color face images of 103 people,53 men and 50 women, representing 17 various images (1 normal face,4 illumination variations,8 pose variations,4 expression variations)per person. All of the people in the database are Asians. There are three kinds of systematic variations, such as illumination, pose, and expression variations in the database. The database is expected to e used to evaluate the technology of face recognition for Asian people or for people with systematic variations.
3. Number of images: 1,751
4. Conditions:

number of subjects	103 (53/50)
number of poses	8
number of expressions	4
number of illuminations	5
number of sessions	1
resolution	1280 x 960
simultaneous	X

5. URL: http://imlab.postech.ac.kr/special/imdb/imdb.html
6. Paper: -
7. Sample images (see Fig. A.8)

Figure A.8. Sample facial expression images. neutral, happy, surprised, irritated, closed-eye

POSTECH FACE DATABASE (07 version)

1. Type: image
2. Description: PF07 database includes 100 male and 100 female subjects captured in 5 different poses under 16 illuminations performing 4 different expressions. The pose variation consists of front, left, right, upper, and down, and the angle between the frontal pose and other poses is 22.5°. The illumination variation consists of no light condition and 15 different light conditions, where each light condition means the turn-on of the light on a specific location, and 15 locations are the intersection points of three vertical positions (high, middle, and low) and five horizontal positions (-90°; -45°; 0°; 45°; 90°). The expression variation consists of neutral, happy, surprise, and angry. Therefore, there are 5 x 4 x 16 = 320 images for a subject. Since 200 subjects are exist in this database, the database contains 64000 images.
3. Number of images: 64,000
4. Conditions:

number of subjects	200 (100/100)
number of poses	5
number of expressions	4
number of illuminations	16
number of sessions	1
resolution	640 x 480
simultaneous	Y

5. URL: http://imlab.postech.ac.kr/~dkim/new_imlab/faceDB/PF07/PF07.html
6. Paper: -
7. Sample images (see Fig. A.9)

XM2VTS Face Database

1. Type: image and video
2. Description: At the Centre for Vision, Speech and Signal Processing we have captured a large multi-modal database which will enable the research community to test their multi-modal face verification algorithms on a high-quality large dataset. In aquiring the XM2FDB database 295 volunteers from the University of Surrey visited our recording studio four times at approximately one month intervals. On each visit (session) two recordings (shots) were made. The first shot consisted of speech whilst the second

Figure A.9. Images of happy facial expression taken under 16 different light condition

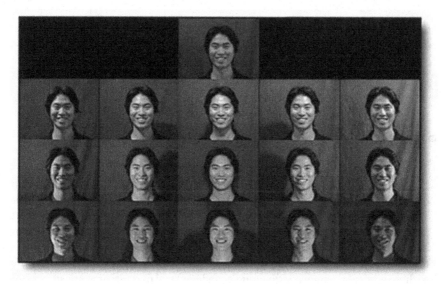

consisted of rotating head movements. Digital video equipment was used to capture the entire database. At the third session a high-precision 3D model of the subjects head was built using an active stereo system provided by the Turing Institute..

3.   Number of images: -
4.   Conditions:

number of subjects	295
number of poses	-
number of expressions	-
number of illuminations	3
number of sessions	4
resolution	720 x 576
simultaneous	X

5.   URL: http://www.ee.surrey.ac.uk/CVSSP/xm2vtsdb/
6.   Paper: K. Messer and J. Matas and J. Kittler and J. Lüttin and G. Maitre, "XM-2VTSDB: The Extended M2VTS Database", Audio- and Video-based Biometric Person Authentication, 72-77, 1999.
7.   Sample images (see Fig. A.10)

YALE FACE DATABASE - A

1.   Type: image
2.   Description: The Yale Face Database (size 6.4MB) contains 165 grayscale images in GIF format of 15 individuals. There are 11 images per subject, one per different facial

Figure A.10. Sequences of rotating head movements from left to right. The sequences are taken 4 times repeatedly. The research of which this (report) is based acknowledges the use of Extended Multimodal Face Database and associated documentation

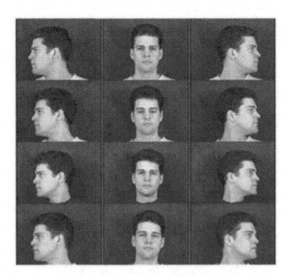

expression or configuration: center-light, w/glasses, happy, left-light, w/no glasses, normal, right-light, sad, sleepy, surprised, and wink.

3. Number of images: 165
4. Conditions:

number of subjects	15
number of poses	1
number of expressions	6
number of illuminations	3
number of sessions	1
resolution	320 x 240
simultaneous	X

5. URL: http://cvc.yale.edu/projects/yalefaces/yalefaces.html/
6. Paper: Belhumeur, P., Hespanha, J., and Kriegman, D, "Eigenfaces vs.fisherfaces: class specific linear projection", IEEE Transactions on Pattern Analysis and Machine Intelligence, 19(7), 711-720, 1997.
7. Sample images (see Fig. A.11)

Figure A.11. Images of 6 different facial expression taken under 3 different illumination conditions

YALE FACE DATABASE - B

1.   Type: image
2.   Description: The database contains 5760 single light source images of 10 subjects each seen under 576 viewing conditions (9 poses x 64 illumination conditions). For every subject in a particular pose, an image with ambient (background) illumination was also captured. Hence, the total number of images is in fact 5760+90=5850. The total size of the compressed database is about 1GB.
3.   Number of images: 5,850
4.   Conditions:

number of subjects	10
number of poses	9
number of expressions	1
number of illuminations	65
number of sessions	1
resolution	640 x 480
simultaneous	Y

5.   URL: http://cvc.yale.edu/projects/yalefacesB/yalefacesB.html
6.   Paper: Georghiades, A.S. and Belhumeur, P.N. and Kriegman, D.J.,"From Few to Many: Illumination Cone Models for Face Recognition under Variable Lighting and Pose", IEEE Trans. Pattern Anal. Mach. Intelligence 26(6), 643-660, 2001.
7.   Sample images (see Fig. A.12)

BJUT (Beijing University of Technology)-3D FACE DATABASE

1.   Type: image
2.   Description:
3.   Number of images: 500
4.   Conditions:

Figure A.12. Images of 10 subjects taken under frontal-view, neutral facial expression

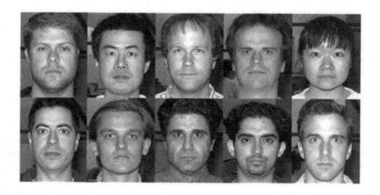

age	16~49
male / female	250 / 250
expressions	Natural without glasses or other accessories

5. URL: http://bjut.edu.cn/sci/multimedia/mul-lab/3dface/face_database.htm
6. Paper: The BJUT-3D Large-Scale Chinese Face Database, MISKL-TR-05-FMFR-001
7. Sample images (see Fig. A.13)

2. Databases for Facial Expression Recognition

MMI FACE DATABASE Type: Image and Video

1. Description:
2. Number of images: 740 images, 848 video sequences (24fps)
3. Conditions:

number of peoples	19 (male, female, 3 ethnics)
views	frontal view and dual-view (combine frontal and profile view of the face)
expressions	facial expression of motion

4. URL: http://www.mmifacedb.com
5. Paper: M. Pantic, M.F. Valstar, R. Rademaker and L. Maat, "Web-based Database for Facial Expression Analysis", Proc. IEEE Int'l Conf. Multmedia and Expo (ICME'05), Amsterdam, The Netherlands, July 2005.
6. Sample imges (see Fig. A.14)

CMU-PITTSBURGH AU-CODED FACE EXPRESSION IMAGE DATABASE

1. Type: image
2. Description:
3. Number of images: frontal view 2105 frames, 30-degree view (videotape only)

Figure A.13. Examples of BJUT database. Each column represents 3D scanner, 3D face, shape data, texture image, from left to right.

Figure A.14. (a) Images of different people, various facial expressions under frontal view. (b) Sequences of 2 different people making a facial expression under profile view. (c) Images of 3 different people under dual-view.

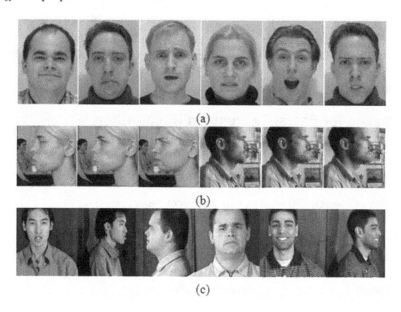

(a)

(b)

(c)

4.   Conditions:

number of peoples	182 (male, female)
age	18~50
number of expressions	23 (varying skin color and facial conformation)

5.   URL: http://vasc.ri.cmu.edu/idb/html/face/facial_expression/index.html
6.   Paper: T. Kanade, J. F. Cohn and Yingli Tian, "Comprehensive Database for Facial Expression Analysis", In Proceedings of the 4th IEEE International Conference on Automatic Face and Gesture Recognition (FG'00) , 2000.
7.   Sample images: (see Fig. A.15)

JAPANESE FEMALE FACIAL EXPRESSION (JAFFE) DATABASE

1.   Type: image
2.   Description:
3.   Number of images: 213
4.   Conditions:

Number of peoples	10 (female)
Number of expressions	7 (6 basic facial expression + 1 neutral)

5.   URL: http://www.kasrl.org/jaffe.html

Figure A.15. some sample images from the CMU Facial Expression Database

6. Paper: J. Michael, Shigeru Akamatsu, Miyuki Kamachi and Jiro Gyoba, "Coding Facial Expressions with Gabor Wavelets", In Proceedings of 3rd International Conference on Automatic Face and Gesture Recognition, pp. 200-205, 2005
7. Sample images (see Fig. A.16)

BU-3DFE (Binghamton University 3D Facial Expression) DATABASE

1. Type: image
2. Description:
3. Number of images: 100 subjects with 2500 3D facial expression models
4. Conditions:

age	18~70
ethnic / racial	White, Black / East-Asian, Middle-east Asian, Indian, and Hispanic Latino
number of expressions	7 (neutral + happiness, disgust, fear, angry, surprise and sadness)

Figure A.16. Images of one subject making 5 different facial expression

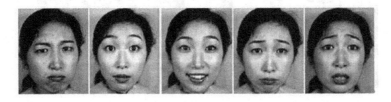

5.   URL: http://www.cs.binghamton.edu/~lijun/Research/3DFE/3DFE_Analysis.html
6.   Paper: Lijun Yin, Xiaozhou Wei, Yi Sun, Jun Wang, and Matthew Rosato, "A 3D Facial Expression Database for Facial Behavior Research", 7th International Conference on Automatic Face and Gesture Recognition (FG2006), IEEE Computer Society TC PAMI, 2006
7.   Sample images (see Fig. A.17 and Fig. A.18)

3. Databases for Hand Gesture Recognition

MASSEY HAND GESTURE (MHG) DATABASE

1.   Type: image
2.   Description : MHG database(2D) contains a variety of hand gesture and hand posture images which is for real-time posture recognition. The data is collected by a digital camera mounted on a tripod from a hand gesture in front of a dark background, and in different lighting environments. Together with the original images, there is a clipped version of each set of images that contains only the hand image. Some of images are consist of black background so that it is quite convenient to detect shape, color of hand.

Figure A.17. Four levels of facial expression from low to high

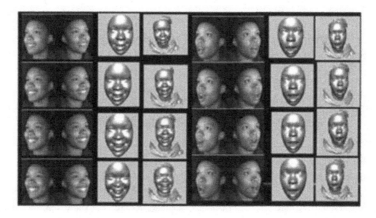

Figure A.18. Seven expressions female with face images and facial models

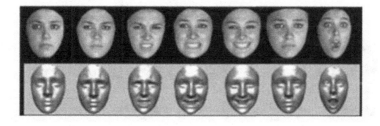

3. Number of images: 15000
4. Conditions

	Dataset	Lighting Condition	Background	Size	Type	Number of files
1	Hand gesture	Normal	Dark background	640x480	Jpeg	169
2	Hand gesture	Normal	RGB(0,0,0)	Varying/ Clipped	jpeg	169
3	Hand palm	Normal	Dark background	640x480	jpeg	145
4	Hand palm	Normal	RGB(0,0,0)	Varying/ Clipped	jpeg	145
5	Hand palm	Artificial light/dark room	Dark background	640x480	jpeg	498
6	Hand palm	Artificial light/dark room	Dark background	Varying/ Clipped	jpeg	498

5. URL:http://tur-www1.massey.ac.nz/~fdadgost/xview.php?page=hand_image_database/default
6. Paper: Farhad Dadgostar, Abdolhossein Sarrafzadeh, Scott P. Overmyer, Liyanage De Silva, *"Is the Hand really quicker than the Eye? Variances of the Mean-Shift algorithm for real-time hand and face tracking"*, IEEE International Conference on Computational Intelligence for Modelling, Control and Automation, 28-30 Nov 2006, Sydney, Australia
7. Sample images (see Fig. A.19)

SÉBASTIEN MARCEL – INTERACTPLAY (SMIP) DATABASE

1. Type: Movie
2. Description: The SMIP database made of a 3D hand trajectories so that one can study hand tracking in 3-dimension space. It will be also possible to recognize gestures b-y tracking the trajectory of the hand. It will be quite suitable for anyone who want to research tracking a hand- trajectory in 3 dimensional space
3. Size of movie: 21 Mb

Figure A.19. Examples of the hand postures of the Massey Hand Gesture Database

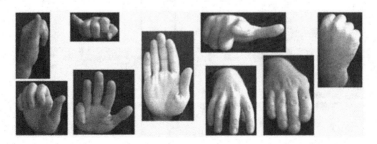

4.   Conditions
     The SMIP database contains 16 hand gestures from 22 persons and provides 5 ses-
     sions and 10 recordings per session. The database contains 3D trajectories, including
     the coordinates of the head and the torso, of segmented gestures. It provides also a
     calibration sequence for every person and every session, and test sequences of con-
     tinuous gestures. Each trajectory is stored in one text file. The naming convention
     is the following [personid]_[gestureid]_[sessionid]_[recordid]. For instance, the file
     01_07_5_9.txt is the record 9 of the gesture 7 performed by person 1 during the ses-
     sion 5. For every session and every person, two additional sequences are provided: a
     calibration sequence called "Vinci" sequence, and a test sequence made of continu-
     ous gestures. Test sequences are labelled and will be available soon. The calibration
     sequence is stored as the gesture 17 and the test sequence as the gesture 18
5.   URL: http://www.idiap.ch/resources/interactplay/
6.   Paper: A. Just, O. Bernier, and S. Marcel. HMM and IOHMM for the recognition
     of mono- and bi-manual 3D hand gestures. In *Proceedings of the British Machine
     Vision Conference (BMVC)*, 2004
7.   Sample images (see Fig. A.20).

POINTING GESTURE: VIDEO SEQUENCE (PGVS) DATABASE

1.   Type: Movie
2.   Description: The PGVS database consists of 24 video sequences of hands pointing
     onto a desk. It will be quite useful providing that you want to recognize a spot which

*Figure A.20. One of the hand gesture sequences. Database contains 16 hand gestures form
22 persons.*

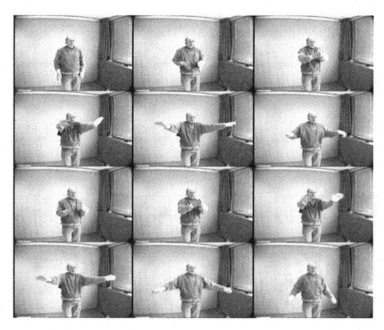

anyone points out. The sequences are provided as a set of PNG format images with lose-less compression. The .png files are named *sequenceType_personID_skinType_sex_frameNumber.png*. The sequence Types are described above, the person ID is a number from 01 to 15, skin Type is either (*White, Yellow, Black*), the sex is either (*Male, Female*), and frame Number is a four digit number (*0000 >> XXXX*).

3. Size of movie: 7 GB
4. Conditions

The scene background is a table covered with a black piece of fabric, a Macbeth color-checker, and two small pieces of light gray rubber. The rubber pieces were placed in the scene to give the test persons some objects to interact with. Doing recordings the light in the scene is switched forth and back between four different light sources, which is described in more details below The scene background is a messy table with a lot of moveable objects, and a Macbeth color-checker. The test persons were asked to interact with as many objects as they felt like, but not to start reading any of the books. The scene background is a messy table with a lot of moveable objects, and a Macbeth color-checker. The test persons were asked to interact with as many objects as they felt like, but not to start reading any of the books. Doing recordings the light in the scene is switched forth and back between four different light sources Lighting

Light 1 :	Philips : TLD 58W/965 (6200K)
Light 2 :	Philips : TLD 58W/950 (4700K)
Light 3 :	Philips : TLD 58W/940 (3680K)
Light 4 :	Philips : TLD 58W/927 (2600K)

5. URL: http://www.cvmt.dk/~fgnet/Pointing04/
6. Paper:

It was originally recorded as part of the Pointing'04 ICPR Workshop, Cambridge, UK, 22th, Aug, 2004

7. Sample images (see Fig. A.21)

Figure A.21. **X:** *The scene background is a messy table with a lot of moveable objects, and a Macbeth color-checker. Doing recordings the light in the scene was fixed to a specific light type;* **Y:** *The scene background is a messy table with a lot of moveable objects, and a Macbeth color-checker. Doing recordings the light in the scene is switched forth and back between four different light sources;* **Z:** *The scene background is a table covered with a black piece of fabric, a Macbeth color-checker, and two small pieces of light gray rubber.*

X   Y   Z

4. Databases for Head Gesture Recognition

HEAD POSE (HP) IMAGE DATABASE

1.   Type: image
2.   Description: HP database proposes a benchmark from head pose estimation system working on static images of known and unknown faces. All images have been taken using the FAME Platform of the PRIMA Team in INRIA Rhone-Alpes. To obtain different poses, we have put markers in the whole room. Each marker corresponds to a pose (h,v). Post-it are used as markers. The whole set of post-it covers a half-sphere in front of the person. In order to obtain the face in the center of the image, the person is asked to adjust the chair to see the device in front of him. After this initialization phase, we ask the person to stare successively at 93 post-it, without moving his eyes. This second phase just takes a few minutes. All images are obtained by using this method (see Fig. A.22 and A.23)
3.   Number of images: 2790 images, 6 movies
4.   Conditions: It consists in 15 sets of images. Each set contains of 2 series of 93 images of the same person at 93 different poses. There are 15 people in the database, wearing glasses or not and having various skin color. The pose, or head orientation is determined by 2 angles (h,v), which varies from -90 degrees to +90 degrees.
5.   URL: http://www-prima.inrialpes.fr/perso/Gourier/Faces/HPDatabase.html
6.   Paper: N. Gourier, D. Hall, J. L. Crowley, "Estimating Face Orientation from Robust Detection of Salient Facial Features", In Proceedings of Pointing 2004, ICPR, International Workshop on Visual Observation of Deictic Gestures, Cambridge, UK
7.   Sample image (see Fig. A.24)

Figure A.22. Top sight

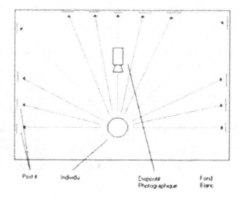

Figure A.23. Side sight

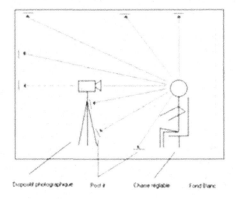

Figure A.24. A sample of a serie, each serie contains 93 images of the same person at 93 different poses

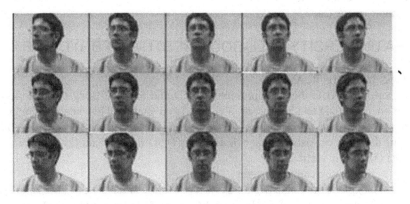

5. Databases for Body Gesture Recognition

CMU MOCAP DATABASE

1. Type: MPEG, c3d, amc
2. Description: MOCAP database is for analyzing the human activities. This DB used a system based on an optical marker-based technology, which yields very clean and detailed motion capture data. Here the actor is equipped with a set of 40-50 retro-reflective markers attached to a suit. There markers are tracked by an array of six to twelve calibrated high-resolution cameras at a frame rate of up to 240 Hz. From the recorded 2D images of the marker positions, the system can then reconstruct the 3D marker positions with high precision. The resulting 3D trajectory data is stored in the C3D mobcap file format.
3. Number of images:

4.   Conditions: 144 subjects (various trials per each subject)
       There are 2605 trials in 6 categories and 23 subcategories.

Subjects	Activities
Human Interaction	2 subjects
Interaction with Environment	Playground, uneven terrain, path with obstacles
Locomotion	Running, walking, jumping, varied
Physical Activities & Sports	Basketball, dance, gymnastics, acrobatics, martial arts, racquet/paddle sports, soccer, boxing, general exercise and stretching, golf, Frisbee
Situations & Scenarios	Common behaviors and expressions, pantomime, communication gestures and signals, cross-category variety
Test Motions	

5.   URL: http://mocap.cs.cmu.edu
6.   Paper: Meinard Muller, Tido Roder, Michael Clausen, Bernhard Eberhardt, Bjorn Kruger, Andres Weber, "Documentation Mocap Databse HDM05" – Computer Graphics Technical Reports CG 2007-2
7.   Sample image (see Fig. A.25)

KOREA UNIVERSITY FULL-BODY GESTURE (FBG) DATABASE

1.   Type: Image, HTR, AVI
2.   Description: KUG database presents the 2D and 3D Full-Body Gesture database for analyzing 2D and 3D gesture and its related studies. This database contains 14 representative gestures in daily life for 10 male and female subjects of 60~80 ages. This database consists of major three parts (1) 3D motion data (2) 2D stereo-video data (3) 2D silhouette data.
       A.   3D Gesture capture system
              It exploits the Eagle Digital System of Motion Analysis Co. The Eagle Digital System consists of Eagle Digital Cameras, the EagleHub, EVaRT software, which can capture subject's motion with high accuracy. The motion capture

Figure A.25. A jumping motion and its animated motion result

camera, Eagle Digital Camera supports a resolution of 1280x1024 pixels at up to 500 frames per second. It totally positioned the 12 cameras. All subjects wear a black and blue color suit, on which 33 markers reflecting light from LED of 3D cameras are attached. All 3D cameras are synchronized and the 3D position of markers is obtained at 60 frames per second. 3D data motion data is saved in Motion Analysis 'HTR (Hierarchical Translation Rotation)' format.

B.   2D Gesture capture system

It captured 2D and 3D gesture data, simultaneously. 2D Video data is captured with stereo camera system (STH-MDCS2) made by Videre Design. 2D stereo camera systems are 4m away from a subject and placed at +45, -45, 0 degrees for obtaining gestures at 3 different directions. It captures uncompressed video at 320x240 resolution, color and 30 frames per second and saved in uncompressed 'AVI' file format.

3.   Number of images: 400 MB for 3D data, 90GB for 2D data.
4.   Conditions:

14 Gestures

(1) sitting on a chair	(8) sitting on the floor
(2) standing up from a chair	(9) getting down on the floor
(3) walking at a place	(10) lying down on the floor
(4) touching a knee and a waist	(11) waving a hand
(5) raising a right hand	(12) running at a place
(6) sticking out a hand	(13) walking forward
(7) bending a waist	(14) walking circularly

5.   URL: http://gesturedb.korea.ac.kr
6.   Paper: B.-W.Hwang, S.Kim and S.-W. Lee, "A Full-Body Gesture Database for Human Gestures Analysis", International Journal of Pattern Recognition and Artificial Intelligence, Vol .21, No. 6, 2007, pp 1069-1084.
7.   Sample image (see Fig. A.26)

APPENDIX B. DEMONSTRATION SYSTEMS

1. Face Detection and Recognition Systems

VISION ACCESS SDK

1.   Author: Bioscrypt
2.   Sales: Commercial
3.   Specification: The SDK tools can be used for development 3D face recognition system. Two versions SDK components are available, BioAPI®-based components and ActiveX® components. From door to desk top computer, many applications are useful.
4.   WWW: http://www.bioscrypt.com/

Figure A.26. 3D motion examples of 14 gestures

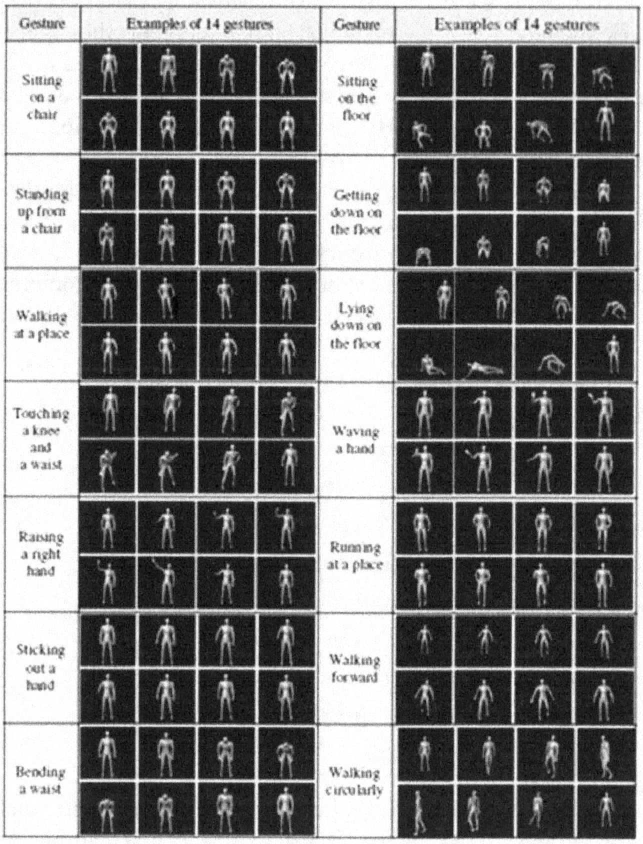

5. Environment:
    A.   Intel Pentium® 4-based PC 2.0+ GHz RAM 512 MB, 60GB HDD
    B.   Microsoft® Windows 2000™ and XP Professional™,
    C.   DirectX®9.0
    D.   Off-the-shelf video capture cards
    E.   Microsoft Visual Studio™ .NET 2003, C++, C#
6. System performance: Perform facial recognition calculations at processing rates of 10 - 12 full capturing- matching cycles per second
7. Available anywhere from 3-6 feet away
8. Demo image (see Fig. B.1)

VISION 3D/2D ENROLLMENT APPLICATION

1. Author: A4vision
2. Sales: Commercial
3. Specification: To perform enrollment of the 3D (optionally 2D) face image. That system is used for a verity of surveillance system such as ePassport programs or

Figure B.1. A sample image

traveler initiatives. The enrollment process is simple. And the system is robust to lighting flexibility

4. WWW: http://www.a4vision.com/
5. Environment:
    A. Intel Pentium® 4 PC 3 GHz or faster, dual processor is supported
    B. RAM 512 MB 1GB preferred, 120MB HDD
    C. Microsoft Windows 2000 Professional / XP Professional
    D. Compatible with ODBC compliant database
    6. System performance
    A. Verification time: less then 1second
    B. Identification time: less then 1seoocnd
    C. Enrollment time: 5~10 seconds
    7. Demo image (see Fig. B.2)

PC-BASED FACE RECOGNITION TECHNOLOGY

1. Author: Neuro technologija
2. Sales: Commercial

Figure B.2. An execution window

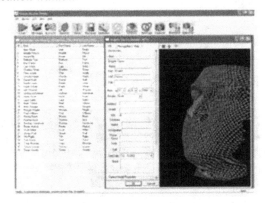

3.   Specification: Like fingerprint biometrics, facial recognition technology is widely used various systems, including physical access control and computer user accounts security. Usually these systems extract cetain features from face images and then perform face matching using these features. A face does not have as many uniquely measurable features as fingerprints and eye irises, so facial recognition reliability is slightly lower than these other biometrical recognition methods. However, it is still suitable for many applications, especially when taking into account its convenience for user. Facial recognition can also be used together with fingerprint recognition or another biometrical method for developing more security-critical applications. The multi-biometrical approach is especially important for identification (1:N) systems. In general, identification systems are very convenient to use because they do not require any additional security information (smart cards, passwords etc.). However, using 1:N-matching routines with only one biometrical method, can result in a higher false acceptance probability, which may become unacceptable for applications with large databases. Using face identification as an additional biometric method can dramatically decrease this effect. This multi-biometrical approach also helps in situations where a certain biometric feature is not optimal for certain groups of users. For example, people who do heavy labor with their hands may have rough fingerprints, which can increase the false rejection rate if fingerprint identification was used alone.

4.   WWW: http://www.neurotechnologija.com/

5.   Environment:
Intel Pentium® PC 1 GHz or faster
Microsoft Windows, Linux, Mac OS   X

6.   System performance:
Multiple faces detection time (640x480) : 0.07 second
Single face processing time(after detecting all faces) : 0.13 second
Matching speed: 100,000 facse/ second
Size of one record in the database: 2.3 Kbytes

7.   Demo image (see Fig. B.3)

Figure B.3. A sample image

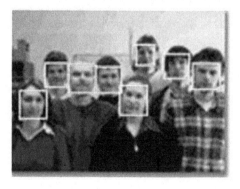

IDFEND SECURITY SHIELD

1. Author: Neuro technologija
2. Sales: Commercial
3. Specification: This system provides biometric authentication to complement standard card entry systems that use magnetic stripe, proximity or smart card technologies. It operates as an intermediary, routing and filtering access card information to and from legacy systems (e.g., Chubb/ADT MIS). It integrates easily with multi-portal security systems and accommodates up to 200 access points and 20,000 users per installation. It can also be integrated with third-party time & attendance systems
4. WWW: http://www.tcc.us.com/
5. Environment:
   A. Client
   B. Intel Pentium® 1.3GHz
   C. RAM 256 MB 512GB preferred, 40MB HDD
   D. Microsoft Windows XP
   E. Server
   F. Intel Pentium® 1.3GHz
   G. RAM 512 MB 1 GB preferred, 40MB HDD
6. System performance:
   A. Speed: less then 2 second
   B. Scalability: Number of access points is not restricted
   C. Reliablility: Reduces fraud compared to card or taken based system
7. Hghly Configurable: Multiple configurations of facial biometric authentication and Wiegand access control devices may be applied within the same installation Unobtrusive Operation-Uses idfend Biometrics Facial Recognition for fast/accurate biometric authentication
8. Demo images (see Fig. B.4)

2. Hand Gesture Recognition Systems

SMART CAR INTERFACE SYSTEM

1. Authors: GM collaborative research lab. And dept. of ECE, Carnegie Mellon Univ.
2. Sales: Commercial

Figure B.4. Sample images

3.   Specification
    A.   A **companion** that recognizes your settings and keeps you alert.
    B.   "**Context aware**" -- responsive to your needs and preferences, road and weather conditions, and information from Internet, on demand.
    C.   Equipped with a "**gesture interface**" that lets you control the car's electronics with a wave of your hand.
    D.   Built with a **speech recognition system** tuned to your voice that connects your car to your handheld computers and cell phone
    E.   Outfitted with the latest **wireless networks** and **Global Positioning Satellite technology** to keep you safe and on time.
    F.   Assembled with a **heads-up display** for operating the radio, navigating, checking email, and your schedule
    G.   Able to automatically **modify its own behavior**, make "**graceful upgrades**" to new versions, monitor mechanical and electrical problems, and repair itself until you can get to the shop
4.   WWW: http://gm.web.cmu.edu/research/index.php
5.   Demo images (see Fig. B.5 and Fig. B.6)

HANDVU

1.   Author: The moves institute
2.   Sales: Non-commercial
3.   Specification: The HandVu is a vision-based hand gesture interface. It detects the hand in a standard posture, then tracks it and recognizes key postures – all in real-time and without the need for camera or user calibration. It is very useful for interfacing between human and machine with only hand gesture combined with virtual reality and warable computer.
4.   WWW: www.movesinstitute.org/~kolsch/HandVu/HandVu.html#overview
5.   Demo images (see Figures B.7, B.8, B.9, and B.10)

Figure B.5. Smart car system using hand gesture

Figure B.6. Training for a certain hand gesture

Figure B.7. Interfacing with virtual objects

Figure B.8. Mouse and button interface with hand gesture

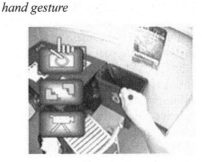

Figure B.9. Rubber band with two handed interaction

Figure B.10. Gesturing to our wearable computing

3. Head Gesture Recognition Systems

USE YOUR HEAD SYSTEM

1. Author: Cybernet Systems Corp.
2. Sales: Commercial
3. Specification: The system makes it possible to assign just about any keyboard command you want to have easily accessible to your head motions. The UseYourHead converts these head movements into user definable keystrokes. In effect, it acts like a second keyboard. This simple implementation allows it to work well with almost all existing games (virtually any game that accepts keyboard input). Additionally, game developers will be able to directly integrate support for UseYourHead (through use of a DirectInput wrapper) to allow a more continuous motion.
4. WWW: http://www.gesturecentral.com/useyourhead/specs.html
5. Demo image: Nothing

WATSON: Real-Time Head Tracking And Gesture Recognition

1. Author: MIT CSAIL, Vision Interfaces Lab
2. Sales: Non-Commercial
3. Specification: The Waton can track rigid objects in real-time with 6 degrees of free-

dom using a tracking framework called Adaptive View-Based Appearance Model. The tracking library can estimate the pose of the object for a long period of time with bounded drift. Our main application is head pose estimation and gesture recognition using a USB camera or a stereo camera. Our approach combines an Adaptive View-based Appearance Model (AVAM) with a robust 3D view registration algorithm. AVAM is a compact and flexible representation of the object that can be used during the tracking to reduce the drift in the pose estimates. The model is acquired online during the tracking and can be adjusted according to the new pose estimates. Relative poses between frames are computed using a hybrid registration technique which combine the robustness of ICP (Iterative Closest Point) for large movement and the precision of the normal flow constraint. The complete system runs at 25Hz on a Pentium 4 3.2GHz.

4.   WWW: http://groups.csail.mit.edu/vision/vip/watson/#top,
     Software manual is available on http://groups.csail.mit.edu/vision/vip/watson/Watson23.pdf
5.   Demo images (see Fig. B.11)

4. Body Gesture Recognition Systems

GESTURE + PLAY

1.   Author: MIT CSAIL, Vision Interfaces Lab
2.   Sales: Non-Commercial
3.   Specification: We are developing a perceptual interface toolkit based on stereo vision sensing. Stereo vision allows accurate estimation of 3-D position and orientation cues, and also allows robust segmentation of the image of a user from other objects or people in a scene. We have developed software that can track users' movement and gesture in real-time and that is robust to crowds, lighting changes, motion, and clothing variation. Our toolkit returns the 3D position and articulated body posture of multiple users as they move in an arbitrary workspace. Gestures, actions, and motions in this space cause motion and action in a virtual workspace, e.g. in a game or avatar-world. For this study we are focusing primarily on game environments, for the playful and evocative nature of their visual content and the variety of possible perceptual interaction styles. The virtual world is created using the HALF-LIFE

Figure B.11. Sample images

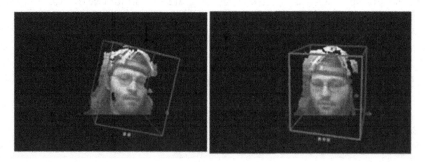

game engine from Sierra/Valve, which enabled us to create rich environments with texture mapping and animations that also contain active objects with behavior. Our installation is physically realized as a simple video projection wall, a stereo-camera and an ample open space in front.

4. WWW: http://groups.csail.mit.edu/vision/vip/index.htm
5. Demo image (see Fig. B.12)

Figure B.12. Sample images

About the Authors

Daijin Kim received the BS degree in electronic engineering from Yonsei University, Seoul, Korea, in 1981, and the MS degree in electrical engineering from the Korea Advanced Institute of Science and Technology(KAIST), Taejon, 1984. In 1991, he received the PhD degree in electrical and computer engineering from Syracuse University, Syracuse, NY. During 1992–1999, he was an associate professor in the Department of Computer Engineering at DongA University, Pusan, Korea. He is currently a professor in the Department of Computer Science and Engineering at POSTECH, Pohang, Korea. His research interests include intelligent systems, biometrics, and human computer interaction.

Jaewon Sung received the BS degree in computer engineering from Chungnam National University, Taejeon, Korea, in 2000, and the MS and PhD degrees in computer science and engineering from Pohang University of Science and Technology (POSTECH), Pohang, Korea, in 2002 and 2007, respectively. He was a postdoctoral researcher at POSTECH in 2007. He is currently a senior research engineer of LG electronics, Korea. His research interests include pattern recognition, machine vision, and video compression and coding.

Index

communication capacity 1
CONDENSATION. see Particle filter 104
conditional density propagation 398
constrained generative model (CGM) 6
CT. see census transform 9
cumukated confidence 16
cumulative density function 398
cylinder head model (CHM) 97, 398

D

DCT 186
detection mode 103, 119, 121, 123, 124
difference of pyramid (DoP) 11, 14, 39
differential-AAM features 273
discrete cosine transform 398

E

EHMM. see Embedded hidden Markov
   model; see Embedded hidden
   Markov model
eigenface 174
eigenface model 45
eigenvalue 57, 77, 80, 171, 174, 178,
   188, 189, 200, 257, 258, 259,
   302, 339
embedded hidden Markov model (EHMM)
   167, 191
entertainment 2
expectation-maximization (EM) 166
expectation-maximization (EM) algorithm
   166
exponential map 54, 99
eye detection 3, 5, 6, 7, 18, 19, 20,
   21, 28, 29, 30, 31, 32, 33, 34,
   35, 36, 38, 39, 40, 41, 44, 94

F

face-to-face human communication 2
face and eye detection 5–44
face authentication 5
face certainty map (FCM) 7, 11, 15, 39,
   160, 251, 393
face detection 2, 3, 4, 5, 6, 7, 9, 10,
   11, 12, 13, 14, 15, 18, 29, 37,
   39, 40, 42, 43, 44, 92, 101,

102, 106, 121, 122, 123, 139,
   160, 174, 225, 228, 251, 255,
   328,
   334, 376, 389, 390, 393
face detection algorithm 11, 12, 13, 15,
   29, 39, 40, 106
face detection research 18
face modeling 3, 45–91, 46, 49, 87,
   167, 225, 227, 245, 265, 320
face modeling technique 46, 245
face recognition 2, 3, 5, 41, 43, 46, 94,
   99, 139, 163, 164, 165, 173,
   174, 179, 180, 181, 182, 184,
   186, 188, 194, 203, 212, 215,
   216, 220, 223, 224, 225, 226,
   247, 248, 250, 251, 252, 254,
   299, 300, 305, 306, 311, 312,
   314, 315, 316, 403, 404, 405,
   406, 408, 423
face recognition vendor test (FRVT) 2
face remote controller (FRC) 322
face roles in human communication 1
face tracking 2, 3, 5, 58, 61, 70, 71,
   72, 73, 88, 92, 93, 94, 97, 101,
   102, 103, 104, 107, 116, 118,
   119, 121, 123, 124, 125, 126,
   127, 128, 129, 137, 139, 140,
   141, 145, 147, 148, 149, 150,
   151, 153, 155, 156, 157, 159,
   160, 161, 250, 251, 314, 324,
   17
face tracking algorithm 3, 93, 94, 104,
   107, 118, 119, 121, 123, 124,
   128, 149, 157, 324
face tracking method 92, 121, 125
face tracking system 101, 103, 148,
   149, 153, 155
facial action coding system (FACS) 255
facial expression recognition 2, 3, 5, 46,
   85, 88, 94, 139, 140, 225, 250,
   253, 255, 255–317, 256, 257,
   265, 266, 271, 272, 273, 279,
   280, 281, 282, 283, 284, 285,
   286, 287, 292, 294, 295, 296,
   298, 300, 311, 312, 314, 315,
   316, 317